PLAYS BY
AMERICAN
1930-1960
WOMEN

Edited and with an introduction by

JUDITH E. BARLOW

APPLAUSE
NEW YORK • LONDON

Also available from Applause Women's Theatre:

Plays by American Women: 1900-1930
edited by Judith E. Barlow

Women on the Verge: 7 Avant-Garde American Plays
edited by Rosette C. Lamont

Womenswork: 5 New Plays from the Women's Project
edited by Julia Miles

Women Heroes: 6 Short Plays from the Women's Project
edited by Julia Miles

I Am a Woman
a dramatic collage conceived and arranged by Viveca
Lindfors and Paul Austin

ACKNOWLEDGEMENTS

For sharing their knowledge of these playwrights with me, I'm indebted to Elizabeth Brown-Guillory, David G. Du Bois, Jean Prinz Korf, Joan Lane, Kathy A. Perkins and Patricia R. Schroeder. I'm grateful to Alice Childress for taking time from her busy schedule to talk and write to me, James V. Hatch and Camille Billops for generously allowing me to use their library, Marcia Morrison for helping with play selection, Judith Fetterley for providing editorial suggestions and encouragement, and my students for continually offering me fresh perspectives on the works of women dramatists. And I am especially thankful to Martha Rozett and Joshua Rozett for support, editorial and research assistance, and chocolate truffles.

The staffs of Yale University's Beinecke Library and Drama School Library, the Federal Theatre Project's Collection at George Mason University, the New York State Library, the S.U.N.Y. Albany Library, the Performing Arts Research Library at Lincoln Center and the Vassar College Rare Book Library have all been enormously helpful.

Research for this book was partly funded by a grant from the Research Foundation of the State University of New York.

This anthology is dedicated to my parents
Lillian Barlow and the late Sidney Barlow
and to my niece, Amanda

JUDITH E. BARLOW

Plays by American Women: 1930-1960
is an original publication of
Applause Theatre Book Publishers

Library of Congress Cataloging-in-Publication Data

Plays by American women, 1930-1960 / edited and with an introduction by Judith E. Barlow.
   p.   cm.
   Sequel to: Plays by American women, 1900-1930.
   Includes bibliographical references.
   ISBN 1-55783-164-5 : $16.95
   1. American drama--Women authors. 2. American drama--20th century. 3. Women--Drama.   I. Barlow, Judith E.
PS628.W6P53   1994
812'.50809287--dc20   94-7760
                                           CIP

British Library of Congress Catalog-in-Publication Data

A catalogue record for this book is available from the British Library

APPLAUSE THEATRE BOOKS
151 W46th Street, 8th Floor
New York, NY 10036
Phone: (212) 575-9265
FAX: (646) 562-5852
email: info@applausepub.com
internet: www.applausepub.com

COMBINED BOOK SERVICES LTD.
Units I/K, Paddock Wood Distribution Centre
Paddock Wood, Tonbridge, Kent TN 12 6UU
Phone: (44) 01892 837171
Fax: (44) 01892 837272

SALES & DISTRIBUTION, HAL LEONARD CORP.
7777 West Bluemound Road, P.O. Box 13819
Milwaukee, WI 53213
Phone: (414) 774-3630 Fax: (414) 774-3259
email: halinfo@halleonard.com
internet: www.halleonard.com

 PRINTED IN CANADA

CONTENTS

JUDITH E. BARLOW is an Associate Professor of English and Women's Studies at the State University of New York at Albany. She received her B.A. from Cornell University and her Ph.D. from the University of Pennsylvania. Dr. Barlow is the editor of *Plays by American Women 1900-1930* and the author of *Final Acts: The Creation of Three Late O'Neill Plays* as well as numerous essays on American Drama.

INTRODUCTION

After women in the United States finally won the vote in 1920, organized feminist activity waned even as the campaign for passage of the Equal Rights Amendment began its long and still unfinished journey. The Great Depression of the 1930s and then the Second World War moved what were considered "women's issues" to the back burner, while the Cold War period ushered in a reactionary attitude toward gender roles as well as politics. Economics, global conflicts and domestic conservatism combined to make the years from 1930 to 1960 even less propitious for women playwrights than the beginning of the century had been for dramatists like Rachel Crothers, Susan Glaspell, Zona Gale, Georgia Douglas Johnson and Sophie Treadwell.[*]

When the stock market plunged in 1929, it took the American theater with it. According to a survey by Burns Mantle, editor of the annual *Best Plays of 19—* volumes, more than two hundred new plays opened in New York City during the 1929-30 season. The following year the number fell by some fifty plays, and the tally continued to drop throughout the Depression and World War II and even into the fifties, when television joined the movies in wooing theater audiences. The situation was similar across the country; theater historian Garff Wilson estimates that "In 1949 there were only 150 legitimate professional theatres serving the entire nation, or approximately one playhouse for every million inhabitants."

In addition to increased competition for professional opportunities in an arena dominated by male producers and directors, women playwrights had to face the demise of many "little theaters" like the Provincetown Players, which in the second and third decades of the century had proved more hospitable to women's work than did the commercial stage. If we look at Mantle's statistics

[*] See *Plays by American Women, 1900-1930.* N.Y.: Applause, 1985.

vii

for women's contributions to the theater, we note that about twenty plays written by women (not counting those co-authored with men) appeared in New York during the 1929-30 season, but the number had decreased significantly a few years later. Even if we acknowledge that Mantle and his successors failed to survey all the smaller theaters and amateur productions, the numbers are still disturbing: in no year from 1934 to 1960 do they record more than fourteen works by women on the New York stage, and in most years there were fewer than ten.

Although a handful of women—including Rosamond Gilder, Edith Isaacs, Mary McCarthy and Kappo Phelan—were reviewing plays during the thirties, forties and/or fifties, the critical establishment remained overwhelmingly the province of White males, as it had been since the birth of the American theater. All too often the critics' attitudes towards women were condescending if not wholly scornful. Joseph Mersand, in his 1937 article "When Ladies Write Plays," belittled all American women dramatists as realistic recorders of the mundane who have succeeded in capturing "the fleeting words of everyday life" but "rarely hit the high note of great drama." (In the course of eight pages he never mentions what he considers one of those "rare" feminine high notes.) Four years later in an essay entitled "Playwrights in Petticoats," the eminent critic George Jean Nathan insisted "that even the best of our women playwrights [by which he meant Lillian Hellman] falls immeasurably short of the mark of our best masculine." Acknowledging that this judgment will probably "cull a smile from the girls at large, since they will attribute it, as is the custom of the dears, to the male's besetting theory of the general superiority of his sex," he concluded that "the beauties...are wrong." Nathan argued that women lack "complete objectivity" because they are too emotional ("Give her an emotion, whether tragic or comic, and she will stretch it not only to its extreme limit, but beyond"). He added that male playwrights like August Strindberg *deliberately* use "over-intensification and elaboration of emotion" while women dramatists do so because it is "unavoidable by nature." Theater critic Norris Houghton managed to combine Nathan's sexism with the post-World War II reactionary gender Zeitgeist in a 1947 *Theatre Arts* article entitled "It's A Woman's World." Houghton cavalierly dismissed all women playwrights except Rachel Crothers and Lillian Hellman and looked with hope toward returning veterans to "hold the ranks against the Amazonian hoards" he feared were threatening to take over the theater.

Despite the odds, however, some female playwrights had substantial hits during these years: Mary Coyle Chase's *Harvey* brought its invisible rabbit to the stage in 1944 for 1775 performances, while Anita Loos' farcical *Happy Birthday* (1946) joined Lillian Hellman's *The Children's Hour* (1934) and Clare Boothe's *The Women* (1936) in achieving more than five hundred performances. And in 1959 Lorraine Hansberry's *A Raisin in the Sun* garnered countless prizes and popular as well as critical success.

Still, the theater remained an uphill battle for women, especially women of color, in the years before 1960. Women writing for the stage between 1930 and 1960 faced such common challenges as the notion that women had gotten all the rights they needed when they won the right to vote, the assumption that economic depression and global war had nothing to do with gender issues, and finally the conviction that all the nation's problems would be solved if the cosmos were returned to its "rightful" order: men at work, women at home, children in the nursery. The eight plays included here—ranging from Hallie Flanagan and Margaret Ellen Clifford's agitprop plea on behalf of starving farmers to Clare Boothe's popular comedy about the urban upper classes, from Lillian Hellman's portrait of greedy White Southerners to Alice Childress' attack on racism in the American theater—represent a broad spectrum of subjects, forms and styles. Half of the plays—*The Women, The Little Foxes, In the Summer House* and *Goodbye, My Fancy*—appeared on Broadway, the Mecca of commercial theater in America; the rest were performed by university, regional, community and/or workers theaters. This anthology is by no means comprehensive, of course; *A Raisin in the Sun* and Carson McCuller's *The Member of the Wedding* are just two of the obvious omissions. But together these eight plays demonstrate the talent and courage of women working in a field where few if any could have felt at home.

*   *   *   *

During the 1930s and even beyond, a few of the older generation of women dramatists—those who began their careers shortly after the turn of the century—were still writing plays. Rachel Crothers' *Let Us Be Gay* (1929) and *When Ladies Meet* (1932) enjoyed long runs, while her last produced work—*Susan and God* (1937)—held the stage nearly a year. All three are witty social comedies that present the dilemma of unhappily married women. Most of the characters in Crothers' late plays comment on the prevalence of affairs and

divorce, reflecting the changing social climate in post-World War I
America, but few of her protagonists find a satisfying alternative to
the flawed institution of marriage. Susan Glaspell retired from the
stage (with the exception of one co-authored work) by winning the
Pulitzer Prize for drama in 1930 with *Alison's House*, a fictionalized
account of the family of Emily Dickinson. Although Sophie
Treadwell never repeated the success she had had with *Machinal*
(1928), she continued her stage career with *Lone Valley* (1933); *Plumes
in the Dust* (1936), a work about Edgar Allan Poe; and *Hope for a
Harvest* (1941), a remarkably contemporary drama about bigotry and
environmental destruction in California.

Zoe Akins won a Pulitzer Prize in 1934-5 for her adaptation of
Edith Wharton's *The Old Maid*, the story of two cousins in love with
the same man. *The Old Maid* explores the pressures on women to
marry well and the stigma on single women, but the stage version
misses many of the novel's subtleties. Clare Kummer continued to
crank out popular farces, the most amusing of which is *Her Master's
Voice* (1933).

Although audiences in the thirties, like audiences in most eras,
preferred comedies and romances that distracted them from their
troubles outside the theater, the most important dramatic work
addressed serious societal problems. There may not have been a
theatrical equivalent to the outpouring of women's proletarian novels
that historian Susan Ware cites, but writers like Hallie Flanagan and
Margaret Ellen Clifford, Lillian Hellman and even Clare Boothe
were exposing both the failures of capitalism at home and the
growing threat from Fascism abroad. At the same time, writers of
color like Shirley Graham were using the stage to examine America's
history of racism.

The woman who had perhaps the greatest effect on the American
theater in the 1930s was Hallie Flanagan, a playwright and director
who would leave her indelible mark as the head of the Federal
Theatre Project. Flanagan was a Vassar professor when she and co-
author Margaret Ellen Clifford wrote *Can You Hear Their Voices?*
(1931), one of the earliest and most compelling agitprop dramas
written in this country. Based on a Whittaker Chambers story about
the Midwest drought, *Voices* uses slides and staged scenes to show
how natural disaster, greed and government indifference combine to
create starvation in the middle of America's most fertile farmland.
Three years later Flanagan was appointed to lead the Federal
Theatre, a program to employ those who lost their jobs during the
Depression. The Federal Theatre had some 12,000 to 15,000

employees and produced over 900 works seen by an estimated 15 to 20 million people throughout the country.

Flanagan administered a mammoth organization that included a number of women in important roles. Rosamond Gilder directed the Bureau of Research and Publications, which printed lists of recommended scripts as well as technical handbooks. Madalyn O'Shea was in charge of community drama and the casting bureau, Kate Drain Lawson headed the technical production division in New York City, while Susan Glaspell ran the Midwest Play Bureau. Rose McClendon, knowing that most theaters in the country were segregated and jobs for people of color scarce, was among the first to suggest separate Black units to produce plays dramatizing African American themes and utilizing African American talent. McClendon had already enjoyed a distinguished acting career and had directed for the Harlem Experimental Theatre when she became co-director (with John Houseman) of the Negro Theatre Unit in Harlem; unfortunately, illness forced her to resign after a few months.

Women found administrative and directing opportunities through the Federal Theatre Project, but they did not necessarily find a forum for new dramatic works. By and large the Federal Theatre had more success inspiring innovative productions of Western "classics"—from Shakespeare to George Bernard Shaw and Eugene O'Neill—than fostering original plays. Federal Theatre productions of works by women were few and scattered, except for stagings of Grace Heyward's *CCC Murder Mystery*, a popular comedy designed for young people in the Civilian Conservation Corps camps. The creation of the National Service Bureau in 1937, however, expanded opportunities for all playwrights. The Bureau was a clearing house that made scripts available not only to the various Federal Theatre units but to schools, colleges, clubs, drama groups and other organizations. According to Lorraine Brown, Director of the Institute on the Federal Theatre Project, "The Bureau read, wrote, rewrote, and translated plays and sent synopses, scripts, and bibliographies to the field. In the first six months, more than thirteen hundred analyses were completed."

A significant percentage of the scripts in the Bureau files are by women, ranging from such Georgia Douglas Johnson anti-lynching dramas as *A Sunday Morning in the South* (ca. 1925) and *Safe* (1929) to a pirate comedy about Jean Lafitte, several marionette works, a spate of Biblical allegories, a Mother's Day tribute, and young people's plays about Native Americans, Norse mythology and Naziism. While most of the plays are short and range in quality from amateurish skits

to polished dramas, all bear witness that women were actively
creating for the stage. Some works were written by dramatists
subsidized by the Federal Theatre, although many were written
before the advent of the Project and simply submitted to the Play
Bureau. Molly Day Thacher's *Blocks* (1933) premiered at Vassar—
where Thacher was a student of Flanagan's—before entering the
Bureau's index and eventually being produced twice by Federal
Theatre units. *Blocks* is an anti-war verse drama reminiscent of Edna
St. Vincent Millay's *Aria da Capo* (1919). Especially compelling is
Thacher's treatment of social class: while it is the leaders who declare
war and promise "Each party, in so far's he can/ Murder like a
gentleman," it is the workers who do the fighting and end up buried
in tombs they themselves built. Betty Smith's *So Gracious Is the Time*
(1936), on the other hand, was written while Smith was employed as
a dramatist by the Federal Theatre. One of a number of plays by
women with religious themes, *Time* is a parable about a young girl—
clearly a modern Virgin Mary—who is nearly forced to have an
abortion because she and her boyfriend cannot afford a child.

Several folk plays by both Black and White authors are in the Play
Bureau archives, including Anne Frierson's Gullah drama *Quagmire*
(1936) which deals, in part, with the clash between Black and White
societies. A play with a socialist message, Margaret Elsworth's
presentational *The Weaver's Story* (nd) follows a group of workers
who create a community-owned store that shares profits among the
customers. Ruth Morris' *The Lowells...Talk Only to God* (nd) exposes
the plight of women and children working in the Lowell,
Massachusetts, mills in dangerous and degrading conditions.
Although *The Lowells*—which focuses on how abusive husbands claim
their wives' wages and how immigrant women in particular are
exploited by employers—is set in the mid-nineteenth century, the
depression of 1848 is obviously a stand-in for the Great Depression
of the 1930s. Simply because a script was offered to the Play Bureau
does not mean it was performed by the Federal Theatre or anyone
else, but several did reach production.

Susan Ware is largely right when she notes that during the 1930s
"so much of the country's attention was focused on the problems of
the Depression that women's issues, which were perceived as having
little relation to the broader problems of the Depression, were
ignored." Still, the Federal Theatre Play Bureau collection reveals
that women, like their male counterparts, were acutely concerned
with social problems. Hunger was certainly a "woman's issue"—as
Flanagan and Clifford had shown earlier in *Can You Hear Their*

Voices? when mothers refused to watch their children starve—as were racism and war. Even more particular to women's concerns were the questions of reproductive rights, addressed in *So Gracious Is the Time*, and the conditions of female employment, the subject of *The Lowells*. The employment rate for women, in fact, did not plunge significantly during the Depression precisely because women were hired for the most menial and lowest paid jobs.

Congress killed the Federal Theatre Project after four years because it did not like the liberal political bent of many productions. Another organization with a liberal agenda was the Group Theater, a major force in the non-commercial stage of the 1930s. Organized in 1931, the Group outlasted the Federal Theater, disbanding in 1940. Despite the fact that Cheryl Crawford was—along with Harold Clurman and Lee Strasberg—one of the founding members of the Group, the company was not noticeably interested in contributions by women. Crawford herself was often overshadowed by her colleagues and relegated to practical matters like raising money, engaging theaters and renting costumes. Wendy Smith, the most recent chronicler of the Group, argues that in the acting ranks "Group women had been feeling like second-class citizens for years," aware that their careers were viewed as less important than those of their male colleagues. Out of more than twenty plays presented by the Group, two were co-authored by women and only two more had women as sole authors. Dawn Powell's *Big Night* (1933; originally entitled *The Party*) ran less than a week; some reviewers suggested that the problem was not with the play, about a salesman so desperate to land an account he offers his wife as a bargaining chip, but with the production, which failed to catch the work's bitter satirical comedy. Nelisse Child's *Weep for the Virgins* (1935), the story of three sisters dominated by their mother, fared equally poorly. Although the Group Theater may have been liberal in the slant of its plays and its communal work methods, its attitudes toward women seem regrettably traditional.

Unstable as the commercial theater was during the Depression, Broadway still offered a venue for some White women, most notably Rose Franken, Clare Boothe (Luce) and Lillian Hellman. Franken garnered success in 1932 with her first Broadway work, *Another Language* (a revised version of *The Hallam Wives*), about a family tyrannized by a mother who rules her sons with an iron hand. While the play provides a sympathetic portrait of Stella, the artistic daughter-in-law who opposes the family's conventional view of women's roles, it is uncomfortably close in theme if not presentation to such "devouring mother" melodramas as Sidney Howard's *The Silver Cord*. Franken's indomitable matriarch was still going strong in the sequel, *The Hallams* (1947), but the dramatist had her biggest hit with *Claudia*, a comedy about a childish young woman who approaches maturity only when her mother is dying and she herself is pregnant. *Claudia*, based on Franken's short stories, is amusing yet scarcely enlightened in its suspect equation of womanhood and motherhood.

Clare Boothe achieved fame with her second stage venture, *The Women*, a comedy about the female upper crust. Attending *The Women* seems to have been an escape from Depression woes and the social event of the season for the middle and upper class Broadway audience: newspaper stories kept them apprised of the costumes (changed seasonally to be *au courant*) and the lives of the stars. Judging by the reviews, few audience members recognized Boothe's critique of a capitalist society that denies women well-paid jobs and pits them against each other in battles to land wealthy mates. Rather, most male critics saw the play as a witty confirmation, from a woman's hand, of their own misogyny. Boothe went on to write other works, including *Kiss the Boys Good-bye* (1938) and the anti-Nazi drama *Margin for Error* (1939), before moving on to the bigger stage of national and world politics. Although both of these plays did well with audiences, neither approached the phenomenal success of *The Women*.

Clare Boothe and Lillian Hellman were not only the most famous women playwrights in the thirties, they were also two of America's most famous women in this century. In some ways the pair were notably different: politically Boothe drifted into conservatism while Hellman stayed staunchly liberal. Not surprisingly, Boothe pursued her political goals within the system—as a Representative in Congress, ambassador, and member of a presidential council—while Hellman remained a gadfly, attacking the system from outside; the closest she came to Congress was her appearance before the House Un-American Activities Committee. Boothe's writing strength was her acid social comedy and witty dialogue, while Hellman's power lay in her strongly dramatic characters and fierce moral indignation.

Yet despite their differences, their lives and their plays share common strands. Critics and political opponents often denigrated Boothe's achievements by attributing them to her "feminine" appeal. Milton McKaye began a long 1939 *Scribner's* profile by noting "Clare Boothe is the glamour girl of letters, the most beautiful living playwright." When she was elected to Congress her opponent sourly complained, "I guess I just haven't got glamour." Ironically, her contemporary Lillian Hellman suffered from the opposite accusation: that her drive and ambition were simply compensation for her lack of conventional beauty. In his biography of the playwright, Carl Rollyson describes her as having "the face of a national monument.... In later years, her craggy face resembled one of the facades etched in stone on Mount Rushmore" and suggests that she used sexual aggressiveness to overcome her cosmetic imperfections. In the biography's index there are twelve page references for Hellman's "physical appearance" but only seven under the heading "place in the American theater"—a startling ratio for America's most eminent female dramatist. Damned if they fulfilled society's expectations for women and damned if they didn't, Boothe and Hellman inevitably harbored deep ambivalence about women and gender roles.

Lillian Hellman's first produced play, *The Children's Hour* (1934), ran nearly two years in New York but reportedly failed even to qualify for a Pulitzer Prize because one member of the awards committee refused to attend a drama in which lesbianism was an issue. Her second theatrical work, *Days to Come* (1936) failed, but her third was *The Little Foxes* (1939), which became her most famous and frequently revived drama. Although set in the South at the turn of the century, *Foxes* is very clearly a thirties work in its portrayal of capitalism as a morally bankrupt system that turns human beings—particularly women—into commodities. Many male critics of *The Little Foxes*, like those of *The Women*, saw in the play a reaffirmation of their own biases: Regina Giddens is a monster because she lacks the "feminine" virtues of reticence, compassion and wifely obedience. Yet these very qualities make Regina's sister-in-law, Birdie Hubbard, a figure of pity and even disdain. In *Foxes* Hellman targets a system that not only sets family members against one another but pretends to reward the cleverest while forbidding the poor, people of color and White women from entering the competition at all. Hellman went on to write *Another Part of the Forest* (1948), the "prequel" to *Foxes*, and saw a total of eight of her original plays and four adaptations performed on the New York stage before she retired from the theater.

Unlike Boothe and Hellman, African American women playwrights during the thirties had no access to Broadway and only limited opportunities in the Federal Theatre Project. The Project employed and trained hundreds of Black actors, directors and technical personnel and sponsored the Negro Dramatists' Laboratory, in which some fifty playwrights participated. But the number of works by African American writers actually performed by Federal Theatre units was relatively small; according to E. Quita Craig in *Black Drama of the Federal Theatre Era*, there was not a single "black representative on the National Play Bureau or the Play Policy Board, which were responsible for the selection of the plays produced by the Black units." At the same time, the economic crisis diminished the ranks of independent Black "little theaters." The original Lafayette Players, begun in 1917, disbanded in 1932, and such groups as the Rose McClendon Players, the Negro Playwrights Company and the American Negro Theatre did not emerge until the last years of the decade or early the next. Elizabeth Brown-Guillory, in her important collection *Wines in the Wilderness: Plays by African American Women from the Harlem Renaissance to the Present*, includes six dramas from the nineteen twenties but only three works written between 1930 and 1960. Similarly, Kathy Perkins' invaluable *Black Female Playwrights: An Anthology of Plays before 1950* comprises a dozen works written in the teens and twenties but just six written later. As Craig observes, "The few [African American] plays that were performed were usually put on by libraries, churches, schools, or clubs within the black community."

Perkins notes that although "Plays and pageants based on the lives of famous black heroes and heroines were...prevalent among black women" during the first half of this century, these writers most often addressed the plight of women and their children. White and Black women had been writing anti-lynching plays since the nineteenth century, and this continued to be a common topic, especially for the latter, at least until World War II. Scholar Judith Stephens points out that these plays usually had domestic settings in order to show how such murders affected "all aspects of life" and to dramatize "connections between motherhood and lynching." Angelina Weld Grimké had made the association in *Rachel* (1916) when the title character refuses marriage and motherhood because she will not offer up more African American children to racist violence. In Georgia Douglas Johnson's *Safe*, Liza Pettigrew is in labor as a White mob drags away a young neighbor who screams for his mother. When Liza discovers she has given birth to a boy, she strangles him: "Now he's safe—safe from the lynchers." May Miller in *Nails and Thorns* (1933) shows the effects of racism on a White mother. When Gladys, the wife of a sheriff in a small town "probably South, probably West," futilely tries to prevent a mob from killing an African American man, the baby she is carrying is trampled to death by the crowd and she herself driven mad. The message is clear:

lynching destroys White families as well as Black.

Among the most extraordinary of this group of African American women writers was Shirley Graham (Du Bois), a musician, composer, playwright, administrator, teacher, biographer, novelist and civil rights activist. In 1932 her opera *Tom-Tom: An Epic of Music and the Negro* played to 25,000 people over two nights at a Cleveland stadium. Graham served as head of the Chicago Negro Unit of the Federal Theatre Project and studied playwriting on scholarship at Yale University. Her powerful *It's Morning*—different versions of which were performed at Yale in 1939 and 1940—is closely linked to the work of her sister dramatists in its focus on the dilemma of an enslaved woman whose teenage daughter has been sold to a vicious trader. Like many other African American dramatists, Graham used the theater to counter White versions of history, to tell the Black woman's story from her own perspective. In this case she cuts through sentimentalized views of the "benevolent" institution of slavery to focus on the destruction of the family and to look at a system that—like the plague of lynchings in subsequent years—denied African American women the ability to protect their own children.

Graham's plays were produced by such major Black companies as the Karamu Theatre in Cleveland, as well as at numerous colleges; both *Track Thirteen* (1940) and selections from *Tom-Tom* were aired on the radio. But despite her faith that she could "break through the barriers" to a Broadway production—something not yet achieved by an African American woman—she was unable to conquer the theater's racism. The prevailing White attitude was made clear in a *Chicago Times* article ironically intended to praise the playwright. "Shirley Graham strives today to make the Negro culturally articulate," the writer maintained; "Her own voice is the voice of her people for a thousand years, a culturally uncomplicated people transplanted into a complicated civilization." Those who could not respect the complexity of African culture nor define "civilization" in other than European terms could scarcely appreciate the works of Shirley Graham, whose re-vision of African American history is rooted in a fusion of non-Western and Western aesthetics.

*   *   *   *

The 1940s saw the end of the Depression with America's entry into World War II, and the situation for women as well as men shifted drastically. In 1940 just over one quarter of American women

were working outside the home, a percentage that had held fairly
steady throughout the thirties, but according to Susan M. Hartmann
by 1945 some 36% of American women were in the marketplace,
many replacing men who had gone to war. Meanwhile, the volume of
theater activity remained far below the 1929 peak, with fewer than a
hundred new plays opening in New York each year. Not surprisingly,
escapist fare was most popular with audiences who daily wondered
whether their world was coming to an end. The American musical
grew to maturity during this decade, with *Oklahoma!* (1943), *Carousel*
(1945), *Annie Get Your Gun* (1946) and later *South Pacific* (1949). The
biggest hit by a woman during the war years was Mary Chase's
Harvey, an entertaining spoof of both conventional society and the
mental health profession centered on a man whose best friend is a
giant invisible rabbit.

Refuting claims that they concerned themselves only with
"domestic trivia," many women playwrights during this era addressed
global conflicts both past and present. In the late 1930s and early
1940s, pacifist dramas like Thacher's *Blocks* were gradually replaced
by anti-Nazi works. An interesting transitional play is Maria M.
Coxe's *If Ye Break Faith* (revised version 1938), which presents the
unknown soldiers of France, England, Italy, Germany, Austria and
the U.S. with a mission to dissuade their compatriots from starting
another war. A distinctly unromantic view of military action, *If Ye
Break Faith* shows Americans as motivated primarily by profit, selling
weapons to the highest bidders, while the Unknown Soldier of
Britain tells his son that he used patriotism to mask his fear and guilt.
The Epilogue, however—presumably added during revisions in
1938—makes clear that a new war is inevitable because of Germany's
aggression. Coxe's play can end only with the hope that perhaps *this*
confrontation will be the last one. Sada Cowan's *Auf Wiedersehen*
(1937), about a Jewish woman in Germany who takes her own life in
an effort to protect the Christian niece and nephew she has lovingly
raised, joined such other anti-Nazi works as Boothe's *Margin for
Error* and Hellman's *Watch on the Rhine*.

Among the most successful women dramatists during the 1940s
was Ruth Gordon, best known to contemporary audiences as a comic
actress. Gordon wrote several star vehicles for herself, including
Years Ago (1947), chronicling a young girl's escape from a small town
to the stage, and *The Leading Lady* (1947), in which an actress realizes
that her beloved late husband was a malicious cad. The best of her
works is *Over Twenty-One* (1944), Gordon's contribution to the war
effort. A farce set near an army base, *Over Twenty-One* follows the

comic trials of Paula Wharton, a feminist novelist and screen-writer, and her husband Max, an overage enlistee. When the hapless Max finally manages to scrape through Officer's Candidate School, Paula agrees to edit the newspaper for which he'd been working. Like many women of the period, she temporarily takes over a man's job to free him to fight.

For the most part the war years were understandably lean ones for the theater. None of the plays in this volume was completed or produced during World War II, and the first to appear in the post-war period—Gertrude Stein's *The Mother of Us All* (completed 1946; premiered 1947)—was by a woman with few ties to the American stage. Stein, who had lived in Europe since the turn of the century, was a "cult" figure most of whose stories, novels, plays, criticism and verbal portraits remained unpublished and unproduced when she died several months before the premiere of *Mother*. Stein was a modernist innovator and plays like "What Happened" (ca. 1913), in which nothing happens, and the enigmatic *Three Sisters Who Are Not Sisters* (1943), a spoof of both murder mysteries and Anton Chekhov's classic *The Three Sisters*, would scarcely have appealed to conventional audiences in those years. Her only American stage successes—the librettos for *Four Saints in Three Acts* (written 1927; premiered 1934) and *The Mother of Us All*—were done at the behest of Virgil Thomson, who invited her to join him in creating the two operas. Without Thomson's influence it is doubtful that any of Stein's work would have seen major productions in this country during her lifetime or the years immediately following her death.

Written just after the Second World War, *Mother* is at least indirectly a comment on the global conflict: making the world "safe for democracy" is one thing, making certain that everyone gets to share in that democracy is another. Looking back at nineteenth century United States history, *The Mother of Us All* is a tribute to Susan B. Anthony and to all who fought (and fight) against laws that deny civil rights to particular groups. But at the same time that Stein was wittily questioning the value of marriage for women—"I will not marry because if I did marry, I would be married," declares her character Jenny Reefer—the nuclear family was being invoked as this nation's greatest asset. In an effort to reinstate "normality," the government offered college educations to returning soldiers while "experts" like psychologists and sociologists urged women to go back to kitchens and nurseries to make room for men in the workplace. Historian Lois Banner observes that "the antifeminism of the postwar 1940s held women responsible for society's ills—either because they were failures as mothers or because they had left the home for work." As women's employment rates sank, so did their median marriage age, which in the nineteen-fifties, according to Rochelle Gatlin in *American Women Since 1945*, "reached an all-time low for the twentieth century." By 1946 the first of the "baby boom" children had begun to arrive, and the dominant gender ideology was overwhelmingly conservative.

In his 1947 "It's A Woman's World," Norris Houghton complained that the American theater had "withdrawn too much from the world of men, because we have been content to reflect the trivialities of domesticity and to enjoy the safe sentimentality of our relations with Mom or the girl-friend rather than face up to the sinewy and exacting life of our time"—that "life" presumably being whatever men do. Ironically, if not surprisingly, several women used the theater to echo Houghton's belief that most spheres of American life should revert to their rightful owners, men. As early as 1944, Rose Franken's *Soldier's Wife* presented the case of Kate, who becomes a popular writer when the letters she sends to her soldier husband are published. Kate's spouse is humiliated to have a wife more successful than he is, and a female friend explains that women must "make it up to men" for what they suffered in the war. All ends happily when Kate decides she'd rather have another baby than a career. Similarly, Esther M. Hawley's brief *On the Way Home* (1945) argues that women are solely responsible for facilitating men's readjustment to civilian life. The female protagonist insists: "*We* have to find the way. For a while we can't matter."

Combined with this renewed gender conservatism was the fact that the end of the war did not significantly improve the theater business; the number of theaters and productions nationwide remained low even as Tennessee Williams and Arthur Miller launched their stage careers with *The Glass Menagerie* (opening a few months before the war ended in 1945) and *All My Sons* (1947) respectively. A few women also had post-war Broadway successes: Lillian Hellman's *The Autumn Garden* (1951) just passed the 100-performance "hit" mark, and Carson McCuller's stage adaptation of her novel *The Member of the Wedding*, the tale of a young girl's rocky journey to maturity, won the Drama Critics Circle Award as best play of 1949-50. Another of the rare successes during this period was Fay Kanin's 1948 comedy *Goodbye, My Fancy* (originally titled *Most Likely to Succeed*) which dared to suggest that women have a place in the world outside the home. Although *Fancy* does have a romantic subplot—something a Broadway-bound comedy could scarcely ignore at the time—the focus is on the accomplishments of Congresswoman Agatha Reed. While the trustees at her alma mater see their institution as a kind of finishing school, a common view in this era, Agatha insists these privileged young women receive a genuine education about the world in which they live. *Fancy* is also part of the tradition of women's anti-war drama, for Agatha opposes Claude Griswold—who would leave military decisions in the hands of those who stand to profit—and makes a film showing the real nature of war.

Kanin faced the challenge of establishing a serious career even while columnists referred to her as "a vital and shapely girl." Perhaps Agatha's film was prophetic, for shortly after she wrote *Goodbye, My Fancy* Kanin turned her major attention to movies and television. She eventually formed an all-woman production company for films, served four terms as president of the Academy of Motion Picture Arts and Sciences, and traveled throughout the world as a representative of the Academy. Married to a writer who was often her co-author, Kanin accomplished all this while still maintaining her role as wife and mother.

If Fay Kanin's life is an American woman's success story, the career of her contemporary Jane Bowles followed a tragically different scenario. Like Gertrude Stein, Bowles was a Jewish lesbian who chose the life of an expatriate, in Bowles' case mostly in Morocco. Also like Stein, for many years Bowles enjoyed the admiration of a coterie of other writers rather than a large audience. Both experimented with a variety of genres of which drama was only one: Stein is best known for *The Autobiography of Alice B. Toklas* (written by Stein), while Bowles first gained recognition with her novel, *Two Serious Ladies*. Although both freely explored lesbian themes in their novels, stories and non-fiction prose, they kept lesbianism muted in their major dramatic work—an acknowledgement of the theater's conservatism. But while Stein wrote prodigiously despite opposition and even ridicule, Bowles managed to complete only one full-length play, one puppet skit, one novel and a handful of short stories—enough to fill a single volume.

The differences may primarily be personal: Bowles spent her short life wrestling with private demons and an almost insurmountable writer's block, complicated by tenuous health and heavy drinking. It is also true, however, that Stein created a comfortable lifestyle for herself in Paris with a life-long lover; she wrote largely if not entirely as she pleased and apparently had only limited concern for the exigencies of commercial publication and production. Bowles, on the other hand, seems always at some level to have courted conventional acceptance: even though she was overt about her lesbianism, she married young and stayed devoted to her gay husband—following him in his wanderings—all her life. And she strove to open *In the Summer House* (1953) on Broadway, despite the fact that this often painful and uncomfortable exploration of women's lives was hardly the kind of play a 1950s Broadway audience would embrace. Perhaps Jane Bowles' attempt to have one foot in Kanin's world and one in Stein's contributed to her creative difficulties.

Of all the plays in this volume, *In the Summer House* (1953) is the most concerned with the emotional resonances of mother-daughter relationships. Maybe because its writing took more than a decade and it was primarily composed far from the United States, *Summer House* seems the least specifically grounded, thematically and stylistically, in the immediate pre- or post-war period. Yet the distinction between personal psychology and societal expectations is arbitrary if not wholly artificial. In Gertrude Eastman Cuevas's story of the younger sister on whom their father doted, for example, we see Bowles's realization of the kind of woman a patriarchy preferred: sickly, dependent, beautifully dressed. Marriage too is a primary subject here and, like *The Women* and *The Little Foxes*, *Summer House* suggests that husbands are mainly useful to support women who cannot support themselves. Most important, while magazines, plays and television comedies in the 1950s were trumpeting the joys of motherhood, *Summer House* was showing how difficult and even dangerous familial bonds can be: mothering and baking cookies are not quite the parallel activities the popular media implied. At least some of the bewilderment expressed by critics of *Summer House* can be attributed to Bowles's radically unsentimental view of maternity, a distinct change from the perspective offered in *I Remember Mama*, *The Donna Reed Show* and *Lassie*.

Not all women, of course, could see themselves as the idealized mothers of 1950s television sit-coms or dramas; the perspective of the shows was not only saccharine, it was also distinctly Caucasian. Except for an occasional servant, women of color hardly existed on television at all. Serious dramatists, however, recognized that the United States could no longer ignore the prejudice that was woven into the very fabric of the country. Among the plays that confronted home-grown bigotry were several by White women, including Doris Frankel's *Journey for an Unknown Soldier* (1943), which addressed the problem of anti-Japanese feeling. Although she was writing while Japanese Americans were still interned in concentration camps,

Frankel was optimistic—overly so—about White Americans' willingness to accept their Asian counterparts. Far less sanguine was Maxine Wood (nom de plume of Maxine Finsterwald), whose *On Whitman Avenue*, first produced in 1946, explores the issue of "restrictive covenants" that prevented people of color from renting or buying homes in many neighborhoods. Loosely based on actual incidents in Detroit, *On Whitman Avenue* shows what happens when a young White woman, Toni, rents an apartment in her house to the family of a disabled Black war hero. In addition to examining the economic roots of restrictive covenants, the drama focuses on Toni's mother, whose prejudice alienates her daughter and husband, infects her young son and devastates the African American family whose only crime is needing a home. Like May Miller's *Nails and Thorns*, *On Whitman Avenue* is designed to show how racism destroys White families as well as Black.

Wood had difficulty getting financing for *On Whitman Avenue* (a play that may have influenced Lorraine Hansberry's *A Raisin in the Sun*) because most White producers considered the material too controversial. It eventually had a moderately successful run in New York largely because of good reviews in the Black press. If post-war White America was not ready to embrace Wood's insights into race relations, they were even less eager to see the world through the eyes of African American dramatists. Most of the Black women who were writing in the teens, twenties and thirties—Angelina Weld Grimké, Georgia Douglas Johnson, Zora Neale Hurston, Marita Bonner, May Miller, Shirley Graham—had either stopped writing plays or died by the end of World War II. It would not be until the 1960s that playwrights like Adrienne Kennedy and Sonia Sanchez would appear as the harbingers of a new wave of African American women's drama. Still, the 1950s did see the emergence of a small number of Black women dramatists who had a profound influence on the theater in this country.

According to Margaret B. Wilkerson, editor of *9 Plays By Black Women*, Beah Richards' impassioned *A Black Woman Speaks* "was first performed in 1950 for a white woman's organization in Chicago, Women for Peace." A verse performance piece, *A Black Woman Speaks* indicts White women for their role in oppressing women of color at the same time pointing out that "White womanhood too is enslaved." In 1951 Richards wrote her first full-length play, *One Is a Crowd*, which Wilkerson characterizes as "a compelling drama about a black singer's lifelong pursuit of revenge against a white man whose casual lust had destroyed her family." *One Is a Crowd* had to wait two full decades before receiving a first production.

Part of the problem facing African American women playwrights during this period was not only the racism of the commercial theater but the decrease, as the fifties progressed, in the number of theaters in Black communities like Harlem. As Doris Abramson points out in *Negro Playwrights in the American Theatre, 1925-1959*, despite restrictive covenants some middle class African Americans were following the postwar American dream to the suburbs, depleting theater audiences in traditionally Black city enclaves. In 1955, for example, Alice Childress' *Trouble in Mind* premiered not in Harlem but in Greenwich Village at the Greenwich Mews, an interracial theater sponsored by the Village Presbyterian Church and the Brotherhood Synagogue.

Childress began her theater career as an actor, so she was well aware of the image of the African American woman on the stage before she began to write. In fact, it was largely those stereotypes—smothering matriarchs, obsequious servants—that inspired her to tell the Black woman's story from her own vantage point. *Trouble in Mind* examines a group of actors as they rehearse a drama about African American life written by a White dramatist. Using a play-within-a-play structure, *Trouble* takes a direct look at the American theater and the racism that exists in the works of even supposedly well-intentioned liberal White writers. *Trouble*'s protagonist, Wiletta Mayer, refuses to be co-opted into enacting still one more stage falsification of the Black woman's life.

In *Their Place on the Stage*, Elizabeth Brown-Guillory reports that Childress' early plays were appreciatively reviewed by Lorraine Hansberry, and she speculates that the young writer took Childress "as a role model." The 1950s closed with the premiere of Hansberry's *A Raisin in the Sun*, the first play by an African American woman to appear on Broadway, the first by an African American to win the New York Drama Critics Circle Award, a cultural and theatrical event of immense importance. Although Hansberry completed only two theater works before her untimely death at age 34, she is probably better known than Childress—author of more than a dozen plays during a still-active forty-year career—among theater audiences, students and the general public. *A Raisin in the Sun* is a dynamic drama that (through stage, film and television productions) has probably touched more Americans than any other play written this century. But it is also a work with which White liberals, especially men, could be comfortable: the values of the Younger family resemble those of most middle class White families;

the crucial family decision is left to Walter Lee, the only adult male; and critics could and did misread *Raisin* as simply a plea for peaceable integration when Mama buys a house in a White neighborhood because she cannot afford the inflated prices in Black ghettoes. Childress' plays are less easy for White audiences to embrace. African American women take center stage in her works, and the nuclear family is rarely the main concern. Moreover, with Mrs. Carter in *Florence* (1949), Al Manners in *Trouble in Mind* and Herman in *Wedding Band* (ca. 1966), Childress repeatedly shows that White liberal hypocrisy can be as dangerous as outright bigotry.

*   *   *   *

Of the nine playwrights represented in this anthology, Alice Childress faced the greatest obstacles: a woman of color with little formal education (poverty forced her to quit high school) she had no economic, race, class or gender privileges. And yet, she is the only one of the nine who devoted her primary attention throughout her life to the writing of plays. Although virtually every one of these women had a truly remarkable career, most chose to abandon dramatic writing. After running the Federal Theatre Project, Hallie Flanagan returned to teaching and academic administration, fields in which her co-author, Margaret Ellen Clifford, also carved her niche; their playwriting activities in later years were minimal. Except for an occasional work, Clare Boothe left the theater after the 1930s for a career in politics and diplomacy, while even Lillian Hellman—the most acclaimed and successful of the group—eventually gave up drama and spent her last years writing memoirs and involving herself in political activities. Shirley Graham, in part because of her frustration with the barriers she faced as an African American women dramatist, turned her hand to biographies, novels and political activism; Fay Kanin opted to exercise her talents in films and television. Gertrude Stein and Jane Bowles were expatriates who wrote far away from the New York "show shop"; Bowles completed only one play and Stein made little effort to see her works staged. Even Childress has branched out into essays and fiction, particularly for children; she may well be better known as the author of *A Hero Ain't Nothin' but a Sandwich*, a novel banned from some school libraries for its frank portrayal of urban adolescent life, than for *Trouble in Mind, Wedding Band* or *Wine in the Wilderness.* The clear implication is that the American theater, longtime home to Eugene O'Neill, Arthur Miller and Tennessee Williams, does little to encourage even its best women playwrights. In their exodus to other careers, they join such earlier women dramatists as Susan Glaspell, Georgia Douglas Johnson and Zona Gale.

Lillian Hellman vehemently objected to being compared to Clare Boothe as a "lady playwright." "Miss Boothe and I don't write about the same things," she asserted, "We don't write the same way and we aren't interested in the same ends. There is no possible basis for comparison except that we are women dramatists with successes to our credit." Hellman is largely right, of course. It is both naive and simplistic to assume that Boothe's and Hellman's styles and concerns are identical, that Kanin's and Childress' characters inhabit kindred worlds, that Bowles' theater is a mirror image of Graham's. And surely Hellman's ire is understandable: she was writing at a time— witness the articles by Mersand, Nathan and Houghton—when "lady playwright" was a denigrating term roughly equivalent to "dancing bear." Yet in that very denigration is the first similarity among all the playwrights included here.

All nine of these dramatists were writing in an era when popular notions of femininity made it difficult for women to imagine themselves as writers. If Shirley Temple was one of the major movie box-office draws in the 1930s, by the 1950s her image was replaced by that of Marilyn Monroe, the quintessential sex kitten, and television's Donna Reed. Both Temple and Monroe projected an aura of immaturity (intellectual if not sexual), vulnerability and dependence; Reed was the symbol of maternal nurturing. All were also, not surprisingly, White. It is against these images that woman playwrights not only had to create their protagonists, but create themselves.

Even the plays that these dramatists did write were often disparaged or ignored, as were the women themselves. Fay Kanin struggled to emerge from the shadow of the theatrical family into which she had married. One reviewer of *Goodbye, My Fancy* wrote that "Michael Kanin's wife and Garson Kanin's sister-in-law have written an ardent, adult play"; that "composite" author was Fay Kanin. Until the publication of *The Collected Works of Jane Bowles* in 1966, Bowles was virtually unknown in her native country; she is still better known as the wife of writer and composer Paul Bowles than an author in her own right. Only a small portion of Gertrude Stein's vast literary output was published during her lifetime, and much of that was subsidized by Stein herself. Even today she is probably more famous as a supporter of Ernest Hemingway and Pablo Picasso than as one of the twentieth century's most important writers. As Kathy

Perkins observes, Shirley Graham was until lately identified as the second wife of W.E.B. Du Bois rather than as an author—despite the fact that she was well into her fifties when she married the civil rights leader. Recent attention to Clare Boothe and Lillian Hellman has been to them as public personae; while there is justification for this in Boothe's case, surely Hellman's canon—a dozen original and adapted plays—is far more than a footnote in her career. Telling a woman's story from a woman's point of view seems the surest way to oblivion. C.W.E. Bigsby's three-volume *A Critical Introduction to Twentieth-Century American Drama*, published in the 1980s, does not mention Graham, Boothe, Kanin or Bowles. Childress is discussed briefly in a chapter entitled "Women's Theatre" and Hellman is accorded some two dozen pages, but an entire three-hundred-fifty-page volume is devoted to just three men: Tennessee Williams, Arthur Miller and Edward Albee.

The plays in the present anthology were chosen to show the range and depth of women's contributions to the stage during this thirty-year period as well as for their individual value as works of art and social documents. Collectively they also reveal what audiences and critics were and were not willing to accept. Clare Boothe's *The Women*, Lillian Hellman's *The Little Foxes* and Fay Kanin's *Goodbye, My Fancy* were overwhelming successes on Broadway; *Foxes* and *Fancy* ran more than 400 performances and *The Women* exceeded 600. *The Women* and *Foxes* are frequently revived, and all three have been turned into Hollywood movies. The popularity of these plays is not surprising. The authors are White women who wrote in these works about the middle and upper class strata that constitute the Broadway audience. *The Women* and *Goodbye, My Fancy* are both witty comedies with clever dialogue, and each includes the romantic triangle so beloved of Broadway theater-goers. Hellman's *Little Foxes* is a wonderfully constructed play that engages viewers with its sheer theatricality. Finally, all three contain the kind of substantial female roles—Regina Giddens, Birdie Hubbard, Sylvia Fowler, Mary Haines, Agatha Reed and Grace Woods—that have attracted stars and brought their fans to the box office.

Surely much of the popularity of *The Women* and *The Little Foxes* over the years is a tribute to their theatrical virtues, yet their success is at least partly due to the fact that some critics and audience members believe they have found their own misogyny confirmed in plays by women writers. From a feminist perspective, *The Women* is the most problematic, for protagonist Mary Haines is scarcely a model of independence and intelligence. Moreover, it is easy enough for viewers to conclude—as many have—that Boothe is showing the way women *always* behave rather than revealing how patriarchal capitalism turns them into adversaries who must use their bodies to compete for wealthy husbands. Similarly, *The Little Foxes* is often taken as the parable of a woman who is monstrous because she values money, power and freedom over family. Only in recent years have critics begun to acknowledge the depth of Hellman's analysis of capitalism and the sexism inherent in that system, a system that grants choices to Oscar Hubbard but denies them to his far more capable sister.

Boothe and Hellman, consciously or unconsciously, may have been catering to Broadway tastes by embedding their critique of gender roles in plays that could be "read" in conventional ways. More likely, both women had ambivalent feelings about their own sex, born and raised as they were in a world in which women were meant to be seen and not heard, an ideal to which neither aspired. Hellman in particular was often hardest on characters—White middle class women—who most resembled herself, as if she were angry at them for fulfilling society's expectations. It is easy to look at these plays through 1990s eyes and to wish that Boothe had made it clearer that women are *not* "natural enemies," that Hellman had better understood the dilemmas of the African American servant and the battered woman, that Kanin hadn't felt obligated to have Matt Cole waiting in the wings for Agatha Reed, that Bowles had created less stereotyped Mexican characters. But these plays were written in eras which, in both gender and racial terms, were overwhelmingly conservative. The challenge for contemporary feminist critics is to recognize the many levels on which these works operate, the contexts in which they were written and performed, and the changing relationship between audiences and these plays over the past half century.

All eight dramas look at social problems such as racism, classism and sexism in the various periods in which they were written: the Depression of the 1930s, the war years of the 1940s, and the post-war years. The three Depression-era plays—*Can You Hear Their Voices?*, *The Women* and *The Little Foxes*—are direct or indirect attacks on a system that fails to provide food for starving families and living wages for working women. *Can You Hear Their Voices?* raises particularly interesting questions about social class, alternating scenes between the very rich and very poor to reveal the economic gap at the heart of our supposedly egalitarian nation. *The Women* shows the chasm between working women and the socialites who employ them, while *Little Foxes* moves back to the turn of the century to reveal how those like the Hubbards ("there are Hubbards all over the country," Ben says) got rich by paying starvation wages to Blacks and poor Whites. *It's Morning*, written as the decade was turning, goes back still further to expose the worst aspect of this country's commodity economy: the literal sale of human beings.

World War II is a factor in at least two of these works. *The Mother of Us All* shows that the real revolutionaries have often been women whose most important campaigns were waged off the battlefield. *Goodbye, My Fancy* suggests that the best way to prevent future bloodshed is to make young people, including women, aware of war's human cost. In the post-war period, *In the Summer House* provides an alternative to the idealized view of motherhood promulgated by the popular media. Appropriately the final work in the volume, *Trouble in Mind*, takes to task White American theater and drama—including that by White women—for its long legacy of racism. In Childress' eyes the theater is indeed a mirror of the society that creates and supports it, not only a *medium* for social critique but a valid *subject* of scrutiny.

Like their female predecessors in the theater, nearly all these authors write predominantly about women's lives. The sole exception is *Can You Hear Their Voices?*—based on a short story written by a man—and Flanagan and Clifford's revisions include the addition of two central female characters: Harriet Bageheot and Rose Drdla. In many ways the plays written by women resemble those penned by men in the same period; the failures of capitalism and the moral consequences of war, for example, loom large in such works as Odets' *Waiting for Lefty* (1935) and *Awake and Sing* (1935), as well as Miller's *All My Sons* and *Death of a Salesman* (1949). The angle of vision, however, is often sharply different. As their very titles suggest, Miller's plays cast the battle between varying moral visions in terms of the struggle between fathers and sons, a distinct contrast to works like *The Little Foxes* and *In the Summer House*, where mother-daughter relationships function as both subject and metaphor. The endings of *Awake and Sing* and *Foxes* are similar, but the voice that rings out to challenge capitalist competition is the male voice of Ralph Berger in the former, the female voice of Alexandra Giddens in the latter. Although during this period men could and did create such richly complex female characters as Mary Tyrone in *Long Day's Journey Into Night* (completed 1942; premiered 1957) and Blanche DuBois in Tennessee Williams' *A Streetcar Named Desire* (1947), more common are the passive, devoted wives that people Miller's universe, or the whores and madonnas that inhabit O'Neill's. One would be hard put to find a woman as witty as Boothe's Nancy Blake, as intelligent as Hellman's Regina Giddens, as intriguing as Bowles' Gertrude Eastman Cuevas or as heroic as Graham's Cassie and Childress' Willeta Mayer.

Norris Houghton complained that women's plays present "the safe sentimentality of our relations with Mom or the girl-friend," yet what is remarkable about most of these works is the *absence* of sentimentality concerning women's conventional roles and relationships. Stein's Susan B. Anthony is a single woman who is a founding "mother" of the feminist movement in this country. Regina Giddens in *The Little Foxes* is anything but a dedicated wife and parent, while her sister-in-law Birdie Hubbard admits she loathes her own son even more than she detests her husband. Marriage in *The Women* is largely a financial arrangement leavened with adultery, and most of the characters view children as annoying but obligatory devices for holding on to spouses. *In the Summer House* suggests that husbands are an economically necessary evil, while mothering is presented as a difficult tug-of-war that yields few winners. Skeptical and often acid in their portrayal of the nuclear family, these plays follow in the tradition of such earlier works as Glaspell's *Trifles* (1916) and *The Verge* (1921), Zona Gale's *Miss Lulu Bett* (1920), Sophie Treadwell's *Machinal* (1928) and many of Crothers' comedies and problem dramas. Finally, *Can You Hear Their Voices?* and *It's Morning* acknowledge that even when mothers genuinely love their children, they are often powerless to protect them from being destroyed by poverty or slavery.

Sadly, few of these works can be seen as celebrations of women's friendship. None shows the kind of female alliances that were established—however tentatively—in such earlier works as Glaspell's *Trifles* (1916), Alice Rostetter's *Widow's Veil* (1919) and Georgia Douglas Johnson's *Plumes* (1927); only with the next wave of the Women's Movement in the sixties and seventies would female communities re-emerge as a major motif in American dramatic literature. Rather, these plays imply the necessity of community by exploring how societal forces keep women separated and powerless. The women do aid each other in *Can You Hear Their Voices?* but when starvation threatens, feeding one's own children must eventually take priority over aiding a neighbor. In *It's Morning* Cassie's friends are helpless to prevent the sale of her daughter, and the White plantation mistress' sympathy is useless. Birdie and Regina take opposite responses to their legal and economic impotence in *The*

Little Foxes, while Boothe shows how societally-induced competitiveness keeps women at each other's throats. Like her colleague Wiletta, Childress' Millie Davis resents the demeaning stereotypes of African American women she is compelled to enact. But Millie's desire for the material goods enjoyed by her White counterparts prevents her from joining Wiletta's protest. The nuclear family in *Summer House* isolates adult women from each other and exacerbates the tensions in the mother-daughter bond. Only Gertrude Stein, in the friendship between Susan B. Anthony and Anne (an echo of her own relationship with Alice B. Toklas), and Fay Kanin, in the camaraderie of Agatha and Woody and the cross-generational connection between Agatha and Ginnie, show what support and strength women can get from each other.

To present their critiques of American society, many of these playwrights chose realism, the dominant theatrical style in this country during the first half of this century. *The Women*, *The Little Foxes*, *Goodbye, My Fancy* and *Trouble in Mind* are cast in the realistic mold. British theater scholar Michelene Wandor argues that "historically, artistic movements which seek to represent the experiences of oppressed groups reach initially for a realistic and immediately recognisable clarity." Building on Wandor's comment, Patricia R. Schroeder adds that "Depicting what is can help create what should be." Alice Childress is one of the most vocal supporters of realism because, as she said in a 1993 seminar, "we never got to see ourselves onstage" before African American women took control over their own theatrical portrayals. *Trouble in Mind*, indeed, is *about* realism, about a Black actress' refusal to play a dramatic role that falsifies how "real" Black women conduct their lives. Childress is not demanding precise mimesis but rather is arguing that the theater has a responsibility to be an honest interpretation of our world. Moreover, when Childress' Wiletta finds herself using in conversation precisely the same lines a White male dramatist created for the character she plays in a racist drama, she realizes that life imitates art as much as art imitates life. Not only does she risk becoming the caricature she enacts, but everyone who sees her portrayal—including the very people being caricatured—are in danger of giving it credence, of seeing the world through the distorted filter of racist and sexist theatrical images. Like many of their female colleagues in the theater in the first half of this century, Childress, Boothe, Hellman and Kanin use realism to explore and expose a society with narrowly inscribed gender roles, and (save perhaps in the case of Boothe) to counter the demeaning portraits of "women" typically proffered by male playwrights.

If female dramatists are writing against the societal notion that women have no story—no lives of their own separate from the lives of the men they serve—narrative can be a crucial tool in the project of affirming women's existence. This battle for a story and voice of one's own is a central issue in *The Little Foxes*, where Birdie is literally silenced by her husband. However questionable her goals, Regina is determined to be heard, to shape a scenario for herself beyond the boundaries set by her husband, brothers and the patriarchal society in which she lives. Regina, like Wiletta Mayer, is in many ways a realist playwright.

The remaining plays are in a diverse mixture of styles, countering the accusation that realism is all women *can* write. *It's Morning* fuses a realistic form with such African theatrical elements as music, dance and verse. Shirley Graham is not only telling a new story about slavery, she is telling it in a new way. Hallie Flanagan and Margaret Ellen Clifford's agitprop *Can You Hear Their Voices?* reflects the dramas Flanagan studied during her European travels. *Voices*, with its multi-media presentational format, looks forward to the political works of dramatists like Odets, Bertold Brecht and recent feminist playwrights and performance artists. Jane Bowles' *In the Summer House* is what one reviewer called "naturalistically surrealistic," a type of poetic realism concerned more with symbol than logic, psychology than plot. *The Mother of Us All* more closely approximates realism than do Gertrude Stein's earlier dramatic works. Still, with its use of repetition and verse, its mix of historical and imaginary characters, and its rejection of the linear concept of time, *Mother* is a strikingly original—and contemporary—work. Finally, the notion of story takes on still another dimension in *The Little Foxes*, *It's Morning* and *The Mother of Us All*, three history plays that use a variety of dramatic modes to re-envision the past from fresh angles. In so doing they accord attention to those—Southern White women who chose not to be "belles," enslaved mothers and fighters for women's rights—whose lives have not been included in the traditional definition of "history."

The contemporary relevance of many of these plays, especially the lesser-known ones, is gradually becoming apparent. Only one of Graham's dramatic works was published during her lifetime, but three more have come into print in the last decade. Community, off-off Broadway and university theaters are increasingly performing such Gertrude Stein dramas as *What Happened* and *Three Sisters Who Are Not Sisters* as well as her longer plays. Nineteen ninety-two saw a highly successful revival of *Trouble in Mind* in London, while a 1993 production of *In the Summer House* at New York's Lincoln Center earned several favorable reviews. When she was preparing the *Summer House* revival, director JoAnne Akalaitis noted: "it's amazing the number of people that I have met who saw the original production and remember it. It did not fade from their memory after 40 years."

With the rise of off-Broadway, off-off Broadway and regional theaters, women writing for the stage in the 1960s and 70s enjoyed opportunities their older sisters missed; of the nine dramatists represented here, only Childress has had a playwriting career that extended significantly into this new era. The increase in non-commercial theaters and the new wave of feminism as well as ethnic and racial pride led to an explosion of feminist theaters across the country, most devoted to performing works by women writers and many providing outlets for the growing number of Latina, Asian American and African American playwrights. Fay Kanin said of *Goodbye, My Fancy*, "I've put into my play my feeling that women should never back away from life, and I think that the women who see it are challenged." The dramatists and other women writers who came of age in the sixties and seventies owe a debt to those who preceded them. Poet Judy Grahn has acknowledged Gertrude Stein's influence on her work, scholars have recognized the links between Clare Boothe's and Wendy Wasserstein's comedies, and Alice Childress has been an inspiration for generations of African American playwrights. When Marsha Norman paid tribute to "the power" of Lillian Hellman's voice "to carry down the dark road, the strength of the example she never meant to set," she could well have been referring to any of these playwrights.

SELECTED BIBLIOGRAPHY

Abramson, Doris E. *Negro Playwrights in the American Theatre 1925-1959*. N.Y.: Columbia UP, 1967.

Austin, Gayle. *Feminist Theories for Dramatic Criticism*. Ann Arbor: U. of Michigan P., 1990.

Banner, Lois W. *Women in Modern America: A Brief History*. N.Y.: Harcourt, 1974.

Betsko, Kathleen, and Rachel Koenig. *Interviews with Contemporary Women Playwrights*. N.Y.: Beech Tree Books, 1987.

Brown-Guillory, Elizabeth. *Their Place on the Stage: Black Women Playwrights in America*. N.Y.: Praeger, 1990.

————— ed., *Wines in the Wilderness: Plays by African American Women from the Harlem Renaissance to the Present*. N.Y.: Praeger, 1990.

Chinoy, Helen Krich, and Linda Walsh Jenkins, eds. *Women in American Theatre*. revised and expanded edition. N.Y.: TCG, 1987.

Craig, E. Quita. *Black Drama of the Federal Theatre Era: Beyond the Formal Horizons*. Amherst: U. of Massachusetts P., 1980.

Gatlin, Rochelle. *American Women Since 1945*. Jackson: UP of Mississippi, 1987.

Goldstein, Malcolm. *The Political Stage: American Drama and Theater of the Great Depression*. N.Y.: Oxford UP, 1974.

Hamalian, Leo and James V. Hatch, eds. *The Roots of African American Drama: An Anthology of Early Plays, 1858-1938*. Detroit: Wayne State UP, 1991.

Hartmann, Susan M. *The Home Front and Beyond: American Women in the 1940s*. Boston: Twayne, 1982.

Perkins, Kathy A., ed. *Black Female Playwrights: An Anthology of Plays before 1950*. Bloomington: Indiana UP, 1989.

Schroeder, Patricia R. "Locked Behind the Proscenium: Feminist Strategies in *Getting Out* and *My Sister in This House*," *Modern Drama* 32 (1989): 104-14.

Stephens, Judith L. "Anti-Lynch Plays by African American Women: Race, Gender, and Social Protest in American Drama," *African American Review* 26 (1992): 329-39.

Wandor, Michelene. "Introduction" to *Strike While the Iron is Hot: Three Plays on Sexual Politics*. London: The Journeyman Press, 1980.

Ware, Susan. *Holding Their Own: American Women in the 1930s*. Boston: Twayne, 1982.

Wilkerson, Margaret B., ed. *9 Plays by Black Women*. N.Y.: New American Library, 1986.

Wilson, Garff B. *Three Hundred Years of American Drama and Theatre*. Englewood Cliffs, N.J.: Prentice-Hall, 1973.

CAN YOU HEAR THEIR VOICES?

A play of our time

HALLIE FLANAGAN
and
MARGARET ELLEN CLIFFORD

Based on a story by Whittaker Chambers

First presented in 1931

FOREWORD

Born Hallie Mae Ferguson on August 27, 1889, in South Dakota, Hallie Flanagan grew up mostly in Grinnell, Iowa, where she graduated from Grinnell College. She joined the college's faculty a few years later, already a widow with a family to support. Flanagan's early attempts at playwriting include *The Curtain* (1920), based on a short story she had written years before. A brief melodrama, *The Curtain* revolves around a young girl who must choose between revealing the whereabouts of her father, an escaped convict, or becoming a criminal herself by sheltering him. Although it won a $100 prize in a state playwriting contest it is obviously the work of a novice dramatist, as is *The Garden of Wishes* (ca. 1921-3), a short fantasy about a middle-aged woman who is granted her wish to regain her youthful beauty but decides that her family is more important than her appearance.

In 1923 Flanagan was admitted to George Pierce Baker's famous "47" playwriting workshop at Harvard University, where she served as his assistant and pursued a master's degree. While studying with Baker, Flanagan worked on *Free* (1924). As Joanne Bentley points out in her biography of Flanagan, her stepmother, *Free* consciously borrows the theme of Rachel Crothers' *He and She* (which was revived in 1920) about a talented woman artist who feels unfulfilled in her marriage. Like Crothers' Ann Herford, Flanagan's Gloria is stifled by family life and decides to compete with her husband in a design contest. Unfortunately, Flanagan's treatment of the situation is far more conventional than Crothers': through a series of complicated plot twists, Gloria's design for a new academic building wins support from a group of conservative plutocrats while her husband's more functional blueprint is favored by the liberal elements on campus. By analogy, Gloria's bid for freedom from domesticity ends up looking, ironically, like a reactionary move. We are not surprised when she renounces her career plans, declaring that all she wants out of life is for her husband to kiss her the way her father kisses her mother—the aptly but unsubtly named "Materna." It is unsettling that Flanagan, who herself had already begun a truly extraordinary career, would consistently write plays so traditional in their views of gender roles. Many years later she would work on a script about Margaret Fuller, a drama apparently begun by Nathalie Wolfe (whose name appears on the script along with Flanagan's). Fuller was a writer, editor and friend of the Transcendentalists, and Wolfe and Flanagan create a character who is brilliant, abrasive, adventurous and committed to fighting for important political causes. Still, the play seems less concerned with Fuller's quest for truth and justice than her quest for "a cure that will make me a worthy object of love." Perhaps in her writing Flanagan romanticizes a domesticity that she—first a young widow, later a woman whose career often kept her apart from her son, stepchildren and second husband—never actually knew.

After her studies at Harvard, Flanagan returned to Grinnell briefly, then moved to Vassar as an associate professor. With the help of a strong if backhanded recommendation from Baker—who wrote that she was "as distinguished a woman student as I have ever had in my 47 Workshop, and she holds her own well with the best of the men"—Flanagan became one of the very first women to earn a Guggenheim Grant, which she used to study theater in Europe. She brought back a familiarity with contemporary stagecraft—she had met Vsevolod Meyerhold, Gordon Craig, and Konstantin Stanislavsky, among others—that would have a profound effect on American productions. She was particularly attracted to the "new drama" in Russia, a country to which she returned in 1930; her experiences abroad are recorded in *Shifting Scenes of the Modern European Theatre* and a series of articles she wrote for *Theatre Guild Magazine*. On her return to Vassar she gained wide attention by staging Anton Chekhov's *The Marriage Proposal* three different ways in one evening: realistically, in an abstract expressionist style, and finally using Meyerhold's constructivist ideas on a largely bare stage.

In March 1931 a former student of Flanagan's, Margaret Ellen Clifford, suggested that she read Whittaker Chambers' story about the drought in the March issue of the left-wing *New Masses*. Born in Portland, Maine, on March 16, 1908, Clifford had received a B.A. from Vassar in 1929 and would later earn an M.A. in drama from the University of Chicago. A teacher, director, actor and playwright with a special interest in children's theater—among her works are a dance-drama entitled *The Secret of the Worn-Out Shoes* and a dramatic adaptation of *Sleeping Beauty*—Clifford was then teaching at Briarcliff Junior College. She had just written a glowing tribute to the Vassar Experimental Theater entitled "Vitality at Vassar" for the journal *Progressive Education*.

"Can You Make Out Their Voices," which Flanagan later called "one of the great American short stories," appealed to both her liberal political views and her interest in "agitprop" (agitation and propaganda) theater. According to Flanagan, the two women completed a scenario for a stage version of the story in one night. Flanagan records in her book *Dynamo* that the final version of *Can You Hear Their Voices?* was a group effort, with additional research done by the Vassar library staff and journalism classes. The play was written rapidly and opened at Vassar on May 2, 1931, just two months after the story's publication. Students, male faculty and townspeople comprised the cast. *Voices* was clearly influenced by the theater Flanagan had seen in the Soviet Union; one Vassar student described the performance as "very stylized," with the action "played on a ramp winding around a pillar with a platform at the top." The drama was presented without an intermission; lighting was used to indicate scene changes, while statistics and newspaper reports were flashed on a screen onstage and placed throughout the lobby. The reviewer for *Theatre Guild Magazine* observed that "the conviction, not the illusion, of reality was aimed at."

Can You Hear Their Voices? received remarkable attention for a college production. The reviewer for the *New Masses*, in which the original story had appeared, called it "the best play of revolutionary interest produced in this country" and added, "written in a college, about farmers, it's a swell play for workers groups." Such groups, the reviewer noted, could obtain the play "free from royalties" (colleges and little theaters were charged a small fee). A letter to the *New York Times* praised the play as "a searing, biting, smashing piece of propaganda." A brief commentary in the July issue of *Theatre Guild Magazine* similarly characterized *Voices* as a "frankly propandist play...[that] deeply moved its audiences." Reviewing the published version, *Theatre Arts Monthly* concluded that *"Can You Hear Their Voices?* is a good play, of important native material, well characterized, handling experimental technical material skillfully, worth any theatre's attention—amateur or professional."

Not everyone, of course, would be pleased by a work so overtly political and theatrically experimental. Although Flanagan insisted that nobody involved with the creation of *Voices* considered it "radical," the conservative press did. Ironically, equally strong objections came from the left, particularly the Communist press which, according to theater historian Malcolm Goldstein, was initially hostile to what may be the first American agitprop drama written by individuals who were not members of the Party. Whittaker Chambers' original story is clearly a work of Communist propaganda; the Party is mentioned more frequently in the story than in the play, and it is evident that for Chambers Communism is the solution to poverty, hunger and inequity. (Many years later Chambers would confess to being a Communist courier and spy, thereby launching the career of Richard Nixon, whose pursuit of Alger Hiss, Chambers' alleged accomplice, catapulted him into the political spotlight.) *Can You Hear Their Voices?*, by contrast, is a liberal cautionary tale: if a democratic government fails to help the poor, then it will be responsible for the rise of Communism and possibly even armed revolution. True democracy is the court of first resort. A. Saks, writing in *Worker's Theatre* magazine in January 1932, complained that "Flanagan and Clifford mutilated the class line of the story and adapted it into play form with a clear liberal ideology." He was particularly incensed about the addition of Harriet Bageheot, a debutante who does not appear in Chambers' story. Nevertheless, the following year the editor of *Worker's Theatre* wrote to Flanagan that he was recommending *Voices* to workers theatre groups and requested five copies of the script. And Ben Blake, the historian of the radical theater movement, conceded that *Voices* "was a shot heard 'round the world" which had "created a sensation in the American little theatre by its courageous and forthright portrayal of a harsh truth in a realm that had been given too much to meaningless or saccharine trifles."

Flanagan records that *Can You Hear Their Voices?* was performed by, among others, the Hedgerow Theatre in Pennsylvania, Smith College, farmers in North Dakota, Black groups in Cleveland, and The Vineyard Shore School for Women Workers in Industry. A group in Vancouver asked permission to rewrite the drama to focus on "the pitiable conditions of many" Canadian farmers; when *Voices* was published, copies were ordered by theaters from Finland to Australia. In a 1933 letter to Henry R. Luce, sent for the purpose of interesting *Fortune* magazine in doing an article on Vassar's Experimental Theatre, Flanagan wrote that *Voices* "has been done by groups as radical as the Artef and the Los Angeles Left Theatre, [and] by groups as conservative as the Old South Church in Boston; it has been mounted on trucks, acted by irate farmers and sent though the back regions of Arkansas, Iowa and Missouri." Her argument, however, failed to impress the conservative Luce.

Can You Hear Their Voices? follows Chambers' tale of a group of starving farmers, led by Communist Jim Wardell, who take matters into their own hands to get food for their families. In both versions a young woman, Hilda, chooses desperate action rather than see her baby starve to death, and both center on battles between farmers and the rich Purcell, who buys up the foreclosed homesteads. Chambers' prescience is particularly striking, for "Can You Make Out Their Voices" is a remarkably early look at the plight of farmers suffering from drought and the Depression, problems that continued to worsen. (John Steinbeck's *The Grapes of Wrath* would not be published for another eight years.) The magazine story was illustrated with cartoons, including President Herbert Hoover in a wagon with the caption "Peddling the Same Old Junk" and a rich employer who takes pity on the jobless by firing his shop workers and offering to hire new ones—at less than half the dismissed men's salaries.

But if much of the power (and the dialogue) of Flanagan and Clifford's play comes from the original source, itself based on actual incidents, the changes they wrought and the way they shaped the material into dramatic form are crucial. Statistics about unemployment and crop losses were flashed on screens, and the play's major events were set at Christmas-time, to deepen the situation's poignancy. Flanagan and Clifford deleted some scenes that would add little to the drama's message, including a physical fight between a starving farm woman and the local Red Cross agent. Other omissions may have sharpened the focus at the expense of narrowing it, for Chambers briefly explored ethnic issues through a homeless Mexican family scorned by most of the local people as alien "greasers" but welcomed by Wardell, who believes that all human beings deserve adequate food and shelter.

Flanagan and Clifford's initial audience for *Can You Hear Their Voices?* was the Vassar community, and they clearly shaped Chambers' original to appeal to these viewers in terms of gender, class and age. Flanagan herself once remarked that the play "portrayed a situation in our country about which college students should know something and do something." The playwrights added the character of Rose, a young woman of Russian origin who is a leader of the protest and in constant conflict with her father, a believer in the government's hollow promises of help. Rose is quick to identify and reject the sexual harassment of the capitalist boss Purcell—"You keep your hands off me, you hear?" she warns him—and preaches both communal gardens and direct action. While the play as a whole does not support Rose's penchant for violence, it does present her raid on the Red Cross office as a necessary action to try to get food for starving children—an action both militant and maternal.

The most obvious new element introduced by Flanagan and Clifford is Harriet Bageheot, whose lavish coming-out party is set against the suffering of the farm families. Congressman Bageheot plays only a tiny role in Chambers' story and Harriet is wholly the playwrights' invention. In the two scenes they created, the Congressman throws a party—ostensibly for his daughter—that costs more than a quarter of a million dollars while the farmworkers can't raise pennies for milk. (Note how casually the Congressman regards the laws of the land: champagne and liquor flow freely despite Prohibition.) Malcolm Goldstein convincingly argues that Bageheot and Wardell "engage in a kind of tug-of-war, with democracy as the fraying rope between them." Still, the Congressman with his trickle-down economic theories—the extravagant gala, he insists, will "keep money in circulation"—is a cardboard villain. Harriet, though scarcely drawn in depth, is considerably more complex. Failing to note the irony of dieting while others are starving, she nevertheless chastises her father's handling of the drought and declares that "Well, personally, if I saw a guy starving I'd rush headlong for a loaf of bread." Harriet echoes Wardell's claim that most people "come into communism... because they can't stand to see the folks they care about go hungry," adding that her coming-out party will surely send the poor into the arms of the Communists. Finally, like Rose she disdains the sexism that is rampant in a country run by "a body of wise, elder men." When the Congressman reveals that he sent her to college not to be educated but to become a lady, she asserts that she is not "left over from the last century" and that, far from being enthralled by the coming-out party, she is appalled by the prospect of being handled and mauled "like a bag of meal."

While Harriet is hardly an exemplary figure—her speech on the horror of the drought is delivered while she is drunk—Flanagan and Clifford give her the play's rallying cry: "Well! We're the educated classes! We're the strength of the nation! What're we going to do about it? What are we going to do about the drought?" Harriet's father will do no more than "appoint an investigating committee," so it is up to young people like her to take direct action. Through Harriet, Flanagan and Clifford wrote their audience into the play, a technique typical of agitprop drama. According to Flanagan's account in *Dynamo* the tactic was successful in arousing Vassar students, who "collected clothes, medical supplies, and money" for the relief of starving farmers and wrote editorials and letters to lawmakers about the problem.

Thematically and stylistically, *Can You Hear Their Voices?* owes a debt to the theater Flanagan had seen in Europe, a political theater just beginning to take root in the United States (Clifford Odets' *Waiting for Lefty* premiered nearly four years later). Flanagan wrote in *Shifting Scenes* that in Russia "the stage...will not be painted or decorated either, but will be constructed by elements of reality from everyday life"—a prescription she followed in the staging of *Voices*. She was also heavily influenced by certain Russian presentations that functioned as "newspapers" for those who could not read. In fact, with its use of slides to provide factual information, quick sketching rather than full development of characters, and reliance on numerous short scenes, *Can You Hear Their Voices?* employs many of the "alienation" techniques that would later come to be identified with the plays of Bertold Brecht. In true agitprop fashion the work both incorporates the audience within it (in the character of Harriet) and ends with a question directed straight at viewers: "These boys [Wardell's sons] are symbols of thousands of our people who are turning somewhere for leaders. Will it be to the educated minority?"

While *Can You Hear Their Voices?* began its journey from Vassar around the world (one of its most popular productions was by the Shanghai People's Theater) its authors moved on in their theatrical careers. Margaret Ellen Clifford founded a children's theater in Portland, Maine, and eventually joined the faculty of Skidmore College, where she served as chair and professor of theater from 1952 until her death in 1971. The last production she directed— during brief furloughs from her hospital bed—was the work of one of America's first woman playwrights, Anna Cora Mowatt's *Fashion*. Hallie Flanagan continued her interest in political theater with productions at Vassar of *We Demand*, a drama about unemployment, and a work entitled *Miners on Strike*, before being tapped in 1935 to head the largest and most important theatrical experiment this country has ever seen: The Federal Theatre Project.

The Federal Theatre Project, a division of the government's Works Project Administration, was primarily designed to employ the legions of theater workers made jobless by the Depression. During confirmation hearings, one senator argued that although there was "no lady in America of higher character than Mrs. Flanagan," the program needed "someone with old-fashioned commonsense rather than some college professor." Flanagan was confirmed anyway, and went on to lead the Project until its dissolution in 1939. In *Arena*, her account of these years, Flanagan wrote that the plays performed under Federal Theatre auspices "showed...the struggle of many different kinds of people to understand the natural, social, and economic forces around them and to achieve through these forces a better life for more people"— a statement that aptly characterizes *Can You Hear Their Voices?* as well. Among the most popular and controversial productions were the "living newspapers," multi-media presentations on such social and political issues as unemployment, syphilis and the exploitation of cotton pickers. Clearly descendants of *Can You Hear Their Voices?*, as Flanagan points out in *Dynamo*, the living newspapers also employed short self-contained scenes, simply drawn characters, factual material and questions aimed directly at audiences. They effectively couched serious issues in an entertaining format while employing large numbers of jobless performers and technical personnel.

As head of the Federal Theatre, Hallie Flanagan oversaw all productions, approved play selections, edited the newsletter and on occasion even painted sets. She weathered a great deal of criticism. Over the four years of its existence, the Project came under increasing attacks from conservatives alarmed by the political content of many of the productions. (They also professed to be concerned about the salaciousness of the works, inferring from the title that Susan Glaspell and George Cram Cook's *Suppressed Desires*, a spoof on Freudianism, was a pornographic play unsuitable for production with government funds.) Flanagan herself was often the subject of these attacks. Once criticized by Communists for *failing* to make *Can You Hear Their Voices?* a Communist tract, Flanagan now found herself pilloried in the press as a "WPA RED" who used the Federal Theatre Project as her forum. Despite her valiant battle against the infamous House Un-American Activities Committee, ignorance and prejudice won: funding for the Federal Theatre Project was terminated.

Flanagan returned to Vassar, then moved on to Smith College, where she served as dean of the college and professor of theater until 1955. She worked on a number of unfinished plays—including her Margaret Fuller drama—during this period, but her strengths continued to be as a director and teacher rather than a dramatist. One of the few works she did complete was a living newspaper, similar to *Can You Hear Their Voices?*, written "with the assistance of" graduate student Sylvia Gassel and Professor Day Tuttle. *E=mc²* (1947), first performed at Smith, traces the history of the atom from its mention in ancient texts through the advent of atomic fission. Flanagan and her co-authors draw heavily on popular magazines and scientific reports to imagine beneficial uses for the atom as well as a possible nuclear holocaust. While much of *E=mc²* seems naive today, the authors' distrust of the motives of power brokers—including the military, politicians, and academics—still rings true.

Flanagan died in a nursing home July 23, 1969; according to Joanne Bentley she was haunted in her later years by memories of her interrogation by the House Un-American Activities Committee. Like many of her colleagues in the thirties, Flanagan knew the power of theater to teach and inspire audiences—a credo that underlies her work as a director, administrator, professor and playwright. Although her canon of plays is small and uneven, her influence on the American theater was and is immense. In *Can You Hear Their Voices?* Hallie Flanagan and Margaret Ellen Clifford fuse theatrical innovation with social conscience to produce a vital dramatic work about poverty and inequity that remains relevant more than half a century later.

SELECTED BIBLIOGRAPHY

Bentley, Joanne. *Hallie Flanagan: A Life in the American Theatre.* N.Y.: Knopf, 1988.

Buttitta, Tony and Barry Witham. *Uncle Sam Presents: A Memoir of the Federal Theatre, 1935-1939.* Philadelphia: U. of Pennsylvania P., 1982.

Clifford, Margaret Ellen. "Vitality at Vassar." *Progressive Education,* VIII (January 1931): 81-4.

Craig, E. Quita. *Black Drama of the Federal Theatre Era: Beyond the Formal Horizons.* Amherst: U. of Massachusetts P., 1980.

Flanagan, Hallie. *Arena.* N.Y.: Duell, Sloan and Pearce, 1940.

————. *The Curtain.* N.Y.: Samuel French, 1923.

————. *Dynamo.* N.Y.: Duell, Sloan and Pearce, 1943.

————. *Shifting Scenes of the Modern European Theatre.* N.Y.: Coward-McCann, 1928.

Flanagan, Hallie. Assisted by Sylvia Gassel and Day Tuttle. *E=mc²: A Living Newspaper about the Atomic Age.* N.Y.: Samuel French, 1948.

Goldstein, Malcolm. *The Political Stage: American Drama and Theater of the Great Depression.* N.Y.: Oxford UP, 1974.

Mathews, Jane DeHart. *The Federal Theatre, 1935-1939: Plays, Relief, and Politics.* Princeton: Princeton UP, 1967.

PEOPLE IN THE PLAY

JIM WARDELL
ANN WARDELL
JOHN WARDELL
SAM WARDELL
MORT DAVIS
SHAY
DRDLA
ROSE DRDLA
DOSCHER
MRS. DOSCHER
BEN DOSCHER
FRANK FRANCIS
HILDA FRANCIS
MARTIN
MRS. MARTIN
MARY MARTIN
PURCELL
RED CROSS WORKER
REPRESENTATIVE BAGEHEOT
HARRIET BAGEHEOT
BILL
FIRST BOY
FIRST GIRL
SECOND BOY
SECOND GIRL
THIRD BOY
THIRD GIRL
FOURTH BOY
FOURTH GIRL
A SENATOR
DOWAGERS
A YOUNG ATTACHÉ
A PAINTED WOMAN
A SECOND SENATOR
A FOREIGN AMBASSADOR

The action of the play takes place on a simple stage construction consisting of two pillars and a flight of circular steps joined by a sloping ramp to a crude doorway and the wall of a house set on a strong diagonal line.

Suggesting power and security on one side of the stage and weakness and poverty on the other, the construction affords playing space for scenes from two totally different worlds existing in juxtaposition but in mutual isolation.

When the audience enters the theatre the construction is lighted. Thereafter shafts of light are directed upon that portion of the stage which best suggests the scene in progress.

The seven scenes, interspersed occasionally with screen projections, are played without a curtain and with no intermission.

By this simplification realism is discarded and reality gained.

Scene I In the drought area, late August, 1930, outside Wardell's house.

Scene II In Washington, late autumn. The breakfast room of Representative Bageheot.

Scene III Frank's kitchen, late autumn.

Scene IV An alcove off the ballroom of the Arden Park Hotel in Washington, Christmas Eve.

Scene V Frank's kitchen, Christmas Eve.

Scene VI Outside the local Red Cross Bureau, dawn of Christmas Day.

Scene VII Outside Wardell's house, Christmas night.

When the audience is seated, the stage lights and auditorium lights dim out, and the screen is lowered to position in darkness.

Slide 1
CAN YOU HEAR THEIR VOICES?

Slide 2
A Play of our time, based on a story by Whittaker Chambers in the *New Masses* for March, 1931; also on material appearing in the *Congressional Record, Time, The Literary Digest, The New Republic, The Nation, The Christian Century,* and *The New York Times.*

Every episode in the play is factual.

Slide 3
Colonel Arthur Woods, Chairman of the President's Emergency Committee for Unemployment, reports to the Appropriations Committee of the Senate:

Total number of totally unemployed
persons in the United States .... 4-5 millions
Approximate number of persons
affected by unemployment .... 25 millions

Of the $2,500,000 to be expended for "Public or private construction" to aid this situation, 40% is still in the plan or contract stage. Machinery is set in operation, but in the meantime people are starving.

Slide 4
No nation has successfully solved the problem of the relation between agriculture and industry.

For ten years American farmers have been growing more and more desperate. The drought of 1930 coincided with the greatest business depression in our history. It made all agricultural problems acute. It demanded immediate measures for relief.

Slide 5
Among the worst sufferers were the farmers of Arkansas, Mississippi, Tennessee, Kentucky, Virginia and the Carolinas. Through these regions the drought stunted the corn, dried the alfalfa, and burned up the kitchen gardens. On August 8 the Department of Agriculture made a preliminary report showing that

1,000,000 farm families were seriously affected. On August 1, 1930 the Department of Agriculture reported a decrease of 690,000,000 bushels in the corn crop up to August 1.

Streams, wells, and ponds went dry. Mules and cattle starved in the fields. Over a hundred banks failed. 250,000,000 people were destitute.

SCENE I

The lights reveal the exterior of Wardell's house. On the steps is FRANK FRANCIS, *a young farmer, slightly built, with a sensitive face. Leaning against the porch post is* DAVIS, *an older farmer.* ANN WARDELL, *wife of Jim Wardell, is standing in the doorway.*

FRANK: It's like a fire. Everything burns up. Nothin' for the cattle to eat.

DAVIS: (*With a drawl*) It's all on account of the sun. Ever notice it up there, Frank? Warms the earth, makes the farmer's crops grow, ripens the apple on the bough! Just now it looks like a red-hot silver cartwheel. Better take a look at it—it's the only cartwheel you'll see this year.

FRANK: My cow died this morning.

ANN: That's the third right around here this week. But you tell Hilda she ain't to worry about milk—we got plenty.

FRANK: That's awful kind of you, Mrs. Wardell.

DAVIS: The water'll go like the corn and the alfalfa. If there's anything left, that'll go too.

FRANK: By the time the snow comes we'll starve.

DAVIS: You got your gun, ain't you?

FRANK: Oh, you mean huntin'?

DAVIS: Yeah, I mean huntin', all right.

(WARDELL, *a quiet man with a kindly, humorous face and a suggestion of latent power, appears in the doorway.*)

DAVIS: Hello, Jim. Just come over to hear the speech over the radio.

WARDELL: Hello, Mort. 'Lo, Frank. Where's the rest of the boys?

DAVIS: They'll be along, glad of an excuse. Don't know what we'd do without the radio.

WARDELL: Best investment the crowd of us ever made.

FRANK: With all the crops burned up there's nothin' to do but sit around and listen to the radio.

(*The two* WARDELL BOYS *have come around the house at the mention of the radio.* JOHN *is fourteen, a strong, sturdy looking boy.* SAM *is twelve, slight and rather frail looking.*)

SAM: We got Tyrone on the radio the other night, Frank.

JOHN: See the rattlesnake I killed, Mr. Davis? It's around here.

WARDELL: Shows what the drought's done. Snakes never come down out of the hills.

ANN: I remember when Purcell started his mines up there, the men drove the snakes down, but when he closed the mines they went back again.

DAVIS: Funny they stayed down here when Purcell was in the hills. I sh'd think Purcell must be right at home with snakes.

(DAVIS *and* WARDELL *laugh.*)

FRANK: What's wrong with Purcell? Nothin' wrong with Purcell. He's the big man in this town all right. I mean beyond he's a little hard-fisted.

DAVIS: You've only been here a year, Frank. You're a newcomer yet.

(*A balalaika is heard offstage.*)

That'll be Drdla. He's taken to playin' his queer Russian fiddle. Makes Rose mad as anything.

SAM: I like it. Why does it make Rose mad?

DAVIS: Well, Sam, Drdla is an old fashioned Russian and his daughter is a new Russian an' that seems to make quite a lot of difference nowadays.

(DRDLA, *a tall, fine looking Russian, enters with his daughter,* ROSE, *a handsome girl of about eighteen. With them are* SHAY, *a young man, and* DOSCHER, *a rather plaintive looking man of middle age.*)

SHAY: 'Lo Jim. 'Lo Mort. Mornin', Mrs. Wardell.

ROSE: Heard you boys killed a rattler. My, ain't he a big one!

DOSCHER: Dead rattler's news these days.

ROSE: 'Lo Mrs. Wardell. We have it pretty easy now, ain't we? Nothin' to do but sit around. Where's Hilda, Frank?

FRANK: Tried to get her to bring the baby and come on over to listen to the radio.

ROSE: She's awful pretty with the baby, Frank. Like to hear her singin' to it.

FRANK: She ain't singin' much these days.

(*He goes back to the bench,* ROSE *with him, and the men gather around the snake, talking about the drought.* DRDLA *approaches* ANN *with a courtesy foreign to the other men.*)

DRDLA: Good day. God bless you. The others talk. I play.

ANN: (*Smiling*) You know I like you music better'n their talk.

(DRDLA *sits down and plays his balalaika softly through the ensuing scene.*)

DOSCHER: How long this weather goin' to last, Davis?

DAVIS: The papers don't tell you. They say there's hope.

SHAY: They've been sayin' that a long time. Besides, it don't make any difference now if it does rain. The corn's done for.

DOSCHER: What do you think, Davis, will the government help us?

DAVIS: What do you think the government'll do for you? Do you think you're the only poor farmer in the country? They's 100,000 of us, remember.

SHAY: I need cheerin', John. How about tunin' in on something?

JOHN: Sure. (*He goes into the house.*)

DOSCHER: The banks'll have to give us some kind of loans.

WARDELL: The banks are just as bad off as we are.

SHAY: If the cows keep on dyin' they'll have to do something about milk.

FRANK: What about winter comin'? What are we goin' to do if there ain't any food? How we goin' to feed the babies?

DAVIS: Anyway, Frank, your cow's dead; you've got one less mouth to feed.

(*The men laugh.*)

ROSE: Aw, that ain't funny!

FRANK: A dead cow ain't no joke.

(*The men laugh again.*)

WARDELL: Well, the government ain't going to do anything, if you want to know. At least not until it's too late.

(*At this minute the radio, after some preliminary static, gets under way with jazz.*)

DAVIS: Well, music! Ain't this gay?

SHAY: Feel like dancin', Rose?

ROSE: No. I'm gonna sit this out.

DAVIS: Try W. G. P. U.

JOHN: (*Appearing at the door*) There's gonna be a talk on farm relief.

WARDELL: Well, I don't know any better place to turn that talk on.

DAVIS: Yes, I feel just like a good, heartnin' talk on farm relief.

(*Through the ensuing scene* DOSCHER *and* DRDLA *listen as if to divine wisdom;* SHAY, FRANK, *and* ANN *eagerly, wanting to believe;* ROSE *skeptically;* WARDELL *and* DAVIS *with frank disbelief.*)

RADIO: Ladies and gentlemen of the radio audience: this program comes to you through the courtesy of U. S. Purse and Co., Fancy Groceries. Ladies and gentlemen, have you ever experienced that hollow feeling that comes over you in the middle of the morning?

DAVIS: Well, I hadn't thought of puttin' it just that way.

RADIO: When that happens, go to the frigidaire and select from your store of Purse's delicacies a crisp hors d'oeuvre or a bottle of U. S. Purse's sparkling fruit punch.

SHAY: Rose, just trot in to the frigidaire and bring me a crisp er derv.

(*Everybody laughs.*)

RADIO: This morning we have a great treat for our radio audience. The fifth of the series of farm-relief talks will be given to you by Mr. Wilton Wordsworth of the business school of Carver University.

DAVIS: This is a treat!

RADIO: Mr. Wordsworth.

(*Another voice says*)
Thank you, Mr. Smythe.

RADIO: Ladies and gentlemen of my radio audience: on this bright, sunny morning it seems malapropos to discuss so sad a subject as the great drought which is affecting our southern farmers. Yet so closely woven is the fabric of American life that what affects one affects all.

(DAVIS *spits.*)
But we cannot allow ourselves to be caught in these crucial days by a feeling of panic.

(SHAY *rubs his stomach.*)

DAVIS: A feelin' of panic, Shay?

RADIO: We must remember the old adage that it is always darkest before dawn. We are now, it is true, on the ebb tide, but the rising tide is gathering even as we speak: has not our Chief Executive recently said that he will call into conference on drought relief the governors of twelve western states?

DAVIS: Well, well.

RADIO: As our great national leader has well said: "Our problems are the problems of growth, not the problems of decay. The fundamental assets of the nation, the education, intelligence, virility, and spiritual strength of our 120,000,000 people have been unimpaired."

WARDELL: Anyway, Davis, we're unimpaired.

RADIO: Although on the surface it seems a curious paradox, is it not true, as our leading economists are pointing out, that the drought is really a blessing in disguise?

DAVIS: Well, I'm blessed.

ROSE: Guess we don't know when we're well off.

RADIO: How is it a blessing, my friends? It has done away with over-production in the rural areas.

WARDELL: It has done away with everything in the rural areas.

RADIO: It has sent up the price of corn on the stock exchange.

DAVIS: Did you clean up much on your last deal on the stock exchange, Wardell?

RADIO: What, after all, my friends, is a brief period of depression, in the history of our vast cavalcade of progress? After each depression of the past—and such depressions are only normal my friends, have we not risen to a new high tide of prosperity? Prosperity is on the way! Let our motto be BUY NOW—

ROSE: Turn that damn thing off!

(JOHN *goes in and the radio stops.*)

DOSCHER: Anyway, he's got a real nice voice.

(*Everybody laughs.*)

WARDELL: I used to wish I could get a good education for my boys but this speech consoles me some.

SHAY: (*Returning to the subject uppermost in the minds of all*) Well, whatever Mr. Wilton Wordsworth says over the radio, I notice they're stoppin' credit at the stores in town.

WARDELL: Think they'd give it all through the winter? To all of us? They've got to make a livin' too.

DOSCHER: You mean there ain't goin' to be nothin' to eat?

WARDELL: There's plenty to eat in the stores in town. All you've gotta have is the money to buy it.

DAVIS: You can eat like a hog—if you're a storekeeper. We only grow the food—they sell it.

WARDELL: But as I haven't got the money to buy and neither have you—

FRANK: We'll starve.

DAVIS: Or take it.

(*There is a moment's silence. They are slow to get this. A shocked look comes slowly over their faces.*)

SHAY: (*In an alarmed voice*) You mean you'd steal it?

DAVIS: I mean that when I'm hungry I like to eat. And when my wife and kids are hungry, I'm likely to take food. If that's stealin', then you can say I like to steal.

(*There is a silence.*)

FRANK: (*Militantly*) Well, I'll be goin' along.

(*He starts off, then turns and looks fixedly at* DAVIS *and* WARDELL.)

And I think all of us better be goin' along and not listenin' to this kind of talk.

SHAY: Frank's right. Come along, Doscher.

DOSCHER: Sure he's right.

(*They start out.*)

DAVIS: You're young, Frank. I felt that way once.

DOSCHER: Whose car is that?

DAVIS: Well, it's no farmer's tin lizzie.

SHAY: It's Purcell. What's the boss doin' down here?

DRDLA: He don't like us to stand around and talk.

DAVIS: Probably get out an injunction against our lookin' at a dead rattlesnake.

SHAY: It's his war trainin' makes him like that. Once a colonel always a colonel.

(PURCELL, *a heavy, prosperous-looking man, comes over to the group which opens slowly.* FRANK, SHAY, DOSCHER *and* DRDLA *nod in somewhat awed and embarrassed greeting.*)

PURCELL: Well, boys, what's this? A meetin'?

DAVIS: Wardell's John killed a rattler in front of the house. The folks came over to see what a dead snake looks like. You like to see?

(PURCELL *walks up to the snake and looks at it idly. On the way he sees* ROSE.)

PURCELL: Well, Rose, gettin' to be a mighty fine lookin' girl, ain't you?

(*He runs his hand down her arm.*)

ROSE: (*Dangerously*) You keep your hands off me, you hear?

PURCELL: Spunk, eh?

(*He winks at the men.*)

I like spunk in horses and women. Well boys—

(*He strolls over to* JOHN *and draws him down-stage.*)

Nice work, John. When you see a snake, kill him. Ain't that right, Frank?

FRANK: (*Pleased at attention from the great man*) That's right.

WARDELL: (*Meaningly*) The drouth killed it—like everything else.

PURCELL: This drought has been a lucky break for you, Wardell. You were runnin' low on your line of trouble talk when the drought—or "drouth" as you call it—(*He winks companionably at the men*) came along.

ANN: We'll call it what we like. It's our babies are dyin'.

WARDELL: (*Facing* PURCELL *and speaking quietly*) Some of us call it drouth, and some of us call it drought, but we all mean the same thing—we mean that the crops are done for, water and forage are dried up, the cattle are dyin', the banks are on the rocks. We mean we'll be needin' food when our credit gives out at the stores in town.

SHAY: You ought to be able to do something about that, Purcell, bein' President of the bank, and all.

PURCELL: (*Turning from* WARDELL *and keeping his good temper with an effort*) I realize you fellows are up against it. All of us are, for the matter of that.

(WARDELL *laughs and turns away.*)

We all have to stick it out together. To do you justice none of you ain't done much whinin' except Wardell here. The trouble with Wardell is that he spends too much time nights readin' those books he has in the house, and lookin' up the words in the dictionary. So he gets sleepy and sore at the world, don't you, Jim?

(*The two* BOYS *glower and draw closer to their father. The rest of the group relaxes its tension and smiles, being let in on a secret by the big boss. All except* ROSE *and* DAVIS *draw toward* PURCELL *and away from the little group on the porch.*)

PURCELL: "Socialism, Utopian and Scientific." (*He laughs.*) Well, every man's got a right to read what he wants in his own house, I guess—if he don't try to force others to think his crazy ways too. (*He starts off, then turns back to them.*) If you get hungry, boys, and he tries to feed you Socialism, Yewtopian and Scientific, and you don't feel full, and I guess you won't, I think the Red Cross will do more for you.

DOSCHER: But the Red Cross won't help you unless you're starvin'.

PURCELL: Well, you wouldn't want to take help unless you were starvin', would you? None of us would. Well, so long, boys. So long, Jim. (*He waves and goes off.*)

(*The men emerge from their speechlessness and say: "The Red Cross." "They did fine work in the Mississippi flood—The Red*

Cross!—maybe the Red Cross'll help us out!")

WARDELL: (*Facing them suddenly*) So! You're goin' to ask for charity?

DOSCHER: Rather take charity than steal.

DRDLA: Always there has been rich and poor. The rich must help the poor. That's the way things are.

ROSE: The way things are don't make 'em right!

SHAY: Charity—hell! We gotta right to live, ain't we?

WARDELL: Think it's goin' to get you any further in your right to live to let the Red Cross hand you out a plate of beans?

SHAY: (*Coming up and facing* WARDELL *antagonistically*) Well, what would you do?

WARDELL: Probably just what you'd do—take the beans. But first I'd like to try to make the government see—

DAVIS: Make the government see—don't make me laugh!

WARDELL: (*Turning from* DAVIS *and facing the crowd*) Then I'd like to try to make you see, all of you, that it ain't charity we want. It's justice. Where's the justice in the Red Cross buyin' Purcell's grain and milk and dealin' it out to us as charity?

DAVIS: It belongs to us, anyway.

SHAY: Whaddaya mean, it belongs to us?

WARDELL: Didn't Purcell make all his money off of us? Hasn't he gone on year after year gettin' richer on the work we do for him? Hasn't he bought up mortgages on our farms and then foreclosed when we couldn't make payments?

DAVIS: We produce and he eats.

FRANK: It ain't no good talkin' against Purcell. He's a smart man—he made this town—and he's hit by the depression just the same as anybody else.

DAVIS: Oh, he is, is he? Well, he yaps a lot about it, but I notice it don't affect the car he drives, the clothes he wears, or the food he eats. Maybe he had to take a few of his securities out of the bank—that'd be just too bad!

FRANK: Well, it's no good you and Wardell gettin' off any of your Socialistic talk here—what you want us to do? Have a revolution, like in Russia?

WARDELL: No, Frank, that's just what Davis and I want to prevent.

DAVIS: Speak for yourself, Jim.

(*Everyone in the group starts and looks at* DAVIS. *The two* WARDELL BOYS, *who have been listening eagerly to all the discussion, draw toward their father.*)

SHAY: You mean you want a revolution?

DAVIS: I ain't sure I wouldn't just as leave die by violent as by natural causes.

DRDLA: What did the revolution do for Russia? Once people laughed in the fields. Everyone was gay. Now, people are hungry there. No one laughs any more.

ROSE: (*Fiercely*) I don't notice any of us splittin' our sides laughin'!

ANN: (*Motions indignantly to the boys, who come to her.*) Well there's one thing I'm sure of. I don't want Sam or John to grow up in this kind of mess. I don't want 'em to be where we are.

SHAY: They're smart boys, Mrs. Wardell. They might get to where Purcell is.

WARDELL: I don't want 'em to get where Purcell is.

ANN: They ain't goin' to get nowhere through this kind of talk! This is the United States of America we live in, and we got a President and a Congress and a government to look after our interests, and I want my boys should respect that government and know that that government ain't goin' to let us down! (*She goes into the house, taking the two boys. There is a pause.*)

SHAY: Your wife's right. We're just shootin' off our faces. We're all right.

DOSCHER: Sure we're all right. We got plenty of beans.

ROSE: Beans!

DRDLA: We're better off than if we had a revolution.

FRANK: Yes, Mrs. Wardell's right. The government won't let anything happen.

DAVIS: This is only August, Frank. Wait till January and see how you feel. Ever notice strikes and revolutions usually break out in winter time?

BLACK OUT

SCENE II

The lights go up revealing CONGRESSMAN BAGEHEOT's *breakfast room. The Congressman is an attractive gentleman past middle age. He has finished breakfast and is absorbing the morning* Times. HARRIET, *his daughter, home from college for a weekend, enters. She is a clean-cut, good-looking young woman who, in the manner of her generation, covers most of her convictions and ideas with a mask of flippancy.*

HARRIET: Good morning, darling. How are you this morning? Up late last night filibustering? Where's Mother?

CONGRESSMAN: She's having her tray. What do you want, my dear?

HARRIET: I want two tremendous fried eggs immediately. I'm going to conquer a young man at golf this morning. What I'm having, however, is orange juice. Must do what we can for the figure. (*She picks up the newspaper and scans the headlines.*) H'm. Jimmie Walker again. One wing of the Fisher Body plant turned into a flop-house for the destitute. (*She looks off into the distance.*) That's not bad. "Bodies by Fisher." How respectable the *New York Times* is. Couldn't you start taking a few tabloids, Father—at least while I'm home for the weekend? Vice investigation continues—more drought suffering. Why don't they do something about the drought, Father?

CONGRESSMAN: (*Tolerantly*) What should you suggest doing, my dear? The bishops have prayed for rain, I believe.

HARRIET: I mean seriously, Father. The Red Cross is a fine, upstanding institution. Why don't you give it a break? If you'll excuse my saying so, the members of the respected body which you adorn are doing as fine a job as I've ever seen done in my life, of parking on their tails and doing absolutely nothing.

CONGRESSMAN: I'll excuse your saying so, my dear, because you don't know what you're talking about. Congress is a body of wise, elder men who have the country's good primarily at heart. It's true we're in the grip of a severe crisis, but just for that reason we have to proceed with caution. We can't rush headlong into things.

HARRIET: Well, personally, if I saw a guy starving I'd rush headlong for a loaf of bread.

CONGRESSMAN: Don't bother your pretty head about it, dear. It takes an economist to understand a crisis as wide in its national import as the drought.

HARRIET: They've got more sense in Russia. When the farmers go on the rocks there, they've got something solidly back of them—they don't have to sit around for the Red Cross to dish them out charity.

CONGRESSMAN: My dear child, what do you know about Russia? Who's been talking to you?

HARRIET: Come out of the fog, old dear. I'm one of the country's educated women. I go to college. I take a course in government and one in charities and corrections.

CONGRESSMAN: College professors—impractical dreamers! Can't even secure an adequate living wage. What do you think they know about world affairs?

HARRIET: I thought it showed a lovely spirit in a young woman to try to get the low-down on what the great ones of her father's profession were doing.

CONGRESSMAN: But my dear child, I didn't send you to college to acquire biased, radical ideas about Russia and collective farming.

HARRIET: (*With a delightful smile but an edge of steel in her voice*) What did you send me for, darling?

CONGRESSMAN: Why, why—that is—of course—I wanted you to have the best education that money could buy. I wanted you to be as beautiful and cultured as your mother is—so that you could do the same credit to your—social position and family, and my name—or your husband's name—that your mother has always done.

HARRIET: You mean you wanted me to learn to be a lady?

CONGRESSMAN: Exactly.

HARRIET: They don't have those any more, dear. If that's what you wanted you should have sent me to one of those emporiums of culture for young ladies. There are a few of them, I believe, left over from the last century, tucked away in the hills.

CONGRESSMAN: Harriet!

HARRIET: I'll never be an ornament to society, Father. You might as well give up the idea now. By the way, speaking of ornaments to society, Mother said I was to chat with you about this burst of glory we're having on Christmas Eve, to introduce me to society.

CONGRESSMAN: (*Expanding with pride*) Yes! Well! Your mother and I have talked a good deal about it, and I told her I wanted to talk to you about it a little.

HARRIET: Sounds like a carnival, from what Mother said. It's very white of you, Father.

CONGRESSMAN: Well, my dear, we wanted our little girl to have the best of everything. Of course it's going to be rather expensive—those things get more and more expensive as people give more and more of them.

HARRIET: How much?

CONGRESSMAN: Well, I haven't figured exactly—I should say—upwards of two hundred and fifty thousand dollars.

HARRIET: Good God, where does it all go? I'm only a simple college girl.

CONGRESSMAN: We have been extremely fortunate in securing the Arden Park Hotel for that night and the services of Mr. Joseph Durban.

HARRIET: Durban? What's this going to be—a musical show? Doesn't the Arden Park satisfy you?

CONGRESSMAN: As a hotel, yes. On this occasion, no. Mr. Durban is going to do it over for your party, a temporary redesigning of the whole lower floor in silver and black. Then your Mother will dress in black shot with silver, and you in silver shot with black.

HARRIET: Shot with black—God!

CONGRESSMAN: Mr. Durban sent the designs yesterday. I thought them a little extreme, but your mother liked them, and as she pointed out, I don't understand these things as she does.

HARRIET: Strikes me I'm nothing but the corpse.

CONGRESSMAN: You don't seem particularly pleased, Harriet. It isn't the attitude I should have expected from a young woman who is having everything done for her.

HARRIET: Well, frankly, I'm not turning handsprings. What do I get out of it? This Durban guy for a preposterous sum of money turns the lower floor of the Arden Park Hotel into a night club; you and Mother glad-hand around with the legislative body and wives; there are pools of champagne in the corners and bathtubs full of hard liquor in the hall; attachés neck debutantes in the foyer; thousands of Harvard and Yale freshmen get drunk and I have to hold up one after another when they dance with me; a few horrid old fat men snuffle amorously down my neck; I get pulled and hauled and slapped on the back, and tossed from hand to hand like a bag of meal; somebody spills gin on my new dress and everybody steps on my feet, and what with too much liquor and caterer's lobster eaten at two in the morning, I'm sick the next day. Personally, the whole thing almost completely feeds me up.

CONGRESSMAN: But my dear, I thought you liked parties. You like to dance, don't you?

HARRIET: Sure, I love to dance. But you don't call that free-for-all, dancing, do you? I like cocktails, too, but I know when to stop, which is more than you can say for most of your friends. I like to go places with some of my friends, and I like to dance and I like to drink, and I like a little love-making—nicely done. But this organizing everything on an automobile factory basis—big business in the debutante world—I don't think it's so hot. Sorry to seem unappreciative, but I thought I'd better let you see how I felt before you went ahead and blew yourself on this Roman orgy.

CONGRESSMAN: I'm frank to say, Harriet, I'm very much surprised. I had hoped we were giving you something you would appreciate—would always remember. I understood from your mother that a girl's coming-out party was something she looked forward to all her girlhood, and treasured the memory of all her life—like her wedding day. Why your mother has a scrap book with all the clippings relating to her coming-out party in it. She had more flowers than any debutante in town ever had.

HARRIET: Mother came out in 1900, Father. An introduction to society meant an introduction to society, then. But I've smoked and drunk and necked with these same boys for five years—or others just like them. Where's the kick?

CONGRESSMAN: But, my dear, society demands of people in our position a certain formality, a certain duty in the graces of living...

HARRIET: The three graces—drinking, cursing, and necking...

CONGRESSMAN: (*Rising, outraged*) I'm very sorry, Harriet. If I had realized how you felt about it I should never have gone ahead with it. I'm frank to admit that your attitude still seems quite incomprehensible to me. I feel worried about the education you are getting. It's expensive enough, heaven knows. I should be disturbed if I thought that all you were getting out of it was to become maladjusted to the life you were born to. But to get back to the question of the party—considering your peculiarly unsympathetic attitude I should throw the whole thing over, but we can't—on account of your mother. She's importing a musical comedy troupe from New York by airplane. She's set her heart on it. Why, she gets almost as much pleasure out of it as if it were her coming-out party. We couldn't disappoint her like that.

HARRIET: Allowing for differences in phraseology, that's exactly what she said about you.

CONGRESSMAN: What? Oh, well, yes—doubtless she doesn't admit it to herself.

HARRIET: (*Facing him, putting her hands on his shoulder, and looking squarely at him*) Look here, Father, if I have to set this in bigger type I will—doesn't it seem a little incongruous to be giving parties with the country in the state it is? With people standing in bread lines and dying of hunger? I don't suppose 250 thousand would be anything but a drop in the bucket, but it ought to feed a mouth here and there. Sounds like Louis XVI at Versailles to me.

CONGRESSMAN: On the contrary, my child, this is just another case of your inability to understand these great economic problems. While this depression affects us all, I feel that it would be selfish to retrench—the thing to do is to keep money in circulation—

Black Out

In the darkness the screen is lowered to position and the following slides projected:

Slide 6

In the meantime, between August and November, the President's State Committees on Drought Relief were investigating. On October 20th they recommended to both Congressional Committees on Agriculture a $60,000,000 appropriation for farm loans. The Senate passed the bill, but the House Committee cut it to $30,000,000.

Slide 7

From early December until Christmas, Congress wrangled with the Administration as to the amount of money needed and its disposition. Should the money be loaned for tools, seed, fertilizer—or should it include food for farmers?

Slide 8

The Senate insisted that since the money was a loan to farmers it should be used when necessary to keep them alive. The President, backed by a majority in the House, maintained that the money should not be used for food because this would constitute a dole. The farmers said, "Millions for mules but not a cent for humans."

In darkness the screen is raised.

SCENE III

The interior of Frank's kitchen. Evening late in autumn. HILDA, *Frank's wife, a slight girl of about twenty, is pacing up and down with the baby in her arms.* FRANK *comes in and sits down. He puts his head in his hands.* HILDA *stands motionless with the baby in her arms. She looks at the baby, then at* FRANK, *turns and puts the baby down in the bunk, crosses to* FRANK *and stands by him awkwardly.*

HILDA: *(Touching his shoulder)* Don't. *(He turns and puts his arms about her, and buries his head against her. They lean against each other and cry without making much sound. Then she wipes the back of her hand across her eyes and goes back to the bunk.* FRANK *gets control of himself. After a while she speaks.)* Did you stop at Wardell's for the milk?

FRANK: Wardell'll be over with it after a while.

HILDA: You don't like Wardell, do you Frank?

FRANK: Wardell's a trouble maker, Hilda.

HILDA: He's kept the baby alive, 'till now.

FRANK: I'm afraid of Wardell. I'm afraid of all these queer ideas he's got. It was easy enough to answer all the things he said in the summer. Things weren't so bad then—we could sit around and listen to the radio. Now we ain't got that no more, there's nobody to tell us everything's alright and the government is going to help us out. It's hard to think straight when you're hungry. *(There is a knock and* WARDELL *comes in.)*

HILDA: Did you bring the milk, Mr. Wardell? *(*WARDELL *slowly shakes his head "no."* HILDA *makes a frightened movement toward* FRANK. WARDELL *goes up to* FRANK.)*

WARDELL: Don't you think the time is comin', Frank, when poor farmers—people like you and me, and the Martins, and Doscher, and Drdla, will have to go and take the food and milk out of the store windows? There's plenty of it there.

FRANK: That's communism you're talkin' about.

WARDELL: Right now communism means free groceries to all poor farmers. No rent for two years, free seed, free milk for babies.

FRANK: You Reds want everything free. (WARDELL *looks at them pityingly, then speaks with gravity.*)

WARDELL: You will, too, before the baby's dead.

HILDA: Frank!

WARDELL: I know what I'm tellin' him, Hilda. We're both tenant farmers. Both came from the same class, so there's no reproach in you takin' something from me when you need it. And there's no reproach meant in my tellin' you that your kid would be dead but for your gettin' the milk from my cow. You couldn't buy it—not from me—I wouldn't sell it to you—we need it too bad ourselves—and you couldn't buy it from Purcell because he would sell it to you, and you haven't the money to buy it. Well, my cow's dead. Now what do you think about having milk free?

FRANK: (*Dully*) Dead?

HILDA: (*In a panic*) What are we going to do?

WARDELL: Some people come into communism through their minds and others through their bellies, but I guess most of 'em come in because they can't stand to see the folks they care about go hungry. (*At this moment the door opens and MRS. WARDELL comes in, followed by SAM and JOHN. She is excited and breathing rapidly. She looks defiant. Three women are with her: ROSE, MRS. DOSCHER, a frightened, little woman, middle-aged, and MRS. MARTIN, a tall, raw-boned woman with a gaunt face. MARY MARTIN, seven years old, and two smaller Martin children huddle near the door.*)

ANN: We got you some milk after all, Hilda.

HILDA: Milk! God bless you, Mrs. Wardell.

MRS. MARTIN: Let's have a look at the baby.

MARY MARTIN: Yes, can we see the baby? (*The women go over and look at the baby and exchange glances.*)

ANN: A funny God that brings babies into the world and takes away their mothers' milk and kills the cows that feed them.

WARDELL: (*To ANN*) You bought milk at Purcell's.

ANN: Yes!

WARDELL: (*Quietly*) You got to stop. We ain't got the money. You got to think of your own boys.

SAM: We don't care, Pa.

JOHN: No, we ain't hungry.

ANN: You can't let a baby die. (WARDELL *goes out without looking around.* FRANK *gets up slowly and goes after him.* SAM *and* JOHN *follow the men. The women and the little girls are left with* HILDA *and the baby.*)

MRS. MARTIN: Does the baby cry much?

HILDA: No. (*There is a pause.*)

MRS. DOSCHER: Well, they say there's folks up the creek that's worse off than us.

ROSE: (*With a hard laugh*) That make you feel any better, Mrs. Doscher? Well, it don't me. It don't seem to cheer me none, to think there's folks yonder in the woods eatin' roots.

MRS. DOSCHER: The thing I mind most is not havin' anything to do. Usually I'm cannin' way into November.

ROSE: I'll bet Purcell's cellar's full of fruit and vegetables. He had enough to get water from outside. If we was all, Purcell and all, workin' together on one big farm, like in Russia, we could a kept our gardens goin'. We could a kept our cows alive.

ANN: This ain't Russia. I been listenin' to this communist talk ever since I married Jim and it ain't never got us nowhere. The ideas of it are all right in some foreign country, but we got a government back of us.

MRS. DOSCHER: Men get a lot of comfort out of talkin' and it don't do them no harm.

ANN: It don't do us no good.

ROSE: (*In a hard voice*) So you're goin' to let Hilda's baby die? (*There is a startled silence.* MRS. DOSCHER *goes over and touches* HILDA *protectingly.*)

MRS. MARTIN: What can we do?

ROSE: We can take the men's guns and we can go to Purcell's, and take the milk. (*There is a silence. The women draw back startled.*)

ANN: (*After a pause*) I ain't goin'. I'd go without milk myself to give it to Hilda and I'd spend the last cent I got to buy it for her, but I ain't goin' to do nothing against the government! (ANN *goes out.*)

MRS. MARTIN: (*Looking at her children*) I'll come with you, Rose. (*She takes the children and goes out.*)

MRS. DOSCHER: Well, I won't go. What do you think I am, a thief?

ROSE: Lend me your husband's gun then, will you? Our farms are too near together. I can't stand hearin' your kids whine themselves to death. (MRS. DOSCHER *starts to cry and goes out.* ROSE *goes out.* HILDA, *left alone, stands motionless. Then she goes over, takes the gun from behind the door and goes out.)*

FADE OUT

SCENE IV

An alcove off the ballroom of the Arden Park Hotel in Washington, Christmas Eve. A flight of steps leads down from the ballroom. Silver and black. Artificiality. Jazz and high laughter. Girls' voices. The actors playing in this scene, as in the breakfast scene, should remember that they represent the upper classes. They should interpret the vulgarity of the lines with staccato brilliance. Four couples dance the climax of "Tiger Rag," ending in a whirl. They go off clapping. Boys and girls walk on lighting cigarettes.

FIRST GIRL: It seems it was one of those parties where everybody jumps into the swimming pool with evening clothes on at five o'clock in the morning. Pool was strung with lanterns. Harriet said it was like animals led to the slaughter, and besides, she had on a new dress, and she was damned if she'd ruin it, what with the depression and all.

FIRST BOY: She's a high grade moron, but she's damn funny.

FIRST GIRL: What more do you want? She gives the town something to talk about, anyway, and that's a godsend—
(The music starts "You're Driving Me Crazy." They dance off. Another couple comes on dancing. The boy sings with the music.)

SECOND BOY: "My love for you makes everything hazy—" *(They stop and indulge in a violent embrace. They emerge.)*

SECOND GIRL: *(Very blasé)* My God, my feet are tired! *(She kicks off her shoes. They walk wearily over to the steps, sit down and embrace again. Enter another couple dancing.)*

THIRD BOY: Can't you Garbo-Gilbert somewhere else, children?

THIRD GIRL: Love may make things hazy for you, but we're all too clear headed.
(The two on the steps uncoil languidly.)

SECOND BOY: May I suggest that the champagne is right around the corner. Possibly that would help you?

THIRD BOY: *(Fastidiously)* Speak to your girl friend, Lemuel. She takes things too seriously. My dear young lady, do you have to take off your shoes when you neck?

(*The* THIRD BOY AND GIRL *go off. The* SECOND BOY AND
GIRL—*the embracing ones—straighten up, and the* BOY *lights the*
GIRL *a cigarette. She strolls over in time to the music and steps into
her slippers.*)

SECOND BOY: (*Listening to the music*) They're playing "Sweet and
Hot"—that music calls me, Genevieve.

SECOND GIRL: (*Composedly*) Sir, you've been drinking. The name is
Katharine.

SECOND BOY: (*Holding her off and looking at her*) Oh, well, you never
can tell, can you? (*They start to dance.*) I've always had a bad
memory for names. Katharine. It's written in fire on my
heart.

SECOND GIRL: Written in lipstick on your shirt-front's more to the
point.

(*They dance off. Enter two* DOWAGERS *with a* SENATOR, *the latter slightly tippled.*)

FIRST DOWAGER: I was saying to Mrs. Harkness, Senator—you'd
never know she was Clarissa Bageheot's daughter.

SENATOR: S'a very pretty girl.

FIRST DOWAGER: Yes, but so reckless. A sort of brazen look. Same
hair as Clarissa's, same eyes—but the expression—I don't
know what it is.

MRS. HARKNESS: I know what it is. It's too much drinking, if you
ask me.

SENATOR: S'a very pretty girl, but she'll never be the girl her mother was.

FIRST DOWAGER: I should think the old senator, Clarissa's father,
must be turning in his grave. I wanted to slap her painted
little face, and tell her she comes of some of the best blood in
the country.

MRS. HARKNESS: And she behaves like a common street woman.

SENATOR: Take it from a man that knows horses, Mrs. Randall—
you can overbreed any stock.

(*They go off. Another dance starts and other people stroll on. A*
SENATOR *and an* AMBASSADOR *enter.*)

SENATOR: Can you look at this scene, my friend, and doubt the
prosperity of these United States?

AMBASSADOR: Yes, it is easy to shorten a dress, but not quite so
easy to make it long. (*He points to the dancers.*) They must be
prosperous to wipe the dust from the floor.

SENATOR: Where in this scene can you find the germs of revolution?

AMBASSADOR: You are right. It is as safe from revolution here as in my own country—in Spain. (*They go off.*)
(*Enter a* PAINTED WOMAN *with a strident voice, speaking to a* YOUNG ATTACHÉ.)
PAINTED WOMAN: Had the most awful day—Young Tom Farrel wanted me to have tea with him.
YOUNG ATTACHÉ: Farrel has all the luck.
PAINTED WOMAN: I told him I had a full day's work to get this aged frame ready for public inspection. I was three hours at the hair dresser's alone—talk about keeping body and soul together—I never have time to get as far as the soul!
YOUNG ATTACHÉ: It's not your soul I'm interested in, darling— let's dance.
PAINTED WOMAN: Oh, you wicked boy!
(*They dance off to the music of "Mood Indigo" which continues through the following scene.* HARRIET *enters, dancing with a boy named* BILL.)
HARRIET: God! (*She sinks down on the steps.*)
BILL: I say, Harriet, why doesn't this barrage of elderly white elephants go home? They ought to be in bed. They've been blocking the traffic too long. I've had my elbow in three women's hair.
HARRIET: I've had my hand in four men's mouths.
BILL: Cigarette?
HARRIET: I think a drink would set me up more.
(*He goes out for a drink.* HARRIET *closes her eyes and proceeds to take a short nap.* BILL *comes back with a silver pitcher of champagne. She comes to and takes it.*)
HARRIET: A pitcher, b' God! (*She drinks.*) I feel better. I feel that I am rapidly becoming drunk, and that I shall rapidly become drunker. (BILL *has sunk, exhausted, onto the steps and is gloomily regarding his legs stuck out straight in front of him.*)
BILL: At this time of the night you have to be drunk or you go to sleep. I usually go to sleep anyway. Being drunk makes it easier.
HARRIET: (*Sentimentally*) We could have gone to a movie tonight, Bill.
BILL: And if we wanted to stay up all night we could have done it privately in a speak-easy or romantically on a hillside.
HARRIET: And if anyone thinks I get any pleasure out of screaming into the leering faces of my mother's girlhood friends, they're

crazy. I could have bitten the lorgnettes off the hatchet-face of that old Mrs. Harkness and chewed them up and swallowed them and never even felt it.

BILL: That's because your stomach's lined with good, hard liquor, dear.

HARRIET: Every Bageheot is either a gourmand or a drunkard, and I have to keep thin so I can wear this kind of dress. I wouldn't be surprised if I just dropped this dress somewhere. I have to keep checking up on myself to make sure it's still with me.

BILL: (*Still regarding his legs gloomily*) I don't think I'd notice if it fell off, myself.

HARRIET: (*Her tone changing as she listens to the waves of shrill laughter from the ballroom*) Sometimes I get so fed up on this stuff I could scream. (*Flippant and hard again*) William, I'm afraid I'm going to have one of those scenes where the poor little rich girl bares her heart to the thoughtless young man who does not understand. I'm going to tell you I wish I were a fish-wife—that you should marry me and we could go to Abyssinia and raise cockle-shells and start all over again—

BILL: Well, it's an interesting version of the old tale. I might ask the orchestra to put on "The Little Things in Life." (*He starts to rise.*)

HARRIET: Don't bother. Or I might be a revolutionary—I look well in red—I might be pretty fascinating with a red flag around my brows and my arms thrust through an Internationale— what is an Internationale, Bill?

BILL: I don't know. Going Bolshevik, huh?

HARRIET: (*Bitterly*) Yeah. Parlor Bolshevik. (*As the music and drunken laughter reach a climax*) Well, if we want the country to go Communist, carrying on stampedes like this one—(*She waves her cigarette towards the ballroom.*)—is the quickest and surest way to do it. If I were a dirt farmer, or a dirt farmer's woman, I know which side I'd be on. (*The orchestra starts to play "Hello Beautiful." The* CONGRESSMAN *enters.*) Well, let's get back to the carnage. Aha, here's the pillar of the State himself. Your health, Pillar!

CONGRESSMAN: Harriet, must you drink like a road-laborer? Really, my dear, at your own party. People are talking—

HARRIET: My, that must be a change.

CONGRESSMAN: It's one thing to take a quiet, ladylike cocktail, but champagne in pitchers—it's perverted!

HARRIET: Come, Father, when did you ever take a quiet, ladylike cocktail? The only reason you never drank champagne in pitchers is because you never thought of it. No, sir, you forget that this is something I've looked forward to all my girlhood, and am going to remember for the rest of my life! And boy, so is everyone else! (*Another dance is over. People begin to come back. Couples One, Two and Three come in, also the* PAINTED WOMAN *and the* YOUNG ATTACHÉ. *A boy calls off-stage,* "*Paging Congressman Bageheot.*" "*Telephone—Long Distance— Congressman Bageheot.*" *The* CONGRESSMAN *goes out. There is a burst of laughter in the group around* HARRIET *who is on the steps. Somebody cries:* "*Speech! Speech!*" *She looks bewildered for a moment and then says*) Drink, please! (*They shout approval and hand her the silver pitcher. She holds it in one hand during the following.*) Listen! I've got something to tell you. Come here, everybody! (*She is quite drunk now. They all gather around shouting,* "*Speech! Speech!*")

FIRST BOY: It's an announcement.

BILL: Who's the lucky man, Harriet?

HARRIET: No, there's nothing tender about this. I want to tell you something important. I want to tell you about the drought. (*One of the men snatches the pitcher and drinks.*)

EVERYONE: Hurrah! The drought! Is there a drought?

HARRIET: (*Under the stress of terrific excitement*) There's a drought— In the United States—In the South. It's a terrible thing—It's killing the crops—It's making people hungry—It's making people thirsty—And you know what it is to be thirsty, my children! (*Chorus of groans and cries of,* "*Give the girl a drink! Let's all have a drink!*" HARRIET *leaps to the top step and her voice crashes through their drunken laughter.*) Well! We're the educated classes! We're the strength of the nation! What're we going to do about it? What're we going to do about the drought?

(*There is a moment of complete silence, then renewed hysteria. Everybody shouts,* "*Down with the drought!*" *The orchestra begins* "*Just a Gigolo.*" *The lights dim to a flood of scarlet. Everyone except* HARRIET *begins to dance. She stands motionless, looking down at them. The jazz is muted and the dancers posture in strange, grotesque positions. Above the jazz a telephone conversation is heard.*)

(*The* CONGRESSMAN'*s voice comes from the general region of the ball scene, and the* GOVERNOR'*s from the other side of the stage.*)

CONGRESSMAN: Hello! Hello! Yes, this is October 1-9-1-7—yes, this is Congressman Bageheot.

GOVERNOR: This is the Governor speaking—Governor Lee.

CONGRESSMAN: Oh, yes, Governor.

GOVERNOR: I'm sorry to disturb you, Bageheot, but the fact is we're having some difficulty here. Central! Central! What's the matter with this connection? Why can't you give me a clear wire? Bageheot!

CONGRESSMAN: Yes.

GOVERNOR: That's better. I say we've had some trouble with the farmers. Because of the drought, you know—and the bank failures.

CONGRESSMAN: Oh, yes, the drought.

GOVERNOR: There's a good deal of talk about communism. A man named Wardell is something of a trouble maker.

CONGRESSMAN: (*Exploding*) A cheap demagogue! Trading on the sufferings of these poor farmers. They always come to the front at times like this.

GOVERNOR: He's just one of a good many in different districts. Even a very little relief—

CONGRESSMAN: What's that? Isn't your local Red Cross functioning?

GOVERNOR: It seems to be tied with orders from higher up.

CONGRESSMAN: (*Coldly*) Well, you know, Governor, I'm opposed to the dole. A few of our Senators seem willing to sacrifice principle to expediency, but I am not one of them. I am opposed to the dole. You know the situation in the House— you know where the President stands. The Red Cross exists to take care of just such situations.

GOVERNOR: Well, I don't want to be responsible—

CONGRESSMAN: (*With irritation*) You really think it's serious, then? Well, I'll see what can be done. I'll appoint an investigating committee tomorrow. I'll send a notice to the press. Now if that's everything I'll ring off now. (*Self-consciously*) It's rather a gala night for us here.

GOVERNOR: Oh, yes—your daughter—Mrs. Lee and I were so sorry—Please present my compliments—

CONGRESSMAN: Thank you, Governor, thank you. How is it down there—cold as it is here?

GOVERNOR: (*His voice receding and dying*) Yes, very cold. We're having snow—(*His voice dies away at the same moment that the dancing figures fade out.*)

FADE OUT

SCENE V

Frank's kitchen, Christmas Eve. The scene opens in darkness. There is a woman's scream, instantly suppressed. Dim figures are revealed in the darkness; HILDA *standing, and* FRANK *lying on the bench. Their movements cast gigantic shadows on the wall.*

FRANK: (*Startled*) What is it, Hil?

HILDA: (*Tonelessly*) Baby's dead.

FRANK: (*In terror*) No. (*He leaps up. He listens for its breathing.*) I'll get someone—I'll get the doctor.

HILDA: What's the use of the doctor? He won't come now.

FRANK: He will!

HILDA: You can't get him in time.

FRANK: I'll go. I'll run.

HILDA: How can you run two miles through all this snow? You haven't even got shoes.

FRANK: I must go.

HILDA: (*With finality*) Don't go. I know she's dead. (*She faces him fiercely.*) What do we mean bringin' a baby into the world when we can't even take care of it? What did we get married for? Folks like us haven't got no right to get married and have kids. (FRANK *sits down at the table and sobs.* HILDA *looks at him and laughs hysterically.* FRANK, *goaded almost to madness, springs to his feet.*)

FRANK: Wardell killed her. She's never been right since he stopped the milk on her. The dirty, lousy Red! He did it! He killed her!

HILDA: Don't be a fool. He gave us the milk as long as his cow lived. And his wife bought milk for her as long as the money held out. She got us milk as long as there was any to get. Now there ain't none. I been to the Red Cross all day long. They say maybe tomorrow. Tomorrow!

FRANK: Then Purcell killed her—that's it. He moved all his cows where he could get more money for the milk. He killed her!

Somebody killed her—God curse 'em!

HILDA: Don't be a fool. I killed her myself. Do you think I wanted to see her tortured to death by inches? I killed her—with the blanket.

(FRANK *shudders away from her.*)

BLACK OUT

SCENE VI

Dawn of Christmas Day outside the local Red Cross Bureau. FRANK *is standing, motionless, gun in hand. He is hard and desperate looking. All traces of boyishness are gone.* WARDELL *comes in right, followed by* DAVIS, SHAY, DRDLA, DOSCHER, ROSE, MRS. DOSCHER, MRS. WARDELL, *the two* BOYS, *and about ten others. They crowd about the entrance and there is confused talk.* ROSE, *in the center of the group, going from one to another, is easily seen to be leading the women.*

WARDELL: (*Speaking off-stage where there is a confused sound of voices*) No need your all comin'—a few of us can handle this! Then we'll all be needed to go to the stores. (*He turns to the group.*) I'm glad to see they're so few of us here.

ROSE: The rest are afraid, the cowards—

WARDELL: It means that only the most reliable and the most needy are here. It means that we can move together easier and have more confidence in each other.

DAVIS: We need a little confidence in something.

WARDELL: Frank, you've decided to come in with us?

FRANK: (*In a hard tone*) I'm in with you.

WARDELL: Good.

ANN: How's the baby, Frank?

FRANK: The baby's—better.

WARDELL: I'm glad you women have brought your babies with you. It's another sign that you're not afraid, and it means that we'll not lose sight of why we're here and what we've decided to do, and why we're movin' from here on the town.

(*There is a murmur, partly of opposition.*)

DRDLA: (*Shaking his head*) There'll be trouble.

ROSE: (*Scornfully*) Go home if you're afraid.

WARDELL: (*His voice gaining firmness*) Because we're movin' on the town next. We're starvin' and we're goin' to the town to get food.

(*At this moment* ANN *forces her way fiercely through the crowd, drawing the* BOYS *with her. She faces* ROSE *and* WARDELL.)

ANN: But first we're goin' to give the Red Cross another chance to help us out!

WARDELL: Best you should keep out of this, Ann. We're here to take the food.

ANN: I say we're givin' the Red Cross one more chance—

ROSE: And you know how they're takin' that chance, Ann Wardell! You know Purcell promised us Red Cross help way back in August and here it is Christmas Day. Christmas Day! You know we been hangin' round here for three weeks signin' blanks to get a mean little drizzle of beans and bread.

DOSCHER: Well, we ain't as bad off as they are in factory towns at that. Look at Detroit.

MRS. DOSCHER: The Red Cross doin' the best they can.

(ROSE *laughs*.)

WARDELL: You're right, Ann, it ain't the fault of the Red Cross; they got to take orders from higher up. But no matter whose fault it is, we've stopped askin'. From now on, we're takin'.

ANN: I say we're givin' the Red Cross one more chance.

ROSE: (*Laughs*.) One more chance! That's a good one! All the kids in this town got rickets and all the sick and old folks has died, and you talk about one more chance. Well, I'll tell you how they'll take their chance. First they'll ask us to prove that we're not impostors. That's what they're callin' some of us now. They'll tell us to prove that we're starvin'. (*She laughs*.) Well, can you prove it?

(*The murmur throughout the crowd grows to an ominous roar.*)

Then when we've proved we're starvin', I'll tell you what they'll give us.

ANN: How do you know what they'll give us?

ROSE: How do I know? Because I ain't got no way of tellin' what's going to happen except by lookin' at what has! What have they give us in the past? One loaf of bread, not one apiece, but one to a family—one bag of flour—same! Maybe some bacon.

MRS. MARTIN: How much milk?

ROSE: Enough for two days.

MRS. MARTIN: What good does two days do? We had a day's before and we made it last three. Now if they give us two days' and we make it last five, what'll we do when it's gone?

ROSE: It's the same with all relief.

WARDELL: It's the same with all charity.

FRANK: (*Menacingly*) We don't want charity.

ROSE: There's food enough in here and in the stores in town to last till spring. The thing to do is to force them to give it to us. How many of you got guns?

(*Murmurs from the crowd, some excited, some in opposition.*)

DAVIS: We got guns and we know how to use 'em.

DRDLA: Rose—Rose...

WARDELL: Wait a minute, Rose. Wait a minute, Mort. You've got to be careful not to use your guns unless somebody starts shootin' at you first.

ROSE: (*Enraged*) There you go, Jim Wardell—tellin' 'em to be careful when what we ought to do is put some guts in 'em.

ANN: We don't want shootin'!

DAVIS: This ain't no time to be careful.

WARDELL: I'll tell you why we got to be careful. If we start fightin' they can call in the police and we'll be outnumbered ten to one, and those of us that ain't killed that way—they can shoot us, you see, because they'd be "in defense of their duty"—will land in the pen—and our children will be hungry just the same—but there'll be nobody to get 'em food.

ROSE: (*Still angry*) You're yellow, Jim Wardell! If I could put a bullet through Purcell I'd go to jail happy!

(*Some of the men shout approval.*)

WARDELL: (*His voice lashing the whole crowd into attention*) Don't you see, Rose, it ain't Purcell that's wrong. It's the plan we live under: it's the whole system. Listen! Maybe I think, like you, that there'll come a time when there'll be shootin'. But today ain't the time. Maybe there'll come a time when we can stand our feet like free men instead of crawlin' on our bellies askin' for help. But that time ain't come yet. Some of us believe in a time comin' when everybody will have to work, and there'll be enough work for everybody. Some of us believe that the land and the crops and the cattle and the factories belong to the men that work 'em. But we ain't strong enough yet to take 'em. And that's why some of us think it's more important to work for that time than to shoot up a few rich guys now.

(*At this moment there is a murmur in the crowd off-stage.* PURCELL *comes through the crowd with a woman, a* RED CROSS WORKER, *who has a kind, troubled face. The crowd makes way for her respectfully, but regards* PURCELL *with suspicion.*)

PURCELL: Another meetin', I see. Wardell, you've taken strong to public speaking, ain't you?

(WARDELL *looks at him, does not reply, does not retreat.*)

RED CROSS WORKER: You're here early, Mrs. Doscher. Good morning, Mrs. Wardell.

(*The women murmur, "Good morning." There is a dead silence as* PURCELL *and the* WOMAN *go up and unlock the door.*)

PURCELL: (*Turning and facing the crowd*) I'm glad to see you're behaving in an orderly way. Everything will be attended to if you just keep quiet and decent. (*They go in and shut the door.*)

ROSE: Quiet and decent! Starve and be quiet and decent about it or you'll go to jail and rot!

(PURCELL *opens the door and appears with a paper in his hand.*)

PURCELL: I've got the names of those who signed blanks yesterday and didn't get food because it gave out before we got to 'em. (*Reading*) Rose Drdla—wouldn't forget you, Rose—

ROSE: Bah!

(*The men murmur ominously as* PURCELL *continues to read.*) Frank Francis, Jim Wardell, Higgins, Carrillo, Gombos, Wells, Sitka—that's all for today.

CROWD: What's that? How about us? We'll sign blanks!

WARDELL: What you mean, Purcell? We're ready to sign blanks.

PURCELL: (*Nervously*) Now I got to ask you to cooperate with us in this. You see—

ROSE: Don't you tell us the food's give out. We know it ain't!

PURCELL: No, the food ain't give out. But the blanks have.

(*A moment's silence.*)

WARDELL: Just what do you mean, Purcell?

PURCELL: You know we got orders not to give out food to anyone who doesn't sign a blank for it. Well, all the blanks have run out and I can't give out no more food until a new lot of blanks come from Washington.

(*A stunned silence*)

ROSE: Well, what do you say to that, Ann Wardell?

SHAY: When'll the blanks get here?

PURCELL: Well, we can't tell. Maybe by tomorrow.

ROSE: And you think we're going to sit around and sing hymns till then, do you? We came here for food.

DAVIS: Yes, and we're takin' what we came for.

WARDELL: What you givin' us?

(*The men surge up around* PURCELL.)

PURCELL: I don't know that we're goin' to give you anything. At least till you put those guns down. I'm chairman of the Red Cross and I'm not takin' orders here. I'm givin' 'em.

(*The men laugh and their laughter is not pleasant to hear.*)

You'll get food when the blanks come and not a second sooner. This place is closed. Get out! (*He goes in and bangs the door.*)

ROSE: Closed! The hell it is! (*She turns to the mob.*) Did you say your kids was dyin'? Come on!

(*Gun in hand she throws herself against the door.* WARDELL *and* DAVIS *are with her. Most of the men and women surge after her shouting.* ANN *tries to hold the two boys back but they follow their father.* DRDLA *remains wringing his hands. The door gives and the crowd rushes in and there is a struggle. The Red Cross worker emerges. She looks ill and frightened, and* PURCELL, *his coat half torn off, is white with rage.* FRANK *comes after him, a fanatic look in his face.*)

PURCELL: It's all the work of that lousy Red!

FRANK: It ain't food I come here for. (*He turns and summons the crowd who spill out of the store in response to the madness in his voice.*) You see that man? He ain't a man—he's a murderer. He's a rattlesnake—that's what he is, a rattlesnake, he and the rest of the ones on top!

(*He fires at* PURCELL *and misses him. The men surround him and take his gun.*)

PURCELL: Well, I'm damned! Tried to kill me, the little shrimp. I'll have you all jailed if it's the last thing I do!

(*He goes out. The men, silent and motionless, watch him.*)

FADE OUT

SCENE VII

Christmas Night, outside Wardell's house. It is very dark. DAVIS *comes in and goes up to the house.*

DAVIS: (*In a low voice*) Jim.

WARDELL: (*Inside*) That you, Mort?

DAVIS: Come out, will you?

    (WARDELL *comes out.*)

WARDELL: Anything new?

DAVIS: State troopers on the way. We'll be under arrest by mornin'.

WARDELL: I know. Ann and I been talkin'. We're sendin' the boys away.

DAVIS: Is Ann willin'?

WARDELL: There ain't anything else she can do. They can hitchhike out over the north road.

DAVIS: They're pretty small for that.

WARDELL: Think I don't know that? What is there for them to do here? Fightin' for food, goin' to jail.

    (*The door opens and* ANN *comes out followed by the two* BOYS. *Their faces look white and frightened in the dim light. They have small bundles on sticks over their shoulders.*)

ANN: (*In a hard, dead voice*) They're ready, Jim.

SAM: (*Suddenly*) Oh, Ma, I don't wanta go.

ANN: (*Still hard*) You'll be all right. Anybody see two boys alone like that'll take you in and maybe even feed you.

WARDELL: You can hitchhike it as far as Tyrone and then you go straight to Communist headquarters and tell 'em Jim Wardell sent you. They'll take care of you. And John, you remember all you're to say to 'em?

JOHN: (*As if reciting from memory*) I'm to say that things have gone too far and that you're organizing, that you may be sent to jail, and that the comrades here need help.

WARDELL: That's right.

ANN: (*Suddenly, desperately*) You boys'll stick together, won't you? You'll try to get jobs and stick together?

SAM: Yes, Ma, we'll stick together—

JOHN: We'll come back in the spring, Ma.

ANN: Yes, in the spring.

(*They start off. Suddenly* WARDELL *goes after them.*)
WARDELL: Try to remember all you've seen here, boys. Try to
    remember it and understand it. Remember that every man,
    every man, mind you, ought to have a right to work and eat.
    Every man ought to have the right to think things out for
    himself. Listen to everything, look at everything, and decide
    for yourselves. Then see if you can't help make a better kind
    of world for kids to live in.
JOHN: Yes, Pa.
SAM: We'll come back in the spring.
    (*The* BOYS *go off.* WARDELL *and* ANN *stand looking at them.*)
WARDELL: (*As if the cry is forced out of him*) Try to remember.
BOYS' VOICES: (*Faintly*) We'll remember.
ANN: Can you—hear their voices?

FADE OUT

In the darkness the screen is lowered.

Slide 9
These boys are symbols of thousands of our people who are turning
somewhere for leaders. Will it be to the educated minority?

CAN YOU HEAR THEIR VOICES?

THE WOMEN

CLARE BOOTHE

First presented in 1936

FOREWORD

Ann Clare Boothe was born in 1903 in New York City to a former chorus "girl" and a violinist who abandoned the family when his daughter was eight. She and her mother moved often; Boothe's haphazard education included short periods at various public schools and some three or four years in exclusive private academies, from which she graduated shortly after her sixteenth birthday. Her ambitious mother had no luck launching Boothe as a child actor beyond getting her understudy spots in plays entitled *A Good Little Devil* and *The Dummy*, as well as a few walk-on film roles. After graduation Boothe attended a business school and also began writing short stories and poems, a few of which appeared in local newspapers. At her mother's urging she enrolled at the Clare Tree Major School of the Drama but left after a few months. Despite her apparent lack of acting talent, Boothe had a strong interest in theater and read widely in modern drama. George Bernard Shaw was a particular favorite and many years later she accepted the title role in a summer playhouse production of his *Candida*; according to the critics, her acting skills had not improved.

After a short stint working as assistant to suffragist Alva Belmont at the Women's National Party headquarters, Boothe made a disastrous marriage to George Brokaw, a wealthy playboy more than twice her age. Brokaw, most of whose high-society family snubbed the young bride, turned out to be a jealous drunk with a violent temper. Boothe eventually divorced him and got a job

writing picture captions for *Vogue*. A short time later she switched
to the trendier *Vanity Fair*, where she rapidly rose through the
ranks to managing editor. Her essays for *Vanity Fair* foreshadow—
in subject matter and often in tone—her most successful play, *The
Women* (1937). In one essay she expounds on the "fine art" of being
"able to slander, criticize and ridicule...friends and acquaintances"
while avoiding their angry recriminations. In another she dubs
lying "the most useful and ornamental, the easiest to practice and
the loveliest" social virtue. She adds, unfortunately, that a woman
"never needs to be instructed in the principles of lying, for being of
the practical sex, it comes quite naturally to her."

Boothe left *Vanity Fair* in 1934, a few years after publishing her
first book, *Stuffed Shirts*, a collection of interconnected stories
about high society, "the rich and badly read" in New York.
Developed from her *Vanity Fair* pieces, *Stuffed Shirts* is a mocking
look at the high society Toppings and Towerlys, the nouveau riche
Crumbs, and assorted hangers-on: physicans and musicians,
painters and clergy. (One debutante has "attended four hundred
parties, wrecked three cars, been in a sanatorium with a nervous
breakdown twice, been engaged three times"—all in the space of
two years.) The society women spend most of the time competing
with each other: friendship is far shallower than "intense,
unpleasant female rivalry." Their male counterparts are infatuated
with the market, their horses and/or young girls. Couples marry for
money or security or because of pregnancy; almost everyone of
both sexes cheats on their spouses, and divorces are as common as
society teas. Boothe was evidently having a good time savaging the
upper crust who snubbed her when she was married to Brokaw, and
also sharpening her pencil for the plays she would shortly begin
composing.

In *Stuffed Shirts* Boothe sketches a publisher whose credo is
"Glamor, amour, humor, furore and horror"—perhaps a jab at
William Randolph Hearst, for whose newspapers she was briefly a
columnist. Also included in the *Shirts* rogues gallery is a drama
critic whose reviews seem to be written "not with the aid of a
typewriter but with a broadsword, a dentist's drill, a pile driver, a
rapier, a dung fork and a bolt of lightening." Boothe was apparently
unintimidated by such critics, however, when she turned her hand
to playwriting. She had first tried writing drama at the age of ten,
and as an adult she composed several unproduced efforts—
including a 1933 satire entitled *O, Pyramids!*—before reaching the

stage with *Abide With Me* in 1934. *Abide With Me* is a melodrama about Nan, a young woman married to a wealthy alcoholic whose viciousness is carefully hidden in public but amply evident in private, where he is emotionally and physically abusive to his wife. Marsden is so despicable to Nan that his long-time servant shoots him and even his own mother helps disguise the death as a suicide. While writing the play may have been cathartic for Boothe—she too had been married to an abusive alcoholic but no one had shot him—*Abide With Me* lacks credible characters, plot, and the sharp wit that distinguishes her best writing. According to biographer Ralph G. Martin it premiered in Westchester County in the summer of 1934; it reopened in New York on November 21, 1935, to consistently negative reviews. Among the disparaging critiques was one in *Time* magazine; legend has it that Boothe herself had a hand in writing the review, although her version was more scathing than the one *Time* printed. Two days after *Abide* opened in New York, she married *Time's* publisher, Henry Luce, one of the industry's most powerful figures.

When Boothe again tried playwriting, she fared considerably better. She claimed she got the idea for *The Women* from a conversation she overheard in a powder room, where a group of women were gossiping about their "friends." According to Faye Henle, who wrote a biography of Boothe in 1943, the first draft was completed in three days. With a cast of more than three dozen women headed by Ilka Chase and Margalo Gillmore, *The Women* arrived in New York December 26, 1936, after a Philadelphia tryout. Line-for-line *The Women* is one of the wittiest—and nastiest—comedies to reach the American stage. Nearly every critic praised the dialogue, usually described as "sparkling," "glittering" or "witty," and the cast received virtually universal acclaim. Otherwise, however, the reviews were mixed, with Brooks Atkinson concluding "Miss Boothe has compiled a workable play out of the withering malice of New York's most unregenerate worldlings. This reviewer disliked it"—a sentiment echoed by Richard Watts, Jr., in the *New York Herald Tribune*, who accurately predicted a long run but "did not care much for" the work. John Mason Brown at the *New York Post* conceded that "as a stunt in showmanship it makes for an arresting and rewarding evening" but dubbed it a "machine made comedy." On the other side of the critical fence, Richard Lockridge at the *Sun* found *The Women* "one of the most fascinating plays of the season, as it is by all odds the most scary," and the reviewer for the *New York American* thought it "sharp, quick, funny, effective."

Audience reception of *The Women* was enthusiastic; the comedy ran 657 performances and reportedly grossed over $900,000, a huge sum in those Depression days. Throughout its New York run *The Women* served as fodder for newspaper and magazine articles about the performers, the costumes (changed each season to keep the fashions current) and the number of watercress sandwiches consumed onstage. The bathroom scene received the most attention, including photo spreads and explanations of how the bathwater was kept bubbling. The New York production spun off two road companies, while Anita Loos and Jane Murfin wrote the screenplay for the very popular film version, starring Joan Crawford as Crystal, Rosalind Russell as Sylvia, and Norma Sheerer as Mary. *The Women* has been produced by hundreds of companies in dozens of countries around the world, even though it ran into censorship difficulties everywhere from Rhode Island to New Zealand. England's Lord Chamberlain demanded changes— reportedly he objected to one of the character's views on motherhood—but even with these revisions a prominent British critic complained that *The Women* was "a frankly vulgar play about frankly vulgar people." Among the odder renditions was a drag production done by soldiers at Camp Lee in 1942, a musical film adaptation entitled *The Opposite Sex* and a performance at the United Nations by diplomatic wives from various nations. A Broadway revival in 1973 was not particularly well received and closed after 63 performances.

When *The Women* premiered, rumors circulated that the play had been written, or at least rewritten, by George S. Kaufman. It seems likely that Kaufman did perform a little "play doctoring"— theater historian Burns Mantle records that Kaufman and Moss Hart "sat in at rehearsals, putting in a suggestion here, pointing up a line there"—but cast members concur the pair's contributions were minor. The massive revision the comedy received during rehearsals, including the excision of extraneous characters, was done by Boothe herself. Kaufman, according to Boothe, settled the matter when he noted: "*The Women* was one of the great hits. If I wrote it, why on earth would I put her name on it?"

The critical comments are particularly useful in showing how audiences interpreted *The Women*. Virtually every reviewer remarked on the absence of men in the cast, a highly unusual if not unique situation for a Broadway play then (and now). In the nineteen thirties the critical establishment—as it had been before and would continue to be—was overwhelmingly male, and some reviewers evidently missed seeing their likeness onstage; one complained that "a strong baritone voice and a pair of tweed trousers would have been welcome to ear and eye." Dorothy Dunbar Bromley, a rare female commentator, had a rather different view of their absence: "Unfortunately, we do not see the men in all their vanity." What we hear about the men is none too positive, but these stories are filtered through the unreliable medium of their wives. In fact, of course, while the men are physically absent it is clear that the women's world revolves around them: men are the constant topic of conversation as the women endure hours of torture in beauty and exercise salons in vain attempts to keep their husbands' eyes from roving. When all else fails they retire to Reno to shed one man and, so they hope, acquire another.

Many critics were alert to the possibility that male and female viewers might see *The Women* differently, and several commented on the disparate reactions, although they didn't always agree. One concluded that "male laughter predominated in the audience, but the ladies enjoyed themselves, too," while Burns Mantle argued that women theater-goers were more receptive. Virtually none of the critics, however, was reluctant to judge the veracity of Boothe's portrait of the female sex. John Mason Brown was unusual in complaining that the comedy was "essentially false in its point of view." One reviewer insisted "Here is more feminine psychology under one roof than in an entire shelf-ful of [psychologist] Havelock Ellis," another claimed that Boothe "holds up [a] mirror" to the female sex, while Sidney B. Whipple in the *New York World-Telegram* recommended that the play be required reading for men but not for women "because it is merely the essence of what all of them instinctively know already."

It's not surprising that male reviewers saw *The Women* as a valid portrait of all women, for there is scarcely a cliché about the sex that Boothe has omitted: women talk too much, women are vain and selfish, women are heartless creatures who care only for money, women are deceitful and untrustworthy, and women are— as Sylvia's therapist assures her—"natural enemies" to each other. Boothe presents us with untamed beasts, ruled by instinct and emotion rather than reason, who wear "jungle red" nail polish and bite each other during fist fights. The opening credits for the film version of *The Women* even assign an animal to each of the characters: Phyllis Povah's Edith is a cow, Norma Shearer's Mary is a doe, while Joan Crawford's Crystal is a leopard.

In the "Foreword" to the published text—in which she is even harder on her characters than she is in the play itself—Boothe proffered a disclaimer, swearing that she was writing about only "a numerically small group of ladies native to the Park Avenues of America." But she added that "an honest misogynist" (whatever that is) "might even be able to prove that all the unkind particularities of *The Women* are generally relevant to the sex." These characters are *worse* than most women, she seems to be saying, but by no means atypical.

Yet Boothe is evidently up to something more than exercising sexist clichés, even if few critics—and certainly the producers of the film—weren't aware of that. *The Women* is fueled by Boothe's deep ambivalence: her personal resentment of the society women who had snubbed her during her disastrous first marriage, her anger at a system that forces intelligent women to waste their time on internecine warfare and permanent waves, as well as her ire at the women who help perpetuate that system. Boothe has (as she claimed) penned a satire of a particular class, the rich, and the consequences of a capitalist system for women. Because these women are seen—by the men and by themselves—as nothing more than decorative accessories to their spouses, their intelligence, time and energy are wasted on frivolous and ultimately self-destructive activities. *The Women* premiered at the height of the Depression, making the selfish antics of the rich wives all the more appalling. But Boothe also makes evident that the women are enmeshed in an economic struggle: a husband represents security. Miss Trimmerback, who has a white-collar office job, proclaims with bitter irony: "A lot of independence you have on a woman's wages," and adds that she'd trade her career "for a decent, or an indecent, home." Mary may be right when she tells her daughter that a woman can enter virtually any profession she chooses—Boothe herself already had a very successful career—but the woman with a creative, lucrative occupation was rare indeed, especially in an era of high unemployment when women were expected to give the best jobs to the men who "needed" them more. Boothe shows us maids, models, governesses, secretaries and manicurists whose work is difficult, poorly paid and often humiliating. The picture we get is particularly disturbing because the society women, recognizing no bond with their less affluent sisters, treat their working-class counterparts like the "creatures" Mrs. Morehead claims they are. Boothe's underlying message, however, is that given the job opportunities open to most women, being kept by a wealthy man—as wife or mistress—is preferable to spending your days sweeping floors or pounding a typewriter for a barely subsistence wage. The female world we see onstage has been designed by the unseen men for their own benefit.

Such a materialist feminist reading of *The Women*, however, has difficulty incorporating Mary and Mrs. Morehead into this critique of capitalism, since these characters' concerns seem largely (though certainly not entirely) situated outside the economic realm. Mary, in fact, has long been a problem for critics. Richard Watts, Jr., claimed that she is "so pure, so innocent, so game, so heroic...that it isn't long before you are inclined to join the innumerable villainesses of the work in an inclination towards mayhem." Eleanor Roosevelt, commenting on *The Women* in her "My Day" column, cut closer to the bone: "I have no patience with the mother [Mrs. Morehead] and her advice, but I have no patience either with the one woman who was supposed to be 'good' and was so 'stupid.'" In her "Foreword" to the published edition Boothe herself admitted that "In spite of her redeeming qualities of faithfulness and sweetness, the difficulty about rooting for Mary is obviously that she is so stupid you hardly give a hoot."

Unlike Eleanor Roosevelt, however, Boothe seems to consider Mrs. Morehead (note her name) a beacon of reason and sanity. Both the play and Boothe argue that Mary's stupidity lies in her allowing herself to be manipulated by her "friends," rather than in her failure to question either her mother's double standard or her own dogged devotion to a man who carried on a notably public affair and conceded that he was only "fond" of his wife. The very structure of *The Women* positions audience members to root for a protagonist who gladly abases herself because pride is "a luxury a woman in love can't afford." Mary hasn't even the motive of Evie Johns, a character in *Stuffed Shirts* who discovers that she longs for her dull ex-husband because "He was the only man I have ever known who made me feel that I was really missing something." True satire not only mocks the way things are but implicitly suggests how they ought to be. Boothe succeeds in critiquing an economic system created to insure that the Sylvias and Miriams spend their time sabotaging each other instead of doing productive work. But if—as *The Women*'s design suggests—Mary is the "ought" to which the others should aspire, Boothe's often brilliant and hilarious satire is at best incomplete.

Stylistically *The Women* is composed of brief scenes and deliberately one-dimensional characters—a technique Boothe may have developed writing magazine sketches of celebrities. Although the character list is considerably smaller, she uses similar techniques in her next play, *Kiss the Boys Good-bye* (1938). Boothe claims in her introduction to *Kiss* that it is an attack on America's closest equivalent to Fascism, "Southernism" and the Ku Klux Klan, but far more obvious is its satirical view of Hollywood and the film industry. Cindy Lou Bethany is a Southern belle being considered for the film role of Velvet O'Toole (a thinly veiled allusion to the search for an unknown to play the lead in *Gone With the Wind*). While this Southern belle may be genuinely repellent, almost no one else in the play is more appealing; employing her usual combination of equal parts wit and vitriol, Boothe trashes everyone: Communist, Fascist, worker, boss. Brooks Atkinson's response to *Kiss the Boys Good-bye* was typical of the critical community: he found the dialogue "bright and devastating" but the characters "rats and lice." The play was popular, nevertheless, running 286 performances.

Margin for Error (1939), like *Kiss the Boys Good-bye*, was chosen by Burns Mantle for the year's *Best Plays* volume. Although it is not, as Boothe's husband claims in the introduction to the published edition, "the first successsful" anti-Nazi play, *Margin* foregrounds the anti-Nazi theme that is muted in *Kiss the Boys Good-bye*. *Margin* is a comedy-mystery-melodrama with its heart in the right place but with a full cast of stereotypes on stage: a villainous German consul straight out of the cartoons; a profoundly stupid American Nazi; a sensitive German secretary who feels guilt over participating in an attack on an elderly Jew and equally horrified to learn that his grandmother was Jewish; and Moses Finkelstein, a Jewish policemen who "in common with most of the people of his race...has the gifts of ready sympathy, loquacity, and inquisitiveness." Despite the play's often compelling first act, Atkinson found *Margin* a "curious and unsatisfactory mixture of political unmasking and detective story." By the time it reached London in the summer of 1940 critics complained that the attacks on the Nazis were already "outdated," but Hollywood disagreed and filmed *Margin for Error* three years later.

With a few minor exceptions, Boothe's playwriting days were over by the end of the 1930s. In an interview she gave many years later she said her husband resented the numerous separations theatrical life caused; although her subsequent careers scarcely guaranteed marital closeness, Henry Luce was at least more interested in politics and diplomacy than theater. The early 1940s found Boothe covering Europe, the Pacific and Africa as a war correspondent and writing her book *Europe in the Spring*. When she returned she inaugurated a new career by becoming the first woman elected to Congress from Connecticut; during her four years on Capitol Hill (after two terms she declined to run for re-election) Boothe was also the first woman appointed to the House Military Affairs Committee. She believed that Congress was one of the few places where a woman "has access to the same amount of power as a man has," and she resented the fact that male reporters often focused on her clothes rather than her ideas. It was also in the forties that Boothe made a very public conversion to Catholicism, a religion to which she turned for solace when her only child was killed in an automobile accident. She earned an Academy Award nomination for her screenplay for the film *Come to the Stable* (1949), a work that reflects her new faith. Boothe's 1951 play *Child of the Morning*—a strange drama about a young girl whose holiness is misdiagnosed as drug addiction—also reveals her skepticism about the psychiatric profession. Starring Margaret O'Brien, *Child* closed after a short out-of-town run but was briefly revived off-Broadway seven years later, to mixed reviews. One of the more receptive critics found it "an interesting play, well-planned, ingeniously constructed and eventful" but complained that the work "comes from the head rather than the heart."

At the age of forty Boothe was already the subject of a two-hundred page biography, even though much of her public career still lay ahead. In 1953 she was chosen in a Gallup Poll as the fourth most admired woman in the world—behind Eleanor Roosevelt, Queen Elizabeth and Mamie Eisenhower. That same year President Eisenhower named her ambassador to Italy, the first woman appointed chief diplomatic representative to a major foreign power. Several years later she was confirmed as ambassador to Brazil but resigned before taking the post because she felt that liberal attacks on her and her politics, which had become increasingly conservative over the years, made it impossible for her to serve effectively. Boothe spent the decades before her death in

1987 writing occasional magazine articles, serving on President Richard Nixon's Foreign Intelligence Advisory Board, painting, scuba diving and collecting accolades ranging from a Lambs Club award for devotion to the theater to the Sylvanus Thayer Award, West Point's highest honor.

Clare Boothe's last foray into stage writing was the one-act *Slam the Door Softly* (originally published in *Life* magazine as *A Doll's House—1970*) which opened in Los Angeles in 1971. A rather didactic rewriting of Ibsen's *A Doll's House*, *Slam the Door Softly* is set in the suburban New York home of insurance executive Thaw Wald and Nora Wald, a well-educated and thoroughly bored modern woman. Tucking her list of grievances and a bill for her services as wife and mother into copies of *The Second Sex* and *The Feminine Mystique*, Nora leaves her obtuse husband to find a job that both challenges and remunerates her. A direct descendant of Stephen Haines from *The Women*, Thaw has been having an affair with a "girl" whom, he implies, he would consider marrying if Nora leaves. But while Nora declares her love for Thaw, she has an answer for his claim that "Marriage is still the best deal that the world has to offer women": "Just now I feel that the best deal I, Nora Wald, can hope to get out of life is to learn to esteem myself as a person." The pride that Mary Haines saw as a "luxury" she couldn't afford, Nora Wald sees as a necessity without which she cannot survive. The times had changed and so had Boothe's female protagonist, perhaps partly in response to the playwright's own notable career.

SELECTED BIBLIOGRAPHY

Boothe, Clare. *Europe in the Spring*. N.Y.: Knopf, 1940.

————. *Kiss the Boys Good-bye*. Foreword Heywood Broun. N.Y.: Random House, 1939.

————. *Margin for Error*. Intro. Henry R. Luce. N.Y.: Random House, 1940.

————. *Slam the Door Softly*. In *A Century of Plays by American Women*, ed. Rachel France. N.Y.: Richards Rosen, 1979.

———— (Brokaw). *Stuffed Shirts*. N.Y.: Horace Liveright, 1931.

Colacello, Bob. "The Many Lives of Clare Boothe Luce." *Parade*, 6 November 1983, 4-7.

Henle, Faye. *Au Clare de Luce: Portrait of a Luminous Lady*. N.Y.: Stephen Daye, 1943.

Mackaye, Milton. "Clare Boothe," *Scribner's Magazine* 105 (March 1939): p. 13.

Martin, Ralph G. *Henry & Clare: An Intimate Portrait of the Luces*. N.Y.: G.P. Putnam's Sons. 1991.

Shadegg, Stephen. *Clare Boothe Luce*. N.Y.: Simon and Schuster, 1970.

Sheed, Wilfrid. *Clare Boothe Luce*. N.Y.: Dutton, 1982.

A NOTE ON THE TEXT

There are two versions of *The Women*: the original 1937 version and a revision Boothe made in 1964. Her revision involved numerous minor changes—some jokes were sharpened (and a few blunted); references to Howard Fowler's supposed impotence, presumably too daring in 1937, were added; the twelve scenes were divided into two rather than three acts—and some more substantial rewriting. Boothe eliminated two minor characters in Scene 2 by replacing Mrs. Wagstaff and Mrs. Phipps with the Countess and Miriam Aarons, who reappear later in the play. She also trimmed Scene 3 by removing the Cook (Ingrid) and her complaint about her philandering husband. While these revisions hone and speed up the comedy, other changes—especially the addition of a physical fight between Crystal and Sylvia at the final curtain—seem egregious. Boothe also felt obliged to "update" the play to the sixties, sometimes with unintentionally ludicrous results: an allusion to silent screen star Rudolph Valentino became an allusion to James Bond, while a reference to Shirley Temple was changed to a comment about the Beatles. Since the two versions of *The Women* are substantially the same, and since the Beatles are clearly out of place in a play set so firmly in the context of the thirties, I decided to reprint the original text. I have, however, included one correction that Boothe herself made in the revision: the Countess' first husband apparently died while they were still married, so she is seeking her third (not her fourth) divorce in Reno.

In both the original and the revised versions of *The Women*, Boothe occasionally referred to a minor character by one title (eg., "First Salesgirl") in the character list and a slightly different one (eg., "First Girl") in the text. At times she even used two different titles (eg., "Second Model" and "Corset Model") for the same character in the course of a scene. To prevent confusion, I have attempted to regularize the character designations. In productions of *The Women*, some of these very minor roles are omitted or combined.

AUTHOR'S PREFACE

The Women is a satirical play about a numerically small group of ladies native to the Park Avenues of America. It was clearly so conceived and patently so executed. The title, which embraces half the human species, is therefore rather too roomy. It was chosen, ungenerously it may seem, from a host of more generic titles— "Park Avenue," "The Girls," "The Ladies"—simply because it was laconic, original and not altogether too remote. Moreover, its very generality seemed to hold a wide audience appeal, a consideration which few commercial dramatists are required to ignore. This having been frankly stated, I am sure that few readers will be distracted by the width of the title from the narrowness of the play's aim: a clinical study of a more or less isolated group, projected, perhaps in bad temper, but in good faith. The reader, who, warned of this, nevertheless claims to discover in it a portrait of *all* womankind, is obviously bound to experience the paradoxical discomfort which ensues to the wearer when the shoe unexpectedly fits.

Of course, an honest misogynist might conceivably make a case for the title's just applicability to the play's content. He might even be able to prove that all the unkind particularities of *The Women* are generally relevant to the sex. With scant research, and the aid of many authorities, he could show that even history's notably nice women have been notably few. He might even ask you to try naming ten famous women of history, famous for their good works, sweet tempers, irreproachable morals and womanly virtues. And the calendar of the church's virgins and saints, once exhausted, you might be hard put to it to find three for your temporal list.

Mr. Heywood Broun, who was unfortunately deceived by the title, paused long enough in his celebrated prosecution of crimes against the body politic to assail what he called this play's "crime against the spirit." He quoted Mr. Burke to sustain his thesis that *The Women* "degraded the whole human race." A good misogynist would begin by quoting Mr. Burke back to him, as the ungallant author of the brute statement: "A woman is an animal, and an animal not of the highest order." Strindberg, Schopenhauer, Ibsen and a great horde of other bilious misogynists, including St. Paul, could then be called upon to uphold speciously, no doubt, but brilliantly that loutish definition. But I have no heart for the easy game of

woman-baiting. Far from resenting Mr. Broun's knightly indignation, I find it adorable. He is, notably and belligerently, a man of
intellectual integrity. It gives one, as a woman, a delicious thrill of
power and contentment to know that he is being truer to his chival-
rous instincts than to his political ideals when he says of *The
Women:* "I would not like it—even if I were informed it had been
financed by Moscow gold." Indeed, like most women, I would not,
if I could, disillusion any of the courtly gentlemen who believe in
the uncloyed sweetness of *Woman*. And I truly, heartily and thank-
fully echo the cry of all who have been revolted by the *specific* bitterness of *The Women* that *"All* women are not like that!" (It would
be a sad world if they were—as indeed it is a sad world anyway.)

And to grow personal, in the fashion of a few critics, none of my
friends is like that—few of my acquaintances. But such mischievous
women have crossed my path, as Hedda Gabler must have crossed
Ibsen's, and, recently, Mary Tilford crossed Lillian Hellman's in
The Children's Hour. (Did Miss Hellman have to face the alarming
accusation that she wrote an indictment of *all* childhood?) I did *not*
like these women. I liked them so little that I put them into this
small Doomsday Book, in order to rid myself once and for all of
their hauntingly ungracious images. (Catharsis which produces
much criticism seldom produces art, but it is, after all, an old and
accepted phenomenon among artists.)

Now, whether or not, this play is a good *play* is any man's business to say. But whether or not it is a true portrait of *such* women is
a matter which no man can adequately judge, for the good reason
that all their actions and emotions are shown forth in places and
times which no man has ever witnessed. "Vas you there,
Charlie?"...The patriotic Daughters of the American Revolution
were notoriously harsh judges of soldiery, as demonstrated in *What
Price Glory?* The fact that their fathers were soldiers did not make
them good judges of life on the Western Front. So all sentimental
gentlemen, young and old, who read this book, are here warned
that the fact that their mothers were women does not constitute
them, ipso facto, able critics of Life in *The Women*'s No-Man's
Land. War and love among *these* women is also an unperfumed
business. Watching it, a man will do well to forget all that he wishes to *think* about "woman," and remember only what, from time to
time, he has *felt* about some. My only feeling, when the curtain rose
on the first night, was that perhaps I had not done justice to the
awfulness of these few. But if I failed to do them justice, I awoke to

find, the following morning, that the critics had not pulled their hunches. Here is a partial list of descriptive nouns and adjectives applied by the Gentlemen of the Press to the Ladies of the Ensemble:

Cats	Cat o'nine tongues	Zoological freaks
Plain cats	Cobras	Harlots
Tiger cats	Female lice	Odious harpies
Supercilious cats	Ostriches	Brazen hussies
Malignant cats	Werewolves	Stalking hussies
Hell cats	Vixens	Lewd hussies
Jades	Acid	Malicious
Sluts	Adder-fanged	Miasmic
Trollops	Avaricious	Murderous
Parasites	Bawdy	Mean-spirited
Poison-tongues	Carbolic	Merciless
Tittle-tattlers	Cynical	Petty
Gossip-peddlers	Evil	Remorseless
Slanderers	Evil-tempered	Repugnant
Fiendish liars	Flashy	Repellent
Insatiables	Flossy	Rotten
Cheats	Frightful	Scurrilous
False friends	Filthy	Silly
Irrepressible	Fiendish	Sinister
interlopers	Feline	Spiteful
Meddlers	Glossy	Stupid
Barbaric savages	Gross	Terrifying
Rogues	Hard-boiled	Two-faced
Fleurs du Mal	Hateful	Venomous
Unregenerate	Wretched souls	Intriguing
worldlings	Vicious	A smelly lot
Lurid	Wicked	

Which, the reader of this book will soon discover, is in the aggregate much harsher language than the dialogue will unfold. I am indebted, however, to this list for a few pertinent epithets which I myself was too faint-hearted to use about *The Women.*

But all this is doing an injustice to the reader who tackles this foreword before he does the play. Such horrendous opprobrium must lead him to anticipate a bloodthirsty gang of Borgias, whose crimes would add another circle to Dante's *Inferno.* His expectations are doomed to disappointment. He will experience, I am

afraid, the same let-down that deflates audiences of mystery plays
which build up to a terrific climax amidst shrieks of "There's a
killer loose in this house," when the fiend incarnate turns out to be
the heretofore comic butler. My villainesses' skullduggery is far
from fiendish, and themselves too unprepossessingly funny to give
the audience a really bang-up shudder. For, as I have confessed, the
case against "the ladies" in *The Women* has been grossly understat-
ed. At worst, they are shown as merely vulgar, silly and futile. Their
infidelities would hardly make good tabloid reading. Their
shrewish gossip is far less inaccurate, wounding, deadly than that of
the masculine columnists you and I enjoy in the daily prints.
Indeed, most Manhattanites, who in speakeasies and night clubs
and restaurants, have so often heard the brighter masculine minds
of Broadway destroy a half dozen friends before cock-crow for the
sake of a frequently not so witty witticism, will certainly find *The
Women*, by comparison, a pathetically tame bunch of tittle-tats.

Again, the reader, titillated by the above-listed spine-prickling
abstract of *The Women*, will be further disappointed to find, among
the inadequate furies, a number of "nice women." He will detect in
the briefly sketched characters of Mrs. Morehead, the cooks,
Nancy, Peggy, the hairdressers, the nurse, Lucy, the cigarette girl
and the maids, at least rudiments of decency, common-sense, generosity and social conscience. Because they are somewhat unwilling
satellites in the garish orbits in which they swing, these traits are
necessarily blurred a bit. Furthermore, an understandable indignation and petulance in them, against the odious principals, mar the
otherwise sweet serenity of their natures. Nevertheless, it is there.

Of course, the heroine, Mary, is nice. Indeed, a reasonable
objection to her may be that she is "too damned nice." She is positively "saccharine." She is "sugar content." It is a sad truism in the
theatre that the customer has got not only to pay his $3.30, but he's
got to root for somebody besides. In spite of her redeeming qualities of faithfulness and sweetness, the difficulty about rooting for
Mary is obviously that she is so stupid you hardly give a hoot.
(Perhaps her very inadequacy provides the play with a good modern moral where none was intended. "Be intelligent, fair maid and
let who will be, good.") But the dilemma which faced me in drawing this central character was this: If she had been drawn three
dimensionally as even a reasonably intelligent woman, she would
have made short shrift of her enemies, and therefore, of my little
play. Creatures like Edith and Sylvia and Crystal can breed no

"worthy antagonists." A "nice" stupid woman is victimized by their nonsense; a "nice" intelligent woman ignores them completely. Indeed, when, in the last act, Mary is penetrated by a belated glimmer of intelligence, and proceeds to act for three minutes with a modicum of common-sense, she brings down the curtain on the utter rout of her enemies. Why, had she been one-tenth as intelligent as her own cook, as far back as Act One, Scene 4, she would have taken her husband from Crystal as Grant took Richmond. Or, to press the logic, if she had been intelligent in Act One, Scene 1, she would have so deliberately eschewed the bridge players that she would have found herself not in *this* play, but across the street in a play by Mr. Coward.

Precisely, alas, what these women are not, are social characters worthy of that gentleman's bright, rapier wit. The women who inspired this play deserved to be smacked across the head with a meat-ax. And that, I flatter myself, is exactly what I smacked them with. They are vulgar and dirty-minded, and alien to grace, and I would not if I could—which, I hasten to say I cannot—gloss their obscenities with a wit which is foreign to them, and gild their futilities with a glamour which by birth and breeding and performance they do not possess. They are the advocates of the hackneyed, devotees of the wisecrack, high priestesses of the banal. That they speak not with the tongues of angels, or even diabolically clever sophisticates, to charm the critical ear from a harsh scrutiny of their indecencies, but with the tongues of fishwives and bartenders, can be laid at the door of good reportage. Everything they say and do is in deplorable taste, because everything I have ever heard such women say and do *is* in deplorable taste. But indeed, if one is not susceptible to their ludicrousness, tickled by their gargantuan absurdities, one is quite justified in being either bored or appalled by them.

The plot, like the heroine, by current dramatic standards, is also "weak." It was knowingly intended to be no more than a peg on which to hang this bedraggled bit of Park Avenue plumage. It is deliberately a commonplace squirrel-cage, full of holes, getting nowhere, serving only the purpose of further emphasizing the minuscule, foolish, whirligig activities of a few cancerous little squirrels, whose little cheeks bulge with rotten little nuts, which in their civilized little cage they have neither the wit, nor the place, to hide.

But that the antics of these women do strike most audiences as

funny, instead of dull or nauseating, as they might quite reasonably
have done, is a very happy accident for me at the box-office. I am
immensely gratified by the play's success, and properly appreciative
of whom I have to thank—the women who are its staunchest advocates and best customers—the women who do *not* think "all women
are like that." These many have gleefully recognized in my harpies,
not themselves, but a certain few deservedly despised, and cursedly
ubiquitous, sisters of theirs, whose chastisement leaves them, as it
left me, content.

To the reader this apology is due: for publishing this play in
book form at all. A book-play, no matter how charitably and imagi-
natively read, is nothing more than the bare bones of a play. Mr.
Max Gordon's unstinted production, Mr. Joseph Mielziner's deft
and authentic sets, Mr. John Hambleton's elegant costumes, beautifully padded these bare bones with seductive dramatic flesh. As
Charita Bauer, the exquisite child-actress who plays Little Mary,
said to me one dark rehearsal day: "Never you mind, even if it's *not*
a success, it's going to *look* lovely!" It did. Above all, that flesh was
made instinct with gay life by the ingenuity and witty tempo of Mr.
Robert Sinclair's direction, and the delicious characterizations of
the forty-odd actresses, too many here to praise severally. And
quickly let me say, who have been accused of adolescent atribilious-
ness and girlish cynicism, that any faith that I may have lost in pre-
vious unfortunate encounters with my sex on Park Avenue was
restored and redoubled by the actresses of *The Women* on
Broadway. With me, and among themselves, and in the midst of
tedious and grueling rehearsals, beset by re-writings and cuttings,
harassed by much scenery and many quick costume changes, they
never failed to display the best in their womanly and professional
natures. To use a word that is current in exclusive Park Avenue circles, but has as yet not been vulgarized by the press, there was not
even one wee bitch in the lot.

CLARE BOOTHE

New York City
February 26, 1937

CHARACTERS

JANE
NANCY   (MISS BLAKE)
PEGGY   (MRS. JOHN DAY)
SYLVIA   (MRS. HOWARD FOWLER)
EDITH   (MRS. PHELPS POTTER)
MARY   (MRS. STEPHEN HAINES)
MRS. WAGSTAFF
FIRST HAIRDRESSER
SECOND HAIRDRESSER
PEDICURIST
OLGA
MUD-MASK   (MRS. PHIPPS)
EUPHIE
COOK   (INGRID)
MISS FORDYCE
LITTLE MARY
MRS. MOREHEAD
FIRST SALESGIRL
SECOND SALESGIRL
FIRST SALESWOMAN   (MISS SHAPIRO)
FIRST MODEL   (MISS MYRTLE)
SECOND SALESWOMAN
CRYSTAL ALLEN
THIRD SALESWOMAN
FIRST FITTER
ANOTHER FITTER
CORSET MODEL
PRINCESS TAMARA
INSTRUCTRESS
MAGGIE
MISS TRIMMERBACK
MISS WATTS
NURSE
LUCY
COUNTESS DE LAGE
MIRIAM AARONS
HELENE
FIRST GIRL

SECOND GIRL
FIRST WOMAN
SECOND WOMAN
SADIE
CIGARETTES   (CIGARETTE GIRL)
DOWAGER
DEBUTANTE
GIRL IN DISTRESS

ACT ONE

Scene I: Mary Haines' living room. A winter afternoon.
Scene II: A hairdresser's. An afternoon, a few days later.
Scene III: Mary's boudoir, an hour later.
Scene IV: A fitting room. An afternoon, two months later.

ACT TWO

Scene I: An exercise room, two weeks later.
Scene II: Mary's kitchen, midnight, a few days later.
Scene III: Mary's living room, a month later.
Scene IV: A hospital room, a month later.
Scene V: A Reno hotel room, a few weeks later.

ACT THREE

Scene I: Crystal's bathroom, early evening, two years later.
Scene II: Mary's bedroom, eleven-thirty, the same night.
Scene III: The Powder Room at the Casino Roof, near midnight,
   the same night.

ACT ONE

SCENE I

Mary Haines' living room. Today, Park Avenue living rooms are deco-
rated with a significant indifference to the fact that ours is still a bi-sexual
society. Period peacock alleys, crystal-hung prima-donna roosts, they reflect
the good taste of their mistresses in everything but a consideration of the
master's pardonable right to fit in his own home decor. Mary Haines' liv-
ing room is not like that. It would be thought a comfortable room by a
man. This, without sacrificing its own subtle, feminine charm. Above the
fireplace, there is a charming portrait of Mary's children—a girl of 11, a
boy of 5 or 6. Right, a door to the living quarters. Left, another to the
hall. Center, a sofa, armchair, tea-table group; and in the good light from
the window, a bridge-table group.
As the curtain rises, JANE, *a pretty, and quite correct little Irish-*
American maid, is arranging the tea-table. Four women are playing
bridge in a smoking-car cloud of smoke. They are:
NANCY, *who is sharp, but not acid; sleek but not smart; a worldly and yet*
virginal 35. And her partner—
PEGGY, *who is pretty, sweet, 25.* PEGGY's *character has not, will never*
quite "jell." And—
SYLVIA, *who is glassy, elegant, feline, 34. And her partner—*
EDITH, *who is a sloppy, expensively dressed (currently, by Lane Bryant)*
matron of 33 or 34. Indifferent to everything but self, EDITH *is incapable*
of either deliberate maliciousness or spontaneous generosity.

SYLVIA: So I said to Howard, "What do you expect me to do? Stay
    home and darn your socks? What do we all have money for?
    Why do we keep servants?"
NANCY: You don't keep them long, God knows— (*Placing the pack*
    of cards) Yours, Peggy.
PEGGY: Isn't it Mrs. Potter's? I opened with four spades. (SYLVIA
    firmly places the pack before PEGGY. PEGGY, *wrong again, deals.*)
SYLVIA: Second hand, you did. And went down a thousand.
    (*Patronizingly*) Peggy, my pet, you can't afford it.
PEGGY: I can too, Sylvia. I'm not a pauper.
SYLVIA: If your bridge doesn't improve, you soon will be.
NANCY: Oh, shut up, Sylvia. She's only playing till Mary comes
    down.
SYLVIA: (*Querulously*) Jane, what's Mrs. Haines doing up there?

JANE: (*Reproachfully*) It's that lingerie woman *you* sent her, Mrs. Fowler.

SYLVIA: I didn't expect Mrs. Haines to buy anything. I was just trying to get rid of the creature. (JANE *exits*) Peggy, bid.

PEGGY: Oh, mine? By.

SYLVIA: (*Looking at* PEGGY) She *won't* concentrate.

NANCY: She's in love, bless her. After the child's been married as long as you girls, she may be able to concentrate on vital matters like bridge.

SYLVIA: (*Bored*) Another lecture on the Modern Woman?

NANCY: At the drop of a hat. By.

SYLVIA: I consider myself a perfectly good wife. I've sacrificed a lot for Howard Fowler—two spades. I devote as much time to my children as any of my friends.

NANCY: Except Mary.

SYLVIA: Oh, Mary, of course. Mary is an exception to all of us.

NANCY: Quite right. (*They are waiting for* PEGGY *again*) Peggy?

PEGGY: (*Uncertainly*) Two no trumps? (EDITH *rises suddenly. Plainly, she feels squeamish.*)

SYLVIA: (*Wearily*) Edith, not *again*?

EDITH: I shouldn't have eaten that alligator pear. Morning sickness! I heave the whole darn day. This is positively the last time I go through this lousy business for any man! Four spades. If men had to bear babies, there'd never be—

NANCY: —more than one child in a family. And he'd be a boy. By. (EDITH *sinks on the edge of her chair, lays down her cards.*)

PEGGY: I wish *I* were having a baby. We can't afford one now.

SYLVIA: And you'll never be able to, until you know Culbertson. (*Arranging* EDITH's *cards*) Honestly, Edith! Why didn't you show a slam?

EDITH: (*Rising hurriedly*) Oh, I *have* got to unswallow. Wait till you've had three, Peggy. You'd wish you'd never gotten past the bees and flowers. (*Exits precipitously.*)

NANCY: (*Disgusted*) Poor, frightened, bewildered madonna!

SYLVIA: I'm devoted to Edith Potter. But she does get me down. You'd think she had a hard time. Dr. Briggs says she's like shelling peas. She ought to go through what I went through. Nobody *knows*!

NANCY: No clubs, partner?

SYLVIA: So when Cynthia came, I had a Cæsarian. You should see my stomach—It's a slam!

NANCY: Are you sure?

SYLVIA: Got the king, Peggy? (PEGGY *obligingly plays the king*) Thanks, dear, it's a slam. And the rubber. (*Rises, lights a fresh cigarette, goes to armchair and perches*) But I've kept my figure. I must say, I don't blame Phelps Potter for playing around.

PEGGY: Oh, does her husband...?

SYLVIA: Oh, Phelps has made passes at all us girls. I do think it's bad taste for a man to try to make his wife's friends, *especially* when he's bald and fat. I told him once, "Phelps Potter," I said, "the next time you grab at me, I'm going straight to Edith."

NANCY: And did you ?

SYLVIA: Certainly not. I wouldn't say anything to hurt Edith for the world. Well, you can't blame the men. But I'll say one thing for Edith. She's not as dumb as *some* of my friends. She's on to her husband.

PEGGY: (*Bravely*) Do you think *he* is on to her?

SYLVIA: What do you mean?

PEGGY: If he could only hear her talk about him!

SYLVIA: Listen, Peggy, do we know how men talk about us when we're not around?

NANCY: I've heard rumors.

SYLVIA: Exactly. Peggy, you haven't been married long enough to form a private opinion of your husband.

PEGGY: Well, if I had one, I'd keep it to myself. Do you think I'd tell anybody in the world about the quarrels John and I have over money? I'd be too proud! (*Enter* EDITH. *Goes to tea-table, and gathers a handful of sandwiches.*)

SYLVIA: All over, dear?

EDITH: Oh, that was a false alarm. What happened?

SYLVIA: Only a slam, dear. You do underbid.

EDITH: I'll bet you had me on the pan.

SYLVIA: I never say behind my friends' backs what I won't say to their faces. I said you ought to diet.

EDITH: There's no use dieting in my condition. I've got to wait until I can begin from scratch. Besides, I've got the most wonderful cook. She was with Mary. She said Mary let her go because she was too extravagant. I think this cook Mary has is too, too homey. (*Examines sandwich*) Watercress. I'd just as soon eat my way across a front lawn.

SYLVIA: I think Mary's gone off terribly this winter. Have you noticed those deep lines, here? (*Draws her finger around her mouth.*)

NANCY: Smiling lines. Tragic, aren't they?

SYLVIA: Perhaps they *are*. Maybe a woman's headed for trouble when she begins to get too—smug.

NANCY: Smug? Don't you mean, happy?

PEGGY: Mr. Haines adores her so!

SYLVIA: (*Snickering and flashing* EDITH *a significant glance*) Yes, doesn't he?

NANCY: (*coldly*) You just can't bear it, Sylvia, can you?

SYLVIA: Bear what?

NANCY: Mary's happiness. It gets you down.

SYLVIA: Nancy Blake, if there's one thing I can say for myself, I've never been jealous of another woman. Why should I be jealous of Mary?

NANCY: Because she's contented. Contented to be what she is.

SYLVIA: Which is what?

NANCY: A woman.

EDITH: And what, in the name of my revolting condition, are we?

NANCY: Females.

SYLVIA: Really. And what are you, pet?

NANCY: What nature abhors, I'm—a virgin—a frozen asset.

EDITH: I wish I were a virgin again. The only fun I ever had was holding out on Phelps. Nancy, you ought to thank God every night you don't have to make sacrifices for some man.

PEGGY: I wish I could make a little money, writing the way you do, Miss Blake.

NANCY: If you wrote the way I do, that's just what you'd make.

SYLVIA: You're not exactly a popular author, are you, dear?

NANCY: Not with you. Well, good news, Sylvia. My book is finished and once again I'm about to leave your midst.

PEGGY: Oh, I wish we could afford to travel. Where do you go this time, Miss Blake?

NANCY: Africa, shooting.

SYLVIA: Well, darling, I don't blame you. I'd rather face a tiger any day than the sort of things the critics said about your last book. (*Enter* MARY *She is a lovely woman in her middle thirties. She is what most of us think our happily married daughters are like. She is carrying several white boxes.*)

MARY: Sorry, girls. (*Teasing*) Sylvia, must you always send me woebegone creatures like that lingerie woman? It's been a very expensive half hour for me.

PEGGY: (*Looking at* SYLVIA) For me too, Mrs. Haines.

MARY: (*Laughing*) Nonsense, Peggy, you were playing for me. Here. (*Hands* PEGGY *a box*) Don't open it now. It's a bed-jacket. Or a tea cozy. Or something padded. I wouldn't know. I was crying so hard.

SYLVIA: You didn't believe that woman's sob story?

MARY: Of course I did. (*She really didn't*) Anyway, she's a lot worse off than you and I. (*Putting down another box*) Edith, wee garments—

EDITH: Darling, how sweet! (*It comes over her again*) Oh, my God! I'm sick as a cat. (*Sits.*)

SYLVIA: It's a girl. Girls always make you sicker.

NANCY: Even before they're born?

EDITH: I don't care what it is. I've lost everything including my curiosity. Why did God make it take nine months?

NANCY: (*Helpfully*) It takes an elephant seven years.

EDITH: I wish I were an elephant. I'll look like one anyway before I'm finished. And it would be heaven not to worry for seven years.

MARY: (*Laughing*) Oh, Edith, it is rather trying. But when it's all over, isn't it the grandest thing in the world to have them?

EDITH: Well, I'd love mine just as much if they came out of cabbages.

NANCY: And I dare say your husband would hardly notice the difference.

JANE: (*Entering with tea-kettle*) Ma'am, Mr. Haines would like to speak to you on the phone.

MARY: Oh, I can feel what it is in my bones, Jane. (*To the others*) Stephen's going to be kept at the office again tonight. (*Exits.*)

SYLVIA: Give him my love, pet.

MARY: (*Off stage*) I will.

SYLVIA: (*She never lets anything pass*) Nancy, you couldn't be more wrong about me and Mary.

NANCY: Still rankling?

SYLVIA: Jealous? As a matter of fact, I'm sorry for her.

NANCY: Oh-ho? Why?

SYLVIA: (*Mysteriously*) Well, for all *we* know she may be living in a fool's paradise with Stephen.

NANCY: Let's check that one for a moment, Sylvia. Jane, are the children in?

JANE: Yes, Miss. Just back from the Park. (EDITH *rises*—SYLVIA, *in pantomime, signals her not to leave room. This is not lost on* NANCY. *For a moment she hesitates at the door.*)

PEGGY: Oh, I'd love to see Mrs. Haines' little girl, Miss Blake—

NANCY: (*Following* PEGGY) Come along, child. Anyway, it's our turn to go on the pan. But we don't have to worry. You've got a poor man. I've got no man at all. (*They exit.*)

EDITH: (*Goes to tea-table—pours two cups.* JANE *empties ash-trays.*) This is positively the last time I play bridge with Nancy. She never misses a chance to get in a dig. What has a creature like her got but her friends? (JANE *exits, closing door, left.* SYLVIA *stealthily closes door, right.*) The way she kept at you about Mary made me so nervous, I thought I'd scream. And in my condition—

SYLVIA: Edith, I've got to tell you! I'll burst if I wait!

EDITH: I *knew* you had something! (*She brings her well-laden plate and tea-cup and settles herself happily beside* SYLVIA *on the sofa.*)

SYLVIA: You'll die!

EDITH: Mary?

SYLVIA: No, Stephen. Guess!

EDITH: You couldn't mean...?

SYLVIA: (*Nodding*) Stephen Haines is cheating on Mary!

EDITH: I don't believe you; is it true?

SYLVIA: Wait till you hear. (*Now she is into it*) You know I go to Michael's for my hair. You ought to go, pet. I despise whoever does yours. Well, there's the most wonderful new manicurist there. (*Shows her scarlet nails*) Isn't that divine? Jungle Red—

EDITH: Simply divine. Go on.

SYLVIA: It all came out in the most extraordinary way, this morning. I tried to get you on the phone—

EDITH: I was in the tub. Go on.

SYLVIA: This manicurist, she's marvelous, was doing my nails. I was looking through *Vogue*, the one with Mary in the Beaux Arts Ball costume—

EDITH: —in that white wig that flattered her so much?

SYLVIA: (*Nodding*) Well, this manicurist: "Oh, Mrs. Fowler," she said, "is that that Mrs. Haines who's so awfully rich?"

EDITH: Funny how people like that think people like us are awfully rich.

SYLVIA: I forget what she said next. You know how those creatures

are, babble, babble, babble, babble, and never let up for a
minute! When suddenly she said: "I know the girl who's
being *kept* by Mr. Haines!"

EDITH: No!

SYLVIA: I swear!

EDITH: (*Thrilled*) Someone *we* know?

SYLVIA: No! That's what's so awful about it. She's a friend of this
manicurist. Oh, it wouldn't be so bad if Stephen had picked
someone in his own class. But a blonde floosie!

EDITH: But how did Stephen ever meet a girl like that?

SYLVIA: How do men ever meet girls like that? That's what they
live for, the rats!

EDITH: But—

SYLVIA: I can't go into all the details, now. They're utterly fantastic—

EDITH: You suppose Mary knows?

SYLVIA: Mary's the kind who couldn't help showing it.

EDITH: (*Nodding, her mouth full of her third cake*) No self-control.
Well, she's bound to find out. If a woman's got any instincts,
she feels when her husband's off the reservation. I know *I*
would.

SYLVIA: Of course you do, darling. Not Mary— (*Rises, and walks
about the room, wrestling with* MARY's *sad problem*) If only there
were some way to *warn* her!

EDITH: (*Horrified, following her*) Sylvia! You're not going to tell
her?

SYLVIA: Certainly not. I'd *die* before I'd be the one to hurt her like
that!

EDITH: Couldn't someone shut that manicurist up?

SYLVIA: A good story like that? A lot those girls care whose life they
ruin.

EDITH: *Isn't* it a dirty trick?

SYLVIA: Isn't it *foul*? It's not as though only Mary's friends knew.
We could keep our mouths shut.

EDITH: I know plenty that I never *breathe* about my friends' husbands!

SYLVIA: So do I! (*They exchange a sudden glance of sharp suspicion.*)
Anyway, the whole thing's disgustingly unfair to Mary. I feel
like a disloyal skunk, just knowing about it—

EDITH: I adore her—

SYLVIA: I *worship* her. She's my dearest friend in all the world—

(Voices, off-stage. They sit down at the card-table and begin to play solitaire hastily. Enter NANCY *and* PEGGY.)

NANCY: Well, Sylvia, feeling better?

SYLVIA: *(Innocently)* Meaning what?

NANCY: Must've been choice. You both look so *relaxed.*

SYLVIA: Nancy, were you listening at that door?

PEGGY: Oh, Mrs. Fowler, we were in the nursery. *(MARY enters.)*

SYLVIA: *(Quickly)* Well, darling, how is Stephen, the old dear? And did you give him my love?

MARY: I did. Stephen's not so well, Sylvia.

SYLVIA: Oh? What's the trouble?

MARY: Nervous indigestion. That's why I have such a plain cook now.

EDITH: Phelps has had indigestion for years. You should hear that man rumble in the night. Like a truck on cobblestones.

SYLVIA: There's nothing—worrying Stephen?

MARY: Oh, no, he's just been working late. He's not coming home tonight. Oh, I wish—*(Abruptly, with an indulgent laugh)* Well, man's love is of man's life a thing apart, 'tis woman's whole— et cetera.

SYLVIA: Are you sure it's *work*, darling, and not a beautiful blonde?

MARY: Stephen? *(Laughing, and perhaps a little smugly, too)* Oh, Sylvia.

EDITH: *(Afraid that* SYLVIA *will go too far)* Sylvia, let's play!

SYLVIA: Stephen's a very attractive man.

MARY: Isn't he? I can't imagine why he hasn't deserted me for some glamorous creature long ago.

NANCY: *(Alarmed)* Mary, you *do* sound smug.

MARY: Oh, let me be, Nancy. How can you be too sure of what you believe in most?

SYLVIA: I wouldn't be sure of the Apostle Paul. I always tell Howard, "If you ever manage to make a fool of me, I'll deserve what I get."

NANCY: You certainly will. *(Faces* SYLVIA *squarely)* Now, Sylvia, let's have it.

SYLVIA: Have what?

NANCY: Just what did you mean when you said Mary was living in a fool's paradise?

MARY: What?

SYLVIA: *(Angrily)* Nancy, don't be absurd. *(A pause. Then, wriggling out of it)* Oh, Mary, I was just trying to make a typical Nancy

Blake wisecrack about marriage. I said, "A woman's paradise is always a fool's paradise!"

MARY: That's not bad, is it, Nancy? Well, Sylvia, whatever I'm living in, I like it. Nancy, cut.

SYLVIA: (SYLVIA *examines her nails minutely, suddenly shows them to* MARY) Mary, how do you like that?

NANCY: (*Not looking*) Too, too adorable.

SYLVIA: You can't imagine how it stays on. I get it at Michael's—you ought to go, Mary!

EDITH: (*Protestingly*) Oh, Sylvia!—

SYLVIA: A wonderful new manicurist. Olga's her name. She's marvelous.

EDITH: Will you cut, Sylvia?

SYLVIA: Look, Jungle Red.

NANCY: Looks as if you'd been tearing at somebody's throat.

SYLVIA: I'll be damned, Nancy, if I'll let you ride me any more!

MARY: Now, Sylvia, Nancy's just being clever too.

SYLVIA: She takes a crack at everything about me. Even my nails!

MARY: (*Laughing*) Well, I like it. I really do! It's new and smart. (*Pats her hand*) Michael's, Olga, Jungle Red? I'll remember that. (*Cuts cards*) You and I, Sylvia. I feel lucky today.

SYLVIA: (*With a sweet, pitying smile*) Do you, darling? Well, you know what they say, "Lucky in cards"—

CURTAIN

SCENE II

An afternoon, a few days later. A hairdressing booth in Michael's. An elegantly functional cubby-hole. Right, a recessed mirror in the wall. Left, from the high partition pole, a curtain to the floor. The rear wall is a plain partition. Center, a swivel hairdressing chair. Above it from an aluminum tree, the hanging thicket of a permanent-wave machine. In the wall, gadgets for curling irons, electric outlets which connect with wires to the drying machine, the hand drier, the manicurists' table-light, stools for the pedicurist, the manicurist, OLGA.
As the curtain rises, the booth is, to put it mildly, full.

MRS. WAGSTAFF, *a fat, elderly woman is in the chair, undergoing the punishment of a permanent. Wires and clamps, Medusa-like, rise from her head, to the cap of the machine.*

OLGA, *at her right, is doing her nails. Her fat bare feet rest in the lap of the* PEDICURIST. *The* FIRST HAIRDRESSER *cools her steaming locks with a hand-drier. The* SECOND HAIRDRESSER, *watch in hand, fiddles with the wires, times the operation. When the machine is working, a small, red light glows among the wires.*

MRS. WAGSTAFF, *apparently inured to public execution, smokes, reads a magazine on her lap, occasionally nibbles a sandwich which* OLGA *passes her from a tray near her instruments. The drier, whenever it is on, makes a loud noise, drowning out voices, which must be harshly raised above it. Now the drier is on, the voices loud.*

MRS. WAGSTAFF: It's burning my neck!

SECOND HAIRDRESSER: Be brave! One minute more!

MRS. WAGSTAFF: (*In pain*) O-o-oo!

FIRST HAIRDRESSER: It's going to be so worth it, Mrs. Wagstaff.

MRS. WAGSTAFF: My ears!

SECOND HAIRDRESSER: Be brave!

MRS. WAGSTAFF: O-o-o-o! My nerves—Oo—my God! (*To* PEDI-CURIST) My sandwich—(OLGA *hands her sandwich.*)

SECOND HAIRDRESSER: Ten seconds. We must suffer to be beautiful. (*The curtain parts;* A FIGURE *in flowing white half-enters. It is, judging by the voice, a woman, but its face is completely obliterated by a mud-mask.*)

MUD-MASK: Oh, pardon—I thought I was in here. Why, hello, Mrs. Wagstaff. (*Coyly*) Guess who I am? (*A second face appears over this intruder's shoulder. At first, it looks like another mud-mask. It's not. It's the colored maid,* EUPHIE. *She clutches the shoulder of the mud-mask.*)

EUPHIE: Mustn't talk, ma'am. You'll crack yo'self. (*Exit* MUD-MASK *followed by* EUPHIE.)

MRS. WAGSTAFF: Who was it?

FIRST HAIRDRESSER: Mrs. Phipps—(*Switches off the drier. Now they all lower their voices to a normal pitch*) There, dear, the agony's over. (*They take the permanent clamps off* MRS. WAGSTAFF'*s hair. A drier is on in the next booth. A voice is heard off-stage, screaming above it.*)

VOICE:—so I feel awful. I ate a lobster at the opening of the Ritz—(*The drier goes off.*)

OLGA: (*To* MRS. WAGSTAFF) Mrs. Mordie Barnes. She's been in the hospital. It wasn't ptomaine at all. It was a mis—

SECOND HAIRDRESSER: Olga! She'll hear you—

MRS. WAGSTAFF: (*Thoughtfully*) I think I'll have a mud-mask.

SECOND HAIRDRESSER: (*Calling outside*) Euphie! Tell the desk Mrs. Wagstaff's working in a mud!

MRS. WAGSTAFF: (*Enviously*) Mrs. Phipps has such a lovely skin.

FIRST HAIRDRESSER: Not lovelier than yours, Mrs. Wagstaff.

CHORUS (SECOND HAIRDRESSER, OLGA, PEDICURIST): Oh, yours is lovely! Why, not nearly as lovely! Lovelier than yours?

MRS. WAGSTAFF: (*Coyly*) I do think it's rather good for a woman my age.

FIRST HAIRDRESSER: You talk as if you were an old woman, dear.

MRS. WAGSTAFF: (*Lying*) I'm 42.

SECOND HAIRDRESSER: Mustn't tell anyone. You don't look a day over 35!

CHORUS (SECOND HAIRDRESSER, PEDICURIST, OLGA): Why, no one would believe it! Why, not a day! Oh, you don't look it!

SECOND HAIRDRESSER: —now you've gotten so much slimmer!

MRS. WAGSTAFF: I have slimmed down, haven't I?

CHORUS (PEDICURIST, OLGA, FIRST HAIRDRESSER): Oh, thin as a shadow! Why, terribly thin! Oh, just right, now!

MRS. WAGSTAFF: (*Admiring her nail polish*) That's lovely.

OLGA: Jungle Red. Everybody loves it. Do you know Mrs. Howard Fowler?

PEDICURIST: (*Rising, gathering up her things*) Don't put your stockings on yet, Mrs. Wagstaff, you'll smear your beautiful big toe—(*Exits.*)

OLGA: They say Mr. Fowler made a fortune in some stock. But one of the ladies Mrs. Fowler sent in was telling me Mr. Fowler does like to drink! Only the other day—

FIRST HAIRDRESSER: (*Sharply*) We're ready now, Mrs. Wagstaff. (*Gets* MRS. WAGSTAFF *up*) We'll unwind you in the shampoo. (*Calling*) Euphie!

SECOND HAIRDRESSER: (*Taking* MRS. WAGSTAFF *to door*) This way, dear. How does your permanent feel? And it's going to look lovely, too—(SECOND HAIRDRESSER *herds* MRS. WAGSTAFF *out of the booth,* MRS. WAGSTAFF *walking on her heels, her toes still wadded with cotton. Enter* EUPHIE, *who, during the ensuing dialogue, cleans up the debris on the floor of the booth.*)

OLGA: That old gasoline truck! Fifty-two if she's a day!

FIRST HAIRDRESSER: One more permanent and she won't have a hair left on her head.

OLGA: There's plenty on her upper lip.

EUPHIE: She sho' does shed, don't she?

OLGA: Any woman who's fool enough to marry a man ten years younger! Know what a client told me? Her husband's a pansy! (FIRST HAIRDRESSER *exits followed by* OLGA.)

SECOND HAIRDRESSER: (*Entering*) Ready?

EUPHIE: Yes, ma'am. (*The* SECOND HAIRDRESSER *holds back the curtain.*)

MARY: (*Off stage*) So I woke up this morning and decided for no reason at all to change the way—(*She enters, followed by* NANCY) I do my hair. (*Exit* EUPHIE.)

SECOND HAIRDRESSER: Mr. Michaels will be ten minutes, ma'am. Anyone in particular for your manicure?

MARY: Who does Mrs. Fowler's nails?

SECOND HAIRDRESSER: Olga. I'll see. (*Exits.*)

NANCY: God, I'd love to do Mrs. Fowler's nails, right down to the wrist, with a nice big buzz saw.

MARY: Sylvia's all right. She's a good friend underneath.

NANCY: Underneath what ?

MARY: Nancy, you don't humor your friends enough.

NANCY: So that's the big idea coming here? You're humoring Sylvia?

MARY: Oh, you did hurt her. I had it all over again at lunch. (*She catches a glimpse of herself in the mirror*) Nancy, am I getting old?

NANCY: Who put that in your head? Sylvia?

MARY: Tell me the truth.

NANCY: Beauty is in the eye of the beholder, and twaddle to that effect.

MARY: But it's such a scary feeling when you see those little wrinkles creeping in.

NANCY: Time's little mice.

MARY: And that first gleam of white in your hair. It's the way you'd feel about autumn if you knew there'd never be another spring—

NANCY: (*Abruptly*) There's only one tragedy for a woman.

MARY: Growing old?

NANCY: Losing her man.

MARY: That's why we're all so afraid of growing old.

NANCY: Are you afraid?

MARY: Well, I was very pretty when I was young. I never thought about it twice then. Now I know it's why Stephen loved me.

NANCY: Smart girl.

MARY: Now I think about it all the time.

NANCY: Love is not love which alters when it alteration finds. Shakespeare.

MARY: Well, he told me, on my birthday, I'd always look the same to him.

NANCY: Nice present. No jewels?

MARY: It rained that day. He brought me a bottle of perfume called "Summer Rain."

NANCY: How many ounces?

MARY: Nancy, you've never been in love.

NANCY: Says who?

MARY: (*Surprised*) Have you?

NANCY: Yes.

MARY: You never told me.

NANCY: You never asked—(*Wistfully*) Neither did *he*. (OLGA *enters with fresh bowl of water.*) Here, innocent. (*Gives a book to* MARY) The book my readers everywhere have been waiting for with such marked apathy.

MARY: "All the Dead Ladies"?

NANCY: Originally called, "From the Silence of the Womb." My publisher thought that would make too much noise.

MARY: What's it about? (OLGA *begins to file* MARY'*s nails.*)

NANCY: Women I dislike: "Ladies"—

MARY: Oh, Nancy!

OLGA: Don't soak it yet. (*Taking* MARY'*s hand out of the water.*)

NANCY: No good? Too bad. It's a parting shot. I'm off.

MARY: Off?

NANCY: Africa.

MARY: But not today?

NANCY: I knew if I told you you'd scurry around and do things. A party. Steamer baskets of sour fruit. Not nearly as sour as the witty cables your girl friends would send me—So don't move. No tears. For my sake—just soak it? Good-bye, Mary—

MARY: Good-bye, Nancy. I'll miss you.

NANCY: I doubt it. Practically nobody ever misses a clever woman. (*Exits.*)

OLGA: Funny, isn't she?

MARY: She's a darling.

OLGA: (*Filing* MARY'*s nails*) She's a writer? How do those writers think up those plots? I guess the plot part's not so hard to think up as the end. I guess anybody's life'd make an interest-

ing plot if it had an interesting end—Mrs. Fowler sent you
in? (MARY, *absorbed in her book, nods.*) She's sent me three
clients this week. Know Mrs. Herbert Parrish that was Mrs.
Malcom Leeds? Well, Mrs. Parrish was telling me herself
about her divorce. Seems Mr. Parrish came home one night
with lipstick on his undershirt. Said he always explained
everything before. But *that* was something he just wasn't
going to try to explain. Know Mrs. Potter? She's awful pregnant—

MARY: (*She wants to read*) I know.

OLGA: Soak it, please. (*Puts* MARY'*s hand in water. Begins on other
hand*) Know Mrs. Stephen Haines?

MARY: What? Why, yes, *I*—

OLGA: I guess Mrs. Fowler's told you about that! Mrs. Fowler feels
awfully sorry for her.

MARY: (*Laughing*) Oh, she does! Well, I don't. I—

OLGA: You would if you knew this girl.

MARY: What girl?

OLGA: This Crystal Allen.

MARY: Crystal Allen?

OLGA: Yes, you know. The girl who's living with Mr. Haines.
(MARY, *starts violently*) Don't you like the file? Mrs. Potter
says it sets her unborn child's teeth on edge.

MARY: (*Indignant*) Whoever told you such a thing?

OLGA: Oh, I thought you knew. Didn't Mrs. Fowler—?

MARY: No—

OLGA: Then you will be interested. You see, Crystal Allen is a
friend of mine. She's really a terrible man-trap. Soak it,
please. (MARY, *dazed, puts her hand in the dish*) She's behind
the perfume counter at Saks. So was I before I got fi—left.
That's how she met him.

MARY: Stephen Haines ?

OLGA: Yeah. It was a couple a months ago. Us girls wasn't busy. It
was an awful rainy day, I remember. So this gentleman walks
up to the counter. He was the serious type, nice-looking, but
kind of thin on top. Well, Crystal nabs him. "I want some
perfume," he says. "May I awsk what type of woman for?"
Crystal says, very Ritzy. That didn't mean a thing. She was
going to sell him Summer Rain, our feature anyway. "Is she
young?" Crystal says. "No," he says, sort of embarrassed. "Is
she the glamorous type?" Crystal says. "No, thank God," he

says. "Thank God?" Crystal says and bats her eyes. She's got those eyes which run up and down a man like a searchlight. Well, she puts perfume on her palm and in the crook of her arm for him to smell. So he got to smelling around and I guess he liked it. Because we heard him tell her his name, which one of the girls recognized from Cholly Knickerbocker's column—Gee, you're nervous—Well, it was after that I left. I wouldn't of thought no more about it. But a couple of weeks ago I stopped by where Crystal lives to say hello. And the landlady says she'd moved to the kind of house where she could entertain her gentleman friend—"What gentleman friend?" I says. "Why, that Mr. Haines that she's had up in her room all hours of the night," the landlady says—Did I hurt? (MARY *draws her hand away*) One coat, or two? (*Picks up a red bottle.*)

MARY: None. (*Rises and goes to the chair, where she has left her purse.*)

OLGA: But I thought that's what you came for? All Mrs. Fowler's friends—

MARY: I think I've gotten what all Mrs. Fowler's friends came for. (*Puts coin on the table.*)

OLGA: (*Picks up coin*) Oh, thanks—Well, good-bye. I'll tell her you were in, Mrs.—?

MARY: Mrs. Stephen Haines.

OLGA: Mrs.—? Oh, gee, gee! Gee, Mrs. Haines—I'm sorry! Oh, isn't there something I can do?

MARY: Stop telling that story!

OLGA: Oh, sure, sure, I will!

MARY: And please, don't tell anyone—(*Her voice breaks*) that you told it to *me*—

OLGA: Oh, I won't, gee, I promise! Gee, that would be kind of humiliating for you! (*Defensively*) But in a way, Mrs. Haines, I'm kinda *glad* you know. Crystal's a terrible girl—I mean, she's terribly clever. And she's terribly pretty, Mrs. Haines—I mean, if I was you I wouldn't waste no time getting Mr. Haines away from her—(MARY *turns abruptly away.*) I mean, now you *know*, Mrs. Haines!

(OLGA *eyes the coin in her hand distastefully, suddenly puts it down on the table and exits.* MARY, *alone, stares blankly in the mirror, then suddenly focusing on her image, leans forward, searching her face between her trembling hands. A drier goes on in the next booth. A shrill voice rises above its drone.*)

VOICE:—Not too hot! My sinus! So *she* said: "I wouldn't want anybody in the world to know," and *I* said: "My dear, you know you can trust *me*!"

CURTAIN

SCENE III

An hour later. MARY's *boudoir. Charming, of course. A door to bedroom, right. A door to the hall, left. A chaise-longue; next to it, a table with books, flowers, a telephone. A dressing table.*
As the curtain rises, MARY *is discovered on the chaise-longue, trying to read.* JANE *enters from the hall. She is upset about something. She keeps daubing at her eyes.*

MARY: Tea, Jane?
JANE: It's coming, ma'am.
MARY: My mother will be here in a few minutes. A cup for her.
JANE: Yes, ma'am. (*Sniffling*) Ma'am—
MARY: And tell Cook please, dinner on time. We're going to the theatre. Mr. Haines likes to be there for the curtain. I'll wear my old black, Jane.
JANE: (*Looking nervously at the door behind her*) Yes, ma'am.
MARY: No, I'll wear my new blue, Jane.
JANE: Ma'am, it's Cook. She wants to see you. (*Defensively*) It's about *me*. She says I—
MARY: Later, Jane.
JANE: Don't you believe a word she says, ma'am. It's all his fault.
MARY: (*Aware of* JANE's *distress for the first time*) Whose fault?
JANE: Her husband's. Ford's.
MARY: (*Surprised*) What's the matter with Ford? He's a very good butler.
JANE: Oh, he does his work, ma'am. But you don't know how he is in the pantry. Always kidding around with us girls. He don't mean any harm, but Cook—(*Enter* COOK *abruptly with* MARY's *tea tray. She is a fat, kind woman, with a strong Scandinavian accent. At the moment she is very mad.*)
COOK: Afternoon, ma'am. (*Glaring at* JANE) I'd like to talk to you alone, ma'am.
JANE: I told you, it isn't my fault.
COOK: You led him on!

JANE: I didn't. (*Bursting into tears*) I've been with Mrs. Haines seven years. She knows I never make trouble downstairs. (*Exits to hall.*)

MARY: Yes, Ingrid?

COOK: Ma'am, you're the nicest I ever had. But I go. I got to get Ford away from that bad girl.

MARY: (*Very firmly*) Jane is not a bad girl.

COOK: (*Bursts into tears*) Oh, course she ain't. He was always like that! Sometimes I could die, for the shame!

MARY: (*Kindly*) I'll send him away. You can stay.

COOK: (*More soberly*) No, I don't do that, ma'am.

MARY: I'll give you a hundred dollars. That's more than half of what you make together.

COOK: Thank you, ma'am. We both go.

MARY: Is that sensible?

COOK: No. It's plain dumb.

MARY: Then why?

COOK: (*She pauses, rocking from foot to foot*) I guess nobody understand. Sure it was no good to marry him. My mother told me he's a lady-killer. Don't marry them, she said. His wife is the lady he kills. Oh, he's terrible. But except for women he's a good man. He always says, "Ingrid, you take the money. You manage good." Oh, he don't want nobody but me for his wife! That's an awful big thing, ma'am.

MARY: Is that the thing that really matters?

COOK: With women like us, yes, ma'am—You give us references? (MARY *nods*) And don't say nothing about his ways?

MARY: I won't.

COOK: (*Moving to the door*) Black bean soup, a fricassee, fried sweets and apple pie for dinner, ma'am—(She *opens the door.* JANE *has been eavesdropping.*)

COOK: (*In a low, fierce voice*) Slut! (*Exit* COOK.)

JANE: (*Entering with extra cup on tray*) Did you hear what she called me, Mrs. Haines?

MARY: Please, Jane.

JANE: (*Cheerfully*) I'd rather be that any day than have some man make a fool of me! (*Enter* MISS FORDYCE. *She is a raw-boned, capable English spinster of 32.*)

MISS FORDYCE: May I see you, Mrs. Haines?

MARY: Of course, Miss Fordyce.

MISS FORDYCE: It's about little Mary—Really, Mrs. Haines, you'll

have to talk to your child. She's just smacked her little brother, hard. Pure temper.

MARY: What did little Stevie do to her, Miss Fordyce?

MISS FORDYCE: Well, you see, it happened while I was down getting my tea. When I came up, she'd had such a tantrum, she'd
made herself ill. She positively refuses to discuss the incident
with me. But I'm quite sure the dear boy hadn't done a thing.

MARY: You're very apt to take the boy's side, Miss Fordyce.

MISS FORDYCE: Not at all. But in England, Mrs. Haines, our girls
are not so wretchedly spoiled. After all, this *is* a man's world.
The sooner our girls are taught to accept the fact *graciously—*

MARY: (*Gently*) Send her in to me, Miss Fordyce. (*Exit* MISS
FORDYCE.) Oh, Jane, I don't understand it. Miss Fordyce
really prefers Mary, but she insists we all make a little god of
Stevie. (*Exits to bedroom, leaving the door open.*)

JANE: Them English ones always hold out for the boys. But they
say since the War, ma'am, there's six women over there to
every man. Competition is something fierce! Over here, you
can treat the men the way they deserve—Men aren't so
scarce. (*Enter* LITTLE MARY. *She is a broad-browed, thoughtful,
healthy little girl, physically well developed for her age.*)

LITTLE MARY: Where's Mother?

JANE: You're going to catch it. Smacking your little brother.
(*Mimicking* MISS FORDYCE) Such a dear, sweet little lad—
shame. (LITTLE MARY *does not answer*) I'll bet you wish you
were Mother's girl, instead of Daddy's girl today, don't you?
(LITTLE MARY *doesn't answer*) What's the matter, the cat got
your tongue? (*Enter* MARY, *wearing a negligée.*)

MARY: Hello, darling—Aren't you going to kiss me? (LITTLE MARY
doesn't move) What red eyes!

LITTLE MARY: I was mad. I threw up. When you throw up, doesn't
it make you cry?

MARY: (*Smiling*) Stevie tease you? (LITTLE MARY, *embarrassed, looks
at* JANE. JANE *snickers, takes the hint and goes out*) Well, darling?

LITTLE MARY: Mother, I don't know how to begin.

MARY: (*Sitting on the chaise-longue, and putting out her hand*) Come
here. (LITTLE MARY *doesn't budge*) Would you rather wait
until tonight and tell Dad?

LITTLE MARY: (*Horrified*) Oh, Mother, I couldn't tell him! (*Fiercely*)
And I'd be killed to death before I'd tell skinny old Miss

Fordyce—

MARY: That's not the way for my dear little girl to talk.

LITTLE MARY: (*Setting her jaw*) I don't want to be a dear little girl. (*She suddenly rushes to her mother's outstretched arms in tears*) Oh, Mother dear, Mother dear!

MARY: Baby, what?

LITTLE MARY: What brother said!

MARY: What did he say, the wretched boy?

LITTLE MARY: (*Disentangling herself*) He said I had bumps!

MARY: Bumps? You don't mean mumps?

LITTLE MARY: No, bumps. He said I was covered with disgusting bumps!

MARY: Mary, *where?*

LITTLE MARY: (*Touching her hips and breasts with delicate, ashamed finger tips*) *Here* and *here!*

MARY: Oh—(*Controlling her relieved laughter, and drawing her daughter to her side*) Of course you have bumps, darling. Very pretty little bumps. And you have them because—you're a little girl.

LITTLE MARY: (*Wailing*) But, Mother dear, I don't want to be a little girl. I hate girls! They're so silly, and they tattle, tattle—

MARY: Not really, Mary.

LITTLE MARY: Yes, Mother, I know. Oh, Mother, what *fun* is there to be a lady? What can a lady do?

MARY: (*Cheerfully*) These days, darling, ladies do all the things men do. They fly airplanes across the ocean, they go into politics and business—

LITTLE MARY: *You* don't, Mother.

MARY: Perhaps I'm happier doing just what I do.

LITTLE MARY: What do you do, Mother?

MARY: Take care of you and Stevie and Dad.

LITTLE MARY: You don't, Mother. Miss Fordyce and the servants do.

MARY: (*Teasing*) I see. I'm not needed around here.

LITTLE MARY: (*Hugging her*) Oh, Mother, I don't mean that. It wouldn't be any fun at all without *you*. But, Mother, even when the ladies *do* do things, they stop it when they get the lovey-doveys.

MARY: The what ?

LITTLE MARY: Like in the movies, Mother. Ladies always end up so *silly*. (*Disgusted*) Lovey-dovey, lovey-dovey all the time!

MARY: Darling, you're too young to understand—

LITTLE MARY: But, Mother—

MARY: "But Mother, but Mother!" There's one thing a woman can do, no man can do.

LITTLE MARY: (*Eagerly*) What?

MARY: Have a child. (*Tenderly*) Like you.

LITTLE MARY: Oh, that! Everybody knows that. But is that any fun, Mother dear?

MARY: Fun? No. But it is—joy. (*Hugging her*) Of a very special kind.

LITTLE MARY: (*Squirming away*) Well, it's never sounded specially exciting to me—I love you, Mother. But I bet you anything you like, Daddy has more *fun* than you! (*She slips away from* MARY. *Then sees her mother's dispirited face, turns and kisses her warmly*) Oh, I'm sorry, Mother. But you just *don't understand*! (*A pause*) Am I to be punished, Mother?

MARY: (*She is thinking about something else*) What do you think?

LITTLE MARY: I smacked him awful hard—Shall I punish myself?

MARY: It will have to be pretty bad.

LITTLE MARY: (*Solemnly*) Then I won't go down to breakfast with Daddy tomorrow, or the next day—O. K., Mother?

MARY: O.K. (LITTLE MARY *walks, crestfallen, to the door as* JANE *enters.* LITTLE MARY *sticks out her tongue.*)

LITTLE MARY: There's my tongue! So what? (*Exits skipping.*)

JANE: (*Laughing*) She never lets anybody get the best of her, does she, Mrs. Haines?

MARY: My poor baby. She doesn't want to be a woman, Jane.

JANE: Who does?

MARY: Somehow, I've never minded it, Jane. (*Enter* MRS. MOREHEAD. *She is a bourgeois aristocrat of 55.* MARY *rises, kisses her.*)

MRS. MOREHEAD: Hello, child. Afternoon, Jane.

JANE: Afternoon, Mrs. Morehead. (*Exits to bedroom.*)

MARY: Mother, dear! (*She walks slowly to the dressing-table.*)

MRS. MOREHEAD: (*Cheerfully*) Well, what's wrong? (*Sits.*)

MARY: (*Turning*) How did you know something's wrong?

MRS. MOREHEAD: Your voice on the phone. Is it Stephen?

MARY: How did you know?

MRS. MOREHEAD: You sent for *Mother*. So it must be he. (*A pause.*)

MARY: I don't know how to begin, Mother.

MRS. MOREHEAD: (*Delighted to find that her instincts were correct*) It's a woman! Who is she?

MARY: Her name is Crystal Allen. She—she's a salesgirl at Saks. (*Her mother's cheerful and practical manner discourages tears, so she begins to cream and tonic her face instead.*)

MRS. MOREHEAD: She's young and pretty, I suppose.

MARY: Well, yes. (*Defensively*) But common.

MRS. MOREHEAD: (*Soothingly*) Of course—Stephen told you?

MARY: No. I—I found out—this afternoon.

MRS. MOREHEAD: How far has it gone?

MARY: He's known her about three months.

MRS. MOREHEAD: Does Stephen know you know?

MARY: (*Shaking her head*) I—I wanted to speak to you first. (*The tears come anyway*) Oh, Mother dear, what am I going to say to him?

MRS. MOREHEAD: *Nothing.*

MARY: Nothing? (*Enter* JANE *with the new dress.*)

JANE: I'll give it a touch with the iron.

MARY: Look, Schaparelli—(JANE *holds dress up*) It's rather trying, though, one of those tight skirts with a flared tunic—

MRS. MOREHEAD: Personally, I always thought you looked best in things not too extreme. (*Exit* JANE.)

MARY: But, Mother, you don't really mean I should say nothing?

MRS. MOREHEAD: I do.

MARY: Oh, but Mother—

MRS. MOREHEAD: My dear, I felt the same way twenty years ago.

MARY: Not Father?

MRS. MOREHEAD: Mary, in many ways your father was an exceptional man. (*Philosophically*) That, unfortunately, was not one of them.

MARY: Did you say nothing?

MRS. MOREHEAD: Nothing. I had a wise mother, too. Listen, dear, this is not a new story. It comes to most wives.

MARY: But Stephen—

MRS. MOREHEAD: Stephen is a man. He's been married twelve years—

MARY: You mean, he's tired of me!

MRS. MOREHEAD: Stop crying. You'll make your nose red.

MARY: I'm not crying. (*Patting tonic on her face*) This stuff stings.

MRS. MOREHEAD: (*Going to her*) Stephen's tired of himself. Tired of feeling the same things in himself year after year. Time comes when every man's got to feel something new—when he's got to feel young again, just because he's growing old.

Women are just the same. But when *we* get that way we change our hair dress. Or get a new cook. Or redecorate the house from stem to stern. But a man can't do over his office, or fire his secretary. Not even change the style of his hair. And the urge usually hits him hardest just when he's beginning to lose his hair. No, dear, a man has only one escape from his old self: to see a different self—in the mirror of some woman's eyes.

MARY: But, Mother—

MRS. MOREHEAD: This girl probably means no more to him than that new dress means to you.

MARY: But, Mother—

MRS. MOREHEAD: "But Mother, but Mother!" He's not giving anything to her that belongs to you, or you would have felt that yourself long ago.

MARY: (*Bewildered*) Oh, I always thought I would. I love him so much.

MRS. MOREHEAD: And he loves you, baby. (*Drawing* MARY *beside her on the chaise-longue*) Now listen to me: Go away somewhere for a month or two. There's nothing like a good dose of another woman to make a man appreciate his wife. Mother knows!

MARY: But, there's never been a lie between us before.

MRS. MOREHEAD: You mean, there's never been a *silence* between you before. Well, it's about time. Keeping still, when you *ache* to talk, is about the only sacrifice spoiled women like us ever have to make.

MARY: But, I'd forgive him—

MRS. MOREHEAD: Forgive him? (*Impatiently*) For what? For being a man? Accuse him, and you'll never get a chance to forgive him. He'd have to justify himself—

MARY: How can he!

MRS. MOREHEAD: (*Sighing*) He can't and he *can*. Don't make him try. Either way you'd lose him. And remember, dear, it's being together at the *end* that really matters. (*Rising*) One more piece of motherly advice: Don't confide in your girl friends!

MARY: I think they all know.

MRS. MOREHEAD: They think you don't? (MARY *nods*) Leave it that way. If you let them advise you, they'll see to it, in the name of friendship, that you lose your husband and your home. I'm an old woman, dear, and I know my sex. (*Moving to the door*) I'm going right down this minute and get our tickets.

MARY: Our—tickets?

MRS. MOREHEAD: You're taking me to Bermuda, dear. My throat's been awfully bad. I haven't wanted to worry you, but my doctor says—

MARY: Oh, Mother darling! Thank you!

MRS. MOREHEAD: Don't thank me, dear. It's rather—*nice* to have you need Mother again. (*Exits. The telephone rings.* MARY *answers it.*)

MARY: Yes?—Oh, Stephen—Yes, dear?—(*Distressed*) Oh, Stephen! Oh, no—I'm not angry. It's—it's just that I wanted to see the play. Yes, I can get Mother. Stephen, will you be very—late? (*It's a bit of a struggle, but she manages a cheerful voice*) Oh, it's—all right. Have a good time. Of course, I know it's just business—No, dear—I won't wait up—Stephen, I love—(*A click. The other end has hung up.* JANE *enters.* MARY *turns her back. Her face would belie the calmness of her voice*) Jane—The children and I will have dinner alone—

CURTAIN

SCENE IV

Two months later. A dressmaker's shop. We see two fitting booths, the same in appointment: triplex pier glasses, dress racks, smoking stands, two small chairs. They are divided by a mirrored partition. At the rear of each booth, a curtain and a door, off a corridor, which leads to "the floor."

As the curtain rises the booth on the left is empty. The other booth it cluttered with dresses. Two SALESGIRLs *are loading them over their arms.*

FIRST SALESGIRL: (*With vivid resentment against a customer who has just departed*) Well, now we can put them all back again. Makes you drag out everything in the damn store, and doesn't even buy a brassiere!

SECOND SALESGIRL: And that's the kind who always needs one.

FIRST SALESGIRL: This isn't her type. That isn't her type. I'd like to tell her what her type is.

SECOND SALESGIRL: I'd like to know.

FIRST SALESGIRL: It's the type that nobody gives a damn about! Gee, I'd like to work in a men's shop once. What can a man try on?

SECOND SALESGIRL: Ever see a man try on hats? What they go through, you'd think a head was something peculiar. (*Both* SALESGIRLs *exit.* FIRST SALESWOMAN *enters the booth on the right, hereafter called "Mary's Booth."*)

FIRST SALESWOMAN: Miss Myrtle, step in here a moment. (*A handsome wench, in a slinky negligée, enters.*)

FIRST MODEL: Yes, Miss Shapiro.

FIRST SALESWOMAN: If I've told you once, I've told you a thousand times, when you're modeling that dress, your stomach must lead. If you walk like this (*Pantomimes*) you take away all the seduction. *This* is seduction! (*Shows* MISS MYRTLE *her rather unconvincing conception of a seductive walk.*)

FIRST MODEL: I'll try, Miss Shapiro. (*Tearfully*) But if you had my appendix!

FIRST SALESWOMAN: Well, Miss Myrtle, you can take your choice: You will either lose your job or lose your appendix! (*Exit* FIRST MODEL. *In left booth, hereafter called "Crystal's Booth," enter* SECOND SALESWOMAN.)

SECOND SALESWOMAN: (*To the* FIRST *and* SECOND SALESGIRLs *who have returned for another load of dresses*) Quickly, please. I have a client waiting. (SECOND SALESGIRL *exits with last of clothes as enter* CRYSTAL, *followed by* SECOND SALESWOMAN. THIRD SALESWOMAN *is seen crossing corridor from right to left.*)

(*Mary's Booth*)

FIRST SALESWOMAN: (*Giving little white slip to the* SALESWOMAN *who passes*) Bring down Mrs. Haines' fittings. (*Exits, leaving booth empty.*)

(*Crystal's Booth*)

SECOND SALESWOMAN: Will you open a charge?

CRYSTAL: (*Taking off her gloves and hat*) Please.

SECOND SALESWOMAN: May I have the name?

CRYSTAL: (*She is quite self-assured*) Allen. Miss Crystal Allen. The Hotel Waverly.

SECOND SALESWOMAN: May I have your other charges? Saks, Bergdorf, Cartier—?

CRYSTAL: (*Putting it on*) Oh, I'll be opening those, in the next few days—

SECOND SALESWOMAN: Then may I have your bank?

CRYSTAL: I've no checking account either, at the moment.

(*Enter* MARY *in her booth, with* FITTER *and* FIRST SALES-
WOMAN, *who carries her try-on gown. During the following scene*
MARY *undresses, gets into gay evening gown, fits.*)
FIRST SALESWOMAN: (*To* MARY, *as they enter*) Shall we show the
   things that came in while you were away?
MARY: Please. But I'd like to see some younger things than I usually
   wear.

(*Crystal's Booth*)
SECOND SALESWOMAN: I'm sorry, Miss Allen. But we *must* ask for
   one business reference—
CRYSTAL: (*Lightly; she was prepared for this*) Oh, of course. Mr.
   Stephen Haines, 40 Wall. He's an old friend of my family.
SECOND SALESWOMAN: (*Writing*) That will do. Mrs. Haines is a
   very good client of ours.
CRYSTAL: (*Unprepared for that*) Oh?
SECOND SALESWOMAN: Will you try on now, or finish seeing the
   collection?
CRYSTAL: By the way, I've never met Mrs. Haines.
SECOND SALESWOMAN: She's lovely.
CRYSTAL: So—I'd rather you didn't mention to her, that I gave her
   husband as reference. (*Beguiling*) Do you mind?
SECOND SALESWOMAN: (*With a faint smile*) Oh, of course not, Miss
   Allen. (*Indulgently*) We understand.
CRYSTAL: (*Angrily*) Do you! What do you understand?
SECOND SALESWOMAN: (*Flustered*) I mean—
CRYSTAL: (*Very injured*) Never mind.
SECOND SALESWOMAN: Please, I hope you don't think I meant—
CRYSTAL: (*Laughing and very charming again*) Of course not. Oh,
   it's dreadful, living in a strange city alone. You have to be so
   careful not to do anything people can misconstrue. You see, I
   don't know Mrs. Haines yet. So I'd hate to get off on the
   wrong foot, before I've met her *socially*.
SECOND SALESWOMAN: (*She sounds convinced*) Naturally. Women
   are funny about little things like that.

(*Mary's Booth—Enter* SYLVIA)
SYLVIA: Yoo-hoo! May I come in?
MARY: (*Not at all pleased to see her*) Hello, Sylvia.

(*In Crystal's Booth*)

SECOND SALESWOMAN: What are you most interested in, Miss Allen, evening gowns?

CRYSTAL: Until I—I organize my social life—I won't have much use for evening gowns.

SECOND SALESWOMAN: I'll show you some smart daytime things. (*Deliberately toneless*) And we have very *exciting* negligées— (*They exit.*)

(*Mary's Booth*)

(SYLVIA *circles around* MARY, *appraising her fitting with a critical eye.*)

MARY: Oh, sit down, Sylvia.

SYLVIA: (*To the* FITTER) I don't like that underslung line. (*Demonstrating on* MARY) It cuts her across the fanny. Makes her look positively duck-bottomed.

MARY: (*Pulling away*) It's so tight, Mrs. Fowler can't sit down.

FIRST SALESWOMAN: Mrs. Fowler, shall I see if your fittings are ready?

SYLVIA: They'll call me.

MARY: (*Pointing to dress* FIRST SALESWOMAN *has over her arm*) Have you seen that?

FIRST SALESWOMAN: (*Holding up dress*) It's a lovely shape on. It doesn't look like a thing in the hand. (*Hands dress to someone outside and calls*) Show this model, girls.

SYLVIA: (*Settling in a chair and smoking a cigarette*) So you had a marvelous time in Bermuda.

MARY: I had a good rest.

SYLVIA: (*With unconscious humor*) Howard wants *me* to take a world cruise. By the way, dear, how is Stephen?

MARY: Splendid. (*Smiling, and very glad to be able to tell* SYLVIA *this*) He's not nearly so busy. He hasn't spent an evening—in the office, since I've come home. (*Enter* FIRST MODEL *in an elaborate negligée.* MARY *shakes her head, very practical*) Pretty, but I never need a thing like that—

SYLVIA: Of course *you* don't. A hot little number, for intimate afternoons. (*Exit* FIRST MODEL) Howard says nobody's seen Stephen in the Club, in the afternoon, for months—

MARY: (*The thought flashes across her mind that* STEPHEN *could, of course, have revised his extra-marital schedule, from an evening to an afternoon one, but she quickly dismisses it;* STEPHEN *has never let anything interfere with his hours downtown)* Don't worry so much about Stephen, Sylvia. He's my concern. *(Enter* MODEL *in a corset. She is prettily fashioned from head to toe. She does a great deal for the wisp of lace she wears. It does nothing that nature didn't do better for her.)*

CORSET MODEL: This is our new one-piece lace foundation garment. *(Pirouettes)* Zips up the back, and no bones. *(She exits.)*

SYLVIA: Just that uplift, Mary, you need. I always said you'd regret nursing. Look at me. I don't think there's another girl our age who has bazooms like mine. I've taken care of them. Ice water every morning, camphor at night.

MARY: Doesn't it smell like an old fur coat? (PRINCESS TAMARA *passes in the corridor.)*

SYLVIA: Who cares?

MARY: Howard?

SYLVIA: *(Laughing harshly)* Howard!

FIRST SALESWOMAN: *(Calling out door)* Princess Tamara, show here. *(Enter* PRINCESS TAMARA *in a very extreme evening gown. She is Russian, regal, soignée.)*

MARY: Oh, Tamara, how lovely!

TAMARA: You must have it. Stephen would be amazed.

MARY: He certainly would. It's too extreme for me.

SYLVIA: *(Rises)* And you really haven't the figure. *(Yanks at gown)* Tamara, you wear it wrong. I saw it in *Vogue.* *(Jerks)* Off here, and down there.

TAMARA: *(Slapping* SYLVIA's *hand down)* Stop mauling me!

FIRST SALESWOMAN: Princess!

TAMARA: What do you know how to wear clothes?

SYLVIA: *I* am not a model, Tamara, but no one disputes how *I* wear clothes!

TAMARA: No one has mistaken you for Mrs. Harrison Williams yet!

FIRST SALESWOMAN: Princess Tamara, you'd better apologize.

MARY: *(To* SALESWOMAN) It's just professional jealousy. They're really good friends!

SYLVIA: *(Maliciously)* You mean Tamara and *Howard* are friends.

TAMARA: *(Disgusted at the thought)* Do you accuse me of flirting with *your* husband?

SYLVIA: *(Pleasantly)* Go as far as you can, Tamara! If I know Howard, you're wasting valuable time.

TAMARA: *(Very angry)* Perhaps I am. But perhaps somebody else is not! (The SALESWOMAN *gives her an angry shove.)* You are riding for a fall-off, Sylvia dear! (*Exit* TAMARA *angrily, followed by* SALESWOMAN.)

SYLVIA: Did you get that innuendo? I'd like to see Howard Fowler put anything over on me. Oh, I've always hated that girl, exploiting her title the way she does! (CRYSTAL *and* SECOND SALESWOMAN *enter Crystal's Booth.*)

SECOND SALESWOMAN: (*Calling down the corridor*) Princess Tamara, show in here, to Miss Allen. (*Mary's* SALESWOMAN *enters Mary's Booth, picking up the call.*)

FIRST SALESWOMAN: Girls, show in Number 3 to Miss Allen.

SYLVIA: (*Alert*) Did you say Miss Allen?

FIRST SALESWOMAN: Yes.

SYLVIA: Not—Crystal Allen?

FIRST SALESWOMAN: Why, yes—I just saw her on the floor. She's so attractive I asked her name.

SYLVIA: (*Watching* MARY *closely*) Oh, so Crystal Allen gets her things here? (MARY *sits down suddenly.*)

FIRST SALESWOMAN: She's a new client—Why, Mrs. Haines, are you ill? (MARY *has caught* SYLVIA's *eye in the mirror.* SYLVIA *knows now that* MARY *knows.*)

MARY: No, no. I'm just tired. (TAMARA *enters Crystal's Booth.*)

FIRST FITTER: We've kept you standing too long—

FIRST SALESWOMAN: I'll get you a glass of sherry. (*Exit* MARY's *FITTER and* SALESWOMAN. SYLVIA *closes door.*)

(*Crystal's Booth*)

CRYSTAL: (*Admiring* TAMARA's *extreme evening gown*) I'm going to have that, if I have to wear it for breakfast.

SECOND SALESWOMAN: Send it in here, Princess. (TAMARA *exits.*)

(*Mary's Booth*)

SYLVIA: Mary, you do know! (*Deeply sympathetic*) Why didn't you confide in me?

MARY: Sylvia, go away.

SYLVIA: (*Fiercely*) Stephen is a louse. Spending your money on a girl like that.

MARY: Sylvia, please mind your own affairs.

SYLVIA: She's already made a fool of you before all your friends. And don't you think the salesgirls know who gets the bills?

MARY: (*Distraught*) I don't care, I tell you. I don't care!

SYLVIA: Oh, yes, you do. (*Pointing to* MARY's *stricken face in the mirror*) Don't be an ostrich, Mary. (*A pause*) Go in there.

MARY: Go in there? I'm going home. (*She rises and begins to dress.*)

FIRST SALESWOMAN: (*Half enters*) Mrs. Haines' sherry—

SYLVIA: (*Taking it from her, and closing the door in her face*) All right. You've caught her cold. It's *your* chance to humiliate her. Just say a few *quiet* words. Tell her you'll make Stephen's life *hell* until he gives her up.

MARY: Stephen will give her up when he's tired of her.

SYLVIA: When he's tired of her? Look where she was six months ago. Look where she is now.

MARY: Stephen's not in love with that girl.

SYLVIA: Maybe not. But you don't know women like that when they get hold of a man.

MARY: Sylvia, please let me decide what is best for me, and my home.

(CRYSTAL, *in her booth, has been undressing, admiring herself as she does so in the mirror. Now she slips into a "really exciting" negligée.*)

SYLVIA: Well, she may be a perfectly marvelous influence for Stephen, but she's not going to do your children any good.

MARY: (*Turning to her*) What do you mean?

SYLVIA: (*Mysteriously*) Never mind.

MARY: (*Going to her*) Tell me!

SYLVIA: Far be it from *me* to tell you things you don't care to hear. I've known this all along. (*Nobly*) Have I *uttered*?

MARY: (*Violently*) What have my children to do with this?

SYLVIA: (*After all,* MARY's *asking for it*) It was while you were away. Edith saw them. Stephen, and that tramp, and your children—together, lunching in the Park.

MARY: It's not true!

SYLVIA: Why would Edith lie? She said they were having a hilarious time. Little Stevie was eating his lunch sitting on that woman's lap. She was kissing him between every bite. When I heard that, I was positively *heart-sick*, dear! (*Sees she has scored. Celebrates by tossing down* MARY's *sherry.*)

(*Crystal's Booth*)

CRYSTAL: Oh, go get that evening gown. This thing bores me.

SECOND SALESWOMAN: Right away, Miss Allen. (*Exits.*)

(*Mary's Booth*)

SYLVIA: But, as you say, dear, it's your affair, not mine. (*Goes to the door, looking very hurt that* MARY *has refused her good advice*) No doubt that girl will make a perfectly good *step-mamma* for your children! (*Exits.* MARY, *now dressed, is alone. She stares at the partition which separates her from that still unmeasured enemy to her well-ordered domesticity, "the other woman." Her common sense dictates she should go home, but now she violently experiences the ache to talk. She struggles against it, then goes, bitterly determined, to the door. Exits. A second later, there is a knock on* CRYS-TAL's *door.* CRYSTAL *is alone.*)

CRYSTAL: Come in! (*Enter* MARY. *She closes door*) I beg your pardon?

MARY: I am—Mrs. Stephen Haines.

CRYSTAL: (*Her poise is admirable*) Sorry—I don't think I know you!

MARY: Please don't pretend.

CRYSTAL: So Stephen finally told you?

MARY: No. I found out. (SECOND SALESWOMAN *half enters.*)

CRYSTAL: Stay out of here! (*Exit* SALESWOMAN.)

MARY: I've known about you from the beginning.

CRYSTAL: Well, that's news.

MARY: I kept still.

CRYSTAL: Very smart of you. (SECOND SALESWOMAN *pantomimes down the corridor, to another girl to join her. Enters* MARY's *booth. One by one, during the rest of this scene, the* FITTERS, SALES-WOMEN *and* MODELS *tip-toe into* MARY's *booth and plaster their ears against the partition.*)

MARY: No, not smart. I wanted to spare Stephen. But you've gone a little too far—You've been seeing my children. I won't have you touching my children!

CRYSTAL: For God's sake, don't get hysterical. What do I care about your children? I'm sick of hearing about them.

MARY: You won't have to hear about them any more. When Stephen realizes how humiliating all this has been to me, he'll give you up instantly.

CRYSTAL: Says who? The dog in the manger?

MARY: That's all I have to say.

CRYSTAL: That's plenty.

MARY: (*More calmly*) Stephen would have grown tired of you anyway.

CRYSTAL: (*Nastily*) Speaking from your *own* experience? Well, he's not tired of me yet, Mrs. Haines.

MARY: (*Contemptuous*) Stephen is just amusing himself with you.

CRYSTAL: And he's amusing himself plenty.

MARY: You're very hard.

CRYSTAL: I can be soft—on the *right* occasions. What do you expect me to do? Burst into tears and beg you to forgive me?

MARY: I found exactly what I expected!

CRYSTAL: That goes double!

MARY: (*Turning to the door*) You'll have to make other plans, Miss Allen.

CRYSTAL: (*Going to her*) Listen, I'm taking my marching orders from Stephen.

MARY: Stephen doesn't love you.

CRYSTAL: He's doing the best he can in the circumstances.

MARY: He couldn't love a girl like you.

CRYSTAL: What do you think we've been doing for the past six months? Crossword puzzles? What have you got to kick about? You've got everything that matters. The name, the position, the money—

MARY: (*Losing control of herself again*) Nothing matters to me but Stephen—!

CRYSTAL: Oh, can the sob-stuff, Mrs. Haines. You don't think this is the first time Stephen's ever cheated? Listen, I'd break up your smug little roost if I could. I have just as much right as you have to sit in a tub of butter. But I don't stand a chance!

MARY: I'm glad you know it.

CRYSTAL: Well, don't think it's just because he's *fond* of you—

MARY: *Fond?*

CRYSTAL: You're not what's stopping him— You're just an old *habit* with him. It's just those brats he's afraid of losing. If he weren't such a sentimental fool about those kids, he'd have walked out on *you* years ago.

MARY: (*Fiercely*) That's not true!

CRYSTAL: Oh, yes, it is. I'm telling you a few plain truths you won't get from Stephen.

MARY: Stephen's always told me the truth—!

CRYSTAL: (*Maliciously*) Well, look at the record. (*A pause*) Listen, Stephen's satisfied with this arrangement. So don't force any issues, unless you want plenty of trouble.

MARY: You've made it impossible for me to do anything else—!

CRYSTAL: (*Rather pleased*) Have I?

MARY: You haven't played fair—!

CRYSTAL: Where would any of us get if we played fair?

MARY: Where do you hope to get?

CRYSTAL: Right where *you* are, Mrs. Haines!

MARY: You're very confident.

CRYSTAL: The longer you stay in here, the more confident I get. Saint or no saint, Mrs. Haines, you are a hell of a *dull woman!*

MARY: (MARY *stares at her wide-eyed at the horrid thought that this may be the truth. She refuses to meet the challenge. She equivocates*) By your standards, I probably am. I—(*Suddenly ashamed that she has allowed herself to be put so pathetically on the defensive*) Oh, why am I standing here talking to you? This is something for Stephen and me to settle! (*Exits.*)

CRYSTAL: (*Slamming the door after her*) Oh, what the hell!

(*Mary's Booth*)

SECOND SALESWOMAN: So that's what she calls meeting Mrs. Haines *socially.*

FIRST SALESGIRL: Gee, I feel sorry for Mrs. Haines. She's so nice.

FIRST MODEL: She should have kept her mouth shut. Now she's in the soup.

FIRST SALESWOMAN: It's a terrible mistake to lay down ultimatums to a man.

FIRST MODEL: Allen's smart. She's fixed it so anything Mr. Haines says is going to sound wrong.

FIRST SALESGIRL: She'll get him sure.

FIRST FITTER: Look at that body. She's got him now.

SECOND SALESGIRL: You can't trust any man. *That's* all they want.

CORSET MODEL: (*Plaintively, her hands on her lovely hips*) What else have we got to give?

CURTAIN

ACT TWO

SCENE I

Two weeks later. A small exercise room in Elizabeth Arden's beauty-salon. Right, a mirrored wall. Rear, a door. Left, a cabinet victrola beneath an open window. On the floor, a wadded pink satin mat. As the curtain rises, SYLVIA, in a pair of shorts, is prone on the mat, describing lackadaisical arcs with her legs, to the sensuous rhythm of a tango record. The INSTRUCTRESS, a bright, pretty girl, in a pink silk bathing suit, stands above her, drilling her in a carefully cultured voice. Until the cue "stretch," the INSTRUCTRESS's lines are spoken through SYLVIA's prattle, which she is determined, for the honor of the salon, to ignore, and, if possible, to discourage. From the word "up," this is a hopeless task.

INSTRUCTRESS: Up—over—up—down. Up—stretch—up—
together. Up—stretch—up—

SYLVIA: Of course, my sympathies are for Mrs. Haines. They
always are for a woman against a man—

INSTRUCTRESS: *(Louder)* Up—over—up—down. Up—stretch—
up—together. Up—

SYLVIA: But she did behave like an awful idiot—

INSTRUCTRESS: Stretch—up—together. Please don't try to talk,
Mrs. Fowler.

SYLVIA: But you know how some women are when they lose their
heads—

INSTRUCTRESS: *(Grimly)* Stretch—up—together—up—

SYLVIA: They do things they regret all their lives—

INSTRUCTRESS: *(Grabs SYLVIA's languid limb and gives it a corrective
yank)* Ster-retch!

SYLVIA: Ouch, my scars!

INSTRUCTRESS: *(Callously)* This is very good for adhesions. Up—

SYLVIA: *(Resolutely inert)* It's got me down.

INSTRUCTRESS: Rest. (SYLVIA *groans her relief*) And relax your
diaphragm muscles, Mrs. Fowler, *(Bitterly)* if you can. *(Goes to
the victrola, changes the record for a fox-trot.)*

SYLVIA: Of course, I do wish Mrs. Haines would make up her mind
if she's going to get a divorce. It's terrible on all her friends,
not knowing. Naturally, you can't ask them anywhere—

INSTRUCTRESS: Of course not. Now, on your side. (SYLVIA *rolls to
her side, reclining on her elbow*) Ready? Up—down—up—

down—(*Snaps her fingers.* SYLVIA *flaps a limp leg up, down*—) Don't bend the knee—

SYLVIA: (*Thoughtfully*) Of course, for the children's sake, I think Mrs. Haines ought to stay. (*Piously*) I know I would. (*Her knees look bent, not to say broken.*)

INSTRUCTRESS: (*Imploring*) Don't crook it, please.

SYLVIA: And she ought not to have faced Mr. Haines with the issue. When a man's got himself in that deep he has to have time to taper it off—

INSTRUCTRESS: (*Straightening out* SYLVIA'*s offending member with considerable force*) Thigh in, not out.

SYLVIA: (*Pained, but undaunted*) But Mrs. Haines never listens to any of her friends. She is a very peculiar woman.

INSTRUCTRESS: She must be. Now, please—up—down—up—down—

SYLVIA: (*Redoubling her efforts, and her errors*) Oh, I tell everybody whatever she wants to do is the right thing. I've got to be loyal to Mrs. Haines, you know... Oh, I'm simply exhausted. (*Flops over, flat on her stomach, panting.*)

INSTRUCTRESS: Then suppose you try something simple—like crawling up the wall? (SYLVIA *lifts a martyred face. The* INSTRUCTRESS *changes the record for a waltz.*)

SYLVIA: (*Scrambling to her feet*) What I go through to keep my figure! Lord, it infuriates me at dinner parties when some fat lazy man asks, "What do you do with yourself all day, Mrs. Fowler?" (*Sits alongside the rear wall.*)

INSTRUCTRESS: You rotate on your buttocks. (SYLVIA *rotates, then lies back, her knees drawn up to her chin, the soles of her feet against the wall*) Arms flat. Now you crawl slowly up the wall.

SYLVIA: (*Crawling*) I wish you wouldn't say that. It makes me feel like vermin—

INSTRUCTRESS: (*Kneeling beside her*) Don't talk.

SYLVIA: There's a couple of people I'd like to exterminate, too—

INSTRUCTRESS: Let's reverse the action. (SYLVIA *crawls down, as* PEGGY *enters in an exercise suit. The* INSTRUCTRESS *brightens.*)

INSTRUCTRESS: How do you do, Mrs. Day? (*To* SYLVIA) Down slowly—

PEGGY: (*Gaily*) How do you do? Hello, Sylvia.

SYLVIA: You're late again, Peggy.

PEGGY: (*Crestfallen*) I'm sorry.

SYLVIA: (*Sitting up*) After all, dear, I am paying for this course.

PEGGY: You know I'm grateful, Sylvia—

SYLVIA: Well, don't cry about it. It's only fifty dollars.

PEGGY: That's a lot to me—

SYLVIA: (*Sweetly*) To you, or just to your husband, dear?

INSTRUCTRESS: Please, ladies. Let us begin with posture. (SYLVIA *rises*) A lady always enters a room erect.

SYLVIA: Lots of my friends exit horizontally. (PEGGY *and* SYLVIA *go to the mirrored wall, stand with their backs to it.*)

INSTRUCTRESS: Now—knees apart. Sit on the wall. (*They sit on imaginary seats*) Relax. (*They bend forward from the waist, finger-tips brushing the floor*) Now, roll slowly up the wall... pressing each little vertebra against the wall as hard as you can... shoulders back, and where they belong. Heads back. Mrs. Fowler, lift yourself behind the ears. Pretend you're just a silly little puppet dangling on a string. Chin up. (*She places her hand at the level of* PEGGY'*s straining chin*) No, Mrs. Day, your chin is resting comfortably on a little table. Elbows bent—up on your toes—arms out—shove with the small of your back— you're off! (SYLVIA *and* PEGGY, *side by side, mince across the room.*)

PEGGY: (*Whispering*) Oh, Sylvia, why do you always insinuate that John is practically a—miser?

INSTRUCTRESS: (*She refers to* PEGGY'*s swaying hips*) Tuck under!

SYLVIA: You have your own little income, Peggy. And what do you do with it? You give it to John—

INSTRUCTRESS: Now, back, please! (*They mince backwards across the room.*)

PEGGY: (*Staunchly*) John makes so little—

INSTRUCTRESS: (*She refers to* SYLVIA'*s relaxed tummy*) Steady center control!

SYLVIA: Peggy, you're robbing John of his manly sense of responsibility. You're turning him into a gigolo. A little money of her own she lets no man touch is the only protection a woman has. (*They are against the mirror again.*)

INSTRUCTRESS: Now, are you both the way you were when you left the wall?

SYLVIA: (*Brightly*) Well, I am.

INSTRUCTRESS: No, Mrs. Fowler, you're not. (*She imitates* SYLVIA'*s posture, showing how* SYLVIA'*s posterior protrudes, against the dictates of fashion, if not of nature.*) Not *this*, Mrs. Fowler— ("*Bumps*") That! (*She leads* SYLVIA *forward*) Try it, please.

(*Facing one another, they do an elegant pair of "bumps"*) Now, relax on the mat.

(*This piece of business defies description, but to do the best one can: the girls stand side by side, arms straight above their heads. At the* INSTRUCTRESS' *count of "one," each drops a hand, limp, from the wrist. At "two," the other hand drops, then their heads fall upon their breasts, their arms flap to their sides, their waists cave in, their knees buckle under, and they swoon, or crumble like boneless things, to the mat.*)

INSTRUCTRESS: (*She has changed the record*) Now, ready? Bend— stretch, you know. Begin—(*They do another leg exercise on the mat*) Bend—stretch—bend—down—plenty of pull on the hamstrings, please! Bend—stretch—bend —down—(*Enter* EDITH. *She is draped in a white sheet. Her head is bound in a white towel. Her face is undergoing a "tie-up," that is, she wears broad white straps under her chin and across her forehead. She appears very distressed.*)

EDITH: Oh, Sylvia! Hello, Peggy—

SYLVIA: (*Sitting up*) Why, Edith, what are you doing up here?

EDITH: Having a facial, downstairs. Oh, Sylvia. I'm so glad you're here. I've done the most *awful* thing, I—

INSTRUCTRESS: We're right in the middle of our exercises, Mrs. Potter—

SYLVIA: (*To* INSTRUCTRESS) Will you tell them outside—I want my paraffin bath now? There's a dear.

INSTRUCTRESS: But, Mrs. Fowler—

SYLVIA: (*Cajoling*) I'm simply exhausted.

INSTRUCTRESS: You've hardly moved a muscle.

SYLVIA: (*With elaborate patience*) Look, whose carcass is this? Yours or mine?

INSTRUCTRESS: It's yours, Mrs. Fowler, but I'm paid to exercise it.

SYLVIA: You talk like a horse-trainer.

INSTRUCTRESS: Well, Mrs. Fowler, you're getting warm. (*Exits.*)

EDITH: I've done the most *ghastly* thing. Move over. (PEGGY *and* SYLVIA *move over*; EDITH *plumps between them on the mat*) But it wasn't until I got here, in the middle of my facial, that I realized it—I could bite my tongue off when I think of it—

SYLVIA: Well, what is it, Edith?

EDITH: I was lunching with Frances Jones, and—

SYLVIA: Edith Potter, I know exactly what you're going to say!

EDITH: I forgot she—

SYLVIA: You forgot she's Dolly de Peyster.

EDITH: But I never read her awful column—

SYLVIA: (*Fiercely*) You told her something about me? What did you tell her?

EDITH: Oh, darling, you know I never give *you* away. (*Remorsefully*) I—I—told her all about Stephen and Mary—

SYLVIA: (*Relieved*) Oh! That!

EDITH: It wasn't until the middle of my facial—

PEGGY: Oh, Edith! It will be in all those dreadful tabloids!

EDITH: I know—I've been racking my brains to recall what I said— I think I told her that when Mary walked into the fitting room, she yanked the ermine coat off the Allen girl—

SYLVIA: You didn't!

EDITH: Well, I don't know whether I said ermine or *sable*—but I know I told her that Mary *smacked* the Allen girl!

PEGGY: Edith!

EDITH: Well, that's what Sylvia told me!

SYLVIA: I didn't!

EDITH: You did, too!

SYLVIA: (*Hurt*) Anyway, I didn't expect you to tell it to a cheap reporter—

EDITH: Well, it doesn't really make much difference. The divorce is practically settled—

SYLVIA: (*Eagerly*) Who says so?

EDITH: You did!

SYLVIA: (*Patiently*) I said, Mary couldn't broadcast her domestic difficulties, and not expect them to wind up in a scandal.

PEGGY: Mary didn't broadcast them!

SYLVIA: Who did?

PEGGY: *You* did. You—you're all making it impossible for her to do anything now but get a divorce!

SYLVIA: You flatter us. We didn't realize how much influence we had on our friends' lives!

PEGGY: Everybody calling her up, telling her how badly she's been treated—

SYLVIA: As a matter of fact, I told her she'd make a great mistake. What has any woman got to gain by a divorce? No matter how much he gives her, she won't have what they have together. And you know as well as I do, he'd marry that girl. What he's spent on her, he'd have to, to protect his investment. (*Sorrowfully*) But, I have as much influence on Mary as I have on *you*, Peggy. (*The* INSTRUCTRESS *re-enters.*)

INSTRUCTRESS: The paraffin bath is ready, Mrs. Fowler.

SYLVIA: (*Rises*) Well, don't worry, Edith, I'll give de Peyster a ring. I can fix it.

EDITH: How?

SYLVIA: (*Graciously*) Oh, I'll tell her you were lying.

EDITH: You'll do no such thing!

SYLVIA: (*Shrugging*) Then let the story ride. It will be forgotten tomorrow. You know the awful things they printed about— what's her name?—before she jumped out the window? Why, I can't even remember her name, so who cares, Edith? (*Exits.*)

INSTRUCTRESS: Mrs. Potter, you come right back where you belong.

EDITH: Why, you'd think this was a boarding school!

INSTRUCTRESS: But, Mrs. Potter, it's such a foolish waste of money—

EDITH: Listen, relaxing is part of my facial.

INSTRUCTRESS: (*Coolly*) Then you should relax completely, Mrs. Potter, from the chin up. (*Exits.*)

EDITH: Honestly, the class feeling you run into these days! (*Struggles to her feet*) I'm so tired of paying creatures like that to insult me—

PEGGY: (*Going to her*) Edith! Let's call Mary up and warn her!

EDITH: About what?

PEGGY: The newspapers!

EDITH: My dear, how could we do that, without involving Sylvia—

PEGGY: But it's *her* fault—Oh, she's such a dreadful woman!

EDITH: Oh, she can't help it, Peggy. It's just her tough luck she wasn't born deaf and dumb. But what can we do about it? She's always gotten away with murder. Why, she's been having an affair for a year with that young customers' man in Howard's office.

PEGGY: (*Shocked*) Edith!

EDITH: Right under Howard's nose! But Howard doesn't care! So what business is it of yours or mine? (*Earnestly*) Peggy, take a tip from me—keep out of other women's troubles. I've never had a fight with a girl friend in all my life. Why? I hear no evil, I see no evil, I speak no evil!

CURTAIN

SCENE II

A few days later.
MARY's *pantry, midnight. Left, a swinging door, to the kitchen. Rear, a sink under a curtained window. A small, built-in refrigerator. Center, a table, two chairs.*
As the curtain rises, JANE, *the maid, and* MAGGIE, *the new cook, are having a midnight snack.* MAGGIE, *a buxom, middle-aged woman, wears a wrapper and felt bedroom slippers.*

JANE: (*Folding a tabloid newspaper which she has been reading to* MAGGIE) So *he* says, "All you can do with a story like that, is live it down, Mary."
MAGGIE: I told you they'd begin all over. Once a thing like that is out between a married couple, they've got to fight it out. Depends which they get sick of first, each other, or the argument.
JANE: It's enough to make you lose your faith in marriage.
MAGGIE: Whose faith in marriage?
JANE: You don't believe in marriage?
MAGGIE: Sure I do. For women. (*Sighs*) But it's the sons of Adam they got to marry. Go on.
JANE: Well, finally he said to the madam, "I gave her up, didn't I? And I was a swine, about the way I did it." How do you suppose he did it, Maggie?
MAGGIE: Maybe he just said, "Scram, the wife is onto us."
JANE: Well, the madam didn't believe him. She says, "Stephen, you really ain't seen her?"
MAGGIE: He lied in his teeth—
JANE: Oh, the way he said it, I kind of believed him. But the madam says, "Oh, but can I ever trust you again?"
MAGGIE: You can't trust none of 'em no further than I can kick this lemon pie.
JANE: Oh, it was terrible sad. He said, "Mary, dear Mary, Mary, dear Mary, Mary—"
MAGGIE: Dear Mary. But it ain't exactly convincing.
JANE: Then, I guess he tried to kiss her. Because she says, "Please don't. I'll never be able to kiss you again, without thinking of her in your arms."
MAGGIE: (*Appreciatively*) Just like in the movies—Imagine him taking

up with a girl like that.

JANE: He was telling the madam: She's a virgin.

MAGGIE: She *is*? Then what's all the rumpus about?

JANE: Oh, she ain't a virgin now. She was.

MAGGIE: So was Mae West—once.

JANE: He told the madam he'd been faithful for twelve years.

MAGGIE: Well, that's something these days, that beats flying the Atlantic. Did the madam believe him?

JANE: She said, "How do I know you've been faithful?"

MAGGIE: She don't.

JANE: But the way he said it—

MAGGIE: Listen, if they lay off six months, they feel themselves busting out all over with haloes.

JANE: Anyway, he says this girl was really a nice girl. So sweet and interested in him and all. And how it happened one night, unexpected, in her room—

MAGGIE: Did he think it was going to happen in Roxy's?

JANE: He said she wouldn't take nothing from him for months—

MAGGIE: Only her education. Oh, that one knew her onions. She certainly played him for a sucker.

JANE: That's what the madam said. She said, "Stephen, can't you see that girl's only interested in you for your money?"

MAGGIE: Tch, tch, tch. I'll bet that made him sore. A man don't like to be told no woman but his wife is fool enough to love him. It drives 'em nutty.

JANE: Did it! "Mary, I told you what kind of girl she is," he says. You know—I just told you—

MAGGIE: I had her number. You didn't convey no information.

JANE: Well, then they both got sore.

MAGGIE: (*Rises, goes out for coffee*) I knew it.

JANE: So, he began to tell her all over, what a good husband he'd been. And how hard he'd worked for her and the kids. And she kept interrupting with what a good wife she'd been and how proud she was of him. Then they began to exaggerate themselves—

MAGGIE: (*Enters with coffee pot*) Listen, anybody that's ever been married knows that line backwards and forwards. What happened?

JANE: Well, somewhere in there the madam says, "Stephen, you do want a divorce. Only you ain't got the courage to ask it." And he says, "Oh, my God, no I don't, Mary. Haven't I told you?"

And she says, "But you don't love me!" And he says, "But oh, my God, Mary, I'm awful *fond* of you." And she says, very icy, "Fond, fond? Is that all?" And he says, "No, Mary, there's the children." Maggie, that's the thing I don't understand. Why does she get so mad every time he says they've got to consider the children? If children ain't the point of being married, what is?

MAGGIE: A woman don't want to be told she's being kept on just to run a kindergarten. (*Goes to the ice box for a bottle of cream.*)

JANE: Well, the madam says, "Stephen, I want to keep the children out of this. I haven't used the children. I ain't asked you to sacrifice yourself for the children." Maggie, that's where he got so terrible mad. He says, "But why, in God's name, Mary? You knew about us all along. Why did you wait until now to make a fool of me?"

MAGGIE: As if he needed her help.

JANE: So then, suddenly she says, in a awful low voice, "Stephen, oh, Stephen, we can't go on like this. It ain't worthy of what we been to each other!" And he says, "Oh, no, it's not, Mary!"

MAGGIE: Quite a actress, ain't you?

JANE: My boy friend says I got eyes like Claudette Colbert's.

MAGGIE: Did he ever say anything about your legs? Have a cup of coffee. (*Pours coffee.*)

JANE: That's when the madam says what you could have knocked me down with a feather! The madam says, "Stephen, I want a divorce. Yes, Stephen, *I* want a divorce!"

MAGGIE: Tch. Tch. Abdicating!

JANE: Well, Maggie, you could have knocked him down with a feather!

MAGGIE: (*Waving coffee pot*) I'd like to knock him down with this.

JANE: "My God! Mary," he says, "you don't mean it!" So she says, in a funny voice, "Yes, I do. You've killed my love for you, Stephen."

MAGGIE: He's just simple-minded enough to believe that.

JANE: So he says, "I don't blame you. My God, how can I blame you?"

MAGGIE: My God, he can't!

JANE: So then she said it was all over, because it was only the children he minded losing. She said that made their marriage a mockery.

MAGGIE: A mockery?

JANE: Something funny.

MAGGIE: I ain't going to die laughing.

JANE: He said she was talking nonsense. He said she was just upset on account of this story in the papers. He said what else could she expect if she was going to spill her troubles to a lot of gabby women? He said she should go to bed until she could think things over. He was going out for a breath of fresh air.

MAGGIE: The old hat trick.

JANE: So the madam says, "You're going to see that girl." And he says, "Oh, for God's sake, Mary, one minute you never want to see me again, the next I can't even go out for a airing!"

MAGGIE: You oughtn't to let none of 'em out except on a leash.

JANE: And she says, "Are you going to see her, or ain't you?" And he says, "Well, what difference does it make, if you're going to divorce me?" And she says, "It don't make no difference to *you*, I guess. Please go, Stephen. And don't come back *ever*." (*Begins to cry.*)

MAGGIE: (*Impatiently*) Yes?

JANE: I didn't hear his last words. Because naturally, when he said he was going, I scooted down the hall. But I heard her call, "Stephen?" And he stops on the landing and says, "Yes, Mary?" and she says, "Nothing. Just don't slam the front door—The servants will hear you!" So I came down here. Oh, Maggie, what's going to happen?

MAGGIE: She's going to get a divorce.

JANE: Oh, dear. I'm so sad for her.

MAGGIE: I ain't.

JANE: What?

MAGGIE: She's indulging a pride she ain't entitled to. Marriage is a business of taking care of a man and rearing his children. It ain't meant to be no perpetual honeymoon. How long would any husband last if he was supposed to go on acting forever like a red-hot Clark Gable? What's the difference if he don't love her?

JANE: How can you say that, Maggie!

MAGGIE: That don't let her off her obligation to keep him from making a fool of himself, does it?

JANE: Do you think he'll marry that girl?

MAGGIE: When a man's got the habit of supporting some woman, he just don't feel natural unless he's doing it.

JANE: But he told the madam marrying her was the furthest thing from his mind.

MAGGIE: It don't matter what he's got in his mind. It's what those two women got in theirs will settle the matter.

JANE: But the madam says it's up to *him*. She said, "You love her, or you love me, Stephen."

MAGGIE: So what did he say to that?

JANE: Nothing for a long time. Just walked up and down—up and down—up and—

MAGGIE: He was thinking. Tch—tch. The first man who can think up a good explanation how he can be in love with his wife *and* another woman, is going to win that prize they're always giving out in Sweden!

CURTAIN

SCENE III

A month later.

MARY'*s living room. The room is now denuded of pictures, books, vases, etc. The rug is rolled up. The curtains and chairs are covered with slips. As the curtain rises,* MARY, *dressed for traveling, is pacing up and down.* MRS. MOREHEAD, *dressed for the street, watches her from the sofa.*

MRS. MOREHEAD: What time does your train go?

MARY: (*Looking at her wrist watch*) An hour. His secretary ought to be here. I never knew there could be so many papers to sign.

MRS. MOREHEAD: You showed everything to your lawyers—

MARY: They always say the same thing! I'm getting a "raw deal"—

MRS. MOREHEAD: (*Alarmed*) But, Mary—

MARY: Oh, I know it's not true. Stephen's been very generous.

MRS. MOREHEAD: Oh, I wouldn't say that. If Stephen is a rich man now, he owes it largely to you.

MARY: Stephen would have gotten where he is, with or without me.

MRS. MOREHEAD: He didn't have a penny when you married him.

MARY: Mother, are you trying to make me bitter, too?

MRS. MOREHEAD: (*Helplessly*) I'm sure I don't know what to say. If I sympathize with Stephen, you accuse me of taking his side. And when I sympathize with you, I'm making you bitter. The thing for me to do is keep still. (*There is a pause. Then, emphatically*) You're both making a terrible mistake!

MARY: Mother, please!

MRS. MOREHEAD: But the children, Mary. The children—

MARY: What good will it do them to be brought up in a home full of quarreling and suspicion? They'll be better off just with me.

MRS. MOREHEAD: No, they won't. A child needs both its parents in one home.

MARY: A home without love?

MRS. MOREHEAD: He's terribly fond of you—

MARY: Mother, don't use that word! Oh, Mother, please. Every argument goes round in circles. And, it's too late now—

MRS. MOREHEAD: It's never too late when you love. Mary, why don't you call this thing off? I'm sure that's what Stephen's waiting for.

MARY: (*Bitterly*) Is it? He hasn't made any sign of it to me. Isn't he the one to come to me?

MRS. MOREHEAD: You're the one, Mary, who insisted on the divorce.

MARY: But don't you see; if he hadn't wanted it, he'd have fought me—

MRS. MOREHEAD: Stephen's not the fighting kind.

MARY: Neither am I.

MRS. MOREHEAD: Damn these modern laws!

MARY: Mother!

MRS. MOREHEAD: Damn them, I say! Fifty years ago, when women couldn't get divorces, they made the best of situations like this. And sometimes, out of situations like this they made very good things indeed! (*Enter* JANE, *right.*)

JANE: Mr. Haines' secretary, ma'am.

MRS. MOREHEAD: Tell her to come in. (*Exit* JANE) Now, go bathe your eyes. Don't let that adding-machine see you like this. And don't be long. Remember, you have one more unpleasant task.

MARY: Mary?

MRS. MOREHEAD: The child must be told.

MARY: (*Miserably, and a little guiltily*) I have been putting it off. Because—

MRS. MOREHEAD: Because you hope at the last minute a miracle will keep you from making a mess of your life. Have you thought: Stephen might marry that girl?

MARY: (*Very confident*) He won't do that.

MRS. MOREHEAD: What makes you so sure?

MARY: Because, deep down, Stephen does love me—But he won't find it out, until I've—really gone away—(*At the door*) You'll take good care of the children, Mother? And make them write to me to Reno, once a week? And please, Mother, don't spoil them so. (*Exits left.*)

MRS. MOREHEAD: Gracious! You'd think I'd never raised children of my own! (Enter MISS WATTS *and* MISS TRIMMERBACK, *right. They are very tailored, plain girls.* MISS WATTS, *the older and the plainer of the two, carries a briefcase*) How do you do, Miss Watts?

MISS WATTS: How do you do, Mrs. Morehead? This is Miss Trimmerback from our office.

MISS TRIMMERBACK: How do you do?

MISS WATTS: She's a notary. We have some papers for Mrs. Haines to sign.

MRS. MOREHEAD: Anything I can do?

MISS WATTS: The children will be with you? (MRS. MOREHEAD *nods*) Any incidental bills, Mrs. Morehead, send to the office. But you understand, bills arriving after the divorce will be assumed by Mrs. Haines under the terms of the settlement.

MRS. MOREHEAD: Mrs. Haines will be with you in a minute. Please don't bother her with unnecessary details. She's—she's pressed for time. (*Exits right.*)

MISS TRIMMERBACK: Gee, don't you feel sorry for Mrs. Haines?

MISS WATTS: (*Bitterly*) I don't feel sorry for any woman who thinks the world owes her breakfast in bed.

MISS TRIMMERBACK: You don't like her.

MISS WATTS: Oh, she never interfered at the office.

MISS TRIMMERBACK: Maybe that's why he's been a success.

MISS WATTS: He'd have gotten further without her. Everything big that came up, he was too cautious, because of her and the kids. (*Opens the briefcase, takes out papers and pen, arranges the papers, for signing, on the table*) Well, thank heavens it's almost over. He and I can go back to work. (*Sits.*)

MISS TRIMMERBACK: What about Allen?

MISS WATTS: (*Guardedly*) What about her?

MISS TRIMMERBACK: Is he going to marry her?

MISS WATTS: I don't butt into his private affairs. Oh, I hold no brief for Allen. But I must say knowing *her* gave him a new interest in his work. Before her, he was certainly going stale. That had me worried.

MISS TRIMMERBACK: (*Sinking on the sofa*) Well, she's lucky, I'll say.

MISS WATTS: Oh?

MISS TRIMMERBACK: I wish I could get a man to foot my bills. I'm sick and tired, cooking my own breakfast, sloshing through the rain at 8 A.M., working like a dog. For what? Independence? A lot of independence you have on a woman's wages. I'd chuck it like that for a decent, or an indecent, home.

MISS WATTS: I'm sure you would.

MISS TRIMMERBACK: Wouldn't you?

MISS WATTS: I have a home.

MISS TRIMMERBACK: You mean Plattsburgh, where you were born?

MISS WATTS: The office. That's my home.

MISS TRIMMERBACK: Some home! I see. The office-wife?

MISS WATTS: (*Defiantly*) He could get along better without Mrs. Haines or Allen than he could without me.

MISS TRIMMERBACK: Oh, you're very efficient, dear. But what makes you think you're indispensable?

MISS WATTS: I relieve him of a thousand foolish details. I remind him of things he forgets, including, very often these days, his good opinion of himself. I never cry and I don't nag. I guess I *am* the office-wife. And a lot better off than Mrs. Haines. He'll never divorce me!

MISS TRIMMERBACK: (*Astonished*) Why, you're in love with him! (*They both rise, face each other angrily.*)

MISS WATTS: What if I am? I'd rather work for him than marry the kind of a dumb cluck I could get—(*Almost tearful*) just because he's a *man*—(*Enter* MARY, *left.*)

MARY: Yes, Miss Watts.

MISS WATTS: (*Collecting herself quickly*) Here are the inventories of the furniture, Mrs. Haines. I had the golf cups, the books, etchings, and the ash stands sent to Mr. Haines' club. (*Pauses*) Mr. Haines asked if he could also have the portrait of the two children.

MARY: (*Looking at the blank space over the mantel*) Oh, but—

MISS WATTS: He said it wouldn't matter, if you really didn't *care* for him to have it.

MARY: It's in storage.

MISS WATTS: (*Laying a paper on the table*) This will get it out. Sign there. The cook's letter of reference. Sign here. (MARY *sits, signs*) The insurance papers. You sign here. (MISS

TRIMMERBACK *signs each paper after* MARY.) The transfer papers on the car. What do you want done with it?

MARY: Well, I—

MISS WATTS: I'll find a garage. Sign here. What do you want done if someone meets your price on this apartment?

MARY: Well, I thought—

MISS WATTS: This gives us power of attorney until you get back. Sign here.

MARY: But—I—

MISS WATTS: Oh, it's quite in order, Mrs. Haines. Now, Mr. Haines took the liberty of drawing you a new will. (*Places a blue, legal-looking document before* MARY.)

MARY: (*Indignantly*) But—really—

MISS WATTS: If anything were to happen to you in Reno, half your property would revert to him. A detail your lawyers overlooked. Mr. Haines drew up a codicil cutting himself out—

MARY: But, I don't understand legal language, Miss Watts. I—I must have my lawyer—

MISS WATTS: As you please. (*Stiffly*) Mr. Haines suggested this for *your* sake, not his. I'm sure you realize, he has nothing but your interests at heart. (*A pause*) Sign here. (MARY *signs*, MISS WATTS *signs*) We need three witnesses. (*Enter* JANE, *right, with a box of flowers*) Your maid will do.

MARY: Jane, please witness this. It's my will.

JANE: (*In tears*) Oh, Mrs. Haines! (*Signs.*)

MISS WATTS: (*Gathering all the papers*) You can always make changes, in the event of your remarriage. (MARY *rises*) And don't hesitate to let me know at the office, if there is anything *I* can ever do for you.

MARY: (*Coldly*) There will be nothing, Miss Watts.

MISS WATTS: (*Cheerfully*) Oh, there are always tag ends to a divorce, Mrs. Haines. And you know how Mr. Haines hates to be bothered with inconsequential details. Good day, Mrs. Haines, and pleasant journey to you! (*Exit* MISS WATTS *right, followed by* MISS TRIMMERBACK.)

JANE: (*Sniveling as she places the box on the table*) Mr. Haines said I was to give you these to wear on the train. (*Exits abruptly.* MARY *slowly opens the box, takes out a corsage of orchids and a card. Reads aloud: "What can I say? Stephen." Then throws them violently in the corner. Enter* MRS. MOREHEAD, LITTLE MARY, *dressed for street.*)

MRS. MOREHEAD: All set, dear?

MARY: (*Grimly*) All set—Mary, Mother wants to talk to you before she goes away.

MRS. MOREHEAD: Brother and I will wait for you downstairs. (*Exit* MRS. MOREHEAD.)

MARY: Mary, sit down, dear. (LITTLE MARY *skips to the sofa, sits down. A pause.* MARY *discovers that it's going to be even more painful and difficult than she imagined.*) Mary—

LITTLE MARY: Yes, Mother?

MARY: Mary—

LITTLE MARY: (*Perplexed by her mother's tone, which she feels bodes no good to her*) Have I done something wrong, Mother?

MARY: Oh, no, darling, no. (*She sits beside her daughter, and takes her two hands*) Mary, you know Daddy's been gone for some time.

LITTLE MARY: (*Sadly*) A whole month.

MARY: Shall I tell you why?

LITTLE MARY: (*Eagerly*) Why?

MARY: (*Plunging in*) You know, darling, when a man and woman fall in love what they do, don't you?

LITTLE MARY: They kiss a lot—

MARY: They get married—

LITTLE MARY: Oh, yes. And then they have those children.

MARY: Well, sometimes, married people don't stay in love.

LITTLE MARY: What, Mother?

MARY: The husband and the wife—fall out of love.

LITTLE MARY: Why do they do that?

MARY: Well, they do, that's all. And when they do, they get unmarried. You see?

LITTLE MARY: No.

MARY: Well, they do. They—they get what is called a divorce.

LITTLE MARY: (*Very matter of fact*) Oh, do they?

MARY: You don't know what a divorce is, but—

LITTLE MARY: Yes, I do. I go to the movies, don't I? And lots of my friends have mummies and daddies who are divorced.

MARY: (*Relieved, kisses her*) You know I love you very much, don't you, Mary?

LITTLE MARY: (*A pause*) Of course, Mother.

MARY: Your father and I are going to get a divorce. That's why I'm going away. That's why—Oh, darling, I can't explain to you quite. But I promise you, when you are older you will understand. And you'll forgive me. You really will! Look at me, baby, please!

LITTLE MARY: (*Her lips begin to tremble*) I'm looking at you, Mother—Doesn't Daddy love you any more?

MARY: No, he doesn't.

LITTLE MARY: Don't you love him?

MARY: I—I—no, Mary.

LITTLE MARY: Oh, Mother, why?

MARY: I—I don't know—But it isn't either Daddy's or Mother's fault.

LITTLE MARY: But, Mother, when you love somebody I thought you loved them until the day you die!

MARY: With children, yes. But grown-ups are different. They can fall out of love.

LITTLE MARY: I won't fall out of love with you and Daddy when I grow up. Will you fall out of love with me?

MARY: Oh, no, darling, that's different, too.

LITTLE MARY: (*Miserable*) I don't see *how*.

MARY: You'll have to take my word for it, baby, it is. This divorce has nothing to do with our love for you.

LITTLE MARY: But if you and Daddy—

MARY: (*Rising and drawing her daughter up to her*) Darling, I'll explain it better to you in the taxi. We'll go alone in the taxi, shall we?

LITTLE MARY: But, Mother, if you and Daddy are getting a divorce, which one won't I see again? Daddy or you?

MARY: You and Brother will live with me. That's what happens when—when people get divorced. Children must go with their mothers. But you'll see Daddy—sometimes. Now, darling, come along.

LITTLE MARY: Please, Mother, wait for me downstairs.

MARY: Why?

LITTLE MARY: I have to go to the bathroom.

MARY: Then hurry along, dear—(*Sees the orchids on the floor, and as she moves to the door stoops, picks them up, goes out. LITTLE MARY stands looking after her, stricken. Suddenly she goes to the back of the chair, hugs it, as if for comfort. Then she begins to cry and beat the back of the chair with her fists.*)

LITTLE MARY: Oh, please, please, Mother dear—Oh! Daddy, Daddy darling! Oh, why don't you do something—*do something*—Mother dear!

CURTAIN

SCENE IV

A month later.
A room in a lying-in hospital. Left, a door to the corridor. Right, a window banked to the sill with expensive flowers. Center, a hospital bed, in which EDITH, *propped up in a sea of lace pillows, lies with a small bundle at her breast. A white-uniformed nurse sits by the window. The droop of her shoulders is eloquent:* EDITH *is a trying patient. As the curtain rises,* EDITH *reaches across the bundle to the bedside table for a cigarette. She can't make it.*

EDITH: (*Whining*) Nurse!
NURSE: (*Rising wearily*) Yes, Mrs. Potter.
EDITH: Throw me a cigarette.
NURSE: Can't you wait, at least until you're through nursing?
EDITH: How many children have you nursed? I've nursed four.
    (NURSE *lights her cigarette;* EDITH *shifts the bundle slightly*)
    Ouch! Damn it! It's got jaws like a dinosaur. (*Enter* PEGGY
    with a box of flowers.)
PEGGY: Hello, Edith.
EDITH: (*In a faint voice*) Hello, Peggy.
PEGGY: (*Putting flowers on bed*) Here—
EDITH: How thoughtful! Nurse, will you ask this damn hospital if
    they're equipped with a decent vase? (NURSE *takes the box,*
    opens flowers and arranges them, with others, in the window.)
PEGGY: (*Leans over baby*) Oh, let me see. Oh, Edith, isn't he divine!
EDITH: I hate that milky smell.
PEGGY: (*Alarmed*) What's that on his nose?
EDITH: What nose? Oh, that's an ash. (*Blows away the ash. Hands*
    PEGGY *a letter from bedside table.*)
PEGGY: Mary?
EDITH: (*Nodding*) All about how healthy Reno is. Not a word about
    how she feels. I thought she cared more about Stephen than
    that. She sends her love to you and John. (PEGGY *reads. The*
    wail of a new-born is heard outside.)
EDITH: Nurse, close that door. (*The* NURSE *closes the door.*) I can't
    tell you what that new-born yodel does to my nerves. (*To*
    PEGGY) What're you so down in the mouth about? I feel as
    badly about it as you do, but it was the thing Mary wanted to
    do, or she wouldn't have done it. Judging by that, she's

reconciled to the whole idea.

PEGGY: She's just being brave!

EDITH: Brave? Why should she bother to be brave with her friends? Here, Nurse, he's through. (*The* NURSE *takes the bundle from her*) I told Phelps to be sure to tell Stephen that Mary's perfectly happy. It will cheer Stephen up. He's been going around like a whipped dog.

PEGGY: Oh, Edith, please let me hold him! (*The* NURSE *gives* PEGGY *the baby.*)

NURSE: (*Smiling*) Careful of his back, Mrs. Day.

PEGGY: (*Goes to the window, hugging the bundle*) Oh, I *like* the feeling so!

EDITH: You wouldn't like it so much if you'd just had it. (*Whimpering*) I had a terrible time, didn't I, Nurse?

NURSE: Oh, no, Mrs. Potter. You had a very easy time. (*She is suddenly angry*) Why, women like you don't know what a terrible time is. Try bearing a baby and scrubbing floors. Try having one in a cold filthy kitchen, without ether, without a change of linen, without decent food, without a cent to bring it up— and try getting up the next day with your insides falling out, to cook your husband's—! (*Controls herself*) No, Mrs. Potter, you didn't have a terrible time at all—I'll take the baby, please. (*Sees the reluctant expression on* PEGGY's *face*) I hope some day you'll have one of your own, Mrs. Day. (*The* NURSE *exits with the baby.* PEGGY *breaks into tears.*)

EDITH: Well, for God's sake, Peggy, that old battle-axe didn't hurt my feelings a bit! They're all the same. If you don't get peritonitis or have quintuplets, they think you've had a picnic— (PEGGY *sits beside the bed, crying*) What's the matter?

PEGGY: Oh, Edith—John and I are getting a divorce!

EDITH: (*Patting her hand*) Well, darling, that's what I heard!

PEGGY: (*Surprised*) But—but we didn't decide to until last night.

EDITH: (*Cheerfully*) Oh, darling, everybody could see it was in the cards. Money, I suppose?

PEGGY: (*Nodding*) Oh, dear! I wish Mary were here—

EDITH: Well, she'll be there. (*Laughs*) Oh, forgive me, dear. I do feel sorry for you. But it is funny.

PEGGY: What's funny?

EDITH: It's going to be quite a gathering of the clan. (*Sitting up in bed, full of energy to break the news*) Howard Fowler's bounced Sylvia out right on her ear! He's threatened to divorce her

right here in New York if she doesn't go to Reno. And name
her young customer's man—
PEGGY: But—Howard's always known—
EDITH: Certainly. He hired him, so he'd have plenty of time for his
own affairs. Howard's got some girl he wants to marry. But
nobody, not even Winchell, knows who she is! Howard's a
coony cuss. (*Laughing*) I do think it's screaming. When you
remember how Sylvia always thought she was putting something over on us girls! (*She laughs so hard, she gives herself a
stitch. She falls back among her pillows, limp and martyred.*)
PEGGY: (*Bitterly*) Life's awfully unattractive, isn't it?
EDITH: (*Yawning*) Oh, I wouldn't complain if that damned stork
would take the Indian sign off me.

CURTAIN

SCENE V

*A few weeks later. Mary's living room in a Reno hotel. In the rear wall, a
bay window showing a view of Reno's squat roof-tops and distant Nevada
ranges. Left, doors to the kitchenette, the bedroom. Right, a door to the
corridor. A plush armchair, a sofa. In the corner, MARY's half-packed
trunks and bags. It is all very drab and ugly. As the curtain rises, LUCY,
a slatternly middle-aged, husky woman in a house-dress, is packing the
clothes that are strewn on the armchair and the table. She is singing in a
nasal falsetto.*

LUCY: Down on ole Smokey, all covered with snow,
   I lost my true lov-ver, from courtin' too slow.
   Courtin' is pul-leasure, partin' is grief,
   Anna false-hearted lov-ver is worse thanna thief—
   (*PEGGY enters, right. She wears a polo-coat and a wool tam. She is
   on the verge of tears.*)
PEGGY: Lucy, where's Mrs. Haines?
LUCY: Down waiting for the mail. You'll miss her a lot when she
   goes tomorrow? (*PEGGY nods, sinks, dejected, on the sofa*) Mrs.
   Haines is about the nicest ever came here.
PEGGY: I hate Reno.
LUCY: You didn't come for fun. (*Goes on with her packing and
   singing.*)
   The grave'll de-cay you, an' change you tuh dust,

Ain't one boy outta twenty, a poor gal kin trust—

PEGGY: You've seen lots of divorcees, haven't you, Lucy?

LUCY: Been cookin' for 'em for ten years.

PEGGY: You feel sorry for us?

LUCY: Well, ma'am, I don't. You feel plenty sorry enough for yourselves. (*Kindly*) Lord, you ain't got much else to do.

PEGGY: (*Resentfully*) You've never been married, Lucy.

LUCY: (*Indignant*) I've had three—

PEGGY: Husbands?

LUCY: Kids!

PEGGY: Oh, then you're probably very happy—

LUCY: Lord, ma'am, I stopped thinking about being happy years
ago.

PEGGY: You don't think about being happy?

LUCY: Ain't had the time. With the kids and all. And the old man
such a demon when he's drinking—Them big, strong, red-
headed men. They're fierce.

PEGGY: Oh, Lucy, he beats you? How terrible!

LUCY: Ain't it? When you think what a lot of women in this hotel
need a beating worse than me.

PEGGY: But you live in Reno. You could get a divorce overnight.

LUCY: Lord, a woman can't get herself worked up to a thing like
that overnight. I had a mind to do it once. I had the money,
too. But I had to call it off.

PEGGY: Why?

LUCY: I found out I was in a family way. (*There is a rap on the door.*)

PEGGY: (*Going to her*) Lucy, tell Mrs. Haines I must talk to her—
alone—before supper—(*Enter* COUNTESS DE LAGE, *left. She is
a silly, amiable, middle-aged woman, with carefully waved,
bleached hair. She wears a gaudily checked riding habit, carries an
enormous new sombrero and a jug of corn liquor.*)

COUNTESS: Ah, Peggy, how are you, dear child?

PEGGY: All right, Countess de Lage.

COUNTESS: I've been galloping madly over the desert all day. Lucy,
here's a wee juggie. We must celebrate Mrs. Haines' divorce.

PEGGY: Oh, Countess de Lage, I don't think a divorce is anything
to celebrate.

COUNTESS: Wait till you've lost as many husbands as I have,
Peggy. (*Wistfully*) Married, divorced, married, divorced! But
where Love leads I always follow. So here I am, in Reno.

PEGGY: Oh, I wish I were anywhere else on earth.

COUNTESS: My dear, you've got the Reno jumpy-wumpies. Did you go to the doctor? What did he say?

PEGGY: He said it was—the altitude.

COUNTESS: Well, la, la, you'll get used to that. My third husband was a Swiss. If one lives in Switzerland, Peggy, one has simply got to accept the Alps. As I used to say to myself, Flora, there those damn Alps are, and there's very little even you can do about it.

PEGGY: Yes, Countess de Lage. (*Exits, hurriedly, left.*)

COUNTESS: Oh, I wish she hadn't brought up the Alps, Lucy. It always reminds me of that nasty moment I had the day Gustav made me climb to the top of one of them. (*Sits in armchair*) Lucy, pull off my boots. (LUCY *kneels, tugs at her boots*) Anyhow, there we were. And suddenly it struck me that Gustav had pushed me. (*Tragically*) I slid halfway down the mountain before I realized that Gustav didn't love me anymore. (*Gaily*) But Love takes care of its own, Lucy. I slid right into the arms of my fourth husband, the Count.

LUCY: (*Rises, with boots*) Ain't that the one you're divorcing now?

COUNTESS: But, of course, Lucy. (*Plaintively*) What could I do when I found out he was putting arsenic in my headache powders. Ah! L'amour! L'amour! Lucy, were you ever in love?

LUCY: Yes, ma'am.

COUNTESS: Tell me about it, Lucy.

LUCY: Well, ma'am, ain't much to tell. I was kinda enjoyin' the courtin' time. It was as purty a sight as you ever saw, to see him come lopin' across them hills. The sky so big and blue and that hair of his, blazing like the be-jesuss in the sun. Then we'd sit on my back fence and spark. But, ma'am, you know how them big, strong, red-headed men are. They just got to get to the point. So we got married, ma'am. And natcheraly, I ain't had no chanct to think about love since—

COUNTESS: (*She has not been listening*) The trouble with me, Lucy, is I've been marrying too many foreigners. I think I'll go back to marrying Americans. (*Enter* MIRIAM, *right. She is a breezy, flashy red-head, about 28 years old. She it wearing a theatrical pair of lounging pajamas.*)

MIRIAM: Hya, Lucy?

LUCY: Evening, Mrs. Aarons. (*Exits, right.*)

MIRIAM: Hya, Countess, how's rhythm on the range? (*Sees the jug on the table, pours the* COUNTESS *and herself drinks.*)

COUNTESS: Gallop, gallop, gallop, madly over the sagebrush! But now, Miriam, I'm having an emotional relapse. In two weeks I'll be free, free as a bird from that little French bastard. But whither, oh, whither shall I fly?

MIRIAM: To the arms of that cowboy up at the dude ranch?

COUNTESS: (*Modestly*) Miriam Aarons!

MIRIAM: Why, he's nuts for you, Countess. He likes you better than his horse, and it's such a damn big horse.

COUNTESS: (*Rises, and pads in her stocking-feet to the sofa*) Well, Buck Winston is nice. So young. So strong. Have you noticed the play of his muscles? (*Reclining*) Musical. Musical.

MIRIAM: He could crack a coconut with those knees. If he could get them together. Say, Countess, that guy hasn't been arousing your honorable intentions, has he?

COUNTESS: Yes, Miriam, but I'm different from the rest of you. I've always put my faith in love. Still, I've had three divorces. Dare I risk a fourth?

MIRIAM: What are you risking, Countess, or maybe I shouldn't ask?

COUNTESS: I mean, Miriam, I could never make a success of Buck at Newport.

MIRIAM: Even Mrs. Astor would have to admit Buck's handsome. If I had your dough, I'd take him to Hollywood first, then Newport.

COUNTESS: Hollywood? Why *not*? I might turn him into a picture star. After all, my second husband was a gondolier, and a month after I married him, a Duchess eloped with him. Ah! L'amour! (*Enter* SYLVIA, *right. She is wearing a smart dinner dress. Her trip to Reno has embittered her, but it has not subdued her.*)

MIRIAM: Hya, Sylvia? Going to a ball?

SYLVIA: (*Pours a drink*) Doing the town with a boy friend.

MIRIAM: Where'd you pick him up?

SYLVIA The Silver State Bar. I'm not going to sit around, moping, like Mary.

COUNTESS: Poor Mary. If her husband gave her the flimsiest excuse, she'd take him back.

SYLVIA: She has no pride. I'd roast in hell before I'd take Howard Fowler back. Kicking me out like that! After all I sacrificed!

MIRIAM: Such as what?

SYLVIA: I gave him my *youth*!

COUNTESS: (*Dreamily*) Hélas, what else can a woman do with her youth, but give it to a man?

MIRIAM: Hélas, she can't preserve it in alcohol.

COUNTESS: (*Practical*) But, Sylvia, how could your husband kick you out, if you were a femme fidèle?

SYLVIA: Of course, I was a faithful wife. (MIRIAM *snorts*) What are you laughing at?

MIRIAM: Two kinds of women, Sylvia, owls and ostriches. (*Raises her glass*) To the feathered sisterhood! To the girls who *get* paid and paid. (*Parenthetically*) And you got paid *plenty*!

SYLVIA: You bet I got plenty! The skunk!

COUNTESS: I never got a sou from any of my husbands, except my first husband, Mr. Straus. He said the most touching thing in his will. I remember every word of it. "To my beloved wife, Flora, I leave all my estate in trust to be administered by executors, because she is an A No. 1 *schlemeil*." (*Touched anew*) Wasn't that sweet?

MIRIAM: (*Enter* MARY, *right. She is subdued. She is carrying some letters*) Hya, queen?

MARY: Fine.

MIRIAM: Ya lie.

COUNTESS: Mary, I'm starved.

(LUCY *enters, left, takes* MARY's *hat*.)

MARY: Supper's nearly ready. As my last official act in Reno, I cooked the whole thing with my hands, didn't I, Lucy?

LUCY: All but the steak and tomatoes and dessert, Mrs. Haines. (*Exits, left*.)

MARY: (*Gives a letter to* SYLVIA, *glancing, as she does so, at the inscription*) For you, Sylvia. From Edith?

SYLVIA: You couldn't miss that infantile handwriting. (*Pointedly*) *You* didn't hear from anyone?

MARY: No.

SYLVIA: Well, darling, Stephen's hardly worth a broken heart.

MARY: The less you have to say about me and Stephen the better I like it!

SYLVIA: I'm only trying to cheer you up. That's more than you do for me.

MARY: I'm doing enough, just being pleasant to you.

SYLVIA: My, you have got the jitters, dear.

MIRIAM: Hey, Sylvia, we're all out here in the same boat. Mary's laid off you. Why don't you lay off her?

SYLVIA: Oh, I'm just trying to make her see life isn't over just because Stephen let her down. (*Opens her letter. A batch of press-clippings falls out. The* COUNTESS *picks them up, reads them idly, as* SYLVIA *goes on with the letter.*)

COUNTESS: You see, Miriam? What else is there for a woman but l'amour?

MIRIAM: There's a little corn whiskey left. (*She pours another drink.*)

COUNTESS: Cynic, you don't believe in Cupid.

MIRIAM: That double-crossing little squirt! Give me Donald Duck. (*To* MARY) Have a drink? (MARY *shakes her head*) Listen, Babe, why not—give out? You'd feel better—

MARY: (*Laughing*) Miriam, you're not very chatty about your own affairs.

COUNTESS: (*Suddenly engrossed by the clippings from* SYLVIA'S *letter*) Miriam, you sly puss, you never told us you even knew Sylvia's husband.

SYLVIA: (*Looking up from her letter*) What?

COUNTESS: (*Rises*) Sylvia, listen to this: "Miriam Vanities Aarons is being Reno-vated. Three guesses, Mrs. Fowler, for whose Ostermoor?" (SYLVIA *snatches the clippings from her.*)

MIRIAM: Why can't those lousy rags leave a successful divorce alone?

COUNTESS: (*Reading another clipping*) "Prominent stockbroker and ex-chorine to marry."

SYLVIA: (*To* MIRIAM) Why, you little hypocrite! (*During this,* PEGGY *has entered and goes back of the sofa. She listens but does not join the group.*)

MARY: (*Going to her*) Now, Sylvia—

SYLVIA: Did you know this?

MARY: Oh, Sylvia, why do you care? You don't love Howard—

SYLVIA: (*Brushing her aside*) That has nothing to do with it. (*To* MIRIAM, *fiercely*) How much did he settle on you?

MIRIAM: I made Howard pay for what he wants; you made him pay what he doesn't want.

SYLVIA: You want him for his money.

MIRIAM: So what do you want him for? I'll stay bought. That's more than you did, Sylvia.

SYLVIA: Why, you dirty little trollop!

MIRIAM: Don't start calling names, you Park Avenue push-over! (SYLVIA *gives* MIRIAM *a terrific smack. In the twinkling of an eye, they are pulling hair.* MARY *seizes* SYLVIA'S *arm;* SYLVIA *breaks loose. The* COUNTESS *tugs at* MIRIAM'S *belt, as* LUCY *comes in, looks at the fight with a rather professional eye, and exits for the smelling-salts.*)

COUNTESS: Tiens! Miriam. Don't be vulgar. (*Her interference enables* SYLVIA *to slap* MIRIAM *unimpeded.*)

MIRIAM: (*Shoving the* COUNTESS *on the sofa*) Out of the way, you fat old—! (SYLVIA *grabs* MIRIAM's *hair*) Ouch, let go! (SYLVIA *is about to use her nails.* MARY *takes a hand.*)

MARY: I won't have this, you hear! (MARY's *interference allows* MIRIAM *to give* SYLVIA *a terrific kick in the shins.*)

SYLVIA: (*Routed, in sobs*) Oh, you hurt me, you bitch, you! (*As she turns away,* MIRIAM *gives her another well-placed kick, which straightens* SYLVIA *up.*)

MIRIAM: Take that! (SYLVIA, *shrieking with rage and humiliation, grabs* MIRIAM *again, sinks her white teeth into* MIRIAM's *arm. At this mayhem,* MARY *seizes her, shakes her violently, pushes her sobbing into the armchair.*)

MARY: (*To* MIRIAM) That's enough.

MIRIAM: Where's the iodine? (MARY *points to bedroom*) Gotta be careful of hydrophobia, you know. (*Exits, right.*)

SYLVIA: (*Blubbering, nursing her wounds*) Oh, Mary, how could you let her do that to me!

MARY: (*Coldly*) I'm terribly sorry, Sylvia.

SYLVIA: The humiliation! You're on her side. After all I've done for you!

MARY: What have you done for me?

SYLVIA: I warned *you*!

MARY: (*Bitterly*) I'm not exactly grateful for that.

SYLVIA: (*Hysterical*) Oh, aren't you? Listen to me, you ball of conceit. You're not the object of pity you suppose. Plenty of the girls are tickled to death you got what was coming to you. You deserved to lose Stephen, the stupid way you acted. But I always stood up for you, like a loyal friend. What thanks do I get? You knew about that woman, and you stood by, gloating, while she—

MARY: Get out of here! (LUCY *enters from the bedroom, with a bottle of spirits of ammonia, as* SYLVIA *gives way completely to hysteria, and, screaming with rage, picks up ash-trays, glasses, and cigarette boxes, and hurls them violently against the wall.*)

SYLVIA: (*At the top of her lungs*) I hate you! I hate you! I hate *every-body*—

LUCY: (*Takes* SYLVIA *firmly by the shoulders, forces the bottle under her nose*) Listen, Mrs. Fowler! You got the hy-strikes! (*Rushes her gasping, sobbing, to the door.*)

SYLVIA: You wait. Some day you'll need a woman friend. Then you'll think of me—(*Exit* LUCY *and* SYLVIA, *struggling helplessly, right.*)

COUNTESS: (*Rising from the sofa*) Poor creatures. They've lost their equilibrium because they've lost their faith in love. (*Philosophically*) L'amour. Remember the song Buck made up, just for me? (*Pours herself a drink, sings*) "Oh, a man can ride a horse to the range above, But a woman's got to ride on the wings of love, Coma a ti-yi-yippi." (*Throws the jug over her shoulder, and exits right, still singing, as* MIRIAM *enters, the ravages of her fight repaired.*)

MIRIAM: The coast clear?

PEGGY: Oh, that was the most disgusting thing I ever saw.

MIRIAM: Right, kid, we're a pair of alley cats—

MARY: You should not be here, Peggy, to see it at all. (*She picks up the ash-trays, etc.*)

MIRIAM: What the hell are you doing here?

MARY: Peggy wanted to buy a car.

PEGGY: With my own money!

MARY: John said they couldn't afford a car.

PEGGY: He couldn't. I could.

MARY: What was his—is yours. What is yours—is your own. Very fair.

PEGGY: A woman's best protection is a little money of her own.

MARY: A woman's best protection is—the right man. (*With gentle sarcasm*) Obviously, John isn't the right man and Peggy will forget all about him in another month.

PEGGY: No, I won't. I can't. Because—because—(*Bursts into tears*) Oh, Mary, I'm going to have a baby. Oh, Mary, what shall I do?

MARY: Peggy, what's his telephone number?

PEGGY: (*Quickly*) Eldorado 5-2075. (MIRIAM *goes at once to the phone. Gets the operator, gives the number*) But, oh, Mary, I can't tell him!

MIRIAM: Why? Isn't it his?

PEGGY: Oh, of course!

MIRIAM: And make it snappy, operator.

PEGGY: I always wanted it. But what can I do with it now?

MIRIAM: Land it with the Marines—

MARY: Peggy, you've shared your love with him. Your baby will share your blood, your eyes, your hair, your virtues—and your faults—But your little pin-money, that, of course, you could not share.

PEGGY: Oh, Mary, I know I'm wrong. But, it's no use—you don't know the things he said to me. I have my pride.

MARY: (*Bitterly*) Reno's full of women who all have their pride.

PEGGY: You think I'm like them.

MIRIAM: You've got the makings, dear.

MARY: Love has pride in nothing—but its own humility.

MIRIAM: (*At telephone*) Mr. Day, please. Reno calling—Mr. Day? My God, he must live by the phone. Just hold the—(PEGGY *leaps to the phone.*)

PEGGY: Hello, John. (*Clears her throat of a sob*) No, I'm not sick. That is, I am sick! That is, I'm sick to my stomach. Oh, John! I'm going to have a baby—Oh, darling, are you?—Oh, darling, do you?—Oh, darling, so am I! So do I! Course, I forgive you.—Yes, precious. Yes, lamb. On the very next train! John? (*A kiss into the phone. It is returned*) Oh, Johnny, when I get back, things are going to be so different—! John, do you mind if I reverse the charges? (*Hangs up*) I can't stay for supper. I've got to pack.

MARY: When you get back—don't see too much of the girls.

PEGGY: Oh, I won't, Mary. It's all their fault we're here.

MARY: Not—entirely.

PEGGY: Good-bye! Oh, I'm so happy, I could cry. (*Exits, right.*)

MIRIAM: Getting wise, aren't you?

MARY: Know all the answers.

MIRIAM: Then, why're you here?

MARY: I had plenty of advice, Miriam. (*The telephone rings.* MIRIAM *goes to it.*)

MIRIAM: Hello. No, we completed that call, operator. (*Hangs up.*)

MARY: Cigarette?

MIRIAM: (*Suddenly*) Listen.

MARY: There's nothing you can say I haven't heard.

MIRIAM: Sure? I come from a world where a woman's got to come out on top—or it's just too damned bad. Maybe I got a new slant.

MARY: (*Wearily*) All right, Miriam. Talk to me about my—lawful husband. Talk to me about security—What does it all come to? Compromise.

MIRIAM: What the hell? A woman's compromised the day she's born.

MARY: You can't compromise with utter defeat. He doesn't want me.

MIRIAM: How do you know?

MARY: How do I know—why else am I here?

MIRIAM: (*A pause. Then, mock-tragically*) Because you've got no guts, Mary Haines. It happened to me—I lost my man, too.

MARY: (*Smiling*) You?

MIRIAM: Oh, it only happened once. Got wise to myself after that. Look, how did I lose him? We didn't have enough dough to get married. I wouldn't sleep with him until we did. I had ideals—God knows where I got 'em. I held out on him— (*Sighs*) Can you beat it? I liked him a lot better than I've ever liked anybody since. I never held out again—What'd my Romeo do? Got himself another girl. I made a terrible stink. Why shouldn't I? I should. But what I ought not to have done was say—good-bye. I was like you.

MARY: I don't understand.

MIRIAM: Then get a load of this. I should of licked that girl where she licked me—in the hay.

MARY: Miriam!

MIRIAM: That's where you win in the first round. And if I know men, that's still Custer's Last Stand. (MARY *walks away from her*) Shocked you? You're too modest. You're ashamed. O.K., sister. But my idea of love is that love isn't ashamed in nothing.

MARY: (*Turning to her*) A good argument, Miriam. So modern. So simple. Sex the cause, sex the cure. It's too simple, Miriam. Your love battles are for—lovers—or professionals. (*Gently*) Not for a man and woman who've been married twelve quiet years! Oh, I don't mean I wouldn't love Stephen's arms around me again. But I wouldn't recapture, if I could, our— young passion. That was the wonderful young thing we had. That was part of our youth, like the—babies. But not the thing that made him my husband, that made me his wife— Stephen needed me. He *needed* me for twelve years. Stephen doesn't need me any more.

MIRIAM: I get it. (*Phone rings*) That's why I'm marrying this guy Fowler. He needs me like hell. If I don't marry him he'll drink himself to death in a month, the poor dope.

MARY: (*At the telephone*) Yes? No, operator, we completed—you say, New York is calling Mrs. Haines? I'll take that call—(*To* MIRIAM) Stephen!

MIRIAM: Listen, make him that speech you just made me!

MARY: (*Radiant*) I knew he'd call. I knew when the last moment came, he'd realize he needed me.

MIRIAM: For God's sake, tell him that *you* need him!

MARY: Hello—hello? Stephen? Mary. Yes. I'm very cheerful. It's so good to hear your voice, Stephen. I—why, yes, it's scheduled for tomorrow at 12—but, Stephen, I can—(*Frightened*) but, Stephen! No—of course—I haven't seen the papers. How could I, out here? (*There is a long pause*) Yes, I'd rather *you* told me. Of course I understand the position you're both in. No, I'm not bitter, not bitter at all—I—I hope you'll both be very happy. No, I have no plans, no plans at all—Stephen, do you mind if I hang up? Good-bye, Stephen—Good-bye—

MIRIAM: He's marrying her?

MARY: Oh, God, why did I let this happen? We were married. We were one person. We had a good life. Oh, God, I've been a *fool*!

MIRIAM: Sure you have. Haven't we all, sister?

MARY: But she doesn't love him. I *do*. That's the way it is. (*She goes to the window, and looks out. There is a pause. Then, violently*) But it's not ended if your heart doesn't say so. It's not ended!

CURTAIN

ACT THREE

SCENE I

Early evening, two years later. CRYSTAL's *bathroom. Left, a black mar-bleized tub with frilled shower-curtains. In a niche, back of the tub, a gilded French telephone. Right, a satin-skirted dressing table, covered with glittering toilet bottles and cosmetic jars. Towel-racks piled with embroidered bath-towels. Center, a door to* CRYSTAL's *bedroom. As the curtain rises,* CRYSTAL *is lolling in the bath, reading a magazine, smoking, as* HELENE, *a chic French maid, enters.*

HELENE: Madame has been soaking an hour.

CRYSTAL: (*Rudely*) So what?

HELENE: But, monsieur—

CRYSTAL: Monsieur is going out with me and my friends, whether he likes it or not. Has that kid gone home yet?

HELENE: Mademoiselle Mary has just finished the supper with her daddy. Madame, monsieur is so anxious that you say good night to her.

CRYSTAL: Listen, that kid doesn't want to bid me beddy-bye any more than I do. He's tried for two years to cram us down each other's throats. Let her go home to her mommer. (*Passes* HELENE *a brush*) Here—scrub—Some day I'm going to slap that kid down. She's too—(*As* HELENE *scrubs too hard*) Ow! You're taking my skin off—Oh, I'm so bored I could—(*Hurls the soap across the room*) Helene, never marry a man who's deserted a "good woman." He's as cheerful as a man who's murdered his poor old mother. (*Telephone rings*) Get out! And, Helene, when Mrs. Fowler comes, keep her downstairs, if you have to *sit* on her. (*Exit* HELENE. CRYSTAL *picks up the telephone. Her voice melts*) Hello, darling, I'm in the tub. I'm shriveled to a peanut waiting for this call. No, I'm not afraid of a shock. You ought to know—Oh, Buck, I'm going to miss you like nobody's business. I can't tell you what it did to me, locking the door on our little apartment—I'll say we had fun! Coma ti-yi-yippy, what? Oh, no, say anything you like. This is the one place where I have some privacy—(CRYSTAL's *back is to the door. She does not hear a brief rap*) Listen, baby, must you really go to the coast? Oh, the hell with Mr. Goldwyn. (*Enter* LITTLE MARY. *She stands hesitantly against the door*)

Listen, you don't have to tell me what you sacrificed to have a movie career. I've seen that cartoon you married. If Flora was ever a Countess, I'm the Duchess of Windsor. Well, Buck, maybe she's not such a half-wit, but—(*Sees* LITTLE MARY) Oh—call me back in two minutes. I've had a small interruption. (*Hangs up*) Who told you to come in here?

LITTLE MARY: (*Politely*) Daddy. Good night. (*Turns to go.*)

CRYSTAL: (*sweetly*) Oh, don't go, darling. Hand me that brush.

LITTLE MARY: (*Gently*) Please?

CRYSTAL: Please. (LITTLE MARY *gives her the brush.*)

LITTLE MARY: Good night. (*Goes to the door.*)

CRYSTAL: My, you're in a hurry to tell Daddy about it.

LITTLE MARY: About what?

CRYSTAL: My talk on the telephone.

LITTLE MARY: I don't understand grown-ups on the telephone. They all sound silly. Good night.

CRYSTAL: Good night, who? (*A pause*) You've been told to call me Aunty Crystal. (*A pause*) Why don't you do it?

LITTLE MARY: (*Still edging to the door*) Yes.

CRYSTAL: Yes, what?

LITTLE MARY: (*Lamely*) Yes, good night.

CRYSTAL: (*Angry*) You sit down!

LITTLE MARY: Oh, it's awfully hot in here. I've got my coat on.

CRYSTAL: You heard me! (LITTLE MARY *sits on the stool before the dressing table, squirms*) We're going to have this out. I've done my damn—my level best to be friends with you, but you refuse to co-operate.

LITTLE MARY: What?

CRYSTAL: Co-operate.

LITTLE MARY: (*Nodding , mechanically*) Co-operate.

CRYSTAL: (*Exasperated*) Answer my question. You don't like me. Why?

LITTLE MARY: (*Rising*) Well, good night, Crystal—

CRYSTAL: I said, why?

LITTLE MARY: (*Very patiently*) Listen, Crystal, my mother told me I wasn't to be rude to you.

CRYSTAL: For the last time, young lady, you give me one good reason why you don't like me.

LITTLE MARY: I never said I didn't like you, Crystal.

CRYSTAL: But you don't like me, do you?

LITTLE MARY: No, but I never *said* so. I've been very polite,

Crystal, considering you're something awful!

CRYSTAL: Wait till your father hears this!

LITTLE MARY: (*Suddenly defiant*) Listen—Daddy doesn't think you're so wonderful any more!

CRYSTAL: Did he tell you that?

LITTLE MARY: No. Daddy always pretends you're all right, but he's just ashamed to have Mother know what a mean, silly wife he's got. And I don't tell Mother what *we* think, because you've made her cry enough, Crystal. So I'm not going to co-operate, *ever!*

CRYSTAL: Get out!

LITTLE MARY: (*Goes to the door, then turns, rather superior*) And *another* thing, I think this bathroom is perfectly ridiculous! Good night, Crystal! (*Exits. The telephone rings.* CRYSTAL *grabs it, irritable.*)

CRYSTAL: Yes, darling—That Haines brat. God, she gets under my skin!—No, she didn't hear anything. What good would it do her, anyhow? You're off in the morning, and Lord knows we've been discreet—What? You are? (*Giggling*) Dining with the first Mrs. Haines?—Well, darling, lay off the gin. It makes you talk too much—Well, just be careful, darling.

(*Enter* SYLVIA, *without knocking. She wears an elaborate evening gown, and carries a cocktail. These two years have had no appreciable effect on* SYLVIA. *She is her old Act One self again.*)

SYLVIA: Yoo-hoo! May I come in?

CRYSTAL: (*In the telephone*) No, this is not the Aquarium. It's Grand Central Station. (*Hangs up.*)

SYLVIA: Who was that?

CRYSTAL: A wrong number.

SYLVIA: You were talking to a man.

CRYSTAL: Pass me that sponge—Please.

SYLVIA: (*Waiting on* CRYSTAL) Oh, Crystal, you know you can trust me.

CRYSTAL: And that eye cup.

SYLVIA: There must be someone. After all, I've known Stephen for years. He's really not your type. I often wonder how you two got together. I was telling my psycho-analyst about it. You know, I've got to tell him everything.

CRYSTAL: That must be an awful effort.

SYLVIA: I don't mind discussing myself. But talking about my friends does make me feel disloyal. He says Stephen has a

Guilt Complex.

CRYSTAL: What?

SYLVIA: (*Cheerfully*) He says men of Stephen's generation were brought up to believe that infidelity is a sin. That's why he allowed Mary to divorce him, and that's why he married you, Crystal. He had to marry you just to convince himself he was not a sexual monster.

CRYSTAL: Yes? Well, if Stephen is a sexual monster, psycho-analysis is through.

SYLVIA: And he says you've got a Cinderella Complex. He says most American women have. They're all brought up to believe that marriage to a rich man should be their aim in life. He says we neither please the men nor function as child-bearing animals—

CRYSTAL: (*Bored and angry*) Will you function yourself into the bedroom?

SYLVIA: (*Hurt*) I don't think that's the way to talk to me, after all I've done for you. When you married Stephen you didn't know a soul. It wasn't easy to put *you* over. Everybody was on Mary's side.

CRYSTAL: They still are. They never miss a chance to remind me what a noble, useful woman Mary has become since she left Stephen.

SYLVIA: (*Comforting*) My dear, she's miserable! Why, she never sees a soul.

CRYSTAL: She's having a dinner party tonight.

SYLVIA: Edith told me. She's going. And Flora.

CRYSTAL: Flora?

SYLVIA: The Countess de Lage. Mrs. Buck Winston? My God, I have to laugh when I think of Flora actually turning that cow-boy into a movie star. Of course he's not my type, but he's positively the Chambermaid's Delight—

CRYSTAL: (*Fiercely*) Will you shut up?

SYLVIA: But, Crystal—

CRYSTAL: I said shut up—(*Calling*) Helene!

SYLVIA: Well, I think you're very ungrateful!

CRYSTAL: Well, take it up with your psycho-analyst. (HELENE *enters*) Helene, draw the curtains. I want to take a shower. (SYLVIA *goes to the door as* HELENE *draws the curtains*) That's right, Sylvia—wait in the bedroom.

SYLVIA: (*Sees the scales, decides to weigh herself*) Oh, dear, I've lost another pound. I must remember to tell my analyst. You know, everything means something. (*The shower goes on.* HELENE *exits.* SYLVIA *gets off the scales. During the following monologue, she goes to* CRYSTAL's *dressing-table, where she examines all the bottles and jars*) But even my analyst says no woman should try to do as much as I do. He says I attach too much value to my feminine friendships. He says I have a Damon and Pythias Complex. I guess I have given too much of myself to other women. He says women are natural enemies—(*Picks up bottle*) Why, Crystal, I thought you didn't touch up your hair—(*Sniffing perfume*) My dear, I wouldn't use this. You smell it on every tart in New York. That reminds me—(*Going to the shower-curtains*)—if you do have an affair, Crystal, for heaven's sake, be discreet. Remember what Howard did to me, the skunk. (*Peeking in*) My, you're putting on weight. (*Going back to dressing-table, she sits down, and begins to pry in all the drawers*) But men are so mercenary. They think they own you body and soul, just because they pay the bills—I tried this cream. It brought out pimples—Of course, Crystal, if you were smart, you'd have a baby. It's the only real hold a woman has—(HELENE *enters.*)

HELENE: Monsieur says will madame be long?

SYLVIA: Can't you see she's rushing?—(HELENE *exits. The shower goes off*) Men are so selfish! When you're only making yourself beautiful for them. (*Opens another drawer*) I wish I could find a man who would understand my need for a companion— (*Finds a key, examines it*) Why, Crystal, what are *you* doing with a key to the Gothic Apartments? (CRYSTAL's *head pops from behind the curtain.*)

CRYSTAL: What?—Oh—(*Nervously*) Oh, that! (*Playing for time*) Throw me a towel, Sylvia!

SYLVIA: (*Bringing her towel*) That's where Howard had me followed. The doorman there is a professional blackmailer! (CRYSTAL *has wrapped herself in a big towel, now steps from behind the shower-curtains and sits on the rim of the tub to dry her legs*) I asked my psycho-analyst about him, and he said blackmailers are really perverts who can't think of a good perversion. So they black-mail people instead.

CRYSTAL: (*Going to the dressing-table*) Really? Well, he can't black-mail me now. (*As she passes* SYLVIA, *she lightly snatches the key from her*) The Gothic Apartments are where Stephen and I

had to go before the divorce. I keep it for sentimental reasons. (*Smiling, she drops the key back in the drawer, locks it.*)

SYLVIA: Poor Stephen! My dear, I thought tonight how tired he
looked, and old. Crystal, I've told you everything. Tell me:
how long do you think you can be faithful to Stephen?

CRYSTAL: (*Making up her face*) Well, life plays funny tricks. The
urge might hit me tomorrow.

SYLVIA: I doubt it, pet. You're a typical blonde.

CRYSTAL: So what?

SYLVIA: (*Loftily*) Most *blondes* are frigid.

CRYSTAL: Really? Well, maybe that's just a dirty piece of *brunette*
propaganda!

CURTAIN

SCENE II

Eleven o'clock the same night. MARY's bedroom. A charming, simple room. Left, a door to the dressing-room. Right, a door to the
hall. As the curtain rises, JANE is arranging a number of evening
wraps on the bed. MIRIAM, MARY and NANCY are entering.

MIRIAM: Thanks, baby, a lot! I never was at a wetter dinner.

MARY: It was a success. I left Reno two years ago today. This was a
memorial dinner for you old Renoites, and your new husbands.

MIRIAM: I get it. Listen, there's no soap eating out your heart, sister!

NANCY: Mary, if I had a heroine in one of my books who behaved
the way you do, my two readers would never believe it. No
one man is worth it.

MIRIAM: Say, the whole Racquet Club's not worth it—Speaking of
my dear husband Howard—the skunk—can I have a whiskey
and soda?

NANCY: Make it two. (JANE *exits, right.*)

MIRIAM: I lay off when Howard's around. I'm weaning him from
the bottle by easy stages. He's in the secondary stage now.

NANCY: What stage is that?

MIRIAM: He puts ice in.

MARY: How's matrimony, Miriam? Making a go of it?

MIRIAM: I'm doing a reconstruction job that makes Boulder Dam look like an egg-cup. (*Enter* PEGGY, *right.*)

PEGGY: Oh, Mary, can't we get off to the party? I have to get home early. Little John always wakes up. Little John said the cutest thing the other day. (*A dramatic pause*) He said da-da—!

NANCY: When does he enter Columbia? (*Enter* JANE *with tray and highballs.*)

MARY: Jane, tell Mrs. Winston the ladies are ready to go.

JANE: Mrs. Winston, ma'am, is drinking with the gentlemen.

MARY: Well, tell her to come up. (*Exit* JANE.)

MIRIAM: What's the hurry? Two more snootfuls, and Flora will float up on her own breath. (*Enter* EDITH, *right.*)

EDITH: (*Petulantly*) Mary, I wish you had an elevator in this house. It's so difficult to walk upstairs in my condition.

MARY: Edith, are you Catholic or just careless?

EDITH: Mary, isn't this your old furniture?

MARY: Yes.

EDITH: I think you should get rid of it. There's nothing that keeps a woman so in the dumps as sleeping in a bed with old associations. Mary, you're carrying this nunnery business too far. How do you expect to find anyone else, if you don't make an effort?

MARY: I don't want anyone, Edith. (*Mock cynical*) I hate men! Men are awful—

EDITH: Oh, they're not all like Stephen, dear.

MARY: I saw plenty of men when I came back from Reno. They're all alike. They never leave you at your own front door without a wrestling-match.

EDITH: You know I asked Phelps about that once. I said, "Why does a man always act like a Don Juan in a taxi?" And he said it was a hang-over from their bachelor days when a man's sex life was conditioned by the click of the meter.

MIRIAM: It beats me how in a taxi, the nicest guy turns into Harpo Marx.

EDITH: Mary, want to hear something about Sylvia? (MARY, MIRIAM, NANCY *and* PEGGY: *chorus*, "*No!*") Well, Sylvia's going to a psycho-analyst. She says you destroyed all her faith in friendship.

MARY: As if any woman needed to go to a psycho-analyst to find out she can't trust women.

EDITH: Mary, you've grown awfully hard since you deserted your old friends.

MARY: Isn't "wise" the word? I'm beginning to understand women.

NANCY: Too bad! It's the beginning of woman's inhumanity to woman.

EDITH: (*Moving to door, left*) Oh, they're going to talk philosophy, Peggy. Come on in here while I powder my nose.

PEGGY: Edith, did I tell you how little John said da-da?

EDITH: Listen, I wouldn't care if *this* one stood up and sang the Star-Spangled Banner! (*They exit, as enter* MRS. MOREHEAD, *in street clothes, right.*)

MRS. MOREHEAD: Oh, hello, girls! Hello, dear. Party over?

MARY: Enjoy the movies, Mother?

MRS. MOREHEAD: I wish I could make up my mind whether or not I like Shirley Temple. (*Enter the* COUNTESS DE LAGE, *right. She is a tangle of tulle and jewels. She has a slight "edge" on.*)

COUNTESS: Such a lovely dinner! It's so wonderful to see all our lives temporarily settled!

MARY: My mother, Mrs. Morehead, Mrs. Winston. Mrs. Buck Winston.

MRS. MOREHEAD: (*Trying to place the name*) Buck Winston?

MARY: The movie star.

MRS. MOREHEAD: Ah, yes! (*Pleasantly*) My granddaughter adores your son on the screen.

COUNTESS: (*Good-naturedly*) I dare say the public does see Buck as just a boy. And it is a trifle absurd *me* being married to a movie star. But, Mrs. Morehead, you wouldn't believe how many of my Newport friends who ridiculed Buck when I married him positively claw for invitations to Hollywood. Mais là, East is East and West is West, but I always say Le Cinema is the Great Leveller!

MRS. MOREHEAD: You don't say! (*Edges to the hall-door.*)

COUNTESS: Mrs. Morehead, do whip into something, and come along with Mary to my party. The Casino Roof. Everyone's clamored to come. I have no idea who's going to be there.

MRS. MOREHEAD: Well, you're sure to know somebody. (*To* MARY) Later, dear? (MARY *nods*, MRS. MOREHEAD *escapes, right.*)

COUNTESS: (*Gathering her wrap*) Mary, you're not coming?

MARY: I'm very tired, Flora.

COUNTESS: Oh, you're cross because Buck's had a wee droppie.

MIRIAM: Don't be modest, Flora. Your ducky is stinko.

COUNTESS: I do wish he wouldn't drink straight gin. You know, he's not allowed to. Mr. Goldwyn put that in the new contract.

MIRIAM: I wish I'd had my marriage license drawn up by Mr. Goldwyn.

COUNTESS: Mary, do come. This is *really* our farewell party. I'm never coming back to New York.

MARY: What's wrong with New York, Flora?

COUNTESS: Well, when Buck isn't working we're not going to live anywhere. (*Whispering*) Mary, can I trust you?

MARY: Of course, Flora!

COUNTESS: (*To the others*) You will keep this just between the four of us?

MIRIAM: Shoot, Flora, it's a nationwide hookup!

COUNTESS: (*Settling herself beside* MARY *on the foot of the bed*) Well, you know how Buck was? (*Wistfully*) So—so impassioné?

MIRIAM: The boy had something.

COUNTESS: (*Tartly*) Well, he hasn't got it any more, Miriam! First, I thought it was just gin, interfering with his libido— (*Tearfully*) But now I think Buck is deceiving me—

NANCY: How incredible!

COUNTESS: Well, I have no proof. Except he comes home every afternoon smelling of a strange perfume.

MARY: Where does he say he's been?

COUNTESS: Visiting his horse. But Trixie was shipped to Hollywood last week. You remember, I was photographed with her in the baggage-car? Now he says he's been going to the Grand Central Gymnasium. But I telephoned today. Some great oaf answered. I said: "Is Buck Winston there?" He said: "Who? No." So I said: "My dear good man, he comes every day." So he said: "My mistake, lady, he's inside now boxing with Rudolph Valentino."

MARY: Poor Flora!

COUNTESS: (*Practical*) That's why I think it's safer just to keep floating around.

MARY: I understand—l'amour.

COUNTESS: L'amour, yes, but jamais, (*She has her lucid moments*) jamais *lopsided* amour!

MARY: (*Laughing*) Lopsided amour is better than no amour at all. Flora, let him make a fool of you. Let him do anything he wants, as long as he stays. He's taking the trouble to deceive you. (*Half to herself*) And if he took the trouble, he really must have cared—

NANCY: The Voice of Experience.

MIRIAM: (*To* COUNTESS) Come on, chin up.

NANCY: That's right. Both of them! (*Enter* PEGGY *and* EDITH.)

COUNTESS: (*Rising*) Oh, cheries, you missed it! I was just saying—now will you keep this just among the six of us?—I suspect Buck of being unfaithful. Of course, it's my own fault. I should have had him watched. The way I did all the others. I wish I'd found out where he's had that apartment!

PEGGY: An apartment—?

COUNTESS: Where would you expect him to go? Central Park? Why, it's winter.

PEGGY: Oh, I've always heard people went to hotels.

COUNTESS: But, cherie, *Buck* couldn't go to a hotel. You know what would happen. At the most inopportune moment someone would say: "Mr. Winston, may I have your autograph?" It happened to us on our wedding night. I would have sent for the manager, but it was the manager asking for the autograph. Ah, well, off to Hollywood in the morning! That's safe! (*Moving to door*) Dear Mr. Hays will protect me from Dietrich and Harlow. (*Exits, right.*)

EDITH: (*Getting her wrap*) Darling, you really won't come to Flora's party?

MARY: No, Edith!

EDITH: Then I can tell you. Of course, I know how you feel about your Ex—and his New Deal—though I think you'd be glad he's so happy.

MARY: I am.

EDITH: Sylvia telephoned tonight. She and Crystal and Stephen are going on to the Roof with a theatre party. Well, darling, I don't feel much like going myself. I loathe this dress. My husband says I look as though I were going to sing in it. (*Exits, right.*)

NANCY: Think I'll go, too, Mary! It's a good chance to study Park Avenue's flora and fauna. And I'm writing a new book. It's called "Gone with the Ice-man," or "Sex Has No Place in the Home." (*Exits with* PEGGY.)

MIRIAM: (*To* MARY) Listen, Queen, change your mind! Let's go on to the party!

MARY: No, Miriam.

MIRIAM: Well, I'm going. Wish you could see the cooing-fest Howard and I put on for Sylvia—Shall I spit in Crystal's eye for you? (MARY *shakes her head.*) You're passing up a swell chance, sister! Where I spit no grass grows ever! (*Exits.* JANE *enters, right.* MARY *begins to unfasten her dress, takes off her jewels, lays them on the dresser.*)

MARY: Jane, turn down my bed.

JANE: Yes, ma'am. (MARY *goes into the boudoir, left.*)

MARY: (*Off-stage*) Did Mary have a nice time with her father?

JANE: (*Turning down the bed*) Well, ma'am, you know how she is when she comes home.

MARY: (*Off-stage*) I'm afraid she's never going to get used to it.

JANE: She takes after you, ma'am, if you'll pardon me. Always brooding. Sometimes, ma'am, I think it would be better if she didn't see her father. Or maybe, ma'am—though it's none of my business—if you could find some nice man—(Enter MRS. MOREHEAD, *right, in a wrapper and slippers.*)

MRS. MOREHEAD: Going to bed, darling?

MARY: (*Off-stage*) Yes, Mother.

MRS. MOREHEAD: Shall we chat for a moment? Jane, I'll have a cigarette.

JANE: (*Surprised*) Mrs. Morehead!

MRS. MOREHEAD: Those dreadful women made me nervous. Why Mrs. Haines tolerates them even once a year is beyond me!

MARY: (*Entering, in a nightgown*) An object lesson. Smoking, Mother?

MRS. MOREHEAD: Oh, you, too?

MARY: Me too?

MRS. MOREHEAD: I just felt that spooky pinch. You'd think after ten years your father's ghost might have grown more tolerant.

JANE: Good night, ma'am. (*Switches off sidelights.*)

MARY AND MRS. MOREHEAD: Good night, Jane. (*Exit* JANE. MARY *gets into bed, opens a book, flips through it.*)

MRS. MOREHEAD: (*Sitting on the bed*) Good book?

MARY: Don't know. Nancy just gave it to me. It's about—love. Poetry. All about love. (*Reads*) "When love beckons to you, follow him, though his ways are hard and steep. And when his wings enfold you, yield to him—Though his voice may shatter your dreams as the North Wind lays waste the garden."

MRS. MOREHEAD: Well, all I can say is, that's very tactless of Nancy. (*Suddenly*) Oh, Mary, I wish you could find—

MARY: (*Slams book shut*) Some nice man. We've been all over that before, Mother. I had the only one I ever wanted, I lost him—

MRS. MOREHEAD: It wasn't entirely your fault.

MARY: If I hadn't listened to everyone, everything but my own heart!

MRS. MOREHEAD: He loved her.

MARY: He still does. Though you know, Mother, I'm just beginning to doubt it.

MRS. MOREHEAD: Why?

MARY: Because so many people, like Edith, make a point of telling me how much he loves her. Oh, Mother, I'm terribly tired.

MRS. MOREHEAD: Well, do cheer up, darling. Living alone has its compensations. You can go where you please, wear what you please and eat what you please. I had to wait twenty years to order the kind of meal I liked! Your father called it bird-food—And, heaven knows, it's marvelous to be able to sprawl out in bed, like a swastika. Good night, darling.

MARY: Good night, Mother.

MRS. MOREHEAD: Don't read by that light. You'll hurt your eyes. (*Exits.* MARY *props herself against the pillows, begins to read.*)

MARY: "But if in your fear you would seek only love's peace and love's pleasure, then it is better for you to pass out of love's threshing-floor, into the seasonless world; where you shall laugh, but not all of your laughter, and weep, but not all of your tears." (*Enter* LITTLE MARY, *in a nightgown, barefooted, and very sleepy.*)

LITTLE MARY: Mother?

MARY: Darling, what's the matter?

LITTLE MARY: (*Goes to the bed*) I had a bad dream!

MARY: Darling, what was it?

LITTLE MARY: I forget. Let me crawl in with you, Mother.

MARY: (*Helping her in*) I'm so restless.

LITTLE MARY: I don't mind if you kick me. You know, that's the only good thing about divorce; you get to sleep with your mother. (*She kisses her. A pause*) I taste lipstick.

MARY: I haven't washed yet. Good night, darling.

LITTLE MARY: You know, you're a very sympathetic mother.

MARY: Am I?

LITTLE MARY: Oh, yes. So would you just tickle my back?

MARY: All right. But go to sleep—(*A pause.*)

LITTLE MARY: She's so silly!

MARY: Who?

LITTLE MARY: Crystal.

MARY: Ssh—

LITTLE MARY: I told Daddy so tonight.

MARY: Oh, you mustn't hurt Daddy's feelings.

LITTLE MARY: Mother?

MARY: Sssh!

LITTLE MARY: I think Daddy doesn't love her as much as you any more.

MARY: What makes you think so, Mary?

LITTLE MARY: He told me so after I saw Crystal.

MARY: What?

LITTLE MARY: But he said I mustn't tell you because, naturally, why do you care how he feels. (*A pause*) Oh, don't stop tickling, Mother. (*A pause*) Mother?

MARY: Yes?

LITTLE MARY: What's anyone want with a telephone in the bathroom?

MARY: I don't know. Sssh!

LITTLE MARY: Crystal has one. She was awful mad when I walked in on her while she was talking.

MARY: Sleep, Mary!

LITTLE MARY: Mother, who's the Duchess of Windsor?

MARY: What a question!

LITTLE MARY: Well, Crystal said on the telephone if somebody else was a Countess, she was the Duchess of Windsor!

MARY: Really!

LITTLE MARY: Good night, Mother.

MARY: Good night, baby. (*A pause.*)

LITTLE MARY: I wonder if it was the same man you had for dinner.

MARY: Maybe, ssh!

LITTLE MARY: I thought so.

MARY: (*Curiously*) If who was the same man?

LITTLE MARY: Crystal was talking to, so lovey-dovey.

MARY: (*Protestingly*) Oh, Mary!

LITTLE MARY: Well, the front part was the same, Mother.

MARY: (*A pause*) The front part of what?

LITTLE MARY: His name, Mother!

MARY: (*Taking her by the shoulders*) What are you talking about?

LITTLE MARY: That man Crystal was talking to in the bathtub.

MARY: (*Half shaking her*) Mary, what do you mean?

LITTLE MARY: I mean his front name was *Buck*, Mother! (MARY *gets quickly out of bed, rings bell on table*) Oh, Mother, what are you doing?

MARY: Go to sleep, darling. (*Begins to pull on her stockings.*)

LITTLE MARY: Grown-ups are so sudden. Are you dressing?

MARY: Yes, Mary.

LITTLE MARY: You forgot you were invited to a party?

MARY: Almost, Mary.

LITTLE MARY: What are you going to do when you get there, Mother?

MARY: I don't know yet. But I've got to do something.

LITTLE MARY: Well, have a good time! (*Rolls over. Then suddenly sits up*) Mother!

MARY: Yes?

LITTLE MARY: I remember now I had something to tell you!

MARY: (*Eagerly*) Yes?

LITTLE MARY: (*Dolefully*) I was awfully rude to Crystal.

MARY: I'll forgive you this time.

(*Enter* JANE.)

JANE: You ring, ma'am?

MARY: Yes. My evening dress, Jane, and a taxi—and don't stand there gaping! Hurry! Hurry!

CURTAIN

SCENE III

Later, the same night. The Powder Room at the Casino Roof. The decoration is rich, tawdry and modernistic. Right, a swinging door from the lobby. Left, another to the washrooms. The rest of the wall-space, left and right, is taken up by counter-like dressing-tables and mirrors. The rear wall is a great window overlooking the glitter of midnight Manhattan. An over-stuffed sofa and an armchair upholstered in modernistic fabric. Near the door, right, a screen hides the coat-rack. By this, a chair for SADIE, *a little old woman in a black maid's uniform and apron. As the curtain rises,* SADIE *is reading a tabloid, which she puts down when two flashily dressed* GIRLS *enter from the lobby. They check their wraps.*

FIRST GIRL: It's jammed.

SECOND GIRL: Oh, my boy-friend'll get a table. (*Enter two* SOCIETY WOMEN. *They move directly across the stage to the washroom.*)

FIRST WOMAN: My dear, won't he let you?

SECOND WOMAN: No, he won't.

FIRST WOMAN: How incredibly foul!

SECOND WOMAN: I'm heartbroken. But I have to be philosophical; after all, missing one winter in Palm Beach really won't kill me. (*Enter* "CIGARETTES," *a pretty girl in a white satin blouse and short black skirt. She carries a tray of cigarettes.*)

FIRST GIRL: (*Moving left*) Thought you and the boy-friend had a row?

SECOND GIRL: We did.

FIRST GIRL: What about?

SECOND GIRL: His wife.

FIRST GIRL: His wife? What right has she got to butt in?

SECOND GIRL: He's got some cockeyed idea that after twenty years he can't kick her out. (*They exit, left.*)

CIGARETTES: Jeepers, why don't they get sick of this joint night after night! Same music, same act, same faces.

SADIE: They like familiarity. It gives them confidence.

CIGARETTES: I'll say they like familiarity. Most of them shoving around that floor would be more comfortable with each other in bed.

SADIE: In bed? If they was to get that over, what would they use for conversation? (*Enter a* DOWAGER *and a* DEBUTANTE, *right. They move directly across stage.*)

DOWAGER: —dancing like that! What can those boys think of you?

DEBUTANTE: (*Wearily*) Oh, Mother.

DOWAGER: Guzzling champagne like that! After all I spent on your education!

DEBUTANTE: Oh, Mother.

DOWAGER: It's one thing to come out. It's quite another to go under the table! (*They exit, left.*)

SADIE: —Getting married, dearie?

CIGARETTES: (*Sinking, very tired, on the arm of a chair*) As soon as Mike gets a job. It ain't fair! Why, we could get married and have a family on that coat—Sadie, wh'd'ya say if I was to tell you I'm a Commyanist?

SADIE: I'd say ya was bats. I was a Townsendite. Where'd it get me? (*Enter the* COUNTESS, *piloted by* NANCY *and* MIRIAM. *She is tight and tearful.* MIRIAM *and* NANCY *get her, with some difficulty, to the sofa.*)

COUNTESS: (*Tacking*) How could Buck do such a thing to me! Oh, the Dr. Jekyll! The Mr. Hyde! Which was which?

MIRIAM: Pipe down or you'll put an awful dent in his career, Flora.

COUNTESS: What of my career? I've had five husbands. Buck's the first one who ever told me what he really thought of me—in public.

NANCY: It takes all kinds of husbands to round out a career like yours, Flora.

COUNTESS: He told me he'd been deceiving me for months. Right in the middle of the Organ-Grinder. (*Kicks off shoes*) Oh, I feel so—superfluous!

MIRIAM: (*To* SADIE) A bromo-seltzer.

COUNTESS: Bromo-seltzer? Qu'est-que c'est que ca?

NANCY: It will settle your—superfluity. Flora, did he tell you the lady's name.

COUNTESS: (*Indignant*) Certainly not, Nancy. He's not that drunk.

MIRIAM: (*As* SADIE *exits, right*) And another drink for Mr. Winston!

COUNTESS: No, Miriam. He wouldn't tell me her name, because she's a married woman. Buck is very proletarian, but he's not a bounder. He just said *she* was a natural blonde.

NANCY: That ought to narrow down the field considerably.

COUNTESS: He said she was pretty as a painted wagon.

MIRIAM: Oh, you're not such a bad calliope. Snap out of it, Flora. You know, you're going to forgive him.

COUNTESS: (*Firmly*) I'd forgive unfaithfulness, but not base ingratitude. I rescued him from those prairies. I married him. What thanks do I get? (*Wailing*) He says he'll be a cockeyed coyote if he'll herd an old beef like me back to the coast!

NANCY: Let this be your lesson. Don't let your next husband become financially independent of you.

COUNTESS: Now, don't lecture me, Nancy. Every time I marry I learn something. This has taught me once and for all—you can't expect *noblesse oblige* from a cowboy—(*Sitting up*) Ohhh, my eyes! They're full of mascara.

NANCY: (*Helping her off the couch. To* MIRIAM) We've got to get her home. Get Buck, and meet us in the lobby.

MIRIAM: (*Exits, right*) We're headin' for the last round-up!

COUNTESS: If there's a telephone in here I'm going to call up Mr. Goldwyn. (*Exits, left, with* NANCY, *as* SADIE, *with a bromo-seltzer, enters, right, followed by* CIGARETTES.)

CIGARETTES: What's it all about?

SADIE (*Picks up* COUNTESS' *shoes, as she crosses, left*) Some man.

CIGARETTES: Bet he isn't worth it.

SADIE: You can always collect on that one. (*Exits, left, as re-enter, left, the* DOWAGER *and the* DEBUTANTE.)

DOWAGER: —Laughing and joking with those boys like that!

DEBUTANTE: Yes, Mother.

DOWAGER: What can they think of you?

DEBUTANTE: Yes, Mother.

DOWAGER: And don't think I didn't overhear that Princeton boy call me an old drizzle-puss, either! (*Exits, right.*)

SADIE: (*Enters, left; to* CIGARETTES) She wants gin in her bromo-seltzer. (*Enter* MARY *and* MIRIAM, *right.*)

MIRIAM: (*Protesting*) Crystal's not in here. I don't think she's in the joint.

MARY: She's coming. I know it.

MIRIAM: So what are you going to do when you find her? (SADIE *takes* MARY's *wrap.*)

MARY: I don't know. But I've got to find her tonight. Buck's going to Hollywood in the morning.

MIRIAM: Say, why don't you settle this matter with Stephen?

MARY: I have no proof, I tell you! But if Buck is as drunk as you say, he'll give away something.

MIRIAM: Listen, he's been trying all night to give Flora away to the doorman. Got a twenty-dollar bill?

MARY: Yes.

MIRIAM: That'll lock him in the men's room till we need him. (*Exits, right, with* MARY, *as enter, left, the two* SOCIETY WOMEN. *They cross the stage.*)

FIRST WOMAN: Not three pounds?

SECOND WOMAN: Three pounds!

FIRST WOMAN: How divine! Aren't you ecstatic?

SECOND WOMAN: Yes, but it's the moral satisfaction. Just bananas and milk for one whole week! That called for enormous character! (*They exit, right.*)

CIGARETTES: (*To* SADIE) Enormous character! Well, she'll need it, all right. Comes the Revolution, she'll diet plenty! (*Enter* PEGGY *and* EDITH, *right. They powder, at the mirror, right.*)

PEGGY: I wish I hadn't come.

EDITH: Well, your husband didn't want you to.

PEGGY: (*Goes for her wrap*) Flora was disgusting!

EDITH: But it was funny. Even the kettle drummer was laughing.

PEGGY: You never miss anything. (SADIE *gives* EDITH *and* PEGGY *their wraps.*)

EDITH: My dear, who could stand the life we lead without a sense of humor? But Flora is a fool. Always remember, Peggy, it's matrimonial suicide to be jealous when you have a really good reason.

PEGGY: Edith, don't you ever get tired of giving advice?

EDITH: Listen, Peggy, I'm the only happy woman you know. Why? I don't ask Phelps or any man to understand me. How could he? I'm a woman. (*Pulls down her corset*) And I don't try to understand them. They're just animals. Who am I to quarrel with the way God made them? I've got security. So I put my faith in the law. And I say: "What the hell?" And let nature take its course—it's going to, anyway. (*They exit, right, as enter the two* GIRLS, *left.*)

SECOND GIRL: (*Powdering at the mirror, left*) —So there we were on Sattiday night and it's Atlantic City. And he says: "I gotta go home tomorrow, baby!" And I says: (*Pulls up her stockings*) "Why dja got to?" And he says: "My wife always expects me home on Easter Sunday." So I says: "What's she expect ya to do? Lay an egg?"

FIRST GIRL: They got no sentiment. (*Enter, right, a* GIRL *in distress. The shoulder strap of her very low décolletage has broken.*)

GIRL IN DISTRESS: (*To* SADIE) Have you got a safety pin? I was never so embarrassed! (SADIE *gets pin.*)

SECOND GIRL: (*Crossing, right*) So I told him, "I had a great career until you made me give up the stage, you lunkhead. For what? A couple of cheesy diamond bracelets? A lousy car, which every time it breaks down you got to have the parts shipped over from Italy." (*The* GIRLS *exit.*)

GIRL IN DISTRESS: So he says, "Don't look now, you've just dropped something!" (*Enter* CRYSTAL *and* SYLVIA, *right. They move to check their wraps with* SADIE.)

SADIE: Just a minute, please.

SYLVIA: (*They go to mirror, left*) Stephen is in a mood.

CRYSTAL: He can take it and like it.

GIRL IN DISTRESS: (*To* SADIE) Does it show now?

SADIE: Not what it did before, miss.

GIRL IN DISTRESS: Thank you. (*She exits, right.* SADIE *takes* CRYSTAL'*s and* SYLVIA'*s wraps.*)

CRYSTAL: Is my mouth on straight?

SYLVIA: Crystal, you didn't come here to see somebody, did you?

CRYSTAL: Oh, Sylvia, can't you lay off that for a minute? (*Enter* MARY *and* MIRIAM, *left.*)

MARY: (*Moving forward resolutely*) Mrs. Haines, this is a great pleasure!

CRYSTAL: (*Turning*) I beg your pardon?

MARY: Such a lovely party! I was afraid you weren't coming. (*Introducing* CRYSTAL *and* MIRIAM, MIRIAM *and* SYLVIA) Mrs. Fowler, Mrs. Haines, Mrs. Fowler, Mrs. Fowler.

MIRIAM: (*Graciously*) Chawmed.

SYLVIA: (*Bridling*) This is humiliating.

MARY: Modern life is complicated. When you came in I was just telling Miriam—

CRYSTAL: Oh, come along, Sylvia. The lady is tight.

SYLVIA: Mary, when did you begin drinking?

MARY: (*To* CRYSTAL) Early in the evening, with Mr. Winston. You *know* Mr. Winston, don't you?

CRYSTAL: (*At the door*) I'm afraid I don't.

SYLVIA: Of course you do, Crystal. I introduced you to him. Don't you remember?

CRYSTAL: Oh, yes, a cocktail party.

MARY: Well, he's in the lobby now, waiting for someone, Mrs. Haines, and drunker than you can possibly imagine. You'd find him very difficult to handle, in front of Stephen. (CRYSTAL *suddenly changes her mind about going into the lobby, moves toward the washroom.*)

SYLVIA: Crystal, where are you going?

CRYSTAL: I won't stand here and listen to drivel!

MARY: I wouldn't go in there, either, Mrs. Haines. His wife's in there now, having hysterics. She's found out that Buck has been deceiving her.

CRYSTAL:. Really! What has that to do with me?

MARY: A good deal, I'm afraid. You seem to be the woman.

SYLVIA: (*Delighted*) Why, Crystal!—*Are* you?

CRYSTAL: If he used my name, it's a lie! He's just the cheap sort— I'll tell my husband.

MARY: You'll have to. Tomorrow it will be common gossip. I don't think Stephen will like it.

SYLVIA: Oh, Crystal, he's going to loathe it! But my psycho-analyst is going to adore it.

CRYSTAL: (*Going to her*) What are you trying to do? Pin something on me, in front of witnesses?

SYLVIA: Whatever she's driving at, Crystal—(*Pointing to* MIRIAM)— that little tramp put her up to it!

CRYSTAL: (*To* SYLVIA) Keep out of this!

MIRIAM: Yeah, check it, Sylvia, we're minor league this evening.

CRYSTAL: All right, Mrs. Haines, you've been listening to the ravings of a conceited fool. What did he tell you?

MARY: (*Playing for time, or inspiration*) Really, Mrs. Haines, this is very embarrassing.

CRYSTAL: (*Brazening it out*) Yes, Mrs. Haines, isn't it? Exactly what do you think you know about me?

MARY: Everything! (*A pause.* CRYSTAL *laughs.*)

CRYSTAL: Then why are you standing here talking to me? You ought to be outside spilling it to Stephen. You're bluffing. Come along, Sylvia!

MARY: (*Also moving to door.* CRYSTAL *stops*) That's very good advice. I will tell Stephen.

CRYSTAL: Oh, he wouldn't believe you.

SYLVIA: Oh, you can't tell, Crystal! He's terribly fond of Mary.

CRYSTAL: Now get this straight, Mrs. Haines. I like what I got, and I'm going to keep it. You handed me your husband on a silver platter. (*Enter* NANCY, *left*) But I'm not returning the compliment. I can't be stampeded by gossip. What you believe and what Stephen believes will cut no ice in a divorce court. You need proof and you haven't got it. When Mr. Winston comes to his senses, he'll apologize. And Stephen will have no choice, but to accept—my explanations. Now that's that! Good night!

MARY: (*Desperately*) I hope Mrs. Winston will accept your explanations.

CRYSTAL: What have I got to explain to her?

MARY: (*With a conviction she does not feel*) What about the apartment?

CRYSTAL: What apartment?

MARY: You know as well as I do.

CRYSTAL: Oh, stop trying to put two and two together—

MARY: Oh, Mrs. Winston did that. She had you watched—she's seen you both.

CRYSTAL: (*Defiantly*) Where?

MARY: Going in, and coming out!

CRYSTAL: Going in and coming out *where*? (*A pause*) You're lying!

SYLVIA: (*Warningly*) I wouldn't be so sure, Crystal!

MIRIAM: Sounds like the McCoy to me, Crystal.

CRYSTAL: Shut up!

SYLVIA: Oh, Crystal, why didn't you confide in me? (CRYSTAL *turns to the door again, triumphant.*)

MARY: (*Dismayed*) Sylvia, didn't she?

SYLVIA: Certainly *not!* (CRYSTAL *smiles, very pleased with herself*) She's the cat that walks alone. (*Goes to* CRYSTAL) Why, Crystal, I could have told you some place *much safer* than the Gothic Apartments!

CRYSTAL: (*Exploding*) Why, you big, loud-mouthed idiot!

SYLVIA: How dare you!

CRYSTAL: I'd like to slap your stupid face.

SYLVIA: (*Backing up*) Oh, Mary, how dare she?

MIRIAM: Oh, I've got a job to do on Flora. (*She pats* SYLVIA *affectionately*) Kiss you when I get back, Sylvia. (*Exits, left.*)

NANCY: And I'll explain the facts of life to Stephen. (NANCY *exits, right.*)

CRYSTAL: (*To* MARY, *fiercely*) You're trying to break up my marriage!

SYLVIA: The way you did hers, you floosie!

CRYSTAL: (*Nasty*) Well, maybe you're welcome to my—left-overs.

MARY: (*Calmly*) I'll take them, thank you.

SYLVIA: Why, Mary, haven't you any *pride?*

MARY: That's right. No, no pride; that's a luxury a woman in love can't afford. (*Enter* COUNTESS *and* MIRIAM, *left.* MIRIAM *goes to* SADIE, *gets the* COUNTESS' *and her own wraps.*)

COUNTESS: (*Rushing for* CRYSTAL) Oh, mon Dieu, mon Dieu!

MARY: (*Stopping her*) Flora, it's really too bad—

COUNTESS: (*To* CRYSTAL) You—you painted wagon!

CRYSTAL: So you're determined to have a scandal, Mrs. Haines.

COUNTESS: I'm the one who's going to have the scandal. Why, Mary, she's no more a blonde naturelle than I am. What's the creature's name? Miriam forgot to tell me.

MARY: Mrs. Stephen Haines, currently.

COUNTESS: Is that the thing Stephen left you for? Well, cherie, all I can say is, you're an idiot! I hope I never live to see the day when an obvious piece like that conquers *me* on the champs d'amour! (*She exits, right, followed by* MIRIAM.)

CRYSTAL: (*To* MARY) That damn fool didn't know. (SADIE *gives* MARY *her wrap.*)

MARY: I'm afraid she didn't. (*Enter* NANCY, *right.*)

NANCY: There's a gentleman called Mr. Haines. He says he's been waiting a long time for his wife—(CRYSTAL *moves to get her wrap.*)

MARY: (*Stepping between her and* SADIE) Tell him, *I* am coming. (*Exit* NANCY *quickly.*)

SYLVIA: Mary, what a dirty female trick!

SYLVIA: Yes! From the great, noble little woman! You're just a cat, like all the rest of us!

MARY: Well, I've had two years to sharpen my claws. (*Waves her hand gaily to* SYLVIA) Jungle-red, Sylvia! Good night, ladies! (*Exits.*)

CURTAIN

THE LITTLE FOXES

"Take us the foxes, the little foxes, that spoil the vines; for our vines have tender grapes."

—*Song of Solomon*

LILLIAN HELLMAN

First presented in 1939

FOREWORD

L illian Hellman is the most famous and possibly the most controversial woman dramatist the United States has ever produced. Her plays are regularly revived by both professional and amateur companies around the world, and several have been turned into feature films. Hellman was elected to the American Academy of Arts and Sciences, served as Vice President of the National Institute of Arts and Letters, and received a National Book Award for a volume of memoirs. When she died in 1984, the *New York Times* ran her obituary on the front page.

Born June 20, 1905, to a German Jewish family in New Orleans, Hellman spent much of her childhood shuttling between her hometown and New York City, where the family lived half of each year from the time Hellman was six. She dropped out of New York University after two years, worked as a manuscript reader for a publishing firm, then as a playreader for Anne Nichols (the author of the fabulously successful comedy *Abie's Irish Rose*, Nichols had turned to producing) and as a script reader for Metro-Goldwyn-Mayer. During this period Hellman also published a few comic short stories and collaborated on a play, *The Dear Queen*, which she was unable to sell.

Hellman was still in her twenties when she made an impressive stage debut with *The Children's Hour* (1934), the story of two owners of a girls' school who are accused of being lesbians. Loosely based on an actual incident that took place in Scotland in the nineteenth century, *The Children's Hour* reportedly failed even to be

considered for a Pulitzer Prize because at least one member of the
Pulitzer committee refused to attend a play about so shocking a
subject. Conservative critic and theater historian Arthur Hobson
Quinn averred that Hellman was "a much more talented playwright
than Clifford Odets," but was bewildered by *The Children's Hour*;
audiences apparently had less trouble and the play ran for 691
performances in New York. Although *The Children's Hour* shows
the marks of the novice dramatist—Hellman's sometimes heavy
hand with plotting and "message" is evident—it perceptively
explores society's fear of women's success and friendship. Her first
produced drama also introduces several themes that will dominate
Hellman's work, particularly the issues of personal responsibility
and the danger posed by self-righteous "good" people who act
without considering the consequences of their deeds. As many
recent feminist critics have complained, *The Children's Hour* is
evasive in its attitude toward lesbianism (a virtual necessity on
Broadway more than a half century ago). Still, both accused women
are positive characters, warm friends and concerned teachers.
Karen and Martha's horror of lesbianism reveals less about
Hellman's own feelings than about the values of a patriarchal
society in which women loving women is the ultimate sin.

Hellman's second play, *Days to Come* (1936), lasted only six
performances. While it offers a compelling analysis of class
differences and capitalist paternalism, the drama is overburdened
with plot and lifeless characters. The failure of *Days* partly explains
Hellman's difficulty in writing *The Little Foxes*. She recalls in
Pentimento, her second book of memoirs, that "*Foxes* was the most
difficult play I ever wrote" and adds that it went through at least
eight drafts. Hellman first got the idea for *Foxes*, partly based on
her mother's family, in 1937. To help clarify her picture of the
South in 1900, Hellman and a researcher compiled more than a
hundred pages of notes on topics including cotton, the industrial
south, and "Historical Background"; in his doctoral dissertation
Glen Whitesides says that she also designed "a representative upper
middle-class house and garden of the period," as well as filling a
notebook with character sketches and plot outlines. According to
the playwright's account, she finished two acts that she thought
"were fine enough to go right into [*King*] *Lear*, as a splendid
addition to that play," but her lover, Dashiell Hammett, had
serious reservations which she came to share. After tearing up what
she'd written and starting "all over again," Hellman still managed

to complete the script by November. Both story and characters had undergone numerous changes—in early versions Horace Giddens (based on a Hellman ancestor) had syphilis rather than heart disease, and at one point Regina and Horace had a son whom his mother adored. The title, suggested by Hellman's friend Dorothy Parker, comes from the Song of Solomon (2:15) and underlines the Hubbards' greed: "Take us the foxes, the little foxes, that spoil the vines: for our vines *have* tender grapes."

After pre-Broadway tryouts *The Little Foxes* opened at the National Theatre in New York on February 15, 1939, with a cast headed by Tallulah Bankhead as Regina Giddens. Ironically, Clare Boothe and Henry Luce gave the opening-night party; Boothe's and Hellman's paths would soon diverge along with their politics. Although it did not achieve quite the initial success of *The Children's Hour—The Little Foxes* closed after 410 performances—it toured the country for years and is the most frequently revived of her works around the world. Simone Signoret translated and starred in a French version, while Marc Blitzstein turned *The Little Foxes* into the operetta *Regina*. Hellman wrote the screenplay for the famous movie version, starring Bette Davis. According to biographer William Wright, however, it was Samuel Goldwyn who demanded that Alexandra be given a suitor in the film; apparently the Hollywood producer feared that audiences would be disturbed (or at least disappointed) to see a young woman leaving home without a man to protect her. Among the most notable revivals was one at Lincoln Center in 1967 starring Anne Bancroft and another in 1981 that marked Elizabeth Taylor's Broadway debut.

Reviews of *The Little Foxes* were mixed but largely positive. The critic for the *New Republic* considered the play a "simple melodrama" and Regina a variation on Lady Macbeth. Brooks Atkinson was less disturbed by both the melodrama and the "malevolent lady" protagonist, calling *Foxes* a "vibrant play." George Jean Nathan managed to condemn Hellman's sister playwrights while praising her for a work that "indicates a dramatic mind, an eye to character, a fundamental strength, and a complete and unremitting integrity that are rare among her native playwriting sex." Richard Watts, Jr., thought *Foxes* a "fine and important American drama."

The term "melodrama" was invoked by nearly every critic, sometimes to condemn, less often to praise. *Time*'s reviewer noted melodrama's "power to excite" and ability to "stir up genuine drama of character and will," concluding that *Foxes* is "powerful drama." And perhaps, as Walter Kerr commented in a review of the 1967 revival, "America *was* melodrama in 1900. It may still be"—as any newspaper will attest. Certainly *Foxes* has what scholar Richard Moody calls "the trappings of melodrama: strongboxes, stolen bonds, spilled medicine..." but it lacks such other requisite ingredients as one-dimensional characters, a plot dependent solely on chance, and a clear victory of the forces of good over those of evil. Hellman's plays are, like all dramatic works, designed to evoke emotional as well as intellectual responses from audiences. Although the mechanisms she uses to manipulate viewers may sometimes be obvious, her dramas are scarcely as "simple" as many critics would like to believe.

Perhaps too it was easier for reviewers to focus on the theatricality of *The Little Foxes* and to see the characters as all-noble or all-evil than to acknowledge Hellman's critique of both capitalism and the gender roles it mandates. Hellman sets *Foxes* in the Deep South at the turn of the century, but it is a South that is coming to resemble the rest of the nation: a society in which state governors can easily be bribed, and nothing—including young women—is exempt as currency in business deals. Even without Ben's speech about "the hundreds of Hubbards" who "will own this country someday" we can clearly see *Foxes* in the anti-capitalist tradition of the 1930s stage and Ben Hubbard as the rapacious businessman already popularized by playwrights like Odets as well as Hallie Flanagan and Margaret Ellen Clifford. Similarly, Alexandra's impassioned vow that she will "be fighting" against the Hubbards of the world is a plea to the audience to do the same, a plea squarely in the thirties tradition and only marginally different from the appeal to the "educated classes" at the end of *Can You Hear Their Voices?*.

By the time seventeen-year-old Alexandra pledges to take action, the play has revealed how corrupt nearly all the adult characters are. Hellman does not intend the avaricious Ben and his spiteful brother Oscar to be the cardboard villains they are sometimes portrayed as; writing in *Pentimento*, she insists "I had meant the audience to recognize some part of themselves in the money-dominated Hubbards." And if Horace Giddens is a fundamentally decent man, he is also a collaborator who tries to refuse further alliance with the Hubbards only *after* he's already done "enough" harm. Hellman allows her characters no second chances: once Horace has helped his brothers-in-law he is forever tainted, and his heart disease is a physical manifestation of his moral weakness.

As in the majority of Hellman's best plays—*The Children's Hour*, *The Autumn Garden*, *Toys in the Attic*—the most interesting characters in *The Little Foxes* are female, and Regina Giddens is one of the dramatist's greatest creations. Over the years critical response to Regina has varied widely. Critics have dubbed her everything from "a kind of single-handed Lady Macbeth" to a "hateful woman [who] has to be respected for the keenness of her mind and the force of her character" to the logical product of a sexist, capitalist system who "could compete in a male-controlled society only by pursuing her own self-interest, and by being more manipulative than the men around her." In a patriarchal world in which the family business is literally and symbolically named "Hubbard Sons," Regina is particularly dangerous because she has no legitimate access to the power and money that society defines as its worthiest prizes. When Regina withholds sex from her husband by telling him she's ill, she's using virtually her only bargaining chip, a tactic at least as old as *Lysistrata*. She has far more brains than Oscar, more drive than her husband; her gender alone bars her from direct participation in their business transactions.

Regina rejects the roles—doting wife and mother, worshipful sister—inscribed for her by society, and the battle for supremacy between Regina and Ben reveals the play's powerful subtext about gender definitions. Ben repeatedly "prompts" his sister in her social role as a woman, invoking tradition and their mother as arbiter and ideal. When Regina dares to voice her own demands, he asks: "For how many years have I told you a good-looking woman gets more by being soft and appealing? Mama used to tell you that." Regina, however, needs no coaching in society's expectations about women and at least temporarily defeats Ben by threatening a bravura performance of poor-helpless-female. If they do not give her the share of the business deal she requests, she will accuse Leo and her brothers of appropriating Horace's bonds. Counting on the very same male chivalry to which Ben constantly refers, she taunts him: "You couldn't find a jury that wouldn't weep for a woman whose brothers steal from her." Regina's goals—money, power, social status—may be no different from her brothers' and certainly we are not meant to approve of her treatment of Horace, but Hellman forces us to admire a woman determined to shape her own life even as we condemn both her means and her specific ends.

By setting *The Little Foxes* in the Giddens' house, Hellman demystifies the relationship between the domestic sphere on the one hand and the economic and political worlds on the other. The hypocrisy of excluding women from direct participation in business negotiations is foregrounded as Birdie, Alexandra and Regina are bought, sold or traded in this home of capitalism. Even the befuddled Birdie Hubbard is aware that marrying her was the "price" Oscar paid to obtain her plantation, and she vows to prevent her niece from being a pawn in a similar bargain. Yet Birdie, unlike Regina, allows the men to turn her into an object—as she herself admits in her third-act "confession" to Alexandra. Hellman writes in *Pentimento*: "I had meant people to smile at, and to sympathize with, the sad, weak Birdie, certainly I had not meant them to cry." In Hellman's eyes, Birdie has the advantages of class privilege (she's the only aristocrat in the family), hence she is partly responsible for her own victimization because she has not fought back against the Hubbards. What Hellman fails to understand fully—in both this comment and the play itself—is the psychology of a woman who is so battered emotionally and physically by a brutal husband that she sees no way out except her own self-destruction through alcoholism.

A far stronger character is Addie, the moral center of the *The Little Foxes*; it is she who speaks Hellman's famous indictment of passivity: "there are people who eat the earth and eat all the people on it like in the Bible with the locusts. And other people who stand around and watch them eat it.... Sometimes I think it ain't right to stand and watch them do it." Working class, Black and female, Addie is the only major character in the play who cannot be implicated in the evil doings because she clearly has no power. Hellman was in many ways ahead of her White colleagues in the 1930s in giving so crucial a role to an African American woman: Addie is a voice of reason throughout, and she is present at the final curtain to provide wisdom and support for Zan. Still, Hellman's own racism is revealed in the fact that Addie, unlike the White women in *Foxes*, has no "story" of her own. It may comfort Whites to believe that the Black women who work for them are dedicated exclusively to their White "families," have no ties to their own kin or African American communities, but it is a fiction grounded in a biased world view. (Interestingly, Richard Moody reveals that in earlier versions of *Foxes* Addie had a daughter named Charlotte, but the Addie of the published play is devoted solely to Zan and Horace.) Years later in her memoir *An Unfinished Woman* Hellman implicitly acknowledged the gaps in her depiction of Addie, noting the ambivalence, perhaps even "hate and contempt," that Southern Black women must feel toward Whites. Addie is a sympathetic character in *Foxes*, but her portrayal reveals a narrowness of vision from which even the most liberal White writers in the 1930s were not exempt.

Despite its flaws, *The Little Foxes* remains a very powerful and complex exploration of the interrelationships between capitalism and gender roles. Writing about films of the Depression era, historian Susan Ware notes that "the number-one box-office attraction between 1935 and 1938 was...a child: Shirley Temple." The child is female, of course, the image of infantilized womanhood. Clinging to her liquor bottle, Birdie Hubbard succumbs to that infantilization. Regina Giddens fights back, even if the price of that fight is much of her humanity. Alexandra vows to combine her mother's strength with her aunt's decency, no mean feat in this world.

Hellman had originally planned *The Little Foxes* as part of a trilogy. Although she never wrote the sequel, she said in an interview that she had intended "to take up with [*Regina*] in about 1920 or 1925, in Europe. And her daughter, Alexandra, was to have become maybe a spinsterish social worker, disappointed, a rather angry woman." But before Hellman became "tired" of the characters she did complete *Another Part of the Forest* (1946), a look at the young Hubbards and their parents in 1880. *Forest* shows how the Hubbard siblings learned their lessons at the knee of their father, Marcus, an arrogant, avaricious man who abuses his wife and disdains his sons. In *Forest* young Ben is a trickster who outsmarts his father with blackmail, Oscar rides with the Ku Klux Klan and professes to be in love with a prostitute, while twenty-year-old Regina finds herself in a difficult bind: her father gives her almost everything she wants but only as long as she returns his nearly incestuous devotion. Even at this young age Regina—like so many other female characters in plays by women dramatists—wants to escape, in this case to flee the South and her family by moving to Chicago with John Bagtry, a cynical veteran of the Civil War.

Another Part of the Forest, which the playwright herself staged in her directing debut, received mixed notices yet ran more than five months in New York. Brooks Atkinson complained that it combined "blackmail, insanity, cruelty, theft, torture, insult, drunkenness, with a trace of incest thrown in for good measure" but others were more receptive and over the years some critics have preferred *Forest* to *Foxes*. In at least one way *Forest* is an advance over *Foxes*: the African American servant Coralee is a more fully rounded character than Addie. While she is infinitely patient with her White "charge," the much-abused Lavinia (mother to the Hubbard siblings), she replies "*wearily*" to Lavinia's chatter about teaching Black children and avers that perhaps she might not be the perfect instructor for them. When Lavinia takes Coralee off to the piney woods with her, she acknowledges she is uprooting her caretaker from a close network of "kinfolk."

In the late nineteen thirties and forties, concerns about the Depression and the collapse of capitalism began to be replaced by worries about the growing Nazi threat in Europe. Certainly because of her liberal politics and perhaps too because of her Jewish heritage (although she had "no religious upbringing," she said in a 1976 interview that being a Jew "became very important to" her with the advent of Nazism), Hellman wrote two plays during this period about American involvement—or lack of involvement—in world events. *Watch on the Rhine* opened at the Martin Beck Theater on April 1, 1941. A critical success (it won the playwright her first Drama Critics Circle Award), *Watch* ran for more than a year as one of the country's most popular anti-Nazi works. Bringing the European war home to Americans, Hellman tries to shock the characters and the audience out of their complacency. When the Farrelly family—safely ensconced in their country house near Washington, D.C.—discover that they are sheltering a Nazi informer, they realize that no one's hands are clean: ignoring evil makes you culpable, even if the main source of that evil is thousands of miles away. Hellman's portrayal of gender roles in *Watch in the Rhine* is unfortunately far more conventional than in *Foxes*. As feminist critic Vivian Patraka points out, Hellman's Kurt Muller is a strong, decisive man, while his wife Sara is endlessly maternal, protective, self-sacrificing; their children follow suit along gender lines. Given this serious limitation, *Watch* remains a passionate plea to oppose the forces of destruction. The United States entered World War II eight months after *Watch on the Rhine* premiered, but only when bombs were dropped in its own backyard.

Another play about the Nazi era, *The Searching Wind* (1944), proved slightly less successful with critics and audiences. Moving back and forth over a period of two decades, *The Searching Wind* exposes the disastrous cowardice of politicians, journalists and private citizens. Once again Hellman allows her characters no excuses: no fear for the happiness and safety of loved ones can justify Alex Hazen's attempts to appease the Nazis, his father-in-law's craven withdrawal from public life, or Cassie Bowman's hypocrisy.

While *The Autumn Garden* (1951) had only a moderate success—at 101 performances it barely achieved the status of a "hit," usually reserved for plays that surpass the hundred-night mark—many people consider it her best work. More than a few critics have called *Garden* "Chekhovian" because, like the works of Anton Chekhov, it concerns a group of mostly middle-aged characters dissatisfied with their lives but unwilling or unable to change them. Hellman admired Chekhov—she edited a volume of his letters a few years later—and certainly *Garden* is more loosely plotted than her earlier plays. But Hellman's introduction to the letters hints at a crucial difference between the two dramatists: where Chekhov almost always shows compassion for his characters, Hellman often treats hers with a certain amount of disdain or at least skepticism. If her characters lead wasted lives, the fault is largely their own.

Neither *Montserrat* (1949), based on Emmanuel Robles' grisly moral parable about loyalty and treachery in nineteenth century Venezuela, nor *The Lark* (1955), Hellman's rendering of Jean Anouilh's drama about St. Joan, is great drama, although the latter has considerable power and proved popular with audiences. It is not surprising that during the post-war period Hellman was intensely concerned with issues of betrayal and martyrdom, for the House Un-American Activities Committee (HUAC) was busy interrogating and indicting left-wing artists and intellectuals solely on the basis of their (usually past) political beliefs. Dashiell Hammett was sentenced to jail in 1951 for refusing to provide the names of contributors to a bail fund for Communists, and Hellman was subpoenaed by the Committee the following year. Refusing to testify about other people, "to hurt innocent people whom I knew many years ago in order to save myself," Hellman wrote to the Committee "I cannot and will not cut my conscience to fit this year's fashions." When the Committee refused to allow her to testify about herself but not others, she pleaded the Fifth

Amendment. Hellman escaped censure for contempt of Congress but joined many colleagues on the Hollywood blacklist, banned from working in films. Several months after her HUAC appearance Hellman directed a revival of *The Children's Hour*, her unfortunately appropriate play about lives ruined by rumors, accusations and smug self-righteousness.

Lillian Hellman's solo foray into the musical world, *Candide* (1956), failed to find an audience and closed after seventy-two performances. Hellman never liked the collaborative aspects of the theater, working with directors and actors, and adding composer Leonard Bernstein and librettist Richard Wilbur into the mix proved entirely too much; she later conceded that *Candide* was probably the decisive moment when she decided to leave the theater. Many critics complained that Hellman's book was too heavy for a comic work, although John Chapman considered the libretto "strong, clear and humorous." In fact, Hellman's text is trenchant and eminently playable; the book, like the lyrics and music, provides a splendid spoof of the whole genre of the American musical (despite war, famine, the Inquisition, earthquakes, shipwrecks, kidnapping and imprisonment, the lovers are eventually reunited). In 1956 the public was simply not ready for Hellman's send-up of that most American of dramatic genres, the musical comedy.

Except for *My Mother, My Father and Me* (1963), an embarrassingly humorless comedy adapted from a Burt Blechman novel, Hellman's final play was *Toys in the Attic* (1960). *Toys* grew from an anecdote, told to her by Hammett, about a feckless young man who surprises those around him when he finally becomes a success. In a revealing comment, Hellman admitted, "I can write about men, but I can't write a play that centers on a man. I've got to tear it up, make it about the women around him, his sisters, his bride, her mother...." *Toys* is a Freudian-Gothic comedy that explores a world where men are valued and women are not, and what happens when three women try to live their lives through the same weak man. Manipulative Carrie may momentarily defeat both her more reasonable sister and the strange Lily (whose name suggests a rather grotesque self-portrait of the artist) but she is largely reenacting the adoration her parents lavished on their spoiled only son; he becomes her life because she has none. Second in popularity only to *The Children's Hour*, *Toys* ran 556 performances, earned Hellman another Drama Critics Circle

Award, and was turned—without Hellman's help—into a Hollywood film.

After she left the theater, Hellman went on to become a successful writer of memoirs: *An Unfinished Woman, Pentimento* and *Scoundrel Time*, all of which were best sellers and all of which evoked enormous controversy. If Hellman based many of her plays on actual people and events, she conversely infused a substantial amount of imagination into her memoirs. (Ironically, Hellman was then attacked for not adhering to the conventions of the memoir genre, much as she had been attacked for adhering *too* closely to dramatic conventions, particularly those of the so-called "well-made play.") The sketch "Julia" from *Pentimento* was made into a popular film, although biographers still seem unable to prove conclusively whether Hellman actually had a friend named Julia; whether she based the character on Muriel Gardiner, a woman she had never met; or whether she created Julia out of whole cloth. *Scoundrel Time*, Hellman's history of the HUAC days, angered many because the focus was not on people like Senator Joe McCarthy and Roy Cohn, who led the persecution of liberals and former Communists, but on the liberals who betrayed their friends or stood by and watched the witch-hunt progress. Consistent to the end, Hellman lays her heaviest censure on the "watchers" who should know better but passively allow evil to happen.

A woman of many talents, Lillian Hellman spent her last years teaching at various prestigious universities while writing *Maybe*, a peculiar book she ambiguously labeled simply "a story," and co-authoring with Peter Feibleman a cookbook entitled *Eating Together: Recollections & Recipes*. She also became embroiled in lawsuits and public battles with writers Mary McCarthy and Martha Gellhorn as well as a host of others who either challenged her veracity or simply found her confrontational style offensive. Like Clare Boothe, Hellman refused the role prescribed for women early in this century; she reaped the rewards but she also paid the price. Her plays earned two Drama Critics Circle Awards, presented by the critics themselves, but despite several nominations she never won a Pulitzer Prize, the establishment recognition of dramatic achievement. Two massive biographies by male authors have appeared in the decade since her death; both are informative and important yet their biases are clear. While William Wright manages to approach Hellman with at least a slightly open mind, Carl Rollyson prefers to see her in terms of the tiredest gender clichés: "There was a tough, masculine quality about Hellman," he asserts, even though deep inside "a vulnerable...female self flowered."

In recent years more attention has been paid to Hellman the public figure than Hellman the dramatist, even as her plays are performed around the world. Perhaps some find it easier to attack the public figure than to grapple seriously with her drama, the themes of which remain strikingly relevant in the 1990s. The recent materialist feminist attack on realism, Hellman's favored dramatic style, may also be partly responsible for the limited scholarly consideration her work receives. Yet while some theorists accuse realistic drama of reifying the very social ills it would condemn, other feminist critics argue that Hellman used realism to unmask the inequities and oppressions inherent in a capitalist society. And one thing is certainly undeniable: after Lillian Hellman, American women playwrights could no longer be ignored.

SELECTED BIBLIOGRAPHY

Austin, Gayle. *Feminist Theories for Dramatic Criticism*. Ann Arbor: U. of Michigan P., 1990.

Bryer, Jackson R., ed. *Conversations With Lillian Hellman*. Jackson: U. of Mississippi P., 1986.

Denham, Cynthia Bailey. "Lillian Hellman's Revisions in *The Collected Plays*. Diss. Auburn University, 1986.

Estrin, Mark W., ed. *Critical Essays on Lillian Hellman*. Boston: G.K. Hall, 1989.

Falk, Doris V. *Lillian Hellman*. N.Y.: Ungar, 1978.

Hellman, Lillian. *The Collected Plays*. Boston: Little, Brown, 1972.

————. *Three: An Unfinished Woman, Pentimento, Scoundrel Time*. Intro. Richard Poirier. Boston: Little Brown, 1979.

Lederer, Katherine. *Lillian Hellman*. Boston: Twayne, 1979.

Moody, Richard. *Lillian Hellman, Playwright*. N.Y.: Bobbs-Merrill, 1972.

Patraka, Vivian M. "Lillian Hellman's *Watch on the Rhine*: Realism, Gender, and Historical Crisis." *Modern Drama* 32 (March 1989): 128-45.

Rollyson, Carl. *Lillian Hellman: Her Legend and Her Legacy*. N.Y.: St. Martin's, 1988.

Wright, William. *Lillian Hellman: The Image, The Woman*. N.Y.: Simon and Schuster, 1986.

A Note on the Text

In 1972 Hellman published a volume entitled *The Collected Plays*, which included a "Publisher's Note" stating "For this edition Miss Hellman has made numerous small revisions and emendations in each of the plays: the texts as given here are henceforth to be regarded as definitive." The text that follows is, accordingly, the 1972 version.

Although *The Little Foxes* underwent less revision than many of the other works in *The Collected Plays*, and many changes simply involve the alteration or deletion of stage directions, there are some modifications worth mentioning. As Cynthia Bailey Denham observes in her dissertation on Hellman's revisions in *The Collected Plays*, most of the changes involve Alexandra and Addie. Hellman's main aim seems to have been to make Zan appear more mature and independent. To this end she cut some of Addie's dialogue that directly refers to her taking care of Zan, removed Addie from the curtain scene of Act II, and slightly modified the final moments of the play, in which Addie had originally moved to the young woman's side. While these changes diminish Addie's role somewhat, they also tone down Addie's maternal devotion to her young White employer. The primary result of the revisions, as Denham notes, is to strengthen Zan's role.

CHARACTERS

ADDIE
CAL
BIRDIE HUBBARD
OSCAR HUBBARD
LEO HUBBARD
REGINA GIDDENS
WILLIAM MARSHALL
BENJAMIN HUBBARD
ALEXANDRA GIDDENS
HORACE GIDDENS

The scene of the play is the living room of the Giddens house, in a small town in the South.

ACT ONE
The spring of 1900, evening.

ACT TWO
A week later, early morning.

ACT THREE
Two weeks later, late afternoon.

There has been no attempt to write Southern dialect. It is to be understood that the accents are Southern.

ACT ONE

SCENE: The living room of the Giddens home, in a small town in the deep South, the spring of 1900. Upstage is a staircase leading to the second story. Upstage, right, are double doors to the dining room. When these doors are open we see a section of the dining room and the furniture. Upstage, left, is an entrance hall with a coatrack and umbrella stand. There are large lace-curtained windows on the left wall. The room is lit by a center gas chandelier and painted china oil lamps on the tables. Against the wall is a large piano. Downstage, right, are a high couch, a large table, several chairs. Against the left back wall are a table and several chairs. Near the window there are a smaller couch and tables. The room is good-looking, the furniture expensive; but it reflects no particular taste. Everything is of the best and that is all.

At rise ADDIE, *a tall, nice-looking Negro woman of about fifty-five, is closing the windows. From behind the closed dining-room doors there is the sound of voices. After a second,* CAL, *a middle-aged Negro, comes in from the entrance hall carrying a tray with glasses and a bottle of port.* ADDIE *crosses, takes the tray from him, puts it on table, begins to arrange it.*

ADDIE: *(Pointing to the bottle)* You gone stark out of your head?

CAL: No, smart lady, I ain't. Miss Regina told me to get out that bottle. *(Points to bottle)* That very bottle for the mighty honored guest. When Miss Regina changes orders like that you can bet your dime she got her reason.

ADDIE: *(Points to dining room)* Go on. You'll be needed.

CAL: Miss Zan she had two helpings frozen fruit cream and she tell that honored guest, she tell him that you make the best frozen fruit cream in all the South.

ADDIE: Did she? Well, see that Belle saves a little for her. She like it right before she go to bed. Save a few little cakes, too, she like—

(The dining-room doors are opened and closed again by BIRDIE HUBBARD. BIRDIE *is a woman of about forty, with a pretty, well-bred, faded face. Her movements are usually nervous and timid, but now, as she comes running into the room, she is gay and excited.* CAL *turns to* BIRDIE.*)*

BIRDIE: Oh, Cal. I want you to get one of the kitchen boys to run home for me. He's to look in my desk drawer and—*(To* ADDIE) My, Addie. What a good supper! Just as good as good can be.

172

ADDIE: You look pretty this evening, Miss Birdie, and young.

BIRDIE: *(Laughing)* Me, young? *(Turns back to* CAL) Maybe you better find Simon and tell him to do it himself. He's to look in my desk, the left drawer, and bring my music album right away. Mr. Marshall is very anxious to see it because of his father and the opera in Chicago. *(To* ADDIE) Mr. Marshall is such a polite man with his manners and very educated and cultured and I've told him all about how my mama and papa used to go to Europe for the music—*(Laughs)* Imagine going all the way to Europe just to listen to music. Wouldn't that be nice, Addie? Just to sit there and listen and—*(Turns)* Left drawer, Cal. Tell him that twice because he forgets. And tell him not to let any of the things drop out of the album and to bring it right in here when he comes back.

(The dining-room doors are opened and quickly closed by OSCAR HUBBARD. *He is a man in his late forties.)*

CAL: Simon he won't get it right. But I'll tell him.

BIRDIE: Left drawer, Cal, and tell him to bring the blue book and—

OSCAR: *(Sharply)* Birdie.

BIRDIE: *(Turning nervously)* Oh, Oscar. I was just sending Simon for my music album.

OSCAR: *(To* CAL) Never mind about the album. Miss Birdie has changed her mind.

BIRDIE: But, really, Oscar. Really I promised Mr. Marshall. I—(CAL *exits.)*

OSCAR: Why do you leave the dinner table and go running about like a child?

BIRDIE: But, Oscar, Mr. Marshall said most specially he *wanted* to see my album. I told him about the time Mama met Wagner, and Mrs. Wagner gave her the signed program and the big picture. Mr. Marshall wants to see that. Very, very much. We had such a nice talk and—

OSCAR: You have been chattering to him like a magpie. You haven't let him be for a second. I can't think he came South to be bored with you.

BIRDIE: *(Quickly, hurt)* He wasn't bored. I don't believe he was bored. He's a very educated, cultured gentleman. *(Her voice rises)* I just don't believe it. You always talk like that when I'm having a nice time.

OSCAR: *(Turning to her, sharply)* You have had too much wine. Get yourself in hand now.

BIRDIE: *(Drawing back, about to cry, shrilly)* What am I doing? I am not doing anything. What am I doing?

OSCAR: *(Taking a step to her)* I said get yourself in hand. Stop acting like a fool.

BIRDIE: I don't believe he was bored. I just don't believe it. Some people like music and like to talk about it. That's all I was doing.

(LEO HUBBARD *comes hurrying through the dining-room door. He is a young man of twenty, with a weak kind of good looks.*)

LEO: Mama! Papa! They are coming in now.

OSCAR: *(Softly)* Sit down, Birdie. Sit down now. (BIRDIE *sits down, bows her head as if to hide her face.*)

(*The dining-room doors are opened by* CAL. *We see people beginning to rise from the table.* REGINA GIDDENS *comes in with* WILLIAM MARSHALL. REGINA *is a handsome woman of forty.* MARSHALL *is forty-five, pleasant-looking, self-possessed. Behind them comes* ALEXANDRA GIDDENS, *a pretty, rather delicate-looking girl of seventeen. She is followed by* BENJAMIN HUBBARD, *fifty-five, with a large jovial face and the light graceful movements that one often finds in large men.*)

REGINA: Mr. Marshall, I think you're trying to console me. Chicago may be the noisiest, dirtiest city in the world but I should still prefer it to the sound of our horses and the smell of our azaleas. I should like crowds of people, and theaters, and lovely women—*Very* lovely women, Mr. Marshall?

MARSHALL: In Chicago? Oh, I suppose so. But I can tell you this: I've never dined there with *three* such lovely ladies.

(ADDIE *begins to pass the port.*)

BEN: Our Southern women are well favored.

LEO: *(Laughs)* But one must go to Mobile for the ladies, sir. Very elegant worldly ladies, too.

BEN: *(Looks at him)* Worldly, eh? *Worldly*, did you say?

OSCAR: *(Hastily, to* LEO) Your Uncle Ben means that worldliness is not a mark of beauty in any woman.

LEO: *(Quickly)* Of course, Uncle Ben. I didn't mean—

MARSHALL: Your port is excellent, Mrs. Giddens.

REGINA: Thank you, Mr. Marshall. We had been saving that bottle, hoping we could open it just for you.

ALEXANDRA: *(As* ADDIE *comes to her with the tray)* Oh. May I *really*, Addie?

ADDIE: Better ask Mama.

ALEXANDRA: May I, Mama?

REGINA: *(Nods, smiles)* In Mr. Marshall's honor.

ALEXANDRA: Mr. Marshall, this will be the first taste of port I've ever had.

MARSHALL: No one ever had their first taste of a better port. *(He lifts his glass in a toast; she lifts hers; they both drink)* Well, I suppose it is all true, Mrs. Giddens.

REGINA: What is true?

MARSHALL: That you Southerners occupy a unique position in America. You live better than the rest of us, you eat better, you drink better. I wonder you find time, or want to find time, to do business.

BEN: A great many Southerners don't.

MARSHALL: Do all of you live here together?

REGINA: Here with me? *(Laughs)* Oh, no. My brother Ben lives next door. My brother Oscar and his family live in the next square.

BEN: But we are a very close family. We've always wanted it that way.

MARSHALL: That is very pleasant. Keeping your family together to share each other's lives. My family moves around too much. My children seem never to come home. Away at school in the winter; in the summer, Europe with their mother—

REGINA: *(Eagerly)* Oh, yes. Even down here we read about Mrs. Marshall in the society pages.

MARSHALL: I dare say. She moves about a great deal. And all of you are part of the same business? Hubbard Sons?

BEN: *(Motions to OSCAR)* Oscar and me. *(Motions to REGINA)* My sister's good husband is a banker.

MARSHALL: *(Looks at REGINA, surprised)* Oh.

REGINA: I am so sorry that my husband isn't here to meet you. He's been very ill. He is at Johns Hopkins. But he will be home soon. We think he is getting better now.

LEO: I work for Uncle Horace. *(REGINA looks at him)* I mean I work for Uncle Horace at his bank. I keep an eye on things while he's away.

REGINA: *(Smiles)* Really, Leo?

BEN: *(Looks at LEO, then to MARSHALL)* Modesty in the young is as excellent as it is rare.

OSCAR: *(To LEO)* Your uncle means that a young man should speak more modestly.

LEO: *(Hastily, taking a step to* BEN) Oh, I didn't mean, sir—

MARSHALL: Oh, Mrs. Hubbard. Where's that Wagner autograph you promised to let me see? My train will be leaving soon and—

BIRDIE: The autograph? Oh. Well. Really, Mr. Marshall, I didn't mean to chatter so about it. Really I—*(Nervously, looking at* OSCAR) You must excuse me. I didn't get it because, well, because I had—I—I had a little headache and—

OSCAR: My wife is a miserable victim of headaches.

REGINA: *(Quickly)* Mr. Marshall said at supper that he would like you to play for him, Alexandra.

ALEXANDRA: *(Who has been looking at* BIRDIE) It's not I who play well, sir. It's my aunt. She plays just wonderfully. She's my teacher. *(Rises. Eagerly)* May we play a duet? May we, Mama?

BIRDIE: Thank you, dear. But I have my headache now. I—

OSCAR: *(Sharply)* Don't be stubborn, Birdie. Mr. Marshall wants you to play.

MARSHALL: Indeed I do. If your headache isn't—

BIRDIE: *(Hesitates, then gets up, pleased)* But I'd like to, sir. Very much. *(She and* ALEXANDRA *go to the piano.)*

MARSHALL: It's very remarkable how you Southern aristocrats have kept together. Kept together and kept what belonged to you.

BEN: You misunderstand, sir. Southern aristocrats have *not* kept together and have *not* kept what belonged to them.

MARSHALL: *(Laughs, indicates room)* You don't call this keeping what belongs to you?

BEN: But we are not aristocrats. *(Points to* BIRDIE *at the piano)* Our brother's wife is the only one of us who belongs to the Southern aristocracy.

*(*BIRDIE *looks toward* BEN.)*

MARSHALL: *(Smiles)* My information is that you people have been here, and solidly here, for a long time.

OSCAR: And so we have. Since our great-grandfather.

BEN: Who was *not* an aristocrat, like Birdie's.

MARSHALL: You make great distinctions.

BEN: Oh, they have been made for us. And maybe they are important distinctions. Now you take Birdie's family. When my great-grandfather came here they were the highest-tone plantation owners in this state.

LEO: *(Steps to* MARSHALL. *Proudly)* My mother's grandfather was *governor* of the state before the war.

OSCAR: They owned the plantation Lionnet. You may have heard of it, sir?

MARSHALL: *(Laughs)* No, I've never heard of anything but brick houses on a lake, and cotton mills.

BEN: Lionnet in its day was the best cotton land in the South. It still brings us in a fair crop. Ah, they were great days for those people—even when I can remember. They had the best of everything. (BIRDIE *turns to them*) Cloth from Paris, trips to Europe, horses you can't raise anymore, niggers to lift their fingers—

BIRDIE: We were good to our people. Everybody knew that. We were better to them than—

REGINA: *(Quickly)* Why, Birdie. You aren't playing.

BEN: But when the war comes these fine gentlemen ride off and leave the cotton, *and* the women, to rot.

BIRDIE: My father was killed in the war. He was a fine soldier, Mr. Marshall. A fine man.

REGINA: Oh, certainly, Birdie. A famous soldier.

BEN: *(To* BIRDIE*)* But that isn't the tale I am telling Mr. Marshall. *(To* MARSHALL*)* Well, sir, the war ends. Lionnet is almost ruined, and the sons finish ruining it. And there were thousands like them. Why? Because the Southern aristocrat can adapt himself to nothing. Too high-tone to try.

MARSHALL: Sometimes it is difficult to learn new ways. (BIRDIE *and* ALEXANDRA *begin to play.* MARSHALL *leans forward, listening.*)

BEN: Perhaps, perhaps. *(He sees that* MARSHALL *is listening to the music. Irritated, he turns to* BIRDIE *and* ALEXANDRA *at the piano, then back to* MARSHALL*)* You're right, Mr. Marshall. It is difficult to learn new ways. But maybe that's why it's profitable. *Our* grandfather and *our* father learned the new ways and learned how to make them pay. *(Smiles) They* were in trade. Hubbard Sons, Merchandise. Others, Birdie's family, for example, looked down on them. *(Settles back in chair)* To make a long story short, Lionnet now belongs to *us.* (BIRDIE *stops playing*) Twenty years ago we took over their land, their cotton, and their daughter. (BIRDIE *rises and stands stiffly by the piano.* MARSHALL, *who has been watching her, rises.*)

MARSHALL: May I bring you a glass of port, Mrs. Hubbard?

BIRDIE: *(Softly)* No, thank you, sir. You are most polite.

REGINA: *(Sharply, to* BEN*)* You are boring Mr. Marshall with these ancient family tales.

BEN: I hope not. I hope not. I am trying to make an important point—(*Bows to* MARSHALL) for our future business partner.

OSCAR: (*To* MARSHALL) My brother always says that it's folks like us who have struggled and fought to bring to our land some of the prosperity of your land.

BEN: Some people call that patriotism.

REGINA: (*Laughs gaily*) I hope you don't find my brothers too obvious, Mr. Marshall. I'm afraid they mean that this is the time for the ladies to leave the gentlemen to talk business.

MARSHALL: (*Hastily*) Not at all. We settled everything this afternoon. (*He looks at his watch*) I have only a few minutes before I must leave for the train. (*Smiles at her*) And I insist they be spent with you.

REGINA: *And* with another glass of port.

MARSHALL: Thank you.

BEN: My sister is right. (*To* MARSHALL) I am a plain man and I am trying to say a plain thing. A man ain't only in business for what he can get out of it. It's got to give him something here. (*Puts hand to his breast*) That's every bit as true for the nigger picking cotton for a silver quarter, as it is for you and me. (REGINA *gives* MARSHALL *a glass of port*) If it don't give him something here, then he don't pick the cotton right. Money isn't all. Not by three shots.

MARSHALL: Really? Well, I always thought it was a great deal.

REGINA: And so did I, Mr. Marshall.

MARSHALL: (*Pleasantly, but with meaning*) Now you don't have to convince me that you are the right people for the deal. I wouldn't be here if you hadn't convinced me six months ago. You want the mill here, and I want it here. It isn't my business to find out why you want it.

BEN: To bring the machine to the cotton, and not the cotton to the machine.

MARSHALL: (*Amused*) You have a turn for neat phrases, Hubbard. Well, however grand your reasons are, mine are simple: I want to make money and I believe I'll make it on you. (*As* BEN *starts to speak, he smiles*) Mind you, I have no objections to more high-minded reasons. They are mighty valuable in business. It's fine to have partners who so closely follow the teachings of Christ. (*Gets up*) And now I must leave for my train.

REGINA: I'm sorry you won't stay over with us, Mr. Marshall, but you'll come again. Anytime you like.

BEN: *(Motions to* LEO, *indicating the bottle)* Fill them up, boy, fill them up. (LEO *moves around filling the glasses as* BEN *speaks)* Down here, sir, we have a strange custom. We drink the *last* drink for a toast. That's to prove that the Southerner is always still on his feet for the last drink. *(Picks up his glass)* It was Henry Frick, your Mr. Henry Frick, who said, "Railroads are the Rembrandts of investments." Well, *I* say, "Southern cotton mills *will be* the Rembrandts of investment." So I give you the firm of Hubbard Sons and Marshall, Cotton Mills, and to it a long and prosperous life. *(They all pick up their glasses.* MARSHALL *looks at them, amused. Then he, too, lifts his glass, smiles.)*

OSCAR: The children will drive you to the depot. Leo! Alexandra! You will drive Mr. Marshall down.

LEO: *(Eagerly, looks at* BEN *who nods)* Yes, sir. *(To* MARSHALL*)* Not often Uncle Ben lets *me* drive the horses. And a beautiful pair they are. *(Starts for hall)* Come on, Zan.

ALEXANDRA: May I drive tonight, Uncle Ben, please? I'd like to and—

BEN: *(Shakes his head, laughs)* In your evening clothes? Oh, no, my dear.

ALEXANDRA: But Leo always—*(Stops, exits quickly.)*

REGINA: I don't like to say good-bye to you, Mr. Marshall.

MARSHALL: Then we won't say good-bye. You have promised that you would come and let me show you Chicago. Do I have to make you promise again?

REGINA: *(Looks at him as he presses her hand)* I promise again.

MARSHALL: *(Moves to* BIRDIE*)* Good-bye, Mrs. Hubbard.

BIRDIE: Good-bye, sir.

MARSHALL: *(As he passes* REGINA*)* Remember.

REGINA: I will.

(MARSHALL *exits, followed by* BEN *and* OSCAR. *For a second* REGINA *and* BIRDIE *stand looking after them. Then* REGINA *throws up her arms, laughs happily.)*

REGINA: And there, Birdie, goes the man who has opened the door to our future.

BIRDIE: *(Surprised at the unaccustomed friendliness)* What?

REGINA: *Our future.* Yours and mine, Ben's and Oscar's, the children—*(Looks at Birdie's puzzled face, laughs)* Our future! *(Gaily)* You were charming at supper, Birdie. Mr. Marshall certainly thought so.

BIRDIE: *(Pleased)* Why, Regina! Do you think he did?

REGINA: Can't you tell when you're being admired?

BIRDIE: Oscar said I bored Mr. Marshall. But he admired *you.* He told me so.

REGINA: What did he say?

BIRDIE: He said to me, "I hope your sister-in-law will come to Chicago. Chicago will be at her feet." He said the ladies would bow to your manners and the gentlemen to your looks.

REGINA: Did he? He seems a lonely man. Imagine being lonely with all that money. I don't think he likes his wife.

BIRDIE: Not like his wife? What a thing to say.

REGINA: She's away a great deal. He said that several times. And once he made fun of her being so social and high-tone. But that fits in all right. *(Sits back, stretches)* Her being social, I mean. She can introduce me. It won't take long with an introduction from her.

BIRDIE: *(Bewildered)* Introduce you? In Chicago? You mean you really might go? Oh, Regina, you can't leave here. What about Horace?

REGINA: Don't look so scared about everything, Birdie. I'm going to live in Chicago. I've always wanted to. And now there'll be plenty of money to go with.

BIRDIE: But Horace won't be able to move around. You know what the doctor wrote.

REGINA: There'll be millions, Birdie, millions. You know what I've always said when people told me we were rich? I said I think you should either be a nigger or a millionaire. In between, like us, what for? *(Laughs)* But I'm not going away tomorrow, Birdie. There's plenty of time to worry about Horace when he comes home. If he ever decides to come home.

BIRDIE: Will we be going to Chicago? I mean, Oscar and Leo and me?

REGINA: You? I shouldn't think so. *(Laughs)* Well, we must remember tonight. It's a very important night and we mustn't forget it. We shall plan all the things we'd like to have and then we'll really have them. Make a wish, Birdie, any wish. It's bound to come true now. (BEN *and* OSCAR *enter.)*

BIRDIE: *(Laughs)* Well. Well, I don't know. Maybe. (REGINA *turns to look at* BEN) Well, I guess I'd know right off what I wanted. (OSCAR *stands by the upper window, waves to the departing carriage.)*

REGINA: *(Looks up at* BEN, *smiles. He smiles back at her)* Well, you did it.

BEN: Looks like it might be we did.

REGINA: *(Springs up)* Looks like it! Don't pretend. You're like a cat who's been licking the cream. *(Crosses to wine bottle)* Now we must all have a drink to celebrate.

OSCAR: The children, Alexandra and Leo, make a very handsome couple, Regina. Marshall remarked himself what fine young folks they were. How well they looked together!

REGINA: *(Sharply)* Yes. You said that before, Oscar.

BEN: Yes, sir. It's beginning to look as if the deal's all set. I may not be a subtle man—but—*(Turns to them. After a second)* Now somebody ask me how I know the deal is set.

OSCAR: What do you mean, Ben?

BEN: You remember I told him that down here we drink the *last* drink for a toast?

OSCAR: *(Thoughtfully)* Yes. I never heard that before.

BEN: Nobody's ever heard it before. God forgives those who invent what they need. I already had his signature. But we've all done business with men whose word over a glass is better than a bond. Anyway it don't hurt to have both.

OSCAR: *(Turns to* REGINA) You understand what Ben means?

REGINA: Yes, Oscar. I understand. I understood immediately.

BEN: *(Looks at her admiringly)* Did you, Regina? Well, when he lifted his glass to drink, I closed my eyes and saw the bricks going into place.

REGINA: And *I* saw a lot more than that.

BEN: Slowly, slowly. As yet we have only our hopes.

REGINA: Birdie and I have just been planning what we want. I know what I want. What will you want, Ben?

BEN: Caution. Don't count the chickens. *(Leans back, laughs)* Well, God would allow us a little daydreaming. Good for the soul when you've worked hard enough to deserve it. *(Pauses)* I think I'll have a stable. For a long time I've had my good eyes on Carter's in Savannah. A rich man's pleasure, the sport of kings, why not the sport of Hubbards? Why not?

REGINA: *(Smiles)* Why not? What will you have, Oscar?

OSCAR: I don't know. *(Thoughtfully)* The pleasure of seeing the bricks grow will be enough for me.

BEN: Oh, of course. Our greatest pleasure will be to see the bricks grow. But we are all entitled to a little side indulgence.

OSCAR: Yes, I suppose so. Well, then, I think we might take a few trips here and there, eh, Birdie?

BIRDIE: *(Surprised at being consulted)* Yes, Oscar. I'd like that.

OSCAR: We might even make a regular trip to Jekyll Island. I've heard the Cornelly place is for sale. We might think about buying it. Make a nice change. Do you good, Birdie, a change of climate. Fine shooting on Jekyll, the best.

BIRDIE: I'd like—

OSCAR: *(Indulgently)* What would you like?

BIRDIE: Two things. Two things I'd like most.

REGINA: Two! I should like a thousand. You are modest, Birdie.

BIRDIE: *(Warmly, delighted with the unexpected interest)* I should like to have Lionnet back. I know you own it now, but I'd like to see it fixed up again, the way Mama and Papa had it. Every year it used to get a nice coat of paint—Papa was very particular about the paint—and the lawn was so smooth all the way down to the river, with the trims of zinnias and red-feather plush. And the figs and blue little plums and the scuppernongs—*(Smiles. Turns to* REGINA*)* The organ is still there and it wouldn't cost much to fix. We could have parties for Zan, the way Mama used to have for me.

BEN: That's a pretty picture, Birdie. Might be a most pleasant way to live. *(Dismissing* BIRDIE*)* What do you want, Regina?

BIRDIE: *(Very happily, not noticing that they are no longer listening to her)* I could have a cutting garden. Just where Mama's used to be. Oh, I do think we could be happier there. Papa used to say that *nobody* had ever lost their temper at Lionnet, and *nobody* ever would. Papa would never let anybody be nasty-spoken or mean. No, sir. He just didn't like it.

BEN: What do you want, Regina?

REGINA: I'm going to Chicago. And when I'm settled there and know the right people and the right things to buy—because I certainly don't now—I shall go to Paris and buy them. *(Laughs)* I'm going to leave you and Oscar to count the bricks.

BIRDIE: Oscar. Please let me have Lionnet back.

OSCAR: *(To* REGINA*)* You are serious about moving to Chicago?

BEN: She is going to see the great world and leave us in the little one. Well, we'll come and visit you and meet all the great and be proud you are our sister.

REGINA: *(Gaily)* Certainly. And you won't even have to learn to be subtle, Ben. Stay as you are. You will be rich and the rich don't have to be subtle.

OSCAR: But what about Alexandra? She's seventeen. Old enough to be thinking about marrying.

BIRDIE: And, Oscar, I have one more wish. Just one more wish.

OSCAR: *(Turns)* What is it, Birdie? What are you saying?

BIRDIE: I want you to stop shooting. I mean, so much. I don't like to see animals and birds killed just for the killing. You only throw them away—

BEN: *(To* REGINA) It'll take a great deal of money to live as you're planning, Regina.

REGINA: Certainly. But there'll be plenty of money. You have estimated the profits very high.

BEN: I have—

BIRDIE: (OSCAR *is looking at her furiously*) And you never let anybody else shoot, and the niggers need it so much to keep from starving. It's wicked to shoot food just because you like to shoot, when poor people need it so—

BEN: *(Laughs)* I have estimated the profits very high—for myself.

REGINA: What did you say?

BIRDIE: I've always wanted to speak about it, Oscar.

OSCAR: *(Slowly, carefully)* What are you chattering about?

BIRDIE: *(Nervously)* I was talking about Lionnet and—and about your shooting—

OSCAR: You are exciting yourself.

REGINA: *(To* BEN) I didn't hear you. There was so much talking.

OSCAR: *(To* BIRDIE) You have been acting very childish, very excited, all evening.

BIRDIE: Regina asked me what I'd like.

REGINA: What did you say, Ben?

BIRDIE: Now that we'll be so rich everybody was saying what they would like, so *I* said what *I* would like, too.

BEN: I said—*(He is interrupted by* OSCAR.)

OSCAR: *(To* BIRDIE) Very well. We've all heard you. That's enough now.

BEN: I am waiting. *(They stop)* I am waiting for you to finish. You and Birdie. Four conversations are three too many. (BIRDIE *slowly sits down.* BEN *smiles, to* REGINA) I said that I had, and I do, estimate the profits very high—for myself, and Oscar, of course.

REGINA: And what does that mean? (BEN *shrugs, looks toward* OSCAR.)

OSCAR: *(Looks at* BEN, *clears throat)* Well, Regina, it's like this. For forty-nine percent Marshall will put up four hundred thousand dollars. For fifty-one percent—*(Smiles archly)* a controlling interest, mind you—we will put up two hundred and twenty-five thousand dollars besides offering him certain benefits that our *(Looks at* BEN*)* local position allows us to manage. Ben means that two hundred and twenty-five thousand dollars is a lot of money.

REGINA: I know the terms and I know it's a lot of money.

BEN: *(Nodding)* It is.

OSCAR: Ben means that we are ready with our two-thirds of the money. Your third, Horace's I mean, doesn't seem to be ready. *(Raises his hand as* REGINA *starts to speak)* Ben has written to Horace, I have written, and you have written. He answers. But he never mentions this business. Yet we have explained to him in great detail, and told him the urgency. Still he never mentions it. Ben has been very patient, Regina. Naturally, you are our sister and we want you to benefit from anything we do.

REGINA: And in addition to your concern for me, you do not want control to go out of the family. *(To* BEN*)* That right, Ben?

BEN: That's cynical. *(Smiles)* Cynicism is an unpleasant way of saying the truth.

OSCAR: No need to be cynical. We'd have no trouble raising the third share, the share that you want to take.

REGINA: I am sure you could get the third share, the share you were saving for me. But that would give you a strange partner. And strange partners sometimes want a great deal. *(Smiles unpleasantly)* But perhaps it would be wise for you to find him.

OSCAR: Now, now. Nobody says we *want* to do that. We would like to have you in and you would like to come in.

REGINA: Yes. I certainly would.

BEN: *(Laughs, puts up his hand)* But we haven't heard from Horace.

REGINA: I've given my word that Horace will put up the money. That should be enough.

BEN: Oh, it was enough. I took your word. But I've got to have more than your word now. The contracts will be signed this week, and Marshall will want to see our money soon after. Regina, Horace has been in Baltimore for five months. I know that you've written him to come home, and that he hasn't come.

OSCAR: It's beginning to look as if he doesn't want to come home.

REGINA: Of course he wants to come home. You can't move around with heart trouble at any moment you choose. You know what doctors are like once they get their hands on a case like this—

OSCAR: They can't very well keep him from answering letters, can they? (REGINA *turns to* BEN) They couldn't keep him from arranging for the money if he wanted to—

REGINA: Has it occurred to you that Horace is also a good businessman?

BEN: Certainly. He is a shrewd trader. Always has been. The bank is proof of that.

REGINA: Then, possibly, he may be keeping silent because he doesn't think he is getting enough for his money. Seventy-five thousand he has to put up. That's a lot of money, too.

OSCAR: Nonsense. He knows a good thing when he hears it. He knows that we can make *twice* the profit on cotton goods manufactured here than can be made in the North.

BEN: That isn't what Regina means. May I interpret you, Regina? (*To* OSCAR) Regina is saying that Horace wants *more* than a third of our share.

OSCAR: But he's only putting up a third of the money. You put up a third and you get a third. What else could he expect?

REGINA: Well, *I* don't know. I don't know about these things. It would seem that if you put up a third you should only get a third. But then again, there's no law about it, is there? I should think that if you knew your money was very badly needed, well, you just might say, I want more, I want a bigger share. You boys have done that. I've heard you say so.

BEN: (*After a pause, laughs*) So you believe he has deliberately held out? For a larger share? Well, I don't believe it. But I do believe that's what *you* want. Am I right, Regina?

REGINA: Oh, I shouldn't like to be too definite. But I could say that I wouldn't like to persuade Horace unless he did get a larger share. I must look after his interests. It seems only natural—

OSCAR: And where would the larger share come from?

REGINA: I don't know. That's not my business. (*Giggles*) But perhaps it could come off your share, Oscar. (REGINA *and* BEN *laugh*.)

OSCAR: (*Rises and wheels on both of them as they laugh*) What kind of talk is this?

BEN: I haven't said a thing.

OSCAR: *(To* REGINA*) You* are talking very big tonight.

REGINA: *(Stops laughing)* Am I? Well, you should know me well enough to know that I wouldn't be asking for things I didn't think I could get.

OSCAR: Listen. I don't believe you can even get Horace to come home, much less get money from him or talk quite so big about what you want.

REGINA: Oh, I can get him home.

OSCAR: Then why haven't you?

REGINA: I thought I should fight his battles for him, before he came home. Horace is a very sick man. And even if *you* don't care how sick he is, I do.

BEN: Stop this foolish squabbling. How can you get him home?

REGINA: I will send Alexandra to Baltimore. She will ask him to come home. She will say that she wants him to come home, and that *I* want him to come home.

BIRDIE: *(Rises)* Well, of course she wants him here, but he's sick and maybe he's happy where he is.

REGINA: *(Ignores* BIRDIE, *to* BEN*)* You agree that he will come home if she asks him to, if she says that I miss him and want him—

BEN: *(Looks at her, smiles)* I admire you, Regina. And I agree. That's settled now and—*(Starts to rise.)*

REGINA: *(Quickly)* But before she brings him home, I want to know what he's going to get.

BEN: What do you want?

REGINA: Twice what you offered.

BEN: Well, you won't get it.

OSCAR: *(To* REGINA*)* I think you've gone crazy.

REGINA: I don't want to fight, Ben—

BEN: I don't either. You won't get it. There isn't any chance of that. *(Roguishly)* You're holding us up, and that's not pretty, Regina, not pretty. *(Holds up his hand as he sees she is about to speak)* But we need you, and I don't want to fight. Here's what I'll do: I'll give Horace forty percent, instead of the thirty-three and a third he really should get. I'll do that, provided he is home and his money is up within two weeks. How's that?

REGINA: All right.

OSCAR: I've asked before: where is this extra share coming from?

BEN: *(Pleasantly)* From you. From your share.

OSCAR: *(Furiously)* From me, is it? That's just fine and dandy.

That's my reward. For thirty-five years I've worked my hands to the bone for you. For thirty-five years I've done all the things you didn't want to do. And this is what I—

BEN: *(Turns to look at* OSCAR. OSCAR *breaks off)* My, my. I am being attacked tonight on all sides. First by my sister, then by my brother. And I ain't a man who likes being attacked. I can't believe that God wants the strong to parade their strength, but I don't mind doing it if it's got to be done. You ought to take these things better, Oscar. I've made you money in the past. I'm going to make you more money now. You'll be a very rich man. What's the difference to any of us if a little more goes here, a little less goes there—it's all in the family. And it will stay in the family. I'll never marry. (ADDIE *enters, begins to gather the glasses from the table)* So my money will go to Alexandra and Leo. They may even marry someday and— (ADDIE *looks at* BEN.)

BIRDIE: *(Rising)* Marry—Zan and Leo—

OSCAR: *(Carefully)* That would make a great difference in my feelings. If they married.

BEN: Yes, that's what I mean. Of course it would make a difference.

OSCAR: *(Carefully)* Is that what *you* mean, Regina?

REGINA: Oh, it's too far away. We'll talk about it in a few years.

OSCAR: I want to talk about it now.

BEN: *(Nods)* Naturally.

REGINA: There's a lot of things to consider. They are first cousins, and—

OSCAR: That isn't unusual. Our grandmother and grandfather were first cousins.

REGINA: *(Giggles)* And look at us. (BEN *giggles.*)

OSCAR: *(Angrily)* You're both being very gay with my money.

BEN: *(Sighs)* These quarrels. I dislike them so. *(To* REGINA) A marriage might be a very wise arrangement, for several reasons. And then, Oscar has given up something for you. You should try to manage something for him.

REGINA: I haven't said I was opposed to it. But Leo is a wild boy. There were those times when he took a little money from the bank and—

OSCAR: That's all past history—

REGINA: Oh, I know. And I know all young men are wild. I'm only mentioning it to show you that there are considerations—

BEN: *(Irritated because she does not understand that he is trying to keep*

OSCAR *quiet)* All right, so there are. But please assure Oscar that you will think about it very seriously.

REGINA: *(Smiles, nods)* Very well. I assure Oscar that I will think about it seriously.

OSCAR: *(Sharply)* That is not an answer.

REGINA: *(Rises)* My, you're in a bad humor and you shall put me in one. I have said all that I am willing to say now. After all, Horace has to give his consent, too.

OSCAR: Horace will do what you tell him to.

REGINA: Yes, I think he will.

OSCAR: And I have your word that you will try to—

REGINA: *(Patiently)* Yes, Oscar. You have my word that I will think about it. Now do leave me alone. *(There is the sound of the front door being closed.)*

BIRDIE: I—Alexandra is only seventeen. She—

LEO: *(Comes into the room)* Mr. Marshall got off safe and sound. Weren't those fine clothes he had? You can always spot clothes made in a good place. Looks like maybe they were done in England. Lots of men in the North send all the way to England for their stuff.

BEN: *(To* LEO) Were you careful driving the horses?

LEO: Oh, yes, sir. I was. (ALEXANDRA *has come in on Ben's question, hears the answer, looks angrily at* LEO.)

ALEXANDRA: It's a lovely night. You should have come, Aunt Birdie.

REGINA: Were you gracious to Mr. Marshall?

ALEXANDRA: I think so, Mama. I liked him.

REGINA: Good. And now I have great news for you. You are going to Baltimore in the morning to bring your father home.

ALEXANDRA: *(Gasps, then delighted)* Me? Papa said I should come? That must mean—(*Turns to* ADDIE) Addie, he must be well. Think of it, he'll be back home again. We'll bring him home.

REGINA: You are going alone, Alexandra.

ADDIE: (ALEXANDRA *has turned in surprise)* Going alone? Going by herself? A child that age! Mr. Horace ain't going to like Zan traipsing up there by herself.

REGINA: *(Sharply)* Go upstairs and lay out Alexandra's things.

ADDIE: He'd expect me to be along—

REGINA: I'll be up in a few minutes to tell you what to pack. (ADDIE *slowly begins to climb the steps. To* ALEXANDRA) I should think you'd like going alone. At your age it certainly would have delighted me. You're a strange girl, Alexandra. Addie has babied you so much.

ALEXANDRA: I only thought it would be more fun if Addie and I went together.

BIRDIE: *(Timidly)* Maybe I could go with her, Regina. I'd really like to.

REGINA: She is going alone. She is getting old enough to take some responsibilities.

OSCAR: She'd better learn now. She's almost old enough to get married. *(Jovially, to LEO, slapping him on shoulder)* Eh, son?

LEO: Huh?

OSCAR: *(Annoyed with LEO for not understanding)* Old enough to get married, you're thinking, eh?

LEO: Oh, yes, sir. *(Feebly)* Lots of girls get married at Zan's age. Look at Mary Prester and Johanna and—

REGINA: Well, she's not getting married tomorrow. But she is going to Baltimore tomorrow, so let's talk about that. *(To ALEXANDRA)* You'll be glad to have Papa home again.

ALEXANDRA: I wanted to go before, Mama. You remember that. But you said *you* couldn't go, and that *I* couldn't go alone.

REGINA: I've changed my mind. *(Too casually)* You're to tell Papa how much you missed him, and that he must come home now—for your sake. Tell him that you *need* him home.

ALEXANDRA: Need him home? I don't understand.

REGINA: There is nothing for you to understand. You are simply to say what I have told you.

BIRDIE: *(Rises)* He may be too sick. She couldn't do that—

ALEXANDRA: Yes. He may be too sick to travel. I couldn't make him think he had to come home for me, if he is too sick to—

REGINA: *(Looks at her, sharply, challengingly)* You *couldn't* do what I tell you to do, Alexandra?

ALEXANDRA: *(Quietly)* No. I couldn't. If I thought it would hurt him.

REGINA: *(After a second's silence, smiles pleasantly)* But you are doing this for Papa's own good. *(Takes Alexandra's hand)* You must let me be the judge of his condition. It's the best possible cure for him to come home and be taken care of here. He mustn't stay there any longer and listen to those alarmist doctors. You are doing this entirely for his sake. Tell your papa that I want him to come home, that I miss him very much.

ALEXANDRA: *(Slowly)* Yes, Mama.

REGINA: *(To the others)* I must go and start getting Alexandra ready now. Why don't you all go home?

BEN: *(Rises)* I'll attend to the railroad ticket. One of the boys will bring it over. Good night, everybody. Have a nice trip, Alexandra. The food on the train is very good. The celery is so crisp. Have a good time and act like a little lady. *(Exits.)*

REGINA: Good night, Ben. Good night, Oscar—*(Playfully)* Don't be so glum, Oscar. It makes you look as if you had chronic indigestion.

BIRDIE: Good night, Regina.

REGINA: Good night, Birdie. *(Exits upstairs.)*

OSCAR: *(Starts for hall)* Come along.

LEO: *(To* ALEXANDRA*)* Imagine your not wanting to go! What a little fool you are. Wish it were me. What I could do in a place like Baltimore!

ALEXANDRA: Mind your business. I can guess the kind of things *you* could do.

LEO: *(Laughs)* Oh, no, you couldn't. *(He exits.)*

REGINA: *(Calling from the top of the stairs)* Come on, Alexandra.

BIRDIE: *(Quickly, softly)* Zan.

ALEXANDRA: I don't understand about my going, Aunt Birdie. *(Shrugs)* But anyway, Papa will be home again. *(Pats Birdie's arm)* Don't worry about me. I can take care of myself. Really I can.

BIRDIE: *(Shakes her head, softly)* That's not what I'm worried about. Zan—

ALEXANDRA: *(Comes close to her)* What's the matter?

BIRDIE: It's about Leo—

ALEXANDRA: *(Whispering)* He beat the horses. That's why we were late getting back. We had to wait until they cooled off. He always beats the horses as if—

BIRDIE: *(Whispering frantically, holding* ALEXANDRA*'s hands)* He's my son. My own son. But you are more to me—more to me than my own child. I love you more than anybody else—

ALEXANDRA: Don't worry about the horses. I'm sorry I told you.

BIRDIE: *(Her voice rising)* I am not worrying about the horses. I am worrying about *you*. You are *not* going to marry Leo. I am not going to let them do that to you—

ALEXANDRA: Marry? To Leo? *(Laughs)* I wouldn't marry, Aunt Birdie. I've never even thought about it—

BIRDIE: But they have thought about it. *(Wildly)* Zan, I couldn't stand to think about such a thing. You and—(OSCAR *has come into the doorway on Alexandra's speech. He is standing quietly, listening.*)

ALEXANDRA: *(Laughs)* But I'm not going to marry. And I'm certainly not going to marry Leo.

BIRDIE: Don't you understand? They'll make you. They'll make you—

ALEXANDRA: *(Takes Birdie's hands, quietly, firmly)* That's foolish, Aunt Birdie. I'm grown now. Nobody can make me do anything.

BIRDIE: I just couldn't stand—

OSCAR: *(Sharply)* Birdie. (BIRDIE *looks up, draws quickly away from* ALEXANDRA. *She stands rigid, frightened.*) Birdie, get your hat and coat.

ADDIE: *(Calls from upstairs)* Come on, baby. Your mama's waiting for you, and she ain't nobody to keep waiting.

ALEXANDRA: All right. *(Then softly, embracing* BIRDIE) Good night, Aunt Birdie. *(As she passes* OSCAR) Good night, Uncle Oscar. (BIRDIE *begins to move slowly toward the door as* ALEXANDRA *climbs the stairs.* ALEXANDRA *is almost out of view when* BIRDIE *reaches* OSCAR *in the doorway. As* BIRDIE *attempts to pass him, he slaps her hard, across the face.* BIRDIE *cries out, puts her hand to her face. On the cry,* ALEXANDRA *turns, begins to run down the stairs)* Aunt Birdie! What happened? What happened? I—

BIRDIE: *(Softly, without turning)* Nothing, darling. Nothing happened. *(Anxious to keep* ALEXANDRA *from coming close)* Now go to bed. (OSCAR *exits)* Nothing happened. I only—I only twisted my ankle. *(She goes out.* ALEXANDRA *stands on the stairs looking after her.*)

CURTAIN

ACT TWO

SCENE: *Same as Act One. A week later, morning.*
At rise the light comes from the open shutter of the right window; the other shutters are tightly closed. ADDIE *is standing at the window, looking out. Near the dining-room doors are brooms, mops, rags, etc. After a second,* OSCAR *comes into the entrance hall, looks in the room, shivers, decides not to take his hat and coat off, comes into the room. At the sound of the door,* ADDIE *turns.*

ADDIE: *(Without interest)* Oh, it's you, Mr. Oscar.

OSCAR: What is this? It's not night. What's the matter here? *(Shivers)* Fine thing at this time of the morning. Blinds all closed. (ADDIE *begins to open shutters)* Where's Miss Regina? It's cold in here.

ADDIE: Miss Regina ain't down yet.

OSCAR: She had any word?

ADDIE: No, sir.

OSCAR: Wouldn't you think a girl that age could get on a train at one place and have sense enough to get off at another?

ADDIE: Something must have happened. If Zan say she was coming last night, she's coming last night. Unless something happened. Sure fire disgrace to let a baby like that go all that way alone to bring home a sick man without—

OSCAR: You do a lot of judging around here, Addie, eh? Judging of your white folks, I mean.

REGINA: *(Speaking from the upstairs hall)* Who's downstairs, Addie? *(She appears in a dressing gown, peers down from the landing.* ADDIE *picks up broom, dustpan and brush and exits)* Oh, it's you, Oscar. What are you doing here so early? I haven't been down yet. I'm not finished dressing.

OSCAR: *(Speaking up to her)* You had any word from them?

REGINA: No.

OSCAR: Then something certainly has happened. People don't just say they are arriving on Thursday night, and they haven't come by Friday morning.

REGINA: Oh, nothing has happened. Alexandra just hasn't got sense enough to send a message.

OSCAR: If nothing's happened, then why aren't they here?

REGINA: You asked me that ten times last night. My, you do fret so, Oscar. Anything might have happened. They may have

192

missed connections in Atlanta, the train may have been delayed—oh, a hundred things could have kept them.

OSCAR: Where's Ben?

REGINA: *(As she disappears upstairs)* Where should he be? At home, probably. Really, Oscar, I don't tuck him in his bed and I don't take him out of it. Have some coffee and don't worry so much.

OSCAR: Have some coffee? There isn't any coffee. *(Looks at his watch, shakes his head. After a second CAL enters with a large silver tray, coffee urn, small cups, newspaper)* Oh, there you are. Is everything in this fancy house always late?

CAL: *(Looks at him, surprised)* You ain't out shooting this morning, Mr. Oscar?

OSCAR: First day I missed since I had my head cold. First day I missed in eight years.

CAL: Yes, sir. I bet you. Simon he say you had a mighty good day yesterday morning. That's what Simon say. *(Brings OSCAR coffee and newspaper.)*

OSCAR: Pretty good, pretty good.

CAL: *(Laughs, slyly)* Bet you got enough bobwhite and squirrel to give every nigger in town a Jesus-party. Most of 'em ain't had no meat since the cotton picking was over. Bet they'd give anything for a little piece of that meat—

OSCAR: *(Turns his head to look at CAL)* Cal, if I catch a nigger in this town going shooting, you know what's going to happen. (LEO *enters.*)

CAL: *(Hastily)* Yes, sir, Mr. Oscar. It was Simon who told me and— Morning, Mr. Leo. You gentlemen having your breakfast with us here?

LEO: The boys in the bank don't know a thing. They haven't had any message. (CAL *waits for an answer, gets none, shrugs, exits.*)

OSCAR: *(Peers at LEO)* What you doing here, son?

LEO: You told me to find out if the boys at the bank had any message from Uncle Horace or Zan—

OSCAR: I told you if they had a message to bring it here. I told you that if they didn't have a message to stay at the bank and do your work.

LEO: Oh, I guess I misunderstood.

OSCAR: You didn't misunderstand. You just were looking for any excuse to take an hour off. (LEO *pours a cup of coffee*) You got to stop that kind of thing. You got to start settling down. You going to be a married man one of these days.

LEO: Yes, sir.

OSCAR: You also got to stop with that woman in Mobile. (*As* LEO *is about to speak*) You're young and I haven't got no objections to outside women. That is, I haven't got no objections so long as they don't interfere with serious things. Outside women are all right in their place, but *now* isn't their place. You got to realize that.

LEO: (*Nods*) Yes, sir. I'll tell her. She'll act all right about it.

OSCAR: Also, you got to start working harder at the bank. You got to convince your Uncle Horace you going to make a fit husband for Alexandra.

LEO: What do you think has happened to them? Supposed to be here last night—(*Laughs*) Bet you Uncle Ben's mighty worried. Seventy-five thousand dollars worried.

OSCAR: (*Smiles happily*) Ought to be worried. Damn well ought to be. First he don't answer the letters, then he don't come home—(*Giggles.*)

LEO: What will happen if Uncle Horace don't come home or don't—

OSCAR: Or don't put up the money? Oh, we'll get it from outside. Easy enough.

LEO: (*Surprised*) But *you* don't want outsiders.

OSCAR: What do I care who gets my share? I been shaved already. Serve Ben right if he had to give away some of his.

LEO: Damn shame what they did to you.

OSCAR: (*Looking up the stairs*) Don't talk so loud. Don't you worry. When I die, you'll have as much as the rest. You might have yours *and* Alexandra's. I'm not so easily licked.

LEO: I wasn't thinking of myself, Papa—

OSCAR: Well, you should be, you should be. It's every man's duty to think of himself.

LEO: You think Uncle Horace don't want to go in on this?

OSCAR: (*Giggles*) That's my hunch. He hasn't showed any signs of loving it yet.

LEO: (*Laughs*) But he hasn't listened to Aunt Regina yet, either. Oh, he'll go along. It's too good a thing. Why wouldn't he want to? He's got plenty and plenty to invest with. He don't even have to sell anything. Eighty-eight thousand worth of Union Pacific bonds sitting right in his safe deposit box. All he's got to do is open the box.

OSCAR: *(After a pause. Looks at his watch)* Mighty late breakfast in this fancy house. Yes, he's had those bonds for fifteen years. Bought them when they were low and just locked them up.

LEO: Yeah. Just has to open the box and take them out. That's all. Easy as easy can be. *(Laughs)* The things in that box! There's all those bonds, looking mighty fine. (OSCAR *slowly puts down his newspaper and turns to* LEO) Then right next to them is a baby shoe of Zan's and a cheap old cameo on a string, and, *and* — nobody'd believe this—a piece of an old violin. Not even a whole violin. Just a piece of an old thing, a piece of a violin.

OSCAR: *(Very softly, as if he were trying to control his voice)* A piece of a violin! What do you think of that!

LEO: Yes, sirree. A lot of other crazy things, too. A poem, I guess it is, signed with his mother's name, and two old schoolbooks with notes and—(LEO *catches Oscar's look. His voice trails off. He turns his head away.)*

OSCAR: *(Very softly)* How do you know what's in the box, son?

LEO: *(Draws back, frightened, realizing what he has said)* Oh, well. Well, er. Well, one of the boys, sir. It was one of the boys at the bank. He took old Manders' keys. It was Joe Horns. He just up and took Manders' keys and, and—well, took the box out. *(Quickly)* Then they all asked me if I wanted to see, too. So I looked a little, I guess, but then I made them close up the box quick and I told them never—

OSCAR: *(Looks at him)* Joe Horns, you say? He opened it?

LEO: Yes, sir, yes, he did. My word of honor. *(Very nervous now)* I suppose that don't excuse *me* for looking—(*Looking at* OSCAR) but I did make him close it up and put the keys back in Manders' drawer—

OSCAR: *(Leans forward, very softly)* Tell me the truth, Leo. I am not going to be angry with you. Did you open the box yourself?

LEO: *No, sir, I didn't.* I told you I didn't. No, I—

OSCAR: *(Irritated, patient)* I am *not* going to be angry with you. *(Watching* LEO *carefully)* Sometimes a young fellow deserves credit for looking round him to see what's going on. Sometimes that's a good sign in a fellow your age. Many great men have made their fortune with their eyes. Did you open the box?

LEO: *(Very puzzled)* No. I—

OSCAR: *(Moves to* LEO) Did you open the box? It may have been —

well, it may have been a good thing if you had.

LEO: *(After a long pause)* I opened it.

OSCAR: *(Quickly)* Is that the truth? (LEO *nods*) Does anybody else know that you opened it? Come, Leo, don't be afraid of speaking the truth to me.

LEO: No. Nobody knew. Nobody was in the bank when I did it. But—

OSCAR: Did your Uncle Horace ever know you opened it?

LEO: *(Shakes his head)* He only looks in it once every six months when he cuts the coupons, and sometimes Manders even does that for him. Uncle Horace don't even have the keys. Manders keeps them for him. Imagine not looking at all that. You can bet if I had the bonds, I'd watch 'em like—

OSCAR: If you had them. *If* you had them. Then you could have a share in the mill, you and me. A fine, big share, too. *(Pauses, shrugs)* Well, a man can't be shot for wanting to see his son get on in the world, can he, boy?

LEO: *(Looks up, begins to understand)* No, he can't. Natural enough. *(Laughs)* But I haven't got the bonds and Uncle Horace has. And now he can just sit back and wait to be a millionaire.

OSCAR: *(Innocently)* You think your Uncle Horace likes you well enough to lend you the bonds if he decides not to use them himself?

LEO: Papa, it must be that you haven't had your breakfast! *(Laughs loudly)* Lend me the bonds! My God—

OSCAR: *(Disappointed)* No, I suppose not. Just a fancy of mine. A loan for three months, maybe four, easy enough for us to pay it back then. Anyway, this is only April—*(Slowly counting the months on his fingers)* and if he doesn't look at them until Autumn he wouldn't even miss them out of the box.

LEO: That's it. He wouldn't even miss them. Ah, well—

OSCAR: No, sir. Wouldn't even miss them. How could he miss them if he never looks at them? *(Sighs as LEO stares at him)* Well, here we are sitting around waiting for him to come home and invest his money in something he hasn't lifted his hand to get. But I can't help thinking he's acting strange. You laugh when I say he could lend you the bonds if he's not going to use them himself. But would it hurt him?

LEO: *(Slowly looking at OSCAR)* No. No, it wouldn't.

OSCAR: People ought to help other people. But that's not always the way it happens. (BEN *enters, hangs his coat and hat in hall.*

Very carefully) And so sometimes you got to think of yourself. (*As* LEO *stares at him,* BEN *appears in the doorway*) Morning, Ben.

BEN: (*Coming in, carrying his newspaper*) Fine sunny morning. Any news from the runaways?

REGINA: (*On the staircase*) There's no news or you would have heard it. Quite a convention so early in the morning, aren't you all? (*Goes to coffee urn.*)

OSCAR: You rising mighty late these days. Is that the way they do things in Chicago society?

BEN: (*Looking at his paper*) Old Carter died up in Senateville. Eighty-one is a good time for us all, eh? What do you think has really happened to Horace, Regina?

REGINA: Nothing.

BEN: You don't think maybe he never started from Baltimore and never intends to start?

REGINA: (*Irritated*) Of course they've started. Didn't I have a letter from Alexandra? What is so strange about people arriving late? He has that cousin in Savannah he's so fond of. He may have stopped to see him. They'll be along today sometime, very flattered that you and Oscar are so worried about them.

BEN: I'm a natural worrier. Especially when I am getting ready to close a business deal and one of my partners remains silent *and* invisible.

REGINA: (*Laughs*) Oh, is that it? I thought you were worried about Horace's health.

OSCAR: Oh, that too. Who could help but worry? I'm worried. This is the first day I haven't been shooting since my head cold.

REGINA: (*Starts toward dining room*) Then you haven't had your breakfast. Come along. (OSCAR *and* LEO *follow her.*)

BEN: Regina. (*She turns at dining-room door*) That cousin of Horace's has been dead for years and, in any case, the train does not go through Savannah.

REGINA: (*Laughs, continues into dining room, seats herself*) Did he die? You're always remembering about people dying. (BEN *rises*) Now I intend to eat my breakfast in peace, and read my newspaper.

BEN: (*Goes toward dining room as he talks*) This is second breakfast for me. My first was bad. Celia ain't the cook she used to be. Too old to have taste anymore. If she hadn't belonged to Mama, I'd send her off to the country. (OSCAR *and* LEO *start to eat.* BEN *seats himself.*)

LEO: Uncle Horace will have some tales to tell, I bet. Baltimore is a lively town.

REGINA: *(To* CAL) The grits isn't hot enough. Take it back.

CAL: Oh, yes'm. *(Calling into the kitchen as he exits)* Grits didn't hold the heat. Grits didn't hold the heat.

LEO: When I was at school three of the boys and myself took a train once and went over to Baltimore. It was so big we thought we were in Europe. I was just a kid then—

REGINA: I find it very pleasant (ADDIE *enters)* to have breakfast alone. I hate chattering before I've had something hot. (CAL *closes the dining-room doors)* Do be still, Leo. (ADDIE *comes into the room, begins gathering up the cups, carries them to the large tray. Outside there are the sounds of voices. Quickly* ADDIE *runs into the hall. A few seconds later she appears again in the doorway, her arm around the shoulders of* HORACE GIDDENS, *supporting him.* HORACE *is a tall man of about forty-five. He has been good looking, but now his face is tired and ill. He walks stiffly, as if it were an enormous effort, and carefully, as if he were unsure of his balance.* ADDIE *takes off his overcoat and hangs it on the hall tree. She then helps him to a chair.)*

HORACE: How are you, Addie? How have you been?

ADDIE: I'm all right, Mr. Horace. I've just been worried about you. (ALEXANDRA *enters. She is flushed and excited, her hat awry, her face dirty. Her arms are full of packages, but she comes quickly to* ADDIE.)

ALEXANDRA: Don't tell me how worried you were. We couldn't help it and there was no way to send a message.

ADDIE: *(Begins to take packages from* ALEXANDRA) Yes, sir, I was mighty worried.

ALEXANDRA: We had to stop in Mobile overnight. Papa didn't feel well. The trip was too much for him, and I made him stop and rest—*(As* ADDIE *takes the last package)* No, don't take that. That's Father's medicine. I'll hold it. It mustn't break. Now, about the stuff outside. Papa must have his wheelchair. I'll get that and the valises—

ADDIE: *(Very happy, holding Alexandra's arms)* Since when you got to carry your own valises? Since when I ain't old enough to hold a bottle of medicine? (HORACE *coughs)* You feel all right, Mr. Horace?

HORACE: *(Nods)* Glad to be sitting down.

ALEXANDRA: *(Opening package of medicine)* He doesn't feel all right. He just says that. The trip was very hard on him, and now he must go right to bed.

ADDIE: *(Looking at him carefully)* Them fancy doctors, they give you help?

HORACE: They did their best.

ALEXANDRA: *(Has become conscious of the voices in the dining room)* I bet Mama was worried. I better tell her we're here now. *(She starts for door.)*

HORACE: Zan. *(She stops)* Not for a minute, dear.

ALEXANDRA: Oh, Papa, you feel bad again. I knew you did. Do you want your medicine?

HORACE: No, I don't feel that way. I'm just tired, darling. Let me rest a little.

ADDIE: They're all in there eating breakfast.

ALEXANDRA: Oh, are they all here? Why do they *always* have to be here? I was hoping Papa wouldn't have to see anybody, that it would be nice for him and quiet.

ADDIE: Then let your papa rest for a minute.

HORACE: Addie, I bet your coffee's as good as ever. They don't have such good coffee up North. Is it as good, Addie? *(ADDIE starts for coffee urn.)*

ALEXANDRA: No. Dr. Reeves said not much coffee. Just now and then. I'm the nurse now, Addie.

ADDIE: You'd be a better one if you didn't look so dirty. Now go take a bath. Change your linens, get out a fresh dress, give your hair a good brushing—go on—

ALEXANDRA: Will you be all right, Papa?

ADDIE: Go on.

ALEXANDRA: *(On stairs, talks as she goes up)* The pills Papa must take once every four hours. And the bottle only when—only if he feels very bad. Now don't move until I come back and don't talk much and remember about his medicine, Addie—*(As she disappears)* How's Aunt Birdie? Is she here?

ADDIE: It ain't right for you to have coffee? It will hurt you?

HORACE: *(Slowly)* Nothing can make much difference now. Get me a cup, Addie. *(She crosses to urn, pours a cup)* Funny. They can't make coffee up North. *(ADDIE brings him a cup)* They don't like red pepper, either. *(He takes the cup and gulps it greedily)* God, that's good. You remember how I used to drink it? Ten, twelve cups a day. So strong it had to stain the cup. *(Then slowly*) Addie, before I see anybody else, I want to know why Zan came to fetch me home. She's tried to tell me, but she doesn't seem to know herself.

ADDIE: I don't know. All I know is big things are going on. Everybody going to be high-tone rich. Big rich. You too. All because smoke's going to start out of a building that ain't even up yet.

HORACE: I've heard about it.

ADDIE: And, er—(*Hesitates, steps to him*) And—well, Zan, maybe she going to marry Mr. Leo in a little while.

HORACE: (*Looks at her, then very slowly*) What are you talking about?

ADDIE: That's right. That's the talk, God help us.

HORACE: (*Angrily*) *What's* the talk?

ADDIE: I'm telling you. There's going to be a wedding—

HORACE: (*After a second, quietly*) Go and tell them I'm home.

ADDIE: (*Hesitates*) Now you ain't to get excited. You're to be in your bed—

HORACE: Go on, Addie. Go and say I'm back. (ADDIE *opens dining-room doors. He rises with difficulty, stands stiff, as if he were in pain, facing the dining room.*)

ADDIE: Miss Regina. They're home. They got here—

REGINA: Horace! (REGINA *quickly rises, runs into the room. Warmly*) Horace! You've finally arrived. (*As she kisses him, the others come forward, all talking together.*)

BEN: (*In doorway, carrying a napkin*) Well, sir, you had us all mighty worried. (*He steps forward. They shake hands.* ADDIE *exits.*)

OSCAR: You're a sight for sore eyes.

HORACE: Hello, Ben.

(LEO *enters, eating a biscuit.*)

OSCAR: And how you feel? Tip-top, I bet, because that's the way you're looking.

HORACE: (*Irritated with Oscar's lie*) Hello, Oscar. Hello, Leo, how are you?

LEO: (*Shaking hands*) I'm fine, sir. But a lot better now that you're back.

REGINA: Now sit down. What did happen to you and where's Alexandra? I am so excited about seeing you that I almost forgot about her.

HORACE: I didn't feel good, a little weak, I guess, and we stopped overnight to rest. Zan's upstairs washing off the train dirt.

REGINA: Oh, I am so sorry the trip was hard on you. I didn't think that—

HORACE: Well, it's just as if I had never been away. All of you here—

BEN: Waiting to welcome you home.

(BIRDIE *bursts in. She is wearing a flannel kimono and her face is flushed and excited.*)

BIRDIE: *(Runs to him, kisses him)* Horace!

HORACE: *(Warmly pressing her arm)* I was just wondering where you were, Birdie.

BIRDIE: *(Excited)* Oh, I would have been here. I didn't know you were back until Simon said he saw the buggy. *(She draws back to look at him. Her face sobers)* Oh, you don't look well, Horace. No, you don't.

REGINA: *(Laughs)* Birdie, what a thing to say—

HORACE: Oscar thinks I look very well.

OSCAR: *(Annoyed. Turns on* LEO*)* Don't stand there holding that biscuit in your hand.

LEO: Oh, well. I'll just finish my breakfast, Uncle Horace and then I'll give you all the news about the bank—(He *exits into the dining room.*)

OSCAR: And what is that costume you have on?

BIRDIE: *(Looking at* HORACE*)* Now that you're home, you'll feel better. Plenty of good rest and we'll take such fine care of you. *(Stops)* But where is Zan? I missed her so much.

OSCAR: I asked you what is that strange costume you're parading around in?

BIRDIE: *(Nervously, backing toward stairs)* Me? Oh! It's my wrapper. I was so excited about Horace I just rushed out of the house—

OSCAR: Did you come across the square dressed that way? My dear Birdie, I—

HORACE: *(To* REGINA, *wearily)* Yes, it's just like old times.

REGINA: *(Quickly to* OSCAR*)* Now, no fights. This is a holiday.

BIRDIE: *(Runs quickly up the stairs)* Zan! Zannie!

OSCAR: Birdie! *(She stops.)*

BIRDIE: Oh. Tell Zan I'll be back in a little while. *(Whispers)* Sorry, Oscar. *(Exits.)*

REGINA: *(To* OSCAR *and* BEN*)* Why don't you go finish your breakfast and let Horace rest for a minute?

BEN: *(Crossing to dining room with* OSCAR*)* Never leave a meal unfinished. There are too many poor people who need the food. Mighty glad to see you home, Horace. Fine to have you back. Fine to have you back.

OSCAR: (*To* LEO *as* BEN *closes dining-room doors*) Your mother has gone crazy. Running around the streets like a woman—(*The moment* REGINA *and* HORACE *are alone, they become awkward and self-conscious.*)

REGINA: (*Laughs awkwardly*) Well. Here we are. It's been a long time. (HORACE *smiles*) Five months. You know, Horace, I wanted to come and be with you in the hospital, but I didn't know where my duty was. Here, or with you. But you know how much I *wanted* to come.

HORACE: That's kind of you, Regina. There was no need to come.

REGINA: Oh, but there was. Five months lying there all by yourself, no kinfolks, no friends. Don't try to tell me you didn't have a bad time of it.

HORACE: I didn't have a bad time. (*As she shakes her head, he becomes insistent*) No, I didn't, Regina. Oh, at first when I—when I heard the news about myself—but after I got used to that, I liked it there.

REGINA: You *liked* it? Isn't that strange. You liked it so well you didn't want to come home?

HORACE: That's not the way to put it. (*Then, kindly, as he sees her turn her head away*) But there I was and I got kind of used to it, kind of to like lying there and thinking. I never had much time to think before. And time's become valuable to me.

REGINA: It sounds almost like a holiday.

HORACE: (*Laughs*) It was, sort of. The first holiday I've had since I was a little kid.

REGINA: And here I was thinking you were in pain and—

HORACE: (*Quietly*) I was in pain.

REGINA: And instead you were having a holiday! A holiday of thinking. Couldn't you have done that here?

HORACE: I wanted to do it before I came here. I was thinking about us.

REGINA: About us? About you and me? Thinking about you and me after all these years. You shall tell me everything you thought—someday.

HORACE: (*There is silence for a minute*) Regina. (*She turns to him*) Why did you send Zan to Baltimore?

REGINA: Why? Because I wanted you home. You can't make anything suspicious out of that, can you?

HORACE: I didn't mean to make anything suspicious about it. (*Hesitantly, taking her hand*) Zan said you wanted me to come home. I was so pleased at that and touched. It made me feel good.

REGINA: *(Taking away her hand)* Touched that I should want you home?

HORACE: I'm saying all the wrong things as usual. Let's try to get along better. There isn't so much more time. Regina, what's all this crazy talk I've been hearing about Zan and Leo? Zan and Leo marrying?

REGINA: *(Turning to him, sharply)* Who gossips so much around here?

HORACE: *(Shocked)* Regina!

REGINA: *(Anxious to quiet him)* It's some foolishness that Oscar thought up. I'll explain later. I have no intention of allowing any such arrangement. It was simply a way of keeping Oscar quiet in all this business I've been writing you about—

HORACE: *(Carefully)* What has Zan to do with any business of Oscar's? Whatever it is, you had better put it out of Oscar's head immediately. You know what I think of Leo.

REGINA: But there's no need to talk about it now.

HORACE: There is no need to talk about it ever. Not as long as I live. (HORACE *stops, slowly turns to look at her*) As long as I live. I've been in a hospital for five months. Yet since I've been here you have not once asked me about—about my health. *(Then gently)* Well, I suppose they've written you. I can't live very long.

REGINA: I've never understood why people have to talk about this kind of thing.

HORACE: *(There is a silence. Then he looks up at her, his face cold)* You misunderstand. I don't intend to gossip about my sickness. I thought it was only fair to tell you. I was not asking for your sympathy.

REGINA: *(Sharply, turns to him)* What do the doctors think caused your bad heart?

HORACE: What do you mean?

REGINA: They didn't think it possible, did they, that your fancy women may have—

HORACE: *(Smiles unpleasantly)* Caused my heart to be bad? I don't think that's the best scientific theory. You don't catch heart trouble in bed.

REGINA: *(Angrily)* I thought you might catch a bad conscience—in bed, as you say.

HORACE: I didn't tell them about my bad conscience. Or about my fancy women. Nor did I tell them that my wife has not wanted me in bed with her for—(*Sharply*) How long is it, Regina? Ten years? Did you bring me home for this, to make me feel guilty again? That means you want something. But you'll not make me feel guilty anymore. My "thinking" has made a difference.

REGINA: I see that it has. (*She looks toward dining-room door. Then comes to him, her manner warm and friendly*) It's foolish for us to fight this way. I didn't mean to be unpleasant. I was stupid.

HORACE: (*Wearily*) God knows I didn't either. I came home wanting so much not to fight, and then all of a sudden there we were.

REGINA: (*Hastily*) It's all my fault. I didn't ask about—about your illness because I didn't want to remind you of it. Anyway, I never believe doctors when they talk about—(*Brightly*) when they talk like that.

HORACE: I understand. Well, we'll try our best with each other. (*He rises.*)

REGINA: (*Quickly*) I'll try. Honestly, I will. Horace, Horace, I know you're tired but, but—couldn't you stay down here a few minutes longer? I want Ben to tell you something.

HORACE: Tomorrow.

REGINA: I'd like to now. It's very important to me. It's very important to all of us. (*Gaily, as she moves toward dining room*) Important to your beloved daughter. She'll be a very great heiress—

HORACE: Will she? That's nice.

REGINA: (*Opens doors*) Ben, are you finished breakfast?

HORACE: Is this the mill business I've had so many letters about?

REGINA: (*To* BEN) Horace would like to talk to you now.

HORACE: Horace would not like to talk to you now. I am very tired, Regina—

REGINA: (*Comes to him*) Please. You've said we'll try our best with each other. I'll try. Really, I will. Please do this for me now. You will see what I've done while you've been away. How I watched your interests. (*Laughs gaily*) And I've done very well too. But things can't be delayed any longer. Everything must be settled this week—(HORACE *sits down.* BEN *enters.* OSCAR *has stayed in the dining room, his head turned to watch them.* LEO *is pretending to read the newspaper*) Now you must tell Horace all about it. Only be quick because he is very tired and must go to bed. (HORACE *is looking at her. His face hardens as she speaks*) But I think your news will be better for him than all the medicine in the world.

BEN: *(Looking at* HORACE) It could wait. Horace may not feel like talking today.

REGINA: What an old faker you are! You know it can't wait. You know it must be finished this week. You've been just as anxious for Horace to get here as I've been.

BEN: *(Very jovial)* I suppose I have been. And why not? Horace has done Hubbard Sons many a good turn. Why shouldn't I be anxious to help him now?

REGINA: *(Laughs)* Help him! Help him when you need him, that's what you mean.

BEN: What a woman you married, Horace. *(Laughs awkwardly when* HORACE *does not answer)* Well, then I'll make it quick. You know what I've been telling you for years. How I've always said that every one of us little Southern businessmen had great things—*(Extends his arm)*—right beyond our fingertips. It's been my dream: my dream to make those fingers grow longer. I'm a lucky man, Horace, a lucky man. To dream and to live to get what you've dreamed of. That's *my* idea of a lucky man. For thirty years I've cried bring the cotton mills to the cotton. (HORACE *opens the medicine bottle*) Well finally I got up nerve to go to Marshall Company in Chicago.

HORACE: I know all this. *(He takes the medicine.* REGINA *rises, steps to him.)*

BEN: Can I get you something?

HORACE: Some water, please.

REGINA: *(Turns quickly)* Oh, I'm sorry. *(Brings him a glass of water. He drinks as they wait in silence)* You feel all right now?

HORACE: Yes. You wrote me. I know all that. (OSCAR *enters from dining room.)*

REGINA: *(Triumphantly)* But you don't know that in the last few days Ben has agreed to give us—you, I mean—a much larger share.

HORACE: Really? That's very generous of him.

BEN: *(Laughs)* It wasn't so generous of me. It was smart of Regina.

REGINA: *(As if she were signaling* HORACE) I explained to Ben that perhaps you hadn't answered his letters because you didn't think he was offering you enough, and that the time was getting short and you could guess how much he needed you—

HORACE: *(Smiles at her, nods)* And I could guess that he wants to keep control in the family.

REGINA: *(Triumphantly)* Exactly. So I did a little bargaining for you and convinced my brothers they weren't the only Hubbards who had a business sense.

HORACE: Did you have to convince them of that? How little people know about each other! *(Laughs)* But you'll know better about Regina next time, eh, Ben? (BEN, REGINA, HORACE *laugh together. Oscar's face is angry)* Now let's see. We're getting a bigger share. *(Looking at* OSCAR) Who's getting less?

BEN: Oscar.

HORACE: Well, Oscar, you've grown very unselfish. What's happened to you? (LEO *enters from dining room.)*

BEN: *(Quickly)* Oscar doesn't mind. Not worth fighting about now, eh, Oscar?

OSCAR: *(Angrily)* I'll get mine in the end. You can be sure of that. I've got my son's future to think about.

HORACE: *(Sharply)* Leo? Oh, I see. *(Puts his head back, laughs.* REGINA *looks at him nervously)* I am beginning to see. Everybody will get theirs.

BEN: I knew you'd see it. Seventy-five thousand, and that seventy-five thousand will make you a million.

REGINA: It will, Horace, it will.

HORACE: I believe you. *(After a second)* Now I can understand Oscar's self-sacrifice, but what did you have to promise Marshall Company besides the money you're putting up?

BEN: They wouldn't take promises. They wanted guarantees.

HORACE: Of what?

BEN: Water power. Free and plenty of it.

HORACE: You got them that, of course.

BEN: Cheap. You'd think the Governor of a great state would make his price a little higher. From pride, you know. (HORACE *smiles.* BEN *smiles)* Cheap wages. "What do you mean by cheap wages?" I say to Marshall. "Less than Massachusetts," he says to me, "and that averages eight a week." "Eight a week! By God," I tell him, "*I'd* work for eight a week myself." Why, there ain't a mountain white or a town nigger but wouldn't give his right arm for three silver dollars every week, eh, Horace?

HORACE: Sure. And they'll take less than that when you get around

to playing them off against each other. You can save a little
money that way, Ben. And make them hate each other just a
little more than they do now.

REGINA: What's all this about?

BEN: *(Laughs)* There'll be no trouble from anybody, white or black.
Marshall said that to me. "What about strikes? That's all
we've had in Massachusetts for the last three years." I say to
him, "What's a strike? I never heard of one. Come South,
Marshall. We got good folks and we don't stand for any fancy
fooling."

HORACE: You're right. *(Slowly)* Well, it looks like you made a good
deal for yourselves, and for Marshall, too. Your father used to
say he made the thousands and you boys would make the millions. I think he was right. *(Rises.)*

REGINA: *(As they look at HORACE. She laughs nervously)* Millions for
us, too.

HORACE: Us? You and me? I don't think so. We've got enough
money, Regina. We'll just sit by and watch the boys grow
rich. *(They watch HORACE as he begins to move toward the staircase. He passes LEO, looks at him for a second)* How's everything
at the bank, Leo?

LEO: Fine, sir. Everything is fine.

HORACE: How are all the ladies in Mobile? (HORACE *turns to*
REGINA, *sharply*) Whatever made you think I'd let Zan
marry—

REGINA: Do you mean that you are turning this down? Is it possible
that's what you mean?

BEN: No, that's not what he means. Turning down a fortune.
Horace is tired. He'd rather talk about it tomorrow—

REGINA: We can't keep putting it off this way. Oscar must be in
Chicago by the end of the week with the money and contracts.

OSCAR: *(Giggles, pleased)* Yes, sir. Got to be there end of the week.
No sense going without the money.

REGINA: *(Tensely)* I've waited long enough for your answer. I'm not
going to wait any longer.

HORACE: *(Very deliberately)* I'm very tired now, Regina.

BEN: *(Quickly)* Now, Horace probably has his reasons. Things he'd
like explained. Tomorrow will do. I can—

REGINA: *(Turns to BEN, sharply)* I want to know his reasons now!

HORACE: *(As he climbs the steps)* I don't know them all myself. Let's leave it at that.

REGINA: We shall not leave it at that! We have waited for you here like children. Waited for you to come home.

HORACE: So that you could invest my money. So that is why you wanted me home? Well, I had hoped—*(Quietly)* If you are disappointed, Regina, I'm sorry. But I must do what I think best. We'll talk about it another day.

REGINA: We'll talk about it now. Just you and me.

HORACE: *(Looks down at her. His voice is tense)* Please, Regina, it's been a hard trip. I don't feel well. Please leave me alone now.

REGINA: *(Quietly)* I want to talk to you, Horace. *(He looks at her for a minute, then moves on, out of sight. She begins to climb the stairs.)*

BEN: *(Softly.* REGINA *turns to him as he speaks)* Sometimes it is better to wait for the sun to rise again. *(She does not answer)* And sometimes, as our mother used to tell you, (REGINA *continues up stairs)* it's unwise for a good-looking woman to frown. (BEN *rises, moves toward stairs)* Softness and a smile do more to the heart of men—*(She disappears.* BEN *stands looking up the stairs. There is a long silence. Then* OSCAR *giggles.)*

OSCAR: Let us hope she'll change his mind. Let us hope. *(After a second* BEN *crosses to table, picks up his newspaper.* OSCAR *looks at* BEN. *The silence makes* LEO *uncomfortable.)*

LEO: The paper says twenty-seven cases of yellow fever in New Orleans. Guess the floodwaters caused it. *(Nobody pays attention)* Thought they were building the levees high enough. Like the niggers always say: a man born of woman can't build nothing high enough for the Mississippi. *(Gets no answer. Gives an embarrassed laugh.)*

(Upstairs there is the sound of voices. The voices are not loud, but BEN, OSCAR, LEO *become conscious of them.* LEO *crosses to landing, looks up, listens.)*

OSCAR: *(Pointing up)* Now just suppose she don't change his mind? Just suppose he keeps on refusing?

BEN: *(Without conviction)* He's tired. It was a mistake to talk to him today. He's a sick man, but he isn't a crazy one.

OSCAR: But just suppose he is crazy. What then?

BEN: *(Puts down his paper, peers at* OSCAR*)* Then we'll go outside for the money. There's plenty who would give it.

OSCAR: And plenty who will want a lot for what they give. The ones who are rich enough to give will be smart enough to want. That means we'd be working for them, don't it, Ben?

BEN: You don't have to tell me the things I told you six months ago.

OSCAR: Oh, you're right not to worry. She'll change his mind. She always has. (*There is a silence. Suddenly Regina's voice becomes louder and sharper. All of them begin to listen now. Slowly* BEN *rises, goes to listen by the staircase.* OSCAR, *watching him, smiles. As they listen Regina's voice becomes very loud. Horace's voice is no longer heard*) Maybe. But I don't believe it. I never did believe he was going in with us.

BEN: (*Turning on him*) What the hell do you expect me to do?

OSCAR: (*Mildly*) Nothing. You done your almighty best. Nobody could blame you if the whole thing just dripped away right through our fingers. You can't do a thing. But there may be something I could do for us. (OSCAR *rises*) Or, I might better say, Leo could do for us. (BEN *turns, looks at* OSCAR. LEO *is staring at* OSCAR) Ain't that true, son? Ain't it true you might be able to help your own kinfolks?

LEO: (*Nervously taking a step to him*) Papa, I—

BEN: (*Slowly*) How would he help us, Oscar?

OSCAR: Leo's got a friend. Leo's friend owns eighty-eight thousand dollars in Union Pacific bonds. (BEN *turns to look at* LEO) Leo's friend don't look at the bonds much—not for five or six months at a time.

BEN: (*After a pause*) Union Pacific. Uh, huh. Let me understand. Leo's friend would—would lend him these bonds and he—

OSCAR: (*Nods*) Would be kind enough to lend them to us.

BEN: Leo.

LEO: (*Excited, comes to him*) Yes, sir?

BEN: When would your friend be wanting the bonds back?

LEO: (*Very nervous*) I don't know. I—well, I—

OSCAR: (*Sharply. Steps to him*) You told me he won't look at them until Autumn—

LEO: Oh, that's right. But I—not till Autumn. Uncle Horace never—

BEN: (*Sharply*) Be still.

OSCAR: (*Smiles at* LEO) Your uncle doesn't wish to know your friend's name.

LEO: (*Starts to laugh*) That's a good one. Not know his name—

OSCAR: Shut up, Leo! (LEO *turns away*) He won't look at them again until September. That gives us five months. Leo will return the bonds in three months. And we'll have no trouble raising the money once the mills are going up. Will Marshall accept bonds? (BEN *stops to listen to the voices from above. The voices are now very angry and very loud.*)

BEN: *(Smiling)* Why not? Why not? *(Laughs)* Good. We are lucky. We'll take the loan from Leo's friend—I think he will make a safer partner than our sister. *(Nods toward stairs. Turns to* LEO) How soon can you get them?

LEO: Today. Right now. They're in the safe-deposit box and—

BEN: *(Sharply)* I don't want to know where they are.

OSCAR: *(Laughs)* We will keep it secret from you. *(Pats Ben's arm.)*

BEN: Good. Draw a check for our part. You can take the night train for Chicago. Well, Oscar *(Holds out his hand)*, good luck to us.

OSCAR: Leo will be taken care of?

LEO: I'm entitled to Uncle Horace's share. I'd enjoy being a partner—

BEN: *(Wheels on him)* You would? You can go to hell, you little— *(Starts toward* LEO.)

OSCAR: *(Nervously)* Now, now. He didn't mean that. I only want to be sure he'll get something out of all this.

BEN: Of course. We'll take care of him. We won't have any trouble about that. I'll see you at the store.

OSCAR: *(Nods)* That's settled then. Come on, son. *(Starts for door.)*

LEO: *(Puts out his hand)* I was only going to say what a great day this was for me and—

BEN: Go on.

(LEO *turns, follows* OSCAR *out. Again the voices upstairs can be heard. Regina's voice is high and furious.* BEN *looks up, smiles, winces at the noise.*)

ALEXANDRA: *(Upstairs)* Mama—Mama—don't...(*The noise of running footsteps is heard and* ALEXANDRA *comes running down the steps, speaking as she comes)* Uncle Ben! Uncle Ben! Please go up. Please make Mama stop. Uncle Ben, he's sick, he's so sick. How can Mama talk to him like that—please, make her stop. She'll—

BEN: Alexandra, you have a tender heart.

ALEXANDRA: *(Crying)* Go on up, Uncle Ben, please—

(*Suddenly the voices stop. A second later there is the sound of a door being slammed.*)

BEN: Now you see. Everything is over. Don't worry. *(He starts for the door)* Alexandra, I want you to tell your mother how sorry I am that I had to leave. And don't worry so, my dear.

Married folk frequently raise their voices, unfortunately. (*He starts to put on his hat and coat as* REGINA *appears on the stairs.*)

ALEXANDRA: (*Furiously*) How can you treat Papa like this? He's sick. He's very sick. Don't you know that? I won't let you.

REGINA: Mind your business, Alexandra. (*To* BEN. *Her voice is cold and calm*) How much longer can you wait for the money?

BEN: (*Putting on his coat*) He has refused? My, that's too bad.

REGINA: He will change his mind. I'll find a way to make him. What's the longest you can wait now?

BEN: I could wait until next week. But I can't wait until next week. (*He giggles, pleased*) I could but I can't. Could and can't. Well, I must go now. I'm very late—

REGINA: (*Coming downstairs toward him*) You're not going. I want to talk to you.

BEN: I was about to give Alexandra a message for you. I wanted to tell you that Oscar is going to Chicago tonight, so we can't be here for our usual Friday supper.

REGINA: (*Tensely*) Oscar is going to Chi—(*Softly*) What do you mean?

BEN: Just that. Everything is settled. He's going on to deliver to Marshall—

REGINA: (*Taking a step to him*) I demand to know what—You are lying. You are trying to scare me. *You haven't got the money.* How could you have it? You can't have—(BEN *laughs*) You will wait until I—(HORACE *comes into view on the landing.*)

BEN: You are getting out of hand. Since when do I take orders from you?

REGINA: Wait, you—(BEN *stops*) How *can* he go to Chicago? Did a ghost arrive with the money? (BEN *starts for the hall*) I don't believe you. Come back here. (REGINA *starts after him*) Come back here, you—(*The door slams. She stops in the doorway, staring, her fists clenched. After a pause she turns slowly.*)

HORACE: (*Very quietly*) It's a great day when you and Ben cross swords. I've been waiting for it for years.

ALEXANDRA: Papa, Papa, please go back! You will—

HORACE: And so they don't need you, and so you will not have your millions, after all.

REGINA: (*Turns slowly*) You hate to see anybody live now, don't you? You hate to think that I'm going to be alive and have what I want.

HORACE: I should have known you'd think that was the reason.

REGINA: Because you're going to die and you know you're going to die.

ALEXANDRA: *(Shrilly)* Mama! Don't—Don't listen, Papa. Just don't listen. Go away—

HORACE: Not to keep you from getting what you want. Not even partly that. I'm sick of you, sick of this house, sick of my life here. I'm sick of your brothers and their dirty tricks to make a dime. Why should I give you the money? *(Very angrily)* To pound the bones of this town to make dividends for you to spend? You wreck the town, you and your brothers, *you* wreck the town and live on it. Not me. Maybe it's easy for the dying to be honest. But it's not my fault I'm dying. I'll do no more harm now. I've done enough. I'll die my own way. And I'll do it without making the world any worse. I leave that to you.

REGINA: *(Looks up at him)* I hope you die. I hope you die soon. *(Smiles)* I'll be waiting for you to die.

ALEXANDRA: *(Shrieking)* Papa! Don't—Don't listen—Don't— (HORACE *turns slowly and starts upstairs.*)

CURTAIN

ACT THREE

SCENE: *Same as Act One. Two weeks later. It is late afternoon and it is raining.*

At Rise HORACE *is sitting near the window in a wheelchair. On the table next to him is a safe-deposit box, and a small bottle of medicine.* BIRDIE *and* ALEXANDRA *are playing the piano. On a chair is a large sewing basket.*

BIRDIE: *(Counting for* ALEXANDRA) One and two and three and four. One and two and three and four. *(Nods—turns to* HORACE) We once played together, Horace. Remember?

HORACE: *(Has been looking out of the window)* What, Birdie?

BIRDIE: We played together. You and me.

ALEXANDRA: *Papa* used to play?

BIRDIE: Indeed he did. (ADDIE *appears at the door in a large kitchen apron)* He played the fiddle and very well, too.

ALEXANDRA: *(Turns to smile at* HORACE) I never knew—

ADDIE: Where's your mama?

ALEXANDRA: Gone to Miss Safronia's to fit her dresses. (ADDIE *nods, starts to exit.)*

HORACE: Addie. Tell Cal to get on his things. I want him to go on an errand. (ADDIE *nods, exits.* HORACE *moves nervously in his chair, looks out of the window.)*

ALEXANDRA: *(Who has been watching him)* It's too bad it's been raining all day, Papa. But you can go out in the yard tomorrow. Don't be restless.

HORACE: I'm not restless, darling.

BIRDIE: I remember so well the time we played together, your papa and me. It was the first time Oscar brought me here to supper. I had never seen all the Hubbards together before, and you know what a ninny I am and how shy. *(Turns to look at* HORACE) You said you could play the fiddle and you'd be much obliged if I'd play with you. *I* was obliged to *you,* all right, all right. *(Laughs when he does not answer her)* Horace, you haven't heard a word I've said.

HORACE: Birdie, when did Oscar get back from Chicago?

BIRDIE: Yesterday. Hasn't he been here yet?

ALEXANDRA: *(Stops playing)* No. Neither has Uncle Ben since— since that day.

BIRDIE: Oh, I didn't know it was *that* bad. Oscar never tells me anything—

HORACE: The Hubbards have had their great quarrel. I knew it would come someday. (*Laughs*) It came.

ALEXANDRA: It came. It certainly came all right.

BIRDIE: (*Amazed*) But Oscar was in such a good humor when he got home, I didn't—

HORACE: Yes, I can understand that.

(ADDIE *enters carrying a large tray with glasses, a carafe of elderberry wine and a plate of cookies, which she puts on the table.*)

ALEXANDRA: Addie! A party! What for?

ADDIE: Nothing for. I had the fresh butter, so I made the cakes, and a little elderberry does the stomach good in the rain.

BIRDIE: Isn't this nice! A party just for us. Let's play party music, Zan. (ALEXANDRA *begins to play a gay piece.*)

ADDIE: (*To* HORACE, *wheeling his chair to center*) Come over here, Mr. Horace, and don't be thinking so much. A glass of elderberry will do more good. (ALEXANDRA *reaches for a cake.* BIRDIE *pours herself a glass of wine.*)

ALEXANDRA: Good cakes, Addie. It's nice here. Just us. Be nice if it could always be this way.

BIRDIE: (*Nods happily*) Quiet and restful.

ADDIE: Well, it won't be that way long. Little while now, even sitting here, you'll hear the red bricks going into place. The next day the smoke'll be pushing out the chimneys and by church time that Sunday every human born of woman will be living on chicken. That's how Mr. Ben's been telling the story.

HORACE: They believe it that way?

ADDIE: Believe it? They use to believing what Mr. Ben orders. There ain't been so much talk around here since Sherman's army didn't come near.

HORACE: (*Softly*) They are fools.

ADDIE: (*Nods, sits down with the sewing basket*) You ain't born in the South unless you're a fool.

BIRDIE: (*Has drunk another glass of wine*) But we didn't play together after that night. Oscar said he didn't like me to play on the piano. (*Turns to* ALEXANDRA) You know what he said that night?

ALEXANDRA: Who?

BIRDIE: Oscar. He said that music made him nervous. He said he just sat and waited for the next note. (ALEXANDRA *laughs*) He wasn't poking fun. He meant it. Ah, well—(*She finishes her glass, shakes her head.* HORACE *looks at her, smiles*) Your papa don't like to admit it, but he's been mighty kind to me all these years. (*Running her hand along his sleeve*) Often he'd step in when somebody said something and once—(*She stops, turns away, her face still*) Once he stopped Oscar from—(*She stops, turns. Quickly*) I'm sorry I said that. Why, here I am so happy and yet I think about bad things. (*Laughs nervously*) That's not right, now, is it? (*She pours a drink.* CAL *appears in the door. He has on an old coat and is carrying a torn umbrella.*)

ALEXANDRA: Have a cake, Cal.

CAL: (*Comes in, takes a cake*) You want me, Mr. Horace?

HORACE: What time is it, Cal?

CAL: 'Bout ten minutes before it's five.

HORACE: All right. Now you walk yourself down to the bank.

CAL: It'll be closed. Nobody'll be there but Mr. Manders, Mr. Joe Horns, Mr. Leo—

HORACE: Go in the back way. They'll be at the table, going over the day's business. (*Points to the deposit box*) See that box?

CAL: (*Nods*) Yes, sir.

HORACE: You tell Mr. Manders that Mr. Horace says he's much obliged to him for bringing the box, it arrived all right.

CAL: (*Bewildered*) He know you got the box. He bring it himself Wednesday. I opened the door to him and he say, "Hello, Cal, coming on to summer weather."

HORACE: You say just what I tell you. Understand? (BIRDIE *pours another drink, stands at table.*)

CAL: No, sir. I ain't going to say I understand. I'm going down and tell a man he give you something he already know he give you, and you say "understand."

HORACE: Now, Cal.

CAL: Yes, sir. I just going to say you obliged for the box coming all right. I ain't going to understand it, but I'm going to say it.

HORACE: And tell him I want him to come over here after supper, and to bring Mr. Sol Fowler with him.

CAL: (*Nods*) He's to come after supper and bring Mr. Sol Fowler, your attorney-at-law, with him.

HORACE: That's right. Just walk right in the back room and say your piece. (*Slowly*) In front of everybody.

CAL: Yes, sir. (*Mumbles to himself as he exits.*)

ALEXANDRA: (*Who has been watching* HORACE) Is anything the matter, Papa?

HORACE: Oh, no. Nothing.

ADDIE: Miss Birdie, that elderberry going to give you a headache spell.

BIRDIE: *(Beginning to be drunk. Gaily)* Oh, I don't think so. I don't think it will.

ALEXANDRA: *(As HORACE puts his hand to his throat)* Do you want your medicine, Papa?

HORACE: No, no. I'm all right, darling.

BIRDIE: Mama used to give me elderberry wine when I was a little girl. For hiccoughs. *(Laughs)* You know, I don't think people get hiccoughs anymore. Isn't that funny? (BIRDIE *laughs.* HORACE *and* ALEXANDRA *smile*) I used to get hiccoughs just when I shouldn't have.

ADDIE: *(Nods)* And nobody gets growing pains no more. That is funny. Just as if there was some style in what you get. One year an ailment's stylish and the next year it ain't.

BIRDIE: I remember. It was my first big party, at Lionnet I mean, and I was so excited, and there I was with hiccoughs and Mama laughing. *(Softly. Looking at carafe)* Mama always laughed. *(Picks up carafe)* A big party, a lovely dress from Mr. Worth in Paris, France, and hiccoughs. *(Pours drink)* My brother pounding me on the back and Mama with the elderberry bottle, laughing at me. Everybody was on their way to come, and I was such a ninny, hiccoughing away. *(Drinks)* You know, that was the first day I ever saw Oscar Hubbard. The Ballongs were selling their horses and he was going there to buy. He passed and lifted his hat—we could see him from the window—and my brother, to tease Mama, said maybe we should have invited the Hubbards to the party. He said Mama didn't like them because they kept a store, and he said that was old-fashioned of her. *(Her face lights up)* And then, and *then*, I saw Mama angry for the first time in my life. She said that wasn't the reason. She said she was old-fashioned, but not that way. She said she was old-fashioned enough not to like people who killed animals they couldn't use, and who made their money charging awful interest to ignorant niggers and cheating them on what they bought. She was very angry, Mama was. I had never seen her face like that. And then suddenly she laughed and said, "Look, I've frightened Birdie out of the hiccoughs." *(Her head drops. Then softly)* And so she had. They were all gone. *(Moves to sofa, sits.)*

ADDIE: Yeah, they got mighty well-off cheating niggers. Well, there are people who eat the earth and eat all the people on it like in the Bible with the locusts. And other people who stand around and watch them eat it. *(Softly)* Sometimes I think it ain't right to stand and watch them do it.

BIRDIE: *(Thoughtfully)* Like I say, if we could only go back to Lionnet. Everybody'd be better there. They'd be good and kind. I like people to be kind. *(Pours drink)* Don't you, Horace; don't you like people to be kind?

HORACE: Yes, Birdie.

BIRDIE: *(Very drunk now)* Yes, that was the first day I ever saw Oscar. Who would have thought—You all want to know something? Well, I don't like Leo. My very own son, and I don't like him. *(Laughs, gaily)* My, I guess I even like Oscar more.

ALEXANDRA: Why did you marry Uncle Oscar?

ADDIE: That's no question for you to be asking.

HORACE: *(Sharply)* Why not? She's heard enough around here to ask anything.

BIRDIE: I don't know. I thought I liked him. He was kind to me and I thought it was because he liked me too. But that wasn't the reason—*(Wheels on* ALEXANDRA*)* Ask why *he* married *me*. I can tell you that: he's told it to me often enough.

ADDIE: Miss Birdie, don't—

BIRDIE: *(Speaking very rapidly)* My family was good and the cotton on Lionnet's fields was better. Ben Hubbard wanted the cotton and Oscar Hubbard married it for him. He was kind to me, then. He used to smile at me. He hasn't smiled at me since. Everybody knew that's what he married me for. (ADDIE *rises)* Everybody but me. Stupid, stupid me.

ALEXANDRA: *(To* HORACE, *softly)* I see. *(Hesitates)* Papa, I mean—when you feel better couldn't we go away? I mean, by ourselves. Couldn't we find a way to go?

HORACE: Yes, I know what you mean. We'll try to find a way. I promise you, darling.

ADDIE: *(Moves to* BIRDIE*)* Rest a bit, Miss Birdie. You get talking like this you'll get a headache and—

BIRDIE: *(Sharply)* I've never had a headache in my life. *(Begins to cry)* You know it as well as I do. *(Turns to* ALEXANDRA*)* I never had a headache, Zan. That's a lie they tell for me. I drink. All by myself, in my own room, by myself, I drink. Then, when they want to hide it, they say, "Birdie's got a headache again"—

ALEXANDRA: *(Comes to her)* Aunt Birdie.

BIRDIE: Even you won't like me now. You won't like me anymore.

ALEXANDRA: I love you. I'll always love you.

BIRDIE: *(Angrily)* Well, don't. Don't love me. Because in twenty years you'll just be like me. They'll do all the same things to you. *(Begins to laugh)* You know what? In twenty-two years I haven't had a whole day of happiness. Oh, a little, like today with you all. But never a single, whole day. I say to myself, if only I had one more *whole* day, then—*(The laugh stops)* And that's the way you'll be. And you'll trail after them, just like me, hoping they won't be so mean that day or say something to make you feel so bad—only you'll be worse off because you haven't got my Mama to remember—*(Turns away, her head drops. She stands quietly, swaying a little, holding to the sofa.)*

ALEXANDRA: *(To* BIRDIE*)* I guess we were all trying to make a happy day. You know, we sit around and try to pretend nothing's happened. We try to pretend we are not here. We make believe we are just by ourselves, someplace else, and it doesn't seem to work. *(Kisses* BIRDIE'S *hand)* Come now, Aunt Birdie, I'll walk you home. You and me. *(She takes* BIRDIE'S *arm. They move slowly out.)*

BIRDIE: *(Softly as they exit)* You and me.

ADDIE: *(After a minute)* Well. First time I ever heard Miss Birdie say a word. Maybe it's good for her. I'm just sorry Zan had to hear it. (HORACE *moves his head as if he were uncomfortable)* You feel bad, don't you? *(He shrugs.)*

HORACE: So you didn't want Zan to hear? It would be nice to let her stay innocent, like Birdie at her age. Let her listen now. Let her see everything. How else is she going to know that she's got to get away? I'm trying to show her that. I'm trying, but I've only got a little time left. She can even hate me when I'm dead, if she'll only learn to hate and fear this.

ADDIE: Mr. Horace—

HORACE: Pretty soon there'll be nobody to help her but you.

ADDIE: What can I do?

HORACE: Take her away.

ADDIE: How can I do that? Do you think they'd let me just go away with her?

HORACE: I'll fix it so they can't stop you when you're ready to go.

You'll go, Addie?

ADDIE: *(After a second, softly)* Yes, sir. I promise. *(He touches her arm, nods.)*

HORACE: *(Quietly)* I'm going to have Sol Fowler make me a new will. They'll make trouble, but you make Zan stand firm and Fowler'll do the rest. Addie, I'd like to leave you something for yourself. I always wanted to.

ADDIE: *(Laughs)* Don't you do that, Mr. Horace. A nigger woman in a white man's will! I'd never get it nohow.

HORACE: I know. But upstairs in the armoire drawer there's thirty-seven hundred-dollar bills. It's money left from my trip. It's in an envelope with your name. It's for you.

ADDIE: It's mighty kind and good of you. I don't know what to say for thanks—

CAL: *(Appears in doorway)* I'm back. *(No answer)* I'm back.

ADDIE: So we see.

HORACE: Well?

CAL: Nothing. I just went down and spoke my piece. Just like you told me. I say, "Mr. Horace he thank you mightily for the safe box arriving in good shape and he say you come right after supper to his house and bring Mr. Attorney-at-law Sol Fowler with you." Then I wipe my hands on my coat. Every time I ever told a lie in my whole life, I wipe my hands right after. Well, while I'm wiping my hands, Mr. Leo jump up and say to me, "What box? What you talking about?"

HORACE: *(Smiles)* Did he?

CAL: And Mr. Leo say he got to leave a little early cause he got something to do. And then Mr. Manders say Mr. Leo should sit right down and finish up his work and stop acting like somebody made him Mr. President. So he sit down. Now, just like I told you, Mr. Manders was mighty surprised with the message because he knows right well he brought the box—*(Points to box, sighs)* But he took it all right. Some men take everything easy and some do not.

HORACE: *(Laughs)* Mr. Leo was telling the truth; he *has* got something to do. I hope Manders don't keep him too long. *(Outside there is the sound of voices. CAL exits. ADDIE crosses quickly to HORACE, begins to wheel his chair toward the stairs)* No. Leave me where I am.

ADDIE: But that's Miss Regina coming back.

HORACE: *(Nods, looking at door)* Go away, Addie.

ADDIE: *(Hesitates)* Mr. Horace. Don't talk no more today. You
   don't feel well and it won't do no good—

HORACE: *(As he hears footsteps in the hall)* Go on. *(She looks at him for
   a second, then picks up her sewing from table and exits as* REGINA
   *comes in from hall. Horace's chair is now so placed that he is in
   front of the table with the medicine.* REGINA *stands in the hall,
   shakes umbrella, stands it in the corner, takes off her cloak and
   throws it over the banister. She stares at* HORACE.*)*

REGINA: *(As she takes off her gloves)* We had agreed that you were to
   stay in your part of this house and I in mine. This room is *my*
   part of the house. Please don't come down here again.

HORACE: I won't.

REGINA: *(Crosses toward bell cord)* I'll get Cal to take you upstairs.

HORACE: Before you do I want to tell you that after all, we have
   invested our money in Hubbard Sons and Marshall, Cotton
   Manufacturers.

REGINA: *(Stops, turns, stares at him)* What are you talking about?
   You haven't seen Ben—When did you change your mind?

HORACE: I didn't change my mind. *I* didn't invest the money.
   (Smiles) It was invested for me.

REGINA: *(Angrily)* What—?

HORACE: I had eighty-eight thousand dollars' worth of Union
   Pacific bonds in that safe-deposit box. They are not there
   now. Go and look. *(As she stares at him, he points to the box)* Go
   and look, Regina. *(She crosses quickly to the box, opens it)* Those
   bonds are as negotiable as money.

REGINA: *(Turns back to him)* What kind of joke are you playing
   now? Is this for my benefit?

HORACE: I don't look in that box very often, but three days ago, on
   Wednesday it was, because I had made a decision—

REGINA: I want to know what you are talking about.

HORACE: Don't interrupt me again. Because I had made a decision,
   I sent for the box. The bonds were gone. Eighty-eight
   thousand dollars gone. *(He smiles at her.)*

REGINA: *(After a moment's silence, quietly)* Do you think I'm crazy
   enough to believe what you're saying?

HORACE: Believe anything you like.

REGINA: *(Slowly)* Where did they go to?

HORACE: They are in Chicago. With Mr. Marshall, I should guess.

REGINA: What did they do? Walk to Chicago? Have you really
   gone crazy?

HORACE: Leo took the bonds.

REGINA: *(Turns sharply, then speaks softly, without conviction)* I don't believe it.

HORACE: I wasn't there but I can guess what happened. This fine gentleman, with whom you were bargaining your daughter, took the keys and opened the box. You remember that the day of the fight Oscar went to Chicago? Well, he went with my bonds that his son Leo had stolen for him. *(Pleasantly)* And for Ben.

REGINA: *(Slowly, nods)* When did you find out the bonds were gone?

HORACE: Wednesday night.

REGINA: I thought that's what you said. Why have you waited three days to do anything? *(Suddenly laughs)* This *will* make a fine story.

HORACE: *(Nods)* Couldn't it?

REGINA: A fine story to hold over their heads. How could they be such fools?

HORACE: But I'm not going to hold it over their heads.

REGINA: *(The laugh stops)* What?

HORACE: *(Turns his chair to face her)* I'm going to let them keep the bonds—as a loan from you. An eighty-eight-thousand-dollar loan; they should be grateful to you. They will be, I think.

REGINA: *(Slowly, smiles)* I see. You are punishing me. But I won't let you punish me. If you won't do anything, I will. Now. *(She starts for door.)*

HORACE: You won't do anything. Because you can't. (REGINA *stops*) It won't do you any good to make trouble because I shall simply say that I lent them the bonds.

REGINA: *(Slowly)* You would do that?

HORACE: Yes. For once in your life I am tying your hands. There is nothing for you to do. *(There is silence. Then she sits down.)*

REGINA: I see. You are going to lend them the bonds and let them keep all the profit they make on them, and there is nothing I can do about it. Is that right?

HORACE: Yes.

REGINA: *(Softly)* Why did you say that I was making this gift?

HORACE: I was coming to that. I am going to make a new will, Regina, leaving you eighty-eight thousand dollars in Union Pacific bonds. The rest will go to Zan. It's true that your brothers have borrowed your share for a little while. After my death I advise you to talk to Ben and Oscar. They won't admit anything and Ben, I think, will be smart enough to see that he's safe. Because I knew about the theft and said nothing. Nor will I say anything as long as I live. Is that clear to you?

REGINA: *(Nods, softly, without looking at him)* You will not say anything as long as you live.

HORACE: That's right. And by that time they will probably have replaced your bonds, and then they'll belong to you and nobody but us will ever know what happened. They'll be around any minute to see what I am going to do. I took good care to see that word reached Leo. They'll be mighty relieved to know I'm going to do nothing and Ben will think it all a capital joke on you. And that will be the end of that. There's nothing you can do to them, nothing you can do to me.

REGINA: You hate me very much.

HORACE: No.

REGINA: Oh, I think you do. *(Puts her head back, sighs)* Well, we haven't been very good together. Anyway, I don't hate you either. I have only contempt for you. I've always had.

HORACE: From the very first?

REGINA: I think so.

HORACE: I was in love with *you*. But why did *you* marry *me*?

REGINA: I was lonely when I was young.

HORACE: *You* were lonely?

REGINA: Not the way people usually mean. Lonely for all the things I wasn't going to get. Everybody in this house was so busy and there was so little place for what I wanted. I wanted the world. Then, and then—*(Smiles)* Papa died and left the money to Ben and Oscar.

HORACE: And you married me?

REGINA: Yes, I thought—But I was wrong. You were a small-town clerk then. You haven't changed.

HORACE: *(Nods)* And that wasn't what you wanted.

REGINA: No. No, it wasn't what I wanted. *(Pleasantly)* It took me a little while to find out I had made a mistake. As for you—I don't know. It was almost as if I couldn't stand the kind of man you were—*(Smiles, softly)* I used to lie there at night, praying you wouldn't come near—

HORACE: Really? It was as bad as that?

REGINA: Remember when I went to Doctor Sloan and I told you he said there was something the matter with me and that you shouldn't touch me anymore?

HORACE: I remember.

REGINA: But you believed it. I couldn't understand that. I couldn't understand that anybody could be such a soft fool. That was when I began to despise you.

HORACE: (*Puts his hand to his throat, looks at the bottle of medicine on table*) Why didn't you leave me?

REGINA: I told you I married you for something. It turned out it was only for this. (*Carefully*) This wasn't what I wanted, but it was something. I never thought about it much, but if I had I'd have known that you would die before I would. But I couldn't have known that you would get heart trouble so early and so bad. I'm lucky, Horace. I've always been lucky. (HORACE *turns slowly to the medicine*) I'll be lucky again. (HORACE *looks at her. Then he puts his hand to his throat. Because he cannot reach the bottle he moves the chair closer. He reaches for the medicine, takes out the cork, picks up the spoon. The bottle slips and smashes on the table. He draws in his breath, gasps.*)

HORACE: Please. Tell Addie—The other bottle is upstairs.

(REGINA *has not moved. She does not move now. He stares at her. Then, suddenly as if he understood, he raises his voice. It is a panic-stricken whisper, too small to be heard outside the room*) Addie! Addie! Come—(*Stops as he hears the softness of his voice. He makes a sudden, furious spring from the chair to the stairs, taking the first few steps as if he were a desperate runner. Then he slips, gasps, grasps the rail, makes a great effort to reach the landing. When he reaches the landing, he is on his knees. His knees give way, he falls on the landing, out of view.* REGINA *has not turned during his climb up the stairs. Now she waits a second. Then she goes below the landing, speaks up.*)

REGINA: Horace. Horace. (*When there is no answer, she turns, calls*) Addie! Cal! Come in here. (*She starts up the steps.* ADDIE *and* CAL *appear. Both run toward the stairs*) He's had an attack. Come up here. (*They run up the steps quickly.*)

CAL: My God. Mr. Horace—

(*They cannot be seen now.*)

REGINA: (*Her voice comes from the head of the stairs*) Be still, Cal. Bring him in here.

(*Before the footsteps and the voices have completely died away,* ALEXANDRA *appears in the hall door, in her raincloak and hood. She comes into the room, begins to unfasten the cloak, suddenly looks around, sees the empty wheelchair, stares, begins to move swiftly as if to look in the dining room. At the same moment* ADDIE *runs down the stairs.* ALEXANDRA *turns and stares up at* ADDIE.)

ALEXANDRA: Addie! What?

ADDIE: *(Takes* ALEXANDRA *by the shoulders)* I'm going for the doctor. Go upstairs. (ALEXANDRA *looks at her, then quickly breaks away and runs up the steps.* ADDIE *exits. The stage is empty for a minute. Then the front doorbell begins to ring. When there is no answer, it rings again. A second later* LEO *appears in the hall, talking as he comes in.)*

LEO: *(Very nervous)* Hello. *(Irritably)* Never saw any use ringing a bell when a door was open. If you are going to ring a bell, then somebody should answer it. *(Gets in the room, looks around, puzzled, listens, hears no sound)* Aunt Regina. *(He moves around restlessly)* Addie. *(Waits)* Where the hell—*(Crosses to the bell cord, rings it impatiently, waits, gets no answer, calls)* Cal! Cal! (CAL *appears on the stair landing.)*

CAL: *(His voice is soft, shaken)* Mr. Leo. Miss Regina says you stop that screaming noise.

LEO: *(Angrily)* Where is everybody?

CAL: Mr. Horace he got an attack. He's bad. Miss Regina says you stop that noise.

LEO: Uncle Horace—What—What happened? (CAL *starts down the stairs, shakes his head, begins to move swiftly off.* LEO *looks around wildly)* But when—You seen Mr. Oscar or Mr. Ben? (CAL *shakes his head. Moves on.* LEO *grabs him by the arm)* Answer me, will you?

CAL: No, I ain't seen 'em. I ain't got time to answer you. I got to get things. (CAL *runs off.)*

LEO: But what's the matter with him? When did this happen—*(Calling after* CAL) You'd think Papa'd be someplace where you could find him. I been chasing him all afternoon. (OSCAR *and* BEN *come quickly into the room.)*

LEO: Papa, I've been looking all over town for you and Uncle Ben—

BEN: Where is he?

OSCAR: Addie just told us it was a sudden attack, and—

BEN: *(To* LEO) Where is he? When did it happen?

LEO: Upstairs. Will you listen to me, please? I been looking for you for—

OSCAR: *(To* BEN) You think we should go up? (BEN, *looking up the steps, shakes his head.*)

BEN: I don't know. I don't know.

OSCAR: But he was all right—

LEO: *(Yelling) Will you listen to me?*

OSCAR: What is the matter with you?

LEO: I been trying to tell you. I been trying to find you for an hour—

OSCAR: Tell me what?

LEO: Uncle Horace knows about the bonds. He knows about them. He's had the box since Wednesday—

BEN: *(Sharply)* Stop shouting! What the hell are you talking about?

LEO: *(Furiously)* I'm telling you he knows about the bonds. Ain't that clear enough—

BEN: *(Grabbing LEO's arm)* You God-damn fool! Stop screaming! Now what happened? Talk quietly.

LEO: You heard me. Uncle Horace knows about the bonds. He's known since Wednesday.

BEN: *(After a second)* How do you know that?

LEO: Because Cal comes down to Manders and says the box came okay and—

OSCAR: *(Trembling)* That might not mean a thing—

LEO: *(Angrily)* No? It might not, huh? Then he says Manders should come here tonight and bring Sol Fowler with him. I guess that don't mean a thing either.

OSCAR: *(To BEN)* Ben—What—Do you think he's seen the—

BEN: *(Motions to the box)* There's the box. *(Both OSCAR and LEO turn sharply. LEO makes a leap to the box)* You ass. Put it down. What are you going to do with it, eat it?

LEO: I'm going to—

BEN: *(Furiously)* Put it down. Don't touch it again. Now sit down and shut up for a minute.

OSCAR: Since Wednesday. *(To LEO)* You said he had it since Wednesday. Why didn't he say something—*(To BEN)* I don't understand—

LEO: *(Taking a step)* I can put it back. I can put it back before anybody knows.

BEN: *(Who is standing at the table, softly)* He's had it since Wednesday. Yet he hasn't said a word to us.

OSCAR: *Why? Why?*

LEO: What's the difference why? He was getting ready to say plenty. He was going to say it to Fowler tonight—

OSCAR: *(Angrily)* Be still. *(Turns to* BEN, *looks at him, waits.)*

BEN: *(After a minute)* I don't believe that.

LEO: *(Wildly) You* don't believe it? What do I care what *you* believe? I do the dirty work and then—

BEN: *(Turning his head to* LEO) I'm remembering that. I'm remembering that, Leo.

OSCAR: What do you mean?

LEO: You—

BEN: *(To* OSCAR) If you don't shut that little fool up, I'll show you what I mean. For some reason he knows, but he don't say a word.

OSCAR: Maybe he didn't know that *we*—

BEN: *(Quickly)* That *Leo*—He's no fool. Does Manders know the bonds are missing?

LEO: How could I tell? I was half crazy. I don't think so. Because Manders seemed kind of puzzled and—

OSCAR: But we got to find out—*(He breaks off as* CAL *comes into the room carrying a kettle of hot water.)*

BEN: How is he, Cal?

CAL: I don't know, Mr. Ben. He was bad. *(Going toward stairs.)*

OSCAR: But when did it happen?

CAL: *(Shrugs)* He wasn't feeling bad early. (ADDIE *comes in quickly from the hall)* Then there he is next thing on the landing, fallen over, his eyes tight—

ADDIE: *(To* CAL) Dr. Sloan's over at the Ballongs. Hitch the buggy and go get him. *(She takes the kettle and cloths from him, pushes him, runs up the stairs)* Go on. *(She disappears.* CAL *exits.)*

BEN: Never seen Sloan anywhere when you need him.

OSCAR: *(Softly)* Sounds bad.

LEO: He would have told *her* about it. Aunt Regina. He would have told his own wife—

BEN: *(Turning to* LEO) Yes, he might have told her. But they weren't on such pretty terms and maybe he didn't. Maybe he didn't. *(Goes quickly to* LEO) Now listen to me. If she doesn't know, it may work out all right. If she does know, you're to say he lent you the bonds.

LEO: Lent them to me! Who's going to believe that?

BEN: Nobody.

OSCAR: *(To* LEO) Don't you understand? It can't do no harm to say it—

LEO: Why should I say he lent them to me? Why not to you?

(Carefully) Why not to Uncle Ben?

BEN: *(Smiles)* Just because he didn't lend them to me. Remember that.

LEO: But all he has to do is say he didn't lend them to me—

BEN: *(Furiously)* But for some reason, he doesn't seem to be talking, does he?

(There are footsteps above. They all stand looking at the stairs. REGINA *begins to come slowly down.)*

BEN: What happened?

REGINA: He's had a bad attack.

OSCAR: Too bad. I'm sorry we weren't here when—when Horace needed us.

BEN: When *you* needed us.

REGINA: *(Looks at him)* Yes.

BEN: How is he? Can we—can we go up?

REGINA: *(Shakes her head)* He's not conscious.

OSCAR: *(Pacing around)* It's that—it's that bad? Wouldn't you think Sloan could be found quickly, just once, just once?

REGINA: I don't think there is much for him to do.

BEN: Oh, don't talk like that. He's come through attacks before. He will now.

*(*REGINA *sits down. After a second she speaks softly.)*

REGINA: Well. We haven't seen each other since the day of our fight.

BEN: *(Tenderly)* That was nothing. Why, you and Oscar and I used to fight when we were kids.

OSCAR: *(Hurriedly)* Don't you think we should grow up? Is there anything we can do for Horace—

BEN: You don't feel well. Ah—

REGINA: *(Without looking at them)* No, I don't. *(Slight pause)* Horace told me about the bonds this afternoon. *(There is an immediate shocked silence.)*

LEO: The bonds. What do you mean? What bonds? What—

BEN: *(Looks at him furiously. Then to* REGINA) The Union Pacific bonds? *Horace's* Union Pacific bonds?

REGINA: Yes.

OSCAR: *(Steps to her, very nervously)* Well. Well what—what about them? What—what could he say?

REGINA: He said that Leo had stolen the bonds and given them to you.

OSCAR: *(Aghast, very loudly)* That's ridiculous, Regina, absolutely—

LEO: I don't know what you're talking about. What would I—
Why—

REGINA: *(Wearily to* BEN) Isn't it enough that he stole them? Do I
have to listen to this in the bargain?

OSCAR: You are talking—

LEO: I didn't steal anything. I don't know why—

REGINA: *(To* BEN) Would you ask them to stop that, please? *(There
is silence.* BEN *glowers at* OSCAR *and* LEO.)

BEN: Aren't we starting at the wrong end, Regina? What did
Horace tell you?

REGINA: *(Smiles at him)* He told me that Leo had stolen the bonds.

LEO: I didn't steal—

REGINA: Please. Let me finish. Then he told me that he was going
to pretend that he had lent them to you (LEO *turns sharply to*
REGINA, *then looks at* OSCAR, *then looks back at* REGINA) as a
present from me—to my brothers. He said there was nothing
I could do about it. He said the rest of his money would go to
Alexandra. That is all. *(There is a silence,* OSCAR *coughs,* LEO
smiles slyly.)

LEO: *(Taking a step to her)* I told you he had lent them—I could
have told you—

REGINA: *(Ignores him, smiles sadly at* BEN) So I'm very badly off, you
see. Horace said there was nothing I could do about it as long
as he was alive to say he had lent you the bonds.

BEN: You shouldn't feel that way. It can all be explained, all be
adjusted. It isn't as bad—

REGINA: So you, at least, are willing to admit the bonds were
stolen?

BEN: (OSCAR *laughs nervously*) I admit no such thing. It's possible
that Horace made up that part of the story to tease you—
(Looks at her) Or perhaps to punish you. Punish you.

REGINA: *(Sadly)* It's not a pleasant story. I feel bad, Ben, naturally. I
hadn't thought—

BEN: Now you shall have the bonds safely back. That was the
understanding, wasn't it, Oscar?

OSCAR: Yes.

REGINA: I'm glad to know that. *(Smiles)* Ah, I had greater hopes—

BEN: Don't talk that way. That's foolish. *(Looks at his watch)* I think
we ought to drive out for Sloan ourselves. If we can't find him
we'll go over to Senateville for Doctor Morris. And don't
think I'm dismissing this other business. I'm not. We'll have

it all out on a more appropriate day.

REGINA: I don't think you had better go yet. I think you had better stay and sit down.

BEN: We'll be back with Sloan.

REGINA: Cal has gone for him. I don't want you to go.

BEN: Now don't worry and—

REGINA: You will come back in this room and sit down. I have something more to say.

BEN: (*Turns, comes toward her*) Since when do I take orders from you?

REGINA: (*Smiles*) You don't—yet. (*Sharply*) Come back, Oscar. You too, Leo.

OSCAR: (*Sure of himself, laughs*) My dear Regina—

BEN: (*Softly, pats her hand*) Horace has already clipped your wings and very wittily. Do I have to clip them, too? (*Smiles at her*) You'd get farther with a smile, Regina. I'm a soft man for a woman's smile.

REGINA: I'm smiling, Ben. I'm smiling because you are quite safe while Horace lives. But I don't think Horace will live. And if he doesn't live I shall want seventy-five percent in exchange for the bonds.

BEN: (*Steps back, whistles, laughs*) Greedy! What a greedy girl you are! You want so much of everything.

REGINA: Yes. And if I don't get what I want I am going to put all three of you in jail.

OSCAR: (*Furiously*) You're mighty crazy. Having just admitted—

BEN: And on what evidence would you put Oscar and Leo in jail?

REGINA: (*Laughs, gaily*) Oscar, listen to him. He's getting ready to swear that it was you and Leo! What do you say to that? (OSCAR *turns furiously toward* BEN) Oh, don't be angry, Oscar. I'm going to see that he goes in with you.

BEN: Try anything you like, Regina. (*Sharply*) And now we can stop all this and say good-bye to you. (ALEXANDRA *comes slowly down the steps*) It's his money and he's obviously willing to let us borrow it. (*More pleasantly*) Learn to make threats when you can carry them through. For how many years have I told you a good-looking woman gets more by being soft and appealing? Mama used to tell you that. (*Looks at his watch*) Where the hell is Sloan? (*To* OSCAR) Take the buggy and— (*As* BEN *turns to* OSCAR, *he sees* ALEXANDRA. *She walks stiffly. She goes slowly to the lower window, her head bent. They all turn to look at her.*)

OSCAR: (*After a second, moving toward her*) What? Alexandra—(*She does not answer. After a second,* ADDIE *comes slowly down the stairs, moving as if she were very tired. At foot of steps, she looks at* ALEXANDRA, *then turns and slowly crosses to door and exits.* REGINA *rises.* BEN *looks nervously at* ALEXANDRA, *at* REGINA. *As* ADDIE *passes him, irritably to* ALEXANDRA) Well, what is— (*Turns into room—sees* ADDIE *at foot of steps*)—what's? (BEN *puts up a hand, shakes his head*) My God, I didn't know—who could have known—I didn't know he was that sick. Well, well—I— (REGINA *stands quietly, her back to them.*)

BEN: (*Softly, sincerely*) Seems like yesterday when he first came here.

OSCAR: Yes, that's true. (*Turns to* BEN) The whole town loved him and respected him.

ALEXANDRA: (*Turns*) Did you love him, Uncle Oscar?

OSCAR: Certainly, I—What a strange thing to ask! I—

ALEXANDRA: Did you love him, Uncle Ben?

BEN: (*Simply*) Alexandra, I—

ALEXANDRA: (*Starts to laugh very loudly*) And you, Mama, did you love him, too?

REGINA: I know what you feel, Alexandra, but please try to control yourself.

ALEXANDRA: I'm trying, Mama. I'm trying very hard.

BEN: Grief makes some people laugh and some people cry. It's better to cry, Alexandra.

ALEXANDRA: (*The laugh has stopped. She moves toward* REGINA) What was Papa doing on the staircase?

(BEN *turns to look at* ALEXANDRA.)

REGINA: Please go and lie down, my dear. We all need time to get over shocks like this. (ALEXANDRA *does not move.* REGINA's *voice becomes softer, more insistent*) Please go, Alexandra.

ALEXANDRA: No, Mama. I'll wait. I've got to talk to you.

REGINA: Later. Go and rest now.

ALEXANDRA: (*Quietly*) I'll wait, Mama. I've plenty of time.

REGINA: (*Hesitates, stares, makes a half shrug, turns back to* BEN) As I was saying. Tomorrow morning I am going up to Judge Simmes. I shall tell him about Leo.

BEN: (*Motioning toward* ALEXANDRA) Not in front of the child, Regina. I—

REGINA: (*Turns to him. Sharply*) I didn't ask her to stay. Tomorrow morning I go to Judge Simmes—

OSCAR: And what proof? What proof of all this—

REGINA: *(Turns sharply)* None. I won't need any. The bonds are missing and they are with Marshall. That will be enough. If it isn't, I'll add what's necessary.

BEN: I'm sure of that.

REGINA: *(Turns to BEN)* You can be quite sure.

OSCAR: We'll deny—

REGINA: Deny your heads off. You couldn't find a jury that wouldn't weep for a woman whose brothers steal from her. And you couldn't find twelve men in this state you haven't cheated and who hate you for it.

OSCAR: What kind of talk is this? You couldn't do anything like that! We're your own brothers. *(Points upstairs)* How can you talk that way when upstairs not five minutes ago—

REGINA: Where was I? *(Smiles at BEN)* Well, they'll convict you. But I won't care much if they don't. Because by that time you'll be ruined. I shall also tell my story to Mr. Marshall, who likes me, I think, and who will not want to be involved in your scandal. A respectable firm like Marshall and Company. The deal would be off in an hour. *(Turns to them angrily)* And you know it. Now I don't want to hear any more from any of you. *You'll do no more bargaining in this house.* I'll take my seventy-five percent and we'll forget the story forever. That's one way of doing it, and the way I prefer. You know me well enough to know that I don't mind taking the other way.

BEN: *(After a second, slowly)* None of us has ever known you well enough, Regina.

REGINA: You're getting old, Ben. Your tricks aren't as smart as they used to be. *(There is no answer. She waits, then smiles)* All right. I take it that's settled and I get what I asked for.

OSCAR: *(Furiously to BEN)* Are you going to let her do this—

BEN: *(Turns to look at him, slowly)* You have a suggestion?

REGINA: *(Puts her arms above her head, stretches, laughs)* No, he hasn't. All right. Now, Leo, I have forgotten that you ever saw the bonds. *(Archly, to BEN and OSCAR)* And as long as you boys both behave yourselves, I've forgotten that we ever even talked about them. You can draw up the necessary papers tomorrow. (BEN *laughs.* LEO *stares at him, starts for door. Exits.* OSCAR *moves toward door angrily.* REGINA *looks at* BEN, *nods, laughs with him. For a second,* OSCAR *stands in the door, looking back at them. Then he exits.)*

REGINA: You're a good loser, Ben. I like that.

BEN: *(Picks up his coat, turns to her)* Well, I say to myself, what's the good? You and I aren't like Oscar. We're not sour people. I think that comes from a good digestion. Then, too, one loses today and wins tomorrow. I say to myself, years of planning and I get what I want. Then I don't get it. But I'm not discouraged. The century's turning, the world is open. Open for people like you and me. Ready for us, waiting for us. After all this is just the beginning. There are hundreds of Hubbards sitting in rooms like this throughout the country. All their names aren't Hubbard, but they are all Hubbards and they will own this country someday. We'll get along.

REGINA: *(Smiles)* I think so.

BEN: Then, too, I say to myself, things may change. *(Looks at ALEXANDRA)* I agree with Alexandra. What is a man in a wheelchair doing on a staircase? I ask myself that.

REGINA: *(Looks up at him)* And what do you answer?

BEN: I have no answer. But maybe someday I will. Maybe never, but maybe someday. *(Smiles. Pats her arm)* When I do, I'll let you know. *(Goes toward hall.)*

REGINA: When you do, write me. I will be in Chicago. *(Gaily)* Ah, Ben, if Papa had only left me his money.

BEN: I'll see you tomorrow.

REGINA: Oh, yes. Certainly. You'll be sort of working for me now.

BEN: *(As he passes ALEXANDRA)* Alexandra, you're turning out to be a right interesting girl. Well, good night all. *(He exits.)*

REGINA: *(Sits quietly for a second, stretches)* What do you want to talk to me about, Alexandra?

ALEXANDRA: *(Slowly)* I've changed my mind. I don't want to talk.

REGINA: You're acting very strange. Not like yourself. You've had a bad shock today. I know that. And you loved Papa, but you must have expected this to come someday. You knew how sick he was.

ALEXANDRA: I knew. We all knew.

REGINA: It will be good for you to get away from here. Good for me, too. Time heals most wounds, Alexandra. You're young, you shall have all the things I wanted. I'll make the world for you the way I wanted it to be for me. *(Uncomfortably)* Don't sit there staring. You've been around Birdie so much you're getting just like her.

ALEXANDRA: *(Nods)* Funny. That's what Aunt Birdie said today.

REGINA: Be good for you to get away from all this. (ADDIE *enters.*)

ADDIE: Cal is back, Miss Regina. He says Dr. Sloan will be coming in a few minutes.

REGINA: We'll leave in a few weeks. A few weeks! That means two or three Saturdays, two or three Sundays. (*Sighs*) Well, I'm very tired. I shall go to bed. I don't want any supper. Put the lights out and lock up. (ADDIE *moves to the piano lamp, turns it out*) You go to your room, Alexandra. Addie will bring you something hot. You look very tired. (*Rises. To* ADDIE) Call me when Dr. Sloan gets here. I don't want to see anybody else. I don't want any condolence calls tonight. The whole town will be over.

ALEXANDRA: Mama, I'm not coming with you. I'm not going to Chicago.

REGINA: (*Turns to her*) You're very upset, Alexandra.

ALEXANDRA: I mean what I say. With all my heart.

REGINA: We'll talk about it tomorrow. The morning will make a difference.

ALEXANDRA: It won't make any difference. And there isn't anything to talk about. I am going away from you. Because I want to. Because I know Papa would want me to.

REGINA: (*Careful, polite*) You *know* your papa wanted you to go away from me?

ALEXANDRA: Yes.

REGINA: (*Softly*) And if I say no?

ALEXANDRA: Say it Mama, say it. And see what happens.

REGINA: (*Softly, after a pause*) And if I make you stay?

ALEXANDRA: That would be foolish. It wouldn't work in the end.

REGINA: You're very serious about it, aren't you? (*Crosses to stairs*) Well, you'll change your mind in a few days.

ALEXANDRA: No.

REGINA: (*Going up the steps*) Alexandra, I've come to the end of my rope. Somewhere there has to be what I want, too. Life goes too fast. Do what you want; think what you want; go where you want. I'd like to keep you with me, but I won't make you stay. Too many people used to make me do too many things. No, I won't make you stay.

ALEXANDRA: You couldn't, Mama, because I want to leave here. As I've never wanted anything in my life before. Because now I understand what Papa was trying to tell me. All in one day: Addie said there were people who ate the earth and other people who stood around and watched them do it. And just now Uncle Ben said the same thing. Really, he said the same thing. (*Tensely*) Well, tell him for me, Mama, I'm not going to stand around and watch you do it. I'll be fighting as hard as he'll be fighting (*Rises*) someplace else.

REGINA: Well, you have spirit, after all. I used to think you were all sugar water. We don't have to be bad friends. I don't want us to be bad friends, Alexandra. (*Starts, stops, turns to* ALEXANDRA) Would you like to come and talk to me, Alexandra? Would you—would you like to sleep in my room tonight?

ALEXANDRA: (*Takes a step toward the stairs*) Are you afraid, Mama? (REGINA *does not answer. She moves up the stairs and out of sight.* ADDIE, *smiling, begins to put out the lamps.*)

CURTAIN

IT'S MORNING

A One-Act Play

SHIRLEY GRAHAM

This version first presented in 1940

FOREWORD

Playwright, composer, musician, teacher, director, biographer, novelist, administrator and international civil rights activist, Shirley Graham lived a truly extraordinary life. The farm on which she was born Lola Bell Graham on November 11, 1896, belonged to her grandfather, a former slave whose home had been part of the underground railroad. Her father was an African Methodist Episcopal minister, and according to Graham scholar Kathy A. Perkins, it was in her father's churches that she "learned to play the piano and pipe organ, sing spirituals and conduct a choir." After graduating from high school in Spokane, Washington, Graham attended business college and obtained a secretarial job. She supplemented her income, Perkins adds, by "playing the pipe organ and singing backstage in a movie house between the changing of movie reels" as well as by giving piano lessons. Graham went on to study in Paris, where she began learning about African music from both Africans she met there and from her brother Lorenz, who—like her father—was working in Liberia. She continued her studies at Howard University while serving as the school's music librarian.

Determined to get a broader educational background to help her support herself and two sons from a brief early marriage, Graham enrolled at Oberlin College in the fall of 1931 as a sophomore. Shortly thereafter Rowena and Russell Jelliffe, founders of the Karamu Playhouse in Cleveland, encouraged Graham to rewrite her short play *Tom-Tom* into an opera. One of the very first all-Black operas professionally produced in this country, as well as the first produced opera by an African American woman, *Tom-Tom: An Epic of Music and the Negro* was presented for two performances at Cleveland's Municipal Stadium in the summer of 1932. The first performance was attended by more than 10,000 people and the second by some 15,000, reportedly including Ohio's governor. Excerpts from *Tom-Tom* were also aired on NBC radio.

Massive in scope, the music drawing on the African rhythms with which Graham had become familiar, *Tom-Tom* covers the history of Blacks who were enslaved in this country. It begins in Africa, where the characters are kidnapped and sold to slave traders. Act II finds them on a plantation during the Civil War: the Voodoo Man of the first act continues to pray to African gods, while others have embraced Christianity and the hope of salvation it offers. Tensions are high and the Voodoo Man kills the overseer just before word rings out that slavery has been abolished. By Act III, the former slaves have moved North to the "Harlem of today." The Voodoo Man exhorts his people to go back to Africa, but his plans are sabotaged by the Real Estate Man and others who try to make a quick dollar from the people's dreams of returning to their homeland. After the Voodoo Man is fatally stabbed, the Boy takes over as leader, vowing to continue the sound of the tom-tom—the heritage of African culture—in the United States.

Shirley Graham graduated from Oberlin in 1935 with a Master's degree in Music History and Fine Arts; her M.A. thesis was entitled "The Survival of Africanism in Modern Music." After a brief stint as head of the Fine Arts Department at Tennessee A & I State College, she joined the Federal Theatre Project as the new director of the Chicago Negro Unit. During her years with the Unit (1936-1938) her work included—in addition to her administrative responsibilities—a very popular production of Charlotte Chorpenning's *Little Black Sambo*, which Graham turned into a musical with African rhythms, directed and helped design, and an equally successful *Swing Mikado*, based on the Gilbert and Sullivan original but with an African beat.

Graham was also chosen to attend the Federal Summer Theater at Vassar College, a gathering of forty stage professionals from around the U.S., where she learned more about acting technique and backstage work. One of two African American members in the group, and the only one on campus full-time, Graham felt she "had to study for, think for and speak for fourteen million brown

Americans." In an essay in *Arts Quarterly*, she encouraged people of color to study theater and castigated her colleagues for having "complacently accepted the white man's standard of what a Negro ought to be on the stage."

According to Hallie Flanagan, head of the Federal Theatre Project, Graham returned to Chicago to initiate "classes in acting, movement and speech." Her work was so outstanding that it earned her a Julius Rosenwald Fellowship in creative writing at Yale University, where between 1938 and 1940 she wrote or revised four plays: *Dust to Earth, I Gotta Home, It's Morning,* and *Track Thirteen.* *Dust to Earth,* a tragedy about coal miners in West Virginia, was first performed in 1930 at Morgan College under the title *Coal Dust.* After Graham revised the play, it was presented at the Yale University Theatre in 1941. *Dust to Earth* is weak on plot but offers telling insights into class and race relations. Black and White miners work and live side by side; tensions exist and children sometimes call each other "dago" and "nigger" but, as one Irish worker puts it, "If lights be out all cats be gray. Coal dust makes us all look alike." Clearer barriers follow class lines, dividing the miners and their families from Clayton, who owns the mine while leaving its operation to dishonest foremen, and his daughter Leslie, a well-meaning liberal whose entrapment in a tunnel helps bring the play to a fiery conclusion. Graham also shows, however, the connections between race and class: the mulatto miner Brick, the drama's hero, hates his light color because it reminds him of his mother's rape by Clayton, whose wealth and White skin allow him to take whatever he wants with impunity.

I Gotta Home (ca. 1939), a full-length comedy, is a revision of *Elijah's Ravens* (ca. 1930); in subsequent years Graham apparently reverted to the original title for the work. Like Ruth Gaines-Shelton's *The Church Fight* (1925) and Eulalie Spence's *Fool's Errand* (1927), *I Gotta Home* is a comedy about Church politics, a popular subject for African American women playwrights and one with which Graham, daughter of a minister, was certainly familiar. Most of the characters are stock figures: the well-meaning reverend afraid of losing his post because of declining church contributions; the hypocritical church elder, who woos the reverend's sister because he mistakenly believes she's an heiress; the reverend's mischievous children; and the snobbish church women, "Daughters of the New Revolution," who bring shabby used furniture as their contributions to the parsonage. Nevertheless, Graham addresses such serious issues as prejudice toward and among the African American community (dark-skinned Mattie notes that "a lady of my complexion does run into complications" trying to get a hotel room, while "high yellows" have fewer problems). All ends fortuitously when an unknown long-shot on whom the family's hopes rest, a black horse symbolically named "Raven," finishes third but still in the money behind "Lone Star" and "Empire" in an Irish Sweepstakes race.

There are at least five extant scripts of *It's Morning* (1939-40), variations of two basic texts, indicating that Graham did a substantial amount of revision on this brief tragedy. *It's Morning* was first presented—perhaps in a staged reading—by the "Drama 140" class at Yale in March of 1939 along with three other short plays. A more formal production of the four works was mounted at the Yale University Theatre the following February 5-7; Frederick Coe directed *It's Morning* while Otto Preminger supervised the entire program. Graham, however, was wary of the project. In a letter written in late December 1939, she told W.E.B. Du Bois: "They are doing a one-act play of mine here at Yale in February. Honestly, I wish they wouldn't. It was written for a Negro cast. It is highly emotional and has an impressive dignity which I do not believe these young students can achieve."

In *Black Female Playwrights: An Anthology of Plays before 1950*, Kathy A. Perkins observes that "The central focus in these women's plays was usually on the children." With its strong sense of fatality, *It's Morning* resembles many other short plays about Black mothers confronting a child's loss, including Georgia Douglas Johnson's *Plumes* (1927) and *A Sunday Morning in the South* (ca. 1925). Often, however, the most difficult questions mothers face concern not simple survival but the *kinds* of lives their children can lead in a racist culture. Angelina Weld Grimké's title character in *Rachel* (1916) refuses marriage and motherhood because she will not offer up more African American children to lynch mobs. Johnson's *Safe* (1929) shows a young Black mother giving birth to a son while a lynch mob murders a neighbor boy. Rather than allow the baby to grow up in such a world, the anguished mother strangles him. *It's Morning* has ties to both plays and also looks forward to Toni Morrison's novel *Beloved*, where another mother must make the terrible choice between killing her child and seeing her brought up in slavery. As Patricia R. Schroeder notes in her forthcoming book on the feminist uses of realism,

African American women feared fates worth than death for those they loved most.

The closest predecessor to *It's Morning* is Graham's own opera *Tom-Tom*. On one of the scripts of *It's Morning* she designates the work "a poetic play" and the dialogue, although irregular in meter, is written as verse—just as it is for most of *Tom-Tom*. Graham wished to indicate that the characters' speech retains a distinct rhythm and cadence that is a legacy of their African language; interestingly, in the third act of *Tom-Tom*—set in modern-day Harlem—the dialogue is partly written in prose, suggesting that African Americans have begun to forget their native tongues. The slave "chorus" in *It's Morning* is also reminiscent of the more formal operatic chorus in *Tom-Tom*, and traditional songs and spirituals—sometimes the very same ones—appear in both the opera and the play. Elizabeth Brown-Guillory in *Wines in the Wilderness: Plays by African American Women from the Harlem Renaissance to the Present* calls *Morning* "a major breakthrough in African American drama." She adds that "Graham's interest in African music and culture is apparent in the structural make up of this tightly compressed one-act play...[which] combines dialogue, music, singing, dancing, and chanting while maintaining the traditional Aristotelian structure." Graham skillfully uses music and dance to build dramatic tension: the party becomes a macabre wake, its celebration of Millie's vitality a painful counterpoint to the impending tragedy. The party also becomes a metaphor for Cissie's frantic plight; her own dancing is reminiscent of Nora's desperate tarantella in Henrik Ibsen's *A Doll's House*.

The notion of a mother killing her child, or allowing her child to be sacrificed, also appears in *Tom-Tom*—in two distinct ways. In Act I, Girl is chosen as a ritual sacrifice to appease the African gods and particularly to protect the community from the slave traders. Her mother is initially aghast but comes to see her daughter as "sacred" and helps prepare her for the ritual killing, which is aborted when Bantu slave hunters attack. Act II of *Tom-Tom*, like *It's Morning*, takes place on a plantation during the Civil War. In both works, the mother learns that her daughter has been sold down the river, and in both she sharpens a knife in preparation for killing the child. The mother in both plays is willing to risk her own damnation to save her daughter.

Where *It's Morning* differs from *Tom-Tom* is in its close focus on what slavery means to women. Cissie was once a beautiful "young colt" who pranced and laughed, until the overseer broke her will—presumably by raping her. Now she sees the same fate about to befall her daughter, sold to a slave trader who looks at Millie as if she were "fresh, young meat." Grannie's story of the proud African mother who beheaded her sons rather than have them sold away from her puts Cissie's action in the context of enslaved women before her, and suggests that she acts from strength rather than weakness. Slavery not only rips apart families but forces mothers to watch daughters suffer the same torture they themselves went through. Cissie believes a swift death is the only escape for Millie.

The brief appearance of the plantation's mistress, Mrs. Tilden, serves little function except to underline the point that the villain is the system of slavery rather than this individual woman, who can do little to oppose the slave merchant. Still, Cissie neither believes the mistress' promise that she will buy back Millie nor accepts her comfort and apologies. (In one version of *It's Morning*, Mrs. Tilden parallels her loss of her son Charles in battle to Cissie's impending loss of Millie, but Cissie points out the crucial difference: Mrs. Tilden's son was free. Cissie adds, "If mah gal could die free-/ Ah would be glad.")

Because it mixes African tradition with Christian elements, *It's Morning* (the title a pun on "mourning") allows us to see the sacrifice of Millie as both a parallel to Christ's sacrifice and an echo of the African ritual in *Tom-Tom*. Millie then becomes both Christ and Girl, the innocent sacrificed to free the community. Critics have suggested that the heavily ironic ending is Cissie's punishment for failing to believe, as Uncle Dave does, in the power of prayer. But "freedom" is a relative term: Emancipation did not free African American women from White men's lust, as Graham surely knew.

Track Thirteen (1940), a comedy about train porters, was produced by Yale over WICC Radio and published in *Yale Radio Plays: The Listener's Theatre*. A mystery-farce centering on a train porter's efforts to appease his demanding passengers while attempting to catch a notorious bank robber, this was the only play of Graham's published during her lifetime. According to Perkins, during her Yale years Graham "frequently" expressed a desire to have a work on Broadway; in one 1940 letter to W.E.B. Du Bois, she writes "everyone expects me to have a play on Broadway soon.... Gradually, I believe I can break through the barriers." Although she persisted for a few years more, she was never to achieve her dream. As late as 1945 she was reworking *Elijah's*

Ravens, which she sent to various producing organizations, including the Theatre Guild. She asked her friend Carl Van Vechten to see if he could help her find a producer, but to no avail.

Like most women playwrights of the period, Graham eventually gave up the stage; perhaps in part because of frustration with the "barriers" she mentions in her letter to Du Bois, she turned to writing books and to social activism. When she protested racism against Black soldiers while director of a Y.W.C.A.-U.S.O. camp at Fort Huachuca in Arizona, she was fired. Her commitment to social justice was further intensified by the death of her older son, who became seriously ill during army basic training and was denied admission to several New York City hospitals. During her later years she was a field secretary for the NAACP, a founding editor of *Freedomways* magazine, and the author of some dozen fictionalized biographies, primarily aimed at young readers, of such famous Africans and Americans of color as Julius K. Nyerere, first president of Tanzania; performer and activist Paul Robeson; poet Phillis Wheatley; and Pocahontas. *There Was Once a Slave: The Heroic Story of Frederick Douglass* won Graham a Julian Messner Award for "the best book combatting intolerance in America." Informative, engaging and upbeat, the biographies stress the subjects' triumphs rather than the disappointments they faced.

Graham's one novel, *Zulu Heart* (1974), is set in South Africa and concerns an Afrikaans doctor named Kirk whose life is saved by a heart transplant; the donor is a Zulu. The doctor begins to dream about the White slaughter of African natives, then to feel guilty about owning mines in which Blacks work for minimal wages under appalling conditions. Kirk gradually becomes a participant in the struggle for African rights, dying in an attempt to rescue political prisoners. He wills his stock in the mines to aid "his" Zulu people and leaves behind a White daughter and a mixed race son, a future "Freedom Fighter like his father" who may live to see the new South Africa that Kirk envisioned.

In 1951 Shirley Graham married her long-time friend and mentor W.E.B. Du Bois, a civil rights leader, scholar, author and founder of the NAACP. Together they were active in the causes of Pan-Africanism and world peace and she helped him successfully defend himself when he was indicted by the United States government for refusing to register as an "agent of a foreign principal." (Such indictments, like the House Un-American Activities Committee hearings, were used during this period to harass those with liberal political views.) They moved in 1961 to Ghana, where Du Bois died two years later. Graham remained there—primarily working to organize Ghana Television—until a military coup forced her out and she settled in Cairo. When she attempted to visit the U.S. Graham was at first denied entry because she had been associated with numerous organizations on the Attorney General's list of supposedly "subversive" groups, but she was eventually granted permission. In 1970 she was honored at a banquet sponsored by the journal *The Black Scholar* followed by a speaking tour of California colleges; this was only one of many accolades—including a Guggenheim Fellowship and an award from the National Institute of Arts and Letters—she received. Shortly afterward she published *His Day is Marching On: A Memoir of W.E.B. Du Bois*, her account of their life together.

During her last years Graham served as English editor of the Afro-Asian Writers Bureau in Beijing, China. According to Leo Hamalian and James V. Hatch, editors of *The Roots of African American Drama*, Graham "was writing a book about the women of China under Mao" when she died March 27, 1977, in Beijing. She had stopped writing plays more than thirty years earlier, but the same passion that sparked dramas like *Tom-Tom* and *It's Morning* informed her other work as well. Her dramas were a part of her life-long commitment to celebrating African and African American culture and building bridges among different peoples. When racism and sexism made her dream of a Broadway play unreachable a half-century ago, she responded by making the world her stage.

SELECTED BIBLIOGRAPHY

Brown-Guillory, Elizabeth, ed. *Wines in the Wilderness: Plays by African American Women from the Harlem Renaissance to the Present.* N.Y.: Praeger, 1990.

"Conversation: Ida Lewis & Shirley Graham Du Bois." *Essence* 1 (January 1971): 21-7.

Graham, Shirley. *I Gotta Home.* In Perkins, *Black Female Playwrights.*

—————. *His Day Is Marching On: A Memoir of W.E.B. Du Bois.* Philadelphia: Lippincott, 1971.

————. *There Was Once a Slave: The Heroic Story of Frederick Douglass.* N.Y.: Messner, 1947.

————. "Tom-Tom." In *The Roots of African American Drama*, ed. Hamalian and Hatch.

————. "Towards an American Theatre." *Arts Quarterly* (October-December 1937): 18-20.

————. *Track Thirteen.* In *Yale Radio Plays: The Listener's Theatre*, ed. Constance Welch and Walter Prichard Easton. Boston: Expression, 1940.

————. *Zulu Heart: A Novel.* N.Y.: Third Press, 1974.

Hamalian, Leo and James V. Hatch, eds. *The Roots of African American Drama: An Anthology of Early Plays, 1858-1938.* Detroit: Wayne State UP, 1991.

Perkins, Kathy A., ed. *Black Female Playwrights: An Anthology of Plays before 1950.* Bloomington: Indiana UP, 1989.

————. "Shirley Graham." *Afro-American Writers, 1940-1955*, ed. Trudier Harris. *Dictionary of Literary Biography.* Vol. 76. Detroit: Gale Press, 1988.

————. "The Unknown Career of Shirley Graham." *Freedomways* 25, 1 (1985): 6-17.

245

A NOTE ON THE TEXT

There are at least five extant scripts of *It's Morning*, variations of two basic texts. The version printed here was used for the 1940 production at Yale University; Yale's script is bound with photographs, groundplans, etc., as well as with texts of the three other plays on the bill.

While the overall plot remains constant in the five scripts, the other variation of *It's Morning*—which I believe is an earlier draft, the basis of the 1939 performance—is divided into two scenes rather than one. Mrs. Tilden does not appear (although the story of Millie's sale is virtually identical) and Cissie has a young son named Pete who is to be sold along with his sister. Since the party is not shown, music and dance play a smaller role in the two-scene version. This version is reprinted in Kathy A. Perkins, *Black Female Playwrights: An Anthology of Plays before 1950.*

In a note attached to one script, Graham comments that the play's dialect is "not uniform" because "many African languages express different meanings by changes in pitch" and volume. According to the playwright, some African Americans "indicate slight changes in meaning by changing vowel sounds" and "the old type of Negro preachers used a biblical mode of expression which cannot be expressed in dialect." Graham adds that the songs in the play include traditional spirituals as well as original music. In his "Introduction" to *The Roots of African American Drama*, James V. Hatch observes that "most African languages, like the French, did not employ the voiced or unvoiced *th* phoneme in English." The dialect in *It's Morning* reflects this fact, a "d" often substituting for "th."

246

CHARACTERS

CISSIE	A slave woman
MILLIE	Her fourteen-year-old daughter
GRANNIE LOU	The oldest slave on the plantation, considered a little crazy
CRIPPLE JAKE	Slave man
ROSE	Slave woman
PHOEBE	Slave woman
AUNT SUE	Slave woman
SALLY	Young slave
PETE	Young slave
SAM	Young slave
FESS	A field-hand, the one able-bodied man on the plantation
MRS. TILDEN	The lonely mistress of the plantation
UNCLE DAVE	The old plantation preacher
SOLDIER	A white soldier
SEVERAL OTHER SLAVES	

PLACE: *A Plantation in the Deep South*

TIME: *The night of December 31st, 1862*

Scene: Interior of CISSIE's *cabin. Before the curtain lifts may be heard music and laughter. When the curtain rises a party in full swing is discovered. It is nearly midnight and the dancing of the young people to* CRIPPLE JAKE's *banjo gives over to the joy of the moment. The bare unplastered room has been decorated with Spanish moss and bunches of holly stuck among the thick greens. In the fireplace down right burn heaps of pine cones. Around the hearth are pots and pans, evidence of much cooking. Drawn close to the fire, as if to warm her shrunken frame, crouches* GRANNIE, *her black, wrinkled face screwed up as she watches the dancers. Between her lips is stuck an old corncob pipe.* PHOEBE *and* ROSE *are in the background talking together. The door center is pushed back on its loose hinges and through this opening as well as through the frameless window may be seen the glow of a bonfire in the yard. Otherwise, it is very dark outside. Above this door hang sprays of mistletoe, the tiny white flowers drooping heavily on wilted stems. Another door or opening up left leads to the other room. On the mantle above the fireplace is a lighted lantern. On a table down right are piled heavy, rude dishes.*

There are shouts of laughter. In the center doorway appears CISSIE. *Her gaunt, black figure seems to fill the frame and even though she claps her hands and her words are joyous there is something strangely harsh about her voice.*

CISSIE: Now den, everybody! Common! Da eats is ready!
    (*Shouts of delight as the dancers stop. Only* MILLIE, *who has been doing a solo dance, continues the rhythm as* JAKE *plays a last chord.*)
SAM: Barbacue! Um-um—Ah can' smell hit!
PETE: Mah mouf am waterin' down!
SALLY: Hurry, 'fore dat smell blow cross da creek an' da soldiers—
PETE: Ain't no soldier gonna git dis ham hock!
SAM: No—suh! Ah'd butt 'im so hard he done t'ink a cannon ball hit 'im!
    (*Laughter*)
MILLIE: (*Still poised to dance*) Jus' one mo' chune, Jake—Jus' one mo' chune!
JAKE: Chile, don' yo' nevah tiya?
CISSIE: (*Who has crossed to hearth*) Sho she do! Hyear, we gotta take

des tings in da ya'd. Ah got conepone dat'll melt 'fore yo' eyes.

JAKE: (*Putting his banjo under his arm*) Lead me to hit!

SALLY: (*In doorway*) Beat yo' to da pit!

(*At this moment* PETE *grabs her and sets a resounding smack full on her lips.*)

PETE: (*Shouts*) Gotcha under da mistletoe!
Oh, yo' Sally!
Ha! Ha!
(*They troop out.*)

BOY: Come long, Jake. Can' eat widout music!

JAKE: (*Hobbling along, banjo under his arm*) Dis sho is some New Year's pahty, Cissie. Sho tis!

MILLIE: (*Gayly*) Hit's *mah* pahty—ain't hit, mammy?

CISSIE: Dat's right. Now, take dis pan o' pone. Dey's gettin' cold.
(*Hands her a pan*)

AUNT SUE: (*Bustling over to table*) Ah'll take da plates.

MILLIE: (*Posing in doorway—her golden brown body half revealed by the thin dress*) Look Sam! Ah'm under da mistletoe!

SAM: Glory be!
(*He dashes towards her only to find his arm caught in the iron clasp of a forbidding* CISSIE.)

CISSIE: No! (*Quietly to* MILLIE) Go long, Millie gal.
(MILLIE *gives her mother a troubled look and disappears.* AUNT SUE, *glancing over her shoulder at* CISSIE, *follows her.*)

CISSIE: (*Savagely*) Don' yo touch mah gal!

SAM: (*Frightened*) No—mam!
(CISSIE *loosens her grasp and he hurries out.*)

ROSE: Sam didn't mean no hahm. Hit's da *pahty*!

GRANNIE: (*Mouthing her words*) Da jack don' call in da moonlight,
An' da young gal's love come down.

CISSIE: Millie don' know nothin' bout—love! (*She goes out with pan*)

PHOEBE: Huh Millie's lak a flower,
She watch huh day an' night.
(*Voices from outside*)

PETE: Cripple Jake's gonna play!

SALLY: An' Millie'll sing!

SEVERAL: Common, Millie's gonna sing!

MILLIE: Ready, Cripple Jake, let's go!
(*singing*)
Oh! Walk togeddar, chillun

(*Group*)
  Don' yo' get weary,
Walk togeddar, chillun,
  Don' yo' get weary,
Walk togeddar, chillun,
  Don' yo get weary,
Dar's a great camp meetin' in da promise lan'.

GRANNIE: (*Shaking her head*)   MILLIE: (*Singing alone*)
  Cissie uster sing lak dat—   Gonna sing an' nevah tiya
  Jes' lak huh gal.   Sing an' nevah tiya
                                          Sing an' nevah tiya— (*All*)
WOMEN: (*Astonished*) Cissie!   Dar's a great camp meetin'
  Sing?   in da promise lan'.

GRANNIE: Yes, Cissie! She war beautiful!
  Black as a berry an' lovely as da night,
  Slender an' swift as a young colt—
  She nevah walk, jes' prance an' run about da place.
  Ah seen da buckra eyein' huh—an' she jes' laf.
  Den come a day when she war very still,
  Ah donno why, till one night seen huh slippin'
      trough shadows lak a hounded coon
  Crawls tuh his hole to lick his bleedin' wounds.
ROSE: Ah heared dat she war proud, an' dat da
  ovahseer swear he break huh will.
GRANNIE: (*Bitterly*) He did—An' when he'd come along da row
  she tremble lak a leaf, an' once she fall
  down cryin' at his feet…. he laf, an' kick
  huh wid his foot, not hard, but lak you kick
  a bitch what's big wid puppy, out o' yo' path.
AUNT SUE: (*Entering from yard bearing platter of food*) Cissie say
  bring our eats inside. Let da chillun play.
ROSE: Ain't she commin?
AUNT SUE: Yes, but she say don' wait.
  (AUNT SUE *is followed by* FESS, *a good-looking slave who is carry-
  ing something in his hand and biting at it.*)
FESS: (*Speaking between bites*) Um-um-um! Us ain't had no eatin'
  laka dis since da stars fall! Mah insides is plume scared.
PHOEBE: Whar Cissie get all des vittualls? How come?
AUNT SUE: (*Comfortably*) Hit's New Year's Eve, ain't hit?
ROSE: Yes—but us ain't had no pahties since Massa Frank went

off to war.

PHOEBE: Sho ain't. What wid ole missie up dar all alone—sittin' lookin' at po' young massa Charles picture—an' turnin' white every time da post come—us ain't had no time fur pahties!

AUNT SUE: Well, Cissie say dat—

PHOEBE: Sh-sh-sh-sh!

(CISSIE *is in the doorway. She is walking very slowly—the life gone out of her movements.*)

AUNT SUE: Cissie—yo' plume tuck out! Com' sit down.

(CISSIE *comes slowly towards the fire.*)

FESS: Dis is gran' eatin'!

PHOEBE: Yo' said someum!...But, Cissie, whar yo' git all dis? Ah ain't seen so much—

FESS: (*Proudly*) Ah gits da meat.

ROSE: (*Anxiously*) Yo' bes' stay outta dem dar woods, Fess. Iffen any dem soldiers cotch yo'—

AUNT SUE: Yes—how we ebbar git da wo'k done. Yo' da only man on da place.

FESS: (*Shaking his head*) Crops failin' anyhow. Massa Charles say—but—tain't no use. Well, long as Ah can hunt we uns won't starve.

ROSE: Da soldiers take yo' off to war.

FESS: Ah ain't scared!

PHOEBE: Dey make yo' fight.

FESS: Maybe dey takes me—maybe dey don'.

(*He draws a long, sharp knife from his side.*)

Ah kin fight—when Ah wan's to.

(CISSIE *is staring at the knife.*)

CISSIE: Hit's sharp.

FESS: (*Boasting*) So sharp dat Ah could draw hit right cross yo' troat—an' you'd not know.

ROSE: Yo' means... ?

FESS: Until yo' saw yo' head come fallin' down! Ha! Ha! Ha!

GRANNIE: (*Joining him*) He! He! He!

(*Their laughter is cut short by a voice coming from the doorway.*)

MRS. TILDEN: Cissie!

(*It is the mistress of the plantation. Four long years have aged her. She has a wrap thrown over a thin dress. She looks at the group with troubled eyes.*)

AUNT SUE: Missie!

FESS: (*Jumping up*) Yo' wan' something, missie?

GRANNIE: (*Severely*) How come yo' runnin' round lak dis at night? You'll cotch yo' death o' cole!

MRS. TILDEN: I—couldn't sleep—I heared music—Cissie, I was sure I heard—Millie—singing—

(CISSIE *turns away*.)

ROSE: We's jus' havin' a lil' New Year pahty, missie.

MRS. TILDEN: A party!

AUNT SUE: Yassum—Fess here wen' huntin' today an' Cissie—

MRS. TILDEN: (*Turning to her*) Cissie—

(*Outside there is a burst of laughter and the banjo sounds again*.)

GRANNIE: Come to da fiah, an' warm yo'self.

MRS. TILDEN: (*Walks slowly to the window and looks out*) They're dancing—Millie's—dancing!

AUNT SUE: Yessum—dat chile sho is a caution!

MRS. TILDEN: (*Slowly*) Cissie, do they know?

CISSIE: (*Very low*) No—missie.

MRS. TILDEN: Oh—Cissie! But—I don't understand—you—a party—They're dancing and singing.

CISSIE: Yassum—dancin' an' singin'—so Millie'll be happy—*one time mo'*.

(*The others look from one to the other not understanding*.)

MRS. TILDEN: (*Sinking into a chair*) Oh, dear God, have mercy on us!

ROSE: (*Alarmed*) Missie, what is it?

AUNT SUE: What's da mattah, missie? Tell us!

MRS. TILDEN: (*After a pause*) Millie's going away—She's going away early in the morning.

WOMEN: Away!

MRS. TILDEN: They're coming for her at daybreak.

FESS: (*Slowly*) Yo' sole—huh?

MRS. TILDEN: I had to. The war's beat us down—our cotton's worthless—there's nothing else.

FESS: (*Softly*) Yo' sole huh to dat man—he'll take huh down da ribbah!

(*A shudder passes over the group. Only* CISSIE *sits like stone*.)

MRS. TILDEN: I'm an old woman—My heart is breaking with your pain—but I'm helpless. Oh! if this war would only end—if our men would only come back—they don't know what it's doing to us—they don't know.

ROSE: No—dey don' know.

MRS. TILDEN: It must end soon.... There's nothing to go on.... Cissie, I'll buy her back—I promise, as God is my judge— we'll get her back.

CISSIE: (*Dully*) Yes, missie.

MRS. TILDEN: (*Getting up*) I—must go now. I—
(*She stops, realizing there's nothing more to say.*)

FESS: (*Taking lantern from mantle*) Ah'll light yo' to da house.
(CISSIE *does not lift her head.* MRS. TILDEN *lays her hand on* CISSIE'*s shoulder and says softly*)

MRS. TILDEN: I'm glad she's happy—tonight—Cissie.
(*She turns quickly and goes out, followed by* FESS. *Only the fire now lights the room. The pause is filled by voices outside.*)

MILLIE: Hav' anodder pone—we dassent leave a scrap.

SALLY: (*Regretfully*) Ah can' eat no mo'.

PETE: Give hit tuh me!

SAM: Boy, yo' gonna fall in da creek an' float!
(*Laughter*)

AUNT SUE: Ah knows now why ole missie cry all day—
Dat man give huh no peace,
He say he will hab Millie gal,
Else tu'n us out tuh starve—
An' missie, too.

PHOEBE: He'd do hit, kase he's cruel an' hard,
He's lak a beast what's scented fresh, young meat,
He's ole—he'll suck huh blood lak damp swamp ting.
(*She shudders.*)

AUNT SUE: His jowls hang down lak empty 'tatah sacks,
An' bacca juice falls drippin' f'om his mouth,
Leavin' a trail o' slime whar he has passed.
(CISSIE *has sat motionless while the others talked. Now, she drops her hand from her face. Her eyes stare straight ahead. She speaks as if from a distance, with difficulty, still looking with horror upon a picture etched on her brain.*)

CISSIE: Ah seed him lick his lips an' smile an' grin,
Ole missie beg him wait till cotton bust,
An' promise him da best bales in da lot.
He say he wait no mo'.... He wan' da gal.
Ah seed his hans'...dey touch huh golden breas',
She war so scared, she couldn't run...
An' den she scream...an' missie tell huh go.
Ah heared him laf...an' spit upon da floah!

PHOEBE: (*rocking her body*) Mussy Jesus! He'p us, Lawd!
(*The prayer is interrupted by* GRANNIE *dropping a spoon on the hearth with a loud clatter. The women give a start.* GRANNIE

breaks into high-pitched, crazy laughter.)
GRANNIE: He! He! He! Ha! Ha!
PHOEBE: Make huh stop! Oh!
ROSE: What's da mattah, grannie,
    Why yo' all laf?
GRANNIE: (*Mocking*) Mussy Jesus! Mussy Jesus!
    (*She snickers while the women gasp.*)
    She don' hab tuh go, Ah tells yo',
    She don' hab tuh go!
AUNT SUE: Let huh talk!
    We allus calls huh crazy, but who knows,
    Maybe da Voodoo wo'k dat way, maybe she
    bile up sompin' dat kin help.
    (*Gently to the old woman*)
    What is it, grannie, what we kin do?
    Might Millie run away?
GRANNIE: (*In a high sing-song voice*)
    Da ribbah's high, da rains dat fall las' week,
    Mak all da ma'shes tick wid mud an' deep.
AUNT SUE: Den what?...Why yo' all laf?
    Hit's Cissie's gal been sole.
PHOEBE: Aw, auntie, why yo' asking' po' ole Lou?
GRANNIE:(*Sharply*) Shut yo' mouf!
    Ah ain't so ole dat Ah don' membah!
    (*Turning to others*)
    Ain't Ah nebbah tole yo' bout dat 'oman
    long time gone? Dey say she straight from jungles
    in da far off Af'ica.... She nevah say.
    Dat war a 'oman—straight lak tree, an' tall,
    Swift as a lion an' strong as any ox.
    Da sugah can wen' down fo' huh big knife,
    Lak cotton stalks under da fierces' gale.
    No mahn could walk wid huh.... An' sing!
    She ustah sing out in da fields....
    Da niggahs wo'k dem days...when Ah war young.
    (*Her voice dies away in a mumble of reminiscences. She turns back
    to her pots, forgetting her audience, lost in the memories of her
    youth.* CISSIE *has been staring at her, but she now drops her head
    again, hopelessly.*)
PHOEBE: Humph!
    Ah tought yo' gonna tell us sompin' we

kin do to help po' Cissie an' huh gal,
An' all yo' all comes talkin' bout is some
cane-choppin' heathen what kin sing!
Gwan!...Anybody kin sing!

GRANNIE: (*Angrily*)
Ain't Ah tol' yo' shut yo' fat mouf, you?
Dat 'oman dar do mo' den sing! Lissen—
She hab tree sons, dey black an' tall lak she,
An' one day news come dat dey sole des sons down
ribbah.... Dey bring good price.
She say dey nebbah go....Da white folk laf,
but niggahs dassent laf...dey see huh face.
She don' say no'tin' mo, but go away,
An' early in da mawnin' call she boys,
An' when dey come, she tell 'em tuh stan' close,
An' watch da sun come up out ob da hill.
Dey sort ob smile at huh an' look,
An' den dat 'oman lift huh big cane knife,
She cry out sompin' in a wild, strange voice,
An' wid one sweep she cut off all dey heads—
Dey roll down at she feet.... All tree ob dem!
(*The women gasp, but* CISSIE *is staring fixedly at the long knife which* FESS *has tossed on the table. Outside* MILLIE *is again singing. Slowly* CISSIE'*s hand approaches the knife.*)

AUNT SUE: No—Cissie!	MILLIE: Oh! see dat sun, See how he run, Don' yo' ebbah let 'im catch yo' Wid yo' wo'k undone.
ROSE: (*Laying her hand on* CISSIE'*s arm*) Cissie!	ALL: Oh! see dat sun, see how he run, Don' yo' ebbah let 'im catch yo' Wid yo' wo'k undone,
PHOEBE: Oh, Jesus!	Oh! I'm gonna shine Lawd, Ah'm a gonna shine.

GRANNIE: (*Leaning towards* CISSIE) She—don'—hab—tuh—go!
CISSIE: (*Her fingers closing about the knife*) No—she don't hab to go.
AUNT SUE: (*Pleading*) Missie say she buy huh back!
CISSIE: Buy huh back? When?...Ah'll tell yo'....
Aftah huh song is dead...when she can' dance no—mo'.
(*She looks at the knife—catching its glint in the firelight.*)
Dis she'll nevah know—Hit's sharp!

(*Putting the knife inside her dress she springs up and rushes to the door calling loudly.*)
Yo'all out dar—da night's mos' gone—jus' time fur one mo' dance!

VOICES: Some pahty!
One mo' dance!
Mah feet jus' won' lay down, nohow!

CISSIE: (*Outside now*) One mo' dance! Now Jake—beat hit down! Make hit a good one! (*The banjo starts.*) Louder! Faster! All togeddar now. Dance, Millie, dance! Everybody dance! Dat's hit! Dance! One mo' dance 'fore yo' go—home! Dance!
(*Sound of clapping hands, furious dancing and loud music. The women watch from the window.*)

PHOEBE: Oh, God! She's crazy!

ROSE: She's dancin', too!
(*The dance comes to an end with much laughter and noise.*)

CISSIE: Now, Millie gal, sing—sing a lil' song!

MILLIE: (*Out of breath*) Mammy! Yo' danced. Ah neva saw yo' dance before!

CISSIE: Come on, gal—sing! Yo'all gotta get some sleep! Look, da stars is goin' out—da moon am gone—mawnin's mos' here.

MILLIE: (*Singing gayly*)
Lil' king David playin' on his harp
(*Group*) Some boy! oh—Some boy!
Lil' king David playin' on his harp
Some boy! oh—Some boy!
Lil' king David playin' on his harp
Laffin' to hisself cause his skirt was so short
Lil' king David playin' on his harp
Some boy! oh—Some boy!

PHOEBE: Ah'll go git Uncle Dave. He'll stop huh.

(*She hurries out.*)

(*Singing continued*)
Ole Goliah comin' right along,
Some boy—oh—Some boy!
Ole Goliah comin' right along,
Some boy—oh—Some boy!
Ole Goliah comin' right along,
Laffin' at David an' his crazy lil' song,

ROSE: Dar's Fess. Ah'll tell 'im.   Ole Goliah comin' right along,
Some boy—oh—Some boy!

(*Exit.* AUNT SUE *begins straightening the room. The fire has died down.*
GRANNIE *is nodding in her corner.* AUNT SUE *shakes her.*)
AUNT SUE: Grannie, da pahty's—ovah. Bes' go to bed.
GRANNIE: (*Starting*) Eh?...eh?...Millie...?
AUNT SUE: N'mine, Grannie—git some sleep.
(*Tottering, the old woman pulls herself up and stumbles through
the doorway up left. She is mumbling to herself. Outside the song
has ended in a burst of final laughter.*)
VOICES: Good night!
Sho had a good time.
Bye, Millie.
T'anks, Cripple Jake.
(*Etc.*)
MILLIE: (*In doorway*) Oh! Mammy, Ah don' wanna sleep yet. Tha
air smells so good—and even da da'kness is sweet!
CISSIE: Yes, gal. Da night am sweet—but—da day am comin'.
Yo' gotta sleep now. Come take yo' rest.
MILLIE: (*Reluctantly as she crosses room*) Ah reckon Ah is sleepy!
'Night, everybody.
(CISSIE *follows her into other room.* MILLIE *is heard laughing
inside.* ROSE, FESS *and another woman have come in.*)
ROSE: (*Whispering*) She'll nebber do hit. She can't.
AUNT SUE: Ah see hit in huh face.
She gotta min' to.
ROSE: Yo' gotta stop huh, Fess, yo' gotta stop huh.
FESS: Ah donno...Ah donno what tuh do...
Sometimes when Ah kills wild tings in da woods—
Ah feels bad—Ah has to tell mahself 'bout all us hungry
Ah hates tuh do hit—But—Millie—
She ain't *free.*
AUNT SUE: But Cissie kain't....
FESS: (*Fiercely*) Why not? Po' Millie's dancin' days am gone. Cissie
know 'bout pain dat breaks an' keep on breakin' till dey ain't
nothin' left.... (*Sadly*) Ah donno. Right now, Ah'm all mixed
up.
CISSIE: (*In doorway of inner room*) Look out, Rose, see if hit's sun-

up, yet.
(*They hold their breath as* ROSE *looks out and says*)
ROSE: No, hit's still dark.
AUNT SUE: (*Fervently*) Tank yo', Jesus!
(CISSIE *comes down to the fire, and squatting on the floor draws the knife from her dress. She tests the blade. Her face has no expression.*)
FESS: (*Bending over her*) Cissie....
CISSIE: (*Dully*) Yo' sho hit's sharp?
FESS: Yes, Cissie, hit's sharp, but...
CISSIE: (*Softly*) She sing an' dance till she kain't dance
no mo'.... Till sleep pull hebby at huh lids,
An' she sink down wid belly full o' joy.
Happy will be huh dreams—huh long, long dreams.
(FESS *turns away. From the doorway* ROSE *speaks.*)
ROSE: Hyear come Uncle Dave!
(*In a moment an old man enters, walking slowly. He is followed by an anxious* PHOEBE. *His hair is white, forming a halo about a gentle, wrinkled face.*)
Howdy, Uncle Dave.
AUNT SUE: Praise da Lawd! Maybe she'll listen to yo', Uncle Dave.
UNCLE DAVE: Yes, chile,
Ah heared da han' ob God lay hebby on yo'.
Whar's Cissie?
(*They draw aside so that he can see* CISSIE *alone at the fire.*)
PHOEBE: (*Loudly*) Hit's all dat black Lou's fault.
VOICES: Sh-sh-sh-sh-sh-!
She'll hyear!
PHOEBE: (*Lower tone*) She put a spell on Cissie,
Shuttin' huh eyes an' stoppin'
up huh ears tuh evahting
dat we kin do an' say.
She gotta evil eye,
Dat's what she got!
UNCLE DAVE: Dar now, daughtah,
De Lawd takes care ob his own.
Us ain't got no cause tuh fret.
(*Several more slaves slip into the room. They have heard.*)
AUNT SUE: (*Shivering*) Shut da door, Fess. Da air's got cold an'
damp.
Talk to huh, Uncle Dave. We gotta stay wid huh.

(FESS closes the door. A wavering wail comes softly from the banjo. It hangs suspended in the air a moment and CRIPPLE JAKE speaks.)

JAKE: Ah'm tinkin' bout dis ting—
    Hebbin is a high an' a holy place,
    Dat gal ain't done no wrong,
    Dying will bring huh joy,
    Da good book say, "Lams
    in His bosom—safe."
    While Cissie know dat
    Livin's jes a slow decay
    Wid worms gnawin' lak nits
    Into huh heart an' soul.

1ST WOMAN: She'll be a murderess!

2ND WOMAN: She'll bu'n in hell!

JAKE: Yes, Cissie will be lonely—now,
    An' maybe fuh a t'ousand yeahs tuh come.
    (They turn at the unexpected sound of CISSIE's voice. It is low and vibrant.)

CISSIE: But, wen da saints ob God go marchin' home
    Mah gal will sing! Wid all da pure, bright stars,
    Togedder wid da mawnin' stars—She'll sing!
    (CISSIE's head is lifted and for one moment a strange beauty illumines her black, gaunt face. A soft chord sounds from the banjo, gentle as wings brushing across the strings.)

UNCLE DAVE: *(Sternly)* We be forgettin' God!
    Didn't he bring Daniel out ob da lion's den,
    An' de Hebrew chillun out da fiery furnace,
    Didn't He open up da Red Sea,
    An' save Jonah from da belly ob da whale?

WOMEN: Yes, mah Lawd!
    Save us, Jesus!
    (They begin to rock back and forth, singing softly.)

WOMAN: *(Humming accompaniment)*
    Ah wan' Jesus tuh walk wid me,
    Ah wan' Jesus tuh walk wid me,
    All along mah hebbenly journey
    Ah wan' Jesus tuh walk wid me.
    (The song sinks to a hum. UNCLE DAVE moves downstage to CISSIE. He places his hand on her shoulder She starts to rise, but when she sees who it is, sinks back. The light has faded from her face.)

UNCLE DAVE: Kain't yo' trus' de Lawd, daughtah?

Hit's wid Him. Yo' kain't stain yo' han's wid
da blood o' yo' own chile.

CISSIE: Ah tought da time is come. Dat man comin' fuh huh
at sun-up.

AUNT SUE: Oh! Lawd! Oh! Lawd!
Hit's mos' time.
(*Singers are humming.*)

UNCLE DAVE: (*Falling on knees*) Oh, Lawd! Our Lawd!
Sittin' on yo' great white throne,
Wid da stars a crown o' beauty
fur yo' haid,
An' de earth a mighty footstool
fur yo' feet,

Lean down ovah da ramparts of
Hebbin' dis mawnin',
An' see us 'umble sinners
kneeling hyear
We been prayin' so long,
We been singin' so...
(*Outside is heard the sound of a galloping horse. It draws rapidly nearer. There is the sound of pawing feet. The horse neighs, running footsteps and in a moment a loud knocking at the door.*)

VOICE: Open the door! Open the door!

CISSIE: Da man! He come!
(*CISSIE clutches the knife. The slaves watch her terrified. Two men spring forward to hold the door. PHOEBE cautiously pulls back the cloth which has been drawn over the window. She jerks back and speaks in a whisper. CISSIE does not hear her. She is intent on what she must do. FESS, standing near her, has his eyes only on CISSIE.*)

PHOEBE: Hit's a soldier!

VOICES: Soldiers?
(*The pounding on the door comes again. The slaves spring up, perplexed, crowd to the window. In that moment CISSIE slips out, noticed only by FESS who takes a step as if to stop her and then hesitates, covering his face with his hands. Just as she disappears the outer door gives way admitting a soldier in torn and dusty blue uniform. He is hardly more than a boy, his face pale with emotion. Behind him the day is breaking. He gazes around surprised at seeing the room filled.*)

SOLDIER: Up—already? You know?

(*There is disappointment in his voice, but the slaves only shrink back. His face breaks with smiles.*)

Don't be scared of me. You don't have to be scared of nobody no more. You're free!

(*They stare at him.*)

This is the day! Abe Lincoln said it. You're free! No more slaves!

FESS: (*Starting up*) Cissie!

(*He rushes into the other room.*)

SOLDIER: Yessir—You been set free! I'm riding ahead of the others, waking folks up—telling 'em. Could I get some water here for my horse?

(*He cannot understand the group before him. In the face of such news they turn towards the other door, anxiously straining forward.*)

UNCLE DAVE: (*Falling on his knees*) Thank God! Oh, thank—

(*His thanksgiving is cut short by a gasping sob. Backing from the room is FESS—his hand before his eyes—his whole body expressing agony. There is a moment of tense waiting. From the distance, borne upon the fresh, morning breeze, comes spirited, marching music. Now, into the room comes CISSIE, holding in her arms the limp body of MILLIE. She advances slowly, her face a mask of ebony, with set, unseeing eyes.*)

CISSIE: Yo' come too late—Mah gal is dead!

See how huh red blood falls hyear in da sun,

Hit's warm an' pure.... Come, dip yo' han's in hit,

She will not shrink away—Huh teahs will nevah

Choke huh song, nor will huh limbs grow hebby

    wid despair....Mah gal is dead!

(*Everyone has crouched back except the young soldier, who stands as if paralyzed, his face white. Now, he finds his voice.*)

SOLDIER: My God! My God! What? What....

UNCLE DAVE: (*Reaching up from his knees*) Cissie! Cissie, dis—dis ain't da man,

Dis am a Yankee soldier, come tuh tell us

    Dat we's....

(*The old man cannot finish. The word chokes in his throat. He buries his face in his hands. Outside a chorus of happy, singing voices is swelling, forming a joyous obligato to the music of the band.*)

VOICES: Free, free, free!

Ah'm free, lil' chillun,
Free! Free!
Da sun o' God does sot us free
    Dis mawnin'!

(Through the door behind CISSIE *has come* GRANNIE LOU. *She stumbles, rubbing her sleep-heavy eyes and shaking her shriveled frame. She sees* CISSIE *facing the white man and her clouded brain can take in only one meaning.)*

SOLDIER: *(Gently to* CISSIE) Do you hear them? It means you're free!

You—

(He is stopped by a burst of wild, loud laughter from GRANNIE, *who points her skinny finger at the limp body.)*

GRANNIE: He! He! He! Ha! Ha! Ha!

Ah tole yo'.... She don' hab tuh go!

He! He! He!

(Several women rush to her, soothing her as they would a child. Only bewilderment shows in CISSIE's *face, but the soldier's poise is completely shattered. Flinging up his hands to shut out the sight, he rushes into the morning sunshine. One of the men follows him. Gradually* GRANNIE *is quieted. The women have dropped to their knees. They rock their bodies and moan.* CISSIE *walks to the door, her inert burden clasped to her breast. For a moment she stands in the bright sunshine, gazing out. The music has diminished into the distance. Somewhere in the yard a cock crows.* CISSIE *looks down into her child's face and speaks quietly.)*

CISSIE: Hit's mawnin'!

(Then from her throat there comes a cry of anguish as she falls to her knees.

Above her, on the door, a single spray of mistletoe sways in the morning breeze and then falls gently on the upturned face of the child.)

CURTAIN

THE MOTHER OF US ALL

GERTRUDE STEIN

First presented in 1947

FOREWORD

"**G**ertrude Stein was born in Allegheny, Pennsylvania. As I am an ardent californian and as she spent her youth there I have often begged her to be born in California but she has always remained firmly born in Allegheny, Pennsylvania." This account of the playwright's birth and childhood comes from *The Autobiography of Alice B. Toklas*—written by Gertrude Stein herself from the perspective of Toklas, her life-long friend, lover and companion. The sense of playfulness apparent in the passage, not to mention in her writing somebody *else*'s autobiography, is one of the hallmarks of Gertrude Stein's writing, which remains among the most original in the twentieth century.

Born February 3, 1874, the youngest of seven children, Stein spent much of her first five years in Europe and most of the rest of her childhood in Oakland, California. Her family, like Hellman's, was German-Jewish. Stein studied psychology at Radcliffe with William James and then attended Johns Hopkins Medical School but left—she claimed she had become "frankly openly bored"— without earning a medical degree. She moved to Paris to live with her older brother Leo and under his guidance began to collect modern art by such largely unknown painters as Pablo Picasso, Henri Matisse, Jean Renoir, Paul Cezanne and Paul Gauguin.

Eventually Leo and Gertrude came to disagree not only about art but about his disdain for her writing; Alice B. Toklas moved in in 1910, and Leo moved out a few years later. The rift soon became permanent and the siblings never spoke to each other again. Stein and Toklas' home at 27 rue de Fleurus was a salon that attracted artists like Picasso and Matisse, as well as writers like Ernest Hemingway, F. Scott Fitzgerald and Sherwood Anderson. Anderson found Stein to be "a woman of striking vigor, a subtle and powerful mind, a discrimination in the arts such as I have found in no other American born man or woman, and a charmingly brilliant conversationalist." Stein spent the rest of her life in Europe, primarily France. She said she liked living among people who spoke a different language: "It has left me more intensely alone with my eyes and my English." Parisians may also have been more accepting of her overtly lesbian lifestyle, and her fascination with innovations in European visual arts, such as expressionism and cubism, are reflected in her writings.

Although Stein's work is difficult to categorize by genres, her canon encompasses what could be classified as plays, novels, stories, poems, scenarios, autobiographies, criticism, meditations on the art of writing and verbal "portraits"—more than five hundred titles in all, ranging from pieces of just a few lines to a massive book like *The Making of Americans*. Her first full-length work, *Q.E.D.* (1903), is an autobiographical novel about a lesbian triangle in which she was involved in medical school; it was not published until four years after her death and even then the names of the principal characters were changed, presumably because of the controversial subject matter. (The original *Q.E.D.* was finally printed in 1971.) *Three Lives* (1909) includes a trio of stories notable for their compassionate treatment of two kindly German servant women and Melanctha, a woman of mixed race who futilely searches for enduring personal relationships. Although marred by racist clichés about the "earth-born, boundless joy of" people of color, "Melanctha" is, as Janis Townsend argues in *American Women Writers*, "remarkable for the time" in being a serious, sympathetic treatment of Black characters by a White author.

Like Susan Glaspell and a number of other talented women, for many years Stein was primarily known for the inspiration and support she gave to male artists and writers rather than for her own literary accomplishments. Only a relatively small part of Stein's immense canon was published during her lifetime, and several works were issued by Toklas in the Plain Editions, which Stein herself subsidized. Although excerpts and shorter pieces—especially her verbal portraits of famous people—appeared in magazines,

Stein's first major book to be issued without this support was *The Making of Americans*, completed in 1911 but not published until 1925.

Gertrude Stein's literary works had a small following primarily among other writers and scholars who admired her experiments with language; in 1926 she was even invited to speak at Oxford and Cambridge universities. Among her works on the subject of composition is *How to Write* (1931), which features such intriguing chapter titles as "Saving the Sentence" and "Arthur A Grammar." Stein finally gained commercial success with *The Autobiography of Alice B. Toklas* (1933), published when she was 59. It remains her most accessible and popular work. A biography of both Stein and Toklas, with more about the former than the latter, *The Autobiography* is a witty book full of amusing if not always reliable stories about the couple and their vast entourage of famous friends and not a few (only partly tongue-in-cheek) examples of Stein's egotism. In the very first chapter we are told that Alice has met only three "geniuses" in her lifetime—one of them, of course, Stein herself. The book wanders and loops back on itself, but Stein keeps her readers clearly in mind; after one digression, for example, she assures us: "But this time I am really going to tell about the pictures."

Following the success of *The Autobiography* and the opera *Four Saints in Three Acts* (1927; performed 1934) Stein and Toklas made a triumphant tour of the U.S. during which, according to scholar Bruce Kellner, they dined with Charlie Chaplin, had tea with Eleanor Roosevelt at the White House and were entertained at a private recital by George Gershwin. If only for a few months, this Jewish lesbian expatriate became the toast of the country. After the tour they returned to Europe, where Stein lived out her last decade.

Gertrude Stein said that she attended the theater and opera frequently when she was a child growing up in California and during her college years in Boston. Her first clear theatrical recollection is of a production of *Uncle Tom's Cabin*, nineteenth century America's most popular play. She was also enthralled with actor Sarah Bernhardt—despite or perhaps because of her own limited knowledge of French at the time—and had a special fondness for Civil War melodramas like William Gillette's *Secret Service* (a fondness echoed in her own theatrical melodramas). But in a lecture on drama Stein conceded, "I when I wrote my first play had completely ceased going to the theatre."

In *The Autobiography of Alice B. Toklas* Stein recalled trying, at about age eight, "to write a Shakespearean drama in which she got as far as a stage direction." Her first adult dramatic effort, "What Happened" (ca. 1913), was written "to express this without telling what happened, in short to make a play the essence of what happened." The result is that nothing happens in "What Happened"—except the very brief play itself, an almost cubist arrangement of words with no characters' names designated beyond "(One)" or "(Four and four more)." Stein published *Geography and Plays* in 1922, a volume that also includes *Ladies Voices*, a work of some fifty lines that seem like fragments of overheard conversations, and *For the Country Entirely*, an epistolary play woven of whole letters as well as bits and pieces, in addition to occasional commentaries on letter writing. Sherwood Anderson wrote the foreword for the volume.

The next group of Stein's dramas, written roughly 1922-1931, are sometimes called "landscape plays" because the words are spatially rather than temporally arranged; words and images are layered rather than following each other in sequence, as they do in realistic theater. Many of these pieces were included in the volume *Operas & Plays*, which Stein and Toklas published in 1932. As James R. Mellow writes in the introduction to a contemporary reissue of this book, Stein's works are all "word plays" where the word itself is more important than plot, character or setting—and, indeed, many of the plays have none of the latter. Not surprisingly Stein is enamoured of puns, including the various meanings of the word "play": she plays with words, our expectations about language, and our notions about what a "play" is. Sometimes the puns begin in the titles, as in *Capital Capitals* (1923) and *They Weighed Weighed-Layed* (1930). Often the word play involves rhymes and/or repetition, as in the opening of *Saints and Singing* (1922): "Saints and singing. I have mentioned them before. Saints and singing need no door they come before, saints and singing, they adore, saints and singing, or, saints and singing...." A work like *They Must. Be Wedded. To Their Wife.* (1931) uses periods throughout to disrupt our sense of how sentences are built and emphasize each word, creating an effect not unlike the line breaks in verse.

Only in Stein's last plays do narrative and story line emerge as important elements, although in some narrative is the subject of the work, not just a part of it, and the concept of character remains slippery. *Three Sisters Who Are Not Sisters* (1943), for example, is a witty parody of murder mysteries in which all the characters are either killed or commit suicide. The title suggests it is also a spoof of Anton Chekhov's classic work; Chekhov's sisters may not have known exactly what they wanted, but Stein's sisters don't even know exactly who they are. Brief and sketchy though they may be, many of Stein's plays foreshadow—as critics have observed—the dramas of Absurd playwrights like Samuel Beckett and Harold Pinter.

Yes Is For a Very Young Man (1944-5; a revision of *In Savoy*) comes perhaps the closest to conventional realism with a recognizable plot, distinct characters and even stage directions. *Yes*, which takes place in occupied France during World War II, involves the clash between a young aristocratic woman who favors whatever government is in power and various male characters who fight against the invading Germans. The play also includes an American woman, Constance, who helps the underground forces resisting the Germans but at the end realizes that it is the "very young" Frenchmen who must bear the brunt of the battle. Interestingly, Constance clearly resembles Stein herself, yet Stein biographer John Malcolm Brinnin suggests that "the character was modeled on Clare Boothe Luce."

It may well be that Stein's commitment "to constantly think about the theatre from the standpoint of sight and sound and its relation to emotion and time, rather than in relation to story and action" makes her work eminently suited to operatic presentation. Composer Virgil Thomson began his association with Stein by writing musical settings for several of her short works. He also makes an appearance as a character in the play *At Present* (1930), but the two are best known for a pair of operas: *Four Saints in Three Acts* and Stein's last work, *The Mother of Us All* (completed 1946; premiered 1947). When Thomson was asked to compose an opera in the late 1920s, he invited Stein to do the libretto. They decided to focus on Spanish saints—especially St. Therese and St. Ignatius—and she wrote the book, which he then set to music. Because the libretto sometimes fails to distinguish stage direction from dialogue or indicate who is speaking or singing, Maurice Grosser developed a scenario from the libretto. An appealing meditation on sainthood, *Four Saints* is also, like all Stein's dramatic work, self-reflexive about language, theater and the process of composition. In a typical Steinian joke on audience expectations, *Four Saints in Three Acts* has—as Saint Therese explains—"many

many saints in it." In case you miss the point, Act *IV* begins: "How many acts are there in it." Performed by an all-Black cast, the premiere of *Four Saints* was an overwhelming success even with what Burns Mantle referred to as "A perfectly mad text...by Gertrude Stein."

When Thomson was commissioned by the Alice M. Ditson Foundation of Columbia University to compose another opera, he suggested Stein join him in a work on nineteenth century America, "with perhaps the language of the senatorial orators quoted." It was Stein who decided on Susan B. Anthony and what Thomson calls her "feminist approach" to the material. Her choice may have been influenced by Toklas, who as a little girl had met Anthony: "the first great woman I met and she made a lasting impression upon me." In Stein's novella *Brewsie and Willie* (1946), a character named Janet announces that she's "been reading a book about Susan B. Anthony." When another character demands "who... might that dame be," Janet replies: "She is the one...that made women vote and have the right to money they earn and to their children, before she came along women were just like Negroes, before they were freed from slavery."

To begin her work on *The Mother of Us All*, Stein researched the nineteenth century in the American Library in Paris, then sent to the New York Public Library for more books. According to Thomson, she began by writing the political meeting scene and the domestic scene, which were completed by late 1945. In March of 1946 she sent the libretto of *Mother* to Thomson. Stein never heard Thomson's score nor saw the production, for she died after cancer surgery on July 27, 1946, and he did not begin composing the score until October. Thomson thought the libretto "very dramatic and very beautiful and very clear and constantly quotable" and set it to music that he characterized as "an evocation of nineteenth-century America, with its gospel hymns and cocky marches, its sentimental ballads, waltzes, darn-fool ditties and intoned sermons." The opera opened at Columbia University on May 7, 1947, as part of the third annual Festival of Contemporary Music, with a cast of students and professionals. *Mother* was also broadcast on radio.

Although in its original production it did not receive the acclaim of *Four Saints*, *The Mother of Us All*—which some reviewers likened to a historical pageant—fared well with the critics and has proved popular with professional and amateur companies. Kappo Phelan in *Commonweal* thought the opera "wholly a delight," while the *New*

Yorker's Robert A. Simon found the libretto "original, entertaining, and provocative." Even critics like Cecil Smith, who called the libretto "uneven" and disliked the second act, considered the text "thoughtful, patriotic, compassionate, stern and witty." Perhaps still more telling are the reviews of revivals. In 1971 Donal Henahan in *The New York Times* called the libretto "as fresh as the day after tomorrow"; five years later, Joan Downs wrote in *Time* that *The Mother of Us All* "seems more pertinent today than in 1947." No less an authority than Leonard Bernstein, despite his belief that Stein's greatest artistic contribution was her effect on others, declared that "Stein has come closer than any other writer except Joyce to the medium of music." The first wholly professional staging of *Mother* was an off-Broadway revival in 1956. It has been revived several times, often in small-scale concert productions. Reviewing a 1983 performance, John Gruen of *The New York Times* wrote of Stein's libretto: "Through language of the starkest and most artful simplicity, she fashioned an historical crazy-quilt of utmost sanity and truth." Perhaps the most notable production was a 1976 performance by the Santa Fe Opera, recorded for New World Records, in which Angel Moore navigated the stage on roller skates and the actress playing Gertrude Stein appeared in a Model T Ford.

Critics have long pointed out that there are strong similarities between Susan B. Anthony as Stein portrays her and Stein herself. Though neither was biologically a mother, both saw themselves as nurturing important movements—Anthony the campaign for women's rights, especially suffrage, and Stein a revolution in art and language. Stein was a lesbian and Anthony's closest relationships were with women; the opera's "Anne" is reminiscent of both Anthony's companion Anna Howard Shaw and Toklas. Stein and Anthony were formidable women whose strength evoked fear and envy; Anthony was derisively dubbed "Saint Anthony," "Bismarck" and "Napoleon" by her opponents, while Stein was characterized as a Roman emperor, a Buddha and "Mother Superior." Whether or not Stein knew she was dying when she wrote *Mother* (she was certainly already suffering the pain of the cancer that would kill her) there is an elegiac tone to the work. The opera's last lines—"My long life, my long life"—hint of this, as does Anthony's famous admonition: "When this you see remember me." Stein had used the same line in several earlier works, but it takes on new poignancy in her final one. Like the Anthony she created, Stein too must have been evaluating her career and hoping her writing would influence others long after her death. Even the "talking" statue of Anthony with which the opera concludes echoes not only George Bernard Shaw's use of a similar image at the end of *St. Joan* but also the well-known portrait of Stein created by Picasso. Stein scholar Lisa Ruddick goes one step further to argue that in *Mother* a dying Stein could be overt about her feminism, which she had self-protectively hidden throughout the years. Ruddick suggests that Anthony's fear of men's retaliation ("they would revenge themselves") is Stein's as well and offers "a retrospective insight" into the obscurity of her early style.

The autobiographical nature of the opera should not, however, mask its importance as an exploration of American history. In an earlier work entitled *Lucy Church Amiably* (1931), Stein had raised the question "Supposing everyone lived at the same time what would they say." While Stein did not go as far as Thornton Wilder had when he set the ice age in suburban New Jersey in *The Skin of Our Teeth*, she assembled a cast of characters—covering roughly a 150 year period—some of whom knew each other, some of whom couldn't possibly have met, and some of whom might have but never did. *Mother* focuses on Susan B. Anthony and famous orator and politician Daniel Webster—about whom Stein had already written a play, "Daniel Webster, Eighteen in America," in 1937. Stein also includes John Adams (who may actually be John Quincy Adams); politician Thaddeus Stevens; Anthony Comstock, known as the "father of American censorship laws"; and a wonderfully conceived Ulysses S. Grant, a Civil War general who hates loud noise and makes comments about Dwight D. Eisenhower. "Anne" is modeled on Anna Shaw, who eventually ascended to the presidency of the National-American Woman Suffrage Association, a post Anthony had held, and Lillian Russell was a flamboyant singer and actor. Into this historical group Stein freely mixes personal friends and acquaintances: Jo the Loiterer is based on a man who was arrested for "loitering" during a demonstration, Constance Fletcher is the name of a writer Stein met in Venice and the subject of a verbal "portrait" included in *Geography and Plays*, and Donald Gallup is a scholar and bibliographer (for many years curator of Yale's Collection of American literature) whom Stein befriended when he was stationed in Paris during World War II. "Virgil T." is the opera's composer and, of course, "Gertrude S." is the playwright herself.

Stein's view of history and Susan B. Anthony's role in it is complex. As Robert K. Martin points out, Stein makes use of Anthony "not so much to depict a specific historic figure at a given point in her career as to capture the essence of a revolutionary spirit that figure incarnates." Though shaken with doubts and at times reluctant to join the fight, Susan regains her determination to win for women the right to vote and to own property. Martin also observes that *Mother* is as much about marriage and property laws as it is about suffrage. Throughout the opera a number of romances are unfolding. Jo the Loiterer woos Indiana Eliot, who weds him but refuses to take his name and thus efface her identity. When she does finally decide that "Indiana Loiterer" has a pleasant ring to it, she demands that Jo adopt her surname in exchange. John Adams is forever wooing "Dear Miss Constance Fletcher" but finds it difficult to kneel to her because of his pride; neither he nor Webster has "kneeling knees." Jenny Reefer's claim "I will not marry because if I did marry, I would be married" is in sharp contrast with John Adams' declaration "I never marry I have been twice divorced but I have never married." For Jenny marriage is a trap into a passive state of "being married," but as a man, Adams has never been defined by his marital status, no matter how many wives he has had. By the end of *The Mother of Us All* even Indiana Eliot declares "how wonderful it is to be never married," apparently a comment on her own wedded state.

In an earlier work entitled *Patriarchal Poetry*, Stein writes: "Patriarchal poetry makes no mistake makes no mistake in estimating the value to be placed upon the best and most arranged of considerations.... Patriarchal poetry to be sure to be sure to be sure...." It is this sense of patriarchal authority and confidence that Stein explores in *The Mother of Us All*, often with humorous results. The great Daniel Webster—congressman, senator and famed orator—is comically inept at wooing; the best he can offer is weak puns: "dear Angel More be my Angel More for evermore." Webster's inarticulateness as a lover is, ironically, pointed up in his political debates as well. Like most of Stein's work, *Mother* is "metalinguistic," focusing on language itself as subject. Stein drew directly from Webster's own writings for his dialogue, embellishing his words with hers. Thus she creates a wonderful juxtaposition between her style and the empty rhetoric of political speech, in addition to contrasting Webster's bombast with Anthony's simplicity. On one level, Stein is answering those critics who throughout her career found her language opaque: by what criteria can one consider her language incomprehensible while bestowing the term "eloquent" on a Daniel Webster who can eulogize "the gorgeous ensign of the republic, still full high advanced, its arms and trophies streaming in their original luster not a stripe erased or polluted not a single star obscured"? On another level, as Robert Martin recognizes, Stein is showing just how ridiculous the "public" language of men can be. Webster is formally correct in referring to Anthony as "he," yet the foolish assumptions behind the use of the generic masculine are glaringly apparent when Webster and Anthony are speaking only to each other. Martin concludes: "Webster must exclude women, since they have not access to speech.... Language in this form has ceased to function, and so quickly becomes the meaningless repeated phrases of patriotic speech."

For a country rooted in patriotic dedication to its forefathers, *The Mother of Us All* not only shows the limitations of those forefathers but the ways in which women have been the true revolutionaries of our country. In the opening moments of the work, all the characters declare: "My father had a name his name was Daniel." Through a happy accident, "Daniel" was not only the name of the renowned orator but also the name of both Susan B. Anthony's and Gertrude Stein's fathers. Daniel—in his opposition to Anthony's pleas for women's rights, in his inability even to see Anthony—thus becomes a conflation of the personal and the political, the (fore)father of us all. When male critics complain about Stein's negative portrayal of men in *Mother*, they miss the point: Stein targets not individuals but a patriarchal system that would keep women as children. Through Anthony she asks how a country born in revolution and pledged to democracy can deny women, as well as men of color, equal rights with White men—a question still alive today. Because this is a world in which "[White] men govern and women know," Andrew G., Thaddeus and Daniel form a hilarious "chorus of the V.I.P.," a group of "Very important persons to every one who can / hear and see." Susan B. Anthony complains: "if I do not come you will never vote my laws, come or not come it always comes to the same thing it comes to their not voting my laws, not voting my laws, tell me all you men tell me you know you will never vote my laws." Stein's beloved repetitions are strikingly apt in a country in which the campaign for women's suffrage lasted well into the twentieth century and in which an

Equal Rights Amendment, proposed decade after decade, is yet to be passed.

In the closing lines of *The Mother of Us All*, Susan B. Anthony wonders: "Do you know because I tell you so, or do/ you know, do you know." As Stein did throughout her life, Anthony is asking questions both about what we know and *how* we know it, about how knowledge is made and conveyed. As lesbian feminist poet Judy Grahn points out, Stein was the ultimate outsider in our culture: a financially independent Jewish lesbian expatriate artist. From this perspective she could see how so much of what we take for granted—language, syntax, dramatic form, literary categories, notions of what constitute "history"—are dependent on male cultural assumptions. Her revolutionary writings force us to confront these conventions. Since her death most of her previously unpublished works have come into print, and she has moved out of the shadow of the famous men who visited her salon. Interest in Stein's work continues to increase and her impact on other women writers is substantial: Grahn's book-length *Really Reading Gertrude Stein*, for example, is a tribute to her literary mentor. According to biographer Carl Rollyson, when Lillian Hellman taught at Yale University in the nineteen sixties, "The first class was devoted to a discussion of Gertrude Stein's lecture at Oxford in 1926, 'How Writing is Written.'"

SELECTED BIBLIOGRAPHY

Bridgman, Richard. *Gertrude Stein in Pieces*. N.Y.: Oxford UP, 1970.

Brinnin, John Malcolm. *The Third Rose: Gertrude Stein and Her World*. 1959. reprint Gloucester, MA: Peter Smith, 1968.

Grahn, Judy. *Really Reading Gertrude Stein*. Freedom, CA.: The Crossing Press, 1989.

Kellner, Bruce. ed. *A Gertrude Stein Companion: content with the example*. Westport: Greenwood, 1988.

Martin, Robert K. "*The Mother of Us All* and American History." In *Gertrude Stein and the Making of Literature*, ed. Shirley Neuman and Ira B. Nadel. Boston: Northeastern UP, 1988.

Marx, Robert. "Thomson, Stein and *The Mother of Us All*." Liner notes to the Santa Fe Opera recording, New World Records, production 1976, recording c. 1977.

Ruddick, Lisa. *Reading Gertrude Stein: Body, Text, Gnosis*. Ithaca: Cornell UP, 1990.

Stein, Gertrude. *The Autobiography of Alice B. Toklas*. N.Y.: Vintage, 1933.

————. *Geography and Plays*. 1922. reissued N.Y.: Something Else Press, 1968.

————. *How to Write*. 1931. reissued West Glover, Vermont: Something Else Press, 1973.

————. *Last Operas and Plays*. ed. and intro. Carl Van Vechten. N.Y.: Rinehart, 1949.

————. *Lectures in America*. 1935. reprint Boston: Beacon Press, 1957.

————. *Operas & Plays*. 1932. reprint with "Foreword" by James R. Mellow. Barrytown, N.Y.: Station Hill Press, 1987.

Sutherland, Donald. *Gertrude Stein: A Biography of her Work*. Westport: Greenwood, 1951.

Thomson, Virgil. *Virgil Thomson*. N. Y.: Knopf, 1966.

Townsend, Janis. "Gertrude Stein." In *American Women Writers*. Vol. 4, ed. Lina Mainiero. N. Y.: Ungar, 1982.

A NOTE ON THE TEXT

This text of *The Mother of Us All* is taken from *Last Operas and Plays by Gertrude Stein*, a volume edited and with an introduction by Carl Van Vechten. This is the libretto as Stein wrote it shortly before her death, including the textual inconsistencies (e.g., stage directions refer to the protagonist sometimes as "Susan B. Anthony," sometimes only as "Susan B.") and idiosyncratic punctuation characteristic of Stein's work. When setting the libretto to music, Virgil Thomson omitted two scenes, turned the "Interlude" into the "Prologue" and made a few more minor revisions. Although in creating the opera Thomson was largely faithful to Stein's original text and composed wonderfully appropriate music, the libretto can stand alone on its own terms.

ACT ONE

Prologue sung by Virgil T.

> Pity the poor persecutor.
>   Why,
> If money is money isn't money money,
>   Why,
> Pity the poor persecutor,
>   Why,
> Is money money or isn't money money.
>   Why.
> Pity the poor persecutor.
> Pity the poor persecutor because the poor persecutor
>   always gets to be poor
>   Why,
> Because the persecutor gets persecuted
> Because is money money or isn't money money,
>   That's why,
> When the poor persecutor is persecuted he has to
>   cry,
>   Why,
> Because the persecutor always ends by being persecuted,
>   That is the reason why.
> (VIRGIL T. *after he has sung his prelude begins to sit*)

VIRGIL T.: Begin to sit.
>   Begins to sit.
>   He begins to sit.
>   That's why.
>   Begins to sit.
>   He begins to sit.
>   And that is the reason why.

ACT ONE § SCENE I

DANIEL WEBSTER: He digged a pit, he digged it deep
>   he digged it for his brother.
>   Into the pit he did fall in the pit
>   he digged for tother.

ALL THE CHARACTERS: Daniel was my father's name,
> My father's name was Daniel.

JO THE LOITERER: Not Daniel.

CHRIS THE CITIZEN: Not Daniel in the lion's den.

ALL THE CHARACTERS: My father's name was Daniel.

G. S.: My father's name was Daniel, Daniel
> and a bear, a bearded Daniel,
> not Daniel in the lion's den not
> Daniel, yes Daniel my father had
> a beard my father's name was Daniel,

DANIEL WEBSTER: He digged a pit he digged it deep
> he digged it for his brother,
> Into the pit he did fall in the pit
> he digged for tother.

INDIANA ELLIOT: Choose a name.

SUSAN B. ANTHONY: Susan B. Anthony is my name to choose a name is feeble, Susan B. Anthony is my name, a name can only be a name my name can only be my name, I have a name, Susan B. Anthony is my name, to choose a name is feeble.

INDIANA ELLIOT: Yes that's easy, Susan B. Anthony is that kind of a name but my name Indiana Elliot. What's in a name.

SUSAN B. ANTHONY: Everything.

G. S.: My father's name was Daniel he had a black beard he was not tall not at all tall, he had a black beard his name was Daniel.

ALL THE CHARACTERS: My father had a name his name was Daniel.

JO THE LOITERER: Not Daniel

CHRIS A CITIZEN: Not Daniel not Daniel in the lion's den not Daniel.

SUSAN B. ANTHONY: I had a father, Daniel was not his name.

INDIANA ELLIOT: I had no father no father.

DANIEL WEBSTER: He digged a pit he digged it deep he
> digged it for his brother,
> into the pit he did fall in the pit
> he digged for tother.

ACT ONE § SCENE II

JO THE LOITERER: I want to tell

CHRIS THE CITIZEN: Very well

JO THE LOITERER: I want to tell oh hell.

CHRIS THE CITIZEN: Oh very well.

JO THE LOITERER: I want to tell oh hell I want to tell about my wife.

CHRIS THE CITIZEN: And have you got one.

JO THE LOITERER: No not one.

CHRIS THE CITIZEN: Two then

JO THE LOITERER: No not two.

CHRIS: How many then

JO THE LOITERER: I haven't got one. I want to tell oh hell about my wife I haven't got one.

CHRIS THE CITIZEN: Well.

JO THE LOITERER: My wife, she had a garden.

CHRIS THE CITIZEN: Yes

JO THE LOITERER: And I bought one.

CHRIS THE CITIZEN: A wife.

No said Jo I was poor and I bought a garden. And then said Chris. She said, said Jo, she said my wife said one tree in my garden was her tree in her garden. And said Chris, Was it. Jo, We quarreled about it. And then said Chris. And then said Jo, we took a train and we went where we went. And then said Chris. She gave me a little package said Jo. And was it a tree said Chris. No it was money said Jo. And was she your wife said Chris, yes said Jo when she was funny, How funny said Chris. Very funny said Jo. Very funny said Jo. To be funny you have to take everything in the kitchen and put it on the floor, you have to take all your money and all your jewels and put them near the door you have to go to bed then and leave the door ajar. That is the way you do when you are funny.

CHRIS THE CITIZEN: Was she funny.

JO THE LOITERER: Yes she was funny.

(*Chris and Jo put their arms around each other*)

ANGEL MORE: Not any more I am not a martyr any more, not any more.

Be a martyr said Chris.

ANGEL MORE: Not any more. I am not a martyr any more.
Surrounded by sweet smelling flowers I
fell asleep three times.
Darn and wash and patch, darn and wash
and patch, darn and wash and patch
darn and wash and patch.

JO THE LOITERER: Anybody can be accused of loitering.

CHRIS BLAKE A CITIZEN: Any loiterer can be accused of loitering.

HENRIETTA M.: Daniel Webster needs an artichoke.

ANGEL MORE: Susan B. is cold in wet weather.

HENRY B.: She swore an oath she'd quickly come to any one to any one.

ANTHONY COMSTOCK: Caution and curiosity, oil and obligation, wheels and appurtenances, in the way of means.

VIRGIL T.: What means.

JOHN ADAMS: I wish to say I also wish to stay, I also wish to go away, I also wish I endeavor to also wish.

ANGEL MORE: I wept on a wish.

JOHN ADAMS: Whenever I hear any one say of course, do I deny it, yes I do deny it whenever I hear any one say of course I deny it, I do deny it.

THADDEUS S.: Be mean.

DANIEL WEBSTER: Be there.

HENRIETTA M.: Be where

CONSTANCE FLETCHER: I do and I do not declare that roses and wreaths, wreaths and roses around and around, blind as a bat, curled as a hat and a plume, be mine when I die, farewell to a thought, he left all alone, be firm in despair dear dear never share, dear dear, dear dear, I Constance Fletcher dear dear, I am a dear, I am dear dear I am a dear, here there everywhere. I bow myself out.

INDIANA ELLIOT: Anybody else would be sorry.

SUSAN B. ANTHONY: Hush, I hush, you hush, they hush, we hush. Hush.

GLOSTER HEMING AND ISABEL WENTWORTH: We, hush, dear as we are, we are very dear to us and to you we hush, we hush you say hush, dear hush. Hush dear.

ANNA HOPE: I open any door, that is the way that any day is to-day, any day is to-day I open any door every door a door.

LILLIAN RUSSELL: Thank you.

ANTHONY COMSTOCK: Quilts are not crazy, they are kind.

JENNY REEFER: My goodness gracious me.

ULYSSES S. GRANT: He knew that his name was not Eisenhower. Yes he knew it. He did know it.

HERMAN ATLAN: He asked me to come he did ask me.

DONALD GALLUP: I chose a long time, a very long time, four hours are a very long time, I chose, I took a very long time, I took a very long time. Yes I took a very long time to choose, yes I did.

T. T. AND A. A.: They missed the boat yes they did they missed the boat.

JO A LOITERER: I came again but not when I was expected, but yes when I was expected because they did expect me.

CHRIS THE CITIZEN: I came to dinner.

(*They all sit down*)

CURTAIN

ACT ONE § SCENE III

(SUSAN B. ANTHONY AND DANIEL WEBSTER *seated in two straight-backed chairs not too near each other.* JO THE LOITERER *comes in*)

JO THE LOITERER: I don't know where a mouse is I don't know what a mouse is. What is a mouse.

ANGEL MORE: I am a mouse

JO THE LOITERER: Well

ANGEL MORE: Yes Well

JO THE LOITERER: All right well. Well what is a mouse

ANGEL MORE: I am a mouse

JO THE LOITERER: Well if you are what is a mouse

ANGEL MORE: You know what a mouse is, I am a mouse.

JO THE LOITERER: Yes well, And she.

(SUSAN B. *Dressed like a Quakeress turns around*)

SUSAN B.: I hear a sound.

JO THE LOITERER: Yes well

DANIEL WEBSTER: I do not hear a sound. When I am told.

SUSAN B. ANTHONY: Silence.

(*Everybody is silent*)

SUSAN B. ANTHONY: Youth is young, I am not old.

DANIEL WEBSTER: When the mariner has been tossed for many days, in thick weather, and on an unknown sea, he naturally avails himself of the first pause in the storm.

SUSAN B. ANTHONY: For instance. They should always fight. They should be martyrs. Some should be martyrs. Will they. They will.

DANIEL WEBSTER: We have thus heard sir what a resolution is.

SUSAN B. ANTHONY: I am resolved.

DANIEL WEBSTER: When this debate sir was to be resumed on Thursday it so happened that it would have been convenient for me to be elsewhere.

SUSAN B.: I am here, ready to be here. Ready to be where. Ready to be here. It is my habit.

DANIEL WEBSTER: The honorable member complained that I had slept on his speech.

SUSAN B.: The right to sleep is given to no woman.

DANIEL WEBSTER: I did sleep on the gentleman's speech; and slept soundly.

SUSAN B.: I too have slept soundly when I have slept, yes when I have slept I too have slept soundly.

DANIEL WEBSTER: Matches and over matches.

SUSAN B.: I understand you undertake to overthrow my undertaking.

DANIEL WEBSTER: I can tell the honorable member once for all that he is greatly mistaken, and that he is dealing with one of whose temper and character he has yet much to learn.

SUSAN B.: I have declared that patience is never more than patient. I too have declared, that I who am not patient am patient.

DANIEL WEBSTER: What interest asks he has South Carolina in a canal in Ohio.

SUSAN B.: What interest have they in me, what interest have I in them, who holds the head of whom, who can bite their lips to avoid a swoon.

DANIEL WEBSTER: The harvest of neutrality had been great, but we had gathered it all.

SUSAN B.: Near hours are made not by shade not by heat not by joy, I always know that not now rather not now, yes and I do not stamp but I know that now yes now is now. I have never asked any one to forgive me.

DANIEL WEBSTER: On yet another point I was still more unaccountably misunderstood.

SUSAN B.: Do we do what we have to do or do we have to do what we do. I answer.

DANIEL WEBSTER: Mr. President I shall enter on no encomium upon Massachusetts she need none. There she is behold her and judge for yourselves.

SUSAN B.: I enter into a tabernacle I was born a believer in peace, I say fight for the right, be a martyr and live, be a coward and

die, and why, because they, yes they, sooner or later go away.
They leave us here. They come again. Don't forget, they
come again.

DANIEL WEBSTER: So sir I understand the gentleman and am happy
to find I did not misunderstand him.

SUSAN B.: I should believe, what they ask, but they know, they
know.

DANIEL WEBSTER: It has been to us all a copious fountain of
national, social and personal happiness.

SUSAN B.: Shall I protest, not while I live and breathe, I shall
protest, shall I protest, shall I protest while I live and breathe.

DANIEL WEBSTER: When my eyes shall be turned to behold for the
last time the sun in heaven.

SUSAN B.: Yes.

JO THE LOITERER: I like a mouse

ANGEL MORE: I hate mice.

JO THE LOITERER: I am not talking about mice, I am talking about
a mouse. I like a mouse.

ANGEL MORE: I hate a mouse.

JO THE LOITERER: Now do you.

CURTAIN

INTERLUDE

Susan B. A Short Story

Yes I was said Susan.
You mean you are, said Anne.
No said Susan no.
When this you see remember me said Susan B.
I do said Anne.
After a while there was education. Who is educated said
Anne.

Susan began to follow, she began to follow herself. I am
not tired said Susan. No not said Anne. No I am not said
Susan. This was the beginning. They began to travel not to
travel you know but to go from one place to another place. In
each place Susan B. said here I am I am here. Well said Anne.
Do not let it trouble you said Susan politely. By the time she
was there she was polite. She often thought about politeness.
She said politeness was so agreeable. It is said Anne. Yes said
Susan yes I think so that is to say politeness is agreeable that
is to say it could be agreeable if everybody were polite but
when it is only me, ah me, said Susan B.

Anne was reproachful why do you not speak louder she
said to Susan B. I speak as loudly as I can said Susan B. I even
speak louder I even speak louder than I can. Do you really
said Anne. Yes I really do said Susan B. it was dark and as it
was dark it was necessary to speak louder or very softly, very
softly. Dear me said Susan B., if it was not so early I would be
sleepy. I myself said Anne never like to look at a newspaper.
You are entirely right said Susan B. only I disagree with you.
You do said Anne. You know very well I do said Susan B.

Men said Susan B. are so conservative, so selfish, so bore-
some and said Susan B. they are so ugly, and said Susan B.
they are gullible, anybody can convince them, listen said
Susan B. they listen to me. Well said Anne anybody would. I
know said Susan B. I know anybody would I know that.

Once upon a time any day was full of occupation. You
were never tired said Anne. No I was never tired said Susan
B. And now, said Anne. Now I am never tired said Susan B.
Let us said Anne let us think about everything. No said Susan

B. no, no no, I know, I know said Susan B. no, said Susan B. No. But said Anne. But me no buts said Susan B. I know, now you like every one, every one and you each one and you they all do, they all listen to me, utterly unnecessary to deny, why deny, they themselves will they deny that they listen to me but let them deny it, all the same they do they do listen to me all the men do, see them said Susan B., do see them, see them, why not, said Susan B., they are men, and men, well of course they know that they cannot either see or hear unless I tell them so, poor things said Susan B. I do not pity them. Poor things. Yes said Anne they are poor things. Yes said Susan B. they are poor things. They are poor things said Susan B. men are poor things. Yes they are said Anne. Yes they are said Susan B. and nobody pities them. No said Anne no, nobody pities them. Very likely said Susan B. More than likely, said Anne. Yes said Susan B. yes.

It was not easy to go away but Susan B. did go away. She kept on going away and every time she went away she went away again. Oh my said Susan B. why do I go away, I go away because if I did not go away I would stay. Yes of course said Anne yes of course, if you did not go away you would stay. Yes of course said Susan B. Now said Susan B., let us not forget that in each place men are the same just the same, they are conservative, they are selfish and they listen to me. Yes they do said Anne. Yes they do said Susan B.

Susan B. was right, she said she was right and she was right. Susan B. was right. She was right because she was right. It is easy to be right, everybody else is wrong so it is easy to be right, and Susan B. was right, of course she was right, it is easy to be right, everybody else is wrong it is easy to be right. And said Susan B., in a way yes in a way yes really in a way, in a way really it is useful to be right. It does what it does, it does do what it does, if you are right, it does do what it does. It is very remarkable said Anne. Not very remarkable said Susan B. not very remarkable, no not very remarkable. It is not very remarkable really not very remarkable said Anne. No said Susan B. no not very remarkable.

And said Susan B. that is what I mean by not very remarkable.

Susan B. said she would not leave home. No said Susan B. I will not leave home. Why not said Anne. Why not said Susan B. all right I will I always have I always will. Yes you always will said Anne. Yes I always will said Susan B. In a little while anything began again and Susan B. said she did not mind. Really and truly said Susan B. really and truly I do not mind. No said Anne you do not mind, no said Susan B. no really and truly truly and really I do not mind. It was very necessary never to be cautious said Susan B. Yes said Anne it is very necessary.

In a little while they found everything very mixed. It is not really mixed said Susan B. How can anything be really mixed when men are conservative, dull, monotonous, deceived, stupid, unchanging and bullies, how said Susan B. how when men are men can they be mixed. Yes said Anne, yes men are men, how can they when men are men how can they be mixed yes how can they. Well said Susan B. let us go on they always listen to me. Yes said Anne yes they always listen to you. Yes said Susan B. yes they always listen to me.

ACT TWO

ANDREW J.: It is cold weather.

HENRIETTA M.: In winter.

ANDREW J.: Wherever I am

(THADDEUS S. *comes in singing a song*)

THADDEUS S.: I believe in public school education, I do not believe in free masons I believe in public school education, I do not believe that every one can do whatever he likes because (*a pause*) I have not always done what I liked, but, I would, if I could, and so I will, I will do what I will, I will have my will, and they, when the they, where are they, beside a poll, Gallup the poll. It is remarkable that there could be any nice person by the name of Gallup, but there is, yes there is, that is my decision.

ANDREW J.: Bother your decision, I tell you it is cold weather.

HENRIETTA M.: In winter.

ANDREW J.: Wherever I am.

CONSTANCE FLETCHER: Antagonises is a pleasant name, antagonises is a pleasant word, antagonises has occurred, bless you all and one.

JOHN ADAMS: Dear Miss Constance Fletcher, it is a great pleasure that I kneel at your feet, but I am Adams, I kneel at the feet of none, not any one, dear Miss Constance Fletcher dear dear Miss Constance Fletcher I kneel at your feet, you would have ruined my father if I had had one but I have had one and you had ruined him, dear Miss Constance Fletcher if I had not been an Adams I would have kneeled at your feet.

CONSTANCE FLETCHER: And kissed my hand.

J. ADAMS: (*Shuddering*) And kissed your hand.

CONSTANCE FLETCHER: What a pity, no not what a pity it is better so, but what a pity what a pity it is what a pity.

J. ADAMS: Do not pity me kind beautiful lovely Miss Constance Fletcher do not pity me, no do not pity me, I am an Adams and not pitiable.

CONSTANCE FLETCHER: Dear dear me if he had not been an Adams he would have kneeled at my feet and he would have kissed my hand. Do you mean that you would have kissed my hand or my hands, dear Mr. Adams.

J. ADAMS: I mean that I would have first kneeled at your feet and then I would have kissed one of your hands and then I would still kneeling have kissed both of your hands, if I had not been an Adams.

CONSTANCE FLETCHER: Dear me Mr. Adams dear me.

ALL THE CHARACTERS: If he had not been an Adams he would have kneeled at her feet and he would have kissed one of her hands, and then still kneeling he would have kissed both of her hands still kneeling if he had not been an Adams.

ANDREW J.: It is cold weather.

HENRIETTA M.: In winter.

ANDREW J.: Wherever I am.

THADDEUS S.: When I look at him I fly, I mean when he looks at me he can cry.

LILLIAN RUSSELL: It is very naughty for men to quarrel so.

HERMAN ATLAN: They do quarrel so.

LILLIAN RUSSELL: It is very naughty of them very naughty.

(JENNY REEFER *begins to waltz with* HERMAN ATLAN)

A SLOW CHORUS: Naughty men, they quarrel so
Quarrel about what.
About how late the moon can rise.
About how soon the earth can turn.
About how naked are the stars.
About how black are blacker men.
About how pink are pinks in spring.
About what corn is best to pop.
About how many feet the ocean has dropped.
Naughty men naughty men, they are always always quarreling.

JENNY REEFER: Ulysses S. Grant was not the most earnest nor the most noble of men, but he was not always quarreling.

DONALD GALLUP: No he was not.

JO THE LOITERER: Has everybody forgotten Isabel Wentworth. I just want to say has everybody forgotten Isabel Wentworth.

CHRIS THE CITIZEN: Why shouldn't everybody forget Isabel Wentworth.

JO THE LOITERER: Well that is just what I want to know I just want to know if everybody has forgotten Isabel Wentworth. That is all I want to know I just want to know if everybody has forgotten Isabel Wentworth.

ACT TWO § SCENE II

SUSAN B.: Shall I regret having been born, will I regret having been born, shall and will, will and shall, I regret having been born.

ANNE: Is Henrietta M. a sister of Angel More.

SUSAN B.: No, I used to feel that sisters should be sisters, and that sisters prefer sisters, and I.

ANNE: Is Angel More the sister of Henrietta M. It is important that I know important.

SUSAN B.: Yes important.

ANNE: An Indiana Elliot are there any other Elliots beside Indiana Elliot. It is important that I should know, very important.

SUSAN B.: Should one work up excitement, or should one turn it low so that it will explode louder, should one work up excitement should one.

ANNE: Are there any other Elliots beside Indiana Elliot, had she sisters or even cousins, it is very important that I should know, very important.

SUSAN B.: A life is never given for a life, when a life is given a life is gone, if no life is gone there is no room for more life, life and strife, I give my life, that is to say, I live my life every day.

ANNE: And Isabel Wentworth, is she older or younger than she was it is very important very important that I should know just how old she is. I must have a list I must of how old every one is, it is very important.

SUSAN B.: I am ready.

ANNE: We have forgotten we have forgotten Jenny Reefer, I don't know even who she is, it is very important that I know who Jenny Reefer is very important.

SUSAN B.: And perhaps it is important to know who Lillian Russell is, perhaps it is important.

ANNE: It is not important to know who Lillian Russell is.

SUSAN B.: Then you do know.

ANNE: It is not important for me to know who Lillian Russell is.

SUSAN B.: I must choose I do choose, men and women women and men I do choose. I must choose colored or white white or colored I must choose, I must choose, weak or strong, strong or weak I must choose.

(All the men coming forward together)

SUSAN B.: I must choose

JO THE LOITERER: Fight fight fight, between the nigger and the white.

CHRIS THE CITIZEN: And the women.

ANDREW J.: I wish to say that little men are bigger than big men, that they know how to drink and to get drunk. They say I was a little man next to that big man, nobody can say what they do say nobody can.

CHORUS OF ALL THE MEN: No nobody can, we feel that way too, no nobody can.

ANDREW JOHNSON.: Begin to be drunk when you can so be a bigger man than a big man, you can.

CHORUS OF MEN: You can.

ANDREW J.: I often think, I am a bigger man than a bigger man. I often think I am.

(ANDREW J. *moves around and as he moves around he sees himself in a mirror*)

Nobody can say little as I am I am not bigger than anybody bigger bigger bigger (*and then in a low whisper*) bigger than him bigger than him.

JO THE LOITERER: Fight fight between the big and the big never between the little and the big.

CHRIS THE CITIZEN: They don't fight.

(VIRGIL T. *makes them all gather around him*)

VIRGIL T.: Hear me he says hear me in every way I have satisfaction, I sit I stand I walk around and I am grand, and you all know it.

CHORUS OF MEN: Yes we all know it. That's that.

AND SAID VIRGIL T.: I will call you up one by one and then you will know which one is which, I know, then you will be known. Very well, Henry B.

HENRY B.: (*Comes forward*) I almost thought that I was Tommy I almost did I almost thought I was Tommy W. but if I were Tommy W. I would never come again, not if I could do better no not if I could do better.

VIRGIL T.: Useless. John Adams. (JOHN ADAMS *advances*) Tell me are you the real John Adams you know I sometimes doubt it not really doubt it you know but doubt it.

JOHN ADAMS: If you were silent I would speak.

JO THE LOITERER: Fight fight fight between day and night.

CHRIS THE CITIZEN: Which is day and which is night.

JO THE LOITERER: Hush, which.

JOHN ADAMS: I ask you Virgil T. do you love women, I do. I love women but I am never subdued by them never.

VIRGIL T.: He is no good. Andrew J. and Thaddeus S. better come together.

JO THE LOITERER: He wants to fight fight fight between.

CHRIS: Between what.

JO THE LOITERER: Between the dead.

ANDREW J.: I tell you I am bigger bigger is not biggest is not bigger. I am bigger and just to the last minute, I stick, it's better to stick than to die, it's better to itch than to cry, I have tried them all.

VIRGIL T.: You bet you have.

THADDEUS S.: I can be carried in dying but I will never quit trying.

JO THE LOITERER: Oh go to bed when all is said oh go to bed, everybody, let's hear the women.

CHRIS THE CITIZEN: Fight fight between the nigger and the white and the women.

(ANDREW J. *and* THADDEUS S. *begin to quarrel violently*)

Tell me said Virgil T. tell me I am from Missouri.

(*Everybody suddenly stricken dumb.*

DANIEL *advances holding* HENRIETTA M. *by the hand*)

DANIEL: Ladies and gentlemen let me present you let me present to you Henrietta M. it is rare in this troubled world to find a woman without a last name rare delicious and troubling, ladies and gentlemen let me present Henrietta M.

CURTAIN

ACT TWO § SCENE III

SUSAN B.: I do not know whether I am asleep or awake, awake or asleep, asleep or awake. Do I know.

JO THE LOITERER: I know, you are awake Susan B.

(*A snowy landscape. A negro man and a negro woman*)

SUSAN B.: Negro man would you vote if you only can and not she.

NEGRO MAN: You bet.

SUSAN B.: I fought for you that you could vote would you vote if they would not let me.

NEGRO MAN: Holy gee.

SUSAN B.: (*Moving down in the snow*) If I believe that I am right and I am right if they believe that they are right and they are not in the right, might, might, might there be what might be.

NEGRO MAN AND WOMAN: (*Following her*) All right Susan B. all right.

SUSAN B.: How then can we entertain a hope that they will act differently, we may pretend to go in good faith but there will be no faith in us.

DONALD GALLUP: Let me help you Susan B.

SUSAN B.: And if you do and I annoy you what will you do.

DONALD GALLUP: But I will help you Susan B.

SUSAN B.: I tell you if you do and I annoy you what will you do.

DONALD GALLUP: I wonder if I can help you Susan B.

SUSAN B.: I wonder.

(ANDREW J., THADDEUS *and* DANIEL WEBSTER *come in together*)

THE THREE V.I.P.'s: We are the chorus of the V.I.P.
Very important persons to every one who can hear and see, we are the chorus of the V.I.P.

SUSAN B.: Yes, so they are. I am important but not that way, not that way.

THE THREE V.I.P.'s: We you see we V.I.P. very important to any one who can hear or you can see, just we three, of course lots of others but just we three, just we three we are the chorus of V.I.P. Very important persons to any one who can hear or can see.

SUSAN B.: My constantly recurring thought and prayer now are that no word or act of mine may lessen the might of this country in the scale of truth and right.

DANIEL WEBSTER: When they all listen to me.

THADDEUS S.: When they all listen to me.

ANDREW J.: When they all listen to him, by him I mean me.

DANIEL WEBSTER: By him I mean me.

THADDEUS S.: It is not necessary to have any meaning I am he, he is me I am a V.I.P.

THE THREE: We are the V.I.P. the very important persons, we have special rights, they ask us first and they wait for us last and wherever we are well there we are everybody knows we are there, we are the V.I.P. Very important persons for everybody to see.

JO THE LOITERER: I wished that I knew the difference between rich and poor, I used to think I was poor, now I think I am rich and I am rich, quite rich not very rich quite rich, I wish I knew the difference between rich and poor.

CHRIS THE CITIZEN: Ask her, ask Susan B. I always ask, I find they like it and I like it, and if I like it, and if they like it, I am not rich and I am not poor, just like that Jo just like that.

JO THE LOITERER: Susan B. listen to me, what is the difference between rich and poor poor and rich no use to ask the V.I.P., they never answer me but you Susan B. you answer, answer me.

SUSAN B.: Rich, to be rich, is to be so rich that when they are rich they have it to be that they do not listen and when they do they do not hear, and to be poor to be poor, is to be so poor they listen and listen and what they hear well what do they hear, they hear that they listen, they listen to hear, that is what it is to be poor, but I, I Susan B., there is no wealth nor poverty, there is no wealth, what is wealth, there is no poverty, what is poverty, has a pen ink, has it.

JO THE LOITERER: I had a pen that was to have ink for a year and it only lasted six weeks.

SUSAN B.: Yes I know Jo. I know.

CURTAIN

ACT TWO § SCENE IV

A Meeting.

SUSAN B.: (On the Platform) Ladies there is no neutral position for us to assume. If we say we love the cause and then sit down at our ease, surely does our action speak the lie. And now will Daniel Webster take the platform as never before.

DANIEL WEBSTER: Coming and coming alone, no man is alone when he comes, when he comes when he is coming he is not alone and now ladies and gentlemen I have done, remember that remember me remember each one.

SUSAN B.: And now Virgil T. Virgil T. will bow and speak and when it is necessary they will know that he is he.

VIRGIL T.: I make what I make, I make a noise, there is a poise in making a noise.

(An interruption at the door)

JO THE LOITERER: I have behind me a crowd, are we allowed.

SUSAN B.: A crowd is never allowed but each one of you can come in.

CHRIS THE CITIZEN: But if we are allowed then we are a crowd.

SUSAN B.: No, this is the cause, and a cause is a pause. Pause before you come in.

JO THE LOITERER: Yes ma'am.

(ALL THE CHARACTERS *crowd in.* CONSTANCE FLETCHER *and* INDIANA ELLIOT *leading*)

DANIEL WEBSTER: I resist it to-day and always. Who ever falters or whoever flies I continue the contest.

CONSTANCE FLETCHER and INDIANA ELLIOT: (*Bowing low say*) Dear man, he can make us glad that we have had so great so dear a man here with us now and now we bow before him here, this dear this dear great man.

SUSAN B.: Hush, this is slush. Hush.

JOHN ADAMS: I cannot be still when still and until I see Constance Fletcher dear Constance Fletcher noble Constance Fletcher and I spill I spill over like a thrill and a trill, dear Constance Fletcher there is no cause in her presence, how can there be a cause. Women what are women. There is Constance Fletcher, men what are men, there is Constance Fletcher, Adams, yes, Adams, I am John Adams, there is Constance Fletcher, when this you see listen to me, Constance, no I cannot call her Constance I can only call her Constance Fletcher.

INDIANA ELLIOT: And how about me.

JO THE LOITERER: Whist shut up I have just had an awful letter from home, shut up.

INDIANA ELLIOT: What did they say.

JO THE LOITERER: They said I must come home and not marry you.

INDIANA: Who ever said we were going to marry.

JO THE LOITERER: Believe me I never did.

INDIANA: Disgrace to the cause of women, out. And she shoves him out.

JO THE LOITERER: Help Susan B. help me.

SUSAN B.: I know that we suffer, and as we suffer we grow strong, I know that we wait and as we wait we are bold, I know that we are beaten and as we are beaten we win, I know that men know that this is not so but it is so, I know, yes I know.

JO THE LOITERER: There didn't I tell you she knew best, you just give me a kiss and let me alone.

DANIEL WEBSTER: I who was once old am now young, I who was once weak am now strong, I who have left every one behind am now overtaken.

SUSAN B.: I undertake to overthrow your undertaking.

JO THE LOITERER: You bet.

CHRIS THE CITIZEN: I always repeat everything I hear.

JO THE LOITERER: You sure do.

(*While all this is going on,* ALL THE CHARACTERS *are crowding up on the platform*)

THEY SAY: Now we are all here there is nobody down there to hear, now if it is we're always like that there would be no reason why anybody should cry, because very likely if at all it would be so nice to be the head, we are the head we have all the bread.

JO THE LOITERER: And the butter too.

CHRIS THE CITIZEN: And Kalamazoo.

SUSAN B.: (*advancing*) I speak to those below who are not there who are not there who are not there. I speak to those below to those below who are not there to those below who are not there.

CURTAIN

ACT TWO § SCENE V

SUSAN B.: Will they remember that it is true that neither they that neither you, will they marry will they carry, aloud, the right to know that even if they love them so, they are alone to live and die, they are alone to sink and swim they are alone to have what they own, to have no idea but that they are here, to struggle and thirst to do everything first, because until it is done there is no other one.

(JO THE LOITERER *leads in* INDIANA ELLIOT *in wedding attire, followed by* JOHN ADAMS *and* CONSTANCE FLETCHER *and followed by* DANIEL WEBSTER *and* ANGEL MORE. *All the other characters follow after.* ANNE *and* JENNY REEFER *come and stand by* SUSAN B. ULYSSES S. GRANT *sits down in a chair right behind the procession.*)

ANNE: Marriage.

JENNY REEFER: Marry marriage.

SUSAN B.: I know I know and I have told you so, but if no one marries how can there be women to tell men, women to tell men.

ANNE: What

JENNY REEFER: Women should not tell men.

SUSAN B.: Men can not count, they do not know that two and two
make four if women do not tell them so. There is a devil
creeps into men when their hands are strengthened. Men
want to be half slave half free. Women want to be all slave or
all free therefore men govern and women know, and yet.

ANNE: Yet.

JENNY REEFER: There is no yet in paradise.

SUSAN B.: Let them marry.

(*The marrying commences*)

JO THE LOITERER: I tell her if she marries me do I marry her.

INDIANA ELLIOT: Listen to what he says so you can answer, have
you the ring.

JO THE LOITERER: You did not like the ring and mine is too large.

INDIANA ELLIOT: Hush.

JO THE LOITERER: I wish my name was Adams.

INDIANA ELLIOT: Hush.

JOHN ADAMS: I never marry I have been twice divorced but I have
never married, fair Constance Fletcher fair Constance
Fletcher do you not admire me that I never can married be. I
who have been twice divorced. Dear Constance Fletcher dear
dear Constance Fletcher do you not admire me.

CONSTANCE FLETCHER: So beautiful. It is so beautiful to meet you
here, so beautiful, so beautiful to meet you here dear, dear
John Adams, so beautiful to meet you here.

DANIEL WEBSTER: When I have joined and not having joined have
separated and not having separated have led, and not having
led have thundered, when I having thundered have provoked
and having provoked have dominated, may I dear Angel More
not kneel at your feet because I cannot kneel my knees are
not kneeling knees but dear Angel More be my Angel More
for evermore.

ANGEL MORE: I join the choir that is visible, because the choir that
is visible is as visible.

DANIEL WEBSTER: As what Angel More.

ANGEL MORE: As visible as visible, do you not hear me, as visible.

DANIEL WEBSTER: You do not and I do not.

ANGEL MORE: What.

DANIEL WEBSTER: Separate marriage from marriage.

ANGEL MORE: And why not.

DANIEL WEBSTER: And.

> (*Just at this moment* ULYSSES S. GRANT *makes his chair pound on the floor*)

ULYSSES S. GRANT: As long as I sit I am sitting, silence again as you were, you were all silent, as long as I sit I am sitting.

ALL TOGETHER: We are silent, as we were.

SUSAN B.: We are all here to celebrate the civil and religious marriage of Jo the Loiterer and Indiana Elliot.

JO THE LOITERER: Who is civil and who is religious.

ANNE: Who is, listen to Susan B. She knows.

THE BROTHER OF INDIANA ELLIOT: (*Rushes in*) Nobody knows who I am but I forbid the marriage, do we know whether Jo the Loiterer is a bigamist or a grandfather or an uncle or a refugee. Do we know, no we do not know and I forbid the marriage, I forbid it, I am Indiana Elliot's brother and I forbid it, I am known as Herman Atlan and I forbid it, I am known as Anthony Comstock and I forbid it, I am Indiana Elliot's brother and I forbid it.

JO THE LOITERER: Well well well, I knew that ring of mine was too large, It could not fall off on account of my joints but I knew it was too large.

INDIANA ELLIOT: I renounce my brother.

JO THE LOITERER: That's right my dear that's all right.

SUSAN B.: What is marriage, is marriage protection or religion, is marriage renunciation or abundance, is marriage a stepping-stone or an end. What is marriage.

ANNE: I will never marry.

JENNY REEFER: If I marry I will divorce but I will not marry because if I did marry, I would be married.

> (ULYSSES S. GRANT *pounds his chair*)

ULYSSES S. GRANT: Didn't I say I do not like noise, I do not like cannon balls, I do not like storms, I do not like talking, I do not like noise. I like everything and everybody to be silent and what I like I have. Everybody be silent.

JO THE LOITERER: I know I was silent, everybody can tell just by listening to me just how silent I am, dear General, dear General Ulysses, dear General Ulysses Simpson dear General Ulysses Simpson Grant, dear dear sir, am I not a perfect example of what you like, am I not silent.

(ULYSSES S. GRANT's *chair pounds and he is silent*)

SUSAN B.: I am not married and the reason why is that I have had to do what I have had to do, I have had to be what I have had to be, I could never be one of two I could never be two in one as married couples do and can, I am but one all one, one and all one, and so I have never been married to any one.

ANNE: But I I have been. I have been married to what you have been to that one.

SUSAN B.: No no, no, you may be married to the past one, the one that is not the present one, no one can be married to the present one, the one, the one, the present one.

JENNY REEFER: I understand you undertake to overthrow their undertaking.

SUSAN B.: I love the sound of these, one over two, two under one, three under four, four over more.

ANNE: Dear Susan B. Anthony thank you.

JOHN ADAMS: All this time I have been lost in my thoughts in my thoughts of thee beautiful thee, Constance Fletcher, do you see, I have been lost in my thoughts of thee.

CONSTANCE FLETCHER: I am blind and therefore I dream.

DANIEL WEBSTER: Dear Angel More, dear Angel More, there have been men who have stammered and stuttered but not, not I.

ANGEL MORE: Speak louder.

DANIEL WEBSTER: Not I.

THE CHORUS: Why the hell don't you all get married, why don't you, we want to go home, why don't you.

JO THE LOITERER: Why don't you.

INDIANA ELLIOT: Why don't you.

INDIAN ELLIOT'S BROTHER: Why don't you because I am here.

    (*The crowd removes him forcibly*)

SUSAN B.: (*Suddenly*) They are married all married and their children women as well as men will have the vote, they will they will, they will have the vote.

CURTAIN

ACT TWO § SCENE VI

(SUSAN B. *doing her housework in her house*)
(*Enter* ANNE)

ANNE: Susan B. they want you.

SUSAN B.: Do they.

ANNE: Yes. You must go.

SUSAN B.: No.

JENNY REEFER: (*Comes in*) Oh yes they want to know if you are here.

SUSAN B.: Yes still alive. Painters paint and writers write and soldiers drink and fight and I I am still alive.

ANNE: They want you.

SUSAN B.: And when they have me.

JENNY REEFER: Then they will want you again.

SUSAN B.: Yes I know, they love me so, they tell me so and they tell me so, but I, I do not tell them so because I know, they will not do what they could do and I I will be left alone to die but they will not have done what I need to have done to make it right that I live lived my life and fight.

JO THE LOITERER: (*At the window*) Indiana Elliot wants to come in, she will not take my name she says it is not all the same, she says that she is Indiana Elliot and that I am Jo, and that she will not take my name and that she will always tell me so. Oh yes she is right of course she is right it is not all the same Indiana Elliot is her name, she is only married to me, but there is no difference that I can see, but all the same there she is and she will not change her name, yes it is all the same.

SUSAN B.: Let her in.

INDIANA ELLIOT: Oh Susan B. they want you they have to have you, can I tell them you are coming I have not changed my name can I tell them you are coming and that you will do everything.

SUSAN B.: No but there is no use in telling them so, they won't vote my laws, there is always a clause, there is always a pause, they won't vote my laws.

(ANDREW JOHNSON *puts his head in at the door*)

ANDREW JOHNSON: Will the good lady come right along.

THADDEUS STEVENS: (*Behind him*) We are waiting, will the good lady not keep us waiting, will the good lady not keep us waiting.

SUSAN B.: You you know so well that you will not vote my laws.

STEVENS: Dear lady remember humanity comes first.

SUSAN B.: You mean men come first, women, you will not vote my laws, how can you dare when you do not care, how can you dare, there is no humanity in humans, there is only law, and you will not because you know so well that there is no humanity there are only laws, you know it so well that you will not you will not vote my laws.

(SUSAN B. *goes back to her housework.* ALL THE CHARACTERS *crowd in*)

CHORUS: Do come Susan B. Anthony do come nobody no nobody can make them come the way you make them come, do come do come Susan B. Anthony, it is your duty, Susan B. Anthony, you know you know your duty, you come, do come, come.

SUSAN B. ANTHONY: I suppose I will be coming, is it because you flatter me, is it because if I do not come you will forget me and never vote my laws, you will never vote my laws even if I do come but if I do not come you will never vote my laws, come or not come it always comes to the same thing it comes to their not voting my laws, not voting my laws, tell me all you men tell me you know you will never vote my laws.

ALL THE MEN: Dear kind lady we count on you, and as we count on you so can you count on us.

SUSAN B. ANTHONY: Yes but I work for you I do, I say never again, never again, never never, and yet I know I do say no but I do not mean no, I know I always hope that if I go that if I go and go and go, perhaps then you men will vote my laws but I know how well I know, a little this way a little that way you steal away, you steal a piece away you steal yourselves away, you do not intend to stay and vote my laws, and still when you call I go, I go, I go, I say no, no, no, and I go, but no, this time no, this time you have to do more than promise, you must write it down that you will vote my laws, but no, you will pay no attention to what is written, well then swear by my hearth, as you hope to have a home and hearth, swear after I work for you swear that you will vote my laws, but no, no oaths, no thoughts, no decisions, no intentions, no gratitude, no convictions, no nothing will make you pass my laws. Tell me can any of you be honest now, and say you will not pass my laws.

JO THE LOITERER: I can I can be honest I can say I will not pass your laws, because you see I have no vote, no loiterer has a vote so it is easy Susan B. Anthony easy for one man among all these men to be honest and to say I will not pass your laws.

Anyway Susan B. Anthony what are your laws. Would it really be all right to pass them, if you say so it is all right with me. I have no vote myself but I'll make them as long as I don't have to change my name don't have to don't have to change my name.

T. STEVENS: Thanks dear Susan B. Anthony, thanks we all know that whatever happens we all can depend upon you to do your best for any cause which is a cause, and any cause is a cause and because any cause is a cause therefore you will always do your best for any cause, and now you will be doing your best for this cause our cause the cause.

SUSAN B.: Because. Very well is it snowing.

CHORUS: Not just now.

SUSAN B. ANTHONY: Is it cold.

CHORUS: A little.

SUSAN B. ANTHONY: I am not well.

CHORUS: But you look so well and once started it will be all right.

SUSAN B. ANTHONY: All right.

CURTAIN

ACT TWO § SCENE VII

(SUSAN B. ANTHONY *busy with her housework*)

ANNE: (*Comes in*) Oh it was wonderful, wonderful, they listen to nobody the way they listen to you.

SUSAN B.: Yes it is wonderful as the result of my work for the first time the word male has been written into the constitution of the United States concerning suffrage. Yes it is wonderful.

ANNE: But

SUSAN B.: Yes but, what is man, what are men, what are they. I do not say that they haven't kind hearts, if I fall down in a faint, they will rush to pick me up, if my house is on fire, they will rush in to put the fire out and help me, yes they have kind hearts but they are afraid, afraid, they are afraid, they are afraid. They fear women, they fear each other, they fear their neighbor, they fear other countries and then they hearten themselves in their fear by crowding together and following each other, and when they crowd together and follow each

other they are brutes, like animals who stampede, and so they
have written in the name male into the United States constitution, because they are afraid of black men because they are
afraid of women, because they are afraid afraid. Men are
afraid.

ANNE: (*Timidly*) And women.

SUSAN B.: Ah women often have not any sense of danger, after all a
hen screams pitifully when she sees an eagle but she is only
afraid for her children, men are afraid for themselves, that is
the real difference between men and women.

ANNE: But Susan B. why do you not say these things out loud.

SUSAN B.: Why not, because if I did they would not listen they not
alone would not listen they would revenge themselves. Men
have kind hearts when they are not afraid but they are afraid
afraid afraid. I say they are afraid, but if I were to tell them so
their kindness would turn to hate. Yes the Quakers are right,
they are not afraid because they do not fight, they do not
fight.

ANNE: But Susan B. you fight and you are not afraid.

SUSAN B.: I fight and I am not afraid, I fight but I am not afraid.

ANNE: And you will win.

SUSAN B.: Win what, win what.

ANNE: Win the vote for women.

SUSAN B.: Yes some day some day the women will vote and by that
time.

ANNE: By that time oh wonderful time.

SUSAN B.: By that time it will do them no good because having the
vote they will become like men, they will be afraid, having the
vote will make them afraid, oh I know it, but I will fight for
the right, for the right to vote for them even though they
become like men, become afraid like men, become like men.

(ANNE *bursts into tears.* JENNY REEFER *rushes in*)

JENNY REEFER: I have just converted Lillian Russell to the cause of
woman's suffrage, I have converted her, she will give all herself and all she earns oh wonderful day I know you will say,
here she comes isn't she beautiful.

(LILLIAN RUSSELL *comes in followed by all the women in the chorus. Women crowding around,* CONSTANCE FLETCHER *in the
background.*)

LILLIAN RUSSELL: Dear friends, it is so beautiful to meet you all, so
beautiful, so beautiful to meet you all.

(JOHN ADAMS *comes in and sees* CONSTANCE FLETCHER)

JOHN ADAMS: Dear friend beautiful friend, there is no beauty where you are not.

CONSTANCE FLETCHER: Yes dear friend but look look at real beauty look at Lillian Russell look at real beauty.

JOHN ADAMS: Real beauty real beauty is all there is of beauty and why should my eye wander where no eye can look without having looked before. Dear friend I kneel to you because dear friend each time I see you I have never looked before, dear friend you are an open door.

(DANIEL WEBSTER *strides in, the women separate*)

DANIEL WEBSTER: What what is it, what is it, what is the false and the true and I say to you you Susan B. Anthony, you know the false from the true and yet you will not wait you will not wait, I say you will you will wait. When my eyes, and I have eyes when my eyes, beyond that I seek not to penetrate the veil, why should you want what you have chosen, when mine eyes, why do you want that the curtain may rise, why when mine eyes, why should the vision be opened to what lies behind, why, Susan B. Anthony fight the fight that is the fight, that any fight may be a fight for the right. I hear that you say that the word male should not be written into the constitution of the United States of America, but I say, I say, that so long that the gorgeous ensign of the republic, still full high advanced, its arms and trophies streaming in their original luster not a stripe erased or polluted not a single star obscured.

JO THE LOITERER: She has decided to change her name.

INDIANA ELLIOT: Not because it is his name but it is such a pretty name, Indiana Loiterer is such a pretty name I think all the same he will have to change his name, he must be Jo Elliot, yes he must, it is what he has to do, he has to be Jo Elliot and I am going to be Indiana Loiterer, dear friends, all friends is it not a lovely name, Indiana Loiterer all the same.

JO THE LOITERER: All right I never fight, nobody will know it's me, but what can I do, if I am not she and I am not me, what can I do, if a name is not true, what can I do but do as she tells me.

ALL THE CHORUS: She is quite right, Indiana Loiterer is so harmonious, so harmonious, Indiana Loiterer is so harmonious.

ALL THE MEN: (*Come in*) What did she say.

JO: I was talking not she but nobody no nobody ever wants to listen to me.

ALL THE CHORUS MEN AND WOMEN: Susan B. Anthony was very successful we are all very grateful to Susan B. Anthony because she was so successful, she worked for the votes for women and she worked for the vote for colored men and she was so successful, they wrote the word male into the constitution of the United States of America, dear Susan B. Anthony. Dear Susan B., whenever she wants to be and she always wants to be she is always so successful so very successful.

SUSAN B.: So successful.

CURTAIN

ACT TWO § SCENE VIII

(*The Congressional Hall, the replica of the statue of* SUSAN B. ANTHONY *and her comrades in the suffrage fight*)

ANNE: (*Alone in front of the statuary*) The Vote. Women have the vote. They have it each and every one, it is glorious glorious glorious.

SUSAN B. ANTHONY: (*Behind the statue*) Yes women have the vote, all my long life of strength and strife, all my long life, women have it, they can vote, every man and every woman have the vote, the word male is not there any more, that is to say, that is to say.

(*Silence.* VIRGIL T. *comes in very nicely, he looks around and sees* ANNE)

VIRGIL T.: Very well indeed, very well indeed, you are looking very well indeed, have you a chair anywhere, very well indeed, as we sit, we sit, some day very soon some day they will vote sitting and that will be a very successful day any day, every day.

(HENRY B. *comes in. He looks all around at the statue and then he sighs*)

HENRY B.: Does it really mean that women are as white and cold as marble does it really mean that.

(ANGEL MORE *comes in and bows gracefully to the sculptured group*)

ANGEL MORE: I can always think of dear Daniel Webster daily.

(JOHN ADAMS *comes in and looks around, and then carefully examines the statue*)

JOHN ADAMS: I think that they might have added dear delicate Constance Fletcher I do think they might have added her wonderful profile, I do think they might have, I do, I really do.

(ANDREW JOHNSON *shuffles in*)

ANDREW JOHNSON: I have no hope in black or white in white or black in black or black or white or white, no hope.

(THADDEUS STEVENS *comes in, he does not address anybody, he stands before the statue and frowns*)

THADDEUS S.: Rob the cradle, rob it, rob the robber, rob him, rob whatever there is to be taken, rob, rob the cradle, rob it.

DANIEL WEBSTER: (*He sees nothing else*) Angel More, more more Angel More, did you hear me, can you hear shall you hear me, when they come and they do come, when they go and they do go, Angel More can you will you shall you may you might you would you hear me, when they have lost and won, when they have won and lost, when words are bitter and snow is white, Angel More come to me and we will leave together.

ANGEL MORE: Dear sir, not leave, stay.

HENRIETTA M.: I have never been mentioned again. (*She curtseys*)

CONSTANCE FLETCHER: Here I am, I am almost blind but here I am, dear dear here I am, I cannot see what is so white, here I am.

JOHN ADAMS: (*Kissing her hand*) Here you are, blind as a bat and beautiful as a bird, here you are, white and cold as marble, beautiful as marble, yes that is marble but you you are the living marble dear Constance Fletcher, you are.

CONSTANCE FLETCHER: Thank you yes I am here, blind as a bat, I am here.

INDIANA ELLIOT: I am sorry to interrupt so sorry to interrupt but I have a great deal to say about marriage, either one or the other married must be economical, either one or the other, if either one or the other of a married couple are economical then a marriage is successful, if not not, I have a great deal to say about marriage, and dear Susan B. Anthony was never

married, how wonderful it is to be never married how wonderful. I have a great deal to say about marriage.

SUSAN B. ANTHONY: (*Voice from behind the statue*) It is a puzzle, I am
not puzzled but it is a puzzle, if there are no children there
are no men and women, and if there are men and women, it is
rather horrible, and if it is rather horrible, then there are children, I am not puzzled but it is very puzzling, women and
men vote and children, I am not puzzled but it is very puzzling.

GLOSTER HEMING: I have only been a man who has a very fine
name, and it must be said I made it up yes I did, so many do
why not I, so many do, so many do, and why not two, when
anybody might, and you can vote and you can dote with any
name. Thank you.

ISABEL WENTWORTH: They looked for me and they found me, I
like to talk about it. It is very nearly necessary not to be noisy
not to be noisy and hope, hope and hop, no use in enjoying
men and women no use, I wonder why we are all happy, yes.

ANNIE HOPE: There is another Anne and she believes, I am hopey
hope and I do not believe I have been in California and
Kalamazoo, and I do not believe I burst into tears and I do
not believe.

(*They all crowd closer together and* LILLIAN RUSSELL *who comes
in stands quite alone*)

LILLIAN RUSSELL: I can act so drunk that I never drink, I can drink
so drunk that I never act, I have a curl I was a girl and I am
old and fat but very handsome for all that.

(ANTHONY COMSTOCK *comes in and glares at her*)

ANTHONY COMSTOCK: I have heard that they have thought that
they would wish that one like you could vote a vote and help
to let the ones who want do what they like, I have heard that
even you, and I am through, I cannot hope that there is dope,
oh yes a horrid word. I have never heard, short.

JENNY REEFER: I have hope and faith, not charity no not charity, I
have hope and faith, no not, not charity, no not charity.

ULYSSES S. GRANT: Women are women, soldiers are soldiers, men
are not men, lies are not lies, do, and then a dog barks, listen
to him and then a dog barks, a dog barks a dog barks any dog
barks, listen to him any dog barks. (*He sits down*)

HERMAN ATLAN: I am not loved any more, I was loved oh yes I was
loved but I am not loved any more, I am not, was I not, I

knew I would refuse what a woman would choose and so I am not loved any more, not loved any more.

DONALD GALLUP: Last but not least, first and not best, I am tall as a man, I am firm as a clam, and I never change, from day to day.

(JO THE LOITERER *and* CHRIS A CITIZEN)

JO THE LOITERER: Let us dance and sing, Chrissy Chris, wet and not in debt, I am a married man and I know how I show I am a married man. She votes, she changes her name and she votes.

(*They all crowd together in front of the statue, there is a moment of silence and then a chorus*)

CHORUS: To vote the vote, the vote we vote, can vote do vote will vote could vote, the vote the vote.

JO THE LOITERER: I am the only one who cannot vote, no loiterer can vote.

INDIANA ELLIOT: I am a loiterer Indiana Loiterer and I can vote.

JO THE LOITERER: You only have the name, you have not got the game.

CHORUS: The vote the vote we will have the vote.

LILLIAN RUSSELL: It is so beautiful to meet you all here so beautiful.

ULYSSES S. GRANT: Vote the vote, the army does not vote, the general generals, there is no vote, bah vote.

CHORUS: The vote we vote we note the vote.

(*They all bow and smile to the statue. Suddenly* SUSAN B.*'s voice is heard*)

SUSAN B.'S VOICE: We cannot retrace our steps, going forward may be the same as going backwards. We cannot retrace our steps, retrace our steps. All my long life, all my life, we do not retrace our steps, all my long life, but.

(*A silence a long silence*)

But—we do not retrace our steps, all my long life, and here, here we are here, in marble and gold, did I say gold, yes I said gold, in marble and gold and where—

(*A silence*)

Where is where. In my long life of effort and strife, dear life, life is strife, in my long life, it will not come and go, I tell you so, it will stay it will pay but

(*A long silence*)

But do I want what we have got, has it not gone, what made it

live, has it not gone because now it is had, in my long life in my long life
(*Silence*)
Life is strife, I was a martyr all my life not to what I won but to what was done.
(*Silence*)
Do you know because I tell you so, or do you know, do you know.
(*Silence*)
My long life, my long life.

CURTAIN

GOODBYE, MY FANCY

A Comedy

FAY KANIN

First presented in 1948

FOREWORD

Despite the gender conservatism of the post-World War II years, when everyone from so-called experts to the popular media were sending women back to the kitchen, Fay Kanin not only had (and still has) an outstanding career but built that career by writing plays, films and television movies about other strong women. Born in 1917 to a Jewish family in New York City, Fay Mitchell lived her early years in Greensburg, Pennsylvania, then moved with her family to Elmira, New York, where she attended Elmira College before graduating from the University of Southern California. Her mother was a retired vaudeville performer, so she already had show business in her blood when she wed playwright Michael Kanin. The writing and acting family into which she married also included author Garson Kanin and Ruth Gordon, a popular actor-playwright in the forties better known today for her roles in such films as *Rosemary's Baby*. Fay Kanin began her career working in Hollywood, where she was a reader and screen writer, and it was in film and television that she would make her greatest mark. She performed for a year with the Hollywood Actors' Laboratory Theatre, and during World War II wrote and did commentary for a network radio program called "The Woman's Angle" that interpreted the war from a female perspective.

Kanin spent two years writing *Goodbye, My Fancy* (originally titled *Most Likely to Succeed*) intermittently because of family responsibilities. She once observed that although she'd written short stories, a short novel and screenplays, she found dramatic writing the hardest, "like playing a game of tennis in a telephone booth." Kanin did extensive revisions—particularly of the last act—during rehearsals and while the work traveled a long tryout circuit. *Goodbye, My Fancy* opened in New York on November 17, 1948, with Madeline Carroll, a screen star making her Broadway debut as Agatha Reed. The comedy proved very popular and ran for 446 performances before a road company began a lengthy tour. It was chosen for the *Ten Best Plays of 1948-9* and a few years later became a Warner Brothers film starring Joan Crawford as Agatha. (Despite her Hollywood experience, Kanin did not write the watered-down screenplay for the movie version.) Agatha has proved an attractive role for many famous performers, including Ann Harding; Kanin herself once played the lead in a Pasadena Playhouse revival of *Fancy*.

While the reviews were generally positive, some critics condescended to the play, the playwright or both. Among the favorable voices, Brooks Atkinson called *Fancy* "a type of comedy that amuses the theatregoer while it is improving his mind." Ward Morehouse in *The Sun* found it "a thoroughly engaging play," John Chapman in the *Daily News* praised what he considered a "pungent, intelligent comedy" and Richard Watts, Jr., despite reservations, dubbed *Fancy* "a bright and entertaining comedy that is far superior to the Broadway average in every way." Robert Garland, reviewing the play when major cast changes were made eight months into the run, saw *Fancy* as an "earnest, adult play with laughter on the surface and underneath, a fierce, almost frightening cry for common-sense."

On the negative side, John Lardner in the *New York Star* thought *Fancy* little more than a "pretty shell." His main objection seemed to be about Agatha: he doubted that "beautiful women" could either learn "the meaning of life and death as war correspondents" or sit in on "high-stake poker games with the boys." Bosley Crowther complained in the *New York Times* that "in its slickly stage-wise jumble of glib sophistication and romance, of sentiment and capsuled propaganda, it is just this side of farce." Most reviewers praised the acting—Shirley Booth as Woody was often singled out—and virtually every critic commented on the beauty of Madeline Carroll, whose looks attracted as much attention as her comedic skills and the role she played. Wollcott

Gibbs in *The New Yorker* described her as "an unusually ornamental girl."

The playwright herself received similar treatment, one columnist referring to her as "a vital and shapely girl in her mid twenties." (The "girl" was actually past thirty.) The combination of having married into a famous family and scoring a Broadway success with her first play made Kanin a celebrity and the subject of numerous articles and interviews. Some writers simply presented her views: "I'm a feminist. I don't think women are better than men, but I think they are just as good. I've put into my play my feeling that women should never back away from life, and I think that the women who see it are challenged." Most journalists, however, emphasized the fact that she was a wife and the mother of a young son as well as a successful author. When she wrote an article for *The Boston Post*, the newspaper's (male) editor suggested the topic: "How to write a play and run a family." Kanin obligingly averred that a professional woman must put family first because "an unfinished manuscript will lie quietly clipped in your file drawer until you come back to it. Your child won't."

The title of *Goodbye, My Fancy* comes from the final section of Walt Whitman's *Leaves of Grass*, his apostrophe to life and to the imagination. This is an appropriate poem for Kanin's protagonist, Agatha Reed, who in saying goodbye to the man she "fancies" is really exorcising a fanciful creation of her mind—a hero not of flesh but of her imagination. Kanin has said that she posed a question to herself when she wrote the play: "what happens to the man or woman who goes back to look at the past and tries to recapture it?" In fact, Agatha does find the past still alive when she returns to Good Hope College: James Merrill, whose cowardice two decades earlier let Agatha take all the blame for their affair, has grown increasingly cautious and hypocritical. When Agatha recites lines from Whitman's poem, she does so in tandem not with her old love but with his daughter, Ginny, who reminds her of the idealistic young woman she once was.

Goodbye, My Fancy may have been inspired by Kanin's own recent trip to Elmira College, the women's school she attended for three years. John Mason Brown was one of the few critics to see the importance of the education issue in the play, although in a *Saturday Review* article comparing *Goodbye, My Fancy* with James Bryant Conant's book *Education in a Divided World* he understandably found Kanin's treatment of the academic freedom issue less probing than Conant's. Kanin (like Flanagan and Clifford in the subplot of *Can You Hear Their Voices?*) emphasizes the education of young *women*, a timely subject in the late 1940s when the G.I. Bill was designed to provide higher education for men returning from war while the value of college study for women was questioned. There is something distinctly amiss at Good Hope College when the young women's curriculum is in the hands of a male college president and a male trustee whose primary aim seems to be to keep them ignorant. The ironic contrast between their professed goal of educating women and their equally strong desire to limit students' knowledge and aspirations foreshadows a similar conflict in Wendy Wasserstein's *Uncommon Women and Others*, written nearly thirty years later.

Kanin herself has said of *Fancy* that "if it has a theme, it is that every adult in this world has to tell the truth to the young." The president and trustees of Good Hope College want to shelter their charges, but the world has just come through a devastating war culminating with the detonation of the first atomic bombs; Kanin is aware that young people will shortly inherit a potentially very dangerous future. Agatha Reed challenges the notion that women's education is simply to prepare them to be homemakers and helpmates. She knows that these young White women—with their tennis rackets and English riding boots—come from the most economically privileged families; as Matt Cole points out, while teenagers at Good Hope are rolling hoops, their counterparts in Rome are selling their bodies to ward off starvation. Not surprisingly, Claude Griswold would prefer the whole of womankind to be like his wife Ellen, who apparently has never heard of the Spanish Civil War even though it occurred only a decade earlier. But just as Flanagan and Clifford place the responsibility for helping suffering farmers on the shoulders of young women like Harriet Bageheot, so Kanin places her faith in the female students at Good Hope, who have the power accorded them by race, class and economic privilege that so many other women are denied.

Claude Griswold's justification for banning the graphic war film is that he does not want to ruin the students' childhood. In fact, having profited handsomely from the last war he smugly pronounces that armed conflict is an inevitable result of "human nature." While *Goodbye, My Fancy* certainly does not question the country's participation in World War II, it is in the tradition of such anti-war dramas as Edna St. Vincent Millay's *Aria da Capo*, Molly Thacher's *Blocks* and Maria M. Coxe's *If Ye Break Faith*. Like many women playwrights before her, Kanin insists that if the world is to be made safe for peace, everyone must know the cost of war.

The spokeswoman for Kanin's viewpoint is Agatha Reed, whom one critic referred to as "a sort of liberal Clare Boothe, if you will pardon the paradox." (Since Boothe had recently been the most prominent woman in Congress, such comparisons were inevitable.) Writing several years later, Judith Olauson suggests that Agatha is "the post-war version of the 'new woman' who represented current feminine ideals." She argues that Agatha "epitomized the post-war image of the educated career woman who had foregone marriage and children during the war and was now ready to complete her busy life with the acquisitions of home and husband." As Agatha puts it, "There's quite a difference between a busy life and a full one."

Agatha, however, has been a career woman for some twenty years, so the war alone could not explain why she has postponed marriage; the late 1940s-1950s image of the ideal female also involved motherhood, a subject Kanin carefully avoids here. But Agatha is in most ways the perfect post-war "new woman": intelligent, witty, aggressive and successful—not to mention blonde, slender, attractive and apparently infinitely charismatic. On the one hand, Agatha is a very appealing character, an ideal toward which teenagers like Ginny can aspire and an antidote to blithely mindless women like Ellen Griswold. On the other hand, she is a fantasy that shows the flaws in an image even remotely approachable only by those born White and at least relatively well-to-do. There is some validity to critic Richard Watts, Jr.'s complaint that Agatha is too quick to condescend to others whose lives have been less successful than hers.

Watts also remains justifiably unconvinced that a woman with such a distinguished political career would fall for Matt Cole, a man who is so "bitingly witty about those serious-minded dreams of hers." Cole refers to women as "dames," declares "*I don't like women!*" and describes Agatha as "the only reporter I ever knew could sit in a poker game, win the biggest pot and still have every guy wondering what she'd be like in bed"—a markedly crude way of describing the new woman who combines "masculine" skill with "feminine" sex appeal. Kanin has struck a bargain with contemporary mores and the Broadway conventions they reflect and reinforce. Cole is in the tradition of the dashing outsider who wins the woman away from the dull suitor, while the verbal jousting between Matt and Agatha places them in the age-old stage pattern of the battling lovers. But instead of fully capitulating to the post-war domestic agenda, Kanin presents Agatha as an intelligent, independent woman who has no intention of letting romance inhibit her career as a liberal member of Congress. *Goodbye, My Fancy* is a compromise, a witty romantic comedy that also manages to ask probing questions about women's education and their roles in the contemporary world.

Kanin's next three plays, all co-written with her husband, include *His and Hers* (1954; a revision of the 1945 *Return Engagement*), an amusing but sentimental comedy about two playwrights whose marriage is jeopardized by their theatrical collaboration. After their first two joint efforts fail the couple divorces, but when they are forced to write a third play together they decide that their love is more important than the success of their work. Although *His and Hers* ran only two months, it may well provide autobiographical insights into the difficulties of writing couples. Fay and Michael Kanin continued collaborating for another decade after *His and Hers* but eventually pursued separate careers. Fay Kanin was quoted in *People Magazine* as saying "We decided we would have to keep the working collaboration or the marriage. We decided on the marriage."

While still writing together, the Kanins developed *Rashomon* (1959), based on the Japanese stories and classic film about a rape and a killing presented from several contradictory points of view. The play did well on Broadway and remains popular with college and little theater groups. They had moderate success with a musical called *The Gay Life* (1961; retitled *The High Life*) based on Arthur Schnitzler's *The Affairs of Anatol*, about a Viennese rake who eventually falls in love with the innocent young woman he was planning to marry as a joke. While *The Gay Life* is certainly clever—in one scene a miniature horse-drawn carriage races a rumor across the stage—it rarely rises above the level of farce.

The Kanins are probably better known for some half-dozen movie scripts on which they collaborated in the 1950s and early 60s, including the musical film version of Clare Boothe's *The Women* entitled *The Opposite Sex* (1956). They had perhaps their greatest success with *Teacher's Pet* (1958), which earned them an Academy Award nomination for best screenplay. A romantic comedy starring the incongruous pair of Doris Day and Clark Gable, *Teacher's Pet* has several similarities to *Goodbye, My Fancy*. Here again there is a triangle involving a newspaperman (Gable as James Gannon), a professor (Gig Young as Dr. Hugo Pine) and a successful career woman, this time a college journalism instructor named Erica Stone (Day). While the tone of the movie is lighter than that of the play—Pine's flaw is not cowardice, as Merrill's is, but a slightly weak head for alcohol—education again plays a central thematic role. The self-taught Gannon proudly announces that he never attended high school and scorns college-trained reporters, but he eventually admits to a prospective journalist: "you won't do any worse with an education and you might do a lot better." The movie ends with a metaphorical (and possibly literal) "wedding of the old pros and the eggheads."

In the 1970s Fay Kanin stopped collaborating with her husband and turned her attention to television; at the same time she began to delve more deeply into social issues, especially those affecting women. In *Notable Women in the American Theatre*, Jean Prinz Korf describes *Tell Me Where It Hurts* (1974) as a story about a middle-aged homemaker who "feeling useless after her children are grown...sets out to find her own place in the world and at the same time re-educates her husband." To prepare for writing the film Kanin did first-person interviews with groups of women; she herself played a small role in *Tell Me Where It Hurts*, which earned her an Emmy Award for best original television drama. *Hustling* (1975)—for which Kanin was associate producer as well—is based on Gail Sheehy's study of prostitution in New York City. Kanin again did her own research, this time by speaking with prostitutes, and her screenplay explores both class and gender issues. The film opens as a group of suburban women leaving a Broadway play encounter several streetwalkers; the theater-goers complain about and laugh at the prostitutes, who return their taunts. In addition to making a point about class antagonisms, Kanin is contrasting the fantasies presented *inside* the Broadway theater with the real life of women on the streets outside. One of the most important questions the film (like the book) asks is why the criminal justice system targets prostitutes rather than their customers, their abusive pimps or the wealthy entrepreneurs who clear huge profits from the hotels in which "business" is transacted—why, in short, women are not only bought and sold but held responsible for a system that uses them. Kanin won the Writer's Guild Award for the *Hustling* script.

She also wrote and co-produced the television movie *Friendly Fire* (1979), based on the book of the same name by C.D.B. Bryan. *Friendly Fire* follows an Iowa farm couple as they try to discover how their son, killed in Vietnam by the ironically named "friendly fire" from American guns, really died. The quest turns them into anti-war activists. While Kanin is faithful to Bryan's account of the actual case, her sympathy with the material is evident: like the fictional Agatha Reed, the real-life Peg Mullen wants both to learn and to publicize the facts of war. *Friendly Fire* garnered several awards, including an Emmy for the best television film of the year.

Kanin joined with Lillian Gallo in the late 1970s to form a production company for television and movies; according to an article in *People Magazine*, they were "the only female team under exclusive contract to a network." Among their productions was *Fun and Games* (1980) about sexual harassment. But Kanin also wanted to take one more try at Broadway, and she did so with the book for the 1985 musical *Grind*, which earned her a Tony nomination. *Grind*, with music by Larry Grossman and lyrics by Ellen Fitzhugh, is set in a Depression-era burlesque house that has both Black and White performers but keeps them segregated offstage as well as on—until racist attacks make them see the necessity of joining together. Like many of Kanin's works *Grind* includes a romantic triangle; this time, however, the triangle is interracial. Kanin's last stage effort was not a success: most reviewers liked neither the show's music nor the lyrics, and more than one complained that the book was "didactic." Still, although the *New York Times*'s Frank Rich had few good things to say about *Grind*, he conceded that "Mrs. Kanin's aspirations are honorable." Perhaps the most positive comment came from John Beaufort in *The Christian Science Monitor*, who felt that this "team of talented collaborators has sought not only to explore the onstage and backstage existence of a show-biz subculture, but to say something meaningful about race and human relations." Apparently Broadway audiences were not anxious to hear something meaningful; *Grind* closed two months later.

In addition to writing, producing and occasionally acting, Kanin served four terms as president of the Academy of Motion Picture Arts and Sciences, only the second woman to hold that post (Bette Davis had previously served for one month in the job), and traveled throughout the world as a representative of the Academy. Among her numerous honors are the Carrie Chapman Catt Award from the League of Women Voters, the Writer's Guild Valentine Davies Award, the Crystal Award from the Women in Film Association, and the Internationalism Award from American Women for International Understanding. When Kanin was honored in 1987 with a Bill of Rights Award by the Southern California American Civil Liberties Union, she was hailed as a woman who "pushed down barriers—not only for herself, but for her contemporaries and for generations of women who followed"—praise that, ironically, fits both Kanin and Agatha Reed. In another example of life imitating art, Kanin was awarded an honorary Doctor of Humane Letters from Elmira College in 1981, just as her fictional character had received an honorary degree from the imaginary Good Hope College some thirty years earlier. In creating Agatha Reed, Fay Kanin appears to have foreseen her own career as a highly successful and influential woman in the male worlds of theater, movies and television.

SELECTED BIBLIOGRAPHY

Brown, John Mason. "Seeing Things: Two College Presidents." *Saturday Review*, 8 January 1949, 30-1.

Dudar, Helen. "Theater: One Foot on Broadway, the Other in Hollywood." *The New York Times.* 14 April 1985, sec. H, 6, 28.

"Fay Kanin Throws a Party for Tout Hollywood and the World: She's Oscar Night's First Lady." *People Magazine*, 21 April 1980, 45-9.

Kanin, Fay. *Hustling.* television film based on book by Gail Sheehy. 1975. (available on videotape)

————. *Friendly Fire.* television film based on book by C.D.B. Bryan. 1979. (available on videotape)

Kanin, Fay, and Michael Kanin. *The High Life.* N.Y.: Samuel French, 1961.

————. *His and Hers.* N.Y.: Samuel French, 1954.

————. *Rashomon.* N.Y.: Samuel French, 1959.

————. *Teacher's Pet.* Paramount, 1958. (available on videotape)

Korf, Jean Prinz. "Fay Mitchell Kanin." In *Notable Women in the American Theatre*, ed. Alice M. Robinson, et al. N.Y.: Greenwood, 1989.

Olauson, Judith. *The American Woman Playwright: A View of Criticism and Characterization.* Troy, N.Y.: Whitson Publishing, 1981.

A NOTE ON THE TEXT

This is the text of *Goodbye, My Fancy* published by Samuel French in 1949. (An acting edition, with a few revisions and additional stage directions, was published in 1950.)

CHARACTERS

GINNY MERRILL
AMELIA
CLARISSE
MARY NELL
MISS SHACKLEFORD
JANITORS
TELEPHONE MAN
SUSAN
GRACE WOODS
AGATHA REED
ELLEN GRISWOLD
PROFESSOR BIRDESHAW
CAROL
JO
DOCTOR PITT
JAMES MERRILL
PROFESSOR DINGLEY
MATT COLE
CLAUDE GRISWOLD

The entire action of the play takes place over Commencement Weekend in early June 1948 in a dormitory room of Good Hope College for Women in Good Hope, Mass.

ACT ONE
Friday morning.

ACT TWO
Scene I: Saturday afternoon.
Scene II: Saturday evening.

ACT THREE
Sunday afternoon.

ACT ONE

SCENE: *With the possible exception of twins and matrimony, there is no relationship closer both spiritually and physically than that peculiar educational phenomenon known as "roommates." Outside the U.S.S.R., communal living has no purer form.*

If you don't believe it, take a look at the sitting room of a student suite in a dormitory of Good Hope College for Women in Good Hope, Mass. There are two of almost everything—two small desks, two reading lamps, two pin-up boards full of a heterogeneous collection of pictures, notes, memos. There's only one portable radio-victrola. But that's all right, because the other portable radio-victrola is in the bedroom, entered through a door down Left. Though you can't see it, you know the bedroom contains two beds, two dressers, two mirrors and so on ad infinitum.

Hope Hall was endowed by a rich and sentimental alumna with a love for old Gothic architecture, and so the room has the grace of a window seat bay with leaded windows and a small but nice stone fireplace. Otherwise it has the kind of simplicity dictated by college dormitory budgets.

Ordinarily, the room is very neatly kept, but today, as the Curtain rises, it's bedlam. There are several suitcases standing in the Center of the room and a couple of heavy cartons obviously in the process of being filled. Some tennis rackets, a bow and a quiver of arrows, and a pair of English riding boots are spilling off a chair. One of the pin-up boards is down and leaning against a desk, and a stocking hanger with four dampish stockings is swinging gently from the neck of a standing lamp. At stage Left, the victrola is playing a jive record.

GINNY MERRILL *enters through the corridor doorway. She's nineteen—alert, intelligent, sensitive. She wears a cotton sundress and sandals, carries a book. She looks around at the state of the room with surprise.* AMELIA, *an excited Senior, races in from the bedroom, carrying an armload of clothes.*

AMELIA: Oh, Ginny! Mary Nell's been trying to find you all over. (*Over her shoulder*) Do we take any of the stuff in here?

MARY NELL'S VOICE: No. Janitors can get that. Thanks.

    (AMELIA *exits as* CLARISSE, *another Senior, enters from the bedroom with her arms full.*)

CLARISSE: (*Excitedly*) You're doubling up with us. (*She goes out.*)

GINNY: Hey! What's going on?

    (MARY NELL *enters from the bedroom, carrying a pair of skis.*

MARY NELL *is very pretty, even in faded jeans and run-over moccasins.*)

MARY NELL: Well, it's about time! Where've you been?

GINNY: At the Libe.

MARY NELL: At the Libe? Finals are all over.

GINNY: People sometimes go to libraries even when they're *not* cramming for exams.

MARY NELL: (*Crossing to put down the skis*) I've got most of your stuff packed anyway.

GINNY: What's the rush? We've got another three days on campus.

MARY NELL: (*Bursting*) Guess who's going to stay here—right in these rooms?

GINNY: (*Turning off the victrola*) Agatha Reed?

MARY NELL: (*Disappointed*) How did you know?

GINNY: That's what I've been doing at the Libe. Reading up on her. (*She holds up the book.*) *Women in the Vanguard.* Tells all about her college days. How she and her roommate had the two corner rooms on the first floor of Hope Hall. (*Looking out the window*) With the windows facing the willow trees.

MARY NELL: Isn't it exciting? Imagine her looking at these same walls, studying at the same desks—

GINNY: Going to the same john.

MARY NELL: Gives me goose pimples.

GINNY: I thought she was going to stay at the Dean's.

MARY NELL: They got a wire this morning not to meet her at the station—a friend's *flying* her down instead. And she hopes they're planning to let her stay in her old rooms at Hope Hall.

GINNY: (*Suddenly noticing the empty space*) Where's our sofa?

MARY NELL: They took it away. Someone got the idea to find the original furniture. You better start on the junk over there. We can sort it out later.

GINNY: I wonder what she's like.

MARY NELL: Busty, probably. Most women with brains, I notice it goes right to their bust.

GINNY: I don't mean what she looks like.

MARY NELL: Well, she's getting an honorary degree, isn't she?

GINNY: Oh, that's just a racket. (*As* MARY NELL *looks at her, shocked*) Well, isn't it? Some celebrity gets a few fancy letters after his name. School gets publicity or a new wing on the science building. Good business.

MARY NELL: You make it sound awful, Ginny. After all, Agatha
Reed is a—

GINNY: Oh, I don't mean her exactly. Matter of fact, she's one of
the few who might deserve it. She's *done* something.

MARY NELL: I should think so, writing for all those newspapers.
And now, being in Congress.

GINNY: Nuts. Anyone can be in Congress these days. It's what they
do there that counts.

MARY NELL: I thought they just voted on things.

GINNY: Really, Mary Nell, for someone who's graduating—
(MISS SHACKLEFORD *enters from the hall, followed by two*
JANITORS *carrying a faded love seat.* MISS SHACKLEFORD *is also
faded, but she makes up for it with an overwhelming air of authority. She is the Alumnae Secretary, and has been as long as practically
anybody can remember.*)

MISS SHACKLEFORD: Put it right over there—in front of the table.
(*As they set it down*) Carefully, now. It's not very sturdy.

MARY NELL: (*Disappointed*) Is *that* it?

MISS SHACKLEFORD: Yes. We did the best we could with it on such
short notice.
(*The* JANITORS *exit.*)

GINNY: (*Trying it*) You mean Agatha Reed sat here? (*Wincing*)
Spring's broken.

MISS SHACKLEFORD: Well, they can't expect sentiment *and* comfort. I've just spent the whole morning tracking it down—to
one of the basement rooms.

GINNY: Such is fame.

MISS SHACKLEFORD: It's very generous of you girls—giving up
your rooms. But then, it's quite an honor. It'll be something
to tell your children.

MARY NELL: Like people who slept in Napoleon's bed. (*Hastily*) I
mean after he was dead, of course.

MISS SHACKLEFORD: Of course. Did your father happen to mention
what time her plane might be arriving, Virginia?

GINNY: (*Freezing*) I don't see Father except on holidays, Miss
Shackleford. I live here in the dorm, you know.

MISS SHACKLEFORD: Well, I just thought he might have. (*As she
exits*) Now where are those men with the rest of the things—?

GINNY: She's a finger-down-the-throat, if I ever saw one.

MARY NELL: Oh, Alumnae Secretaries have to gush around. The
Alums like it. Besides, you're too sensitive about your father,

Ginny. Everybody knows you don't take advantage of it. If *my* father was president of this college, I'd have lived in a penthouse on top of the Libe and never taken gym—

GINNY: Is that all?

MARY NELL: And had men imported from Princeton every weekend.

(MISS SHACKLEFORD *re-enters with the* JANITORS *who are carrying a framed reproduction, a small step-ladder and a Windsor chair.*)

MISS SHACKLEFORD: (*Giving orders*) Over the fireplace. You can take the other one down. Put that chair there—and move the dictionary stand over there.

GINNY: Why, that's Uncle Willy!

(*She's staring at the picture one* JANITOR *is hanging.*)

MISS SHACKLEFORD: I think you're mistaken, Virginia. That's "The Laughing Cavalier" by—(*Stuck*)

GINNY: Frans Hals. I know. But father has one just like it in his study. We always called him Uncle Willy.

MISS SHACKLEFORD: This is your father's. We borrowed it. Somebody remembered one like it used to hang in this room.

(*A* TELEPHONE MAN *enters. He's quite young, nice-looking—a fact* MARY NELL *doesn't miss.*)

TELEPHONE MAN: This where the phone extension goes?

MISS SHACKLEFORD: Yes, put it—well, wherever telephones go.

(*As the* TELEPHONE MAN *goes about wiring the extension to one of the desks,* MISS SHACKLEFORD *turns to the* JANITORS.)

You can take the rest of those things.

MARY NELL: There's still some stuff we haven't taken down—

GINNY: Let's leave a little. It'll make her feel more at home.

(*There's a moment in which everyone seems to get in everyone else's way. A box crashes to the floor.*)

MISS SHACKLEFORD: Organization, everyone! We'll never get through the weekend like this without organization.

(*The* JANITORS *exit.*)

GINNY: I'd better take a last look in the bedroom.

(*She exits into bedroom as* SUSAN, *a Junior student, enters through the hall doorway.*)

SUSAN: Miss Shackleford, there's a man outside with a tree.

MISS SHACKLEFORD: Oh yes, for the Tree Planting Ceremony.

SUSAN: He says, "Where do you want it?"

MISS SHACKLEFORD: Well, let me see—someplace near the Ivy

Arch. (*Looking out the window*) My goodness, not that monster! I distinctly told him a very young tree—practically a branch. (*Heading for the door*) I told him we wanted to plant it ourselves. Well, he'll just have to take it right back—
(*She exits,* SUSAN *after her.*)

TELEPHONE MAN: (*Into telephone*) Hello, Ed? It's all set.
(GINNY *enters from the bedroom.*)

MARY NELL: Find anything else?

GINNY: (*Throwing her a shower cap*) Behind the radiator.

MARY NELL: My God! I lost it Junior Year.

TELEPHONE MAN: (*Crossing to the door*) You can use that phone now.

MARY NELL: Thank you.

TELEPHONE MAN: Mind if I keep the telephone number?
(MARY NELL *gives him a freeze. He turns up his coat collar, exits.*)

MARY NELL: He's cute. (*Turning immediately to the telephone*) Wouldn't it have been wonderful if we'd had it all last year? I could have talked to Sam without the whole floor listening in.

GINNY: It never seemed to inhibit you any.

MARY NELL: (*Draping herself across the window seat*) I don't know. There's something about talking to a man when you're lying down—(*She languidly picks up the phone.*) Da-arling—Of course I love you, you silly fool. Last night? Da-arling, let's have no regrets. Until tomorrow, then—Au revoir.
(*Wearily, she drops the telephone back on its hook. It rings, suddenly. They both jump as if they've never heard a telephone before. It rings again.*)

GINNY: Well—answer it.

MARY NELL: (*Picking it up gingerly*) Hello? Hello—What? Oh. (*Cupping her hand over the mouthpiece*) It's long distance. New York! (*Into telephone*) No, she isn't here yet. I said, she isn't here yet.—Who? (*Her eyes widen and she cups her hand over the mouthpiece again.*) It's *Life Magazine*! (*Into telephone*) No. No, this is Mary Nell Dodge. —Mary Nell Do—I don't think you'd know even if you *could* hear me. —Yes, they're expecting her very soon. —Yes, I'll tell her. I'll write it down. (GINNY *notes it on a pad as* MARY NELL *says it.*) *Matt Cole.* Delayed.—Yes, I certainly will. (*She hangs up.*)

GINNY: *Life Magazine?*

MARY NELL: They're sending a man over to cover the whole weekend!

(*A woman appears in the doorway, carrying a briefcase, a portable typewriter, and one small suitcase. She's in her late forties, almost exactly* MARY NELL'*s description of a brainy woman—plenty busty. It just so happens, though, that she's not* AGATHA REED *but her secretary,* GRACE WOODS, *better known around Washington circles as* WOODY.)

MARY NELL: (*Recognizing her as* AGATHA) Oh, they just hung up! Maybe you could still get the Operator.

WOODY: Who just hung up?

MARY NELL: *Life Magazine!*

WOODY: Oh.

MARY NELL: Their man got held up in New York, but he'll be here as soon as he can. (*She hands* WOODY *the paper.*) It's all written down.

WOODY: (*Taking the paper unexcitedly*) Uh-huh.
(*She crosses to the desk, and puts down her briefcase and typewriter. The girls stare at her, fascinated.*)

GINNY: I'm Ginny Merrill. And this is my roommate, Mary Nell Dodge.

WOODY: How are you?

GINNY: It's a great pleasure to have you here—in our rooms.

MARY NELL: We would have been out sooner. Except things got a little mixed up.

WOODY: (*Walking toward the bedroom door*) This the bedroom?

GINNY: Yes. (*After* WOODY *exits into it*) Doesn't she remember?

MARY NELL: It's been a long time.

GINNY: (*Bleakly*) Anyway, you were right.

MARY NELL: About what?

GINNY: (*Pantomiming the bust profile*) And I thought—
(MARY NELL *quiets her as* WOODY *re-enters, crosses to the desk, opens the briefcase and starts to take out some papers.*)

MARY NELL: (*Tentatively*) I suppose you've noticed—

WOODY: What?

MARY NELL: (*Pointing to it*) The sofa.

WOODY: Could stand recovering.

GINNY: They thought you'd like it this way.

MARY NELL: Carted it all the way up from the basement.

GINNY: (*Indicating "The Laughing Cavalier"*) And the picture—

WOODY: They cart that up from the basement, too?

GINNY: (*A little angry*) We'd better go, Mary Nell. And leave Miss Reed alone—with her memories.

WOODY: Miss Reed *is* alone with her memories. Outside, under a tree.

MARY NELL: Then, who—?

WOODY: Me? I just carry the typewriter.

GINNY: Oh, her secretary! (*Happily*) How do you do?

MARY NELL: She must be under the willows!

(*They dash to the window and hang out. Not much of them except two excited behinds is visible as* AGATHA REED *enters. As far from* MARY NELL's *expectations as possible, she's undoubtedly the best thing that's happened to the United States Congress in a long time. She wears a smart lightweight suit and carries her hat and a small suitcase.*)

WOODY: (*Indicating the two behinds*) Your reception committee.

(*The girls turn at the voice. But* AGATHA *doesn't even notice. She's drinking in the room, her face suffused with nostalgia. She wanders around touching the sofa, fingering the desk, standing for a second under the picture of "Uncle Willy." They all watch her—the girls respectfully,* WOODY *disgustedly. Finally, she disappears into the bedroom.*)

MARY NELL: Gosh! I felt like I was in church!

GINNY: Doesn't anybody know she's here?

WOODY: I doubt it. She had the taxi stop two blocks away so we could take some short cut.

MARY NELL: Through the alfalfa field—behind the gym!

WOODY: Yeah—! (*Irritably picks things off her stockings*)

GINNY: (*Picking up the skis*) We'd better tell them she's here. (*She exits.*)

WOODY: Give her five minutes. Let her have a good cry.

MARY NELL: We'll give her *ten* minutes.

WOODY: Five's enough. Let's not overdo it.

MARY NELL: I'm leaving her my vic. There's some Sinatras and Comos. And a keen Stan Kenton.

WOODY: Oh—peachy! (MARY NELL *hurries out.* WOODY *picks up the telephone.*) Hello. How late does Western Union stay open?— I see. What about the switchboard here? Somebody on it all night? (AGATHA *enters from the bedroom.*) —Well, could we arrange that? Miss Reed may have to be in touch with Washington at any hour. Fine. (*She hangs up.*)

AGATHA: (*Wiping her eyes*) I haven't cried in years. It feels wonderful.

WOODY: It looks lousy.

AGATHA: You don't understand. You just see a collection of build-
    ings, a gate, some ivy—
WOODY: What do *you* see?
AGATHA: Myself at eighteen—eager, expectant, a little frightened.
    Asking—what is life? What am I? This is where it all starts.
WOODY: You sound like an alumnae bulletin.
AGATHA: Don't you even believe in colleges?
WOODY: I don't believe in looking at the past. I was born in
    Newark, New Jersey. Every time I go through on a train, I
    pull down the shade.
AGATHA: You ought to see a psychoanalyst.
WOODY: I just don't get it, that's all. A crowded calendar, two
    important bills coming out of committee, an election just four
    months off—and we're braiding a daisy chain.
AGATHA: Look, Woody, let's get this settled right now. I've come
    down here to *enjoy* this weekend. I'm going to cry, I'm going
    to be silly, I'm going to be sentimental, I'm going to walk
    barefoot down memory lane with ivy entwined in my hair. If
    you don't like it, you don't have to look.
WOODY: (*Shrugs and picks up her notebook*) What do you want to do
    about that Madison Square Garden rally ? There's a choice of
    dates.
AGATHA: (*Plaintively*) Not now—
WOODY: The world doesn't stop, even for Honorary Degrees.
AGATHA: (*With a sigh*) All right, tell them I think it should be the
    earliest date they can get. (*Sitting on the sofa, she winces*) They
    never fixed it!
WOODY: Fixed what?
AGATHA: The spring. Ellie broke it when she got her junior grades.
    She thought old Dennis was going to flunk her. When she
    got the C, she jumped up and down on the sofa for ten min-
    utes.
WOODY: I'll wire them you'll speak—if they can make it next week.
    Who's Ellie?
AGATHA: My roommate, Ellen Thatcher. She was a beautiful girl.
    They called us Sugar and Spice. (*Crossing to the window seat*)
    We used to sit over here—on this window seat—spring nights
    after Lights Out and talk about Life. (*Smiling*) We had a pact.
    Wherever in the world we were, we'd send each other a
    telegram when we lost our respective virginities.
WOODY: Well?

AGATHA: Whatever happens to all girlhood pacts?

WOODY: (WOODY *grunts eloquently and turns over to the next sheet of paper.*) Mrs. S. Arthur Poinceford invites you for a cruise on her yacht the week of the twenty-ninth. Down to Florida—back by Monday.

AGATHA: That's the oil lobby. Tell her oil and water don't mix. (*At the desk*) There's a little secret panel in this desk. (*She pulls out a drawer and feels around behind it.*) I used to hide brownies in it. You share your clothes, your perfume, even your themes with your roommate. But not your brownies. Not the— (*She reacts suddenly, draws out a small box, opens it.*) Brownies!

WOODY: God, they must be stale.

AGATHA: (*She tastes one. Relieved*) Fresh this week. (*She offers the box to* WOODY.)

WOODY: (*Grimacing*) Horrible stuff. Sticks to the roof of your mouth.

AGATHA: Now I *know* you need a psychoanalyst.

WOODY: (*Consulting the paper in her hand*) Hope you feel photogenic. *Life*'s covering the weekend.

AGATHA: Oh, that's nice.

WOODY: You *must* be getting important. They're sending Matt Cole down.

AGATHA: (*Turning abruptly*) Who?

WOODY: Matt Cole, the war photographer.

AGATHA: You're joking.

WOODY: That's what it says here. (*Reading*) "Matt Cole delayed." One of the kids took the message.

AGATHA: Why should they send *him* down here? This isn't his kind of thing at all. It's—it's ridiculous.

WOODY: (*Shrugging*) Maybe he needs a vacation.

AGATHA: (*Obviously perturbed*) You call Henry Luce. They've got twenty men that can do a better job on this sort of thing. Tell him I *don't want Matt Cole*—I'd consider it a personal favor if he'd see to it.

WOODY: Why bother?

AGATHA: (*Firmly*) I *want* to bother.

WOODY: (*Shrugging*) You're the boss. Might've been interesting, though. (*Picking up the telephone*) Get me New York. — Yeah—*Life Magazine*.—All right, put it through whenever the circuits *are* free. (*She hangs up.*) The circuits are busy.

AGATHA: Well, keep after it.

GINNY: (GINNY *has appeared in the hallway. She knocks against the framework to attract their attention.*) I'm sorry to disturb you—

AGATHA: Oh, that's all right—

GINNY: But I forgot something. (*She starts toward the desk.*)

AGATHA: I'm afraid I found them. I've been a pig about it, too.
(*She holds the box of brownies toward* GINNY.)

GINNY: Oh, you keep them.

AGATHA: You won't have to twist my arm. I don't get brownies very often. Not good ones like these.

GINNY: I made them myself.

AGATHA: Really? What do you use—whole chocolate or ground?

GINNY: Chocolate *syrup*. That's the secret. It's what makes them so wet.

WOODY: Oh, brother! (*She crosses to the bedroom and exits.*)

GINNY: (*Going to the desk*) I didn't really come for the brownies. I always hide the book I'm reading in here. It's the only way I can get to finish it without somebody waltzing in and borrowing it. (*She fishes a book out of the secret panel.*)

AGATHA: Is it good, the book?

GINNY: It's *Leaves of Grass* by Walt Whitman.

AGATHA: Oh, I'm very fond of Walt Whitman.

GINNY: (*Pleased*) Are you?

AGATHA: Matter of fact, I have a favorite.

GINNY: Which one?

AGATHA: It's a rather obscure one. "Goodbye, my fancy, Farewell, dear mate, dear love. I'm going away, I know not where—"

GINNY: "—Or to what fortune, or whether I may ever see you again. So goodbye, my fancy." (*They look at each other in mutual appreciation.*) I like that one, too. I'd never read much Whitman till Dr. Pitt gave me the book.

AGATHA: Your English teacher?

GINNY: No, Physics.

AGATHA: Oh. (*Smiling*) Walt Whitman seems a little far afield.

GINNY: You don't know Dr. Pitt. When he teaches, you learn about everything.

AGATHA: Sounds as if I'd like to know him. (*Examining* GINNY) Do you want to be a poet?

GINNY: Oh, no.

AGATHA: What *do* you want to be?

GINNY: I don't know yet. I guess that sounds odd from a college Senior. Only—I think it's more important to know what you want than what you want to be. Does that make sense?

AGATHA: (*Impressed*) Yes, of course. (*Then*) You know, I don't know your name.

GINNY: I'm sorry. It's Ginny. Ginny Merrill.

AGATHA: How do you do? (*They shake hands.*)

GINNY: Mary Nell's telling them you're here. I'd better be going. I guess they'll all be in soon.

AGATHA: Sounds very formal. Better comb my hair. (*She starts toward the bedroom, suddenly stops herself.*) Merrill. (*Turning*) Your parents—will they be here for Commencement?

GINNY: There's just my father.

AGATHA: Oh. Does he—have to come very far?

GINNY: (*Uncomfortably*) No. As a matter of fact—

AGATHA: You're Jim Merrill's daughter!

GINNY: Yes.

AGATHA: I should have known.

GINNY: Why?

AGATHA: You look like him. Something you do with your mouth when you talk— (*Feeling it suddenly necessary to explain*) I knew your father very well. He was *my* favorite professor.

GINNY: I always forget Father once taught History 101A. (*Then*) What was he like?

AGATHA: Very handsome. All the girls were in love with him.

GINNY: They still are. Old as he is.

AGATHA: Not so old.

GINNY: In his forties.

AGATHA: (*Amused*) I guess it depends on your point of view.

GINNY:. Was he a good teacher?

AGATHA: Very. He had a way of making history come to life. Not just dates and battles but real things that happened to real people. I remember once I cried all night when he told us about John Brown. It was the most wonderful thing that happened to me my whole Freshman year.

GINNY: Did he know about it?

AGATHA: Yes. I wrote him a note and told him. And he wrote me back a note. I remember what it said. (*Smiling*) "My dear Miss Reed—I'm sorry I made you cry. I shall try to make up for it next month when we discuss the Coolidge administration."

GINNY: (*After a moment*) I wish he was still a teacher.

AGATHA: Why? Is being President of the College so bad?

GINNY: It's—different.

AGATHA: A little heavier on the dignity side, I guess.

GINNY: Yes.

(*A woman appears in the doorway. She has the look of a beauty who has eaten too many finger sandwiches at too many afternoon teas. She wears an expensive print dress and a much-too-fancy hat, and carries a large paper hat box. This, I'm sorry to say, is* ELLEN GRISWOLD, *née Thatcher.*)

AGATHA: (*Seeing her*) Ellie—!

ELLIE: Ag—! (*They come together and embrace in a very genuine rush of emotion.*) It's so good to see you. I heard you'd arrived and I had to hurry over before the others.

GINNY: (*Rising*) I'd better be going.

ELLEN: Oh, hello Ginny.

GINNY: Hello, Mrs. Griswold.

AGATHA: (*Crossing to* GINNY) Wait a minute. I'll be seeing you again, won't I?

GINNY:. Oh yes. Matter of fact, I'm supposed to be getting dressed right now to be introduced to you.

AGATHA: Well, let's call this a rehearsal.

(GINNY *smiles and exits.* AGATHA *turns to* ELLEN *who's looking up at the picture of "Uncle Willy."*)

ELLEN: Uncle Willy doesn't look a day older, docs he?

AGATHA: Wasn't it nice of them to remember? (*Noticing the box Ellen's carrying*) What's all that?

ELLEN: Just some old things I've saved. I dug them out when I heard you were coming. (*She takes them out of the box one by one and hands them to* AGATHA.) That sketch I made of Smitty in art class. You put the mustache on it, with real hair. Remember? (*As* AGATHA *nods, she takes out a stuffed doll with red wool hair.*) Clara Bow. You forgot to take her when you left. (*Another piece of paper*) The theme you wrote for me when I had the hangover from Dartmouth Winter Carnival. (*She takes out a victrola record.*) And one of our old victrola records. Betty Boop. Our favorite. (*She sees the victrola and, crossing, puts the record on the turntable.*) Let's hear it again.

AGATHA: (*Stopping her*) Later, later— (*Holding her off*) I haven't had a chance to look at you.

ELLEN: (*Defensively*) I've put on some weight, I know. Too many bridge luncheons. And Claude won't let me diet.

AGATHA: Claude. That's your husband.

ELLEN: Yes.

AGATHA: (*Trying to remember*) I never met him, did I?

ELLEN: No, I didn't meet him myself till a few years after I'd left school. We had one of those big church weddings—I sent you an invitation.

AGATHA: I was in Spain. I found it when I got back.

ELLEN: Claude and I nearly went to Spain on our honeymoon. (*Searching*) There was some reason—

AGATHA: The war.

ELLEN: (*Vaguely*) War—?

AGATHA: The Spanish Civil War. That was my first big newspaper job.

ELLEN: Oh, that's right. That's the one where the Russians were fighting it out with the Nazis or something.

AGATHA: Well, not quite.

ELLEN: Oh, it's all too much for me. I don't bother with those things. If there's anything I want to know I just ask Claude. (*As AGATHA looks at her*) It's convenient having a husband.

AGATHA: So I've been told.

ELLEN: (*With a touch of embarrassment*) You know, I never did send you that telegram—like we promised. I guess I figured the wedding invitation would—

AGATHA: It did.

ELLEN: (*Archly*) I've never gotten one from you either.

AGATHA: Must have slipped my mind at the moment. (*As Ellen's back straightens ever so slightly, she changes the subject.*) I hear you have a child.

ELLEN: *Two.* Both boys. I'd like to have a girl but it's so much trouble at my age. Maybe you can come to dinner and see them. We have a big barn of a house—eighteen rooms. I could have just a few people, the Mayor and the Falkners—that's Falkner Tools. And most of the trustees are in town. Claude's Chairman of the Board of Trustees, you know.

AGATHA: No, I didn't.

ELLEN: Ever since the year I was elected President of the Alumnae Association. It's so cute—the interest he takes in the school. Gets a big kick out of it when the girls call him Daddy Griswold. He's always giving them things. This year it's a projection booth and movie equipment. They're renaming the theatre—*Griswold* Theatre.

AGATHA: Oh yes, Miss Shackleford wrote and asked me to bring down a documentary film from Washington—for the program this weekend. So I brought my own.

ELLEN: Your own?

AGATHA: Yes. *Fight to the Finish*. It's based on a speech of mine.

ELLEN: Isn't that wonderful? You know, I always talk about how I knew you when. How we all voted you the-girl-most-likely-to-succeed. (*A pause*) Of course, I never say anything about your being expelled.

AGATHA: Thank you. (*Amused*) I guess there won't be much said about that this weekend.

ELLEN: I never did understand it, Agatha. Student Court was so hush-hush about it, nobody could find out a thing. Of course, everyone knew there was a man connected with it. You don't get expelled for staying out all night unless there's a man connected with it.

AGATHA: (*Staring at her*) You know, I've got the most peculiar feeling, Ellen. That you haven't changed—at all.

ELLEN: Thank you! That's what Claude says. He says if I ever change he'll divorce—(*Suddenly reacting to something she sees out the window*) Here they come—the whole delegation! (*To* AGATHA, *reproachfully*) You upset the applecart, you know. They had an elaborate welcome planned for you at the railroad station.

AGATHA: Oh, I'm sorry.

ELLEN: (*Peering through the window*) Miss Shackleford, leading the way, and the Student Committee. Miss Birdeshaw—you remember her—?

AGATHA: Old Fun-in-Bed Birdeshaw?

ELLEN: Still here. And still teaching Physiology. Only now they call it Sex Hygiene. (*Squinting*) And a man— (*Surprised*) Why, it's Dr. Pitt. Isn't it just like Shackleford to pull a boner and put him on the Reception Committee?

AGATHA: Dr. Pitt? Physics professor?

ELLEN: Yes.

AGATHA: Why, a boner?

ELLEN: Well, Claude says he's a troublemaker. Jim's going to get rid of him next year. (*Then*) You knew they made Jim Merrill President, the year after you left?

AGATHA: Yes, I read it in the papers.

ELLEN: It was quite an honor—he was pretty young for it. And generally they bring in a President from outside. But he was so terribly popular. And he's done a great job. (*She straightens*

her hat.) I'm glad I came ahead, Agatha. I wanted this cozy little chat with you alone, just like old times. I've enjoyed it.

AGATHA: I have too, Ellen. (*Wryly*) It's the first time in years I've
been alone with anyone that I haven't been asked what's
going on in Washington.

ELLEN: Oh, you never have to worry about that from me. I always
say the less women worry about the government, the better.
(*Realizing it's a faux pas*) Except *Congresswomen*, of course.
(AGATHA *is looking at her, almost as if she can't believe it, as the
whole delegation enters the room. The girls are in white dresses—
each carries a bouquet of flowers.* MISS SHACKLEFORD, *in the
vanguard, sweeps up to* AGATHA *and shakes her hand.*)

MISS SHACKLEFORD: (*Resoundingly*) Welcome home, Agatha Reed!

AGATHA: Thank you, Miss Shackleford.

MISS SHACKLEFORD: Or should I call you—the Honorable?

AGATHA: Definitely not.

MISS SHACKLEFORD: (*Chidingly*) I see Mrs. Griswold's been the
early bird. But I'm sure she's been telling you how honored
Good Hope is to welcome back one of its *favorite* graduates.

AGATHA: Not *quite* a graduate.

MISS SHACKLEFORD: (*Thrown for a moment*) Well—practically.
(*Turning quickly to the rest who have grouped themselves inside the
door*) You remember Miss Birdeshaw?
(MISS BIRDESHAW *flutters forward.*)

AGATHA: Of course. (*As* MISS BIRDESHAW *shakes her hand*) How
could I forget Miss Birdeshaw? She taught me the facts of life.

MISS BIRDESHAW: (*Embarrassed*) I never really thought of it that
way.

AGATHA: You look wonderful, Miss Birdeshaw.

MISS BIRDESHAW: So do you, Agatha. Of course, a bit older—I
mean, a woman instead of a—

MISS SHACKLEFORD: (*Hastily*) Miss Birdeshaw means you look so
young to be in Congress.

AGATHA: Maybe Congress was equally deceived, Miss Birdeshaw.
At least for the first few months.

DR. PITT: September fourteenth, to be exact, wasn't it? (AGATHA
turns to look at him in surprise.) Your atom-bomb speech on
the House floor.

MISS SHACKLEFORD: (*Delighted at the coup*) I don't believe you know
Dr. Pitt, Agatha. Our Physics professor. He came to us a little
after your time.

AGATHA: How do you do, Dr. Pitt? (*They shake hands.* DR. PITT *is around fifty—tall, a little drawn. There is the look about him of a man who knows a great deal, so much that there is no necessity to be constantly proving it.*) It's very gratifying, your knowing my speech. Sometimes you get a feeling on the floor of Congress, something like being on the radio—you're not quite sure anyone's listening.

DR. PITT: I know what you mean. Get somewhat the same feeling in my classroom.

(*There is a general laugh at this, especially from the Student Committee.* MISS SHACKLEFORD *beckons them forward. The girls are eager and excited.*)

MISS SHACKLEFORD: And this is your "honor guard"—chosen to represent the activities of the college this weekend. (*Beckoning the first one forward*) Carol Friedman—President of Student Government.

CAROL: (CAROL *steps forward, clearing her throat nervously.*) Student Government wishes to present you this bouquet, Miss Reed, as a token of their respect for one who has so well demonstrated the principle that Women can take their rightful place beside Men in the Government of this Great Nation. (*She hands* AGATHA *the bouquet and shakes hands with her.*)

AGATHA: Thank you.

MISS SHACKLEFORD: Jo Wintner—Physical Education.

JO: (JO *steps forward. She is a sturdy girl with a gruff voice.*) Phys Ed welcomes Agatha Reed, who has the spirit of Good Sportsmanship and Fair Play in all that she does.

(JO *shakes* AGATHA's *hand in a grip that makes her wince. She hands her some flowers.*)

AGATHA: That's very sweet.

(*During this last,* WOODY *has come out of the bedroom to see what all the commotion is about. She leans against the door frame enjoying* AGATHA's *increasing discomfiture.*)

MISS SHACKLEFORD: Mary Nell Dodge—May Queen.

MARY NELL: (*Stepping forward*) These flowers are for you, Miss Reed, who combines the qualities that make for True Beauty and—(*She's suddenly stuck.*)

MISS SHACKLEFORD: (*Prompting*) Wom—

MARY NELL: (*Gratefully*)—Womanhood Glorified! (*She hands* AGATHA *a bunch of roses and shakes her hand.*)

AGATHA: (AGATHA *avoids* WOODY's *eyes.*) Really, I—

MISS SHACKLEFORD: (*Indomitable*) Clarisse Carter—Dramatics Club.

CLARISSE: (CLARISSE *steps forward dramatically. Her voice is a combination of Bernhardt and Duse.*) In the Theatre of Life, you have made Woman's Role more important and more truly rich. We of the Dramatic Club—applaud you, Agatha Reed!
(*She hands* AGATHA *a bouquet.* WOODY *applauds. They all turn and stare at her.* AGATHA *gives her a stern look. She stops.*)

MISS SHACKLEFORD: And last—Virginia Merrill, representing the graduating Seniors.

GINNY: (GINNY *steps forward.*) The Seniors have asked me to thank you for coming to our Commencement, Miss Reed, because your presence here gives us courage and reassurance when we need it most.
(*She and* AGATHA *exchange a warm smile as she shakes* AGATHA's *hand and hands her the flowers.*)

AGATHA: Thank you. (*To all*) I'm not sure I deserve all the extremely nice things you've said about me—but I'm not going to let you take back a single one of them. (*There's an appreciative laugh from the group.*) I've thought a great deal about Good Hope in the past few years. Because of a growing feeling that the "good hope" of our world lies in the young and, most importantly, in the places where they're taught to think. Standing under the willows beside Hope Hall, and now, here in these rooms with all of you, I feel that more strongly than ever. And a fine, warm feeling of coming—home.
(*At the end of* AGATHA's *speech,* DR. MERRILL *appears and stops in the doorway.* JAMES MERRILL *is a handsome man with the combination of virility and charm that can survive the difficult atmosphere of a girls' college. The dignity of the Presidency is undeniably on his shoulders, but there is a sense of humor with it that rescues it from pedantry.*)

MISS SHACKLEFORD: (*Crossing to him excitedly*) Oh, Dr. Merrill! You missed our little ceremony. Miss Reed has just given our girls a very inspiring speech.

MERRILL: Yes, I heard the end of it from the hall. (*Crossing to* AGATHA) We're very pleased to have you back, Miss Reed.

AGATHA: Thank you, Dr. Merrill.
(*She attempts to shake his outstretched hand but in the effort some of the bouquets tumble to the floor.* MERRILL *tries to help recover them—it's an awkward moment.*)

WOODY: I'll take them. (*She relieves* AGATHA *of all the flowers*.)

AGATHA: (*Gratefully*) Thank you, Woody. (*Generally*) My secretary, Miss Woods. (*There is an exchange of how-do-you-do's*.)

MISS SHACKLEFORD: (*Taking charge*) Now I hate to break this up, but I'm afraid we'd better all run along. We've a very full day ahead.

(*She herds her brood toward the door and* AGATHA *crosses to shake hands and say goodbye.* DR. PITT *is the last*.)

AGATHA: Thank you so much for coming today, Dr. Pitt.

DR. PITT: I've enjoyed it, Miss Reed. (*He looks pointedly at* MERRILL.) I never expected to be put on your Reception Committee. It was a "pleasant surprise." (*To* MISS SHACKLEFORD) Thank you, Miss Shackleford. (*He exits*.)

(*There is a strained moment.*)

ELLEN: (*Bristling*) Well, that certainly was uncalled-for! Now I see what Claude means—

MERRILL: (*Politely but firmly*) They tell me the Alumnae Luncheon's a sellout, Ellen.

ELLEN: Oh, yes. I'd better go and check my guest lists. I've lost part of the class of '24. See you at the speaker's table, Ag.

AGATHA: Fine.

(ELLEN *exits*.)

MISS SHACKLEFORD: Oh, Agatha. I hope you haven't forgotten that movie you promised us.

AGATHA: Didn't the print get here?

MISS SHACKLEFORD: Print?

AGATHA: Of the film. We sent it out a few days ago.

MISS SHACKLEFORD: Sent it? Oh, dear. I thought you'd *bring* it. What does it look like?

WOODY: It's round—in a tin can.

MISS SHACKLEFORD: Like sardines?

MERRILL: (*Controlling a smile*) Maybe they delivered it right to the theatre, Miss Shackleford.

MISS SHACKLEFORD: (*Distraught*) I'd better go down and see. (*She hurries out*.)

AGATHA: You'd better go along, Woody. She might not recognize it.

WOODY: Recognize it? She probably *ate* it. (*She exits*.)

AGATHA: (*Apologetically*) You mustn't mind Woody. Her mind's always on the tip of her tongue.

MERRILL: It's refreshing.

AGATHA: I stole her from a Senator who stole her from a Cabinet Member. She knows more about Washington than the FBI. (*There is a silence for a moment, a rather awkward one. As if these two people are very aware that they are alone in a room together*)

MERRILL: You're looking very well, Agatha.

AGATHA: Thank you, Jim. I'm tired. This session of Congress has been a little exhausting.

MERRILL: I'm afraid you're not in for much of a rest this weekend. Miss Shackleford seems to have outdone even herself.

AGATHA: Yes, I've seen the agenda.

MERRILL: I can turn my back if you'd still like to escape.

AGATHA: (*Shaking her head*) Vanity, I guess. Secretly everyone dreams of coming back to his college for an honorary degree. It's a popular ambition—like wanting a mink coat.

MERRILL: Or to be President.

AGATHA: Yes. (*Then*) How does it feel?

MERRILL: What?

AGATHA: To be—President.

MERRILL: (*Smiling*) It's never dull—the faces change too often. And with so much youth around, you actually get the feeling you're preserving your own.

AGATHA: Your daughter has you "tottering" on the brink of senility. (*As he reacts*) We had a talk. She's a lovely child. No, that's wrong. She's not a child. What are we at that age, Jim? At that wonderful, terrible in-between time? You've seen so many of us.

MERRILL: Wait a minute. Now you *are* dating me.

AGATHA: Even with most of the student body in love with you? (*As he looks surprised*) Ginny's my authority.

MERRILL: Well, I serve a function. They sigh wistfully over my grayed temples—until it's time to trot off to proms and have some fun. Then they come back and sigh some more. It gives their lives an interesting dimension.

AGATHA: There must be more to this business of being college President than that.

MERRILL: Not much. A few good Latin phrases and one slightly risqué story for Alumnae dinners. *Very* slightly, you understand. And, of course, a cap and gown in fairly-good condition.

AGATHA: That's an accurate description of some college Presidents I know. I won't accept it for you.

MERRILL: No?

AGATHA: (*Shaking her head*) I have a pretty vivid recollection of your contempt for educators with banquet-side manners. What was it you called them—Educaterers? (*She laughs. He's looking at her oddly.*) You seem surprised I remember so well what you said.

MERRILL: I am. You've heard a lot of people say a lot of things.

AGATHA: Yes. (*Then, quietly*) Only you were the first. The first who ever said anything that mattered. (*She meets his eyes for a moment, then walks to the window.*) Do they still skate on Horner's Pond—in the winter?

MERRILL: Yes. We've got a lodge now, with a stove for hot coffee.

AGATHA: That sounds nice. (*After a moment*) Once I found a little pond just like it, near a university outside Leningrad. I even wrote a piece about it. I called it—

MERRILL: Horner's Pond, U.S.S.R. (*As she turns, surprised*) You were syndicated, you know.

AGATHA: Odd, though. That you should have read *that* one.

MERRILL: I read them all. (*She looks at him.*) Spain, China, Poland, Russia—Washington.

AGATHA: Isn't that Miss Shackleford's job—keeping track of the alumnae?

MERRILL: Sometimes she's careless.

AGATHA: (*With an attempt at casualness*) Well, it's a good thing. Now I don't have to catch you up on all I've been doing the past twenty years.

MERRILL: No. (*Then*) Except the first one. I've never quite—caught up on the first one. (AGATHA *reaches for a cigarette. Her hand is not quite steady.*) You don't mind my being curious?

AGATHA: No, I don't mind.

MERRILL: Maybe it's *my* vanity. But all these years I've wondered—what happened. Why you just—disappeared.

AGATHA: It was very stupid of me to get caught climbing in my window at six a.m. (*Smiling*) I trust this generation is more adroit.

MERRILL: (*Turning away*) I'm not up on the statistics.

AGATHA: Obviously I'm not saying this very well.

MERRILL: I shouldn't have brought it up.

AGATHA: (*Earnestly*) It would have made no difference to the trustees that you were the man, and that we were planning to be married. I would have been kicked out just the same, only you would have been kicked out with me. Not many young professors would have been so willing to give up a chance to be President.

MERRILL: We'd decided to take that chance.

AGATHA: I know. (*Simply*) But I couldn't let you, Jim.

MERRILL: Where did you go?

AGATHA: My mother had to get over the humiliation of having a daughter expelled. I stayed with an aunt in Detroit. She'd been an old suffragette and there wasn't anything could humiliate her.

MERRILL: My letters came back. When I phoned your home, they said they didn't know where you were.

AGATHA: I made them promise that.

MERRILL: It all sounds so—

AGATHA: Cold-blooded? (*Shaking her head*) It wasn't. At eighteen, it's very difficult to be cold-blooded. Once, I almost wrote you a letter. (*She takes a deep draw on her cigarette.*) I didn't finish it. A little later I read about your marriage in the newspaper.

MERRILL: (*After a moment*) Did Ginny tell you anything about her mother?

AGATHA: No.

MERRILL: I'd like to.

AGATHA: It's not necessary, Jim. I didn't mean—

MERRILL: (*Firmly*) I'd like to. (*She nods, turning away from him.*) I met her at Columbia. I'd gone down there for the summer. She was a little older than I was—but we had a lot of things in common. They helped to balance the things we—didn't have. She—well, she died when Ginny was born.

AGATHA: Why did you feel you had to tell me that?

MERRILL: I don't know exactly.

AGATHA: (*Turning to him*) What are you trying to say, Jim?

MERRILL: You came down here this weekend. (*Searching her face*) Why?

AGATHA: Have you forgotten? You invited me.

MERRILL: That invitation—I carried it around two years before I sent it. (*A pause*) I thought about it five years before that.

AGATHA: That was silly. I answered it five minutes after I got it.

(*He stares at her. As if he can't quite believe it. Then, almost simultaneously, they start toward each other. WOODY enters. They stop in their tracks.*)

WOODY: The weekend is saved. We found the film.
> (*There's a pause.* AGATHA *and* MERRILL *turn away from each other with elaborate casualness.*)

AGATHA: Oh—fine.

WOODY: (WOODY *looks from one to the other.*) I've got orders to tell you the Alumnae look hungry.

AGATHA: (*To* MERRILL) Creamed chicken and peas?

MERRILL: You learn to accept the inevitable.

AGATHA: (*Crossing toward the bedroom*) I'd better fix my face.

MERRILL: (*Coming up to her*) Miss Reed, did I tell you—it's wonderful to have you back?

AGATHA: Yes, Dr. Merrill. But it's good to hear it again.
> (*They smile at each other. Then* MERRILL *turns and starts to the door.*)

MERRILL: It's wonderful to have you, too, Miss Woods.
> (*He exits.* WOODY, *looking after him curiously, crosses to the door and closes it. There is a silence.*)

WOODY: Nice looking—

AGATHA: Who?

WOODY: Prexy.

AGATHA: (AGATHA *is fixing her hair at the mirror.*) Yes, isn't he?

WOODY: Looked mighty cozy in here when I came in.

AGATHA: Mmm.

WOODY: Talking over old History exams?

AGATHA: (*Laughing*) You know what's wrong with you? You're spoiled. You're so used to having your thumb in every Washington pie you can't stand missing—

WOODY: Stop filibustering.

AGATHA: All right. (*She sits down deliberately.*) It's so.

WOODY: What's so?

AGATHA: Just what you're thinking.

WOODY: Oh. (*Then*) Well, I guess you've got to do something to give this weekend a lift. Has he got a friend for tonight?

AGATHA: (*Laughing*) You're warm, darling. But not warm enough.

WOODY: Wait a minute! Let me get this straight—

AGATHA: It's quite simple. He was the first man I ever loved. Maybe the only one. (*As* WOODY *stares at her*) Don't look so shocked. I'm going to marry him.

WOODY: *Marry* him?

AGATHA: He hasn't asked me yet. But he will—tonight.

WOODY: (*Hopefully*) You're kidding.

AGATHA: Why ? Are you against marriage, too?

WOODY: Good God, Agatha, I'm not against marriage. But there's a time and place for everything. (*Then*) You're smack in the middle of an election campaign—a *hundred* things. Your life's too busy.

AGATHA: There's quite a difference between a busy life and a full one.

WOODY: (*Shaking her head*) That's funny—coming from you. Do you know what you are to millions of American women? The embodiment of an ideal. The woman they think they'd like to be. Not just reading about history, but helping to shape it.

AGATHA: Am I all that? Sounds wonderful.

WOODY: (*Belligerently*) It *is* wonderful!

AGATHA: You've missed the point, Woody. I don't want to be any less. I'm greedy. I want to be more.

WOODY: And he's the man to do it?

AGATHA: Yes.

WOODY: For God's sake, Agatha, when I was fourteen, *I* fell in love with the fellow who sold peanuts on our block. I'm not going to marry him.

AGATHA: Maybe you should. Maybe you have a deep and consuming need for peanuts. (*There is a silence.* AGATHA *turns away.*) I'm a little—disappointed. I hoped you'd be happy for me.

WOODY: What did you expect? I don't even *know* the guy.

AGATHA: Well, *I* know him. (*Earnestly*) Woody, this isn't a whim. It's something I've waited for—thought about for twenty years. It may be the most important thing in my whole life. That's why I don't want anything to spoil it. I don't—(*She stops suddenly.*) What about that telephone call?

WOODY: Telephone—?

AGATHA: To *Life*. Henry Luce. About Matt Cole.

WOODY: I told you. The circuits were busy. They said they'd call me back.

AGATHA: (AGATHA *crosses abruptly to the telephone and picks it up. Into telephone.*) Hello— What happened on that call to New York? *Life Magazine*.

WOODY: What's the rush?

AGATHA: (*Into telephone*) Oh good. Then put it right through.

WOODY: I told you I'd take care of it.

AGATHA: When? When we get back to Washington?

WOODY: I didn't know it was life and death.

AGATHA: (*Into telephone*) Hello, is Mr. Henry Luce in?— Will you tell him it's Agatha Reed? It's very important.—Yes, I'll wait.

SUSAN: (SUSAN *comes rushing in, excitedly*.) Oh, Miss Reed! Mr. Cole just came and he's taking pictures of everybody! He wants one of you—with the graduating class!

(AGATHA'*s hand with the telephone in it drops slowly to her side. She sits down in the desk chair. The squeak of a voice is heard through the telephone. It seems to be saying "Hello" over and over.* WOODY *crosses and takes the telephone from* AGATHA.)

WOODY: (*Into telephone*) Hello. Mr. Luce?—You'll be delighted to know. We're renewing our subscription.

CURTAIN

ACT TWO

SCENE I

SCENE: *It is late afternoon of the following day. Some of the flowers of the day before are arranged tastefully around the room, giving the place a kind of festive air. The last afternoon sun is slanting through the windows.*

The room is empty. Through the open corridor door can be heard dimly the sound of voices and the tinkle of glass. This is AGATHA's *"tea" going on in the Lounge of Hope Hall. After a moment* AGATHA *and two Merry Larks enter. The Merry Larks wear maroon flannel blazers with large yellow notes appliquéed on them. They're talking excitedly.*

FIRST MERRY LARK: —And we tried to look for Dr. Merrill.

SECOND MERRY LARK: But then Professor Dingley came along and he said he'd take care of her—

AGATHA: I think he brought her in here. (*A rather elderly man enters from the bedroom. This is* PROFESSOR DINGLEY *who teaches Botany, and looks it.*) Oh there you are, Professor Dingley. Is Miss Birdeshaw all right?

DINGLEY: I don't know. She's resting on the bed. She looks quite pale.

AGATHA: I'm sure it's nothing serious.

DINGLEY: I've sent the janitor to bring my car around. So we can take her home.

AGATHA: Good.

DINGLEY: (*Heading for the door*) I hope he remembers to bring it to the service entrance—(*He exits.*)

FIRST MERRY LARK: It was all so sudden. All of us Merry Larks were lined up in the hall, just starting in to the lounge to serenade you—

SECOND MERRY LARK: And Miss Birdeshaw came along and insisted on singing with us—

FIRST MERRY LARK: And we didn't know what to do. Then—she just sort of—collapsed!

AGATHA: Well, don't worry about it. She probably forgot to eat lunch. (WOODY *enters from the bedroom, a wet towel in her hand*) Now you run along and reassure the rest of the Merry Larks. (*They exit.* AGATHA *turns to* WOODY.) Poor little Birdeshaw.

348

I'm afraid she never had a cocktail before.

WOODY: (*Mopping her own brow with the towel*) *A* cocktail ? After the second one, she started on doubles.

AGATHA: How is she?

WOODY: Stinking!

AGATHA: Oh well, I'm glad. She might've gone on all her life quietly drinking tea and died one day without ever knowing what she'd missed.

WOODY: She's missed a lot more than that. (*Then*) What the devil does she teach around here anyway?

AGATHA: Sex Hygiene.

WOODY: Oh—no!

DINGLEY: (*Entering and crossing to the bedroom*) It's here.

AGATHA: Fine.

(*He exits into bedroom.*)

WOODY: Did you see the way she was snuggling up to that—butterfly chaser?

AGATHA: Professor Dingley is a *botanist*. (*Smiling reminiscently*) She's had what was known as a crush on him since way back when I was here. We used to make jokes about how she could never even say hello to him without blushing.

WOODY: That ole debbil rum! I think she's going to hate herself in the morning.

AGATHA: (*As* PROFESSOR DINGLEY *enters carrying the prostrate form of* MISS BIRDESHAW.) Don't you need some help?

DINGLEY. No, thank you. I'll just take her home and— (*He stops, suddenly realizing what he's saying.*) Well, perhaps, it would be better if— (*He's embarrassed.*)

WOODY: Okay. You put her *on* the bed. I'll be along in a few minutes and put her *in* it.

DINGLEY: Thank you. (*He shifts the dead weight a little to get a better grip and manages to make it out the door.*)

AGATHA: (*Enjoying it*) You're a regella Florence Nightingale.

WOODY: You know, nobody but you could get away with this. Turning a tea into a cocktail party.

AGATHA: Well, it's one of those things you promise yourself to do before you die.

WOODY: There's a lot you're getting away with this weekend. (*Chidingly*) Keeping Prexy out till three in the morning. You know, that isn't done.

AGATHA: It's all right, Woody. You're now speaking to the future

Mrs. James Merrill.
(*There is a pause.*)
WOODY: It's all—set?
AGATHA: All set.
(*There is a moment while* WOODY *struggles with her own feelings.*
AGATHA *watches her expectantly.*)
WOODY: Agatha, I've been with you a long time. You always knew
what you wanted. If this is it—congratulations.
AGATHA: (*Warmly*) Thank you, Woody. Nothing's going to be dif-
ferent. Just better.
WOODY: You mean—I get a raise? (AGATHA *laughs.*) When's the
great day?
AGATHA: Oh, we haven't talked about that yet. Matter of fact, we're
going to keep it all pretty quiet until after this whole
Commencement business is over.
WOODY: (*Looking out the window*) What was all that fuss about Matt
Cole? He's out there—doing his job, taking pictures like
crazy.
AGATHA: Yes. I'm afraid I exaggerated that whole thing. Forget it.
(MERRILL *appears in the doorway.*) Oh—Jim.
MERRILL: They told me Miss Birdeshaw had an "accident."
AGATHA: Just a little too much picnic lemonade.
MERRILL: (*Smiling*) That's what I figured. (*Then*) Did anyone
notice?
AGATHA: I don't think so. If you have to pass out, you should do it
like Miss Birdeshaw—quietly and in the hall.
(WOODY *is studying* MERRILL *with great interest.*)
MERRILL: It's a good thing the *Life* man wasn't around. (*Then*) He
told me you worked together in China.
AGATHA: Yes.
MERRILL: Is he discreet?
AGATHA: (*Shaking her head*) I'm afraid not, but don't worry. He
specializes in major indiscretions. I don't think he'll make
anything of it.
MERRILL: Oh yes—he wants a picture of you, Miss Woods. Said
you'd been dodging him.
WOODY: I hate *Life* photographers. They're always trying to catch
you picking your nose. (*She exits pointedly closing the door.*)
(MERRILL *and* AGATHA *stand looking at each other.*)
AGATHA: You can lock the door, if you want to.
MERRILL: It's against dormitory rules. (*He crosses the room and catches*

her in his arms.) And so is this. (*He kisses her.*)

AGATHA: I hate dormitory rules.

MERRILL: So do I.

AGATHA: Who makes them anyway?

MERRILL: I do. (AGATHA *laughs.*) I can't believe it.

AGATHA: What?

MERRILL: That you're here. That everything's the same. You won't run away again?

AGATHA: Not a chance. Never on second proposals.

MERRILL: Incidentally—how did they compare?

AGATHA: Well, the first one was a bit more colorful. It had one lovely quotation from Shelley.

MERRILL: Shelley! I don't believe it!

AGATHA: Would you like me to quote?

MERRILL: No! Women have such frighteningly-long memories.

AGATHA: *Some* women—for the words of *some* men. Have you any idea how many times I remembered things you said?

MERRILL: No—

AGATHA: That's how I got into politics. (*As he looks at her questioningly*) I have a little farm in Pennsylvania where I go whenever things get too complicated. Some women change their hairstyle or take an ocean voyage. I put up chow-chow. In jars. With labels. (*Suddenly*) Do you *like* chow-chow?

MERRILL: Very much.

AGATHA: (*Relieved*) It's lucky. We have four hundred jars. Anyway, I was up there when a local delegation called on me. They wanted to run me for Congress—with an assist from Mr. Roosevelt. There wasn't any machine, or much money, but there seemed to be a lot of plain people who wanted to go out and ring doorbells for me. (*She pauses, remembering.*) It was all very flattering—but I didn't want to run for Congress. I just wanted to relax and get some sleep for a while. Only all that night I kept remembering something you'd once said when there was first talk of their offering you the Presidency. You were a teacher, you said, and you wanted to teach. I asked you if that meant you'd turn it down, and you said, of course not. You said that "not to go forward was to go back. That no man could afford the luxury of standing still, no matter how comfortable it was." (*A pause*) Do you remember?

MERRILL: Yes.

AGATHA: I called them up the next morning and told them they had a candidate.

MERRILL: (*Quietly*) That's quite a responsibility. I'm not sure I would have wanted it. (*He rises.*) I think we'd better get back in there.

AGATHA: Maybe *everybody's* passed out by now.

MERRILL: I wouldn't count on it. I'm sure Miss Shackleford hasn't passed out.

AGATHA: Or Claude Griswold.

MERRILL: What do you think of Claude?

AGATHA: He's a charm-boy, all right.

MERRILL: Well, he has his faults. But he's pleasant—and he's really interested in the school. Oddly enough, he's a great admirer of yours.

AGATHA: Oddly enough is right. My voting record can't exactly have endeared me to him.

MERRILL: (*Laughs*) No, but he seems to like you in spite of it. (*Then*) Maybe I'll go on ahead. It'll look less— (*He searches for the correct word.*)

AGATHA: (*Kissing him*) Is that what you mean?

MERRILL: That's what I mean.

(*There is a knock on the door.* MERRILL *releases her quickly.*)

AGATHA: Yes?

GINNY'S VOICE: It's Ginny, Miss Reed. Are you busy?

MERRILL: (MERRILL *reacts to this information nervously. He gets out his handkerchief and dabs at his lips.*) I'd rather we didn't mention anything about this to Ginny at the moment. I'd like to tell her later—in my own way.

AGATHA: Of course, Jim. Just as you like. (*Crossing to the door, she opens it.*) Come in, Ginny.

GINNY: (*Urgently*) Oh, Miss Reed, I'd like to ask a favor of—(*She stops as* AGATHA *indicates her father, turns and sees him.*) Oh. I didn't know you were with someone.

(AGATHA *looks from father to daughter, aware of a kind of tension.*)

MERRILL: Nothing wrong out there, is there?

GINNY: No. I—I just wanted to tell Miss Reed something.

MERRILL: (*Starting to the door*) Well, I can take a hint. (*Noticing*) You look very lovely today, Ginny. Is that a new dress?

GINNY: I got it last year—for Dean's Tea.

MERRILL: Oh. Didn't the flowers go well with it?

GINNY: No, the color was wrong. Maybe I can wear them tonight.

Thank you for sending them. (*She stands there, tense.*)

MERRILL: Well—(*He exits.*)

GINNY: (GINNY *shuts the door. Talking fast*) Miss Reed, there isn't much time. I told Dr. Pitt you wanted to see him. He'll be in any minute.

AGATHA: Dr. Pitt? I don't—

GINNY: I hope you don't mind. I did it without asking you—but I had to get him away. Claude Griswold's in there, sounding off all about "the next war" and Dr. Pitt's getting mad. His hands are beginning to shake like the last time. That was at Sophomore Reception and he'd been drinking that time, too.

AGATHA: (*Smiling*) Wait a minute. I'm sure Dr. Pitt can manage a cocktail or two without—

GINNY: It's more than a cocktail or two. (*As* AGATHA *reacts*) Oh, don't get the wrong idea. It's just lately. Since they've been trying to get him out of here. It's so unfair. He's what all teachers should be.

AGATHA: I'm sure your father appreciates that. (GINNY *withdraws.*) Why don't you tell him how you feel about Dr. Pitt? (GINNY *doesn't answer. There's a knock on the door.*)

GINNY: (*Desperately*) You *will* pretend you asked to see him, won't you, Miss Reed? I wouldn't want him to know I—(*She stops.*)

AGATHA: Yes. Of course. (*She calls.*) Come in.

(GINNY *hurries to the desk, picks up the Walt Whitman book as* DR. PITT *enters. He looks at her, then* AGATHA.)

DR. PITT: Ginny said you wanted to see me.

AGATHA: Yes.

GINNY: (*Elaborately*) You're quite sure you're finished with the book, Miss Reed?

AGATHA: Oh—yes.

GINNY: Well, then, I'll just take it along with me.

(*She walks past* DR. PITT, *smiles hesitantly, exits. There's a moment.*)

DR. PITT: I have a feeling I'm being saved.

AGATHA: (*Smiling*) Well, I did want a chance to talk to you again before the weekend was over.

DR. PITT: Why?

AGATHA: Because you told me my speech was wonderful, of course. And because I have great respect for good teachers. Physics professors who give their students Walt Whitman to read.

(DR. PITT *bows, a bit ironically. He loses his balance imperceptibly and grabs the back of a chair for support.*)

AGATHA: (*Gently*) Would you like to sit down, Dr. Pitt? (He smiles and sits.) You know, I've always been curious. About what makes someone become a teacher.

DR. PITT: So have I. What do *you* think?

AGATHA: Well, it can't be the pay. It must be that one day you decide the mind of a person is the most exciting thing in the world.

DR. PITT: Isn't that a little romantic?

AGATHA: (*Laughing*) Maybe. But I think all of us who believe in the future have to be a little "romantic."

DR. PITT: Future? I thought that word had become obsolete.

AGATHA: (AGATHA *stops smiling and looks at him for a moment.*) Ginny tells me there's some question of your staying on here. She seems to feel it's important that you do.

DR. PITT: Ginny's a nice girl. She has the eager, intense convictions of youth.

AGATHA: Isn't it good? That there's so much of it around ?

DR. PITT: Not very. Not when you can't get to it.

AGATHA: You're a teacher. If anyone can get to it, you can.

DR. PITT: Can I? (*He smiles as if at a child.*) I teach Physics, Miss Reed. Only sometimes I don't. Sometimes I talk about other things. The daily headlines—the atom bomb—the world. You see, I have the dangerous misconception that the object of education is to teach the young to think. That's dangerous, because they might get to like it. (*He sits, lost for a moment, staring.*)

AGATHA: (*Gently*) You were making a point, Dr. Pitt.

DR. PITT: Oh, yes—the point. The point is that I now teach Physics—and I stay safely within the covers of the textbook.

AGATHA: Why?

DR. PITT: Why? Because I've been given an ultimatum. I either do—or I resign. (*He smiles again.*) Oh, I thought of it. I even wrote a letter to a friend of mine at the head of the Science Department of a Texas university. He once offered me a job. The letter came back with a polite note from the Dean. My friend had "resigned" two weeks before.

AGATHA: (*Quietly*) That can't be the end of the story, Dr. Pitt. Or you wouldn't be challenging Mr. Griswold at tea parties.

DR. PITT: (*Rising*) Don't worry, I'm working on it. By next year, I'll be able to listen to him and not even hear.

AGATHA: And in two years you might even be agreeing with him.

DR. PITT: (DR. PITT *turns and looks squarely at* AGATHA.) I'm forty-five years old, Miss Reed! For twenty-two of those years I've fought every way I knew against ignorance, against indifference. Because I believe that people really wanted to learn. (*The anger drains out of him.*) Now I say to hell with them. If they don't care enough about it, why should I? Let their daughters bring their knitting to classes and read movie magazines inside their notebook covers. Let them all be wiped off the face of the earth without even knowing why. Like the pigs and the mice at Bikini. Maybe it's better to die stupid, like an animal.

AGATHA: (*Quietly*) Dr. Pitt, I respect your fears. I'm frightened myself. Anyone who isn't frightened today is a fool. But I never get angry at the fools. Just at the wise men, who see the danger and run away.

DR. PITT: What would you have me do?

AGATHA: (*Encouragingly*) First of all, stop feeling sorry for yourself. We all know there are men who're afraid to let education have a mind and voice. But you're in a better position than at most colleges. You can get the support of your President— and then make a real fight of it.

DR. PITT: (*After a pause*) Merrill?

AGATHA: Yes.

DR. PITT: (DR. PITT *crosses to the window and looks out.*) Have you seen our library, that monument to learning? And the shiny gymnasium? Our eminent President gave up battles for buildings a long time ago. (*He notices the look on* AGATHA's *face.*) You don't believe me?

AGATHA: No.

DR. PITT: Why? It can't be a surprise to you that a man who gets position gets comfortable and careful. It's a fine old tradition.

AGATHA: I know Jim Merrill.

DR. PITT: Do you?

AGATHA: Yes!

DR. PITT: (*Shrugging*) Then there's nothing to say.

AGATHA: (*Coldly*) I'm beginning to realize I also know you, Dr. Pitt. The weary liberal, the defeatist. I know why you can't go to Jim Merrill. Because the weakness is in *you*—not him!

MISS SHACKLEFORD: (*The corridor door suddenly bursts open under the vigorous hand of* MISS SHACKLEFORD. *Booming*) —and this is

the room where it all started. We've tried to restore the original— (*She sees* AGATHA *and* DR. PITT.) Oh, I had no idea anyone was in here.

(MATT COLE *has appeared in the doorway behind* MISS SHACKLE-
FORD. *He's in his forties, a large man with an easy body and a
hard head. He wears a Leica camera in a case and an extra lens
case over his shoulder. When he uses the camera later, it becomes
part of his body, like a third hand.*)

COLE: We can come back later.

AGATHA: No, come ahead, Cole. Dr. Pitt and I were just finishing.

DR. PITT: (*A tired man*) If you'll excuse me—(*He starts toward the
door.*)

AGATHA: Dr. Pitt— (*As he turns*) You'll probably be looking for
your drink.
(*With quiet irony, she hands him the glass he's left on the table. He
looks at her, then takes it silently and exits.*)

MISS SHACKLEFORD: Mr. Cole thought it would be nice to get
some pictures of your room. It's such a coincidence—you and
he being old friends.

AGATHA: Yes. We've run into each other all over the world.

MISS SHACKLEFORD: Photography is such a fascinating profession.
Several of our girls have taken it up. Perhaps you've run
across them—Mary Jessup, she was Class of '32? And
Phyllis—no, it was *Evelyn* Tate, Class of '40?

COLE: Must've missed them.

MISS SHACKLEFORD: Oh well, I think they both had babies and
gave it up. (*Coyly*) Mr. Cole, I know you have things all figured out, but I was wondering if I could make *one little* suggestion?

COLE: Sure. Go ahead.

MISS SHACKLEFORD: Well, I was thinking it would be a darling idea
to do a picture of Miss Reed and Mrs. Griswold in this room
with the two girls who live here now. You know, past and
present?

COLE: (*To* AGATHA) How do you feel about being—past?

MISS SHACKLEFORD: (*Hastily*) Oh, I didn't mean that *literally*.

AGATHA: It's quite all right, Miss Shackleford. Can you get the
other three rounded up?

MISS SHACKLEFORD: (*Delightedly*) I'm sure they're all right in the
lounge. (*Heading for the door*) It won't take a minute.
(*She exits.*)

COLE: (COLE *is wandering around the room.*) So this is the cocoon.

AGATHA: I've never exactly thought of myself as a butterfly. (*He picks up the record on the victrola.*) Make yourself at home.

COLE: Thank you. (*Reading*) Betty Boop. A memento?

AGATHA: Yes.

COLE: Touching. (*He replaces the record and snaps a quick picture of the victrola.*)

AGATHA: Have you been getting anything decent?

COLE: All *very* decent. Will you sit on the sofa, please?

AGATHA: (*As she crosses and sits*) How did you come to get on this assignment anyway? Isn't it a little out of your line?

COLE: I asked for it.

AGATHA: Why?

COLE: Thought it might be interesting to see Agatha Reed and how she grew. (*He's wandering around her, getting an angle.*)

AGATHA: Is it?

COLE: Very. It's such a paradox.
(*She looks at him.* COLE *gets the shot.*)

AGATHA: Why paradox?

COLE: Because I don't get *you* coming out of this.

AGATHA: (*Riled*) You've been on war fronts so long, an atmosphere like this is bound to seem a little incongruous.

COLE: Dated is the word. A kind of old-world feeling you used to connect with Europe in the twenties. The graceful yet desperate attempt to maintain the status quo.

AGATHA: Generalities are so easy.

COLE: All right, then I'll be specific. I got a shot yesterday of some of the girls here—how old are they, nineteen, twenty? (*As she nods*) They were rolling hoops down the lawn. An old tradition. Very cute. I've got a picture I took in Rome five weeks ago. A couple of fourteen-year-old girls, soliciting on the streets. I'd like to print them side by side. Higher Education—1948.

AGATHA: Why don't you?

COLE: It's another set for Cole's Gallery. All the pictures not fit to print.

AGATHA: You must have quite a collection by now.

COLE: Enough for a book—this winter.

AGATHA: Cole, that's wonderful.

COLE: I'll send you an autographed copy. (*He sits on the arm of the sofa.*) I never got a chance to ask you—did you ever get that stuff I sent you from China?

AGATHA: Oh yes. I—(*She doesn't look at him.*)—I was so glad to have the pictures of Lao San and the kids. And the schoolhouse. I'm sorry. I didn't know where to write to thank you.

COLE: I went on to Cairo. (*After a moment*) Did you like the one of yourself?

AGATHA: I'm not sure. The one place you don't expect to be photographed is in bed—asleep.

COLE: Why not? It's the best time. Nothing false. No attitudes.

AGATHA: (AGATHA *gets up and crosses away from him.*) I wasn't thinking as a photographer.

COLE: Neither was I. (*She turns and looks at him quickly.*)

AGATHA: The occasion wasn't exactly the kind of thing I wanted recorded for posterity.

COLE: No? I thought it had the makings of one of the big moments of history. As I remember, you did, too.

AGATHA: War has a way of making little moments seem big at the time.

(*There is a pause.* COLE *just stares at her.*)

COLE: (*Quietly*) Can I quote you on that, Miss Reed?

AGATHA: I'm sorry. I didn't mean that quite the way it sounded. (*Then*) But it's true, isn't it, Cole? It's what I tried to say that day in Paris—but didn't. That it was a nice snapshot, but never a family portrait.

COLE: Such subtle distinctions escape me.

AGATHA: Oh, I'm sure you didn't come down here to dig all that up. (*Brightly*) Come on—what'll you take for the negative?

COLE: I'll give it to you. Tied up with a pink bow. For a wedding present.

AGATHA: (*Startled*) What kind of talk is that?

COLE: There's an overpowering odor of orange blossoms in the air.

AGATHA: How on earth?—(*Getting it*) You took pictures of Woody just now—

COLE: She's not a bad subject. Once you pin her down.

AGATHA: (*Angrily*) How could she?

COLE: She didn't. Just gave me a hint. Now you've confirmed it.

AGATHA: Cole, if you breathe a word of this in that article—

COLE: Don't worry. It's purely for my personal files. (*Then*) He must be quite a guy to keep a woman like you on the hook for twenty years.

AGATHA: How did you know I—

COLE: He told me. What a brilliant History student you were.

AGATHA: You haven't wasted a minute, have you?

COLE: (*Shaking his head*) Mmm—no.

AGATHA: (*Confidently*) Yes, he *is* quite a guy.

COLE: Or else you must be getting tired.

AGATHA: What does that mean?

COLE: This overwhelming desire to return to the womb.

AGATHA: You're revolting!

COLE: Girlhood memories. Old pictures, old sofas, old records—pardon me if I throw up.

AGATHA: (*Icily*) Have you finished?

COLE: Who're you kidding? (*Crossing to her*) You can't bury yourself in a graveyard like this. Or on a corpse like Merrill. Anyone can see he's got no blood. They've sucked him dry.

AGATHA: Will you get out of here!

COLE: Sure. But here's another memento. Since you've gone in for collecting them.

(*He pulls her to him and kisses her. She pushes away from him.*)

AGATHA: (*Furious*) You can't take it, can you, Cole? That he could be more exciting, more desirable than you?

COLE: That's right. I'm vain as hell.

AGATHA: Let's get this straight. You were sent up here to take pictures. Anything else is none of your damned business!

(*The door bursts open.*)

MISS SHACKLEFORD: (*Gaily*) Here we come, ready or not! (*There's no answer.* MISS SHACKLEFORD *doesn't even notice. She has* ELLEN, GINNY *and* MARY NELL *in tow.*) Does everyone know everyone?

COLE: (*To* AGATHA'*s back, with a smile*) All friends.

ELLEN: Miss Shackleford didn't even give me a chance to comb my hair. How does it look, Ag?

AGATHA: (*Automatically*) Fine.

ELLEN: It's your fault if it doesn't. I'm just a wee bit tipsy. (*Reproachfully*) Cocktails at a school tea. Of course, Claude made it clear to Mr. Cole we don't do this sort of thing all the time. He's going to make a point of that in the story, aren't you, Mr. Cole?

COLE: Yes, indeed.

MARY NELL: (*Crossing to him*) I'm awfully excited, Mr. Cole. I never thought I'd get my picture in *Life*.

COLE: Just stick around long enough and *Life's* bound to catch up with you.

MISS SHACKLEFORD: (*Busy planning*) Now let me see—don't you think one of Ellen and Agatha here on the sofa?

COLE: I think we can do better than that. (*To* AGATHA) Can you suggest a "representative" pose of your student days, Miss Reed?

AGATHA: (*Icily*) I wouldn't remember.

COLE: Maybe Mrs. Griswold could help us out.

ELLEN: Well, Ag always loved to lie on her stomach on the floor, with a pillow under her—

AGATHA: (*Hastily*) Something in a chair near the desk would do.

COLE: Inspired. (*As* AGATHA *complies*) And Mrs. Griswold—leaning on the desk, I think, talking. Just talking easily.

ELLEN: (ELLEN *crosses and leans stiffly against the desk.*) Now you'll tell me when, won't you, Mr. Cole? I always have to be told when.

COLE: Sure. But you can just relax now. It'll be a minute till I get the camera set. (*He sights.*)

ELLEN: (*Slumping comfortably*) Claude has one of those expensive cameras with all the gadgets, but he never gets anything in focus. And I just pick up my little box Brownie and push the button and out come—

COLE: (COLE *takes his shot.*) Thank you.

ELLEN: (*Horrified*) You didn't take it, did you?

COLE: Afraid I did.

ELLEN: (*Almost in tears*) But you didn't say when. I wasn't even trying to look nice.

COLE: I have a theory about women, Mrs. Griswold. (*He looks at* AGATHA.) I think they look nicest when they're not trying.

AGATHA: (*Arising abruptly*) Are you finished?

COLE: I think so. (*Turning to* GINNY *and* MARY NELL) Now let's have 1948. (*As they come forward*) I think in the same positions. Leaning against the desk, Miss—

MARY NELL: (*Selling it*) Dodge.

COLE: (*With an appreciative appraisal of* MARY NELL) Dodge. (*Then*) And in Miss Reed's place, the other young lady.

MISS SHACKLEFORD: Ginny is the daughter of our President, you know.

COLE: No, I didn't. (*He looks at her with interest.*)

GINNY: (*Uncomfortably*) I'd rather Mr. Cole didn't mention that, Miss Shackleford. If you don't mind.

(AGATHA *gives* GINNY *a disturbed glance which* COLE *doesn't miss.*)

COLE: Whatever you say. (*Sighting through his camera*) Oh, I meant to ask you, Mrs. Griswold. Did your husband ever get hold of Dr. Merrill?

ELLEN: I think so. (*To* AGATHA) Claude was a little worried about the movie you brought down, Agatha. Mr. Cole was telling him something about it.

(AGATHA *looks quickly at* COLE. *He smiles.*)

COLE: Woody said you were showing *Fight to the Finish* here tomorrow.

AGATHA: Yes.

COLE: I was telling Mr. Griswold it's one of the few pictures I ever saw that had real guts. Wished I'd made it myself.

AGATHA: (*To* ELLEN) Why should Claude be worried?

ELLEN: Something about wanting to be sure it was right for our girls to see. I don't know—I never get those things straight.

MARY NELL: (*Eagerly*) Is it censorable?

MISS SHACKLEFORD: (*Now she's worried.*) Oh, dear!

ELLEN: Well, don't everybody worry about it. Claude's taking it up with Jim now.

COLE: (*Clicking*) That's it. (*The girls get up.* GINNY *looks in* AGATHA's *direction apprehensively.*) I'm sorry. I hope I haven't started any trouble.

AGATHA: Not at all, Mr. Cole. I'm sure Dr. Merrill is quite capable of handling the situation.

COLE: Good. (*Unloading his camera*) Otherwise I'd have this on my conscience.

(MERRILL *appears in the doorway.*)

MISS SHACKLEFORD: (*Dolorously*) Oh, Dr. Merrill. I hope there isn't any trouble.

MERRILL: Trouble?

MISS SHACKLEFORD: About the movie.

MERRILL: Oh. (*His eyes go immediately to* AGATHA.)

AGATHA: (*Smiling steadily*) Ellen tells us Mr. Griswold was concerned about it.

MERRILL: A little.

AGATHA: (*Confidently*) I trust you reassured him.

MERRILL: Well, I had to admit I didn't know too much about it myself.

(*There is an awkward pause.*)

COLE: Shall we get on to those other pictures you suggested, Miss Shackleford?

MISS SHACKLEFORD: What other—? (*She gets it.*) Oh yes. Those *other* pictures. Come along, girls.

ELLEN: (*Taking the cue*) Claude'll be looking for me.

(*As they all exit,* COLE *pauses in the doorway for one significant glance back at* AGATHA *and* MERRILL. *Then he goes out, closing the door. There is a little silence.*)

MERRILL: Darling, I'm very sorry this happened. I forgot to ask you anything about the picture and when it came up, I didn't really know what to say.

AGATHA: You don't think I'd have brought down anything unsuitable?

MERRILL: Of course not.

AGATHA: You know how I feel about what another war would mean. That's what this movie is—some newsreel film, illustrating a speech I once made. I even narrated it myself.

MERRILL: Agatha, I'm not questioning it at all. It's just that—all the trustees are in town. Your springing the cocktail party this afternoon got their feathers a little ruffled. So Claude feels we ought to take a look at the picture. There's just time enough to run it now. (*She's quiet.*) Darling, don't get upset. It's a shame Mr. Cole brought this whole matter up. But we'll straighten it out. (*She's still quiet.*) Look, you come with me. We'll both—

AGATHA: No. I'd rather not. I'm just a little tired.

MERRILL: Of course. You must be. I won't even see the picture. (*At her questioning look*) Something must be wrong with my eyes. I can't seem to see anything but you. (*She smiles. He leans down and kisses her tenderly and reassuringly.*) You haven't forgotten. There's a step-sing before the Prom. I'll pick you up.

(*She nods and he exits. She stands there for a moment, then turns—her face unsmiling and troubled. Then she starts back across the room, automatically removing her earrings, unfastening her dress. As she does, her eye falls on the victrola. She stares at it, slowly lifts the hand and starts it. The voice of Betty Boop bounces out. It sounds pathetically and irretrievably dated, like the era it represents. Suddenly,* AGATHA *is afraid to listen any more. She stops the record and shuts the victrola lid as*)

THE CURTAIN FALLS

ACT TWO

SCENE II

SCENE: *It is two hours later.*
The room is the same, except that all the lamps are now on, and some candles are lit on the mantel. The windows are open and lights from the building across the quad are twinkling in the summer night. The corridor door is open and through it the noise of the dormitory can be heard—a radio remotely playing a popular tune, occasional voices.
WOODY *is seated at the desk downstage, typing briskly, wearing a formal dress and her working glasses. In a second,* SUSAN *appears in the corridor doorway carrying two corsage boxes. As she starts to look in,* CLARISSE *intercepts her in the hall.* CLARISSE *is in an evening slip and stocking feet.*

CLARISSE: Hey Susie, do you remember who I loaned my gold
    shoes to?
SUSAN: No.
CLARISSE: Dammit, I can't find them. (*She disappears on down the
    hall.*)
    (SUSAN *enters the room as* WOODY *continues typing. She coughs,
    but gets no response. Finally, she knocks on the door frame.*)
WOODY: (*Stopping the typing*) Yeah?
SUSAN: These just came for you and Miss Reed. (*She hands* WOODY
    the boxes.) Flowers.
WOODY: Thanks. (*She puts one down, and opens hers.*)
SUSAN: (*Chattily*) Orchestra just arrived. Twenty-two men. Last
    year they only had eighteen.
WOODY: Inflation.
SUSAN: Well, if Miss Reed needs anything, I'll be on the switch-
    board all night.
WOODY: Fine.
SUSAN: (SUSAN *starts to go out, then stops.*) Oh—that call you're
    expecting from Washington—?
WOODY: (*Expectantly*) Yeah?
SUSAN: It hasn't come yet.
WOODY: (*Looking at her sourly*) Oh. (*Then*) It'll come. Look, even if
    I'm at this—what is it—?
SUSAN: Step-sing ?
WOODY: Now wait a minute, don't tell me. They *sing*—on the *steps*?

363

SUSAN: Yes.

WOODY: That's what I thought. Anyway, you come out there and get me. It's important.

(*There's the remote sound of a buzzer off-stage.*)

SUSAN: There goes the board now—(*She dashes out.*)

(*Alone,* WOODY *sets her orchid down while she examines the card dangling from* AGATHA's *box. Unfortunately, it's in a sealed envelope. She's holding it up to the light when* COLE *appears outside the window. He leans on the window sill, watching* WOODY *with interest.*)

COLE: Uh—uh—uh!

WOODY: (WOODY *jumps guiltily, sets the box down. Turning, she sees* COLE.) Oh—it's you.

COLE: Why don't you try a little steam?

WOODY: I forgot my tea kettle.

COLE: Where's the Honorable?

WOODY: In the "date room"—being interviewed by the local press.

COLE: (*As he swings his leg over the sill and sits on it*) Too bad. Thought I might pick up a little cheesecake for the piece. How a Congresswoman dresses for a Senior Prom. Does she put her shoes on *before* her girdle or *after*?

WOODY: She doesn't wear a girdle.

COLE: The rubber lobby won't like that.

WOODY: (*Sharply*) That's not for publication.

COLE: Who, me—?

WOODY: Don't give me those baby blues. You're about as innocent as a rattlesnake.

COLE: What'd I do now?

WOODY: I haven't forgiven you yet for spilling that marriage business.

COLE: I didn't tell her you told me. Just that you gave me a little hint.

WOODY: That's great. (*Shaking her head*) And now this thing with Griswold—about the picture. What'd you go and start *that* for?

COLE: All I said was it was a good picture. Is there anything wrong with that?

WOODY: I don't dig it, Cole. What are you in this for?

COLE: (*Smiling*) I'm in the employ of a foreign government.

WOODY: Quit stalling.

COLE: I'm in it for the same thing you are. I think she's making a mistake. I'd like to stop her.

WOODY: But why should *you* care?

COLE: (*Getting up and coming into the room*) That ought to be an easy one for a smart girl like you.

WOODY: (*After a pause*) Oh, God. It all adds up. (*Staring at him*) How long has *this* been going on? Twenty-*five* years?

COLE: No. He's got a few years seniority on me.

WOODY: Where did it start?

COLE: Yugoslavia. The first time I saw her she was up to her hips in mud in a shell hole. I thought she was a native, got a shot of her. That night the siege broke and she took a bath—came out a blonde from the *Detroit Free Press*.

WOODY: (*Enjoying it*) Was she a good reporter then?

COLE: The only reporter I ever knew could sit in a poker game, win the biggest pot and still have every guy wondering what she'd be like in bed.

WOODY: How long did it take you to find out?

COLE: (COLE *gives her a look, crosses away.*) I'll write my biography some day. You can read it.

WOODY: Hey, wait a minute, you can't do that to me—leave me with my tongue hanging out. What happened? I've been with her four years and you never turned up. Then all of a sudden, this weekend—

COLE: I'm on an assignment.

WOODY: Just your stuff—(COLE *turns away.*) For God's sake, Cole, I'm not being nosey. I don't just work for this woman. I like her. I care what happens to her.

COLE: (COLE *turns and looks at her for a long moment. He believes her. Quietly*) I haven't seen her since Paris—August 26, 1944. The day of the liberation. Me and every other newspaper hack in Europe had "liberated" the city—with a little help, of course, from the Allied Forces. I shot two hundred and forty-one pictures by six o'clock and sent them off. Then I went over to the Scribe Bar. The "cream" of American Journalism was there—and all way ahead of me. The place was a madhouse—I wanted to get out fast. (*Pause*) Then I saw Agatha. I hadn't seen her in six months. She had a red flower in that blonde hair—it stood out against the khaki and smoke. She was talking with some officer. She saw me and she stopped talking—I could tell it was in the middle of a sentence. It took us ten minutes to push our way through to each other, and another five minutes to get outside. That was even more hectic. The French people were celebrating outside—with champagne they'd hoarded in cellars for four years. Men wept in the streets, strangers kissed like lovers. Nobody talked—they yelled. (*He stops, remembering.*) I had to fight off two French Maquis to hang on to Agatha. Then I saw two more coming. I pushed in a door and pulled her after me. It was a barber shop. I could smell the hair tonic when I kissed her. And when I did, I knew it didn't matter that she'd ducked out on me in China—that she'd been a little remote in Algiers. I knew I wasn't going to ask her why—I was just going to ask her to marry me. She knew it, too. She had a room at the Ritz and she gave me the key while she went to her office to file her story. I bought up all the flowers I could find in ten blocks and sent them up to the room. Then I went up. (*Wryly*) I sprinkled rose petals in the doorway— (*A long pause*) They were a little brown around the edges when I got the cable from London. It said there'd been an urgent message calling her back to New York. Would I have the hotel send her bag on to her? (*He stops, smiles without humor.*) Well, I did. But I looked in it first. She traveled light. A tooth brush, a clean khaki blouse, a pair of stockings, two cakes of soap, her newspaper credentials, a flashlight—and a snapshot of a man. Not a very good one—overexposed. But good enough for me to remember. I recognized the face last week in a New York newspaper announcing the return of the "Honorable Agatha Reed" to her college for an honorary degree.

WOODY: (WOODY *just looks at him, not saying anything. Finally*) I'm sorry, Cole.

COLE: What are you sorry about? Now that I've seen him, I'm not worried. He's no competition—he's a memory. Something she's pressed in a book through the years. Like a goddam rose.

WOODY: Maybe you're right, but she doesn't know it.

COLE: She will. She's a realist—she can lie to herself just so much. Then she'll see him for what he is. (*Confidently*) And then she'll see me.

WOODY: You're expecting a lot from her in just two days.

COLE: Maybe. That's why I'm giving her a little help. A little sleight-of-hand. Something I picked up from an old Hindu fakir. Watch closely now—a word here, a word there—and

right before your very eyes, I turn the memory back into—a
man.

WOODY: Very clever, if it works.

COLE: It's working already, isn't it? Isn't it?

WOODY: Yes, she's getting worried. (*Suddenly*) Look, I don't know.
Maybe it's better for you to sit back and let the thing happen
by itself. Like I am—(*The phone rings.* WOODY *goes to it, picks it
up.*) Hello?—Oh. (*She looks at* COLE *for a second.*) All right. Put
him through. (*A pause*) Hello?—Oh, hello, George. Have you
got that stuff for me?—Good. That was quick work. (COLE
stretches out on the sofa.) Just a minute till I get a pencil.
(*Picking up pad and pencil*) All right, George. All set. —What?
You're kidding. I don't believe it. On the other hand, maybe I
do. —Don't be silly, that's a big help, George. Much obliged.
—Yes, and we ought to be back next week. I'll drop in to see
you. And thanks again. (*She hangs up, looks at the pad in her
hand for a moment meditatively.*)

COLE: Trouble?

WOODY: (*Casually*) No. Just routine stuff.

COLE: (COLE *sits up, looks straight at her.*) Don't give me those "baby
blues." Sit back—see what happens. Butter wouldn't melt in
your mouth.

WOODY: Well, I—

COLE: (*Crossing to her*) You've been busy as a little bee!

WOODY: It's nothing. I just asked a friend to do a little research for
me.

COLE: Don't apologize. You're terrific! What research?

WOODY: He looked up Merrill for me.

COLE: What about him?

WOODY: Well, it's mighty interesting. He—

COLE: (*Stopping her*) Wait a minute—don't tell me. I've got this guy
all figured out. He's one of these—
(*There's a sudden squealing outside in the hall.*)

GIRL'S VOICE(*Off stage*) Oh, Miss Reed, have some candy!
(*Other girls' voices chime in.*)

WOODY: (*Over it*) That's Agatha. Look, you better get out of here.

COLE: Why?

WOODY: She thinks we're in cahoots as it is. If she sees you in here
she'll blow her top.

COLE: (*Crossing to the window*) Okay.

WOODY: No. They can see that window from the hall. (*Pushing him toward the bedroom*) There are a couple of windows in there on the other side. Be sure no one sees you climbing out.

COLE: (*As he exits*) This takes me back to my youth.

(WOODY *closes the bedroom door.* AGATHA *enters, followed by* MARY NELL, CLARISSE, AMELIA, *and* CAROL. *They're all in evening dress, and the girls are very excited.* MARY NELL *is holding out a box of candy.*)

MARY NELL: —And I'd consider it a great honor for you to have a piece, Miss Reed.

AGATHA: (*Taking one*) Why, thank you, Mary Nell.

MARY NELL: Sam didn't understand. He laughed. And I got awfully mad. I didn't talk to him all the way home. But then he explained. He said he only laughed because he had other plans for me. Such as asking me to be Mrs. Sam Carter.

AMELIA: Wasn't that darling?

MARY NELL: And we're going to live in Bangor, Maine, and have a wood-burning fireplace in every room practically.

AGATHA: Sounds wonderful.

MARY NELL: (*Expansively*) Everybody have another piece of candy! (*Passing it, her face sobers.*) Miss Reed. You don't think I made a mistake, do you? Giving up the Government and Congress and all that.

AGATHA: Do you feel as if you've made a mistake?

MARY NELL: No.

AGATHA: Then you haven't. Most mistakes you make you can feel. (*She avoids* WOODY's *piercing glance.*)

MARY NELL: Gosh. I just remembered. This is probably the last time I'll be in this room. (*She looks around, swallowing.*)

CLARISSE: It was always the nicest room in the Dorm.

MARY NELL: Wasn't it? Ginny made the curtains. I was going to make spreads. But I never got to it.

AMELIA: Seems just yesterday we were Freshmen.

CAROL: And tomorrow it'll all be over.

MARY NELL: I can hardly believe it.

(*There's a silent, poignant moment*)

JO: (*Appearing in the doorway*) Hey! The men are here!

(*It's electrifying. Lumps in throats are gone, and there's a mad dash for the door. All exit.*)

WOODY: I'll give you one guess what *they* majored in. (*Then*) How was the interview?

AGATHA: Oh, the usual. Is Congress going to do anything to stop inflation? Has the United Nations got a chance and how do I feel about the Draft.

WOODY: Did you tell them?

AGATHA: I went easy.

WOODY: Easy? Since when have you started pulling your punches?

AGATHA: Well, after all, I'm not down here for political purposes.

WOODY: I know, but—

AGATHA: Well, I'm not. It would just create more embarrassment—

WOODY: (WOODY *stares at her, then turns abruptly and walks to the desk.*) I finished typing the notes you dictated for your Commencement speech. You better look them over tonight. (*She pulls the sheet out of the typewriter.*)

AGATHA: Good idea. (*She takes the pages, then sets them down absently.*)

WOODY: (*Suddenly making up her mind*) I have some other notes you might like to look over. (*She picks up her shorthand pad.*)

AGATHA: Other notes?

WOODY: I called George Cameron and asked him to see what dope there might be around on Merrill.

AGATHA: You did—what?

WOODY: Yeah, I'm funny that way. I like to know everything I can about everybody. You always said that's what makes me such a good secretary.

AGATHA: Stop making excuses. It's inexcusable! (*As* WOODY *shrugs and starts to put down the pad*) What did he find out?

WOODY: (*Handing her the pad*) It's right here. You can read it.

AGATHA: (*Almost unwillingly* AGATHA *crosses to her, takes the pad. She looks at it, turns over the page, goes back to the first one in confusion.*) I don't understand.

WOODY: Just what you see there.

AGATHA: (*Looking again*) There's nothing here.

WOODY: That's what I mean. Nothing. An unblemished record. (*As* AGATHA *relaxes*) That's what bothers me.

AGATHA: Bothers you?

WOODY: Yes. Don't you think it's funny? He's a prominent educator. Yet he's never been a member of one committee that took a stand on any issue. Not a single endorsement of anything the least bit political, controversial. Never even been investigated *once.*

AGATHA: What are you trying to say?

WOODY: We've just been through a war. People took stands on things. *You've* been investigated.

AGATHA: (*Icy*) Very nice, Woody. Only don't forget. I've seen you work before.

WOODY: For God's sake, Agatha. If you want to get married, it's your own business. I just want you to be happy.

AGATHA: (*With mounting anger*) What makes you think I won't be?

WOODY: I'm not saying you won't. I'm just asking. After all, you haven't seen this man for twenty years. And now in just two days, you think—

AGATHA: (*Violently*) I'm *tired* of all this—

GINNY: (GINNY *knocks on the door frame.*) Miss Reed, could I talk to you?

AGATHA: Yes, of course.

 (*There is an awkward pause. Then, as* GINNY *enters,* WOODY *starts to the door.*)

WOODY: I forgot to tell you. There's some flowers there for you. (*She exits.*)

 (AGATHA *stands, looking after her. Then, pulling herself together, she turns to* GINNY.)

AGATHA: Shouldn't you be dressed by now? (*She opens the flower box, reads the card.*)

GINNY: I had to drop some things off at my father's house.

AGATHA: (*Lifting out the orchids*) These are from him. He's my date for the Step-sing and the Prom. And he's late.

GINNY: Yes, I know. They're having a meeting over there.

AGATHA: (*Looks at her*) A meeting?

GINNY: Yes. (*Abruptly*) Is it a good picture? The one you brought down?

AGATHA: Yes, I think it is.

GINNY: Would you call it—propaganda?

AGATHA: It's a picture against war. If that's propaganda, it's like propaganda against cancer. (*Quietly*) Why, Ginny?

GINNY: Nothing.

AGATHA: What are you trying to tell me?

GINNY: (*Facing her*) Some people think the President of a college has the right to make decisions on things. But he doesn't. He has to check everything with the trustees. Whatever he may feel himself, that doesn't matter.

AGATHA: You mean, they may not show the movie?

GINNY: (*Fervently*) It's like you said yourself. Being President is different from just being a professor. You have more responsibility, so you have to make more concessions. He's done wonderful things for the school. Seven new buildings in ten years. And last year they named him the most successful college administrator east of the Rockies. Isn't that something to be proud of? I'm so proud I could—(*She turns away, fighting back the sobs. They come anyway—the dam finally run over.*)

AGATHA: (*She crosses to her*) It's all right, Ginny. It's all right.

GINNY: I'm so ashamed. I've been ashamed for a long time now. (*She starts blindly for the door.*)

AGATHA: Where are you going?

GINNY: I don't know. Anywhere—away from here—

AGATHA: (*Catching her*) Stop it, Ginny! Stop it!

GINNY: Why? Why should I stay? To stand up there and let him hand me a diploma when I know it doesn't mean anything?

AGATHA: That's not so. It's yours for what you've learned here.

GINNY: What have I learned? That my father's a coward? That he's so afraid of losing his job he's lost everything else he ever believed in? Oh, I've made apologies. I've made them till I can't look at him any more. But there've been too many things. (*Pulling away*) Dr. Pitt wasn't the first, and your movie won't be the last.

AGATHA: Wait, Ginny. You may be wrong.

GINNY: I'm not wrong.

AGATHA: When you left the house, had they finished? Had they decided not to show the picture?

GINNY: No, but—

AGATHA: Then how do you know? How do you know he hasn't fought them on this?

GINNY: He's forgotten how to fight.

AGATHA: Sometimes a man needs a certain moment. Maybe this is it.

GINNY: I can't listen any more, Miss Reed, I can't—
(She starts for the door, but Agatha catches her arm and holds her.)

AGATHA: Ginny, you must listen! You probably know I was expelled from this college. I want you to know why. Because I stayed out all night with a man. We were very much in love—we were planning to be married. But I ran away—so I wouldn't hurt his chances of becoming President. (GINNY's *face pales.*) Even at eighteen, I felt it was important for a man

like him to be the President of a college. I think your father
remembers that today. Whatever's happened in between, I
think he'd like to be that man again. (GINNY *crosses away from
her.*) Maybe you resent me now. That was the chance I had to
take. But I want you to know why I told you this. It's because
I've grown very fond of you. You have a good mind and a
whole life ahead of you. You mustn't throw it away by being
bitter and disillusioned. (*There's a long moment.* AGATHA *turns
away in defeat.*)

GINNY: I don't resent you. (AGATHA *wheels.*) I think I just grew up a
little, though.

AGATHA: I'm sorry.

GINNY: Don't be. It's good. I should have known. Whenever he
talked about you, he was different. That's why Uncle Willy—
It's been in his study ever since I can remember.

AGATHA: (*Encouraged herself*) I didn't know.

GINNY: (*Suddenly smiling*) I feel better. I feel so much better.
(*The telephone rings.* AGATHA *crosses to answer it.*)

AGATHA: (*Into telephone*) Hello—Yes, this is Miss Reed. Will you
ask Dr. Merrill to come in, please? (*She hangs up.* GINNY *has
started for the door.*) Where are you going?

GINNY: Don't worry. Just to get dressed.

AGATHA: Good.

GINNY: (*Turning*) I want you to know, I never gave him up, really. I
just needed someone else to believe in him, too. (*She goes out.*)
(AGATHA *hurries across the room to her flower box. She's tense,
expectant. She fumbles putting the flower on, sticks herself, finally
gets it. There's a knock on the door. She turns, takes a deep breath.*)

AGATHA: Come in. (*The door opens and* MERRILL *stands there. He's in
tails, exceedingly distinguished and exceedingly handsome.* AGATHA
smiles.) I'd begun to feel jilted. As if—
(*There is a strident, hysterical giggle from the corridor.*)

MERRILL: (*Apologetically*) Claude and Ellen dropped by. They
thought we might as well make it a foursome.
(*The* GRISWOLDS *enter behind him.* CLAUDE GRISWOLD *is a
personable, jovial man in his late forties. He wears an impeccable
tuxedo. He also wears the indefinable air which a great deal of
money and power give to a man. Too many people have told*
CLAUDE GRISWOLD *he's right for him ever again to believe that
he's wrong.* ELLEN *wears an evening gown that seems carefully
designed to accentuate all the worst points of her figure—the kind*

that always costs a lot of money. She has obviously kept up the pace from the afternoon's cocktail party because by now she's really sailing.)

ELLEN: Just like old times, Ag. (*To* CLAUDE) We always went on double dates.

GRISWOLD: Well, how do we stack up against the 1928 wolves?

ELLEN: They had more hair.

GRISWOLD: But less money, eh, Jim?

MERRILL: Speak for yourself, Claude.

GRISWOLD: Now, don't let him give you the impression education doesn't pay, Miss Reed. I know. I sign his checks. (*At* MERRILL*'s obvious discomfort*) Don't get embarrassed, Jim. It's worth every cent to have a President who can wear tails like that.

ELLEN: Claude could wear them too, but he just won't.

GRISWOLD: They flap against my legs.

ELLEN: That's silly. If you were too short, I could understand it. (*Suddenly*) Ag, remember the buzzer? (*To the men*) You could buzz from the lounge to the rooms. When one of us had a blind date, the other always went in first. One buzz—he was short, low heels. Two buzzes, tall—high heels. (*Looking at Claude complacently*) Remember, I always said I'd marry a two-buzz.

GRISWOLD: I've been called a lot of things in my time—

MERRILL: You seem full of reminiscences tonight, Ellen.

GRISWOLD: And martinis.

ELLEN: I guess it's being back in the old room with Uncle Willy—and Ag and everything. (*The remote sound of instruments tuning up floats through the open window.*) Oh, listen, the orchestra's warming up. (*Her eye catches the victrola.*) We've got to warm up, too.

GRISWOLD: Now, Ellen, there's plenty of time—

ELLEN: Now, don't be a kill-joy. (*Picking up a record*) Stan Kenton. He's super. Isn't that the word now? (*She puts the record on.*)

GRISWOLD: Ellen, we're going to be dancing all evening.

ELLEN: Oh, come on. (*She sways up to him—her arms outstretched.*)

GRISWOLD: This is silly.

ELLEN: It's awful to be married to a man with no imagination. (*That does it.* GRISWOLD *grasps his wife firmly and swings her into a fox trot.*) Where's your manners, Jim? Aren't you going to ask Ag to dance?

(MERRILL *looks at* AGATHA *helplessly.*)

GRISWOLD: (*Puffing a bit*) Every year dance music keeps—getting—faster and faster.

ELLEN: Could be you're just getting slower and slower.

GRISWOLD: (*He stops, puffing slightly.*) Can't do it—I'm out of condition.

AGATHA: (*Gratefully*) I think we're all out of condition. (*She takes advantage of the opportunity to cross and turn off the victrola.*)

GRISWOLD: (*Pressing his chest*) Besides, I ate too fast tonight.

ELLEN: Well, it's your own fault. (*Irritably*) If we hadn't had to rush off and see that movie in the middle of everything—(*She stops herself.*)

(MERRILL *and* GRISWOLD *exchange glances.* AGATHA*'s back is turned. There is a silent, strained moment. Then she turns slowly.*)

AGATHA: Too bad. Sounds like it's all my fault.

ELLEN: Oh, I didn't mean that, Ag. I just meant—(*She looks helplessly at her husband.*)

AGATHA: (*Crossing to* GRISWOLD) How did you like the picture?

GRISWOLD: Well—it's no Abbott and Costello.

ELLEN: They're Claude's favorites.

MERRILL: Don't you think we ought to get along now? It's getting rather late. (*It's obvious he's trying to avoid a discussion.*)

AGATHA: (*She makes up her mind.*) Don't rush us, Jim. We've plenty of time. The Seniors aren't even out on the steps yet. Besides, this is the first time I've had a chance to talk with Mr. Griswold.

GRISWOLD: Make it Claude.

AGATHA: Claude. I haven't even had a moment to compliment you on all the signs of your interest around the campus. The motion picture machine, for instance. How did it occur to you?

GRISWOLD: Well, I'd like to take credit for that, but it was really Jim's idea.

MERRILL: Visual education's been one of our pet projects for a long time.

GRISWOLD: Jim's got to make it sound important. But what made me reach my hand in my pocket was the thought of the kick those kids were going to get, seeing movies right on campus.

ELLEN: It's a good thing you haven't got a daughter. She'd be spoiled silly.

GRISWOLD: I've got six hundred and twenty-two daughters. *All* spoiled silly. And why not? They've got time enough to start worrying their heads when they're *out* of college.

AGATHA: That's an interesting theory of education.

GRISWOLD: No. I leave the theories to the experts like Jim here. I just know what I like and what I don't like.

AGATHA: (*Doggedly*) Which brings us back to what you thought of the picture.

MERRILL: (*Quickly*) Well, of course, Claude understands what you're trying to do with this picture.

GRISWOLD: It's a good thing to make pictures like this about outlawing war. As long as—

AGATHA: Nobody sees them? (*There's something in her tone.*)

GRISWOLD: (GRISWOLD *looks at her, laughs.*) I was going to say as long as you're careful who you show them to. For instance, if I'd known some of those strong scenes were going to be in that picture, I wouldn't have wanted Ellen here to see it.

ELLEN: It's all right, Claude. I turned my head away at the bad parts.

AGATHA: That's a shame, Ellen. They're worth seeing and remembering.

ELLEN: I just meant—

GRISWOLD: Don't forget, you're a very special kind of woman, Miss Reed. You've been out on the field, on the war fronts. You've gotten a kind of toughness about this sort of thing. More like—well, more like a man.

AGATHA: I'm sure you intended that as a compliment.

MERRILL: Miss Reed, you realize what Claude meant was—

AGATHA: —That I'm a very superior woman because I can face ugly things without turning my head away. But those other poor creatures, the rest of my sex, we must be very careful to spare them. Because they have such delicate stomachs.

GRISWOLD: Well, haven't they?

AGATHA: What do you think of that description of women, Ellen? (ELLEN *looks from* AGATHA *to her husband in disturbed bewilderment.*)

GRISWOLD: Miss Reed, I'm a great admirer of yours—even if we don't always agree politically. I say thank God we've got the right to disagree with each other here in this country. But I don't like propaganda—

MERRILL: (*Crossing to him*) Claude!

GRISWOLD: (*Resolutely*) —whether it's from Congresswomen, or scientists or the President of the United States!

AGATHA: That's become such an easy word. Is it propaganda to show that the results of another war will be the most devastating the world's ever known?

GRISWOLD: There's too much scaremongering going on. All these scientists getting hot under the collar. All this loose talk. You're not going to stop wars that way.

AGATHA: How *are* you going to stop them?

GRISWOLD: There've always been wars. There always will be. It's human nature and we may as well face it.

AGATHA: (*Something explodes inside her.*) You own Great Northern Textiles, don't you? (GRISWOLD *faces her.*) I sit on the Jameson Committee. We've been reviewing war profits.

GRISWOLD: (*With a steady smile*) What are you trying to say, Miss Reed? That I made money out of the war? Sure I did. So did everyone. I'd have been a fool not to. But if you're accusing me of doing anything to start another war—

AGATHA: No, Mr. Griswold, I don't believe that. But what are you doing to stop another one?

GRISWOLD: That's beyond my power.

AGATHA: Maybe. Maybe it's really in the power of your six hundred and twenty-two daughters. But only if they know what war means. If they look at it—if they understand it.

GRISWOLD: You mean, cheat these kids out of their youth? No, sir! Life's tough enough. Let them have these few years of fun instead of drumming their heads full of war—

AGATHA: And then just hand them one and say—don't understand it. Fight it. Die for it.

GRISWOLD: (*Admiringly*) Miss Reed, I can understand why you start so much fireworks down there in Congress. But it all boils down to one thing. *We* know what's best for our school—

MERRILL: (*Warningly*) Claude—

GRISWOLD: Now, let's stop this beating around the bush, Jim.

MERRILL: (*Desperately*) Claude, if you'll just let me handle this—

GRISWOLD: There's no handling to it. (MERRILL *crosses away from them.*) I like to be frank, Miss Reed. We've canceled the showing of the film—the trustees took a vote an hour ago. There'll be a statement that the schedule got overcrowded. (*There's a pause.*)

AGATHA: I see. (*She turns to* MERRILL.) And the President, did he agree? (MERRILL'*s face is strained. He starts to say something, but*

GRISWOLD *says it for him.*)

GRISWOLD: The President and the trustees always agree. (AGATHA *looks at* MERRILL, *waiting for him to deny it. He doesn't.*) I'm sorry this had to happen, Miss Reed. Nothing personal in it at all. I hope it won't spoil an extremely pleasant weekend.

MERRILL: Claude, I'd like to speak to Miss Reed alone.

GRISWOLD: Now, stop worrying, Jim. You're making too much of this thing. Miss Reed's a sensible woman.

MERRILL: (*Insistently*) We'll join you.

GRISWOLD: (*Annoyed*) All right. Only, don't be too long. It wouldn't look well if you were late—(*It's an order. He turns to* ELLEN.) Come on, Ellen. (*For the first time in her marriage,* ELLEN *looks at her husband with the suspicion that he may be less than perfect. She looks back at* AGATHA. *Then, quietly, she exits.* GRISWOLD *bows to* AGATHA.) Miss Reed. (*He exits, closes the door.*)

(*It seems very still for a moment.*)

AGATHA: I feel a little—sick.

MERRILL: Agatha, you're not giving me a chance to explain.

AGATHA: Did you feel that movie shouldn't be shown?

MERRILL: It wasn't a question of—

AGATHA: Be frank with me, Jim. Did you think it was wrong for your Seniors to see?

MERRILL: (*After a struggle*) No.

AGATHA: And you didn't stand up and say that?

MERRILL: Agatha, you're not being very objective. I know it's embarrassing for you to bring a film down here—

AGATHA: (*Aghast*) Could you possibly believe my vanity is concerned in this?

MERRILL: I didn't say that. I'm just asking you to try and see my position. I can't always bluster through my own opinions. There are moments when I have to bow to—

AGATHA: Claude?

MERRILL: You're exaggerating Claude's whole importance in this affair.

AGATHA: Am I? When he, not you, seems to be the real judge of what should be taught in this college. By what right? Do you respect him as an educator?

MERRILL: He doesn't pretend to be that. He's a business man. And a very successful one.

AGATHA: Fine, but a college isn't a business.

MERRILL: Then who's going to pay for it? Don't forget, he's the man who foots the bills. And he's very generous.

AGATHA: Yes, I know. Give a college a Science building—then tell the professors what they can say in it. Give them a motion picture machine but tell them what to run on it. That's not generosity. That's an investment—with damned good dividends!

MERRILL: All right. It's a business deal. He gives money. He wants his say. It's as simple as that. (*At* AGATHA'*s look*) Why do you look so shocked?

AGATHA: Not shocked. Frightened. That *you* stand here and say that, and *accept* it.

MERRILL: Good God, Agatha, I have to run a college. That means I have to get money, endowments, buildings. It's part of the job. So I've learned to compromise. I give in on smaller things here and there so I can win on larger ones.

AGATHA: (*Facing him*) What *are* the larger ones? Or have you been waiting for them so long you don't recognize them anymore?

MERRILL: You mean Dr. Pitt? This film? Suppose I fought Griswold on them? To a showdown. It would be a heroic gesture. But I'd be out of here tomorrow.

AGATHA: Would you? You used to fight very well.

MERRILL: (*Slight pause*) Things are quite different now. I have Ginny to think of.

AGATHA: You don't know your daughter very well, do you, Jim?

MERRILL: We have a very good relationship.

AGATHA: There's no need to lie to me. I've seen you together.

MERRILL: (*Turning away*) I don't care to discuss it any more.

AGATHA: You've got to discuss it. You've got a bigger stake in this than you think. (*He wheels, looks at her.*) You're going to lose her, Jim. I don't know how important that is to you. I suspect it's very important.

MERRILL: (*Angrily*) What have you been telling her?

AGATHA: Terrible things. That you have courage. That you have integrity. (MERRILL *turns away to the window. She knows she's reaching him.*) I didn't just say it. I believe it, Jim. Stand up to Griswold. Not for me. Not even for Ginny. For yourself.

(*There is a poignant silence.* AGATHA *can see the struggle mirrored in his back. Suddenly there's a sharp knock on the door. Neither of them moves. The knock repeats.*)

CAROL: (*Offstage*) Dr. Merrill. (MERRILL *crosses, opens the door.*) Mr.

Griswold sent me, Dr. Merrill. They're waiting for you and Miss Reed.

(*Just the name does it. The name and all the years of acquiescence. You can see it happen. In one long moment.*)

MERRILL: We'll be right there.

CAROL: I'll tell him. (*She disappears.*)

(AGATHA *has sunk into a chair, her face white, like a woman who's been slapped.*)

MERRILL: We'd better go. (*She's quiet.*) We're late.

AGATHA: You've jumped through the hoop too long, haven't you?

MERRILL: (*Harshly*) Are you coming?

AGATHA: In a moment. I have a few more things to say.

MERRILL: Agatha, I'm sorry, but there's no use in pursuing the matter any—

AGATHA: (*Rising*) Oh, I'm not going to plead with you any more. No more appeals to your better nature. I know when I'm licked. (*She smiles.*) I'm going to make a deal with you. A business deal. That's more in your line.

MERRILL: What are you talking about?

AGATHA: A few minutes ago I assured your daughter that you'd run this picture tomorrow. I don't like to think of her finding out that you won't. So I'm afraid you're going to do it. With or without Mr. Griswold's consent. I'll leave procedure up to you.

MERRILL: Is this your idea of a joke?

AGATHA: —And in exchange for that small service, I'll give you my personal guarantee that the *Life* article won't even hint at the colorful events leading up to my expulsion from this seat of higher learning. (MERRILL *stares at her.*) You can imagine how excited Cole would be, stumbling across such a juicy morsel. Such a beautiful tale of love and sacrifice. A daring young girl caught climbing in her dormitory window—see picture of window on preceding page—braving the perils of expulsion rather than blight the budding career of her lover. And now, twenty years later—the girl, a Congresswoman, asked back to her college for an honorary degree. And the lover—hold on to your hats now, folks—the President of the college!

MERRILL: I can't believe you'd—

AGATHA: Why not? You see, I'm willing to take a chance on you, Jim. I know now that you're a coward, and with a coward it's only a question of the lesser of two evils. Whether you *risk*

being removed from here by running the picture or whether you
accept the *certainty* of being removed when this story breaks.

MERRILL: You'd really do a thing like this?

AGATHA: Yes. You learn all kinds of dirty tricks in my work. The
most important one being never to play fair except when you
respect the men you're playing with. (*She picks up her scarf
from the chair.*)

(*From outside, the clear young voices of the Senior Class have broken into the Alma Mater as the step-sing obviously begins.*)

VOICES (*Off*)

"Good Hope, Our Alma Mater
Thy wisdom and thy truth
Shall grow forever greater
In the years beyond our youth—

AGATHA: The Alma Mater. Appropriate, isn't it?

VOICES (*Off*)

"Whate'er may be our station,
Whate'er the storm and strife—
(MERRILL *stands there for a second. Then he turns without a word
and goes out.*)
"Thy shining inspiration
Shall light our way through life—
(AGATHA *looks after him. Then she walks slowly to the door, turns
off the lights and exits. The room is in darkness except for the
moonlight streaming in the windows.*)
"So we raise up our voices and we shout Good Hope,
Good old Good Hope—
All the praise of our voices is about Good Hope,
Good old Good Hope—
(*The bedroom door opens, and* COLE *comes out. There is a calm sat-
isfaction about even his silhouette which makes it obvious that he
hasn't missed a word.*)
"We hope to be
Worthy of thee
And we plight love undying
To thy bright colors flying
In our hearts, brave and bold—
(COLE *lights a cigarette and starts slowly across the stage toward
the window.*)
"Maroon and Gold—

Good old—
GOOD HOPE!

THE CURTAIN HAS FALLEN

ACT THREE

SCENE: *It's early the next afternoon. Half an hour before the*
Commencement procession is scheduled to start.
The room looks much the same except for a bed pillow crushed at one end
of the sofa, and on the table an ash tray spilling over with cigarette butts.
WOODY *is alone in the room and on the telephone.*

WOODY: (*Into telephone*) —No, I think it would be better if we
drove into Boston and made that seven o'clock plane. That
would get us back to Washington tonight. See if you can
arrange that. —Good. (*She hangs up, takes a few papers from the
desk and puts them in her open briefcase. The telephone rings. She
picks it up.*) Hello? —No, she's not back yet, Miss
Shackleford. I haven't seen her since eight o'clock. —I really
don't know. She just said she was going for a walk. (*She puts
the telephone down as* MISS SHACKLEFORD *continues talking, locks
the typewriter case, then picks the telephone up again.*) Yes, I know
the procession starts in half an hour. I'm sure she does, too—
Yes, all right. (*She hangs up, takes her typewriter case from the
desk, crosses to Center and sets it down beside the chair. She continues on toward the bedroom, singing "Goodbye, My Alma Mater—."*
WOODY *gives every appearance of a happy woman as she exits into
the bedroom. In a moment,* MISS BIRDESHAW *appears in the door-
way and looks around timidly. She is in a cap and gown and seems a
little pale around the edges. Hesitantly, she steps into the room.*)
MISS BIRDESHAW: Anybody here?
WOODY: (*Offstage*) Agatha? I've been worrying about— (*As she
enters, carrying* AGATHA's *small suitcase*) Oh, it's *you.*
MISS BIRDESHAW: The door was open. So I just came on in.
(*Timidly*) Is Miss Reed back yet?
WOODY: No.
MISS BIRDESHAW: Do you mind if I wait?
WOODY: (*Setting down* AGATHA's *suitcase*) I don't mind, if you don't.
(MISS BIRDESHAW *sits down on the sofa with a minimum of dis-
turbance as* WOODY *crosses toward the desk.*)
MISS BIRDESHAW: I hope Agatha's feelings aren't hurt. I didn't get
to her film showing this morning. I had a little—ah,
headache.
WOODY: (*With grim satisfaction*) Didn't you know? The film show-
ing was canceled last night. (*She drops* AGATHA's *wilted corsage*

of the night before in the waste basket.)

MISS BIRDESHAW: Oh, I'm glad. (*Hastily*) I mean, I'm glad I didn't miss it. (*After a slight pause*) I—I don't think I got to say goodnight to you yesterday at the tea, Miss Woods.

WOODY: Not in so many words.

MISS BIRDESHAW: I—I had to leave early.

WOODY: Kind of early.

MISS BIRDESHAW: Did I leave with anyone? I mean—(*Swallowing*) It was very nice of Professor Dingley to accompany me—wasn't it?

WOODY: (WOODY *turns, amused, suddenly understanding what* MISS BIRDESHAW *is worrying about.*) Very. He wouldn't let anyone else carry you.

MISS BIRDESHAW: *Carry* me?

(WOODY *nods.* MISS BIRDESHAW *emits a little moan.*)

WOODY: You felt a little—sleepy. We took you home.

MISS BIRDESHAW: We? *You* undressed me?

WOODY: Yes.

MISS BIRDESHAW: (*Sinking back with a sigh of relief*) Thank you, Miss Woods.

WOODY: Not at all. Some day you can return the favor.

MISS BIRDESHAW: I must have acted pretty silly yesterday.

WOODY: Don't you remember?

MISS BIRDESHAW: I remember some things.

WOODY: You told some great stories. About your Aunt Deborah. The time she locked herself in the carriage house all night with two of the stable boys—

MISS BIRDESHAW: Oh, no! (*Faintly*) Did Professor Dingley laugh at that?

WOODY: He choked. That was when you took him out in the garden for some deep breaths of fresh air. Do you remember that?

MISS BIRDESHAW: A little. (*Blushing*) I suppose I ought to be ashamed of myself.

WOODY: Why?

MISS BIRDESHAW: At my age—(*Then, remembering*) But I had a wonderful time. The best time I ever had in my life.

WOODY: (*Touched*) Good. That's the way to talk.

MISS BIRDESHAW: I wonder—maybe you'd tell Agatha I'm sorry. In case she feels badly about yesterday. I've been worrying about that.

WOODY: Sure, I'll tell her.

MISS BIRDESHAW: Thank you. Then I think I'll run along. (*Rising*) Professor Dingley's waiting for me outside. We're walking in the procession together, you know.

WOODY: No, I didn't.

MISS BIRDESHAW: He dropped by this morning, to see how I felt. He brought me some roses—yellow roses. Two dozen.

WOODY: That was very thoughtful.

MISS BIRDESHAW: Wasn't it? (*Then*) Do you know something, Miss Woods? Professor Dingley and I have walked in twenty-three Commencement processions at this college. But this is the first time we'll have ever walked—together.
(*She smiles at* WOODY, *her eyes bright, her cheeks flushed.* MISS BIRDESHAW *looks almost pretty.* MISS SHACKLEFORD *bustles in.*)

MISS SHACKLEFORD: Is Agatha back yet?

WOODY: Not yet.

MISS SHACKLEFORD: My goodness, I hope she realizes what time it—(*She notices* MISS BIRDESHAW.) Oh.

MISS BIRDESHAW: I—I had some business with Miss Reed.

MISS SHACKLEFORD: I see. (*She crosses past* MISS BIRDESHAW *to* WOODY.)

MISS BIRDESHAW: (*Timidly—the old reflex*) Miss Shackleford, I—uh—

MISS SHACKLEFORD: (*Ignoring her, to* WOODY) You don't suppose anything—

WOODY: Look, she's got the best attendance record in Congress! (*Indicating the papers on her desk*) There's her Commencement speech.

MISS SHACKLEFORD: (*Convinced*) Well, then maybe you can explain to her. We've made a very important change in the procession formation. Her honor guard will come to pick her up *here*. They'll escort her to the Ivy Arch rather than Hope Hall gate. Which means that they'll *follow* the President and the Dean instead of *preceding* them. Is that clear?

WOODY: Perfectly.

MISS SHACKLEFORD: Good. Now—(*She notices* MISS BIRDESHAW *still standing there.*) Hadn't you better run along, Miss Birdeshaw? The Associate Professors are starting to form right now.

MISS BIRDESHAW: I think I should tell you, Miss Shackleford. (*Quietly*) Professor Dingley and I are walking together in the procession.

MISS SHACKLEFORD: (*Aghast*) Why, that's ridiculous, Miss Birdeshaw! You know the full professors are always *several hundred* feet—

MISS BIRDESHAW: —ahead of the associate professors. Yes, I know. But Professor Dingley and I prefer it the other way. And there's no rule that says we can't. (MISS SHACKLEFORD'*s* mouth is open. MISS BIRDESHAW *turns at the door*) I looked it up. (*She exits.*)

MISS SHACKLEFORD: (*She stares after her.*) Well, I'll certainly be glad when *this* weekend is over!

WOODY: It had its moments.

MISS SHACKLEFORD: Everyone's been acting so strangely. I just don't understand it. First Dr. Merrill, and now Miss Birdeshaw, of all people—

WOODY: Dr. Merrill?

MISS SHACKLEFORD: Yes, with that whole film business. Last night he tells me to cancel it. Then this morning at half past nine he calls and says I'm to go ahead.

WOODY: (*Dumbfounded*) You mean—Dr. Merrill ordered the film shown?

MISS SHACKLEFORD: Yes. (*Sighing*) And then Mr. Griswold, calling me up and barking at me like that. As I told him, this is not *my* responsibility. I just do what the President tells me. Really, it's been extremely difficult for me. Now if Commencement goes off without the speakers' platform collapsing or something—(WOODY *is a picture of incredulity and disappointment, but* MISS SHACKLEFORD *hardly notices.* COLE *appears in the doorway.*) Oh, Mr. Cole, did you get what you needed at the film showing?

COLE: Just what I needed, Miss Shackleford.

MISS SHACKLEFORD: Well, thank goodness for you. It's such a comfort to have *someone* going around doing his job. (*As* COLE *leans over and smells the corsage she is wearing*) Sweet, aren't they?

COLE: (*In high spirits*) Lovely! You look wonderful, Miss Shackleford. Is that a new hat?

MISS SHACKLEFORD: (*Overcome*) Oh no, it's—

COLE: It's beautiful. Miss Shackleford, don't you be surprised if you wind up on the cover of *Life*!

MISS SHACKLEFORD: Oh, come now, Mr. Cole! You're pulling my leg.

COLE: No, but it's an idea.

MISS SHACKLEFORD: (*Gulping*) Why, Mr. Cole—(*She exits in a flurry of embarrassment.*)

COLE: (*Turning to* WOODY) I *love* that dame.

WOODY: (*Looking at him narrowly*) Wait a minute—didn't you just come from the film showing?

COLE: Mm-hm.

WOODY: Then what the hell are you so happy about?

COLE: I'm not happy. I'm sad. But—I'm philosophical. Something I learned from—

WOODY AND COLE: (*Together*) An old Hindu fakir—yeah!

WOODY: The same jerk who taught you to turn a memory into a man?

COLE: What do you want me to do—go around dragging my tail? That's the way it goes. Got to take the bad with the good. You're up—you're down—

SUSAN: (*Hurrying in*) Oh, Miss Woods—

WOODY: Yeah. Anything?

SUSAN: Well, I asked around. Like you said. Casual. And Kip Martin—she was picking up her mother at the railroad station, and she thinks she saw Miss Reed—at least it looked like Miss Reed, walking along the road.

WOODY: When was that?

SUSAN: About an hour ago.

WOODY: (*Starts her toward the door*) Okay. Good work but keep on asking. See if anyone's seen her since then.

SUSAN: Casual—?

WOODY: That's right. Real casual. (SUSAN *exits.* WOODY *stalks around, troubled.*) An hour ago! I don't like it. *She* sits up all night. *He* runs the picture. And *you're* philosophical. There's something fishy about all this. I don't know—(*She looks across at* COLE. *He shrugs. She comes to a decision.*) I'm not going to wait—I'm going to go out and find her myself. (*She exits.*)

COLE: (*His unconcerned pose disappears. He hurries across to the telephone. Into telephone*) Hello, get me the railroad station. — Yeah—ticket office. (*A pause*) Hello? Has a tall blonde bought a ticket to anywhere in the past hour? —I see. Are you the only ticket clerk? —So you'd know. Well, thanks. (*He hangs up, starts meditatively across the room. The telephone rings. He wheels and races back to it.*) Hello. —No, Miss Woods just stepped out. But you can give me the message. (*Injured*) —

Oh, you can trust me—Yeah, I got it. Coming through the Ivy Arch. About five minutes ago—Well, that's great work, Casual. I'll see that you're mentioned for a citation. (*He hangs up, looks out the window. She isn't in sight yet. Then, like an expectant lover examining the scene of a rendezvous, he looks around the room. Crossing to the door, he opens it a bit wider. As he wheels, he sees the Clara Bow doll on the radiator shelf. Violently he turns its face to the wall. On the sofa, he sees the crumpled bedpillow. With an attempt at neatness, he picks it up and tosses it through the bedroom door. His eye falls on the victrola—it's an idea. Background music. He drops the needle on the record, starts away. The voice of Betty Boop oozes out in one of her coyest boop-boop-a-doops. He stops, pained, goes back, takes the record off, breaks it. Searching through a stack of records, he finds a more suitable love song, puts it on—low. As he wanders back across the room, surveying his handiwork with pleasure, he notices a vase of roses. A reminiscent smile lights his face. Taking out a couple of the roses, he tears off the petals and strews a handful in the doorway. Pleased, he continues a path of rose petals to the window seat where he plumps up a pillow and stretches out comfortably, awaiting AGATHA's imminent arrival. In a moment, she enters. She's tense and jittery, doesn't even notice the rose petals. Crossing to the mantel, she leans her head against it wearily. COLE sits up—watches her for a few seconds.*)

COLE: Tired?

AGATHA: (*She starts at the sound of his voice, turns around.*) What are you doing here?

COLE: Woody went out to look for you. Asked me to stick around in case the phone rang.

AGATHA: Oh.

COLE: (*Rising*) Well—what's new? (AGATHA *turns away from him. He tries a different tack.*) Heard about the film showing?

AGATHA: Yes. I just met Ginny outside. She told me how—wonderful it was.

COLE: Congratulations. (*She doesn't say anything.*) What's the matter? Aren't you glad?

AGATHA: (*Trying*) Yes, of course.

COLE: (*Crossing to her*) Seems you were right about Merrill. Weren't you?

AGATHA: (*Crossing away from him*) Really, there's no need to—

COLE: Eat crow? Oh, I don't mind. Where you're concerned, I've got no pride. You ought to know that by now. I gave it up when I came down here. (*Approaching her again*) Of course, I did have a feeling you might like it—

AGATHA: (*Eluding him again*) We went through all this yesterday.

COLE: (*Coming around to face her*) I know. But that was so long ago. I thought you might have changed your mind.

AGATHA: Why should I?

COLE: (*Gently*) People do. All the time. (*Brushing his face against her hair*) Besides, I once saw it in a movie—how the bride turned at the last moment and ran off with the best man.

AGATHA: (*For one moment*, AGATHA *stands there. Then she breaks away from him.*) Cole, leave me alone—

COLE: (*There is a pause as* COLE *looks at her, unable to believe that she isn't going to tell him the truth.*) You mean—you've got nothing to say to me?

AGATHA: I thought we said it all.

COLE: (*Slowly*) Yeah, but I'm stupid. I've got to have it spelled out for me. He's a great guy. He's all you've dreamed about— waited for—for twenty years. You're gonna go right ahead and marry him—?

AGATHA: (*Her back to him*) The date hasn't been set—yet.

COLE: But it will be?

AGATHA: (*Turning—desperately*) I don't see that this is any of your business!

COLE: You don't? (*Abruptly, he crosses, turns off the victrola. Then he strides to the telephone, picks it up.*) Get me Dr. Merrill's office.

AGATHA: What are you doing?

COLE: I'm gonna ask Merrill to come over here. I'd like to congratulate him. (*Into telephone*) Is Dr. Merrill there? I'd like to talk to him—(AGATHA *runs across the room and wrenches the telephone out of his hand, slams it down on the desk.* COLE *stands looking at her.*) You couldn't face that, could you? Because you know it's a lie. You threw away six years we could have had together because of a lie, but you can't be honest enough now to admit it to me. You've got to hang on to your precious ego. Well, you can keep it. I'm a big boy now. I've got bigger and better things to do with my life. (*He turns and goes out.*)

(AGATHA *stands motionless for a moment, her face white, fighting for control. The telephone squeaks "Hello—Hello"— She picks up the receiver and bangs it back on the hook. Lying on the desk beside the telephone is her Commencement speech. She picks it up, reads the first few lines. In her face you can see the disgust at what she's reading. She crumples it violently and throws it into the waste basket. At almost the same moment her eye falls on her suitcase. She stares at it, then makes an impulsive decision, crosses and opens it. It's packed. She shuts it and hurries into the bedroom. MERRILL appears in the corridor doorway. He's in his gown, the colors of his degrees rich against the black. AGATHA comes hurrying out of the bedroom, carrying her jacket, her hat and purse. She's about to pick up the suitcase when she sees MERRILL and stops. He looks at her, taking in her obvious intent.)*

MERRILL: Where are you going?

AGATHA: I can't stay here and go through with this lie any more. I can't.

MERRILL: You realize what you're doing?

AGATHA: Yes. There's my speech in the waste basket—where it belongs. I couldn't get up there and say it. I'd choke on every word! *(She picks up the bag and starts for the door.)* I'll send you a telegram. That I'm sick. Or that I'm needed in Washington. You can read it.

MERRILL: *(Quietly)* Just like twenty years ago, isn't it, Agatha? *(She stops abruptly.)* Running away again.

AGATHA: *(The effect of his words can be seen in her back. And when she turns to him, it's obvious that she's moved.)* Jim, you don't understand. I was wrong last night—to expect you to be the same man I remembered. Nothing stays the same. And I was wrong to think I could "save" your daughter. I can't blackmail you for the rest of your life. It's better for her to know the truth— now, while she's young.

MERRILL: Would you tell her that?

AGATHA: If I had to, yes.

MERRILL: You'll have your chance. I just saw her running across the Quad. *(There's a knock on the door.)* She's probably there now. *(The knock comes again.)*

GINNY'S VOICE: It's Ginny.

MERRILL: You'd better answer.

AGATHA: *(Setting down her suitcase quickly and putting her other things on a chair)* Come in.

GINNY: *(GINNY enters. There are no words to describe her radiance. She smiles at AGATHA, then at her father, and it shines out of her.)* I went to your office. They told me you'd come here. *(Crossing to MERRILL)* We just saw the picture. I wish you'd been there.

Some of the girls cried. Some were shocked. They didn't all understand it—but I don't think any of them'll ever forget it. It was the best graduation present you could have given the Senior Class. And me. (*She kisses him without shyness or apology.*) Thank you. (MERRILL *stands rigid, looking at* AGATHA.) I have to go now. They're all waiting for me. (*She starts to the door.*)

MERRILL: Ginny—

GINNY: (*Stops*) Yes.

MERRILL: I'd like you to stay for a moment.

GINNY: The Seniors are starting to form—

MERRILL: This won't take long. Miss Reed and I have been discussing something I think you should know. (*He looks at* AGATHA.)

GINNY: Yes?

AGATHA: (*With great difficulty*) Ginny—Yesterday I told you—(*She can't. She turns away.*)

MERRILL: If you won't tell her, I will.

GINNY: Tell me—what?

(AGATHA *is silent.*)

MERRILL: (*To* GINNY) You kissed me just now. You haven't done that in a long time. I'm very grateful. But I can't accept it under false pretenses.

GINNY: False pretenses?

MERRILL: I had the movie shown—but not for the reasons you think. I did it because Miss Reed forced me to. Because she gave me an alternative that left me no choice. That's the truth and I want you to know it. (GINNY *just stands, looking at him.*) I don't want any more lies between us—there've been too many already. I can't wipe them out. But you're graduating today and the best present I can give you is a fresh start. I'm afraid I haven't been much of a father for quite a while. I'm sorry. (GINNY *turns her head to choke back the tears.* MERRILL *crosses to her.*) Ginny, I didn't tell you this to hurt you. I've never meant to hurt you—

GINNY: (*Turning to face him*) You've forgotten a lot of things about me, haven't you? That I just don't cry when I'm sad. That I cry just as much when I'm happy. (*Embracing him*) I don't care why you showed the picture. I never wanted you to be a hero. I just wanted you to be honest. With me. And with yourself.

ELLEN: (ELLEN *comes hurrying in. Breathless*) Oh, there you are, Jim.

I've been all over—

AGATHA: (*Pained at the interruption*) Ellen, maybe you and I could come back—

ELLEN: Well, not until I've had one moment with Jim. (*She crosses to him.*) Now what is all this nonsense? Claude's terribly upset. I sneaked away and left him home on the telephone. He's been on it all morning. First when he heard about the movie—and then, right out of the blue—this *resignation* thing—

AGATHA: Resignation?

(*As* GINNY *and* AGATHA *look at him,* MERRILL *moves from them to the window.*)

ELLEN: (*Crossing to* AGATHA) I haven't seen Claude so worked up since they had a strike in one of the plants.

AGATHA: When did this happen?

ELLEN: The letter came half an hour ago. (*To* MERRILL) Oh, I read it, Jim. It was lying on Claude's desk—and it was just beautiful. Especially that part about self-respect. About your feeling like a—what was it? It had something to do with eating—

AGATHA: An—educaterer?

ELLEN: That's it! Why, Ag, how clever of you!

AGATHA: (*Crossing to him*) What happened, Jim?

MERRILL: (*Simply*) I *did* see the picture. I stood in the back of the theatre and watched them watching it. And I realized I almost hadn't let them see it. That's when I knew everything you said about me last night was true. That I had no right to be the President of this college—or any college.

ELLEN: (*Shocked*) Ag, how could you say such a thing? I can't think of this college without Jim! And neither can the Board. You should hear them all arguing back there at home. About how much Jim's done for the school. And how it would look in the papers. And what a row the students would raise if they ever heard about it. Wouldn't they, Ginny?

GINNY: (*Happily*) They'd raise a heck of a row!

ELLEN: Why, I'd even resign as Alumnae President!

(*Some Seniors, going by the window to the Commencement parade, are chanting a class song. A voice calls, "Hey,* GINNY! *Did you forget? It's Commencement!"*)

GINNY: (*Shouting through the window*) Okay—! (*Then*) I've got to go now. (*She hurries to the door, then turns back for a moment.*) I always wondered why they called it Commencement. Now I know. (*She goes out.*)

ELLEN: I really have to go, too. I'm late already. But I just wanted to come and ask you to reconsider, Jim. (*Then, hesitantly*) You won't mention this to Claude, will you? That I came over? He'll like thinking it was his own idea. It's kind of important for a man like Claude, you know. To think everything's his own idea.

MERRILL: (MERRILL *looks at her, then smiles.*) I'm afraid I've been underestimating you, Ellen.

ELLEN: You forgot, *I* was in your History class, too. I even got a B-plus.

MERRILL: A *B.*

ELLEN: Well, it's still the best mark I ever got. (*She smiles and exits.*) (AGATHA *and* MERRILL *are left alone. There's a quiet moment.*)

AGATHA: I'm overwhelmed, Jim. I never expected all this.

MERRILL: We're even. Neither did I.

AGATHA: You know the trouble with most of us? We give up too easily. We forget that when you fight—you very often win. (*Then*) *Will* you reconsider, Jim?

MERRILL: I don't know.

AGATHA: I think it's important to this college that you stay on.

MERRILL: I'm glad you do. But I want to be sure. (*Slowly*) I've got a lot of thinking to do. A lot of catching up—

AGATHA: I've got a bit of catching up, myself. (*She sees a rose petal on the floor, picks it up, smiles in sudden appreciation.*)

MERRILL: Agatha—(*As she turns*) When I came in here, it was because I wanted to tell you again that I was in love with you. That I didn't have much hope for it—after last night. But that somehow, today—(*He pauses, searching her face.*) I know we're different people than we were twenty years ago. I know a lot of things have changed. But I wouldn't want to kick myself for the rest of my life—for not trying. Do I have a chance?

AGATHA: (*After a moment*) You might have had a hell of a chance, Jim. Except that I've had a standing offer for six years. And I think I'd better take it up before it runs out. If it hasn't run out already.

MERRILL: I see. (*Then*) He's lucky. I wish I'd met you six years ago.

WOODY: (WOODY *enters. She stops short as she sees them in such close proximity. This is where she came in.*) Oh, I'm sorry. (*Backing up*) I'll come back later.

MERRILL: It's all right, Miss Woods. I was just leaving. (*As he passes* WOODY, *she holds out her hand.*)

WOODY: I'd like to say—I think it's—

MERRILL: Thanks. (*Turning to* AGATHA) See you in a few minutes?

AGATHA: I'll be there, Jim. (*He goes out.*)

WOODY: (WOODY *looks after him, sighing resignedly.*) Want to get into your cap and gown?

AGATHA: Yes.

(WOODY *starts toward the bedroom.* AGATHA *has been looking around the room with new eyes. Suddenly, she sees the sofa—laughs to herself.*)

WOODY: (*Turning at the bedroom door*) What's the matter?

AGATHA: The sofa. It's so faded.

WOODY: Carted it all the way up from the basement. (*She exits.*)

AGATHA: (AGATHA *finishes her inspection of the room with real enjoyment. Suddenly she feels free—her mind begins to function at top speed. Briskly*) What arrangements did you make for getting us out of here?

WOODY: (*Appearing like a shot in the door*) Getting us—out—?

AGATHA: (AGATHA *takes her gown from the amazed* WOODY *and starts putting it on.*) We can drive into Boston and get the seven o'clock plane. Better call Wister tonight to set up that committee meeting in the morning. (WOODY *just stares at her.*) And call Senator Haines. Tell him he was right. I'll make a swing through the whole state before the election—get the Washington lead out of my pants. (*Enjoying it*) Shut your mouth. You look like a fish.

WOODY: But, I thought—

AGATHA: That's your trouble. You think too much. You're so busy trying to figure things out ahead, you're always miles behind. (COLE *enters. He looks angry and full of resolve.*)

COLE: I want to talk to you!

AGATHA: (*Seeing him for the first time*) Not now—later.

COLE: Not later—now! (*To* WOODY) Leave us alone. (As she stands there) I said—leave us alone!

(WOODY *drops* AGATHA's *cap on the sofa, and heads for the door. As she passes* COLE, *she gives him an approving nod. She doesn't know what the hell's going on, but she's for it. She shuts the door.*)

AGATHA: I thought you were on your way to bigger and better things.

COLE: You're not going to do it!

AGATHA: Do what?

COLE: You're the stubbornest dame I ever saw in my life. You're so goddam stubborn, you'd go ahead and *marry* him—(*With grim resolution*) But you're not going to do it!

AGATHA: (*Enjoying it*) Really?

COLE: Look, let's get one thing straight. I don't expect you to fall into my arms. I wouldn't even catch you if you did. One thing I found out this weekend. I *don't like women!*

AGATHA: (*If she could only laugh.*) Then why all the bother?

COLE: Because I'm neat! I straighten pictures— I put the tops on toothpaste tubes. I don't like leaving unfinished things around. You're not going to go through with this!

AGATHA: Aren't you being a little over-confident?

COLE: I don't think so. I'm offering you a deal. A business deal. (AGATHA's *smile fades.*) In exchange for such a small service, I'm giving you my personal guarantee that the *Life* article won't even hint at the colorful events leading up to your expulsion from this seat of higher learning. (AGATHA *takes an angry step toward him. He holds up his hand.*) See pictures on preceding page.

AGATHA:, So you even eavesdrop!

COLE: Sure. (*With a smile*) You learn all kinds of dirty tricks in *my* work, too.
(*There's a moment while* AGATHA *struggles between anger and appreciation. The latter wins, but* COLE *doesn't know it.*)

AGATHA: (*Elaborately*) Well, then it seems I have no choice. (*She crosses to the door, opens it, calls.*) Woody! (WOODY *enters almost immediately. She looks toward* COLE, *eagerly.*) Woody, there's been a change of plans. We'll drive into Boston and catch the seven o'clock plane. And call Wister tonight to set up that committee meeting in the morning. Oh yes—call Senator Haines and tell him I'll make a swing through the whole state before the election.

WOODY: (*Bewildered*) But you just told me to—

AGATHA: I know. But there's been a *change of plans.* (AMELIA, MARY NELL, CLARISSE *and* JO *enter, all capped and gowned, and very excited.*)

AMELIA: We're your honor guard, Miss Reed!

AGATHA: I'm honored.

MARY NELL: Everything's on schedule. We're supposed to leave here as soon as the bells start to—
(*The college bells start peeling—all of them—all over campus, rich and mellow.*)

AMELIA: There they go.

AGATHA: (*Starting to the door*) I'm ready.

CLARISSE: (*Hastily*) Your cap—

AGATHA: (*Feeling her head*) Oh, yes. (*She rushes back to the sofa and gets her cap, puts it on.*)

WOODY: Your speech! Where's your speech?

AGATHA: (*Hurrying to the desk*) I left it on the desk. What did you do with it, Woody?

WOODY: (*Crossing behind her*) It was there a minute ago.

(AGATHA *suddenly remembers. She stoops, fishes it triumphantly out of the waste basket, as they all watch her.*)

AGATHA: (*Smoothing out the wrinkles*) I found it! (*She starts to the door.*)

AMELIA: Got everything now?

AGATHA: (*As she passes* COLE, *a little smile.*) Everything.

(*She goes out, followed by the four girls. There's a pause as* WOODY *looks after her, shaking her head.*)

WOODY: One weekend. (*Turning to* COLE) A woman couldn't go crazy in one weekend, could she?

COLE: What's so crazy about changing her mind?

WOODY: Changing her mind? She told me the *same damned thing* five minutes ago!

COLE: (*Slowly*) She—what?

WOODY: What do they put in the food around here? (*Comprehension sweeps over* COLE. *He reaches for* WOODY *and gives her a resounding kiss. She comes up for air.*) Now what's the matter with *you*?

COLE: Sweetheart, don't try to understand it. Just relax and enjoy it. *He heads for the door like crazy as the*

CURTAIN FALLS

IN THE SUMMER HOUSE

JANE BOWLES

First presented in 1953

FOREWORD

In the Summer House is the only full-length play written by Jane
Auer Bowles, whose small canon also includes a novel and
several short stories. Born February 22, 1917, in New York
City, Bowles was educated at public and private schools and for two
years by a tutor in Switzerland, where she was being treated for a
leg ailment—exacerbated by a fall from a horse—that left her with
a pronounced limp all her life. Like Stein, Hellman and Kanin she
came from a Jewish family; she did not actively practice her
religion, although her Jewish roots seem to have been still one
more factor that made her feel like an outsider: according to friends
she would sometimes refer to herself as "Crippie, the Kike Dyke."
A woman of profound contradictions, Bowles was a lesbian who
married Paul Bowles—a gay composer, poet and novelist—just
before she turned twenty-one and remained devoted to him
throughout her life even as both were involved in serious
relationships with lovers of their own sex. The two lived all over
the world (sometimes together, sometimes apart) but most of Jane
Bowles's adult years were spent in Morocco.

Bowles once said, "I started to 'write' when I was about fifteen
and was obliged to do composition in school. I always thought it
the most loathsome of all activities, and still do. At the same time, I
felt even then that I had to do it." The manuscript of her first
novel, *Le Phaeton Hypocrite*, has been lost. Bowles' second, *Two
Serious Ladies*, was published by Knopf in 1943 and despite a
generally negative reception became a cult classic. Over the years

399

reviewers have called the novel everything from "incredibly bad" to "a landmark in twentieth century American literature."

Like all of her work, *Two Serious Ladies* is filled with actual or threatened violence; secretive, alienated characters hoping to escape their lives but terrified to do so; substantial quantities of liquor consumed by nearly everyone; and a good deal of bleak humor. *Ladies* encompasses two stories—Mrs. Copperfield's and Miss Goering's—that connect only at tenuous points. Mrs. Copperfield goes with her husband to Panama, where she falls in love with a prostitute, Pacifica, whom she brings back to the United States. Miss Goering is a wealthy woman who as a child played bizarre religious games and as an adult collects odd acquaintances: her companion Miss Gamelon, the slothful Arnold and his father. On what she believes is a journey to salvation, she gives herself to a series of repulsive men who mistreat her. In society's eyes Mrs. Copperfield's lesbian liaison with a prostitute is clearly sinful, while Miss Goering's masochistic relationships with men are more nearly acceptable. Accordingly, while Mrs. Copperfield sees herself as "gone to pieces," Miss Goering believes she is moving "nearer to becoming a saint." In Bowles' view, however, the differences between sin and salvation (both favorite words in her canon) are never clear, a point Miss Goering acknowledges at the book's conclusion: "but is it possible that a part of me hidden from my sight is piling sin upon sin as fast as Mrs. Copperfield?" What is clear is that love—lesbian or heterosexual, maternal or filial—has little chance of yielding lasting happiness in Bowles' grim world.

Jane Bowles' short stories—both those completed and the fragments collected posthumously in a volume entitled *Feminine Wiles* (from a line in one of the stories)—share a remarkable similarity of subject and structure; they are also clearly of a piece with *In the Summer House*. Typically one or more characters are on the move: to a summer camp, an exotic locale, a hotel, or just on a business trip or a bus journey. Harriet in "Camp Cataract" tries to flee from her family by settling at the camp of the title. "Emmy Moore's Journal" is a first-person fragment about a woman who goes to a hotel to escape her husband but obsessively writes him letters as she tries to clarify her feelings. The male protagonist in the ironically named "A Guatemalan Idyll" concedes, "I don't see what you're supposed to get out of traveling."

The characters—usually presented in pairs—are unsure about

what they are running from and what they are running toward, which may be salvation or sin, the self or someone else (or both). Harriet hopes that by spending time at Camp Cataract she can slowly slip into the "outside world," although she has no idea what that world might be. Her sister Sadie, who follows her to the camp, is horrified by the duplicity she finds in her first excursion beyond her family circle; the story's ambiguous ending implies that her journey may be fatal. In "Going to Massachusetts" Janet sends her lover Bozoe away and attempts to seduce another woman, but the other woman is disdainful and Bozoe peppers Janet with portentous letters: "I don't feel that I can allow you to sink into the mire of contentment and happy ambitious enterprise." Relationships both support and trap the mostly female characters in Bowles' canon, and independence is as frightening as dependence. If readers are puzzled about the aims of the various quests, they share the characters' perplexity; like Sadie, for whom "secrecy was the real absolution from guilt," they often hide their motives from themselves.

Bowles's earliest completed theater work is "A Quarreling Pair," a brief puppet show performed in 1945. Ostensibly about feuding sisters, Harriet and Rhoda, the play is even more obviously than her other works about two characters who represent two sides of the same conflicted self. Harriet sings about an ominous dream from which the dreamer "wakened not yet knowing/ If the name she bore was my sister's name/ Or if it was my own." The dream is about a cliff (a repeated image of danger in Bowles' work, including *In the Summer House*) from which the dreamer searches for her home, a futile activity because women are inevitably exiles in Bowles' literary terrain.

Paul Bowles recalls that "For some years, Oliver Smith had been telling Jane that with her gift for dialogue she would write a play and he would produce it. She did and he did." According to biographer Millicent Dillon, Bowles began *In the Summer House* while living in Vermont in 1943 and 1944 and continued working on it for roughly a decade as she moved from Vermont to New York and finally to Tangier in 1948. An early version of the first scene—substantially similar to the final version—was published in *Harper's Bazaar* in 1947, and in 1949 her friend Tennessee Williams, who admired what he had read of the play, secured for her a thousand dollar grant from the Author's League. A planned 1950 production in Westport, Connecticut, never materialized, but

In the Summer House reached the stage August 23, 1951, at the Hedgerow Theater in Moylan, Pennsylvania. Bowles continued to work on the second act when the play reopened two years later in a new production at the Mendelssohn Theater at the University of Michigan with Miriam Hopkins as Gertrude Eastman Cuevas, Mildred Dunnock as Mrs. Constable and Anne Jackson as Vivian. Williams contributed a testimonial for publicity purposes in which he called *Summer House* "not only the most original play I have ever read, I think it also the oddest and funniest and one of the most touching." Michigan critics were not so kind. One insisted that "all the important characters were, in varying degrees, mentally deranged" while another saw it as a saga of "female crackpots."

The production moved to Hartford, where it opened on Thanksgiving Day with Judith Anderson now cast as Gertrude, and then on to Boston, where José Quintero took over as director and Bowles continued making changes. Paul Bowles claims that Anderson was perplexed by her role and "occasionally stopped everything, saying piteously: 'Who am I? Who am I supposed to be?'" *In the Summer House*, with a musical score by Paul Bowles, finally opened in New York on December 29, 1953, at the Playhouse Theater. It ran for 55 performances. The reviews were mixed but far more positive than they had been in Michigan. Henry Hewes thought *Summer House* "a memorable piece of theatre" if not a "very satisfactory play." Harold Clurman in *The Nation* praised the first act as "truthful, sharp, and wittily poignant… lovely, colorful, and strangely evocative" and called *Summer House* "a kind of wryly comic lyric poem in a minor key." Richard Hayes in *Commonweal* also likened it to a poem as well as to music: "a work of intricate and seductive beauty, harmonious and subtle in its impact on the sensibility as a musical composition."

More than a few critics felt the play was uneven: John Chapman, for one, called it "brilliant at times and baffling at other times," while Walter Kerr came perhaps closest to the truth when he characterized it as a "tantalizingly imperfect play…possessed of a number of unusual virtues." Even reviewers like Eric Bentley, who was not impressed with the work itself, called Bowles "an authoress [sic] of uncommon talent." Like William Hawkins of the *New York World-Telegram*, who dubbed Bowles "the most original American dramatist of her generation," Bentley and others sensed that Bowles' talents had not been fully realized in this fascinating and sometimes maddening play. Despite misgivings, Louis

Kronenberger chose *Summer House* for inclusion in his *Best Plays of 1953-4* volume.

Critics struggled to find established writers with whom to compare Bowles, and the names of such disparate authors as William Saroyan, Anton Chekhov and Dorothy Parker were invoked. Several likened *Summer House* to the work of Tennessee Williams, a more apt comparison, but few knew that Bowles began writing the play before Williams completed *The Glass Menagerie* and long before he composed such surrealistic nightmare visions as *Suddenly Last Summer*, *Night of the Iguana* and *Camino Real*. Since Williams had met Bowles in 1940, it is as likely that early drafts of *Summer House* influenced his work as that his plays influenced hers.

In the Summer House was briefly revived off-Broadway in 1964; Bowles did not leave Tangier to see the production and was upset by its short run. More recent revivals have been staged at the Manhattan Theater Club, La Mama E.T.C. and in 1993 at the Vivian Beaumont Theater at New York's Lincoln Center. Reviewing the 1980 La Mama production, critic Thomas Ryan argues, "While it is not a great play, for a first—and only—play it is often emotionally true and its language has a bright ring to it." The Lincoln Center staging earned widely divergent responses from New York's two most influential critics; although both had reservations about the acting, Clive Barnes hoped this would be the very last revival of an "odd ghost of a play" he considered "a muddled bore," while Frank Rich praised *Summer House* as an "unjustly neglected piece" with a "poetic subtext."

Some female directors and critics have embraced the play, others have not. JoAnne Akalaitis chose to direct a production of *Summer House* because the work "understands women." On the other hand, Tish Dace in the *Soho Weekly* has charged that *Summer House* contains "representation of 10 utterly irredeemable women." Despite the very obvious differences between Boothe's *The Women* and Bowles' *In the Summer House*, the accusations leveled against them are sometimes remarkably similar. Both works present us with "women's worlds" (the male characters in *Summer House* are little more than thematic symbols and plot devices) and both worlds are marked by jealousy and conflict. But just as Boothe is well aware of the patriarchal societal structures that create and condone this competition, so Bowles is alert to the very complex relationships—psychological, sociological and physical—between mothers and daughters.

In the Summer House explores all the permutations and combinations of this most primal bond. The central pair is Gertrude Eastman Cuevas, "a beautiful middle-aged" widow, and her eighteen year old daughter, Molly. Act I is set in a ragged garden that is obviously post-Edenic. The passive Molly has no interest in growing up; her favorite haunt is the summer house, a vine-covered womb where she likes to read comic books. Gertrude, who commands Molly to express her thoughts then cuts her off the moment she begins to do so, is the controlling figure in this mother-daughter dyad.

Walter Kerr complained about "the author's reluctance to pry beneath a painstakingly accurate surface" but William Hawkins was more astute in noting that "Bowles writes in terms of [the characters'] inner essence," leaving it up to the audience "to assume what visible surface they expose to the world." Part of the shock and the humor of *Summer House* comes from the fact that Bowles is operating on a number of levels simultaneously. In some ways Gertrude is the clichéd middle-class parent. As she advises Molly to get out of the house more, walk more gracefully and keep the mustard off her dress, we hear the age-old maternal paradox: the command to be an adult which, in its very phrasing, suggests that in a mother's eyes no woman is ever grown up. (Like all Bowles' work, *Summer House* is heavily autobiographical. When Bowles was in her forties her mother was still writing to advise her to see her dentist and hairdresser regularly, keep clean and remember to wind the clock.)

On still another level, Gertrude and Molly are acting out psychological dramas that usually remain subconscious or unconscious. In her very first speech, for example, Gertrude threatens to burn down the summer house in which her daughter is hiding, and threats and accusations of violence echo through the work. Playwright Tina Howe once commented that "As a mother, you experience moments of excruciating tenderness and love, but there is also great savagery." Bowles doesn't hesitate to show the savagery.

Gertrude's ostensible reason for wanting Molly married is because she will be wedding Mr. Solares and Molly must find either a job or a husband. It is clear, however, that Gertrude has little interest in Mr. Solares or in marriage; indeed, she tells her daughter that she would have left her first husband "but I couldn't. I was carrying you. I had no choice. All my hopes were wrapped up in you then, all of them." Now Gertrude has decided it is time for Molly—who understandably feels inadequate to her mother's high expectations—to leave the womb-nest she has created for her. Gertrude's second marriage is both a way to escape from a stifling bond and an attempt to force her daughter to grow up, one version of the classic mother-daughter struggle. Perhaps too Gertrude is frightened by the intensity of that bond, the obviously sexual overtones that Bowles attributes to it. As scholar Gayle Austin observes, the wedding seems to be between the two brides rather than between the women and their fiancés.

The second mother-daughter "couple" is composed of Mrs. Constable and Vivian. The aptly-named Vivian ("full of life") is trying her hardest to run away from her mother, Mrs. Constable (whose name suggests Vivian's view of her as her jailer). Three years younger than Molly but already more independent, she won't even stay in the same building as her mother, who hovers at a hotel nearby. Vivian poses a direct threat to Molly in part because she models for her the appropriate behavior of a maturing girl: "She has to escape from her mother too" Vivian says of Molly. From another perspective, Molly and Vivian may be seen as enacting the age-old rite of sibling rivalry. The younger Vivian taunts Molly by taking possession of the summer house, and stage directions repeatedly place Vivian in the same position that Molly held a few moments earlier. Like Gertrude, who is still so jealous of her father's attentions to her younger sister that she cannot even admit his partiality, Molly seethes in envious rage as Vivian courts Gertrude.

Looked at another way, Vivian's attachment to Gertrude may be seen as the consequence of her escape from Mrs. Constable: Having denied one mother, she spends her time pursuing a substitute. As much as adolescents may want freedom, so much do they fear it; hence Vivian seeks in Gertrude the security she needs without the threat of smothering that Mrs. Constable's fierce affection portends. These readings, of course, are scarcely mutually exclusive, for in most mother-daughter relationships the longing for closeness and the desire for freedom are inextricably mixed. *Summer House* is a play of mirrors and echoes, doubles and doppelgangers; Henry Hewes rightly sees Mrs. Constable and Vivian as "alter egos" of Gertrude and Molly. (In one script of *Summer House* the echoes are multiplied when Gertrude reveals that Molly is named after her own youngest sister.)

The third mother-daughter relationship is that of Mrs. Lopez and Frederica. Critics have justifiably complained about Bowles' stereotyping of the Mexican characters, a raucous crew whose days are spent playing, sleeping and eating huge meals. Bowles seems to have swallowed whole the notion that Latin peoples are closer to nature than their alienated Northern neighbors. Still, there is joy in these characters and strength in the mother-daughter bond that the others lack. If Mrs. Lopez occasionally treats her daughter roughly, it is because she fears Frederica will be cheated, as when she is reluctant to ask for a toy lobster like Molly's.

Further, Frederica's dependence on her mother seems less problematic than Molly's attachment to Gertrude. On the one hand Bowles' highly questionable vision of Mexicans as children may suggest that growing up is less difficult when even adults are allowed to play with toys. On the other hand, Bowles implies that this mother-daughter bond need not be so abruptly severed because there is a community of women to which both may belong. The extended Mexican family about which Gertrude complains is a largely female society where a woman can be married and still not separated from her mother. And perhaps too their participation in this community allows both Mrs. Lopez and Frederica to better understand women of different generations. It is Mrs. Lopez who goes into the summer house after the wedding to hug and gently coax Molly out, and in the final moments of the play Frederica gives her small bouquet of flowers to a grieving Gertrude.

Critics rightly find the second act of *Summer House* less successful than the first, but the rupture between the acts is smaller than some would suggest. Because she has failed to protect Vivian, Mrs. Constable feels responsible for what has happened and tries to escape into alcoholism; her guilt is echoed in Gertrude's dream of bringing Molly a gift of macaroons that turn out to be "just a shell filled with dust." With this dream Bowles choreographs the final confrontation between Molly and Gertrude, the section of the play that she endlessly wrote and rewrote without ever being satisfied.

According to Millicent Dillon, Bowles tried at least three endings of *Summer House*: "In one version...Gertrude drags Molly away, after convincing her that she is violent and dangerous to others, and Lionel is left alone. In another version, Molly runs out and kills herself. In the published play Molly rushes off after Lionel, and Gertrude is left alone." Dillon sees strong autobiographical elements in the final scene, and surely Bowles' inability to decide on the "right" way to separate from one's mother mirrored confusion in her own life; even as a middle-aged woman she was accustomed to receiving maternal letters that insisted "he [Paul] loves you so much—but no one can love you as much as I do." Molly's suicide appears in a script dated October 1953, but as early as 1947 Bowles had envisioned a final separation between mother and daughter: an "Editor's Note" appended to the scene published in *Harper's Bazaar* indicates that Molly chooses Lionel rather than Gertrude. Gayle Austin, drawing on Nancy Chodorow's theories about mothering, persuasively argues that the three endings "represent three different ways a daughter may attempt separation from her mother." Austin adds that the published ending is the "Freudian scenario" in which the young woman goes off with a man. It is also the classic conclusion to popular drama, the daughter married to her young suitor, hence likely the ending favored by Broadway producers. (Lillian Hellman managed to move Alexandra away from Regina at the end of *The Little Foxes* without a man for her to lean on, but the requisite suitor was written into the screen version.)

Finally, if we follow Austin's theory that all the mothers and daughters are fragments of one whole, we can also say that Bowles actually has included in *Summer House* all three "resolutions" to the mother-daughter bond: Vivian may have killed herself, Frederica remains with her mother, and Molly chooses Lionel. And even the "conventional" ending is heavily ironic since Molly's suitor is a figure so sketchily drawn that he seems more caricature than character. Although Lionel is first seen dressed as Neptune, the Roman God of the sea associated with fertility, he does not appear godlike, potent or (as his name would suggest) kingly. A parody of the American male—he imagines he'll be a politician or a religious leader but doesn't relish either choice—Lionel is a questionable savior.

When the original production of *Summer House* was floundering in rehearsals, according to Dillon "a psychiatrist was brought in to explain the motivation of the play. Paul Bowles recalls that the therapist 'kept wanting to know more about Gertrude's father.'" This might have influenced the final ending Bowles wrote, with its references to that father, but the psychiatrist's questions also reveal why many male reviewers were bewildered by the play: *Summer House* is overwhelmingly about the psychological dynamics of mother-daughter relationships, a bond they found alien and confusing. Brooks Atkinson wondered aloud in the *Times*, "Is it enough to present one aspect of life with insight into the motives of a handful of drifting people?"—ignoring the fact that this "one aspect," the relationship between mothers and daughters, is central to the lives of half the world's people. Unlike *Two Serious Ladies* and many of Bowles' short stories, *In the Summer House* contains no overtly lesbian relationships; she must have known how difficult it would be in the conservative 1950s to find a producer for a lesbian play. But *In the Summer House* presents a wide spectrum of the ways women love other women that many male critics could not comprehend. Reviewers may also have been baffled by the style of Bowles' play, which one aptly called "naturalistically surrealistic." Concerned more with symbol than logic, psychology than plot, Bowles frustrated those who demanded to know exactly what had happened to Vivian. Some of the mystery in her work arises from its deeply personal nature: Bowles writes without the objective distance to which audiences are accustomed. But the mystery is also part of her art. In an interview in *Vogue* in 1954, Bowles said that the long revision period on *In the Summer House* was intended "to increase 'magic as opposed to construction.'"

It isn't necessary to agree with Tennessee Williams that Jane Bowles was "quite the greatest writer of our century in the English language" to understand how little of her potential was realized. Millicent Dillon reveals that Bowles filled notebook after notebook with stories and various ideas, even scenes, for plays she was never able to complete. *At the Jumping Bean*, published posthumously in *Feminine Wiles*, is "a scene from a play Jane Bowles was writing in Ceylon in 1955." A two-character fragment, *Jumping Bean* presents the obviously autobiographical Beryl Jane, who sees herself as "more like a child than most girls," and Gabriel, a poet. The most poignant note in these few pages is Beryl Jane's desire to convince Gabriel that she is like other people, that she loves what "the world loves."

In 1957, at the age of forty, Jane Bowles suffered a stroke, which increased her anxiety and depression. Still trying to write, she spent her last fifteen years in and out of hospitals and sanitaria. As late as December of 1961 she was awarded a $3000 playwriting grant from the Ingram Merrill Foundation, and Dillon relates that in desperation Bowles tried to use *Summer House* as the springboard for a new dramatic work, comparing each character to one in *Summer House*, imagining the same actors performing the new play.

Ironically, as her physical and mental health deteriorated, Bowles' literary reputation grew. Like Gertrude Stein, Bowles had had for years an underground reputation among other artists. In a famous tribute, poet John Ashbery called Bowles "a writer's writer's writer." Bowles gathered a wider audience in the 1960s when *Two Serious Ladies* was reissued, Paul compiled a volume of her stories entitled *Plain Pleasures*, and *The Collected Works of Jane Bowles* (with an introduction by Truman Capote) appeared. It was too late, however, for her to resume her career or even enjoy the new fame. Jane Bowles died May 4, 1973, in Malaga, Spain.

We can only speculate to what extent Bowles' inability to write, or to conceive of herself as a writer, was caused by her own private demons and/or her failure to conform to society's ideas of what a writer should be. Her husband, whose life was as unsettled as hers, turned out a far larger corpus of literary as well as musical compositions and acknowledged the importance of Jane as his muse. She blamed Morocco for her writing difficulties—"It's good for Paul, but not for me"—although her output was scarcely prodigious even before she moved to the Middle East. In a long review of Bowles' biography and letters in the *Village Voice* in 1981, Laurie Stone offers a particularly chilling perspective on her career: "The world, in fact, was satisfied, for little pleases it more than to see a woman fail at art, unless it is also seeing her take refuge in being Mr. Artist's wife." Whatever the reason so much of her talent was wasted, Jane Bowles left a very small but brilliant collection of works mined out of the pain she could never escape.

SELECTED BIBLIOGRAPHY

Austin, Gayle. *Feminist Theories for Dramatic Criticism.* Ann Arbor: U. of Michigan P., 1990.

Bowles, Jane. *Feminine Wiles.* Intro. Tennessee Williams. Santa Barbara, CA: Black Sparrow Press, 1976.

——. *Out in the World: Selected Letters of Jane Bowles, 1935-1970.* ed. Millicent Dillon. Santa Barbara, CA: Black Sparrow Press, 1985.

——. *My Sister's Hand in Mine: An Expanded Edition of the Collected Works of Jane Bowles.* Intro. Truman Capote. N.Y.: Ecco Press, 1978.

Bowles, Paul. "Paul Bowles and the Long Reach of Memory." *New York Times.* 25 July 1993, Sec. 2, 5.

——. *Without Stopping: An Autobiography.* N.Y.: G.P. Putnam's Sons, 1972.

Dillon, Millicent. "Jane Bowles: Experiment as Character." In *Breaking the Sequence: Women's Experimental Fiction.* Intro. and ed. Ellen G. Friedman and Miriam Fuchs. Princeton: Princeton UP, 1989.

——. *A Little Original Sin: The Life and Work of Jane Bowles.* N.Y.: Holt, Rinehart and Winston, 1981.

Green, Michelle. *The Dream at the End of the World: Paul Bowles and the Literary Renegades in Tangier.* N.Y.: HarperCollins, 1991.

Jaher, Diana. "Building the Summer House." *TheaterWeek* (August 16-22, 1993): 23-7.

Williams, Tennessee. *Memoirs.* Garden City, N.Y.: Anchor/Doubleday, 1983.

CHARACTERS

GERTRUDE EASTMAN CUEVAS
MOLLY, *her daughter*
MR. SOLARES
MRS. LOPEZ
FREDERICA
ESPERANZA
ALTA GRACIA
QUINTINA
LIONEL
A FIGURE BEARER
ANOTHER FIGURE BEARER
VIVIAN CONSTABLE
CHAUFFEUR
MRS. CONSTABLE
INEZ

ACT ONE
Scene I: Gertrude Eastman Cuevas' garden on the coast, Southern
    California
Scene II: The beach. One month later
Scene III: The garden. One month later

ACT TWO
Scene I: The Lobster Bowl. Ten months later, before dawn
Scene II: The same. Two months later, late afternoon

Time: the present

ACT ONE

SCENE I

GERTRUDE EASTMAN CUEVAS' *garden somewhere on the coast of Southern California. The garden is a mess, with ragged cactus plants and broken ornaments scattered about. A low hedge at the back of the set separates the garden from a dirt lane which supposedly leads to the main road. Beyond the lane is the beach and the sea. The side of the house and the front door are visible. A low balcony hangs over the garden. In the garden itself there is a round summer house covered with vines.*

GERTRUDE: (*A beautiful middle-aged woman with sharply defined features, a good carriage and bright red hair. She is dressed in a tacky provincial fashion. Her voice is tense but resonant. She is seated on the balcony*) Are you in the summer house?

(MOLLY, *a girl of eighteen with straight black hair cut in bangs and a somnolent impassive face, does not hear* GERTRUDE *'s question but remains in the summer house.* GERTRUDE, *repeating, goes to railing*)

Are you in the summer house?

MOLLY: Yes, I am.

GERTRUDE: If I believed in acts of violence, I would burn the summer house down. You love to get in there and loll about hour after hour. You can't even see out because those vines hide the view. Why don't you find a good flat rock overlooking the ocean and sit on it? (MOLLY *fingers the vine*) As long as you're so indifferent to the beauties of nature, I should think you would interest yourself in political affairs, or in music or painting or at least in the future. But I've said this to you at least a thousand times before. You admit you relax too much?

MOLLY: I guess I do.

GERTRUDE: We already have to take in occasional boarders to help make ends meet. As the years go by the boarders will increase, and I can barely put up with the few that come here now; I'm not temperamentally suited to boarders. Nor am I interested in whether this should be considered a character defect or not. I simply hate gossiping with strangers and I don't want to listen to their business. I never have and I never will. It disgusts me. Even my own flesh and blood saps my vitality—

412

particularly you. You seem to have developed such a slow and gloomy way of walking lately...not at all becoming to a girl. Don't you think you could correct your walk?   *nitpicking*

MOLLY: I'm trying. I'm trying to correct it.

GERTRUDE: I'm thinking seriously of marrying Mr. Solares, after all. I would at least have a life free of financial worry if I did, and I'm sure I could gradually ease his sister, Mrs. Lopez, out of the house because she certainly gets on my nerves. He's a manageable man and Spanish men aren't around the house much, which is a blessing. They're almost always out...not getting intoxicated or having a wild time...just out...sitting around with bunches of other men...Spanish men...Cubans, Mexicans...I don't know...They're all alike, drinking little cups of coffee and jabbering away to each other for hours on end. That was your father's life anyway. I minded then. I minded terribly, not so much because he left me alone, but he wasn't in his office for more than a few hours a day...and he wasn't rich enough, not like Mr. Solares. I lectured him in the beginning. I lectured him on ambition, on making contacts, on developing his personality. Often at night I was quite hoarse. I worked on him steadily, trying to make him worry about sugar. I warned him he was letting his father's interests go to pot. Nothing helped. He refused to worry about sugar; he refused to worry about anything. (*She knits a moment in silence*) I lost interest finally. I lost interest in sugar...in him. I lost interest in our life together. I wanted to give it all up...start out fresh, but I couldn't. I was carrying you. I had no choice. All my hopes were wrapped up in you then, all of them. You were my reason for going on, my one and only hope...my love. (*She knits furiously. Then, craning her neck to look in the summer house, she gets up and goes to the rail*) Are you asleep in there, or are you reading comic strips?

MOLLY: I'm not asleep.

GERTRUDE: Sometimes I have the strangest feeling about you. It frightens me... I feel that you are plotting something. Especially when you get inside that summer house. I think your black hair helps me to feel that way. Whenever I think of a woman going wild, I always picture her with black hair, never blond or red. I know that what I'm saying has no connection with a scientific truth. It's very personal. They say red-haired women go wild a lot but I never picture it that way. Do you?

MOLLY: I don't guess I've ever pictured women going wild.

GERTRUDE: And why not? They do all the time. They break the bonds...Sometimes I picture little scenes where they turn evil like wolves...(*Shuddering*) I don't choose to, but I do all the same.

MOLLY: I've never seen a wild woman.

GERTRUDE: (*Music*) On the other hand, sometimes I wake up at night with a strange feeling of isolation...as if I'd fallen off the cliffs and landed miles away from everything that was close to my heart...Even my griefs and my sorrows don't seem to belong to me. Nothing does—as if a shadow had passed over my whole life and made it dark. I try saying my name aloud, over and over again, but it doesn't hook things together. Whenever I feel that way I put my wrapper on and I go down into the kitchen. I open the ice chest and take out some fizzy water. Then I sit at the table with the light switched on and by and by I feel all right again. (*The music fades. Then in a more matter-of-fact tone*) There is no doubt that each one of us has to put up with a shadow or two as he grows older. But if we occupy ourselves while the shadow passes, it passes swiftly enough and scarcely leaves a trace on our daily lives...(*She knits for a moment. Then looks up the road*) The girl who is coming here this afternoon is about seventeen. She should be arriving pretty soon. I also think that Mr. Solares will be arriving shortly and that he'll be bringing one of his hot picnic luncheons with him today. I can feel it in my bones. It's disgraceful of me, really, to allow him to feed us on our own lawn, but then, their mouths count up to six, while ours count up to only two. So actually it's only half a disgrace. I hope Mr. Solares realizes that. Besides, I might be driven to accepting his marriage offer and then the chicken would be in the same pot anyway. Don't you agree?

MOLLY: Yes.

GERTRUDE: You don't seem very interested in what I'm saying.

MOLLY: Well, I...

GERTRUDE: I think that you should be more of a conversationalist. You never express an opinion, nor do you seem to have an outlook. What on earth is your outlook?

MOLLY: (*Uncertainly*) Democracy...

GERTRUDE: I don't think you feel very strongly about it. You don't listen to the various commentators, nor do you ever glance at the newspapers. It's very easy to say that one is democratic, but that doesn't prevent one from being a slob if one is a slob. I've never permitted myself to become a slob, even though I sit home all the time and avoid the outside world as much as possible. I've never liked going out any more than my father did. He always avoided the outside world. He hated a lot of idle gossip and had no use for people anyway. "Let the world do its dancing and its drinking and its inter-killing without me," he always said. "They'll manage perfectly well; I'll stick to myself and my work." (*The music comes up again and she is lost in a dream*) When I was a little girl I made up my mind that I was going to be just like him. He was my model, my ideal. I admired him more than anyone on earth. And he admired me of course. I was so much like him—ambitious, defiant, a fighting cock always. I worshipped him. But I was never meek, not like Ellen my sister. She was very frail and delicate. My father used to put his arms around her, and play with her hair, long golden curls...Ellen was the weak one. That's why he spoiled her. He pitied Ellen. (*With wonder, and very delicately, as if afraid to break a spell. The music expresses the sorrow she is hiding from herself*) Once he took her out of school, when she was ten years old. He bought her a little fur hat and they went away together for two whole weeks. I was left behind. I had no reason to leave school. I was healthy and strong. He took her to a big hotel on the edge of a lake. The lake was frozen, and they sat in the sunshine all day long, watching the people skate. When they came back he said, "Look at her, look at Ellen. She has roses in her cheeks." He pitied Ellen, but he was proud of me. I was his true love. He never showed it...He was so frightened Ellen would guess. He didn't want her to be jealous, but I knew the truth...He didn't have to show it. He didn't have to say anything. (*The music fades and she knits furiously, coming back to the present*) Why don't you go inside and clean up? It might sharpen your wits. Go and change that rumpled dress.

MOLLY: (MOLLY *comes out of the summer house and sniffs a blossom*) The honeysuckle's beginning to smell real good. I can never remember when you planted this vine, but it's sure getting thick. It makes the summer house so nice and shady inside.

GERTRUDE: (*Stiffening in anger*) I told you never to mention that vine again. You know it was there when we bought this house. You love to call my attention to that wretched vine because it's the only thing that grows well in the garden and you know it was planted by the people who came here before us and not by me at all. (*She rises and paces the balcony*) You're mocking me for being such a failure in the garden and not being able to make things grow. That's an underhanded Spanish trait of yours you inherit from your father. You love to mock me.

MOLLY: (*Tenderly*) I would never mock you.

GERTRUDE: (*Working herself up*) I thought I'd find peace here...with these waving palms and the ocean stretching as far as the eye can see, but you don't like the ocean...You won't even go in the water. You're afraid to swim...I thought we'd found a paradise at last—the perfect place—but you don't want paradise...You want hell. Well, go into your little house and rot if you like...I don't care. Go on in while you still can. It won't be there much longer...I'll marry Mr. Solares and send you to business school. (*The voices of MR. SOLARES and his family arriving with a picnic lunch stop her. She leans over the railing of the balcony and looks up the road*) Oh, here they come with their covered pots. I knew they'd appear with a picnic luncheon today. I could feel it in my bones. We'll put our own luncheon away for supper and have our supper tomorrow for lunch...Go and change...Quickly... Watch that walk. (MOLLY *exits into the house.* GERTRUDE *settles down in her chair to prepare for* MR. SOLARES' *arrival*) I wish they weren't coming. I'd rather be here by myself really. (*Enter Spanish people*) Nature's the best company of all. (*She pats her bun and rearranges some hairpins. Then she stands up and waves to her guests, cupping her mouth and yelling at the same time*) Hello there!

(*In another moment* MR. SOLARES, MRS. LOPEZ *and her daughter,* FREDERICA, *and the three servants enter, walking in single file down the lane. Two of the servants are old hags and the third is a young half caste,* ESPERANZA, *in mulberry-colored satin. The servants all carry pots wrapped with bright bandannas.*)

MR. SOLARES: (*He wears a dark dusty suit. Pushing ahead of his sister,* MRS. LOPEZ, *in his haste to greet* GERTRUDE *and thus squeezing his sister's arm rather painfully against the gate post*) Hello, Miss Eastman Cuevas! (MRS. LOPEZ *squeals with pain and rubs her arm. She is fat and middle-aged. She wears a black picture hat and black city dress. Her hat is decorated with flowers;* MR. SOLARES *speaks with only a trace of an accent, having lived for many years in this country. Grinning and bobbing around*) We brought you a picnic. For you and your daughter. Plenty of everything! You come down into the garden.

(*The others crowd slowly through the gate and stand awkwardly in a bunch looking up at* GERTRUDE.)

GERTRUDE: (*Perfunctorily*) I think I'll stay here on the balcony, thank you. Just spread yourselves on the lawn and we'll talk back and forth this way. It's all the same. (*To the maids*) You can hand me up my food by stepping on that little stump and I'll lean over and get it.

MRS. LOPEZ: (*Her accent is much thicker than her brother's, smiling up at* GERTRUDE) You will come down into the garden, Miss Eastman Cuevas?

MR. SOLARES: (*Giving his sister a poke*) Acaba de decirte que se queda arriba. ¿Ya no oyes? (*The next few minutes on the stage have a considerable musical background. The hags and* ESPERANZA *start spreading bandannas on the lawn and emptying the baskets. The others settle on the lawn.* ESPERANZA *and the hags sing a raucous song as they work, the hags just joining in at the chorus and a bit off key.* ESPERANZA *brings over a pot wrapped in a Turkish towel and serves the family group. They all take enormous helpings of spaghetti.* MR. SOLARES *serves himself*) Italian spaghetti with meat balls! Esperanza, serve a big plate to Miss Eastman Cuevas up on the porch. You climb on that.

(*He points to a fake stump with a gnome carved on one side of it.*)

ESPERANZA: (*Disagreeably*) ¡Caramba!

(*She climbs up on the stump after filling a plate with spaghetti and hands it to* GERTRUDE, *releasing her hold on the plate before* GERTRUDE *has secured her own grip.* ESPERANZA *jumps out of the way immediately and the plate swings downward under the weight of the food, dumping the spaghetti on* MRS. LOPEZ' *head.*)

GERTRUDE: Oh! (*To* ESPERANZA) You didn't give me a chance to get a firm hold on it!

MR. SOLARES: ¡Silencio!

(ESPERANZA *rushes over to the hags and all three of them become hysterical with laughter. After their hysterics they pull themselves together and go over to clean up* MRS. LOPEZ *and to restore* GERTRUDE's *plate to her filled with fresh spaghetti. They return to their side of the garden in a far corner and everyone starts to eat.*)

MR. SOLARES: (*To* GERTRUDE) Miss Eastman Cuevas, you like chop suey?

GERTRUDE: I have never eaten any.

MRS. LOPEZ: (*Eager to get into the conversation and expressing great wonder in her voice*) Chop suey? What is it?

MR. SOLARES: (*In a mean voice to* MRS. LOPEZ) You know what it is. (*In Spanish*) Que me dejes hablar con la señora Eastman Cuevas por favor. (*To* GERTRUDE) I'll bring you some chop suey tomorrow in a box, or maybe we better go out to a restaurant, to a dining and dancing. Maybe you would go to try out some chop suey...Would you?

GERTRUDE: (*Coolly*) That's very nice of you but I've told you before that I don't care for the type of excitement you get when you go out...You know what I mean—entertainment, dancing, etc. Why don't you describe chop suey to me and I'll try and imagine it? (MRS. LOPEZ *roars with laughter for no apparent reason.* GERTRUDE *cranes her neck and looks down at her over the balcony with raised eyebrows*) I could die content without ever setting foot in another restaurant. Frankly, I would not care if every single one of them burned to the ground. I really love to sit on my porch and look out over the ocean.

MRS. LOPEZ: You like the ocean?

GERTRUDE: I love it!

MRS. LOPEZ: (*Making a wild gesture with her arm*) I hate it!

GERTRUDE: I love it. It's majestic...

MRS. LOPEZ: I hate!

GERTRUDE: (*Freezing up*) I see that we don't agree.

MR. SOLARES: (*Scowling at* MRS. LOPEZ) Oh, she loves the ocean. I don't know what the hell is the matter with her today. (GERTRUDE *winces at his language*) Myself, I like ocean, land, mountain, all kinds of food, chop suey, chili, eel, turtle steak...Everything. Solares like everything. (*In hideous French accent*) Joie de vivre! (*He snaps his fingers in the air.*)

GERTRUDE: (*Sucking some long strands of spaghetti into her mouth*) What is your attitude toward your business?

MR. SOLARES: (*Happily*) My business is dandy.

GERTRUDE: (*Irritably*) Yes, but what is your attitude toward it?

MR. SOLARES: (*With his mouth full*) O.K.

GERTRUDE: Please try to concentrate on my question, Mr. Solares. Do you like business or do you really prefer to stay home and lazy around?

MRS. LOPEZ: (*Effusively*) He don't like no business—he likes to stay home and sleep—and eat. (*Then in a mocking tone intended to impress* MR. SOLARES *himself*) "Fula, I got headache...I got bellyache...I stay home, no?" (*She jabs her brother in the ribs with her elbow several times rolling her eyes in a teasing manner and repeats*) "Fula, I got headache...I got bellyache...I stay home, no?"
(*She jabs him once again even harder and laughs way down in her throat.*)

MR. SOLARES: ¡Fula! Esta es la última vez que sales conmigo. Ya, déjame hablar con la señora *Eastman Cuevas!*

MRS. LOPEZ: Look, *Miss* Eastman Cuevas?

GERTRUDE: (*Looking disagreeably surprised*) Yes?

MRS. LOPEZ: You like to talk to me?

GERTRUDE: (*As coolly as possible short of sounding rude*) Yes, I enjoy it.

MRS. LOPEZ: (*Triumphantly to* MR. SOLARES) Miss Eastman Cuevas *like* talk to me, so you shut your mouth. He don't want no one to talk to you, Miss Eastman Cuevas because he think he gonna marry you.
(FREDERICA *doubles over and buries her face in her hands. Her skinny shoulders shake with laughter.*)

MR. SOLARES: (*Embarrassed and furious*) Bring the chicken and rice, Esperanza.

ESPERANZA: You ain't finished what you got!

MR. SOLARES: Cállate, y tráigame el arroz con pollo.
(ESPERANZA *walks across the lawn with the second pot wrapped in a Turkish towel. She walks deliberately at a very slow pace, throwing a hip out at each step, and with a terrible sneer on her face. She serves them all chicken and rice, first removing the spaghetti plates and giving them clean ones. Everyone takes enormous helpings again, with the exception of* GERTRUDE *who refuses to have any.*)

GERTRUDE: (*While* ESPERANZA *serves the others*) If Molly doesn't come out soon she will simply have to miss her lunch. It's very tiring to have to keep reminding her of the time and the other realities of life. Molly is a dreamer.

MRS. LOPEZ: (*Nodding*) That's right.

GERTRUDE: (*Watching* FREDERICA *serve herself*) Do you people always eat such a big midday meal? Molly and I are in the habit of eating simple salads at noon.

MRS. LOPEZ: (*Wiping her mouth roughly with her napkin. Then without pausing and with gusto*) For breakfast: chocolate and sugar

bread; for lunch: soup, beans, eggs, rice, roast pork with potatoes and guava paste...(*She pulls on a different finger for each
separate item*) Next day: soup, eggs, beans, rice, chicken with
rice and guava paste—other day: soup, eggs, beans, rice, stew
meat, roasted baby pig and guava paste. Other day: soup, rice,
beans, grilled red snapper, roasted goat meat and guava paste.

FREDERICA: (*Speaking for the first time, rapidly, in a scarcely audible
voice*) Soup, rice, beans, eggs, ground-up meat and guava
paste.

GERTRUDE: (*Wearily*) We usually have a simple salad.

MR. SOLARES: She's talkin' about the old Spanish custom. She only
come here ten years ago when her old man died. I don't like a
big lunch neither. (*In a sudden burst of temerity*) Listen, what
my sister said was true. I hope I am gonna marry you some
day soon. I've told you so before. You remember?

MRS. LOPEZ: (*Laughing and whispering to* FREDERICA, *who goes off
into hysterics, and then delving into a shopping bag which lies beside
her on the grass. In a very gay voice*) This is what you gonna get
if you make a wedding. (*She pulls out a paper bag and hurls it at*
GERTRUDE's *head with the gesture of a baseball pitcher. The bag
splits and spills rice all over* GERTRUDE. *There is general hilarity
and even a bit of singing on the part of* ESPERANZA *and the hags.*
MRS. LOPEZ *yells above the noise*) Rice!

GERTRUDE: (*Standing up and flicking rice from her shoulders*) Stop it!
Please! Stop it! I can't stand this racket...Really. (*She is genuinely upset. They subside gradually. Bewildered, she looks out over
the land toward the road*) Something is coming down the
road...It must be my boarder...No...She would be coming in
an automobile. (*Pause*) Gracious! It certainly is *no* boarder,
but what is it?

MRS. LOPEZ: Friend come and see you?

GERTRUDE: (*Bewildered, staring hard*) No, it's not a friend.
It's...(*She stares harder*) It's some sort of king—and others.

MRS. LOPEZ: (*To her brother*) ¿Qué?

MR. SOLARES: (*Absently absorbed in his food*) King. Un rey y otros
más...

MRS. LOPEZ: (*Nodding*) Un rey y otros más.

(*Enter* LIONEL, *bearing a cardboard figure larger than himself,
representing Neptune, with flowing beard, crown and scepter, etc.
He is followed by two or more other* FIGURE BEARERS, *carrying
representations of a channel swimmer and a mermaid.* LIONEL

stops at the gate and dangles into the garden a toy lobster which he has tied to the line of a real fishing rod. The music dies down.)

LIONEL: Advertisement.

(*He bobs the lobster up and down.*)

GERTRUDE: For what?

LIONEL: For the Lobster Bowl…It's opening next week. (*Pointing*) That figure there represents a mermaid and the other one is Neptune, the sea god. This is a lobster…(*He shakes the rod*) Everything connected with the sea in some capacity. Can we have a glass of water?

GERTRUDE: Yes. (*Calling*) Molly! Molly!

MOLLY: (*From inside the house*) What is it?

GERTRUDE: Come out here immediately. (*To* LIONEL) Excuse me but I think your figures are really awful. I don't like advertising schemes anyway.

LIONEL: I have nothing to do with them. I just have to carry them around a few more days and then after that I'll be working at the Bowl. I'm sorry you don't like them.

GERTRUDE: I've always hated everything that was larger than life size.

(LIONEL *opens the gate and enters the garden, followed by the other* FIGURE BEARERS. *The garden by now has a very cluttered appearance. The servants,* MRS. LOPEZ *and* FREDERICA *have been gaping at the figures in silence since their arrival.*)

MRS. LOPEZ: (*Finding her tongue*) ¡Una maravilla!

FREDERICA: Ay, sí.

(*She is nearly swooning with delight. Enter* MOLLY. *She stops short when she sees the figures.*)

MOLLY: Oh…What are those?

LIONEL: Advertisements. This is Neptune, the old god.

(MOLLY *approaches the figures slowly and touches Neptune.*)

MOLLY: It's beautiful…

LIONEL: Here's a little lobster.

(*He dangles it into* MOLLY's *open palm.*)

MOLLY: It looks like a real lobster. It even has those long threads sticking out over its eyes.

GERTRUDE: Antennae.

MOLLY: Antennae.

LIONEL: (*Pulling another little lobster from his pocket and handing it to* MOLLY) Here. Take this one. I have a few to give away.

MOLLY: Oh, thank you very much.

(There follows a heated argument between FREDERICA *and* MRS.
LOPEZ, *who is trying to force* FREDERICA *to ask for a lobster too.
They almost come to blows and finally* MRS. LOPEZ *gives*
FREDERICA *a terrific shove which sends her stumbling over toward*
LIONEL *and* MOLLY.)

MRS. LOPEZ: *(Calling out to* LIONEL) Give my girl a little fish please!
*(*LIONEL *digs reluctantly into his pocket and hands* FREDERICA *a
little lobster. She takes it and returns to her mother, stubbing her
toe in her confusion.)*

GERTRUDE: *(Craning her neck and looking out over the lane toward the
road)* There's a car stopping. This really must be my boarder.
*(She looks down into the garden with an expression of consternation
on her face)* The garden is a wreck. Mr. Solares, can't your servants organize this mess? Quickly, for heaven's sake. *(She looks
with disgust at* MR. SOLARES, *who is still eating, but holds her
tongue. Enter* VIVIAN, *a young girl of fifteen with wild reddish
gold hair. She is painfully thin and her eyes appear to pop out of her
head with excitement. She is dressed in bright colors and wears high
heels. She is followed by a* CHAUFFEUR *carrying luggage)* And get
those figures out of sight!

VIVIAN: *(Stopping in the road and staring at the house intently for a
moment)* The house is heavenly!
*(*MOLLY *exits rapidly.)*

GERTRUDE: Welcome, Vivian Constable. I'm Gertrude Eastman
Cuevas. How was your trip?

VIVIAN: Stinky. *(Gazing with admiration into the garden packed with
people)* And your garden is heavenly too.

GERTRUDE: The garden is a wreck at the moment.

VIVIAN: Oh, no! It's fascinating.

GERTRUDE: You can't possibly tell yet.

VIVIAN: Oh, but I can. I decide everything the first minute. It's a
fascinating garden.
(She smiles at everyone. MR. SOLARE's *spits chicken skin out of his
mouth onto the grass.)*

MRS. LOPEZ: Do you want some spaghetti?

VIVIAN: Not yet, thank you. I'm too excited.

GERTRUDE: *(To* MR. SOLARES) Will you show Miss Constable and
the chauffeur into the house, Mr. Solares? I'll meet you at the
top of the stairs.
(She exits hurriedly into the house, but MR. SOLARES *continues
gnawing on his bone not having paid the slightest attention to*

JANE BOWLES 423

GERTRUDE's *request. Enter* MRS. CONSTABLE, VIVIAN's *mother. She is wearing a distinguished city print, gloves, hat and veil. She is frail like her daughter but her coloring is dull.*)

VIVIAN: (*Spying her mother. Her expression immediately hardens*) Why did you get out of the taxi? You promised at the hotel that you wouldn't get out if I allowed you to ride over with me. You promised me once in the room and then again on the porch. Now you've gotten out. You're dying to spoil the magic. Go back...Don't stand there looking at the house. (MRS. CONSTABLE *puts her fingers to her lips entreating silence, shakes her head at* VIVIAN *and scurries off stage after nodding distractedly to the people on the lawn*) She can't keep a promise.

GERTRUDE: (*Coming out onto the balcony again and spotting* MR. SOLARES, *still eating on the grass*) What is the matter with you, Mr. Solares? I asked you to show Miss Constable and the chauffeur into the house and you haven't budged an inch. I've been waiting at the top of the stairs like an idiot.
(MR. SOLARES *scrambles to his feet and goes into the house followed by* VIVIAN *and the* CHAUFFEUR. *Enter* MRS. CONSTABLE *again.*)

MRS. CONSTABLE: (*Coming up to the hedge and leaning over. To* MRS. LOPEZ) Forgive me but I would like you to tell Mrs. Eastman Cuevas that I am at the Herons Hotel. (MRS. LOPEZ *nods absently.* MRS. CONSTABLE *continues in a scarcely audible voice*) You see, Mrs. Eastman Cuevas comes from the same town that I come from and through mutual friends I heard that she took in boarders these days, so I wrote her that Vivian my daughter was coming.

MRS. LOPEZ: Thank you very much.

MRS. CONSTABLE: My daughter likes her freedom, so we have a little system worked out when we go on vacations. I stay somewhere nearby but not in the same place. Even so, I am the nervous type and I would like Mrs. Eastman Cuevas to know that I'm at the Herons...You see my daughter is unusually high spirited. She feels everything so strongly that she's apt to tire herself out. I want to be available just in case she collapses.

MRS. LOPEZ: (*Ruffling* FREDERICA's *hair*) Frederica get very tired too.

MRS. CONSTABLE: Yes, I know. I suppose all the young girls do. Will you tell Mrs. Eastman Cuevas that I'm at the Herons?

MRS. LOPEZ: O.K.

passive

MRS. CONSTABLE: Thank you a thousand times. I'll run along now or Vivian will see me and she'll think that I'm interfering with her freedom...You'll notice right away what fun she gets out of life. Good-bye.

MRS. LOPEZ: Good-bye, Mrs. Vamos; despiértense. Esperanza. (MRS. CONSTABLE *exits hurriedly. To* MR. SOLARES) Now we go home.

MR. SOLARES: (*Sullenly*) All right. (*Spanish group leaves*) Esperanza! Esperanza! Frederica!
(*Enter from the house* VIVIAN, GERTRUDE *and the* CHAUFFEUR, *who leaves the garden and exits down the lane.*)

VIVIAN: (*To* GERTRUDE, *continuing a conversation*) I'm going to be sky high by dinner time. Then I won't sleep all night. I know myself.

GERTRUDE: Don't you use controls?

VIVIAN: No, I never do. When I feel myself going up I just go on up until I hit the ceiling. I'm like that. The world is ten times more exciting for me than it is for others.

GERTRUDE: Still I believe in using controls. It's a part of the law of civilization. Otherwise we would be like wild beasts. (*She sighs*) We're bad enough as it is, controls and all.

VIVIAN: (*Hugging* GERTRUDE *impulsively*) You've got the prettiest hair I've ever seen, and I'm going to love it here. (GERTRUDE *backs away a little, embarrassed.* VIVIAN *spots the summer house*) What a darling little house! It's like the home of a bird or a poet. (*She approaches the summer house and enters it.* MRS. LOPEZ *motions to the hags to start cleaning up. They hobble around one behind the other gathering things and scraping plates very ineffectually. More often than not the hag behind scrapes more garbage onto the plate just cleaned by the hag in front of her. They continue this until the curtain falls. Music begins. Calling to* GERTRUDE) I can imagine all sorts of things in here, Miss Eastman Cuevas. I could make plans for hours on end in here. It's so darling and little.

GERTRUDE: (*Coldly*) Molly usually sits in there. But I can't say that she plans much. Just dozes or reads trash. Comic strips. It will do no harm if someone else sits in there for a change.

VIVIAN: Who is Molly?

GERTRUDE: Molly is my daughter.

VIVIAN: How wonderful! I want to meet her right away...Where is she?

(*The boys start righting the cardboard figures.*)

LIONEL: Do you think we could have our water?

GERTRUDE: I'm sorry. Yes, of course. (*Calling*) Molly! (*Silence*) Molly! (*More loudly*) Molly! (*Silence*)

LIONEL: I think we'll go along to the next place. Don't bother your daughter. I'll come back if I may. I'd like to see you all again…and your daughter. She disappeared so quickly.

GERTRUDE: You stay right where you are. I'll get her out here in a minute. (*Screaming*) Molly! Come out here immediately! Molly!

VIVIAN: (*In a trilling voice*) Molly! Come on out!…I'm in your little house…Molly!

GERTRUDE: (*Furious*) Molly!

(*All the players look expectantly at the doorway.* MOLLY *does not appear and the curtain comes down in silence.*)

SCENE II

One month later.

A beach and a beautiful backdrop of the water. The SOLARES *family is again spread out among dirty plates as though the scenery had changed around them while they themselves had not stirred since the first act.* GERTRUDE *is kneeling and rearranging her hair near the* SOLARES *family,* VIVIAN *at her feet.* MOLLY *and* LIONEL *a little apart from the other people,* MOLLY *watching* VIVIAN. *The two old hags are wearing white slips for swimming.*

The music is sad and disturbing, implying a more serious mood.

MRS. LOPEZ: (*Poking her daughter who is lying next to her*) A ver si tú y Esperanza nos cantan algo…

FREDERICA: (*From under handkerchief which covers her face*) Ay, mamá.

MRS. LOPEZ: (*Calling to* ESPERANZA) Esperanza, a ver si nos cantan algo, tú y Frederica.

(*She gives her daughter a few pokes. They argue a bit and* FREDERICA *gets up and drags herself wearily over to the hags. They consult and sing a little song. The hags join in at the chorus.*)

ESPERANZA: Bueno—sí…

GERTRUDE: (*When they have finished*) That was nice. I like sad songs.

VIVIAN: (*Still at her feet and looking up at her with adoration*) So do

I...(MOLLY *is watching* VIVIAN, *a beam of hate in her eye.* VIVIAN *takes* GERTRUDE'*s wrist and plays with her hand just for a moment.* GERTRUDE *pulls it away, instinctively afraid of* MOLLY'*s reaction. To* GERTRUDE) I wish Molly would come swimming with me. I thought maybe she would. (*Then to* MOLLY, *for* GERTRUDE'*s benefit*) Molly, won't you come in, just this once. You'll love it once you do. Everyone loves the water, everyone in the world.

GERTRUDE: (*Springing to her feet, and addressing the Spanish people*) I thought we were going for a stroll up the beach after lunch. (*There is apprehension behind her words*) You'll never digest lying on your backs, and besides you're sure to fall asleep if you don't get up right away.

(*She regains her inner composure as she gives her commands.*)

MRS. LOPEZ: (*Groaning*) ¡Ay! ¡Caray! Why don't you sleep, Miss Eastman Cuevas?

GERTRUDE: It's very bad for you, really. Come on. Come on, everybody! Get up! You too, Alta Gracia and Quintina, get up! Come on, everybody up! (*There is a good deal of protesting while the servants and the* SOLARES *family struggle to their feet*) I promise you you'll feel much better later on if we take just a little walk along the beach.

VIVIAN: (*Leaping to* GERTRUDE'*s side in one bound*) I *love* to walk on the beach!

(MOLLY *too has come forward to be with her mother.*)

GERTRUDE: (*Pause. Again stifling her apprehension with a command*) You children stay here. Or take a walk along the cliffs if you'd like to. But be careful!

FREDERICA: I want to be with my mother.

GERTRUDE: Well, come along, but we're only going for a short stroll. What a baby you are, Frederica Lopez.

MR. SOLARES: I'll run the car up to my house and go and collect that horse I was telling you about. Then I'll catch up with you on the way back.

GERTRUDE: You won't get much of a walk.

(FREDERICA *throws her arms around her mother and gives her a big smacking kiss on the cheek.* MRS. LOPEZ *kisses* FREDERICA. *They all exit slowly, leaving* VIVIAN, LIONEL, MOLLY *and the dishes behind.* MOLLY, *sad that she can't walk with her mother, crosses wistfully back to her former place next to* LIONEL, *but* VIVIAN—*eager to cut her out whenever she can—rushes to*

LIONEL'*s side, and crouches on her heels exactly where* MOLLY *was sitting before.* MOLLY *notices this, and settles in a brooding way a little apart from them, her back to the pair.*)

VIVIAN: Lionel, what were you saying before about policies?

LIONEL: When?

VIVIAN: Today, before lunch. You said, "What are your policies" or something crazy like that?

LIONEL: Oh, yes. It's just…I'm mixed up about my own policies, so I like to know how other people's are getting along.

VIVIAN: Well, I'm for freedom and a full exciting life! (*Pointedly to* MOLLY'*s back*) I'm a daredevil. It frightens my mother out of her wits, but I love excitement!

LIONEL: Do you always do what gives you pleasure?

VIVIAN: Whenever I can, I do.

LIONEL: What about conflicts?

VIVIAN: What do you mean?

LIONEL: Being pulled different ways and not knowing which to choose.

VIVIAN: I don't have those. I always know exactly what I want to do. When I have a plan in my head I get so excited I can't sleep.

LIONEL: Maybe it would be a stroke of luck to be like you. I have nothing but conflicts. For instance, one day I think I ought to give up the world and be a religious leader, and the next day I'll turn right around and think I ought to throw myself deep into politics. (VIVIAN, *bored, starts untying her beach shoes*) There have been ecclesiastics in my family before. I come from a gloomy family. A lot of the men seem to have married crazy wives. Five brothers out of six and a first cousin did. My uncle's first wife boiled a cat alive in the upstairs kitchen.

VIVIAN: What do you mean, the upstairs kitchen?

LIONEL: We had the top floor fitted out as an apartment and the kitchen upstairs was called the upstairs kitchen.

VIVIAN: (*Hopping to her feet*) Oh, well, let's stop talking dull heavy stuff. I'm going to swim.

LIONEL: All right.

VIVIAN: (*Archly*) Good-bye, Molly.

(*She runs off stage in the direction of the cove.* MOLLY *sits on rock.*)

LIONEL: (*Goes over and sits next to her*) Doesn't the ocean make you feel gloomy when the sky is gray or when it starts getting dark out?

MOLLY: I don't guess it does.

LIONEL: Well, in the daytime, if it's sunny out and the ocean's blue it puts you in a lighter mood, doesn't it?

MOLLY: When it's blue...

LIONEL: Yes, when it's blue and dazzling. Don't you feel happier when it's like that?

MOLLY: I don't guess I emphasize that kind of thing.

LIONEL: I see. (*Thoughtfully*) Well, how do you feel about the future? Are you afraid of the future in the back of your mind?

MOLLY: I don't guess I emphasize that much either.

LIONEL: Maybe you're one of the lucky ones who looks forward to the future. Have you got some kind of ambition?

MOLLY: Not so far. Have you?

LIONEL: I've got two things I think I should do, like I told Vivian. But they're not exactly ambitions. One's being a religious leader, the other's getting deep into politics. I don't look forward to either one of them.

MOLLY: Then you'd better not do them.

LIONEL: I wish it was that simple. I'm not an easygoing type. I come from a gloomy family...I dread being a minister in a way because it brings you so close to death all the time. You would get too deep in to ever forget death and eternity again, as long as you lived—not even for an afternoon. I think that even when you were talking with your friends or eating or joking, it would be there in the back of your mind. Death, I mean...and eternity. At the same time I think I might have a message for a parish if I had one.

MOLLY: What would you tell them?

LIONEL: Well, that would only come through divine inspiration, after I made the sacrifice and joined up.

MOLLY: Oh.

LIONEL: I get a feeling of dread in my stomach about being a political leader too...That should cheer me up more, but it doesn't. You'd think I really liked working at the Lobster Bowl.

MOLLY: Don't you?

LIONEL: Yes, I do, but of course that isn't life. I have fun too, in between worrying...fun, dancing, and eating, and swimming...and being with you. I like to be with you because you seem to only half hear me. I think I could say just the opposite and it wouldn't sound any different to you. Now why do I like that? Because it makes me feel very peaceful. Usually if I tell my feelings to a person I don't want to see them any more. That's another peculiar quirk of mine. Also there's something very familiar about you, even though I never met you before two months ago. I don't know what it is quite...your face...your voice...(*Taking her hand*) or maybe just your hand. (*Holds her hand for a moment, deep in thought*) I hope I'm not going to dread it all for too long. Because it doesn't feel right to me, just working at the Lobster Bowl. It's nice though really...Inez is always around if you want company. She can set up oyster cocktails faster than anyone on the coast. That's what she claims, anyway. She has some way of checking. You'd like Inez.

MOLLY: I don't like girls.

LIONEL: Inez is a grown-up woman. A kind of sturdy rock-of-Gibraltar type but very high strung and nervous too. Every now and then she blows up. (MOLLY *rises suddenly and crosses to the rock*) Well, I guess it really isn't so interesting to be there, but it is outside of the world and gloomy ideas. Maybe it's the decorations. It doesn't always help though, things come creeping in anyway.

MOLLY: (*Turning to* LIONEL) What?

LIONEL: Well, like what ministers talk about...the valley of the Shadow of Death and all that...or the world comes creeping in. I feel like it's a warning that I shouldn't stay too long. That I should go back to St. Louis. It would be tough though. Now I'm getting too deep in. I suppose you live mainly from day to day. That's the way girls live mainly, isn't it?

MOLLY: (*Crossing back to* LIONEL) I don't know. I'm all right as long as I can keep from getting mad. It's hard to keep from getting mad when you see through people. Most people can't like I do. I'd emphasize that all right. The rest of the stuff doesn't bother me much. A lot of people want to yank you out and get in themselves. Girls do anyway. I haven't got anything against men. They don't scheme the way girls do. But I keep to myself as much as I can.

LIONEL: Well, there's that angle too, but my point of view is different. Have you thought any more about marrying me if your mother marries Mr. Solares? I know we're both young, but you don't want to go to business school and she's sure to send you there if she marries him. She's always talking about it. She'd be in Mexico most of the year and you'd be in business school. We could live over the Lobster Bowl and get all the food we wanted free, and it's good food. Mr. Solares and Mrs. Lopez liked it when they went to eat there.

MOLLY: Yes, I know they did.

LIONEL: Well?

MOLLY: I won't think of it until it happens. I can't picture anything being any different than it is. I feel I might just plain die if everything changes, but I don't imagine it will.

LIONEL: You should look forward to change.

MOLLY: I don't want anything different.

LIONEL: Then you *are* afraid of the future just like me.

MOLLY: (*Stubbornly*) I don't think much about the future.

(VIVIAN *returns from her swim.*)

LIONEL: (*To* MOLLY) Well, even if you don't think much about the future you have to admit that...

(*He is interrupted by* VIVIAN *who rushes up to them, almost stumbling in her haste.*)

VIVIAN: (*Plopping down next to* LIONEL *and shaking out her wet hair*) Wait 'til you hear this...! (LIONEL *is startled.* VIVIAN *is almost swooning with delight, to* LIONEL) It's so wonderful...I can hardly talk about it...I saw the whole thing in front of my eyes...Just now while I was swimming...

LIONEL: What?

VIVIAN: Our restaurant.

LIONEL: What restaurant?

VIVIAN: *Our restaurant.* The one we're going to open together, right now, as soon as we can. I'll tell you about it...But only on one condition...You have to promise you won't put a damper on it, and tell me it's not practical.

(*Shaking him.*)

LIONEL: (*Bored*) All right.

VIVIAN: Well, this is it. I'm going to sell all the jewelry my grandmother left me and we're going on a trip. We're going to some city I don't know which but some big city that will be as far from here as we can get. Then we'll take jobs and when we have enough money we'll start a restaurant. We could start it on credit with just the barest amount of cash. It's not going to be just an ordinary restaurant but an odd one where everyone sits on cushions instead of on chairs. We could dress the waiters up in those flowing Turkish bloomers and serve very expensive oriental foods, all night long. It will be called

Restaurant Midnight. Can you picture it?

LIONEL: (*Very bored*) Well, yes…in a way…

VIVIAN: Well, I can see the whole thing…very small lamps and perfume in the air, no menus, just silent waiters…bringing in
elaborate dishes one after the other…and music. We could
call it "Minuit"…as it is in French…But either way we must
leave soon…I can't go on this way with my mother snooping
around…I can't be tied down…I've tried running off before,
when I felt desperate…But things didn't work out…maybe
because I never had a real friend before…But *now* I have
you— (*She stops, suddenly aware of* MOLLY—*then with a certain
diffidence*) and Molly, of course, she must come too—we
understand each other even if she is still waters run deep. She
has to escape from her mother too…

(MOLLY *starts at the word "mother." Her face blackens.*)

LIONEL: Molly, you're shivering…Why didn't you say something?
(*Looking up*) The sun's gone behind a cloud, no wonder you're
cold…I can go back to the house and get you a jacket, unless
you want to come along and go home now too. (MOLLY *does
not move*) I'll go and get it. Sit nearer the rocks you'll be out
of the wind. Vivian, do you want something heavier than
that? (*Points to her robe.*)

VIVIAN: No, thanks. I'm much too excited about Restaurant
Midnight to notice anything. Besides I'm not very conscious
of the physical. (LIONEL *exits.* MOLLY *gets up and walks to the
rocks leading to the cliff*) Have you ever eaten Armenian vine
leaves with little pine nuts inside of them?

(MOLLY *is climbing the rocks.*)

MOLLY: Don't follow me…

VIVIAN: Or their wonderful flaky desserts with golden honey
poured…

MOLLY: Don't follow me!

VIVIAN: (*Tapering off*)…all over them…

MOLLY: The day you came I was standing on the porch watching
you. I heard everything you said. You put your arm around
my mother, and you told her she had beautiful hair, then you
saw my summer house and you told her how much you loved
it. You went and sat in it and you yelled, Come out, Molly.
I'm in your little house. You've tried in every way since you
came to push me out. She hates you.

VIVIAN: What?

MOLLY: My mother hates you! She hates you!

VIVIAN: (*After recovering from her shock starts out after her in a rage*) That's a lie, a rotten lie...She doesn't hate me...She's ashamed of *you*...ashamed of you. (*Exits, then repeating several times off stage*) She's ashamed of you...ashamed of you...

(*Her voice is muffled by the entrance of the Mexicans and* GERTRUDE. *The servants head the procession, chattering like magpies and singing.* MR. SOLARES *and* FREDERICA *bring up the rear carrying a tremendous pink rubber horse with purple dots. The hindquarters are supported by* FREDERICA.)

MRS. LOPEZ: (*Signaling to one of the hags who puts a fancy cushion down on the bench, which she sits on, then yelling to* GERTRUDE) Well, how do you like our gorgeous horse? Pretty big, eh?

MR. SOLARES: It's worth thirty-two dollars.

(*They all seat themselves.*)

GERTRUDE: Now that you've asked me I'll tell you quite frankly that I would never dream of spending my money on a thing like that.

MRS. LOPEZ: (*Popping a mint into her mouth*) Pretty big, eh?

GERTRUDE: (*Irritably*) Yes, yes, it's big all right but I don't see what that has to do with anything.

MRS. LOPEZ: That right. Big, lots of money. Little not so much.

GERTRUDE: (*Bitterly*) All the worse.

MRS. LOPEZ: (*Merrily*) Maybe next year, bigger. You got one? (GERTRUDE, *bored, does not answer*) You got one?

GERTRUDE: What?

MRS. LOPEZ: A rubber horse?

GERTRUDE: Oh, for heaven's sake! I told you I thought it was silly. I don't believe in toys for grownups. I think they should buy other things, if they have money to spare.

MRS. LOPEZ: (*Complacently folding her hands*) What?

GERTRUDE: Well, I guess a dresser or a chair or clothing or curtains. I don't know but certainly not a rubber horse. Clothing, of course, one can always buy because the styles change so frequently.

MR. SOLARES: Miss Eastman Cuevas, how many dresses you got?

GERTRUDE: (*Icily*) I have never counted them.

MRS. LOPEZ: (*To her brother*) Cincuenta y nueve, dile.

MR. SOLARES: She got fifty-nine back at the house.

GERTRUDE: (*In spite of herself*) Fifty-nine!

MR. SOLARES: I bought them all for her, since her husband died. He was a no good fellow. No ambition, no brain, no pep.

MRS. LOPEZ: (*Smiling, and nodding her head to* GERTRUDE *sweetly*) Fifty-nine dresses. You like to have that many dresses?

(*Enter* MRS. CONSTABLE *carrying a fishing pole and basket, although she is immaculately dressed in a white crocheted summer ensemble. She has on a large hat and black glasses.*)

MRS. CONSTABLE: (*Trying to smile and appear at ease*) I hope I'm not interrupting a private discussion.

MR. SOLARES: Happy to see you on this beautiful day. Sit down with us. We weren't having no discussion. Just counting up how many dresses the ladies got.

MRS. CONSTABLE: (*A little shocked*) Oh! I myself was hunting for a good spot to fish and I passed so near to your house that I dropped in to call, but you weren't there, of course. Then I remembered that you told me about a bathing spot, somewhere in this direction, so I struck out hoping to find you. Where are the children?

GERTRUDE: They were here a little while ago…They'll be back.

MRS. CONSTABLE: I think I might sit down for a few minutes and wait for my bird to come back. I call Vivian my bird. Don't you think it suits her, Mrs. Eastman Cuevas?

GERTRUDE: (*Bored*) Yes.

MRS. CONSTABLE: (*She sits down on a cushion*) I miss her very badly already. It's partly because she has so much life in her. She finds so many things of interest to do and think about. (*She speaks with wonder in her voice*) I myself can't work up very much interest. I guess that's normal at my age. I can't think of much to do really, not being either a moviegoer, or a card player or a walker. Don't you think that makes me miss her more?

GERTRUDE: (*Icily*) It might.

MRS. CONSTABLE: This morning after I was cleaned and dressed I sat on the porch, but I got so tired of sitting there that I went to the front desk and asked them to tell me how to fish. They did and I bought this pole. The clerk gave me a kit with some bait in it. I think it's a worm. I'm not looking forward to opening the kit. I don't like the old hook either. I'll wager I don't fish after all. (*She sighs*) So you see what my days are like.

GERTRUDE: Don't you read?

MRS. CONSTABLE: I would love to read but I have trouble with concentration.

MR. SOLARES: (*Coming over and crouching next to* MRS. CONSTABLE
   on his heels) How are you feeling today, Mrs. Constable?
   What's new?

MRS. CONSTABLE: Not very well, thank you. I'm a little bit blue.
   That's why I thought I'd get a look at my bird.

MR. SOLARES: (*Still to* MRS. CONSTABLE) You're looking real good.
   (*Studying her crocheted dress*) That's handwork, ain't it?

MRS. CONSTABLE: (*Startled*) Why, yes.

MR. SOLARES: You like turtle steak?

MRS. CONSTABLE: What?

MR. SOLARES: Turtle steak. You like it, Mrs. Constable?

MRS. CONSTABLE: (*Stammering, bewildered*) Oh, yes...

GERTRUDE: Mr. Solares!

MR. SOLARES: (*Looking up*) What is it?

GERTRUDE: Perhaps I might try chop suey with you, after all. Did
   it originate in China or is it actually an American dish?

MR. SOLARES: I don't know, Miss Eastman Cuevas.
   (*Quickly turns again to* MRS. CONSTABLE.)

MRS. LOPEZ: (*Loudly to* GERTRUDE) Now you want to go eat chop
   suey because he's talkin' to the other lady. You be careful,
   Señora Eastman Cuevas or you gonna lose him. (*She chuckles.*)

GERTRUDE: (*Furious but ignoring* MRS. LOPEZ) I thought we might
   try some tonight, Mr. Solares—that is, if you'd like
   to...(*Bitterly*) Or have you lost your taste for chop suey?

MR. SOLARES: No, it's good. (*Turning to* MRS. CONSTABLE *again*) I'll
   call you up in your hotel and we'll go eat a real good turtle
   steak with fried potatoes one night. One steak would be too
   big for you, Mrs. Constable. You look like a dainty eater. Am
   I right?

GERTRUDE: (*Turns and sees* MOLLY *sitting on the rock*) Molly, we met
   Lionel. He's bringing the coats. (*She sees* MOLLY's *stricken face
   and questions her*) Molly, what's happened? (MOLLY *doesn't
   answer*) What is it, Molly? What's happened to you...Molly...
   what happened? What is it, Molly? (*Looking around for*
   VIVIAN) Where's Vivian? (MOLLY *still does not answer*)
   Molly...Where is she? Where's Vivian?

MOLLY: (*In a quavering voice*) She's gathering shells...
   (MRS. CONSTABLE *rises and starts looking vaguely for* VIVIAN.
   Then she sits down again. GERTRUDE *gathers her composure after
   a moment and speaks to* MR. SOLARES.)

GERTRUDE: (*Starts off and meets* LIONEL) Mr. Solares, I'm going home. It's windy and cold...The clouds are getting thicker every minute...The sun's not coming out again. I'm going back to the house.

LIONEL: (*Entering with the coats*) I brought these...I brought one for Vivian too.... Where's Vivian?

GERTRUDE: (*Takes sweater from* LIONEL) She's gathering shells. (*She puts sweater on* MOLLY'*s shoulders*) Molly, put this on, you'll freeze. (*She starts off and calls to* MR. SOLARES) I'm going home.

(MOLLY *rises and starts to leave and comes face to face with* MRS. CONSTABLE. *They look at each other a moment.* MOLLY *then rushes off following her mother.* MRS. CONSTABLE *goes back to the rock.* MR. SOLARES *and the Spanish people start to gather up their stuff and prepare to leave.*)

MR. SOLARES: We're coming right away, Miss Eastman Cuevas. (*He gives the servants orders in Spanish. Then to* MRS. CONSTABLE) Come on back to the house and I'll mix up some drinks.

MRS. CONSTABLE: No, thank you.

MRS. LOPEZ: (*Butting into the conversation*) You don't come?

MR. SOLARES: (*To* MRS. LOPEZ) Acaba de decir, no thank you...¿no oyes nunca?

(*The Spanish people all exit noisily.*)

LIONEL: (*As he leaves, sees* MRS. CONSTABLE *alone*) Aren't you coming Mrs. Constable?

MRS. CONSTABLE: I think I'll sit here and wait for my bird.

LIONEL: But she might climb up the cliffs and go home around the other way. It's getting colder Mrs. Constable...I could wait with you...

MRS. CONSTABLE: I don't want to talk. No, I'll just sit here and wait a little while.

LIONEL: (*Going off*) Don't worry, Mrs. Constable. She'll be all right.

MRS. CONSTABLE: (*Left alone on the stage*) I get so frightened, I never know where she's going to end up.

(*The curtain falls slowly*)

SCENE III

Same as Scene I. There is an improvised stand in the upper right-hand corner of the garden (the corner from the house), festooned with crepe paper and laden with a number of hot dogs, as well as part of a wedding cake and other things. MOLLY *is leaning against the stand wearing a simple wedding dress with a round shirred neck. She has removed her veil and she looks more like a girl graduating from school than like a bride. She is eating a hot dog. The stage is flooded with sunlight.*

GERTRUDE: (*Also in bridal costume. She is sitting on a straight-backed chair in the middle of the garden, with her own dress hiked above her ankles, revealing bedroom slippers with pompons. Eyeing* MOLLY) Molly! You don't have to stuff yourself just because the others stuffed so much that they had to go and lie down! After all, you and I are brides even if I did take off my shoes. But they pinched so, I couldn't bear it another minute. Don't get mustard spots all over your dress. You'll want to show it to your grandchildren some day.
(MOLLY's *mouth is so full that she is unable to answer. The hags and* ESPERANZA *are lying with their heads under the stand, for shade, and their legs sticking way out into the garden.* MRS. CONSTABLE *is wandering around in a widow's outfit, with hat and veil. She holds a champagne glass in her hand.*)
MRS. CONSTABLE: (*Stopping beside* GERTRUDE's *chair*) I don't know where to go or what to do next. I can't seem to tear myself away from you or Mr. Solares or Mrs. Lopez or Molly. Isn't that a ridiculous reaction? (*She is obviously tight*) I feel linked to you. That's the only way I can explain it. I don't ever want to have any other friends. It's as if I had been born right here in this garden and had never lived anywhere before in my life. Isn't that funny? I don't want ever to have any other friends. Don't leave me please. (*She throws her arms around* GERTRUDE) I don't know where to go. Don't leave me.
(*She squeezes* GERTRUDE *for a moment in silence.*)
GERTRUDE: Now you must stop brooding. Can't you occupy yourself with something?
MRS. CONSTABLE: (*Firmly*) I'm not brooding. I can think about it without feeling a thing, because if you must know it's just not real to me. I can't believe it. Now what does seem real is that

you and Mr. Solares are going away and deserting me and Mrs. Lopez and Molly and Lionel too. And I don't want to be anywhere except in this garden with all of you. Isn't it funny? Not that I'm enjoying myself, but it's all that I want to do, just hang around in this garden. (*She goes over to the stand rather unsteadily and pours some champagne into her glass out of a bottle. She takes a few sips, then bitterly in a changed tone*) I want to stay right here, by this stand.

GERTRUDE: (*Looking over her shoulder at* MRS. CONSTABLE) Drinking's not the answer to anything.

MRS. CONSTABLE: Answer? Who said anything about answers? I don't want any answers. It's too late for answers. Not that I ever asked much anyway. (*Angrily*) I never cared for answers. You can take your answers and flush them down the toilet. I *want* to be able to stay here. Right here where I am, and never, never leave this garden. Why don't you have a drink, or one of these lousy hot dogs? (*She brushes a few hot dogs off the stand, onto the grass.* MOLLY *stoops down and picks them up*) Let's stay here, Gertrude Eastman Cuevas, please.

GERTRUDE: You're being silly, Mrs. Constable. I know you're upset, but still you realize that I've sold the house and that Molly and I are going on honeymoons.

MRS. CONSTABLE: (*Vaguely*) What about Mrs. Lopez?

GERTRUDE: Well, now, I guess she has her own affairs to attend to, and Frederica. Mrs. Constable, I think a sanatorium would be the best solution for you until you are ready to face the world again.

MRS. CONSTABLE: (*Thickly*) What world?

GERTRUDE: Come now, Mrs. Constable, you know what I mean.

MRS. CONSTABLE: I know you're trying to be a bitch!

GERTRUDE: Mrs. Constable...I...(*She turns to* MOLLY *who has come to her side*) Molly, go inside. At once...(MOLLY *runs into the house*) Mrs. Constable, you ought to be ashamed. I won't tolerate such...

MRS. CONSTABLE: You have no understanding or feeling. Mrs. Lopez is much nicer than you are. You're very coarse. I know that even if I do hate to read. You're coarse, coarse and selfish. Two awful things to be. But I'm stuck here anyway so what difference does it make?

GERTRUDE: (*Refusing to listen to any more of her rambling*) Mrs. Constable, I'm surprised at you. I'm going in. I won't put up with this. What would Vivian think...

MRS. CONSTABLE: Vivian was a bird. How do you know what Vivian would feel? Do you know anything about birds? Vivian understood everything I did. Vivian loved me even if she did answer back and act snippy in company. She was much too delicate to show her true feelings all over the place like you do and like I do.

GERTRUDE: (*Crossing to* MRS. CONSTABLE) I've never in my life shown my feelings. I don't know what you're talking about!

MRS. CONSTABLE: (*Reeling about at the wedding table*) I don't know what I'm talking about...(*She grabs a bottle of champagne and offers it to* GERTRUDE) Have another drink, Miss Eastman Cuevas.

GERTRUDE: (*In disgust grabs the bottle from her and puts it on the table*) I don't like to drink!

MRS. CONSTABLE: Then have a hot dog. (*She drops it at* GERTRUDE's *feet.* GERTRUDE *starts toward the house.* MRS. CONSTABLE *stops her*) You and I grew up believing this kind of thing would never happen to us or to any of ours.

GERTRUDE: What?

MRS. CONSTABLE: We were kept far away from tragedy, weren't we?

GERTRUDE: No, Mrs. Constable. None of us have been kept from it.

MRS. CONSTABLE: Yes, well, now it's close to me, because Vivian hopped off a cliff—just like a cricket.

GERTRUDE: Life is tragic, Mrs. Constable.

MRS. CONSTABLE: I don't want tragic.

GERTRUDE: (*Can't put up with it any more*) Why don't you lie down on the grass and rest? It's dry. (GERTRUDE *starts toward the door of the house.* MRS. CONSTABLE *takes the suggestion and falls in a heap behind the stump under the balcony of the house*) Take your veil off. You'll roast! (MRS. CONSTABLE *complies and* GERTRUDE *goes into the house. The two old hags appear from behind the wedding table and start to take some hot dogs. They are stopped by* MOLLY *coming out of the house.* MOLLY *looks for a moment at the garden and then runs into her summer house. A moment later* GERTRUDE *calls to the garden from the balcony*) Molly? Molly, are you in the summer house?

MOLLY: Yes, I am.

GERTRUDE: They're getting ready. After we've left if Mrs.

Constable is still asleep, will you and Lionel carry her inside and put her to bed in my room? Tomorrow when you leave for the Lobster Bowl you can take her along and drop her off at her hotel. Poor thing. Be sure and clean up this mess in the morning. I have a list of things here I want you to attend to. I'll leave it on the table downstairs. Mr. Solares and I will be leaving soon.

MOLLY: No!

GERTRUDE: Yes.   *change in attitude*

MOLLY: <u>Please don't go away.</u> — *change in attitude*

GERTRUDE: Now, Molly, what kind of nonsense is this? You know we're leaving, what's the matter with you?

MOLLY: No, I won't let you go!

GERTRUDE: Please, Molly, no mysteries. It's very hard getting everyone started and I'm worn out. And I can't find my pocketbook. I think I left it in the garden. I'm coming down to look. (GERTRUDE *leaves the balcony to come downstairs.* MOLLY *comes out of the summer house and stands waiting with a small bunch of honeysuckle in her hands.* GERTRUDE *comes out of the house and crosses to the wedding table. She looks at* MOLLY *and sees her crying and goes to her*) What on earth is wrong, Molly? Why are you crying? Are you nervous? You've been so contented all day, stuffing yourself right along with the others. What has happened now?

MOLLY: <u>I didn't picture it.</u>

GERTRUDE: Picture what?

MOLLY: What it would be like when the time came. <u>Your leaving…</u>

GERTRUDE: Why not?

MOLLY: I don't know. I don't know…I couldn't picture it, I guess. I thought so long as we were here we'd go right on being here. So I just ate right along with the others like you say.

GERTRUDE: Well, it sounds like nonsense to me. Don't be a crybaby, and <u>wipe your tears.</u> *→ switched places*
(GERTRUDE *starts toward the table when she is stopped by* MOLLY *who puts the flowers in her hands.*)

MOLLY: Stay!

GERTRUDE: Molly. Put them back. They belong on your wedding dress.

MOLLY: No, they're from the vine. I picked them for you!

GERTRUDE: They're for your wedding. They belong to your dress. Here, put them back…

MOLLY: No...No...They're for you...They're flowers for you!
(GERTRUDE *does not know what to make of this strange and sud-*
den love and moves across the garden) I love you. I love you.
Don't leave me. I love you. Don't go away!

GERTRUDE: (*Shocked and white*) Molly, stop. You can't go on like
this!

MOLLY: I love you. You can't go!

GERTRUDE: I didn't think you cared this much. If you really feel
this way, why have you tormented me so... ⁊

MOLLY: I never have. I never have.

GERTRUDE: You have. You have in a thousand different ways.
What about the summer house?

MOLLY: Don't leave me!

GERTRUDE: And the vine?

MOLLY: I love you!

GERTRUDE: What about the vine, and the ocean, what about that?
If you care this much why have you tormented me so about
the water...when you knew how ashamed I was...Crazy,
unnatural fear...Why didn't you try to overcome it, if you
love me so much? Answer that!
(MOLLY, *in a frenzy of despair, starts clawing at her dress, pulling*
it open.)

MOLLY: I will. I will. I'll overcome it. I'm sorry. I'll go in the water
right away. I'm going now. I'm going...
(MOLLY *rips off her veil and throws it on the wedding table and*
makes a break for the gate to the ocean. GERTRUDE *in horror*
grabs MOLLY's *arm and drags her back into the garden.*)

GERTRUDE: Stop it! Come back here at once. Are you insane?
Button your dress. They'll see you...they'll find you this way
and think you're insane...

MOLLY: I was going in the water...

GERTRUDE: Button your dress. Are you insane! This is what I
meant. I've always known it was there, this violence. I've told
you again and again that I was frightened. I wasn't sure what I
meant...I didn't want to be sure. But I was right, there's
something heavy and dangerous inside you, like some terrible
rock that's ready to explode...And it's been getting worse all
the time. I can't bear it any more. I've got to get away, out of
this garden. That's why I married. That's why I'm going
away. I'm frightened of staying here with you any more. I
can't breathe. Even on bright days the garden seems like a

dark place without any air. I'm stifling!

(GERTRUDE *passes below the balcony on her way to the front door,* MRS. LOPEZ *tilts a vessel containing rice and pours it on* GERTRUDE'*s head.*)

MRS. LOPEZ: That's for you, bride number one! Plenty more when you go in the car with Solares. Ha ha! Frederica, ándele, ¡tú también!

(FREDERICA, *terribly embarrassed, tosses a little rice onto* GERTRUDE *and starts to giggle.*)

GERTRUDE: (*Very agitated, ill-humoredly flicking rice from her shoulders*) Oh, really! Where is Mr. Solares? Is he ready?

MRS. LOPEZ: My brother is coming right away. Where is bride number two?

GERTRUDE: (*Looking around for* MOLLY *who is back in the summer house*) She's gone back into the summer house.

(*She goes out.*)

MRS. LOPEZ: I got rice for her too! (*Calling down to the servants who are still lying with their heads under the food stand*) ¡Quinta! ¡Alta Gracia! ¡Esperanza! ¡Despiértense!

(*The servants wake up and come crawling out from under the food stand.*)

ESPERANZA: (*Scowling*) ¡Caray!

(*She takes an enormous comb out of her pocket and starts running it through her matted hair. There is a sound of a horn right after* ESPERANZA *begins to comb her hair.*)

FREDERICA: (*Beside herself with excitement*) It's Lionel back with the automobile, mama! It must be time. Tell the musicians to start playing!

MRS. LOPEZ: Yes, querida. ¡Música! (*She kisses her daughter effusively and they both exit from the balcony into the house talking and laughing.* LIONEL *enters from the lane, hurries across the lawn and into the house, just as* FREDERICA *and* MRS. LOPEZ *enter through the front door onto the lawn.* MRS. LOPEZ *calling to the servants*) Cuando salga la señora Eastman Cuevan de la casa, empezarán a cantar. (*She sings a few bars herself counting the time with a swinging finger and facing the servants, who rise and line up in a row. Calling to* MOLLY) Bride number two! Bride number two! Molly!

(*She takes a few steps toward the summer house and throws some rice at it. The rice gets stuck in the vines instead of reaching* MOLLY *inside. After a few more failures, she goes around to the front of the summer house and, standing at the entrance, she hurls handful after handful at* MOLLY. *Enter from the house* LIONEL, *and* MR. SOLARES. *The men are carrying grips.* MRS. CONSTABLE *is still stretched out in a corner where she won't interfere with the procession. Some very naive music starts back stage [sounding, if possible, like a Taxco band], as they proceed across the lawn; then the maids begin to sing. While this happens* MRS. LOPEZ *gradually ceases to throw her rice and then disappears in the summer house where she takes the weeping* MOLLY *into her arms.*)

LIONEL: Where's Molly?

MRS. LOPEZ: (*Over the music, from inside the summer house*) She don't feel good. She's crying in here. I cried too when I had my wedding. Many young girls do. I didn't want to leave my house neither.

(*She steps out of the summer house.*)

LIONEL: (*Calling*) I'll be back, Molly, as soon as I load these bags.

(*Enter* GERTRUDE *as* MRS. LOPEZ *comes out of the summer house. The music swells and the singing is louder.* GERTRUDE *walks rapidly through the garden in a shower of rice and rose petals.* MOLLY *comes out of the summer house and* GERTRUDE *stops. They confront each other for a second without speaking.* GERTRUDE *continues on her way.* MOLLY *goes back into the summer house.*)

GERTRUDE: (*From the road, calling over the music*) Good-bye, Molly! (*The wedding party files out, singing,* MRS. LOPEZ *bringing up the rear. She throws a final handful of rice at the summer house, but it does not reach. They exit.* MOLLY *is left alone on the stage. The music gradually fades.*)

LIONEL: (*Returning and coming into the garden*) Molly! (*There is no answer. He walks around to the front of the summer house and looks in*) Molly, I'm sorry you feel bad. (*Pause*) Why don't you come out? There's a very pretty sunset. (*He reaches in and pulls her out by the hands. He puts his arm around her shoulder and leads her toward the house*) We can go upstairs on the balcony and look at the sunset.

(*They disappear into the house and reappear on the balcony, where they go to the balustrade and lean over it.*)

MOLLY: (*Staring down into the garden, in a very small voice*) It looks different.

LIONEL: (*After gazing off into the distance very thoughtfully for a minute*) I've always liked it when something that I've looked at every day suddenly seems strange and unfamiliar. Maybe not always, but when I was home I used to like looking out my window after certain storms that left a special kind of light in the sky.

MOLLY: (*In a whisper*) It looks different...

LIONEL: A very brilliant light that illuminated only the most distant places, the places nearest to the horizon. Then I could see little round hills, and clumps of trees, and pastures that I didn't remember ever seeing before, very, very close to the sky. It always gave me a lift, as if everything might change around me but in a wonderful way that I wouldn't have guessed was possible. Do you understand what I mean?

(MOLLY *shakes her head, negatively. He looks at her for a moment, a little sadly.*)

MOLLY: (*Anguished, turning away from him*) I don't know. I don't know. It looks so different...

CURTAIN

ACT TWO

SCENE I

The Lobster Bowl, ten months later.
Just before dawn. The oyster-shell door is open and the sound of waves breaking will continue throughout this scene. MOLLY *and* LIONEL *are playing cards at one of the tables, Russian Bank or its equivalent. They are sitting in a circle of light. The rest of the stage is in darkness.* MRS. CONSTABLE *is lying on a bench but can't be seen.*

MOLLY: You just put a king on top of another king.

LIONEL: I was looking for an ace.

MOLLY: (*Smiling*) It's right here, silly, under your nose.

LIONEL: It's almost morning.

MOLLY: (*Wistful*) Can't we play one more game after this?

LIONEL: All right.

(*They play for a while in silence, then* LIONEL *stops again.*)

MOLLY: What is it?

LIONEL: Nothing.

MOLLY: I don't think you want to play at all. You're thinking about something else.

LIONEL: I had a letter from my brother...again.

MOLLY: (*Tense*) The one who's still in St. Louis?

LIONEL: That's right, the popular one, the one who'd like us to come back there.

MOLLY: He's big and tall.

LIONEL: Yes, he's big and tall, like most boys in this country. I've been thinking a lot about St. Louis, Molly...

MOLLY: Inez says we've got bigger men here than they have in Europe.

LIONEL: Well, Swedes are big and so are Yugoslavians...

MOLLY: But the French people are little.

LIONEL: Well, yes, but they're not as little as all that. They're not midgets. And they're not the way people used to picture them years ago, silly and carefree and saying Oo...la...la...all the time.

MOLLY: They're not saying Oo...la...la?

LIONEL: I don't know really, I've never been there. (*Dreaming, neglecting his cards*) Molly, when you close your eyes and

444

picture the world do you see it dark? (MOLLY *doesn't answer right away*) Do you, Molly? Do you see the world dark behind your eyes?

MOLLY: I...I don't know...I see parts of it dark.

LIONEL: Like what?

MOLLY: Like woods...like pine-tree woods.

LIONEL: I see it dark, but beautiful like the ocean is right now. And like I saw it once when I was a child...just before a total eclipse. Did you ever see a total eclipse?

MOLLY: I never saw any kind of eclipse.

LIONEL: I saw one with my brother. There was a shadow over the whole earth. I was afraid then, but it stayed in my memory like something that was beautiful. It made me afraid but I knew it was beautiful.

MOLLY: It's my game.

(*They start shuffling.*)

LIONEL: (*Tentative*) Did you ever worry about running far away from sad things when you were young, and then later getting older and not being able to find your way back to them ever again, even when you wanted to?

MOLLY: You would never want to find your way back to sad things.

LIONEL: But you might have lost wonderful things too, mixed in with the sad ones. Suppose in a few years I wanted to remember the way the world looked that day, the day of the eclipse when I saw the shadow.

MOLLY: (*Stops dealing her cards out very slowly, steeped in a dream*) She had a shadow.

LIONEL: And suppose I couldn't remember it. What Molly?

MOLLY: She had a shadow.

LIONEL: Who?

MOLLY: My mother.

LIONEL: Oh... (*He deals his cards out more rapidly, becoming deeply absorbed in his game.*)

MOLLY: It used to come and pass over her whole life and make it dark. It didn't come very often, but when it did she used to go downstairs and drink fizzy water. Once I went down when I was twelve years old. I waited until she was asleep and I sneaked down into the kitchen very quietly. Then I switched the light on and I opened the ice chest and I took out a bottle of fizzy water just like she did. Then I went over to the table and I sat down.

LIONEL: (*Without looking up from his cards*) And then...

MOLLY: I drank a little water, but I couldn't drink any more. The water was so icy cold. I was going to drink a whole bottle full like she did, but nothing...really nothing turned out like I thought it would. (LIONEL *mixes all his cards up together in a sudden gesture.* MOLLY *comes out of her dream*) Why are you messing up the cards? We haven't begun our game...(LIONEL *doesn't answer*) What's the matter?

LIONEL: Nothing.

MOLLY: But you've messed up the cards.

LIONEL: I was trying to tell you something...It meant a lot to me...I wanted you to listen.

MOLLY: I was listening.

LIONEL: You told me about fizzy water...and your mother. (MOLLY *automatically passing her hand over her own cards and messing them up*) I wanted you to listen. I don't want you to half hear me any more. I used to like it but...

MOLLY: (*Pathetic, bewildered*) I listen to you. We had a nice time yesterday...when...when we were digging for clams.

LIONEL: (*Looking back at her unable to be angry, now with compassion*) Yes, Molly, we did. We had a very good time...yesterday. I like digging for clams...(*They hold, looking at each other for a moment*) I'm going upstairs. I'm tired. I'm going to bed.
(LIONEL *exits up stairs.* MRS. CONSTABLE *comes out of the darkness, where she has been sleeping on her bench, into the circle of light.*)

MOLLY: You woke up.

MRS. CONSTABLE: I've been awake...for a while. I was waiting.

MOLLY: I won the game, but it wasn't much fun. Lionel didn't pay attention to the cards.

MRS. CONSTABLE: I was waiting because I wanted to tell you something...a secret...I always tell you my secrets...But there's one I haven't told you...I've known it all along...But I've never said anything to you...never before...But now I'm going to...I must.

MOLLY: (*Wide-eyed, thinking she is referring to* VIVIAN) It wasn't my fault! I didn't mean to...

MRS. CONSTABLE: My husband never loved me...Vivian?

MOLLY: Vivian! It wasn't my fault...I didn't...She...I didn't...
(MOLLY *starts to sob.*)

MRS. CONSTABLE: (*Clapping her hand over* MOLLY'*s mouth*)

Shhhhhh...They belonged to each other, my husband and Vivian. They never belonged to me...ever...But I couldn't admit it...I hung on hard to the bitter end. When they died...nothing was left...no memories...Everything vanished...all the panic...and the strain...I hardly remember my life. They never loved me...I didn't really love them...My heart had fake roots...when the strain was over, they dried up...they shriveled and snapped and my heart was left empty. There was no blood left in my heart at all...They never loved me! Molly...your mother...It's not too late...She doesn't...

MOLLY: (*Interrupting, sensing that* MRS. CONSTABLE *will say something too awful to hear*) My mother wrote me. I got the letter today. She *hates* it down in Mexico. She hates it there.

MRS. CONSTABLE: Molly, if you went away from here, I'd miss you very much. If you went away there wouldn't be anyone here I loved...Molly, go away...go away with Lionel...Don't stay here in the Lobster Bowl...

MOLLY: (*Commenting on her mother's letter and then reading from it*) She doesn't know how long she can stand it...She says she doesn't feel very well..."The climate doesn't suit me...I feel sick all the time and I find it almost impossible to sleep...I can't read very much...not at night...because the light is too feeble here in the mountains. Mrs. Lopez has two of her sisters here at the moment. Things are getting more and more unbearable. Mrs. Lopez is the least raucous of the three. I hope that you are occupying yourself with something constructive. Be careful not to dream and be sure..."

MRS. CONSTABLE: Why shouldn't you dream?

MOLLY: I used to waste a lot of time day-dreaming. I guess I still do. She didn't want me to dream.

MRS. CONSTABLE: Why shouldn't you dream? Why didn't she want you to?

MOLLY: Because she wanted me to grow up to be wonderful and strong like she is. Will she come back soon, Mrs. Constable? Will she make them all leave there? Will she?

MRS. CONSTABLE: I don't know dear...I don't know...I suppose she will...If she needs you, she'll come back. If she needs you, I'm sure she will.

MOLLY: Are you going to walk home along the edge of the water?

MRS. CONSTABLE: I like wet sand...and I like the spray.

MOLLY: You'll get the bottom of your dress all soaking wet. You'll catch cold.

MRS. CONSTABLE: I love the waves breaking in this early light...I run after them. I run after the waves...I scoop up the foam and I rub it on my face. All along the way I think it's beginning...

MOLLY: What?

MRS. CONSTABLE: My life. I think it's beginning, and then...

MOLLY: And then?

MRS. CONSTABLE: I see the hotel.

(MRS. CONSTABLE *exits through oyster-shell door.*)

MOLLY: (*She reads again part of her mother's letter*) "Two days ago, Fula Lopez went into the city and came back with a hideous white dog. She bought it in the street. The dog's bark is high and sharp. It hasn't stopped yapping since it came. I haven't slept at all for two nights. Now I'm beginning a cold..."

(*The lights fade as the curtain falls.*)

SCENE II

The Lobster Bowl. Two months later.

INEZ: (*She is middle-aged, full bosomed, spirited but a little coarse. She cannot see into* MOLLY'*s booth from where she stands behind the bar*) I'd rather hit myself over the head with a club than drag around here the way you do, reading comic books all day long. It's so damp and empty and quiet in here.

(*She shakes a whole tray of glasses in the sink, which makes a terrific racket.*)

MOLLY: It's not a comic book. It's a letter from my mother.

INEZ: What's new?

MOLLY: It came last week.

INEZ: What are you doing reading it now?

MOLLY: She's coming back today. She's coming back from Mexico.

INEZ: Maybe she'll pep things up a little. I hear she's got more personality than you. (*Shifts some oysters*) You didn't model yourself after her, did you?

MOLLY: No.

INEZ: Ever try modeling yourself after anyone?

MOLLY: No.

INEZ: Well, if you don't feel like you've got much personality yourself, it's an easy way to do. You just pick the right model and you watch how they act. I never modeled myself after anyone, but there were two or three who modeled after me. And they weren't even relatives—just ordinary girls. It's an easy way to do. (*Shifts some oysters*) Anyway, I don't see poring over comic books. I'd rather have someone tell me a good joke any day. What's really nice is to go out—eight or nine—to an Italian dinner, and sit around afterwards listening to the different jokes. You get a better selection that way! Ever try that?

MOLLY: I don't like big bunches of people.

INEZ: You could at least live in a regular home if you don't like crowds, and do cooking for your husband. You don't even have a hot plate in your room! (*Crash of stool to floor, followed by some high giggles*) There goes Mrs. Constable again. You'd think she'd drink home, at her hotel, where no one could see her. She's got a whole suite to herself there. It's been over a year since her daughter's accident, so I could say her drinking permit had expired. I think she's just on a plain drunk now. Right? (MOLLY *nods*) You sure are a button lip. As long as you're sitting there you might as well talk. It don't cost extra. (*She frowns and looks rather mean for a moment. There is more offstage racket*) I think Mrs. Constable is heading this way. I hope to God she don't get started on Death. Not that I blame her for thinking about it after what happened, but I don't like that topic.

(*Enter* MRS. CONSTABLE.)

MRS. CONSTABLE: (*She has been drinking*) How is everyone, this afternoon?

MOLLY: My mother's coming back today.

INEZ: I'm kind of rushing, Mrs. Constable. I've got to have three hundred oyster cocktails ready by tonight and I haven't even prepared the hot sauce yet.

MRS. CONSTABLE: Rushing? I didn't know that people still rushed...

INEZ: Here we go, boys!

MRS. CONSTABLE: Then you must be one of the fortunate ones who has not yet stood on the edge of the black pit. There is no rushing after that, only waiting. It seems hardly worthwhile even keeping oneself clean after one has stood on the edge of the black pit.

INEZ: If you're clean by nature, you're clean.

MRS. CONSTABLE: Oh, really? How very interesting!

INEZ: Some people would rather be clean than eat or sleep.

MRS. CONSTABLE: How very interesting! How nice that they are all so terribly interested in keeping clean! Cleanliness is so important really, such a *deep deep* thing. Those people who are so interested in keeping clean must have very deep souls. They must think a lot about life and death, that is when they're not too busy *washing*, but I guess washing takes up most of their time. How right they are! Hoorah for them! (*She flourishes her glass.*)

INEZ: (*With a set face determined to ignore her taunts*) The tide's pretty far out today. Did you take a look at the...

MRS. CONSTABLE: They say that people can't live unless they can fill their lives with petty details. That's people's way of avoiding the black pit. I'm just a weak, ordinary, *very ordinary* woman in her middle years, but I've been able to wipe all the petty details from my life...all of them. I never rush or get excited about anything. I've dumped my entire life out the window...like that! (*She tips her whisky glass and pours a little on the floor.*)

INEZ: (*Flaring up*) Listen here, Mrs. Constable, I haven't got time to go wiping up slops. I've got to prepare three hundred oyster cocktails. That means toothpicks and three hundred little hookers of hot sauce. I haven't got time to talk so I certainly haven't got time to wipe up slops.

MRS. CONSTABLE: I know...toothpicks and hot sauce and hookers. Very interesting! How many oysters do you serve to a customer? Please tell me.

INEZ: (*Only half listening to* MRS. CONSTABLE, *automatically*) Five.

MRS. CONSTABLE: (*Smirking as much as she can*) Five! How fascinating! Really and truly, I can't believe it!

INEZ: Balls! Now you get out and don't come back here until I finish my work. Not if you know what's good for you. I can feel myself getting ready to blow up! (*Shifts some more oysters*) I'm going upstairs now and I'm going to put a cold towel on my head. Then, I'm coming down to finish my oyster cocktails, and when I do I want peace and quiet. I've got to have peace and quiet when I'm doing my oyster cocktails. If I don't I just get too nervous. That's all.

MRS. CONSTABLE: I'm going...whether you're getting ready to blow up or not. (*She walks unsteadily toward exit. Then from the doorway*) I happen to be a very independent woman...But you are just plain bossy, Mrs. Oyster Cocktail Sauce.

(*Exit* MRS. CONSTABLE.)

INEZ: Independent! I could make her into a slave if I cared to. I could walk all over her if I cared to, but I don't. I don't like to walk all over anyone. Most women do...they love it. They like to take some other man or woman and make him or her into a slave, but I don't. I don't like slaves. I like everybody to be going his own independent way. Hello. Good-bye. You go your way and I'll go my way, but no slaves. I'll bet you wouldn't find ten men in this town as democratic as I am. (*Shifts some oysters*) Well, here I go. I guess I'll give myself a fresh apron while I'm up there. Then I'll be ready when they come for their oysters. (*Vaguely touching her head*) I don't like to eat oysters any more. I suppose I've seen too much of them, like everything else in life.

(*She pulls the chain on the big light behind the bar so that the scene darkens. There is a little light playing on* MOLLY's *booth and on the paper flowers and leaves.* MOLLY *puts her book of comics down, sits dreaming for a moment. There is summer house music to indicate a more lyrical mood. She pulls a letter out of her pocket and reads it. Enter* LIONEL.)

LIONEL: Hey.

MOLLY: Where were you?

LIONEL: I was walking along the beach thinking about something. Molly, listen. I got a wire this morning!

MOLLY: A wire?

LIONEL: Yes, from my brother.

MOLLY: The one in St. Louis? The one who wants us to come...

LIONEL: Yes, Molly. He has a place for me in his business now. He sells barbecue equipment to people.

MOLLY: To people?

LIONEL: Yes, to people. For their back yards, and he wants my help.

MOLLY: But...but you're going to be a religious leader.

LIONEL: I didn't say I wouldn't be, or I may end up religious without leading anybody at all. But wherever I end up, I'm getting out of here. I've made up my mind. This place is a fake. ✳

MOLLY: These oyster shells are real and so is the turtle. He just hasn't got his own head and feet. They're wooden.

LIONEL: To me this place is a fake. I chose it for protection, and it doesn't work out.

MOLLY: It doesn't work out?

LIONEL: Molly, you know that. I've been saying it to you in a thousand different ways. You know it's not easy for me to leave. Places that don't work out are ten times tougher to leave than any other places in the world.

MRS. CONSTABLE: My sisters used to have cherry contests. They stuffed themselves with cherries all week long and counted up the pits on Saturday. It made them feel exuberant.

[handwritten margin note: When reappear]

MOLLY: I can't eat cherries.

MRS. CONSTABLE: I couldn't either. I'd eat a few and I'd feel sick. But that never stopped me. I never missed a single contest. I despised cherry contests, but I couldn't stand being left out. Never. Every week I'd sneak off to the woods with bags full of cherries. I'd sit on a log and pit each cherry with a knife. Then I'd bury the fruit in a deep hole and fill it up with dirt. I cheated so hard to be in them, and I didn't even like them. I was so scared to be left out.

LIONEL: They are harder to leave, Molly, places that don't work out. I know it sounds crazy, but they are. Like it's three times harder for me to leave now than when I first came here, and in those days I liked the decorations. Molly, don't look so funny. I can explain it all some other way. (*Indicates oyster-shell door*) Suppose I kept on closing that door against the ocean every night because the ocean made me sad and then one night I went to open it and I couldn't even find the door. Suppose I couldn't tell it apart from the wall any more. Then it would be too late and we'd be shut in here forever once and for all. It's not going to happen, Molly. I won't let it happen. We're going away—you and me. We're getting out of here. We're not playing cards in this oyster cocktail bar until we're old.

MOLLY: (*Turns and looks up the stairs and then back to* LIONEL) If we had a bigger light bulb we could play in the bedroom upstairs.

LIONEL: (*Walking away*) You're right Molly, dead right. We could do just that. We could play cards up there in that God-forsaken bedroom upstairs.

(*Exits.*)

MRS. CONSTABLE: (*Gets up and goes to* MOLLY) Molly, call him back.

MOLLY: No, I'm going upstairs.

MRS. CONSTABLE: It's time...Go...go with Lionel.

MOLLY: My mother's coming. I'm going to her birthday supper.

MRS. CONSTABLE: Don't go there...

MOLLY: I'm late. I must change my dress. (*She exits up the stairs.*)

MRS. CONSTABLE: (*Stumbling about and crossing to the bar*) You're hanging on just like me. If she brought you her love you wouldn't know her. You wouldn't know who she was. (MRS. CONSTABLE *sinks into a chair below the bar.* GERTRUDE *enters. She is pale, distraught. She does not see* MRS. CONSTABLE) Hello, Gertrude Eastman Cuevas.

GERTRUDE: (*Trying to conceal the strain she is under*) Hello, Mrs. Constable. How are you?

MRS. CONSTABLE: How are you making out?

GERTRUDE: Molly wrote me you were still here. Where is she?

MRS. CONSTABLE: You look tired.

GERTRUDE: Where is Molly? (LIONEL *enters*) Lionel! How nice to see you! Where's Molly?

LIONEL: I...I didn't know you were coming.

GERTRUDE: Didn't you?

LIONEL: I didn't expect to see you. How are you, Mrs. Eastman Cuevas? How was your trip? When did you arrive?

GERTRUDE: Well, around two...But I *had* to wait...They were driving me here...Didn't you *know* I was coming?

LIONEL: No, I didn't.

GERTRUDE: (*Uneasily*) But I wrote Molly. I told her I was coming. I wanted to get here for my birthday. I wrote Molly that. Didn't she tell you about it? I sent her a letter. The paper was very sweet. I was sure that she would show it to you. There's a picture of a little Spanish dancer on the paper with a real lace mantilla pasted round her head. Didn't she show it to you?

LIONEL: (*Brooding*) No.

GERTRUDE: That's strange. I thought she would. I have others for her too. A toreador with peach satin breeches and a macaw with real feathers.

LIONEL: (*Unheeding*) She never said anything about it. She never showed me any letter.

GERTRUDE: That's strange. I thought...I thought...(*She hesitates, feeling the barrier between them. Tentative*) Macaws are called guacamayos down there.

LIONEL: Are they?

GERTRUDE: Yes, they are. Guacamayos...

LIONEL: What's the difference between them and parrots?

GERTRUDE: They're bigger! Much bigger.

LIONEL: Do they talk?

GERTRUDE: Yes, they do, but parrots have a better vocabulary. Lionel, my birthday supper's tonight. I suppose you can't come. You work late at night, don't you?

LIONEL: I work at night, but not for long...

GERTRUDE: You'll work in the day then?

LIONEL: No.

GERTRUDE: Then when will you work?

LIONEL: I'm quitting.

GERTRUDE: What?

LIONEL: I'm quitting this job. I'm getting out.

GERTRUDE: Getting out. What will you do? Where will you work?

LIONEL: I'm quitting. I'm going. (*He exits.*)

GERTRUDE: Lionel...Wait...Where are you going?

MRS. CONSTABLE: Come on over here and talk to me...You need a drink.

GERTRUDE: Where is she? Where's Molly?

MRS. CONSTABLE: She's gone down on the rocks, hunting for mussels.

GERTRUDE: Hunting for mussels? But she knew I was coming. Why isn't she here? I don't understand. Didn't she get my letter?

MRS. CONSTABLE: (*Dragging* GERTRUDE *rather roughly to a table*) Sit down...You look sick.

GERTRUDE: I'm not sick...I'm just tired, exhausted, that's all. They've worn me out in a thousand different ways. Even today...I wanted to see Molly the second we arrived, but I had to wait. I tried to rest. I had a bad dream. It's hanging over me still. But I'll be all right in a little bit. I'll be fine as soon as I see Molly. I'm just tired, that's all.

MRS. CONSTABLE: I'm glad you're well. How is Mrs. Lopez? If I were a man, I'd marry Mrs. Lopez. She'd be my type. We should both have been men. Two Spanish men, married to Mrs. Lopez.

GERTRUDE: She was part of the whole thing! The confusion...the racket...the pandemonium.

MRS. CONSTABLE: I like Mrs. Lopez, and I'm glad she's fat.

GERTRUDE: There were twelve of us at table every meal.

MRS. CONSTABLE: When?

GERTRUDE: All these months down in Mexico. Twelve of us at

least. Old ladies, babies, men, little girls, everyone jabbering, the noise, the screeching never stopped...The cooks, the maids, even the birds...

MRS. CONSTABLE: Birds?

GERTRUDE: Dirty noisy parrots, trailing around loose. There was a big one called Pepe, with a frightening beak.

MRS. CONSTABLE: (*Rather delighted*) Pepe?

GERTRUDE: Their pet, their favorite...Crazy undisciplined bird, always climbing up the table leg and plowing through the food.

MRS. CONSTABLE: (*Ingenuous*) Didn't you like Pepe?

GERTRUDE: (*Dejected, as if in answer to a sad question, not irritated*) No, I didn't like Pepe. I didn't like anything. Where's Molly? (*Going to oyster-shell door.*)

MRS. CONSTABLE: When are you going back?

GERTRUDE: Back? I'm never going back. I've made up my mind. From now on I'm staying in the house up here. It was a terrible mistake. I told him that. I told him that when he had to be there he could go by himself. We had a terrible fight...It was disgusting. When he stood there saying that men should never have given us the vote, I slapped him.

MRS. CONSTABLE: I never voted. I would vote all right if I could only register.

GERTRUDE: He's a barbarian. A subnormal human being. But it doesn't matter. He can stay down there as long as he likes. I'll be up here, where I belong, near Molly. (*Face clouding over*) What was he saying before? What did he mean?

MRS. CONSTABLE: Who?

GERTRUDE: Lionel. He said he was quitting. He said he was leaving, getting out of here.

MRS. CONSTABLE: Lionel's sick of the Lobster Bowl. I'm not. Molly likes it too, more than Lionel.

GERTRUDE: Molly. She couldn't like it here, not after our life in the ocean house.

MRS. CONSTABLE: Tell me more, Gertrude Eastman Cuevas. Did you enjoy the scenery?

GERTRUDE: What?

MRS. CONSTABLE: Down in Mexico.

GERTRUDE: I didn't enjoy anything. How could I, the way they lived? It wasn't even civilized.

MRS. CONSTABLE: (*Merrily*) Great big lunches every day.

GERTRUDE: There were three or four beds in every single room.

MRS. CONSTABLE: Who was in them?

GERTRUDE: Relatives, endless visiting relatives, snapping at each other, jabbering half the night. No wonder I look sick. (*Sadly to herself*) But I'll be fine soon. I know it. I will...as soon as I see Molly. If only she'd come back...(*To* MRS. CONSTABLE) Which way did she go? Do you think I could find her?

MRS. CONSTABLE: She always goes a different way.

GERTRUDE: She couldn't like it in this ugly place. It's not true!

MRS. CONSTABLE: They take long walks down the beach or go digging for clams. They're very polite. They invite me along. But I never accept. I know they'd rather go off together, all by themselves.

GERTRUDE: (*Alarmed*) All by themselves!

MRS. CONSTABLE: When they play cards at night, I like to watch them. Sometimes I'm asleep on that bench, but either way I'm around. Inez doesn't know about it. She goes to bed early. She thinks I leave here at a reasonable hour. She's never found out. I take off my shoes and I wade home at dawn.

GERTRUDE: I don't know what's happening to the people in this world.

(*Leaves* MRS. CONSTABLE)

MRS. CONSTABLE: Why don't you go back to Mexico, Gertrude Eastman Cuevas, go back to Pepe? (GERTRUDE *looks in disgust at* MRS. CONSTABLE. *More gently*) Then have a drink.

GERTRUDE: (*Fighting back a desire to cry*) I don't like to drink.

MRS. CONSTABLE: Then what do you like? What's your favorite pleasure?

GERTRUDE: I don't know. I don't know. I don't like pleasures. I...I like idealism and backbone and ambition. I take after my father. We were both very proud. We had the same standards, the same ideals. We both loved grit and fight.

MRS. CONSTABLE: You loved grit and fight.

GERTRUDE: We were exactly alike. I was his favorite. He loved me more than anyone in the world!

MRS. CONSTABLE: (*Faintly echoing*) More than anyone in the world...

GERTRUDE: (*Picking up one of the two boxes she brought with her and brooding over it*) It was a senseless dream, a nightmare.

MRS. CONSTABLE: What's in the box?

GERTRUDE: Little macaroons. I bought them for Molly on the way up. I thought she'd like them. Some of them are orange and some are bright pink. (*Shakes the box and broods again, troubled, haunted by the dream*) They were so pretty...

MRS. CONSTABLE: Aren't they pretty any more?

GERTRUDE: I had a dream about them just now, before I came. I was running very fast through the night trying to get to Molly, but I couldn't find the way. I kept losing all her presents. Everything I'd bought her I kept scattering on the ground. Then I was in a cold room with my father and she was there too. I asked him for a gift. I said, "I want something to give to my child," and he handed me this box...(*Fingering the actual box*) I opened it up, and took out a macaroon and I gave it to Molly. (*Long pause. She looks haunted, deeply troubled*) When she began to eat it, I saw that it was hollow, just a shell filled with dust. Molly's lips were gray with dust. Then I heard him...I heard my father. (*Excited*) He was laughing. He was laughing at *me*! (*She goes away from* MRS. CONSTABLE *to collect herself*) I've loved him so. I don't know what's happening to me. I've never been this way. I've always thrown things off, but now even foolish dreams hang over me. I can't shake anything off. I'm not myself...I...(*Stiffening against the weakness*) When I was in the ocean house...(*Covering her face with her hands and shaking her head, very softly, almost to herself*) Oh, I miss it so...I miss it so.

MRS. CONSTABLE: Houses! I hate houses. I like public places. Houses break your heart. Come and be with me in the Lobster Bowl. They gyp you, but it's a great place. They gyp you, but I don't care.

GERTRUDE: It was a beautiful house with a wall and a garden and a view of the sea.

MRS. CONSTABLE: Don't break your heart, Mrs. Eastman dear, don't...

GERTRUDE: I was happy in my house. There was nothing wrong. I had a beautiful life. I had Molly. I was busy teaching her. I had a full daily life. Everything was fine. There was nothing wrong. I don't know why I got frightened, why I married again. It must have been...it must have been because we had no money. That was it...We had so little money, I got frightened for us both...I should never have married. Now my life's lost its meaning...I have nightmares all the time. I lie awake in the night trying to think of just one standard or one ideal but something foolish pops into my head like Fula Lopez wearing city shoes and stockings to the beach. I've lost my daily life, that's all. I've lost Molly. My life has no meaning now. It's their fault. It's because I'm living their way. But I'm back now with Molly. I'm going to be fine again...She's coming with me tonight to my birthday supper...It's getting dark out. Where is she? (LIONEL *enters at bar with basket of glasses*) Lionel. Wait...

LIONEL: What is it?

GERTRUDE: What did you mean just now?

LIONEL: When?

GERTRUDE: Before...when I came in. You said you were going, getting out.

LIONEL: I am. I sent a wire just now.

GERTRUDE: Wire?

LIONEL: Yes, to my brother. I'm going to St. Louis. He has a business there.

GERTRUDE: But you can't do that! I've come back. You won't have to live in this stupid Lobster Bowl. You're going to be living in a house with *me*.

LIONEL: We'll never make a life, sticking around here. I've made up my mind. We're going away...

GERTRUDE: You talk like a child.

LIONEL: (*Interrupting*) I'm not staying here.

GERTRUDE: You're running away...You're running home to your family...to your brother. Don't you have any backbone, any fight?

LIONEL: I don't care what you think about me! It's Molly that...

GERTRUDE: What about Molly!

LIONEL: I've got to get Molly out of here, far away from everything she's ever known. It's her only chance.

GERTRUDE: You're taking her away from *me*. That's what you're doing.

LIONEL: You're like a wall around Molly, some kind of shadow between us. She lives...

GERTRUDE: (*Interrupting, vehement*) I'm not a shadow any more. I've come back and I'm staying here, where I belong with Molly! (LIONEL *looks at her with an expression of bitterness and revulsion*) What is it? Why do you look at me that way?

LIONEL: What way?

GERTRUDE: As if I was some terrible witch...That's it, some

terrible witch!

LIONEL: You're using her. You need Molly. You don't love her.
You're using her...

GERTRUDE: You don't know what you're talking about. You don't
know anything about me or Molly. You never could. You
never will. When she married she was desperate. She cried
like a baby and she begged me to stay. But you want to drag
her away from me—from her mother. She loves me more
than anyone on earth. She needs me. In her heart she's still a
child.

LIONEL: If you get what you want she'll stay that way. Let her go, if
you love her at all, let her go away...Don't stop her...

GERTRUDE: I can't stop her. How can I? She'll do what she likes,
but I won't stand here watching while you drag her away. I'll
talk to her myself. I'll ask her what she wants, what she'd really like to do. She has a right to choose.

LIONEL: To choose?

GERTRUDE: Between going with you and staying with me!
    (LIONEL *is silent. After a moment he walks away from*
    GERTRUDE. *Then to himself as if she were no longer there.*)

LIONEL: This morning she was holding her wedding dress up to
the light.

GERTRUDE: (*Proud*) She's going to wear it to my birthday supper.
It's a party dress, after all.

LIONEL: (*Not really answering*) She didn't say anything to me. She
just held her dress up to the light.

GERTRUDE: Go and find her. Get her now. Bring her back...tell
her I'm here.

LIONEL: If you go half way up those stairs and holler...

GERTRUDE: No, Mrs. Constable said she was hunting mussels on
the beach.

LIONEL: She's upstairs. (LIONEL *goes up to landing and calls*) Molly!
Your mother's here. She wants you. Come on down. Your
mother's back.
    (MOLLY *enters down stairs*. LIONEL *backs away and lurks in the
    shadows near the bar.*)

GERTRUDE: (*Tentative, starts forward to embrace her, but stops*) Molly,
how pretty you look! How lovely...and your wedding dress.

MOLLY: (*Spellbound, as if looking at something very beautiful just behind*
    GERTRUDE) I took it out this morning for your birthday.

GERTRUDE: I'm glad, darling. How are you? Are you well, Molly?

Are you all right?

MOLLY: Yes, I am.

GERTRUDE: (*Going to table*) I have something for you. A bracelet! (*She hooks necklace around* MOLLY's *neck*) And a necklace! They're made of real silver. Oh, how sweet you look! How pretty you look in silver! Just like a little girl, just as young as you looked when we were in the ocean house together. The ocean house, Molly! I miss it so. Don't you?

MOLLY: I knew you'd come back.

(*They sit down.*)

GERTRUDE: I knew it, too, from the beginning. They were strangers—all of them. I couldn't bear it. Nothing, really nothing meant anything to me down there, nothing at all. And you, darling, are you happy? What do you do in this terrible ugly place?

MOLLY: In the afternoon we hunt for mussels, sometimes, and at night we play cards...Lionel and me.

GERTRUDE: (*Uneasily*) I spoke to Lionel just now.

MOLLY: Did you?

GERTRUDE: Yes, about St. Louis.

MOLLY: (*Darkening*) Oh!

LIONEL: (*Coming over to them from the bar*) Yes, Molly. I'm arranging things now for the trip tomorrow. My mind's made up. If you're not coming with me, I'm going by myself. I'm coming down in a little while and you've got to tell me what you're going to do.

(LIONEL *exits upstairs.*)

GERTRUDE: You see. With or without you he's determined to go. Don't look frightened, Molly. I won't allow you to go. You're coming with me, with your mother, where you belong. I never should have let you marry. I never should have left you. I'll never leave you again, darling. You're mine, the only one I have...my own blood...the only thing I'm sure of in the world. (*She clasps* MOLLY *greedily to her breast*) We're going soon, but we've got to wait for them, Mrs. Lopez and Frederica. They're calling for us here. You're coming with me and you're never going back. Tonight, when you go to bed, you can wear my gown, the one you've always loved with the different colored tulips stitched around the neck. (*She notices* MOLLY's *strange expression and the fact that she has recoiled just a little*) What is it, dear? Don't you like the gown with the tulips any more? You used to...

MOLLY: (*As if from far away*) I like it.

GERTRUDE: Tomorrow, after Lionel has gone, I'll come back to pack you up. (*Fingering the necklace*) Did you like the paper with the dancing girl on it?

MOLLY: I have your letter here.

GERTRUDE: There are different ones at home—a toreador with peach satin breeches and a macaw with real feathers...(*It is obvious to her that* MOLLY *is not listening*) You've seen them, dear...Those big parrots...(*Anxiously*) Haven't you?

MOLLY: What?

GERTRUDE: (*Trying to ignore* MOLLY's *coldly remote behavior*) How could you bear it here in this awful public place after our life together in the ocean house?

MOLLY: I used to go back and look into the garden...over the wall. Then the people moved in and I didn't go there any more. But, after a while...

GERTRUDE: (*Cutting in*) I'll make it all up to you, darling. You'll have everything you want.

MOLLY: It was all right after a while. I didn't mind so much. It was like being there...

GERTRUDE: What, Molly? What was like being there?

MOLLY: After a while I could sit in that booth, and if I wanted to I could imagine I was home in the garden...inside the summer house.

GERTRUDE: That's over, Molly. That's over now. All over. I have a wonderful surprise for you, darling. Can you guess?

MOLLY: (*Bewildered*) I don't know. I don't know.

GERTRUDE: I ordered the platform built, and the trellis, and I know where I can get the vines. Fully grown vines, heavy with leaves...just like the ones...(*She is stopped again by* MOLLY's *expression. Then, touching her face apologetically*) I know, I know. I don't look well. I look sick. But I'm not...I'm not sick.

MOLLY: No, you don't look sick. You look...different. *prejudice*

GERTRUDE: It's their fault. It's because I'm living their way. But soon I'll be the same again, my old self.

(*Enter* MRS. LOPEZ *and* FREDERICA *carrying paper bags.*)

MRS. LOPEZ: ¡Inez! ¡Inez! Ya llegamos...

GERTRUDE: Here they are.

INEZ: (*Coming downstairs with a heavy tread*) Something tells me I hear Fula Lopez, the girl I love...

MRS. LOPEZ: (*Grabbing* INEZ *and whirling her around*) Inez...
Guapa...Inez. Aquí estamos...que alegría...We are coming
back from Mexico, Frederica, Fula...(*She spots* GERTRUDE)
and Eastman Cuevas. (*Then to* MOLLY, *giving her a big smacking kiss*) Molly...Hello, Molly! Inez, guapa, bring us three
limonadas, please...two for Fula and one for Frederica. Look,
look, Eastman Cuevas. We got gorgeous stuff. (*She pulls a
chicken out of a bag she is carrying and dangles it for* GERTRUDE)
Look and see what a nice one we got...Feel him!

GERTRUDE: No, later at home.

MRS. LOPEZ: Pinch him, see how much fat he got on him.

GERTRUDE: (*Automatically touching chicken for a second*) He's very
nice...(*Then swerving around abruptly and showing a stern fierce
profile to the audience*) Why is he here?

MRS. LOPEZ: (*Looking stupid*) Who?

GERTRUDE: The chicken. Why is he here?

MRS. LOPEZ: The chicken? He go home. We put him now with his
rice and his peas.

GERTRUDE: (*In a fury manifestly about the chicken. But her rage conceals panic about* MOLLY) But *what* rice and peas. You know
what we're having...I ordered it myself...It was going to be a
light meal...something *I* liked...for once...we're having jellied consommé and little African lobster tails.

MRS. LOPEZ: (*Crossing back to center tables and stopping near* MRS.
CONSTABLE) That's right, jelly and Africa and this one too.
(*She hoists chicken up in the air with a flourish. Enter* MRS.
CONSTABLE.)

MRS. CONSTABLE: A chicken. I hate chickens. I'd rather have a dog.
(FREDERICA *pulls a thin striped horn out of one of the paper bags
and blows on it.*)

GERTRUDE: Frederica, stop that. Stop that at once! I told you I
didn't want to hear a single horn on my birthday. This is a
party for adults. Put that away. Come along, we're leaving.
We'll leave here at once.

FREDERICA: (*In her pallid voice*) And Umberto? My uncle...

GERTRUDE: What about him?

FREDERICA: Uncle Umberto say he was calling for us to ride home
all together.

GERTRUDE: (*Automatically*) Where *is* he?

FREDERICA: He is with Pepe Hernández, Frederica Gómez, Pacito
Sánchez, Pepito Pita Luga...

GERTRUDE: No more names, Frederica...Tell him we're coming. We'll be right along...

MRS. LOPEZ: And the limonadas...

GERTRUDE: Never mind the limonadas. We're leaving here at once...Collect your bundles...Go on, go along.

(*The Mexicans start to collect everything, and there is the usual confusion and chatter.* FREDERICA *spills some horns out of her bag.* MRS. LOPEZ *screams at her, etc. They reach the exit just as* INEZ *arrives with the limonadas.*)

MRS. LOPEZ: (*Almost weeping, in a pleading voice to* GERTRUDE) Look, Eastman Cuevas, the limonadas!

FREDERICA: (*Echoing*) The limonadas...¡Ay!

GERTRUDE: No! There isn't time. I said we were leaving. We're leaving at once...

INEZ: (*To* MRS. LOPEZ *as they exit, including* MRS. CONSTABLE) Take them along...Drink them in the car, for Christ's sake.

MRS. LOPEZ: (*Off stage*) But the glasses...

INEZ: (*Off stage*) To hell with the glasses. Toss them down the cliff.

GERTRUDE: Molly, it's time to go. (MOLLY *starts for stairway*) Molly, come along. We're going. What is it, Molly? Why are you standing there? You have your silver bracelet on and the necklace to match. We're ready to leave. Why are you waiting? Tonight you'll wear my gown with the tulips on it. I told you that...and tomorrow we'll go and I'll show you the vines. When you see how thick the leaves are and the blossoms, you'll know I'm not dreaming. Molly, why do you look at me like that? What is it? What did you forget?

(LIONEL *comes downstairs.* GERTRUDE *stiffens and pulls* MOLLY *to her side with a strong hand, holding her there as a guard holds his prisoner.*)

GERTRUDE: Lionel, we're going. It's all settled. We're leaving at once. Molly's coming with me and she's not coming back.

MOLLY: (*Her voice sticking in her throat*) I...

LIONEL: (*Seeing her stand there, overpowered by her mother, as if by a great tree, accepts the pattern as utterly hopeless once and for all. Then, after a moment*) Good-bye, Molly. Have a nice time at the birthday supper...(*Bitterly*) You look very pretty in that dress.

(*He exits through oyster-shell door.*)

GERTRUDE: (*After a moment. Calm and firm, certain of her triumph*) Molly, we're going now. You've said good-bye. There's no point in standing around here any longer.

MOLLY: (*Retreating*) Leave me alone...

GERTRUDE: Molly, what is it? Why are you acting this way?

MOLLY: I want to go out.

GERTRUDE: Molly!

MOLLY: I'm going...I'm going out.

GERTRUDE: (*Blocking her way*) I'll make it all up to you. I'll give you everything you wanted, everything you've dreamed about.

MOLLY: You told me not to dream. You're all changed...You're not like you used to be.

GERTRUDE: I will be, darling. You'll see...when we're together. It's going to be the same, just the way it was. Tomorrow we'll go back and look at the vines, thicker and more beautiful...

MOLLY: I'm going...Lionel!

GERTRUDE: (*Blocking her way, fiendish from now on*) He did it. He changed you. He turned you against me. *life is change*

MOLLY: Let me go...You're all changed.

GERTRUDE: You can't go. I won't let you. I can stop you. I can and I will.

(*There is a physical struggle between them near the oyster-shell door.*)

MOLLY: (*Straining to get through the door and calling in a voice that seems to come up from the bottom of her heart*) Lionel!

GERTRUDE: I know what you did...I didn't want to...I was frightened, but I knew...You hated Vivian. I'm the only one in the world who knows you. (MOLLY *aghast ceases to struggle. They hold for a moment before* GERTRUDE *releases her grip on* MOLLY. *Confident now that she has broken her daughter's will forever*) Molly, we're going...We're going home.

MOLLY: (*Backing away in horror*) No!

GERTRUDE: Molly, we're going! (MOLLY *continues to retreat*) If you don't (MOLLY, *shaking her head still retreats*) If you don't, I'll tell her! I'll call Mrs. Constable.

MOLLY: (*Still retreating*) No...

GERTRUDE: (*Wild, calling like an animal*) Mrs. Constable! Mrs. Constable! (*To* MOLLY, *shaking her*) Do you see what you're doing to me! Do you? (MRS. CONSTABLE *appears in doorway.* GERTRUDE *drags* MOLLY *brutally out of her corner near the staircase and confronts her with* MRS. CONSTABLE) I have something to tell you, Mrs. Constable. It's about Molly. It's about my daughter...She hated Vivian. My daughter hated yours and a terrible ugly thing happened...an ugly thing happened on the cliffs...

MRS. CONSTABLE: (*Defiantly*) Nothing happened...Nothing!

GERTRUDE: (*Hanging on to* MOLLY, *who is straining to go*) It *had* to happen. I know Molly...I know her jealousy...I was her whole world, the only one she loved...She wanted me all to herself...I know that kind of jealousy and what it can do to you...I know what it feels like to wish someone dead. When I was a little girl...I...(*She stops dead as if a knife had been thrust in her heart now. The hand holding* MOLLY's *in its hard iron grip slowly relaxes. There is a long pause. Then, under her breath*) Go...(MOLLY's *flight is sudden. She is visible in the blue light beyond the oyster-shell door only for a second. The Mexican band starts playing the wedding song from Act One.* GERTRUDE *stands as still as a statue.* MRS. CONSTABLE *approaches, making a gesture of compassion*) The band is playing on the beach. They're playing their music. Go, Mrs. Constable...Please.

(MRS. CONSTABLE *exits through oyster-shell door.*)

FREDERICA: (*Entering from street, calling, exuberant*) Eastman Cuevas! Eastman Cuevas! Uncle Umberto is ready. We are waiting in the car...Where's Molly? (*She falters at the sight of* GERTRUDE's *white face. Then, with awe*) Ay dios...¿Qué pasa? ¿Qué tiene? Miss Eastman Cuevas, you don't feel happy? (*She unpins a simple bouquet of red flowers and puts it into* GERTRUDE's *hand*) For your birthday, Miss Eastman Cuevas...your birthday...

(*She backs away into the shadows, not knowing what to do next.* GERTRUDE *is standing rigid, the bouquet stuck in her hand.*)

GERTRUDE: (*Almost in a whisper, as the curtain falls*) When I was a little girl...

TROUBLE IN MIND

A Comedy-Drama in Two Acts

ALICE CHILDRESS

First presented in 1955

FOREWORD

In an essay entitled "A Woman Playwright Speaks Her Mind," Alice Childress observes that "the Negro woman has almost been omitted as important subject matter in the general popular American drama, television, motion pictures and radio." She adds: "The Negro woman will attain her rightful place in American literature when those of us who care about truth, justice and a better life tell her story, with the full knowledge and appreciation of her constant, unrelenting struggle against racism and for human rights." That is the project to which Childress has dedicated her long and distinguished career.

Childress traces her roots back to "a particular American slave, my great grandmother, Annie," about whom she is currently writing a book. The playwright was born in Charleston, South Carolina, October 12, 1920, and grew up in Harlem. After economic necessity forced her to drop out of high school, she educated herself by reading prodigiously in the library—perhaps one reason she is committed to writing works for young people. Childress spent a decade performing and directing with the American Negro Theatre, which she helped found; she appeared on Broadway in *Anna Lucasta*, and also did radio and television work. Like virtually all actors of color, however, Childress consistently confronted racism when she ventured outside Black theater companies; in her case she was told that she was "too light" to be cast in Black roles but of course could not be cast in "White roles." She revealed in an essay "I never planned to become a writer" but decided she would have more artistic freedom if she herself were creating the plays. Recalling the days of slavery, Childress also notes the ironic satisfaction she got from such a career, because African Americans "are the only racial group within the United States ever forbidden by law to read and write."

Although Childress' teachers had urged her to focus on African Americans who were "accomplishers," she chose instead "to write about those who come in second, or not at all.... My writing attempts to interpret the 'ordinary' because they are not ordinary." Her first play, the one-act *Florence* (1949), was written quickly to prove that such "ordinary" people and events could be the substance of compelling drama. Set in a segregated railway station waiting room in "a very small town in the South," *Florence* depicts a confrontation between Mama, a Black woman going to New York City to bring home her daughter, and Mrs. Carter, an apparently well-meaning White woman. When Mrs. Carter, who claims to be an actor, learns that Mama's daughter Florence has failed to establish an acting career, she offers to help the young woman get a job. But Mama soon discovers that the promised "job" is, in reality, as a domestic servant; angry and moved to action, she sends money to Florence to "keep trying" to fulfill her dream despite the Mrs. Carters of the world. *Florence*, which Childress herself directed and in which she later starred, was followed by *Just a Little Simple* (1950), an adaptation of a Langston Hughes work that was the first play by a Black woman professionally produced (i.e., with union contracts) on the American stage. In 1952 she wrote *Gold Through the Trees;* according to Doris Abramson in *Negro Playwrights in the American Theatre, 1925-1959*, this work includes "an Ashanti warrior's dance, modern dance, the Blues, sketches about Harriet Tubman and about the present-day freedom movement."

Trouble in Mind, billed in press releases as a "comedy-drama," was Childress' first original full-length play. *Trouble* premiered at the Greenwich Mews Theatre on West 13th St. on November 3, 1955, co-directed by Childress and Clarice Taylor, who starred as Wiletta Mayer. According to critic Harry Raymond, the audience "applauded and shouted bravos, and would not leave their seats until the author was brought on stage." Raymond called *Trouble* "a sparkling play of protest...which bubbles with humor and at the same time has deep meaning," and Arthur Gelb of the *New York Times*, although unhappy with what he considered the didacticism of the last few minutes of the evening, agreed that it is "a fresh, lively and cutting satire." Gelb added that *Trouble* "has some witty and penetrating things to say about the dearth of roles for Negro actors in the contemporary theatre, the cutthroat competition for these parts and the fact that Negro actors often find themselves playing stereotyped roles in which they cannot bring themselves to believe." Slated for a limited run, *Trouble* was extended through February 19, 1956, a total of ninety-one performances; it also garnered an Obie Award for the best original off-Broadway play of the season.

Trouble in Mind was optioned for Broadway and announcements appeared in New York newspapers that the play, retitled *So Early Monday Morning*, would reopen in the spring of 1957. It never did. According to Childress, "They had me rewrite for two years" but were never satisfied with the results because she refused to give them the "heart-warming little story" they wanted. Not surprisingly, Broadway was wary of a play whose very subject is the racism of the American commercial theater. Like Shirley Graham before her, Childress found her goal of a Broadway production unreachable. *Trouble* has, however, been revived numerous times in this country and abroad, including productions at Cleveland's Karamu Theatre and New York's Woman's Interart Center, a B.B.C. broadcast in England in 1964 and a London stage premiere in October of 1992. Reviewing a 1967 revival, Abiola Sinclair pronounced *Trouble* as "fresh, vibrant and timely as it ever was." The London production received nearly unanimous approbation from critics who wondered why it took nearly four decades for the work to reach the British theater. Jane Searle in the *Tribune* found *Trouble*'s arguments about speaking out "as relevant now as ever" and Jeremy Kingston in *The Times* called it a "fascinating and spirited play"; among the most enthusiastic was Irving Wardle in the *Independent*, who praised *Trouble* as "a humane and well-characterised study of artistic compromise" in which "for once, the theater is telling the truth about itself."

As critic Samuel A. Hay suggests, *Trouble* is in many ways an extension of *Florence*, not only in its concern with the theater but in its firm rooting in the political events of the period. *Trouble* is clearly set in the context of the social upheavals of the fifties: Sheldon can't find a decent place to live in the overcrowded, segregated post-war housing market; references are made to the Montgomery, Alabama, bus boycott and the violence that accompanied desegregation of Little Rock's Central High School.

Interestingly, some of these references were added after the original production (the Little Rock riots didn't occur until 1957), suggesting how future events would expand the play rather than render it obsolete.

Allusions to current events are common in Childress' canon, for she knows that all art is political and that art not only reflects but helps create the "reality" outside the theater's walls. Childress was on the stage for many years and *Trouble in Mind*—a largely plotless work about a group of performers rehearsing a play entitled "Chaos in Belleville"—grows out of her own experience as an African American woman told how to look and act by White male dramatists and directors. Comparing *Florence* to *Trouble*, Hay adds: "Mama...was simply asking Mrs. Carter to help Florence survive. But in 1955, Willetta demands that Manners let Black people control their own projected images." The White director Al Manners in *Trouble* is not quite the one-dimensional villain some critics have implied; he is a 1950s liberal forced to confront both his own hypocrisy and the damage caused by his cowardice. Manners clings to the liberal claim "there is only one race...the human race" until, in a moment of passion, he reveals that he is giving lip-service to a concept in which he doesn't finally believe: his son, he is convinced, has "nothing in common" with the lynched young man in "Chaos in Belleville"—or, by extension, the children being stoned in Little Rock. Even more important, however, is his involvement with "Chaos in Belleville," a play written, directed and produced by Whites that claims to portray the unhappy plight of poor African Americans. By using metatheater—a play-within-a-play—Childress forces us to explore the nature of the theatrical image being created; the complex connections among characters, actors and audience members; and the extent to which relationships between Blacks and Whites inside and outside the theater are based on carefully scripted roles.

Manners is surely right that few directors in the period would be willing to work on a show about racial themes with a predominantly Black cast, and that White audiences "don't want to believe" or see people of color as they really are and "want to be seen." (The failure of Broadway producers to risk showing *Trouble in Mind* is ironic proof of his claim.) Yet he cannot understand that a White liberal "version" of African American life is no substitute for Black people defining who they are and what they have experienced. The fraudulence of "Chaos in Belleville" is most obvious when the elderly actor Sheldon offers a moving account of the lynching that he witnessed as a child, a description at sharp odds with the sanitized melodrama of "Belleville." The ring of authenticity in Sheldon's account points up the shabby clichés of the interior drama.

"Chaos in Belleville" is not only a bad reflection of reality, it is an example of how drama by White authors differs from, and usurps the place of, drama by playwrights of color. "Chaos in Belleville" purports to contain "an anti-lynch theme," yet it bears little resemblance to the anti-lynch dramas written by African Americans, particularly women. In Angelina Weld Grimké's *Rachel* (1916), Rachel's mother is helpless against the mob that brutally murders her husband and son. The mother in Georgia Douglas Johnson's *Blue-Eyed Black Boy* (ca. 1930) appeals to the governor of the state (who raped her long ago) to save their child, while the grandmother in Johnson's *A Sunday Morning in the South* (ca. 1925) desperately tries to rescue her unjustly accused grandson. In none of these plays does a mother blame her son for White bigotry and turn him over to an angry mob, and none offers as hero a White man like Renard, who preaches tolerance and pity *after* Job has been killed. "Chaos in Belleville" is a distorted mirror not only of actual events but of the way those events have been interpreted for the stage by African Americans themselves.

The metatheatrical structure of *Trouble* thus allows Childress to write a critique of the history of the American stage, where plays by (usually male) White writers purporting to show the Black experience have been embraced while dramas by African American writers are ignored. Wiletta advises John to please Manners by saying he was in a revival of *The Green Pastures*, White author Marc Connelly's immensely popular play in which "Mammy Angels" prepare fish fries in heaven. Like its "real" dramatic predecessors, "Chaos" silences Black voices by pretending to tell their story, thus insuring that the works of Black writers will never see the light of the stage. (Why tell a tale that's already been told?) In writing *Trouble in Mind*, Alice Childress simultaneously explores the hypocrisy of having White playwrights interpret African American life and also writes herself into the long line of African American women dramatists—Angelina Weld Grimké, Georgia Douglas Johnson, May Miller, Alice Dunbar-Nelson, Regina Andrews—whose plays have served to expose one of White America's most heinous cultural crimes.

Childress once said in an interview, "I certainly consider myself a feminist writer," and "Chaos" also explores the parallels between paternalism toward White women and paternalism toward people of color. Elizabeth Brown-Guillory, in *Their Place on the Stage: Black Women Playwrights in America*, identifies the ways in which Manners attempts to silence the female and the African American cast members, waving his arms at them dismissively, ignoring their suggestions for script changes while agreeing to discuss Bill O'Wray's comments with the playwright. Following a lecherous look at Judy's "nice shoulders," Manners is intimidated to learn that she's been to Yale Drama School (he apparently likes both his female and his Black actors to be "natural" talents) and thereafter mockingly calls her "Yale." When Wiletta disagrees with him he insists she's "confused," even threatening to spank her as if she were a wayward child.

The woman to whom Manners condescends, Wiletta Mayer, is one of Childress' many strong, independent female characters — and to some extent a spokesperson for the playwright herself. While Wiletta's protective attitude toward John could be considered maternal, she is clearly not one of the passive Black "mammies" of which White dramatists were so fond. Wiletta foreshadows such Childress heroes as Julia Augustine in *Wedding Band* and Tommy in *Wine in the Wilderness* who go through a learning process as their plays progress at the same time as they educate those around them. The first acting lesson in *Trouble* is not given by Manners but by Wiletta, who instructs young John to agree with everything the director says and laugh at anything that might be construed as a joke because it "makes 'em feel superior." This way of dealing with racism is associated with Sheldon, who long ago learned that appeasement was the route to survival. Sheldon's approach cannot easily be dismissed—he's now an old man who needs this acting job to pay for groceries and rent—but Wiletta eventually realizes how dangerous it can be. Childress' characters often have a moment of revelation and Wiletta's comes when she hears herself saying, "Lord, have mercy, don't ask me 'cause I don't know"—the exact same line the author of "Chaos in Belleville" wrote for Ruby. Wiletta sees that by agreeing to play the acquiescent mammy, she is perpetuating the stereotype that is used to keep Black women powerless. From this point on she becomes increasingly vociferous about her objections to "Chaos in Belleville" and eventually urges John, who has begun to imitate his

White "master," Manners, to join in her protest. Wiletta also offers a brief retrospective of the "character parts" she has enacted during her career: mothers asking Whites to help keep Black sons from demanding equality; loyal wives to "lazy, no-good, two-timin" men; and devoted nursemaids (not unlike Hellman's Addie in *The Little Foxes*) who hand over to their White charges their "whole damn life."

There are several versions of the conclusion of *Trouble in Mind* and the outcome of Wiletta's protest differs in each. Childress has said that the Board of the Greenwich Mews Theater, where the play premiered, wanted a happy ending, a rapprochement. She adds, "I kept doing rewrites" until everyone in the cast "walked off hand in hand as friends. It was and is a formula thing of the time." While they were not as determined on a pat, sanguine conclusion as potential Broadway producers apparently were, the Board members encouraged Childress to create an upbeat, racially unified curtain scene. The ending performed at the Greenwich Mews is presumably similar to that of the script Doris Abramson discusses in *Negro Playwrights*, in which "Wiletta tells the director that she forgives him and loves him" and Manners replies, "I, a prejudiced man, ask you, a prejudiced cast, to wait until our prejudiced author arrives tomorrow. I propose that we sit down in mutual blindness and try to find a way to bring some splinter of truth to a prejudiced audience." Abramson adds, "The play ends on a note of optimism, although there is little doubt that the soldiers have many battles ahead of them." It's likely that Childress always intended a note of hope at the curtain; virtually all her literary works end with the *possibility* of change and reconciliation among the characters. In addition, the popular Richard M. Jones blues song which gave the play its title opens and closes with the stanza:

> Trouble in mind
> I'm blue
> But I won't be blue always
> The sun will shine in my back door someday.

Still, when Childress allowed *Trouble in Mind* to be published, she included the ending reprinted in this volume, which neither implies that the African American actors are "prejudiced" nor suggests that Wiletta will have the support of all her colleagues. This ending shows the differences among the actors—Sheldon feels he cannot afford to join Wiletta's protest and Millie is unlikely to sacrifice her material desires to her principles—while questioning any possibility of "conversion" in Manners. It also acknowledges a bond among all oppressed peoples, for Wiletta finds a sympathetic listener in the Irish doorman, Henry.

Trouble in Mind does suffer at times from didacticism—a sense that, as Abramson suggests, "the author [is] pulling strings, putting her own words into a number of mouths"—a problem that reoccurs in some of Childress' later work as well. But it is crucial to realize how revolutionary *Trouble in Mind* is in its sweeping critique of American drama and its insistence that African American women have the right—as Ntozake Shange would insist two decades later in *for colored girls*—to "sing a black girl's song." Commenting on a 1979 revival of *Trouble*, Sally R. Sommer in the *Village Voice* notes "its double cutting edge: It predicts not only the course of social history but the course of black playwriting."

Trouble in Mind came early in what would be an illustrious career for Alice Childress. She has written more than a dozen plays, including *Wedding Band: A Love/Hate Story in Black and White*, which explores the different ways a group of African American women cope in a segregated society that grants them neither economic nor legal power. Set in South Carolina during World War I, *Wedding Band* focuses on the story of Julia Augustine, who learns how much she has in common with the other Black women in her community and how complicated it is to love a White man whose racism—bred in him by his family and culture—hovers just below the surface. Childress in an interview insisted, "It was a play I did not want to write, about people few others wanted to hear from." Although an early version of *Wedding Band* was performed at the University of Michigan in 1966 to what Ruby Dee characterizes as "rave reviews," the play did not open on the New York stage until nearly seven years later. Childress co-directed the 1972-3 production at the off-Broadway Public Theater, which earned mixed notices from White critics. Clive Barnes of the *New York Times* rather bewilderingly characterized *Wedding Band* as "a sweet old love story" but also candidly acknowledged: "We are so used to the black stereotypes thrust on us" by literature and films of the World War I era "that it is difficult to judge the credibility of a black play deliberately set more than half a century ago." In the same newspaper, Walter Kerr reverted to the condescending vocabulary male critics frequently use in writing about women's plays when he concluded that "there are both pleasant and bitter little home-truths bobbing about" in *Wedding Band*. The Public Theater production ran for six months; according to Rosemary Curb in *Notable Women in the American Theatre*, *Wedding Band* also "was optioned for Broadway several times but never produced because it was controversial." A 1974 television adaptation broadcast by ABC was banned by some local stations and received delayed airing—after the late news—on others, presumably because of its unflinching look at interracial relationships and racial conflict.

Originally written as a television drama, *Wine in the Wilderness* (1969) is set against the urban riots of the sixties and offers Tomorrow Marie as still another indomitable Childress hero. Tommy is uneducated and has lost her few belongings in the riot, yet she is more than a match for Bill, Cynthia and Sonny-man— African American artists and intellectuals whose talk of "brothers" and "sisters" masks a deep disdain for ordinary people who lack their advantages. Particularly important in *Wine*—as in the one-act *Mojo: A Black Love Story* (1970)—is the relationship between African American women and the men who absorb White society's contempt for them; in Childress' plays neither White men like Manners nor Black men like Bill have the right to define what Black women are and, even worse, how they *ought* to be.

The role of social class in African American relationships is also central in these works. Teddy in *Mojo*, for example, fills his house with "expensive junk and gadgetry" and spends his time with a wealthy White girlfriend. His former wife, Irene, forces Teddy to see how difficult love is for people who earn their living cleaning toilets and carrying garbage, but love is all the more important because they *don't* have the advantages that "white folks write stories bout." Finally, Childress' dramatic works are deeply rooted in the history of Black Americans and in changing attitudes toward that history. The middle-aged Irene teaches a skeptical Teddy to appreciate the richness of African culture, a lesson about "a good blackness...a blackness I never knew" that she has learned from the young people in her neighborhood. Among Childress' more recent plays are two musical works, *Gullah* (also called *Sea Island Song*; ca. 1979) about the lives of Blacks on the South Carolina Sea Islands, and *Moms: A Praise Play for a Black Comedienne* (1986), with lyrics and music by Childress and her husband, musician Nathan Woodard.

Childress acknowledges that even her fictional works—

including *Like One of the Family* (1956), *A Hero Ain't Nothin' but a Sandwich* (1973) and *Rainbow Jordan* (1982)—read like plays because "I think mainly in terms of visual, staged scenes and live actors in performance—even in a novel." *Like One of the Family*, subtitled "conversations from a domestic's life," is a series of dramatic monologues in which Mildred talks to her friend Marge about her White employers. Mildred touches on every subject from subway signs to Harriet Tubman as she explores the uneasy relationship between herself and these women, some of whom are truly considerate while others are blatantly insulting. The ironic title refers to the White women's claim that Mildred is "like one of the family"—despite the fact that she cleans the house, cooks and serves the dinner, and eats her own meals in the kitchen. *A Short Walk* (1979) traces the career of Cora James, born in South Carolina at the turn of the twentieth century, whose life encapsulates much of African American history from 1900-1950. When Cora moves to Harlem, she finds a more subtle Northern form of segregation: in Broadway theaters, for example, people of color are herded "all together in one section, with not a sign in sight." Cora becomes involved with Marcus Garvey's Black separatist movement, but her main commitment is necessarily to her own survival: "Papa said one hope a woman has is a good provider. Well, my provider might just turn out to be me." Before she dies, Cora sees her daughter take advantage of opportunities never available to her.

A Hero Ain't Nothin' but a Sandwich is the most famous of Childress' works for children, in part because—despite earning numerous honors, including a National Book Award nomination and a Best Young Adult Book citation from the American Library Association—it was banned from several school libraries. Some parents objected to the fact that *Hero* tells the story of a thirteen-year-old drug addict who talks knowledgeably about skinpopping and mainlining, while others protested a scene in which a teacher points out that his classroom walls feature a picture of slave-holder George Washington but no portraits of African Americans. Along with eight other books, including works by Kurt Vonnegut and Bernard Malamud, *Hero* was returned to one Long Island school's library shelves only after a ruling by the Supreme Court. Like Benjie Johnson in *Hero*, the title character in *Rainbow Jordan* finds an adult willing to help her try to regain control of her young life. Childress' powerful children's books and dramas—which include

When the Rattlesnake Sounds (1975), a play about Harriet Tubman—address the same issues of racism, classism and sexism that she confronts in her writings for adults, and they likewise disturb those who would prefer to pretend these problems don't exist.

In addition to her work in fiction and theater, Childress has written the award-winning screenplay for *A Hero Ain't Nothin' but a Sandwich* and television adaptations of *Wedding Band* and her short play *String*. When *Sea Island Song* premiered, "Alice Childress Week" was observed in both Columbia and Charleston, South Carolina, and over the years Childress has received numerous honors, including a Rockefeller grant, the Sojourner Truth Award from the National Association of Negro Business and Professional Women's Clubs, the Coretta Scott King Award and the first Paul Robeson Award for Outstanding Contributions to the Performing Arts from the Black Filmmaker's Hall of Fame. She has lectured widely at schools and universities and was a visiting scholar at the Radcliffe Institute for Independent Study (now the Mary Ingraham Bunting Institute).

Alice Childress' exceptional career in the theater has spanned more than half a century. She has always known the odds against her. "There aren't any black critics who can close a white play," she said recently, "But in black theater, black experience has been fought against by white critics. The white critic feels no obligation to prepare himself to judge a black play." Such obstacles, however, have not stopped her from making her voice heard in print and on stage. Childress has fought against racism and sexism to provide audiences with truthful depictions of the lives of African Americans, particularly women—an achievement that has helped change the American theatrical landscape.

SELECTED BIBLIOGRAPHY

Abramson, Doris E. *Negro Playwrights in the American Theatre 1925-1959*. N.Y.: Columbia UP, 1967.

Austin, Gayle. "Alice Childress: Black Woman Playwright as Feminist Critic." *Southern Quarterly* (Spring 1987): 53-62.

Betsko, Kathleen, and Rachel Koenig. *Interviews with Contemporary Women Playwrights*. N.Y.: Beech Tree Books, 1987.

Brown-Guillory, Elizabeth. *Their Place on the Stage: Black Women Playwrights in America*. N.Y.: Praeger, 1990.

Childress, Alice. "A Candle in a Gale Wind." In *Black Women Writers (1950-1980)*, ed. Mari Evans.

————. "For a Negro Theatre." *Masses and Mainstream*, Feb. 1951, 61-4.

————. *Like One of the Family: Conversations from a Domestic's Life*. Brooklyn, N.Y.: Independence Publishers, 1956.

————. *Mojo* and *String*. N.Y.: Dramatists Play Service, 1971.

————. *A Short Walk*. N.Y.: Coward, McCann & Geoghegan, 1979.

————. *Wedding Band*. In *9 Plays By Black Women*, ed. Margaret B. Wilkerson. N.Y.: New American Library, 1986.

————. *Wine in the Wilderness*. In *Plays by and about Women*, ed. Victoria Sullivan and James Hatch. N.Y.: Vintage/Random House, 1973.

————. "A Woman Playwright Speaks Her Mind." In Lindsay Patterson, comp. and ed. *Anthology of the American Negro in the Theatre: A Critical Approach*. N.Y.: Publishers Co., 1967.

Curb, Rosemary. "Alice Childress." In *Dictionary of Literary Biography*, ed. John MacNicholas. Vol. 7: *Twentieth-Century American Dramatists*. Part I. Detroit: Gale, 1981.

————. "Alice Childress." In *Notable Women in the American Theatre*, ed. Alice M. Robinson, et al. N.Y.: Greenwood, 1989.

Evans, Mari, ed. *Black Women Writers (1950-1980): A Critical Evaluation*. N.Y.: Anchor/Doubleday, 1984.

Hay, Samuel A. "Alice Childress' Dramatic Structure." In *Black Women Writers (1950-1980)*, ed. Mari Evans.

Mitchell, Loften. *Voices of the Black Theatre*. Clifton, N.J.: James T. White & Co., 1975.

A NOTE ON THE TEXT

This is the definitive text of *Trouble in Mind*, provided by Alice Childress' agent, Flora Roberts. It includes a short scene, Wiletta Mayer's recapitulation of the character parts she has played in her career, that was accidentally omitted when *Trouble in Mind* was first published. The text printed here also includes a few minor changes Ms. Childress made elsewhere in Act II.

CHARACTERS

WILETTA MAYER
HENRY
JOHN NEVINS
MILLIE DAVIS
SHELDON FORRESTER
JUDY SEARS
AL MANNERS
EDDIE FENTON
BILL O'WRAY

ACT ONE

TIME: Ten o'clock Monday morning, fall, 1957.

PLACE: A Broadway theater in New York City. BLUES MUSIC in—out after LIGHTS UP.

SCENE: The stage of the theater. Stage Left leads to the outside entrance, Stage Right to upstairs dressing rooms. There are many props and left-overs from the last show: a plaster fountain with a cupid perched atop, garden furniture, tables, benches, a trellis, two white armchairs trimmed with gold gilt. Before the Curtain rises we hear BANGING SOUNDS from offstage Left, the banging grows louder and louder. CURTAIN RISES. WILETTA MAYER, a middle-aged actress, appears. She is attractive and expansive in personality. She carries a purse and a script. At the moment, she is in quite a huff.

WILETTA: My Lord, I like to have wore my arm off bangin' on that
    door! What you got it locked for?
    (*LIGHTS up brighter*)
    Had me standin' out there in the cold, catchin' my death of
    pneumonia!
    (HENRY, *the elderly doorman, enters.*)
HENRY: I didn't hear a thing...I didn't know...
WILETTA: (*Is suddenly moved by the sight of the theater. She holds up
    her hand for silence, looks out and up at the balcony. She loves the
    theater. She turns back to* HENRY.) A theater always makes me
    feel that way...gotta get still for a second.
HENRY: (*Welcomes an old memory*) You...you are Wiletta
    Mayer...more than twenty years ago, in the old Galy
    Theater....
    (*Is pleased to be remembered*)
    You was singin' a number, with the lights changin' color all
    around you.... What was the name of that show?
WILETTA: *Brownskin Melody.*
HENRY: That's it...and the lights...
WILETTA: Was a doggone rainbow.
HENRY: And you looked so pretty and sounded so fine, there's no
    denyin' it.
WILETTA: Thank you, but I...I...(*Hates to admit she doesn't remem-
    ber him*)

HENRY: I'm Henry.

WILETTA: Mmmmm, you don't say.

HENRY: I was the electrician. Rigged up all those lights and never missed a cue. I'm the doorman here now. I've been in show business over fifty years. I'm the doorman...Henry.

WILETTA: That's a nice name. I...I sure remember those lights.

HENRY: Bet you can't guess how old I am, I'll betcha.

WILETTA: (*Would rather not guess*) Well...you're sure lookin' good.

HENRY: Go ahead, take a guess.

WILETTA: (*Being very kind*) Ohhhhh, I'd say you're in your...late fifties.

HENRY: (*Laughs proudly*) I fool 'em all! I'm seventy-eight years old! How's that?

WILETTA: Ohhhh, don't be tellin' it. (*She places her script and purse on the table, removes her coat.*)

(HENRY *takes coat and hangs it on a rack.*)

HENRY: You singin' in this new show?

WILETTA: No, I'm actin'. I play the mother.

HENRY: (*Is hard of hearing*) How's that?

WILETTA: I'm the mother!

HENRY: Could I run next door and get you some coffee? I'm goin' anyway, no bother.

WILETTA: No, thank you just the same.

HENRY: If you open here, don't let 'em give you dressin' room "C." It's small and it's got no "john" in it...excuse me, I mean...no commode...Miss Mayer.

WILETTA: (*Feeling like the star he's made her*) Thank you, I'll watch out for that.

HENRY: (*Reaches for a small chair, changes his mind and draws the gilt armchair to the table*) Make yourself comfortable. The old Galy. Yessir, I'm seventy-eight years old.

WILETTA: Well, I'm not gonna tell you my age. A woman that'll tell her age will tell anything.

HENRY: (*Laughs*) Oh, that's a good one! I'll remember that! A woman that'll tell her age...what else?

WILETTA: Will tell anything.

HENRY: *Will* tell. Well, I'll see you a little later. (*He exits stage Left.*)

WILETTA: (*Saying goodbye to the kind of gentle treatment she seldom receives*) So long. (*Rises and walks downstage, strikes a pose from the "old Galy" and sings a snatch of an old song*)
Oh, honey babe

Oh, honey babe...
(*She pushes the memory aside.*) Yes indeed!
(JOHN NEVINS, *a young Negro actor, enters. He tries to look self-assured but it's obvious that he is new to the theater and fighting hard to control his enthusiasm.*)
Good morning. Another early bird! I'm glad they hired you, you read so nice er...ah...

JOHN: John, John Nevins.

WILETTA: This is new for you, ain't it?

JOHN: Yes, ma'am

WILETTA: Yes, ma'am? I know you're not a New Yorker, where's your home?

JOHN: Newport News, that's in Virginia.

WILETTA: HOT DOG, I shoulda known anyone as handsome and mannerly as you had to come from my home. Newport News! Think of that! Last name?

JOHN: Nevins, John Nevins.

WILETTA: Wait a minute...do you know Estelle Nevins, used to live out on Prairie Road...fine built woman?

JOHN: Guess I do, that's my mother.

WILETTA: (*Very touched*) No, she ain't!

JOHN: (*Afraid of oncoming sentiment*) Yes...ah...yes she is.

WILETTA: What a day! I went to school with Estelle! She married a fella named Clarence! Used to play baseball. Last time I hit home she had a little baby in the carriage. How many children she got?

JOHN: I'm the only one.

WILETTA: You can't be that little baby in the carriage! Stand up, let me look at you! Brings all of yesterday back to my mind! Tell me, John, is the drugstore still on the corner? Used to be run by a tall, strappin' fella...got wavy, black hair...and, well, he's kind of devilish...Eddie Bentley!

JOHN: Oh, yes, Mr. Bentley is still there...

WILETTA: Fresh and sassy and...

JOHN: But he's gray-haired and very stern and businesslike.

WILETTA: (*Very conscious of her age*) You don't say. Why you want to act? Why don't you make somethin' outta yourself?

JOHN: (*Is amazed at this*) What? Well, I...

WILETTA: You look bright enough to be a doctor or even a lawyer maybe.... You don't have to take what I've been through...don't have to take it off 'em.

JOHN: I think the theater is the grandest place in the world, and I plan to go right to the top.

WILETTA: (*With good humor*) Uh-huh, and where do you think I was plannin' to go?

JOHN: (*Feeling slightly superior because he thinks he knows more about the craft than* WILETTA) Ohhhh, well...

WILETTA: (*Quick to sense his feeling*) Oh, well, what?

JOHN: (*Feels a bit chastised*) Nothing. I know what I want to do, I'm set, decided, and that's that. You're in it, aren't you proud to be a part of it all?

WILETTA: Of what all?

JOHN: Theater.

WILETTA: *Show business*, it's just a business. Colored folks ain't in no theater. You ever do a professional show before?

JOHN: Yes, some off-Broadway...and I've taken classes.

WILETTA: Don't let the man know that. They don't like us to go to school.

JOHN: Oh, now.

WILETTA: They want us to be naturals...you know, just born with the gift. 'Course they want you to be experienced too. Tell 'em you was in the last revival of *Porgy and Bess*.

JOHN: I'm a little young for that.

WILETTA: They don't know the difference. You were one of the children.

JOHN: I need this job but...must I lie?

WILETTA: Yes. Management hates folks who *need* jobs. They get the least money, the least respect, and most times they don't get the job.

JOHN: (*Laughs*) Got it. I'm always doing great.

WILETTA: But don't get too cocky. They don't like that either. You have to cater to these fools too....

JOHN: I'm afraid I don't know how to do that.

WILETTA: Laugh! Laugh at everything they say, makes 'em feel superior.

JOHN: Why do they have to feel superior?

WILETTA: You gonna sit there and pretend you don't know why?

JOHN: I...I'd feel silly laughing at everything.

WILETTA: You don't. Sometimes they laugh, you're supposed to look serious, other times they serious, you supposed to laugh.

JOHN: (*In polite disagreement*) Sounds too complicated.

WILETTA: (*Warming to her subject*) Nothin' too it. Suppose the director walks in, looks around and says...(*She mimics* MANNERS.) "Well, if the dust around here doesn't choke us to death, we'll be able to freeze in comfort."

JOHN: Yes?

WILETTA: We laugh and dispute him. (*She illustrates.*) "Oh, now, Mr. Manners, it ain't that bad!"...White folks can't stand unhappy Negroes...so laugh, laugh when it ain't funny at all.

JOHN: Sounds kind of Uncle Tommish.

WILETTA: You callin' me a "Tom"?

JOHN: No, ma'am.

WILETTA: Stop sayin' ma'am, it sounds countrified.

JOHN: Yes.

WILETTA: It is Tommish...but they do it more than we do. They call it bein' a "yes man." You either do it and stay or don't do it and get out. I can let you in on things that school never heard of...'cause I know what's out here and they don't.

JOHN: Thank you. I guess I'll learn the ropes as I go along.

WILETTA: I'm tellin' you now! Oh, you so lucky! Nobody told me, had to learn it for myself.

(JOHN *is trying to hide the fact that he does not relish her instructions.*)

Another thing, he's gonna ask your honest opinion about the play. Don't tell him, he don't mean it...just say you're crazy about it...butter him up.

JOHN: (*This remark really bothers him.*) What *do* you think of our play?

WILETTA: Oh, honey, it stinks, ain't nothin' atall. Course, if I hear that again, I'll swear you lyin'.

JOHN: Why are you doing it? A flop can't make you but so rich.

WILETTA: Who said it's gonna flop? I said it ain't nothin', but things that aggravate me always *run* for a long time...cause what bugs me is what sends somebody else, if you know what I mean.

JOHN: (*Defensively*) I studied it thoroughly and...

WILETTA: Honey, don't study it, just learn it.

JOHN: I wouldn't, couldn't play anything I didn't believe in...I couldn't.

WILETTA: (*Understands he's a bit upstage now*) Oh, well, you just a lost ball in the high grass.

(MILLIE DAVIS, *an actress about thirty-five years old, enters. She breezes in, beautifully dressed in a mink coat, pastel wool dress and hat, suede shoes and bag.*)

MILLIE: Hi!

WILETTA: Walk, girl! Don't she look good?

MILLIE: Don't look too hard, it's not paid for. (*Models the coat for*
WILETTA *as she talks to* JOHN) You got the job! Good for you.
(WILETTA *picks up* MILLIE'*s newspaper.*)

JOHN: And congratulations to you.

MILLIE: (*Taking off her coat and hanging it up*) I don't care one way
or the other 'cause my husband doesn't want me workin' anyway.

WILETTA: Is he still a dining-car waiter?

MILLIE: I wanted to read for your part but Mr. Manners said I was
too young. They always say too young...too young.

WILETTA: Hear they're lookin' for a little girl to play Goldilocks,
maybe you should try for that.

MILLIE: Oh, funny.

WILETTA: (*Commenting on the headlines*) Look at 'em! Throwin'
stones at little children, got to call out the militia to go to
school.

JOHN: That's terrible.

MILLIE: (*Quite proud of her contribution to Little Rock*) A woman
pushed me on the subway this mornin' and I was ready for
her! Called her everything but a child of God. She turned
purple! Oh, I fixed her!
(JUDITH SEARS, *a young actress, is heard offstage with* SHELDON
FORRESTER, *an elderly character man.*)

JUDY: This way....

SHELDON: Yes, ma'am. Don't hurt yourself.
(SHELDON *and* JUDY *enter,* JUDY *first.*)

JUDY: Good morning.
(*Others respond in unison.*)

JOHN: Hello again, glad you made it.

MILLIE: Hi! I'm Millie, that's John, Wiletta, and you're?

JUDY: Judith, just call me Judy.

SHELDON: (*Bundled in heavy overcoat, two scarves, one outer, one inner*)
And call me Shel!

WILETTA: Sheldon Forrester! So glad to see you! Heard you was
sick.

MILLIE: I heard he was dead.

SHELDON: Yeah! Some fool wrote a piece in that *Medium Brown
Magazine* 'bout me bein' dead. You can see he was lyin'. Bet I

lost a lotta work on accounta that. Doctor says that with plenty of rest and fresh air, I oughta outlive him.

WILETTA: Bet you will, too.

SHELDON: Mr. Manners was lookin' all over for me, said nobody could play this part but me.

MILLIE: Not another soul can do what you're gonna do to it.

SHELDON: Thank you.

(JOHN *starts over to* JUDY *but* SHELDON *stops him.*)

Didn't you play in er...ah...er...

WILETTA: He was in the last revival of *Porgy and Bess*. Was one of the children. (*She watches* JOHN's *reaction to this.*)

SHELDON: Yeah, I know I remembered you. He ain't changed much, just bigger. Nice little actor.

JOHN: (*Embarrassed*) Thank you, sir.

WILETTA: Sheldon got a good memory.

MILLIE: (*To* JUDY) What're you doing?

SHELDON: She's *Miss* Renard, the Southerner's daughter. Fights her father 'bout the way he's treatin' us.

MILLIE: What I want is a part where I get to fight him.

WILETTA: Ha! That'll be the day!

SHELDON: Bill O'Wray is the father, he's awful nice.

MILLIE: Also wish I'd get to wear some decent clothes sometime. Only chance I get to dress up is offstage. I'll wear them baggy cotton dresses but damn if I'll wear another bandanna.

SHELDON: That's how country people do! But go on the beach today, what do you see? Bandannas. White folks wear 'em! They stylish!

MILLIE: That's a lot of crap!

SHELDON: There you go! You holler when there's no work, when the man give you some, you holler just as loud. Ain't no pleasin' you.

(JOHN *starts toward* JUDY *again, this time* MILLIE *stops him.*)

MILLIE: Last show I was in, I wouldn't even tell my relatives. All I did was shout "Lord, have mercy!" for almost two hours every night.

WILETTA: Yes, but you did it, so hush! She's played every flower in the garden. Let's see, what was your name in that T.V. mess?

MILLIE: Never mind.

WILETTA: Gardenia! She was Gardenia! 'Nother thing...she was Magnolia, Chrysanthemum was another....

MILLIE: And you've done the jewels...Crystal, Pearl, Opal! (Millie *laughs.*)

JOHN: (*Weak, self-conscious laughter*) Oh, now...

(JUDY *has retreated to one side, is trying to hide herself behind a book.*)

SHELDON: Do, Lord, let's keep peace. Last thing I was in, the folks fought and argued so, the man said he'd never do a colored show again...and he didn't!

WILETTA: I always say it's the man's play, the man's money and the man's theater, so what you gonna do? (*To* MILLIE) You ain't got a pot nor a window. Now, when you get your own...

(SHELDON *clears his throat to remind them that* JUDY *is listening.*)

Honey, er...what you say your name was?

JUDY: Judy.

WILETTA: (*Sweeps over to* JUDY *and tries to cover the past argument*) I know I've seen you in pictures, didn't you make some pictures?

JUDY: No, this is my first job.

JOHN: (*Joshing* WILETTA) Oh, you mustn't tell that because...

WILETTA: (*Cutting him off*) You're just as cute as a new penny.

SHELDON: Sure is.

(*A brief moment of silence while they wait for* JUDY *to say something*)

JUDY: (*Starts hesitantly but picks up momentum as she goes along*) Thank you, and er...er...I hope I can do a good job and that people learn something from this play.

MILLIE: Like what?

JUDY: That people are the same, that people are...are...well, you know...that people are people.

SHELDON: There you go...brotherhood of man stuff! Sure!

WILETTA: Yes, indeed. I don't like to think of theater as just a business. Oh, it's the art...ain't art a wonderful thing?

MILLIE: (*Bald, flat statement to no one in particular*) People aren't the same.

JUDY: I read twice for the part and there were so many others before me and after me...and I was so scared that my voice came out all funny.... I stumbled on the rug when I went in...everything was terrible.

MILLIE: (*Another bald, flat statement*) But you got the job.

JUDY: (*Uneasy about* MILLIE's *attitude*) Yes.

JOHN: (*To the rescue*) And all the proud relatives will cheer you on opening night!

JUDY: (*Nothing can drown her spirits for long.*) Yes! My mother and father...they live in Bridgeport...they really don't want me here at all. They keep expecting something *terrible* to happen to me...like being murdered or something! But they're awfully sweet and they'll be so happy. (*Abrupt change of subject*) What do you think of the play?

WILETTA: Oh, I never had anything affect me so much in all my life. It's so sad, ain't it sad?

JUDY: Oh, there's some humor.

WILETTA: I'm tellin' you, I almost busted my sides laughin'.

(SHELDON *is busy looking in the script.*)

JOHN: It has a social theme and something to say.

JUDY: Yes.

WILETTA: Art! Art is a great thing!

MILLIE: It's all right except for a few words here and there...and those Gawd-awful clothes....

JOHN: Words, clothes. What about the very meaning?

SHELDON: (*Startles everyone by reading out loud. His finger runs down the page, he skips his cues and reads his lines.*) Mr. Renard, sir, everything is just fine.... Yes, sir.... Thank you, sir.... Yes, sireee, I sure will...I know.... Yes, sir.... But iffen, iffen...(*He pauses to question the word.*) Iffen? (*Now he understands.*) Iffen you don't mind, we'd like to use the barn.

MILLIE: Iffen.

SHELDON: Hush, Millie, so I can get these lines, I'm not a good reader, you know.

MILLIE: Iffen you forget one, just keep shakin' your head.

(*Offstage we hear a door slam.* AL MANNERS, *the director [white] is giving* EDDIE FENTON, *the stage manager [white] a friendly chastising.*)

MANNERS: (*Offstage*) Eddie, why? Why do you do it?

EDDIE: (*Offstage*) I didn't know.

SHELDON: (*Assumes a very studious air and begins to study his script earnestly*) Mr. Manners.

(EDDIE *and* MANNERS *enter, followed by* HENRY. EDDIE *is eager and quick. He carries a portfolio and a stack of scripts.* MANNERS *is in his early forties, hatless, a well-tweeded product of Hollywood. He is a bundle of energy, considerate and understanding after his own fashion; selfish and tactless after ours.* HENRY *is following him around, ready to write out a coffee order.*)

EDDIE: (*With a smile*) You asked my opinion.

MANNERS: That, my friend, was a mistake.

EDDIE: (*Laughing while cast smiles in anticipation of* MANNERS' *words*) Okay, I admit you were right, you were.

MANNERS: (*Enjoying himself*) Of course I was. (*To company*) All of his taste is in his mouth!

(*Burst of company laughter, especially from* SHELDON *and* WILETTA)

EDDIE: (*Playfully correcting* MANNERS) All right, Al, play fair...uncle...a truce.

MANNERS: (*To company*) Greetings to New York's finest.

ALL: Good morning.... Flatterer.... Hello.... Good Morning.

MANNERS: (*To* HENRY) Coffee all around the room and count yourself in. (*Hands him a bill*) Rolls? Cake? No...how about Danish...all right?

ALL: Yes.... Sure.... Anything.... O.K.

SHELDON: I like doughnuts, those jelly doughnuts.

MANNERS: Jelly doughnuts! What a horrible thought. Get Danish...all right?

ALL: Sure.... Anything.... That's fine.

MANNERS: (*After* HENRY *exits*) If you were looking for that type, you could never find it! A real character.

JOHN: One of the old forty-niners.

MANNERS: No, no...not quite that.... (*Turns off that faucet and quickly switches to another*) Everyone on speaking terms?

ALL: Of course.... Old friends.... Oh, yes.... Sure.

MANNERS: (*Opens the portfolio with a flourish*) Best scenic design you've ever laid eyes on.

(*All gasp and sigh as they gather around him. They are quite impressed with the sketch.* JUDY *is very close and* MANNERS *looks down at her hair and neck which is perched right under his nostrils.* JUDY *can feel his breath on her neck. She turns suddenly and* MANNERS *backs away a trifle.*)

You er...wear a beautiful dress in the third act and I wanted to see if you have nice shoulders.

(JUDY *backs away slightly.*)

I wasn't planning to attack you.

(*Cast laughs.*)

MILLIE: I got nice shoulders. You got one of those dresses for me?

SHELDON: (*Determined to enjoy everything*) Ha! He wasn't gonna attack her!

MANNERS: (*Suddenly changes faucets again*) Oh, I'm so weary.

EDDIE: (*Running interference*) He was with Melton on this sketch until four a.m.

MANNERS: Four-thirty.

EDDIE: Four-thirty.

MANNERS: (*Swoops down on* WILETTA) Ahhhhh, this is my sweetheart!

WILETTA: (*With mock severity*) Go on! Go 'way! Ain't speakin' to you! He won't eat, he won't sleep, he's just terrible! I'm mad with you.

SHELDON: Gonna ruin your health like that!

WILETTA: Gonna kill himself!

MANNERS: Bawl me out, I deserve it.

EDDIE: Melton is so stubborn, won't change a line.

MANNERS: But he did.

EDDIE: Yes, but so stubborn.

MANNERS: A genius should be stubborn. (*Points index finger at* SHELDON) Right?

SHELDON: (*Snaps his finger and points back*) There you go! (*Cast laughs.*)

MANNERS: (*To* WILETTA) You'd better speak to me. This is my girl, we did a picture together.

CAST: (*Ad lib*) Really? How nice. She sure did. That's right.

MANNERS: (*As though it's been centuries*) Ohhhhhh, years and years ago. She and I worked together, too.

MILLIE: (*To* WILETTA) Remember that?

SHELDON: (*Proudly*) I was helpin' the Confederate Army.

MANNERS: And what a chestnut, guns, cannons, drums, Indians, slaves, hearts and flowers, sex and Civil War...on wide screen!

JUDY: Oh, just horrible.

MANNERS: (*Touchy about outside criticism*) But it had something, wasn't the worst.... I twisted myself out of shape to build this guy's part. It was really a sympathetic character.

SHELDON: Sure, everybody was sorry for me.

MANNERS: (*To* JOHN) Hear you went to college. You're so modest you need a press agent.

SHELDON: He was one of the children in the last revival of *Porgy and Bess*.

MANNERS: Ohhhh, yes...nice clean job.

JUDY: I'm not modest. I finished the Yale drama course.

Girls...girls...can go to the Yale drama....

MANNERS: Yale. I'm impressed.

JUDY: You're teasing.

MANNERS: No, you are. Well, where are we? Bill O'Wray is out until tomorrow, he's in a rehearsal for a TV show tonight.

(*Proper sighs of regret from the cast*)

WILETTA: Oh, I was lookin' forward to seein' him today.

SHELDON: Yeah, yeah, nice fella.

MANNERS: Works all the time.

(*Now some attention for* MILLIE)

You look gorgeous. This gal has such a flair for clothes. How do you do it?

(MILLIE *is pleased.* MANNERS *changes the subject.*)

Ted Bronson is one of our finest writers.

WILETTA: Knows art, knows it.

EDDIE: He was up for an award.

MANNERS: Really, Eddie, I wish you'd let me tell it.

EDDIE: I'm sorry.

MANNERS: Ted's been out on the coast batting out commercial stuff... meat grinder...he's in Europe now...Italy...about a week before he can get back...he did this "Chaos in Belleville" a while back. Producers gave him nothing but howls.... "It's ahead of the times!" "Why stick your neck out?" "Why You?"

SHELDON: (*Raises his hand, speaks after* MANNERS *gives him a nod*) Who is chaos?

EDDIE: Oh, no.

JOHN: *Who*?

MANNERS: (*Holds up his hand for silence*) Chaos means er...ah, confusion. Confusion in Belleville, confusion in a small town.

SHELDON: Ohhhhhh.

MANNERS: I was casually talking to Ted about the er...er, race situation, kicking a few things around...dynamic subject, hard to come to grips with on the screen, TV, anywhere...explosive subject. Suddenly he reaches to the bottom shelf and comes up with "Chaos." I flipped a few pages...when I read it bells rang. This is *now*, we're living this, who's in the headlines these days?

(*Eloquent pause*)

SHELDON: How 'bout that Montgomery, Alabama? Made the bus company lose one, cold, cash, billion dollars!

JOHN: Not a billion.

MANNERS: Here was a contribution to the elimination of...

SHELDON: I know what I read!

MANNERS: A story of Negro rights that...

SHELDON: How 'bout them busses!

JUDY: And they're absolutely right.

MILLIE: Who's right?

MANNERS: A contribution that really...

JUDY: The colored people.

MANNERS: Leads to a clearer understanding...

MILLIE: Oh. I thought you meant the other people.

MANNERS: A clearer understanding.

JUDY: I didn't mean that.

MANNERS: Yale, please!

> (*All silent*)
> I placed an option on this script so fast....
> (SHELDON *raises his hand.*)
> I tied it up, Sheldon, so that no one else could get hold of it.
> When I showed it to Hoskins...

WILETTA: (*To* SHELDON) The producer. Another nice man.

MANNERS: Well, the rest is history. This is my first Broadway
> show....
> (*Applause from cast*)
> But I definitely know what I want and however unorthodox
> my methods, I promise never to bore you.

SHELDON: (*Popping his fingers rapidly*) He's like that.

MANNERS: I bring to this a burning desire above and beyond any-
> thing I've...well, I'm ready to sweat blood. I want to see you
> kids drawing pay envelopes for a long time to come and...
> (SHELDON *applauds, the others join him.* SHELDON *aims his
> remark at* MILLIE.)

SHELDON: Listen to the man! Listen.

MANNERS: (*Holds up his hand for silence*) At ease. (*Mainly for* JOHN
> *and* JUDY) I ask this, please forget your old methods of work
> and go along with me. I'll probably confuse the hell out of
> you for the first few days but after that...well, I hope we'll be
> swingin'. Now, you're all familiar with the story....

WILETTA: Oh, I never had anything affect me so much in all my
> life.

ALL: (*Ad lib*) There was one part.... I have a question.... Uh-huh....
> A question....

MANNERS: We will *not* discuss the parts.

(JOHN *groans in mock agony.*)

JUDY: One little thing.

MANNERS: We will not discuss the parts.

(EDDIE *smiles knowingly.*)

We will not read the play down from beginning to end.

SHELDON: (*Popping his fingers*) There he goes!

MANNERS: We will *not* delve into character backgrounds...not now. Turn to act one, scene two, page fifteen.

(*Actors scramble madly for places in scripts.*)

Top of the page. Eddie, you read for O'Wray. Judy! Stand up!

(JUDY *stands hesitantly while* MANNERS *toys with a sheet of paper.*)

Walk downstage!

(JUDY *is startled and nervous, she walks upstage. The others are eager to correct her but* MANNERS *will not tolerate cast interference. He crumbles the paper, throws it to the floor, takes* JUDY *by the shoulders and speedily leads her around the stage.*)

Downstage! Center stage! Left Center! Right Center! Up Right! Up Left! Down Center, Down Right, Down Left, Upstage...DOWNSTAGE!

JUDY: I know, I forgot....

MANNERS: Don't forget again. Take downstage. (*Notices the paper he threw on the floor*) A trashy stage is most distracting.

(JUDY *starts to pick up the paper.*)

Hold your position! Wiletta, pick up the paper!

(JOHN *and* SHELDON *start for the paper.*)

I asked Wiletta! (*Catches* WILETTA's *eye*)

Well?

WILETTA: (*Shocked into a quick flare of temper*) Well, hell! I ain't the damn janitor! (*Trying to check her temper*) I...well, I...shucks... I...damn.

MANNERS: (*Even though he was trying to catch them off-guard, he didn't expect this.*) Cut! Cut! It's all over.

(*Everyone is surprised again.*)

What you have just seen is...is...is fine acting. (*He is quite shaken and embarrassed from* WILETTA's *action.*) Actors struggle for weeks to do what you have done perfectly...the first time. You gave me anger, frustration, movement, er...excitement. Your faces were alive! Why? You did what came naturally, you believed.... That is the quality I want in your work...the firm texture of truth.

JUDY: Oh, you tricked us.

MILLIE: I didn't know what to think.

JOHN: Tension all over the place.

WILETTA: (*Still having a hard time getting herself under control. She fans herself with a pocket handkerchief and tries to muster a weak laugh.*) Yes indeed.

MANNERS: (*Gingerly touches* WILETTA *and shivers in mock fear*) She plays rough. "Well, hell!" Honey, I love you, believe me.

SHELDON: Oh, she cut up!

WILETTA: (*Tries to laugh along with them but it's hard going. From this point on, she watches* MANNERS *with a sharp eye, always cautious and on the look-out.*) Yes...well, let's don't play that no more.

MANNERS: Top of the page. Judy, you're appealing to your father to allow some of his tenant farmers...(*He glances at script to find the next direction.* SHELDON *leans over and whispers to* WILETTA.)

WILETTA: Sharecroppers.

SHELDON: Oh.

MANNERS:...hold a barn dance. Now! Some of them have been talking about voting.

SHELDON: Trouble.

MANNERS: (*Points first to* MILLIE, *then* WILETTA) Petunia and Ruby are in your father's study...er...er...(*Consults script again*)

SHELDON: (*Without consulting script*) Cleanin' up. Sure, that's what they're doin'.

MANNERS: Tidying up. Your father is going over his account books, you're there...

SHELDON: (*With admiration*) Lookin' pretty.

MANNERS: There's an awful echo coming from our assistant director.

SHELDON: (*Laughs*) 'Sistant director! This man breaks me up all the time!

MANNERS: (*Liking the salve*) What, what did you say?

SHELDON: Say you tickle me to death.

WILETTA: Tickles me too.

MANNERS: Take it!

JUDY: (*Reading*) Papa, it's a good year, isn't it?

EDDIE: (*With a too-broad Southern accent*) I'd say fair, fair to middlin'.

(*Cast snickers.*)

MANNERS: All right, Barrymore, just read it.

JUDY: Papa, it's Petunia's birthday today.

EDDIE: That so? Happy birthday, Petunia.

MILLIE: (*Wearily*) Thank you, sir.

MANNERS: (*Correcting the reading*) You feel good, full of ginger...your birthday!

MILLIE: (*Remembers the old, standard formula. Gives the line with a chuckle and extra warmth*) Thank you sir.

JUDY: It would be nice if they could have a stomp in the barn.

MILLIE: (*Her attitude suggests that* JUDY *thought up the line.*) Hmmph.

EDDIE: No need to have any barn stomp until this election business is over.

MILLIE: What the hell is a stomp?

JUDY: I can't see why.

MANNERS: A barn dance. You know that, Millie.

EDDIE: Ruby, you think y'all oughta use the barn?

WILETTA: (*Pleasantly*) Lord, have mercy, Mr. Renard, don't ask me 'cause I don't know nothin'.

EDDIE: Well, better forget about it.

JUDY: Oh, papa, let the...let the...

MILLIE: (*For* JUDY's *benefit*) Mmmmmmmmmmmph. Why didn't they *call* it a barn dance?

JUDY:...let the...(*Stops reading*) Oh, must I say that word?

MANNERS: What word?

MILLIE: *Darkies.* That's the word. It says, "Papa, let the darkies have their fun."

MANNERS: *What* do you want to say?

MILLIE: She could say..."Let *them* have their fun."

MANNERS: But that's Carrie. (*To* SHELDON) Do you object?

SHELDON: Well, no, not if that's how they spoke in them days.

MANNERS: The time is now, down south in some remote little county, they say those things...now. Can you object in an artistic sense?

SHELDON: No, but you better ask him, he's more artistic than I am.

JOHN: No, I don't object. I don't like the word but it is used, it's a slice of life. Let's face it, Judy wouldn't use it, Mr. Manners wouldn't...

MANNERS: (*Very pleased with* JOHN's *answer*) Call me Al, everybody. Al's good enough, Johnny.

JOHN: Al wouldn't say it but Carrie would.

(MANNERS *gives* WILETTA *an inquiring look.*)

WILETTA: Lord, have mercy, don't ask me 'cause I don't know.... (*She stops short as she realizes she is repeating words from the script. She's disturbed that she's repeating the exact line the author indicated.*)

MANNERS: (*Gives* JUDY *a light tap on the head*) Yale! Proceed.

EDDIE: (*Reads*) Ruby and Petunia leave the room and wait on the porch.

JUDY: Please, Papa, I gave my word. I ask one little thing and...

EDDIE: All right! Before you know it, them niggers will be runnin' me!

JUDY: Please, don't use that word!

MANNERS: Oh, stop it!

WILETTA: That's her line in the play, Mr. Manners, Carrie says...

ALL: Please, don't use that word.

(MANNERS *signals* EDDIE *to carry on.*)

EDDIE: (*Reads*) Carrie runs out to the porch.

JUDY: You can use the barn!

MILLIE: Lord, have mercy...

EDDIE: (*Intones*) Wrong line.

MILLIE: (*Quickly corrects line*) Er...er, somethin' seems to trouble my spirit, a troublous feelin' is in old Petunia's breast. (*Stops reading*) Old Petunia?

WILETTA: Yes, *old* Petunia!

JUDY: (*Reads*) I'm going upstairs to lay out my white organdy dress.

WILETTA: No, you ain't, I'm gonna do that for you.

JUDY: Then I'll take a nap.

MILLIE: No, you ain't, I'm gonna do that for you.

EDDIE: Wrong line.

MILLIE: Sorry. (*Corrects line*) Yes, child, you rest yourself, you had a terrible, hard day. Bless your soul, you just one of God's golden-haired angels.

MANNERS: (*Frantically searching for that certain quality. He thinks everything will open once they hit the right chord.*) Cut! Top of page three, act one, as it's written. Ruby is shelling beans on the back porch as her son Job approaches.

JOHN: If I can read over...

MANNERS: Do as I ask, do it. Take it, Wiletta.

SHELDON: (*Popping his fingers*) He's just like that.

WILETTA: (*Reads*) Boy, where you goin'?

JOHN: Down to Turner's Corner.

WILETTA: You ain't lost nothin' down there. Turner and his brother is talkin' 'bout votin', I know.

JOHN: They only talkin', I'm goin'.

SHELDON: Mr. Renard say to stay outta that.

JOHN: I got a letter from the President 'bout goin' in the army, Turner says when that happens, a man's sposed to vote and things.

(MILLIE and JUDY *are very pleased about this line*.)

SHELDON: Letter ain't from no President, it come from the crackers on the draft board.

JOHN: It *say* from the President.

WILETTA: Pa say you don't go.

(MANNERS *is jotting down a flood of notes*.)

JOHN: Sorry, but I say I'd be there.

SHELDON: I don't know who that boy take after.

EDDIE: Ruby dashes from the porch and Sam follows her. Carrie comes outside and Renard follows her. (EDDIE *reads Renard*.) You pamper them rascals too much, see how they do? None of 'em's worth their weight in salt, that boy would steal the egg out of a cake.

JUDY: (*Tries to laugh while* MILLIE *watches coldly.* MANNERS *is amazed at the facial distortion*.) It says laugh.

MANNERS: Well?

JUDY: (*Laughs and continues reading*) But I can't help feeling sorry for them, they didn't ask to be born.

MILLIE: (*Just loud enough for* JUDY's *ears*) Hmmmmmph.

JUDY: I keep thinking, there but for the grace of God go I. If we're superior we should prove it by our actions.

SHELDON: (*Commenting on the line*) There you go, prove it!

(MANNERS *is taking more notes.* JUDY *is disturbed by the reactions to her reading. She hesitates,* MANNERS *looks up. The PHONE RINGS.* EDDIE *goes off to answer*.)

JUDY: She *is* their friend, right? It's just that I feel reactions and...

MANNERS: What reactions?

MILLIE: I was reacting.

MANNERS: Ohhhhh, who pays Millie any attention, that's her way.

MILLIE: There you go.

SHELDON: Sure is.

JUDY: (*Tries again but she's very uncomfortable*) I...I keep thinking...there but for the grace of God...

MANNERS: Are you planning to cry?

JUDY: No, but...no. (*She's fighting to hold back the tears.*)

SHELDON: Millie is pickin' on her.

MANNERS: Utter nonsense!

JUDY: My part seems...she seems so smug.

MILLIE: (*To* SHELDON) Keep my name out of your mouth.

WILETTA: (*To* SHELDON) Mind your business, your own affairs.

MANNERS: This is fantastic. What in the hell is smug?

> (HENRY *enters with a cardboard box full of coffee containers and a large paper bag.*)

> Cut! coffee break! (*To* JUDY) Especially you.

HENRY: Told the waiter feller to fix up everything nice.

MANNERS: (*Looks in bag*) What's this?

HENRY: That's what you said. I heard you. "Jelly doughnuts!" you said.

> (SHELDON *gets a container of coffee for* JUDY *and one for himself.*)

MANNERS: I won't eat it!

HENRY: But I heard you.

MANNERS: Take your coffee and leave.

> (HENRY *starts to leave without the coffee.*)

> Don't play games, take it with you.

> (HENRY *snatches a container and leaves in a quiet huff.* SHELDON *hands coffee to* JUDY *but* MILLIE *snatches it from his hand.*)

MILLIE: I know you brought that for me.

MANNERS: Where do they find these characters? All right, he's old but it's an imposition...he's probably ninety, you know.

WILETTA: (*Laughs and then suddenly stops*) We all get old sometime.

EDDIE: (*Hurries onstage. Looks worried*) It's Mrs. Manners...she...she says it's urgent. She has to talk to you *now*...immediately.

MANNERS: Oh, you stupid jerk. Why did you say I was here? You and your big, stupid mouth. Couldn't you say "He isn't here now, I'll give him your message"?

EDDIE: I'm sorry. She was so...so...Well, she said right off "I *know* he's there." If I had any idea that she would...

MANNERS: I don't expect you to have *ideas*! Only common sense, just a little common sense. Where do you find a stage manager these days?

EDDIE: I can tell her you can't be disturbed now.

MANNERS: No, numbskull, don't do another thing, you've done enough. (*With wry humor*) Alimony is not enough, every time I make three extra dollars she takes me to court to get two-thirds of it. If I don't talk to her I'll have a subpoena. You're stupid. (*He exits to the telephone. During the brief silence which follows,* EDDIE *is miserably self-conscious.*)

WILETTA: (*Tries to save the day*) Well...I'm glad it's getting a little like winter now. We sure had a hot summer. Did you have a nice summer?

EDDIE: (*Choking back his suppressed anger*) I worked in stock...summer theater. It was O. K.

WILETTA: That's nice. What did you do?

EDDIE: (*Relaxing more*) Kind of Jack of all trades...understudied some, stage managed, made sets....

MILLIE: And did three people out of a job.

JUDY: I spent the summer with my folks. Soon as we open, I want everyone to come up to Bridgeport and have a glorious day! (MANNERS *returns, looks up briefly.*) Daddy makes the yummiest barbecue, you'll love it.

WILETTA: You better discuss it with your folks first.

JUDY: Why?

MILLIE: 'Cause we wouldn't want it discussed after we got there.

SHELDON: No, thank you, ma'am. I'm plannin' to be busy all winter lookin' for an apartment, I sure hate roomin'.

EDDIE: I have my own apartment. It's only a cold-water walk-up but I have it fixed real nice like the magazines show you... whitewashed brick and mobiles hanging in the kitchen and living room. I painted the floors black and spattered them with red and white paint...I learned that in stock...then I shellacked over it and waxed it...and I scraped all of the furniture down to the natural wood....

MILLIE: Oh, hush, you're making me tired. Cold-water flat!

EDDIE: It gives a cheery effect....

MILLIE: And it'll give you double pneumonia.

SHELDON: Yeah, that's the stuff you got to watch.

EDDIE: Well, it's only thirty dollars a month.

SHELDON: They got any colored livin' in that buildin'?

EDDIE: I...I...I don't know. I haven't seen any.

SHELDON: Well, there's none there then.

EDDIE: (*Slightly ill at ease*) Sheldon, I'll gladly ask.

SHELDON: (*In great alarm*) Oh, no, no, no! I don't want to be the first.

MILLIE: Damn cold-water flats! I like ease, comfort, furs, cars, big, thick steaks. I want everything.

EDDIE: (*Trying to change the subject*) Aren't there a lot of new shows this season?

JUDY: My mother says...gosh, every time I open my mouth it's something about my parents. It's not stylish to love your parents...you either have a mother-complex or a father-fixation! (*She laughs and* MANNERS *looks up again. He doesn't care for her remarks.*)

But I'm crazy about my parents, but then maybe that's abnormal. I probably have a mother-father-fixation.

WILETTA: What did your mother say?

JUDY: "Never have limitations on your horizon, reach for infinity!" She also feels that everyone has a right to an equal education and not separate either.

JOHN: She sounds like a wonderful woman who...

JUDY: (*Raising her voice*) Oh, I get so mad about this prejudice nonsense! It's a wonder colored people don't go out and *kill* somebody, I mean actually, really do it...bloody murder, you know?

SHELDON: There's lotsa folks worse off than we are, Millie.

MILLIE: Well, all I hope is that they don't like it, dontcha know.

MANNERS: (*Boastful about his trials and troubles*) The seven-year-old kid, the seven-year-old kid...to hear her tell it, our son is ragged, barefoot, hungry...and his teeth are lousy. The orthodontist says he needs braces...they wanta remake his mouth. The kid is falling to pieces. When I go for visitation...he looks in my pockets before he says hello. Can you imagine? Seven years old. The orthodontist and the psychiatrist...the story of my life. But he's a bright kid...smart as a whip...you can't fool him. (*A big sigh*) Oh, well, let's go. Suppose you were all strangers, had never heard anything about this story except the snatches you heard today. What would you know?

MILLIE: It's my birthday.

(WILETTA *is following him closely; she doesn't care to be caught off-guard again.*)

JOHN: Carrie's father has tenant farmers working for him.

MANNERS: Yes and...

JUDY: They want to hold a barn dance and he's against it because...

JOHN: Some of the Negroes are planning to vote for the first time and there's opposition...

SHELDON: His ma and pa don't want him mixed in it 'cause they smell trouble.

JUDY: And my father overheard that John is in it.

SHELDON: And *he don't like it*, that's another thing.

WILETTA: (*Amazed that they have learned so much*) Mmmmmm, all of that.

JOHN: But Job is determined.

JUDY: And he's been notified by the draft board.

SHELDON: And the paper, the paper!

MANNERS: Paper?

WILETTA: You know, upstage, downstage and doin' what comes natural.

MANNERS: Not bad for an hour's work.

EDDIE: Amazing.

SHELDON: (*Popping his fingers*) Man is on the ball. Fast.

MANNERS: Now we can see how we're heading for the lynching.

SHELDON: (*Starts to peep at back page of script*) Lynchin'?

MANNERS: We're dealing with an anti-lynch theme. I want it uncluttered, clear in your mind, you must see the skeleton framework within which we're working. Wiletta, turn to the last page of act one.

EDDIE: Fifty.

MANNERS: Wiletta, dear heart...the end of the act finds you alone on the porch, worried, heartsick...

WILETTA: And singin' a song, sittin', worryin', and singin'.

MANNERS: It's not simply a song, it's a summing up. You're think-ing of Renard, the threats, the people and your son....

(WILETTA *is tensely listening, trying to follow him.* MANNERS *stands behind her and gently shakes her shoulders.*)

Loosen up, let the thoughts flood over you. I know you have to read....

WILETTA: Oh, I know the song, learned it when I was a child.

MANNERS: Hold a thought, close your eyes and think aloud...get a good start and then sing...speak your mind and then sing.

WILETTA: (*Not for thinking out loud*) I know exactly what you want.

MANNERS: Blurt out the first thing that enters your mind.

WILETTA: (*Sings a mournful dirge of despair*) come and go with me to that land, come and go with me to that land...

MANNERS: Gosh, that guy can write.

WILETTA: Come and go with me to that land where
    I'm bound
No confusion in that land, no confusion
    in that land

No confusion in that land where I'm
    bound...
MILLIE: (*Wipes her eyes*) A heart-breaker.
EDDIE: Oh, Wiletta, it's so...so...gosh.
JOHN: Leaves you weak.
MANNERS: Beautiful. What were you thinking?
WILETTA: (*Ready to move on to something else*) Thank you.
MANNERS: What were you thinking?
WILETTA: I thought...I...er, er...I don't know, whatever you said.
MANNERS: Tell me. You're not a vacuum, you thought something.
JOHN: Your motivation. What motivated...
MANNERS: (*Waving* JOHN *out of it*) You thought *something*, right?
WILETTA: Uh-huh.
MANNERS: And out of the thought came song.
WILETTA: Yeah.
MANNERS: What did you think?
WILETTA: I thought that's what you wanted. (*She realizes she is the center of attention and finds it uncomfortable.*)
MANNERS: It won't do. You must know why you do a thing, that way you're true to me, to the part and yourself....
WILETTA: Didn't you like it?
MANNERS: Very much but...I'm sure you've never worked this way before, but you're not carrying a tray or answering doorbells, this is substance, meat. I demand that you *know* what you're doing and *why*, at all times. I will accept nothing less.
WILETTA: (*To* JOHN *and* JUDY) I know, you have to justify.
SHELDON: (*Worried and trying to help* WILETTA) You was thinkin' how sad it was, wasn't you?
WILETTA: Uh-huh.
MANNERS: It's new to you but it must be done. Let go, think aloud and when you are moved to do so...sing.
    (WILETTA *looks blank.*)
    Start anywhere.
WILETTA: Ah, er...it's so sad that folks can't vote...it's also sad that er, er...
MANNERS: No. (*Picks up newspaper*) We'll try word association. I'll give you a word, then you say what comes to your mind and keep on going...one word brings on another.... Montgomery!
WILETTA: Alabama.
MANNERS: Montgomery!
WILETTA: Alabama

MANNERS: Montgomery!!

WILETTA: Reverend King is speakin' on Sunday.

MANNERS: Colored.

WILETTA: Lights changin' colors all around me.

MANNERS: Colored.

WILETTA: They...they...

MANNERS: Colored.

WILETTA: "They got any colored in that buildin'?"

MANNERS: Children, little children.

WILETTA: Children...children.... "Pick up that paper!" Oh, my...

MANNERS: Lynching.

WILETTA: Killin'! Killin'!

MANNERS: Killing.

WILETTA: It's the man's theater, the man's money, so what you gonna do?

MANNERS: Oh, Wiletta...I don't know! *Darkness!*

WILETTA: A star! Oh, I can't, I don't like it....

MANNERS: Sing.

WILETTA: (*Sings a song of strength and anger*) Come and go with me to that land

(*The song is overpowering, we see a woman who could fight the world.*)

Come and go with me to that land

Come and go with me to that land—

where I'm bound.

JUDY: Bravo! Magnificent!

MANNERS: Wiletta, if you dare! You will undo us! Are you out of your senses? When you didn't know what you were doing...perfection on the nose. I'll grant you the first interpretation was right, without motivating. All right, I'll settle for that.

WILETTA: (*Feeling very lost*) I said I *knew* what you wanted.

MANNERS: Judy! I...I want to talk to you about...about Carrie. (*He rises and starts for the dressing room.*) Eddie, will you dash out and get me a piece of Danish? Okay, at ease.

(EDDIE *quickly exits.* MANNERS *and* JUDY *exit Stage Right toward dressing rooms.*)

MILLIE: (*To* JOHN) Look, don't get too close to her.

SHELDON: Mind your own business.

JOHN: What have I done?

MILLIE: You're too friendly with her.

WILETTA: Justify. Ain't enough to do it, you got to justify.

JOHN: I've only been civil.

MILLIE: That's too friendly.

WILETTA: Got a splittin' headache.

SHELDON: (*To* WILETTA) I wish I had a aspirin for you.

MILLIE: (*To* JOHN) All set to run up and see her folks. Didn't you hear her say they expect something terrible to happen to her? Well, you're one of the terrible things they have in mind!

SHELDON: Mind your business.

MILLIE: It is my business. When they start raisin' a fund for his defense, they're gonna come and ask me for money and I'll have to be writin' the President and signin' petitions...so it's my business.

SHELDON: I tell you, son, I'm friendly with white folks in a distant sorta way but I don't get too close. Take Egypt, Russia, all these countries, why they kickin' up their heels? 'Cause of white folks. I wouldn't trust one of 'em sittin' in front of me on a merry-go-round, wouldn't trust 'em if they was laid up in bed with lockjaw and the mumps both at the same time.

JOHN: Last time I heard from you, you said it was the colored who made all the trouble.

SHELDON: They do, they're the worst ones. There's two kinda people that's got the world messed up for good, that's the colored and the white, and I got no use for either one of 'em.

MILLIE: I'm going to stop trying to help people.

JOHN: Hell, I'm though with it. Oh, I'm learning the ropes!

SHELDON: *That's* why they don't do more colored shows...trouble makers, pot boilers, spoon stirrers . . and sharper than a serpent's tooth! Colored women wake up in the mornin' with their fists ball up...ready to fight.

WILETTA: What in the devil is all this justifyin'? Ain't necessary.

MILLIE: (*To* SHELDON) And you crawlin' all over me to hand her coffee! Damn "Tom."

SHELDON: You talkin' 'bout your relatives, ain't talkin' 'bout me, if I'm a "Tom," you a "Jemima."

JOHN: I need out, I need air. (*He exits Stage Left.*)

SHELDON: White folks is stickin' together, stickin' together, stickin' together...we fightin'.

WILETTA: Hush, I got a headache.

MILLIE: I need a breath of air, too, before I slap the taste out of somebody's mouth. (MILLIE *grabs her coat and exits Stage Left.*)

SHELDON: I hope the wind blows her away. They gonna kick us until we all out in the street...unemployed...get all the air you want then. Sometimes I take low, yes, gotta take low. Man say somethin' to me, I say..."Yes, sure, certainly." You 'n' me know how to do. That ain't *tommin'*, that's common sense. You and me...we don't mind takin' low because we tryin' to accomplish somethin'....

WILETTA: I mind...I do mind...I mind...I mind....

SHELDON: Well, yeah, we all mind...but you got to swaller what you mind. What you mind won't buy beans. I mean you gotta take what you mind to survive...to eat...to breathe....

WILETTA: (*Tensely*) *I mind*. Leave me alone.

(SHELDON *exits with a sigh*.)

HENRY: (*Enters carrying a lunch box. WILETTA turns, she looks so distressed*.) They've all flown the coop?

WILETTA: Yes.

HENRY: What's the matter? Somebody hurt your feelin's?

WILETTA: Yes.

HENRY: Don't fret, it's too nice a day. I believe in treatin' folks right. When you're just about through with this life, that's the time when you know how to live. Seems like yesterday I was forty years old and the day before that I wasn't but nineteen.... Think of it.

WILETTA: I don't like to think...makes me fightin' mad.

HENRY: (*Giving vent to his pent-up feelings*) Don't I know it? When he yelled about jelly doughnuts, I started to land one on him! Oh, I almost did it!

WILETTA: I know it!

HENRY: But..."Hold your temper!" I says. I have a most ferocious temper.

WILETTA: Me too. I take and take, then watch out!

HENRY: Have to hold my temper, I don't want to kill the man.

WILETTA: Yeah, makes you feel like fightin'.

HENRY: (*Joining in the spirit of the discussion*) Sure I'm a fighter and I come from a fightin' people.

WILETTA: You from Ireland?

HENRY: A fightin' people! Didn't we fight for the home rule?

WILETTA: Uh-huh, now you see there.

(WILETTA *doesn't worry about making sense out of* HENRY's *speech on Ireland, it's the feeling behind it that counts*.)

HENRY: O, a history of great men, fightin' men!

WILETTA: (*Rallying to the call, she answers as though sitting on an amen bench at a revival meeting.*) Yes, carry on.

HENRY: Ah, yes, we was fightin' for the home rule! Ah, there was some great men!

WILETTA: I know it.

HENRY: There was Parnell! Charles Stewart Parnell!

WILETTA: All right!

HENRY: A figure of a man! The highest! Fightin' hard for the home rule! A parliamentarian! And they clapped him in the blasted jail house for six months!

WILETTA: Yes, my Lord!

HENRY: And Gladstone introduced the bill...and later on you had Dillon and John Redmond...and then when the home rule was almost put through, what do you think happened? World War One! That killed the whole business!

WILETTA: (*Very indignant*) Oh, if it ain't one thing, it's another!

HENRY: I'm descended from a great line! And then the likes of him with his jelly doughnuts! Jelly doughnuts, indeed, is it? What does he know? Tramplin' upon a man's dignity! Me father was the greatest, most dignified man you've ever seen...and he played vaudeville! Oh, the bearin' of him! (*Angrily demonstrating his father's dignity*) Doin' the little soft-shoe step...and it's take your hat off to the ladies...and step along there....

WILETTA: Henry, I want to be an actress, I've always wanted to be an actress and they ain't gonna do me the way they did the home rule! I want to be an actress 'cause one day you're nineteen and then forty and so on...I want to be an actress! Henry, they stone us when we try to go to school, the world's crazy.

HENRY: It's a shame, a shame....

WILETTA: Where the hell do I come in? Every damn body pushin' me off the face of the earth! I want to be an actress...hell, I'm gonna be one, you hear me? (*She pounds the table.*)

HENRY: Sure, and why not, I'd like to know!

WILETTA: (*Quietly*) Yes, dammit...and why not? Why in the hell not?

(*BLUES RECORD in. Woman singer*)

CURTAIN

ACT TWO

Time: Ten o'clock Thursday morning.

Place: Same as Act One. BLUES MUSIC—in—up and out.

Scene: Same as Act One, except furniture has been changed around; some of the old set removed. BILL O'WRAY, a character actor (white) stands upstage on a makeshift platform. He radiates strength and power as he addresses an imaginary audience. MANNERS stands Stage Left, tie loosened, hair ruffled. He is hepped up with nervous energy, can barely stand still. EDDIE is Stage Right, in charge of the script and a tape recorder; he follows the script and turns up the tape recorder on cue from MANNERS. O'WRAY is delivering a "masterful" rendition of Renard's speech on "tolerance." MANNERS is elated one moment, deflated the next. EDDIE is obviously nervous, drawn and lacking the easy-going attitude of Act One.

BILL: (*Intones speech with vigor and heartfelt passion*) My friends, if all the world were just, there would be no need for valor.... And those of us who are of a moderate mind...I would say the majority...
(*Light applause from tape recorder*)
... we are anything but light-hearted. But the moving finger writes and having writ moves *on*. No, you can't wash out a word of it. Heretofore we've gotten along with our Nigra population...but times change.
(*Applause from tape recorder*)
I do not argue with any man who believes in segregation. I, of all people, will not, cannot question that belief. We all believe in the words of Henry Clay—"Sir, I would rather be right than be president."
(EDDIE *sleeps his cue.*)
MANNERS: Dammit! Eddie!
(EDDIE *suddenly switches to loud applause.*)
BILL: But difficulties are things that show what men are, and necessity is still the mother of invention. As Emerson so aptly pointed out—"The true test of civilization is not the—census, nor the size of cities, nor the crops—but the kind of man the country turns out." Oh, my friends, let every man look before he leaps, let us consider submitting to the present evil lest a

greater one befall us— say to yourself, my honor is dearer to
me than my life.
(*Very light applause*)
I say moderation—for these are the times that try men's
souls! In these terrible days we must realize—how oft the
darkest hour of ill breaks brightest into dawn. Moderation,
yes.
(*Very light applause*)
Even the misguided, infamous Adolph Hitler said—"One
should guard against believing the great masses to be more
stupid than they actually are!"
(*Applause*)
Oh, friends, moderation. Let us weigh our answer very carefully when the dark-skinned Oliver Twist approaches our
common pot and says: "Please, sir, I want some more." When
we say "no," remember that a soft answer turneth away wrath.
Ohhh, we shall come out of the darkness, and sweet is pleasure after pain. If we are superior, let us show our superiority!
(MANNERS *directs* EDDIE *to take applause up high and then out.*)
Moderation. With wisdom and moderation, these terrible
days will pass. I am reminded of the immortal words of
Longfellow. "And the night shall be filled with music and the
cares that infest the day shall fold their tents like the Arabs
and silently steal away."
(*Terrific applause*)

MANNERS: (*Slaps* BILL *on back. Dashes to* EDDIE *and turns the applause
up and down*) Is this such a Herculean task? All you have to do
is listen! Inattention—aggravates the hell out of me!

BILL: (*When* BILL *drops out of character we see that he is very different
from the strong Renard. He appears to be worried at all times. He
has a habit of negatively shaking his head even though nothing is
wrong.* BILL O'WRAY *is but a shadow of a man—but by some miracle he turns into a dynamic figure as Renard. As* BILL—*he sees
dragons in every corner and worries about each one.*) I don't know,
I don't know....

MANNERS: (*Fears the worst for the show as he watches* BILL) What?
What is it?

BILL: (*Half dismissing the thought*) Oh, well...I guess....
(EDDIE *is toying with the machine and turns the applause up by
accident.*)

MANNERS: Hell, Eddie, a little consideration! Why do you do it?

Damned childish!

(EDDIE *turns off machine.*)

What's bothering you?

BILL: Well, you never can tell...but I don't know....

MANNERS: Bill, cut it out, come on.

BILL: That *Arab* stuff...you know, quietly folding his tent...you're gonna get a laugh...and then on the other hand you might offend somebody...well, we'll see....

MANNERS: Eddie, make a note of that. Arab folding his tent. I'll take it up with Bronson.

(EDDIE *is making notes.*)

BILL: I'm tellin' you, you don't need it...wouldn't lose a thing...the Longfellow quote...I don't know, maybe I'm wrong but...

MANNERS: You act like you've lost your last friend! I'm the one holding the blasted bag.

BILL: (*Taking "Show Business" out of his coat pocket*) Well, maybe I shouldn't have said...

MANNERS: I'm out of my mind! When I think of the money borrowed, and for what! Oh, I'm just talking. This always happens when the ship leaves port. The union's making me take three extra stage hands. (*Laughs*)...they hate us! *Co-produce*, filthy word! You know who I had to put the bite on for an extra ten thousand? My ex-wife's present boyfriend. Enough to emasculate a man for the rest of his life!

BILL: How is Fay? Sweet kid. I was sure surprised when you two broke it off. Oh, well, that's the way....

MANNERS: She's fine and we're good friends. Thank God for civilization.

BILL: That's nice. Ten thousand? She must have connected up with a big wheel, huh?

MANNERS: I've known you long enough to ask a favor.

BILL: All depends.

MANNERS: Will you stop running off at lunch hour? It looks bad.

BILL: Now, wait a minute....

EDDIE: I eat with them all the time.

MANNERS: Drop it, Eddie. Unity in *this* company is very important. Hell, I don't care, but it looks like you don't want to eat with the colored members of the cast.

BILL: I don't.

EDDIE: I guess you heard him.

MANNERS: Bill, this is fantastic. I never credited you with this kind of...silly, childlike...

BILL: There's not a prejudiced bone in my body. It is important that I eat my lunch. I used to have an ulcer. I have nothing against anybody but I can't eat my damn lunch...people *stare*. They sit there glaring and staring.

MANNERS: Nonsense.

BILL: Tuesday I lunched with Millie because I bumped into her on the street. That restaurant...people straining and looking at me as if I were an old lecher! God knows what they're thinking. I've got to eat my lunch. After all...I can't stand that...

MANNERS: (*Laughs*) All right but mix a little...it's the show...do it for the show.

BILL: Every time I open my mouth somebody is telling me don't say this or that...Millie doesn't want to be called "gal"...I call *all* women "gal"...I don't know...I'm not going into analysis about this...I'm not. How do you think my character is shaping up?

MANNERS: Great, no complaints...fine.

(WILETTA *drags in, tired and worn.*)

'Morning, sweetie.

EDDIE: Good morning.

WILETTA: (*Indicating script*) I been readin' this back and forth and over again.

MANNERS: (*Automatic sympathy*) Honey, don't...

WILETTA: My neighbor, Miss Green, she come up and held the book and I sat there justifyin' like you said....

MANNERS: Darling, don't think. You're great until you start thinking. I don't expect you to....

WILETTA: (*Weak laugh*) I've been in this business a long time, more than twenty-five years and...

MANNERS: Don't tell it, you're beautiful.

WILETTA: Guess I can do like the others. We was justifyin' and Miss Green says to me...

BILL: (*Gets in his good deed*) Wiletta, you look wonderful, you really do.

WILETTA: Huh?

BILL: You...you're looking well.

WILETTA: Thank you, Miss Green says...

MANNERS: (*Wearily*) Oh, a plague on Miss Green. Darling, it's too early to listen to outside criticism, it can be dangerous if the person doesn't understand...

WILETTA: Miss Green puts on shows at the church...and she had an uncle that was a sharecropper, so she says the first act...

MANNERS: (*Flips the script to Act Three*) We're hitting the third today.

WILETTA: Miss Green also conducts the church choir...

MANNERS: Wiletta, don't complicate my life. (*To* BILL *and* EDDIE) Isn't she wonderful? (*To* WILETTA) Dear heart, I adore you.

WILETTA: (*Feels like a fool as she limply trails on*) She...she did the Messiah...*Handel's* Messiah...last Easter...and folks come from downtown to hear it...all kinds of folks...white folks too.

MANNERS: Eddie! Did I leave the schedule at home?

EDDIE: (*Hands him the schedule*) I have a copy.

WILETTA: Miss Green says, now...she said it...she says the third act doesn't justify with the first...no, wait...her exact words was, "The third act is not the natural outcome of the first." I thought, I thought she might be right.

MANNERS: (*Teasing*) Make me a solemn promise, don't start thinking.

SHELDON: (*Enters in a rush and hastily begins to remove scarves, coat etc.*) Good mornin', there ain't no justice.

(BILL O'WRAY *glances at "Show Business" from time to time.*)

EDDIE: What a greeting.

SHELDON: I dreamed six, twelve, six, one, two...just like that. You know what come out yesterday? Six, one, three. What you gonna do?

MANNERS: Save your money.

BILL: Hey, what do you know?

MANNERS: Did we make the press?

SHELDON: (*To* WILETTA) Friend of mine died yesterday, went to see about his apartment...gone! Just like that!

BILL: Gary Brewer's going into rehearsal on *Lost and Lonely*.

MANNERS: Been a long time.

BILL: He was in that Hollywood investigation some years ago.

SHELDON: (*To* EDDIE) They musta applied whilst the man was dyin'.

MANNERS: He wasn't really in it, someone named him I think.

BILL: You knew him well, didn't you?

MANNERS: Me? I don't know him. I've worked with him a couple of times but I don't really know him.

BILL: A very strange story reached me once, some fellow was planning to name me, can you imagine?

(MILLIE *enters wearing a breathtaking black suit. She is radiant.*)

EDDIE: That's ridiculous.

BILL: Nothing ever happened, but that's the story. Naming *me*.

MANNERS: (*As he studies schedule*) Talking about the coast, I could be out there now on a honey of a deal...but this I had to do, that's all.

SHELDON: Y'all ever hear any stories 'bout people namin' me?

MANNERS: What?

BILL: Oh, Shel!

SHELDON: (*This is a burden he has carried for quite some time.*) I sang on a program once with Millie, to help some boy that was in trouble...but later on I heard they was tryin' to overthrow the gov'ment.

(MANNERS, EDDIE *and* BILL *are embarrassed by this.*)

MILLIE: Oh, hush! Your mouth runs like a race horse!

SHELDON: Well, ain't nothin' wrong with singin' is there? We just sang.

MILLIE: (*As she removes her hat*) A big fool.

MANNERS: (*Making peace*) Oh, now... we're all good Americans.

BILL: (*To ease the tension*) I...I...er, didn't know you went in for singing, Sheldon.

SHELDON: Sure, I even wrote me a coupla tunes. Can make a lotta money like that but you gotta know somebody, I ain't got no pull.

WILETTA: (*To* MILLIE) He talks too much, talks too much.

MANNERS: Ah, we have a composer, popular stuff?

SHELDON: (*Stands and mechanically rocks to and fro in a rock and roll beat as he sings*) You-oo-hoo-oo are my hon-honey

Ooo-oo-ooo-oo, you smile is su-hu-hunny

My hu-hu-hunny, Bay-hay-hay-bee-e-e-e-e

... and it goes like that.

MANNERS: Well!

SHELDON: Thank you.

BILL: I don't know why you haven't sold it, that's all you hear.

(SHELDON *is pleased with* BILL'*s compliment but also a little worried.*)

MILLIE: Hmmmmmmph.

EDDIE: Really a tune.

SHELDON: (*To* BILL) My song...it...it's copyrighted.

BILL: Oh?

SHELDON: I got papers.

MILLIE: (*Extends her wrist to* WILETTA) Look. My husband is in off the road.

WILETTA: What's the matter?

MILLIE: A new watch, and I got my suit out...brought me this watch. We looked at a freezer this morning...food freezer...what's best, a chest freezer or an upright? I don't know.

JUDY: (*She enters dressed a little older than Act One, her hair is set with more precision. She is reaching for a sophistication that can never go deeper than the surface. She often makes graceful, studied postures and tries new attitudes, but very often she forgets.*) Greetings and salutations. Sheldon, how are you dear?

SHELDON: Thank you.

JUDY: (*As* MILLIE *displays her wrist for inspection*) Millie, darling, how lovely, ohhhhh, exquisite...

WILETTA: (*Really trying to join in*) Mmmm, ain't it divine.

(HENRY *and* JOHN *enter together.* HENRY *carries a container of coffee and a piece of Danish for* MANNERS. HENRY *is exact, precise, all business. He carries the container to* MANNERS' *table, places pastry, taps* EDDIE *on the shoulder, points to* MANNERS, *points to container, nods to* MANNERS *and company, turns and leaves, all while dialogue continues.*)

JOHN: (*Enters on a cloud. He is drifting more and more toward the heady heights of opportunism. He sees himself on the brink of escaping* WILETTA, MILLIE *and* SHELDON. *It's becoming very easy to conform to* MANNERS' *pattern.*) I'm walking in my sleep. I was up all hours last night.

MANNERS: At Sardi's no doubt.

JOHN: No!

JUDY: Exposed! We've found you out.

(*General laughter from* MILLIE, JUDY, BILL, EDDIE *and* MANNERS. JUDY *is enjoying the intangible joke to the utmost but as she turns to* WILETTA *her laughter dies...but* WILETTA *quickly picks it up.*)

WILETTA: Oh, my, yes indeed!

JOHN: I struggled with the third act. I think I won.

(MILLIE *sticks out her wrist for John's inspection.*)

Exquisite, Millie, beautiful. You deserve it.

(*During the following the conversation tumbles criss-cross in all directions and the only clear things are underscored.*)

MANNERS: Tell him what I told you this morning.

BILL: Why should I swell his head?

MANNERS: (*Arm around John's shoulder*) Hollywood's going to grab you so fast! I won't drop names but our opening night is going to be the end.

MILLIE: (*To* WILETTA) *Barbara died!*

JUDY: (*To* MANNERS) Oh, you terrify me!

MILLIE: *Died alone in her apartment*. Sudden-like.

JOHN: I've got to catch Katherine's performance, I hear it's terrific!

BILL: She's great, only great.

MILLIE: *I wouldn't live alone!*

MANNERS: She's going to get the award, no doubt about it!

JUDY: Marion Hatterly is good.

MANNERS: Marion is as *old as the hills!* I mean, she's so old it's embarrassing.

JOHN: But she has a quality.

SHELDON: (*To* MILLIE *and* WILETTA) *People dyin' like they got nothin' else to do!*

JUDY: She has, John, a real quality.

SHELDON: *I ain't gonna die*, can't afford to do it.

MANNERS: You have to respect her.

EDDIE: Can name her own ticket.

JOHN: Imperishable talent.

MILLIE: *Funeral is Monday*.

WILETTA: (*Weakly, to no one in particular*) Mmmmm, fascinatin'....

MANNERS: Picnic is over! Third Act!

SHELDON: I know my lines.

BILL: Don't worry about lines yet.

MANNERS: No, let him worry...I mean it's okay. Beginning of third!

WILETTA: (*Feels dizzy from past conversation. She rises and walks in a half-circle, then half-circles back again. She is suddenly the center of attraction.*) It...it's night time and I'm ironin' clothes.

MANNERS: Right. We wander through it. Here's the ironing board, door, window...you iron. Carrie is over there crying.

JUDY: Oh, poor, dear, Carrie, crying again.

MANNERS: Petunia is near the window, looking out for Job. Everyone is worried, worried, worried like crazy. Have the lynchers caught Job? Sam is seated in the corner, whittling a stick.

SHELDON: (*Flat statement*) Whittlin' a stick.

MANNERS: Excitement. Everyone knows that a mob is gathering.

SHELDON: (*Seated and busy running one index finger over the other*) I'm whittlin' a stick.

MANNERS: (*Drumming up excitement*) The hounds can be heard baying in the distance.

(SHELDON *bays to fill in the dog bit.* MANNERS *silences him with a gesture.*)

Everyone *listens*! They are thinking—has Job been killed? Ruby begins to sing.

WILETTA: (*Begins to sing with a little too much power but* MANNERS *directs her down*) Lord, have mercy, Lord have mercy…(*Hums*)

MILLIE: (*In abject, big-eyed fear*) Listen to them dogs in the night.

(MANNERS *warns* SHELDON *not to provide sound effects.*)

WILETTA: (*Trying to lose herself in the part*) Child, you better go now.

(BILL *whispers to* EDDIE.)

EDDIE: *Line. Miss Carrie*, you better go now.

MANNERS: Oh, bother! Don't do that!

(EDDIE *feels resentful toward* BILL *as* BILL *acts as though he had nothing to do with the correction.*)

WILETTA: This ain't no place for you to be.

JUDY: (*Now plays* CARRIE *in a different way from Act One. There is a reserved kindliness, rather than real involvement.*) I don't want to leave you alone, Ruby.

SHELDON: Thassa mistake, Mr. Manners. She can't be alone if me and Millie is there with her.

MANNERS: Don't interrupt!

SHELDON: Sorry.

(BILL *shakes his fist at* SHELDON *in playful pantomime.*)

WILETTA: Man that it born of woman is but a few days and full of trouble.

JUDY: I'm going to drive over to the next county and get my father and Judge Willis.

MILLIE: No, you ain't. Mr. Renard would never forgive me if somethin' was to happen to you.

(SHELDON *is very touched and sorry for all concerned as he whittles his stick.*)

JUDY: I feel so helpless.

SHELDON: (*Interrupts out of sheer frustration*) Am I still whittlin' the stick?

WILETTA: Dammit, yes.

MANNERS: (*Paces to control his annoyance*) Shel.

SHELDON: I thought I lost my place.

WILETTA: (*Picks up* MANNERS' *signal*) Nothin' to do now but pray!

SHELDON: (*Recognizes his cue*) Oh, yeah, that's me. (*Knows his lines almost perfectly*) Lord, once and again and one more time...

(MILLIE *moans in the background.* WILETTA's *mind seems a thousand miles away.* MANNERS *snaps his fingers and she begins to moan background for* SHELDON's *prayer.*)

Your humble servant calls on your everlastin' mercy...

MILLIE: Yes, Lord!

SHELDON:...to beseech, to beseech thy help for all your children this evenin'....

MILLIE: This evenin', Lord.

(MANNERS *is busy talking to* JOHN.)

SHELDON: But most of all we ask, we pray...that you help your son and servant Job....

WILETTA: Help him, Lord!

SHELDON: (*Doing a grand job of the prayer*) Walk with Job! Talk with Job! Ohhhhh, be with Job!

JUDY: Yes!

(MANNERS *and* BILL *give* JUDY *disapproving looks and she clasps her hand over her mouth.*)

WILETTA: (*Starts to sing and is joined by* SHELDON *and* MILLIE) Death ain't nothin' but a robber, cantcha see, cantcha see...

MANNERS: (*Is in a real tizzy, watching to catch* BILL's *reaction to the scene, and trying with his whole body to keep the scene up and going*) Eddie! Direction!

EDDIE: The door opens and Job enters!

WILETTA: Job, why you come here?

(MANNERS *doesn't like her reading. It is too direct and thoughtful.*)

MILLIE: (*Lashing out*) They after you! They told you 'bout mixin' in with Turner and that votin'!

MANNERS: Oh, good girl!

WILETTA: I'm the one to talk to my boy!

JOHN: (*A frightened, shivering figure*) If somebody could get me a wagon, I'll take the low road around Simpkin's Hollow and catch a train goin' away from here.

WILETTA: Shoulda gone 'fore you started this misery.

(MANNERS *indicates that she should get rougher; she tries.*)

Screamin' 'bout your rights! You got none! You got none!

JOHN: I'm askin' for help, I gotta leave!

MANNERS: (*To* JOHN) Appeal, remember it's an appeal.

JOHN: (*As though a light has dawned*) Ah, you're so right. (*Reads with tender appeal*) I gotta leave.

MANNERS: Right.

WILETTA: You tryin' to tell me that you runnin' away?

SHELDON: (*Worried about* JOB's *escape and getting caught up outside of the scene*) Sure! That's what he said in the line right there!

(MANNERS *silences* SHELDON *with a gesture*.)

WILETTA: You say you ain't done nothin' wrong?

(MANNERS *looks at* EDDIE *and* BILL *with despair*.)

JOHN: I ain't lyin'...

WILETTA: Then there's no need to be runnin'. Ain't you got no faith?

SHELDON: (*Sings in a shaky voice as he raps out time*) Oh, wella, time of trouble is a lonesome time.

Time of trouble is a lonesome time...

(*Joined by* MILLIE)

Feel like I could die, feel like I could die...

WILETTA: Tell 'em you sorry, tell 'em you done wrong!

MANNERS: Relate, Wiletta. Relate to what's going on around you!

(*To* JOHN)

Go on.

JOHN: I wasn't even votin' for a black man, votin' for somebody white same as they. (*Aside to* MANNERS) Too much? Too little? I fell off.

(MANNERS *indicates that he's on the beam*.)

WILETTA: I ain't never voted!

SHELDON: No, Lord!

WILETTA: I don't care who get in! Don't make no nevermind to us!

MILLIE: The truth!

JOHN: (*All afire*) When a man got a decent word to say for us down here, I gonna vote for him.

WILETTA: A decent word! And that's all you ever gonna get outta him. Dammit! He ain't gonna win nohow! They done said he ain't and they gonna see to it! And you gonna be dead...for a decent word!

JOHN: I ain't gonna wait to be killed.

WILETTA: There's only one right thing to do!

(*Everyone turns page in unison*.)

You got to go and give yourself up.

JOHN: But I ain't done nothin'.

SHELDON: (*Starts to sing again*) Wella, trouble is a lonesome thing...lonesome...lonesome...

MANNERS: (*The song even grates on him.*) Cut it, it's too much.

JUDY: My father will have you put in the county jail where you'll be safe.

JOHN: But I ain't done nothin'!

JUDY: I'm thinking of Ruby and the others, even if you aren't. I don't want murder in this community.

WILETTA: (*Screams*) Boy, get down on your knees.

MANNERS: (*To* EDDIE) Muscular tension.

(EDDIE *makes a note.*)

WILETTA: Oh, Lord, touch this boy's heart!

SHELDON: Mmmmmm, Hmmmmmmmm. Hmmmmmm...

WILETTA: Reach him tonight! Take the fear and hatred out of his soul!

MILLIE: Mercy, Lord!

JOHN: Stop, I can't stand no more. Whatever you say, anything you say.

SHELDON: Praise the Lord!

EDDIE: Renard enters.

BILL: Carrie, you shouldn't be here.

WILETTA: I told her. I'm beggin' you to help my boy, sir.... (*She drops script and picks it up.*)

JOHN: Ohhh, I can't sustain.

MANNERS: Don't try. We're breaking everything down to the simplest components...I want simple reactions to given circumstances in order to highlight the outstanding phases.

(WILETTA *finds her place.*)

Okay, let it roll.

WILETTA: I'm beggin' you to help my boy.

BILL: Boy, you're a mighty little fella to fly in the face of things people live by 'round here. I'll do what I can, what little I can.

WILETTA: Thank you, sir.

JUDY: Have Judge Willis put him in jail where he'll be safe.

BILL: Guess it wasn't his fault.

WILETTA: He don' know nothin'.

BILL: There are all kinds of white men in the world.

SHELDON: The truth.

BILL: This bird Akins got to sayin' the kind of things that was bound to stir you folks up.

MILLIE: I ain't paid him no mind myself.

BILL: Well, anything you want to take to the jail house with you? Like a washcloth and…well, whatever you might need.

JOHN: I don't know, don't know what I'm doin'.

BILL: Think you learned a lesson from all this?

MILLIE: You hear Mr. Renard?

SHELDON: He wanna know if you learned your lesson.

JOHN: I believed I was right.

SHELDON: Now you know you wasn't.

BILL: If anything happens, you tell the men Mr. Akins put notions in your head, understand?

SHELDON: He wanna know if you understand.

BILL: Come along, we'll put you in the jail house. Reckon I owe your ma and pa that much.

JOHN: I'm afraid, I so afraid….

MILLIE: Just go, 'fore they get here.

EDDIE: Job turns and looks at his father.

(SHELDON *places one finger to his lips and throws up his arms to show that he has no line.*)

Finally he looks to his mother, she goes back to her ironing.

BILL: Petunia, see that Miss Carrie gets home safe.

MILLIE: Yes sir.

EDDIE: Job follows Renard out into the night as Ruby starts to sing.

WILETTA: (*Sings*)

Keep me from sinkin' down

O, Lord, O, my Lord

Keep me from sinkin' down….

MANNERS: Cut, relax, at ease!

MILLIE: (*Brushes lint from her skirt*) I'll have to bring work clothes.

SHELDON: (*To* MILLIE) I almost hit the number yesterday.

MILLIE: I'm glad you didn't.

(BILL *crosses to* MANNERS, *we hear snatches of their conversation as the others cross-talk.*)

JUDY: (*To* JOHN) did you finish my book?

(JOHN *claps his hand to his forehead in a typical* MANNERS *gesture.*)

BILL: (*A light conference on* WILETTA) A line of physical action might…

SHELDON: (*To* MILLIE) I almost got an apartment.

MANNERS: Limited emotional capacity.

MILLIE: (*To* SHELDON) *Almost* don't mean a thing.

MANNERS: Well, it's coming. Sheldon, I like what's happening.

SHELDON: Thank you, does he give himself up to Judge Willis and get saved?

MANNERS: (*Flabbergasted, as are* JOHN, JUDY, BILL *and* EDDIE) Shel, haven't you read it? Haven't you heard us read it?

SHELDON: No, I just go over and over my own lines, I ain't in the last of the third act.

JUDY: Are my motivations coming through?

MANNERS: Yeah, forget it. Sit down, Sheldon...just for you...Renard drives him toward jail, deputies stop them on the way, someone shoots and kills Job as he tries to escape, afterward they find out he was innocent, Renard makes everyone feel like a dog...they realize they were wrong and so forth.

SHELDON: And so forth.

MANNERS: He makes them realize that lynching is wrong. (*He refers to his notes.*)

SHELDON: (*To* WILETTA) What was he innocent of?

WILETTA: I don't know.

JOHN: About the voting.

SHELDON: Uh-uh, he was guilty of that 'cause he done confessed.

MANNERS: Innocent of wrong-doing, Sheldon.

SHELDON: Uh-huh, oh, yeah.

MANNERS: Yale, you're on the right track. John, what can I say? You're great. Millie, you're growing, gaining command...I begin to feel an inner as well as the outer rendering.

JOHN: If we could run the sequence without interruption.

SHELDON: Yeah, then we could motorate and all that.

MANNERS: (*To* WILETTA) Dear heart, I've got to tell you...

WILETTA: I ain't so hot.

MANNERS: Don't be sensitive, let me help you, will you?

WILETTA: (*Trying to handle matters in the same way as* JOHN *and* JUDY) I know my relations and motivation may not be just so...

SHELDON: (*Wisely*) Uh-huh, *motivation*, that's the thing.

WILETTA: They not right and I think I know why...

MANNERS: Darling, that's my department, will you listen?

(JOHN *is self-conscious about* WILETTA *and* SHELDON. *He is ashamed of them and has reached the point where he exchanges knowing looks with* BILL, EDDIE *and* MANNERS.)

WILETTA: You don't ever listen to me. You hear the others but not me. And it's 'cause of the school. 'Cause they know 'bout justifyin' and the...antagonist...I never studied that, so you don't want to hear me, that's all right.

JUDY: (*Stricken to the heart*) Oh, don't say that.

SHELDON: He listen to me, and I ain't had it.

JOHN: (*Starts to put his arm around* WILETTA) Oh, Wiletta...

WILETTA: (*Moving away from him*) Oh, go on.

MANNERS: Wiletta, dear, I'm sorry if I've complicated things. I'll make it as clear as I can. You are pretending to act and I can see through your pretense. I want truth. What is truth? Truth is simply whatever you can bring yourself to believe, that is all. You must have integrity about your work...a sense of...well, sense.

WILETTA: I'm tryin' to lose myself like you say but...

JOHN: (*Wants to help but afraid to interrupt*) Oh, no...

MANNERS: (*Sternly*) You can't lose yourself, you are you...and you can't get away. You, Wiletta, must relate.

SHELDON: That's what I do.

WILETTA: I don't see why the boy couldn't get away...it's the killin' that...something's wrong. I may be in fast company but I got as much integrity as any. I didn't start workin' no yesterday.

MANNERS: No, Wiletta, no self-pity. Look, he can't escape this death. We want audience sympathy. We have a very subtle point to make, very subtle....

BILL: I hate the kind of play that bangs you over the head with the message. Keep it subtle.

MANNERS: (*Getting very basic*) We don't want to antagonize the audience.

WILETTA: It'll make 'em mad if he gets away?

MANNERS: This is a simple, sweet, lovable guy. Sheldon, does it offend you that he gives himself up to Judge Willis?

SHELDON: No, not if that's how they do.

MANNERS: We're making one beautiful, clear point...violence is wrong.

WILETTA: My friend, Miss Green, say she don't see why they act like this.

JOHN: (*Thinks he knows how to handle* WILETTA. *He is about to burst with an idea.* MANNERS *decides to let* JOHN *wade in.*) Look, think of the intellectual level here...they're under-privileged, uneducated....

WILETTA: (*Letting* JOHN *know he's treading on thin ice*) Look out, you ain't so smart.

JOHN: (*Showing so much of* MANNERS) They've probably never seen a movie or television...never used a telephone. They...they're not like us. They're good, kind, folksy people...but they're ignorant, they just don't know.

WILETTA: You ain't the director.

SHELDON: (*To* JOHN) You better hush.

MANNERS: We're dealing with simple, backward people but they're human beings.

WILETTA: 'Cause they colored, you tellin' me they're human bein's.... I *know* I'm a human bein'.... Listen here...

MANNERS: I will not listen! It does not matter to me that they're Negroes. Black, white, green or purple, I maintain there is only one race...the human race.

(SHELDON *bursts into applause.*)

MILLIE: That's true.

MANNERS: Don't think "Negro," think "people."

SHELDON: Let's stop segregatin' ourselves.

JOHN: (*To* WILETTA) I didn't mean any harm, you don't understand....

BILL: (*To* MILLIE *as he looks heavenward and acts out his weariness*) Oh, honey child!

MILLIE: Don't call me no damn honey child!

BILL: Well, is my face red.

MILLIE: Yeah, and on you it looks good.

MANNERS: What's going on?

MILLIE: Honey child.

WILETTA: (*Mumbling as all dialogue falls pell-mell*) Justify.

BILL: (*With great resignation*) Trying to be friendly.

WILETTA: Justify.

MILLIE: Get friendly with someone else.

MANNERS: May we have order!

SHELDON: (*In a terrible flash of temper*) That's why they don't do more colored shows! Always fightin'! Everybody hush, let this man direct! He don't even have to be here! Right now he could be out in Hollywood in the middle of a big investigation!

EDDIE: The word is production!

SHELDON: That's what I said, production.

EDDIE: No, you didn't.

SHELDON: What'd I say?

MANNERS: (*Bangs table*) I will not countenance another outbreak of this nature. I say to each and every one of you...I am in charge and I'll thank you to remember it. I've been much too lax, too informal. Well, it doesn't work. There's going to be order.

WILETTA: I was only sayin'...

MANNERS: I said *everyone*! My patience is at an end. I demand your concentrated attention. It's as simple as A, B, C, if you will apply yourselves. The threat of this horrible violence throws you into cold, stark fear. It's a perfectly human emotion, anyone would feel it. I'm not asking you to dream up some fantastic horror...it's a lynching. We've never actually seen such a thing, thank God...but allow your imagination to soar, to take hold of it...think.

SHELDON: I seen one.

MANNERS: (*Can't believe he heard right*) What?

BILL: What did you see?

SHELDON: A lynchin', when I was a little boy 'bout nine years old.

JUDY: Oh, no.

WILETTA: How did it happen? Tell me, Sheldon did you really?

MANNERS: Would it help you to know, Wiletta?

WILETTA: I...guess...I don't know.

BILL: (*Not eager to hear about it*) Will it bother you, Sheldon? It could be wrong for him...I don't know....

(EDDIE *gives* MANNERS *a doubtful look.*)

MILLIE: That must be something to see.

MANNERS: (*With a sigh*) Go on, Sheldon.

(MANNERS *watches cast reactions.*)

SHELDON: I think it was on a Saturday, yeah, it had to be or elsewise I woulda been in the field with my ma and pa.

WILETTA: What field?

SHELDON: The cotton field. My ma said I was too little to go every day but some of 'em younger'n me was out there all the time. My grandma was home with me.... (*Thinks of grandma and almost forgets his story*)

WILETTA: What about the lynchin'?

SHELDON: It was Saturday and rainin' a sort of sifty rain. I was standin' at the window watchin' the lilac bush wavin' in the wind. A sound come to my ears like bees hummin'...was voices comin' closer and closer, screamin' and cursin'. My granny tried to pull me from the window. "Come on, chile." She said, "They gonna kill us all...hide!" But I was fightin' to

keep from goin' with her, scared to go in the dark closet.
(JUDY *places her hands over her ears and bows her head.*)
The screamin' comin' closer and closer...and the screamin'
was laughin'.... Lord, how they was laughin'...louder and
louder. (SHELDON *rises and puts in his best performance to date.
He raises one hand and creates a stillness...everyone is spellbound.*)
Hush! Then I hear wagon wheels bumpin' over the wet, stony
road, chains clankin'. Man drivin' the wagon, beatin' the
horse...Ahhhhhhhh! Ahhhhhhhh! Horse just pullin'
along...and then I saw it! Chained to the back of the wagon,
draggin' and bumpin' along.... (*He opens his arms wide.*) The
arms of it stretched out...a burnt, naked thing...a burnt,
naked thing that once was a man...and I started to scream but
no sound come out...just a screamin' but no sound.... (*He
lowers his arms and brings the company back to the present.*) That
was Mr. Morris that they killed. Mr. Morris. I remember one
time he come to our house and was laughin' and talkin' and
everything...and he give us a fruit cake that his wife made.
Folks said he was crazy...you know, 'bout talkin' back...quick
to speak his mind. I left there when I was seventeen. I don't
want to live in no place like that.

MANNERS: When I hear of barbarism...I feel so wretched, so guilty.

SHELDON: Don't feel that way. You wouldn't kill nobody and do
'em like that...would you?

MANNERS: (*Hurt by the question*) No, Sheldon.

SHELDON: That's what I know.

(BILL *crosses and rests his hand on* SHELDON's *shoulder.*
SHELDON *flinches because he hadn't noticed* BILL's *approach.*)
Oh! I didn't see you. Did I help y'all by tellin' that story?

MANNERS: It was quite an experience. I'm shot. Break for lunch,
we'll pick up in an hour, have a good afternoon session.

MILLIE: Makes me feel like goin' out in the street and crackin'
heads.

JUDY: (*Shocked*) Oh!

EDDIE: Makes my blood boil...but what can you do?

MANNERS: We're doing the play.

MILLIE: (*To* JUDY) I'm starved. You promised to show us that
Italian place.

JUDY: (*Surprised that* MILLIE *no longer feels violent*) Why...sure, I'd
love to. Let's have a festive lunch, with wine!

SHELDON: Yeah, that wine that comes in a straw bottle.

JUDY: Imported wine.

MILLIE: And chicken cacciatore…let's live!

WILETTA: (*Crosses to* MANNERS *while others are getting coats. She has hit on a scheme to make* MANNERS *see her point.*) Look here, I ain't gonna let you get mad with me. You supposed to be my buddy.

JOHN: Let's go!

MANNERS: (*Opens his arms to* WILETTA) I'm glad you said that. You're my sweetheart.

MILLIE: Bill, how about you?

BILL: (*Places his hand on his stomach*) The Italian place. Okay, count me in.

EDDIE: (*Stacking scripts*) I want a king-size dish of clams…raw ones.

WILETTA: Wouldn't it be nice if the mother could say, "Son, you right! I don't want to send you outta here but I don't know what to do.…"

MANNERS: Darling, darling…no.

MILLIE: Wiletta, get a move on.

WILETTA: Or else she says "Run for it, Job!" and then they catch him like that…he's dead *anyway*, see?

MANNERS: (*Trying to cover his annoyance*) It's not the script, it's *you*. Bronson does the writing, you do the acting, it's that simple.

SHELDON: One race, the human race. I like that.

JUDY: Veal Parmesan with oodles and oodles of cheese!

WILETTA: I was just thinkin' if I could…

MANNERS: (*Indicating script*) Address yourself to this.

JUDY: (*To* JOHN) Bring my book tomorrow.

JOHN: Cross my heart.

WILETTA: I just wanted to talk about…

MANNERS: You are going to get a spanking. (*He leaves with* EDDIE *and others.*)

MILLIE: Wiletta, come on!

WILETTA: (*Abruptly*) I…I'll be there later.

MILLIE: (*Miffed by the short answer*) Suit yourself.

JUDY: (*To* WILETTA) It's on the corner of Sixth Avenue on this side of the street.

JOHN: Correction. Correction, Avenue of the Americas.

(*Laughter from* MANNERS, MILLIE, SHELDON *and* BILL *offstage*)

JUDY: (*Posturing in her best theatrical style*) But no one, absolutely no one, ever says it. He's impossible, absolutely impossible!

WILETTA: Oh, ain't he though.

JOHN: (*Bows to* JUDY *and indicates that she goes first*) Dear Gaston, Alphonse will follow.

WILETTA: John, I told you everything wrong 'cause I didn't know better, that's the size of it. No fool like a old fool. You right, don't make sense to be bowin' and scrapin' and tommin'.... No, don't pay no attention to what I said.

JOHN: (*Completely* MANNERS) Wiletta, my dear, you're my sweetheart, I love you madly and I think you're wonderfully magnificent!

JUDY: (JUDY *suddenly notices his posturing and hers, she feels silly. She laughs, laughter bordering on tears.*) John, you're a puppet with strings attached and so am I. Everyone's a stranger and I'm the strangest of all. (*She quickly leaves.*)

JOHN: Wiletta, don't forget to come over! (*He follows* JUDY.)

WILETTA: (*Paces up and down, tries doing her lines aloud*) Only one thing to do, give yourself up! Give yourself up...give up...give up...give up...give up...give up.

(*LIGHTS WHIRL AND FLICKER. BLUES RECORD comes in loud—then down—LIGHTS FLICKER to indicate passage of time.* WILETTA *is gone. Stage is empty.*)

(BILL *enters, removing his coat. He has a slight attack of indigestion and belches his disapproval of pizza pie. Others can be heard laughing and talking offstage.*)

BILL: Ohhhhhh, Ahhhhh....

MANNERS: (*Enters with* EDDIE. EDDIE *proceeds to the table and script.* MANNERS *is just getting over the effects of a good laugh...but his mirth suddenly fades as he crosses to* BILL.) I am sorry you felt compelled to tell that joke about the colored minister and the stolen chicken.

BILL: Trying to be friendly...I don't know...I even ate pizza.

EDDIE: I always *think*...think first, is this the right thing to say, would I want anyone to say this to me?
(*Burst of laughter from offstage*)

BILL: Oh, you're so noble, you give me a pain in the ass. Love thy neighbor as thyself, now I ask you, is that a reasonable request?

MANNERS: (*For fear the others will hear*) All right. Knock it off.

BILL: Okay, I said I was sorry, but for what...I'll never know.
(SHELDON, MILLIE, JUDY *and* JOHN *enter in a hilarious mood.* JUDY *is definitely feeling the wine.* SHELDON *is supplying the fun.*)

SHELDON: Sure, I was workin' my hind parts off...Superintendent of the buildin'...

JOHN: But the tenants, Shel! That's a riot!

SHELDON: One day a man came along and offered me fifty dollars a week just to walk across the stage real slow. (*Mimics his acting role*) Sure, I took it! Hard as I worked I was glad to slow down!

(*Others laugh.*)

JUDY: (*Holds her head*) Ohhhhhh, that wine.

MILLIE: Wasn't it good? I wanna get a whole *case* of it for the holidays. All that I have to do! My liquors, wreathes, presents, cards...I'm gonna buy my husband a tape recorder.

JUDY: (*To* JOHN) I'm sorry I hurt your feelings but you are a little puppet, and I'm a little puppet, and all the world....(*She impresses the lesson by tapping* JOHN *on his chest.*)

MANNERS: Judy, I want to go over something with you....

JUDY: No, you don't...you're afraid I'm going to...hic. 'Fraid I'll go overboard on the friendship deal and *compli*cate matters...complications....

MANNERS: Two or three glasses of wine, she's delirious. Do you want some black coffee?

JUDY: No, no, I only have hiccups.

MILLIE: (*To* JOHN) Which would you rather have, a tape recorder or a camera?

JOHN: I don't know.

SHELDON: I'd rather have some money, make mine cash.

MANNERS: (*To* JUDY) Why don't you sit down and get yourself together? (She sits.)

JOHN: (*To* MANNERS) I...I think I have some questions about Wiletta and the third act.

MANNERS: It's settled, don't worry, John, she's got it straight.

JOHN: I know but it seems...

MANNERS: Hoskins sat out front yesterday afternoon. He's mad about you. First thing he says, "Somebody's going to try and steal that boy from us."

JOHN: (*Very pleased*) I'm glad I didn't know he was there.

MANNERS: Eddie, call it, will you? Okay, attention!

EDDIE: Beginning of the third.

(*Company quiets down, opens scripts.* WILETTA *enters.*)

MANNERS: You're late.

WILETTA: I know it. (*To* MILLIE) I had a bowl of soup and was able to relate to it and justify, no trouble at all. (*To* MANNERS) I'm not gonna take up your time now but I wanta see you at the end of the afternoon.

MANNERS: Well...I...I'll let you know...we'll see.

WILETTA: It's important.

MANNERS: (*Ignoring her and addressing entire company*) Attention, I want to touch on a corner of what we did this morning and then we'll highlight the rest of three!
(*Actors rise and start for places.*)
John, top of page four.

JOHN: When a man has a decent word to say for us down here, I gonna vote for him.

WILETTA: (*With real force. She is lecturing him rather than scolding.*) A decent word? And that's all you ever gonna get out of him. Dammit, he ain't gonna win nohow. They done said he ain't and they gonna see to it! And you gonna be dead for a decent word.

MANNERS: (*To* EDDIE) This is deliberate.

JOHN: I gotta go, I ain't gonna wait to be killed.

WILETTA: There's only one right thing to do. You got to go and give yourself up.

JOHN: I ain't done nothin'.

JUDY: My father will have Judge Willis put you in the County Jail where you'll be safe.
(MANNERS *is quite disheartened.*)

WILETTA: Job, she's tryin' to help us.

JUDY: I'm thinking of the others even if you aren't. I don't want murder in this community.

WILETTA: Boy, get down on your knees.
(JOHN *falls to his knees.*)
Oh, Lord, touch this boy's heart. Reach him tonight, take the fear and hatred out of his soul!

SHELDON: Hmmmmmmm, mmmmmmm, mmmmmmmm....

MILLIE: Mercy, Lord.

JOHN: Stop, I can't stand anymore.... (WILETTA *tries to raise* JOHN.)

MANNERS: No, keep him on his knees.

JOHN: I can't stand anymore...whatever you say...(*Again* WILETTA *tries to raise him.*)

SHELDON: (*To* WILETTA) He say keep him on his knees.

WILETTA: Aw, get up off the floor, wallowin' around like that.
(*Everyone is shocked.*)

MANNERS: Wiletta, this is not the time or place to...

WILETTA: All that crawlin' and goin' on before me...hell, I ain't the one tryin' to lynch him. This ain't sayin' nothin', don't make sense. Talkin' 'bout the truth is anything I can believe...well, I don't believe this.

MANNERS: I will not allow you to interrupt in this disorganized manner.

WILETTA: You been askin' me what I think and where things come from and how come I thought it and all that. Where is this comin' from?! (*Company murmuring in background*) Tell me, why this boy's people turned against him? Why we sendin' him out into the teeth of a lynch mob? I'm his mother and I'm sendin' him to his death. This is a lie.

JOHN: But his mother doesn't understand. There have been men dragged from their homes for....

WILETTA: But they was dragged...they came with guns and dragged them, they weren't sent to be killed by their mama! Writer wants the damn white man to be the hero and me the villain.

MILLIE: I think we're all tired.

SHELDON: Outta order, outta order, you outta order.

MANNERS: Wiletta, there are some who may deserve this from you but I'm not the one.

SHELDON: No, you ain't.

MANNERS: As long as I've known you, you've never given me any trouble.

WILETTA: And that's what's the matter.

MANNERS: What do you want to do when the mob comes after Job? Shoot it out? That's sheer violence.

WILETTA: Yeah, kill my child and call me violent, that's what comes of all the justifyin'.

MANNERS: I'm going to tell you something you've never known before now. Remember the last picture we made together? You played a character part. I had to sweat blood, stayed up all night with the writers...getting them to change a stereotype, mammy role into something decent for you....

WILETTA: And when you got through, dammit, it was still a mammy part. Character part! Lemmie tell you 'bout them character parts.

(*She startles company by falling into character.*)

"Oh, Miss Wentworth, I'm so distress, I don't know what to do."

(*Falls out of character*)

Always distressed and don't know a damn thing to do!

(*Back into character*)

"It's 'bout my son, he's a good boy but he's got notions that's gonna get him in trouble."

(*Out of character*)

Our sons always got notions that they as good as anybody else, and we always askin' the white folks we work for to change their minds for 'em! We got husbands too, you may not see 'em but you hear 'bout 'em in those character parts.

(*In character*)

"I don't know why I stays with that man, he won't work, he won't come home, I don't know why I loves him, guess it's 'cause he keeps me laughin' all the time."

(*Out of character*)

You ever hear of a lazy, no-good, two-timin' man keepin' a woman laughin' all the time? Character part!

(*In character*)

A baby in my arms. "You're my little angel, and just like I raised your mama, I'm gonna raise you to be a little lady."

(*Making up her own act*)

Dear little baby of the folks I work for, I got a present for you...my whole damn life! I'm handin' it over to you and your ma and pa. If you got no money to pay me, I wanna stay anyhow, my pleasure is to wait on you forever. To hell with my children and hooray for you!

(*Out of character*)

You stayin' up all night fixin' up character parts for me! Givin' 'em what you call dignity! Dignity! You know what your dignity is? A old black straw hat with a flower stickin' up in front, hands folded cross my stomach, sayin' the same damn fool things...only nice and easy and proper!

(*In character*)

"I know it's none of my business, Mrs. Sanders, but I just got to say it. You haven't been yourself lately and it grieves me to see you eatin' your heart out 'bout Mr. John. I try to pretend I don't see it, but I do. It's almost more than a body can stand."

MANNERS: I'm sorry you've had to play maids but it's not my fault....

WILETTA: They're not maids. What you call maids aren't even

people! I got news for you. We don't give a damn 'bout Mr.
John or Mr. Renard either. I don't sit down and eat with 'em
and I ain't sittin' up nights worryin' 'bout 'em. Dignity! All
them lyin' pictures I seen with white folks pretendin' they
passin' for white? When they wanta show a colored girl
passin', they go and get this child to do it. (*Points to* JUDY)

MILLIE: Exactly.

WILETTA: Who gets to play the Indian chief? Look close and you'll
see he's got blue eyes, and you gonna tell me 'bout truth and
justifyin'? And don't dare be BLACK...then you got to
scratch your head (*Demonstrates*) every time you start to
think...plowin' up thoughts. Justify! Oh, I'm holdin' class
today.

BILL: Wiletta, I've had to do roles that I found objectionable.

WILETTA: I'm wise. But you don't give a damn 'cause a lynch mob
ain't after you! I know what you play... turnin' into a fanged
wolf when the moon is full, turnin' into a vampire bat, a
blood-sucker! You *had* to go to school to justify that. On that
tee-vee box y'all shootin' down each other every night, all
night long. Shootin' and kissin', that's all you know...how big
is your bust and murder, murder, murder. Yes indeed, that's
your stereotype. Suit yourself, but I'm sick-a mine. I'm full,
my cup runneth over. (*Points to script*) Would you...could you
do this to a son of yours?

MANNERS: She places him in the hands of Judge Willis because....

WILETTA: And I tell you she knows better.

BILL: It's only because she trusts and believes in someone. Couldn't
you trust and believe in Al?

MANNERS: Bill, please.

WILETTA: No, I would not trust him with my son's life.

MANNERS: Thank you.

SHELDON: She don't mean it.

WILETTA: Judge Willis! Why don't his people help him?

MANNERS: The story goes a certain way and...

WILETTA: It oughta go another way.

ENTIRE COMPANY: (*In unison*) Talk about it later. We're all tired.
Yes. We need a rest. Sometime your own won't help you.

MANNERS: Leave her alone! (MANNERS *is on fire now. He loves the
challenge of this conflict and is determined to win the battle...he
must win.*) Why this great fear of death? Christ died for something and...

WILETTA: Sure, they came and got him and hauled him off to jail. His mother didn't turn him in, in fact; the one who did it was one of them so-called friends.

MANNERS: His death proved something. Job's death brings him the lesson...

WILETTA: That they should stop lynchin' *innocent* men! Fine thing! Lynch the guilty, is that the idea? The dark-skinned Oliver Twist. (*Points to* JOHN) That's you. Yeah, I mean, you got to go to school to justify this!

MANNERS: Wiletta, I've listened, I've heard you out....

WILETTA: (*To* SHELDON) And you echoin' every damn word he says..."Keep him on his knees."

MANNERS: I've heard you out and even though you think you know more than the author...

WILETTA: You don't want to hear. You are a prejudiced man. (*Gasp from the company.*)

MANNERS: (*Caught off-guard*) I will not accept that from you or anyone else.

WILETTA: I told this boy to laugh and grin at everything you said, well...I ain't laughin'.

MANNERS: While you give me hell-up-the-river, I'm supposed to stand here and take it with a tolerance beyond human endurance. I'm white! You think it's so wonderful to be white? I've got troubles up to here! But I don't expect anyone to hand me anything and it's high time you got rid of that notion. No, I never worked in a cotton field, I didn't. I was raised in a nice, comfortable, nine room house in the midwest...and I learned to say nigger, kike, sheeny, spick, dago, wop and chink...I heard 'em plenty! I was raised by a sweet, dear, kind, old aunt, who spent her time gathering funds for missionaries...but she almost turned our town upside down when Mexicans moved in on our block. I know about troubles...my own! I've never been *handed* any gifts. Oh, it's so grand to be white! I had to crawl and knuckle under step by step.... What I want and what I believe, indeed! I directed blood, guts, fist-fights, bedroom farces and the lowest kind of dirtied-up sex until I earned the respect of this business.

WILETTA: But would you send your son out to...

MANNERS: I proclaim this National Truth Week! Whites! You think we belong to one great, grand fraternity? They stole and snatched from me for years...and I'm a club member!

Ever hear of an idea man? They picked my brains! They stripped me! They threw me cash and I let the credit go! My brains milked, while somebody else climbed on my back to take bows. But I didn't beg for mercy...why waste your breath? But I learned one thing that's the only damned truth worth knowing...you get nothin' for nothin', but nothin'! No favors, no dreams served up on silver platters. Now...finally I get...something for all of us...but it's not enough for you! I'm prejudiced! Get wise, there's damned few of us interested in putting on a colored show at all, much less one that's going to say anything. It's rough out here, it's a hard world! Do you think I can stick my neck out by telling the truth about you? There are billions of things that *can't* be *said*...do you follow me, billions! Where the hell do you think I can raise a hundred thousand dollars to tell the unvarnished truth? (*Picks up the script and waves it*) So, maybe it's a lie...but it's one of the finest lies you'll come across for a damned long time! Here's bitter news, since you're livin' off truth...The American public is not ready to see you the way you want to be seen because, one...they don't believe it, two...they don't want to believe it...and three...they're convinced they're superior...and that, my friend, is why Carrie and Renard have to carry the ball! Get it? Now you wise up and aim for the soft spot in that American heart, let 'em pity you, make 'em weep buckets, be helpless, make 'em feel so damned sorry for you that they'll lend a hand in easing up the pressure. You've got a free ride...coast, baby, coast.

WILETTA: Would you send your son out to be murdered?

MANNERS: (*So wound up, he answers without thinking*) Don't compare yourself to me! What goes for my son doesn't necessarily go for yours! Don't compare him (*Points to* JOHN)... with three strikes against him, don't compare him with my son, they've got nothing in common...not a Goddamn thing! (*He realizes what he has said, also that he has lost company sympathy. He is utterly confused and embarrassed by his own statement.*) I tried to make it clear.

JOHN: It is clear.

(MANNERS *quickly exits to dressing room.* EDDIE *follows him.* JUDY *has an impulse to follow.*)

BILL: No, leave him alone.

JOHN: (*To* WILETTA) I feel like a fool.... Hmmph, "Don't think

Negro, think *people*."

SHELDON: (*To* BILL) You think he means we're fired?

BILL: I don't know...I don't know...

MILLIE: Wiletta, this should have been discussed with everyone first.

SHELDON: Done talked yourself out of a job.

BILL: Shel, you don't know that.

SHELDON: (*During the following scene,* SHELDON *is more active and dynamic than ever before.*) Well, he didn't go out there to bake her no birthday cake.

(JUDY *is quietly crying.*)

MILLIE: We got all the truth we bargained for and then some.

WILETTA: Yes, I spoke my mind and he spoke his.

BILL: We have a company representative, Sheldon is the deputy. Any complaints we have should be handled in an orderly manner. Equity has rules, the rule book says...

SHELDON: I left my rule book home. Furthermore, I don't think I want to be the deputy.

MILLIE: He was dead right about some things but I didn't appreciate that *last* remark.

SHELDON: (*To* WILETTA) You can't spit in somebody's eye and tell 'em you was washin' it out.

BILL: Sheldon, now is not the time to resign.

SHELDON: (*Taking charge*) All right, I'm tryin' to lead 'em, tryin' to play peace-maker. Shame on y'all! Look at the U.N.!

MILLIE: The U.N.?

SHELDON: Yes, the United Nations. You think they run their business by blabbin' everything they think? No! They talk sweet and polite 'til they can out-slick the next feller. Wisdom! The greatest gift in the world, they got it! (*To* WILETTA) Way you talked, I thought you had the 'tomic bomb.

WILETTA: I'm sick of people signifyin' we got no sense.

SHELDON: I know. I'm the only man in the house and what am I doin'? Whittlin' a doggone stick. But I whittled it, didn't I? I can't write a play and I got no money to put one on.... Yes! I'm gonna whittle my stick! (*Stamps his foot to emphasize the point*)

JOHN: (*Very noble and very worried*) How do you go about putting in a notice?

SHELDON: (*To* JOHN) Hold on 'til I get to you. (*To* WILETTA) Now, when he gets back here, you be sure and tell him.

WILETTA: Tell him what?

SHELDON: Damn, tell him you *sorry*.

BILL: Oh, he doesn't want that.

WILETTA: Shame on him if he does.

MILLIE: I don't want to spend the rest of the day wondering why he walked out.

WILETTA: I'm playin' a leadin' part and I want this script changed or else.

SHELDON: Hush up, before the man hears you.

MILLIE: Just make sure you're not the one to tell him. You're a great one for runnin' to management and telling your guts.

SHELDON: I never told management nothin', anybody say I did is lyin'.

JUDY: Let's ask for a *quiet* talk to straighten things out.

BILL: No. This is between Wiletta and Manners and I'm sure they can...

JOHN: We all ought to show some integrity.

SHELDON: Integrity...got us in a big mess.

MILLIE: (*To* JOHN) You can't put in your notice until after opening night. You've got to follow Equity rules....

SHELDON: Yeah, he's trying to defy the union.

WILETTA: (*Thumping the script*) This is a damn lie.

MILLIE: But you can't tell people what to write, that's censorship.

SHELDON: (*To* WILETTA) And that's another point in your disfavor.

JOHN: They can write what they want but we don't have to do it.

SHELDON: You outta order!

BILL: (*To* JOHN) Oh, don't keep stirring it up, heaping on coals...

JUDY: Wiletta, maybe if we appeal to Mr. Hoskins or Mr. Bronson...

SHELDON: The producer and the author ain't gonna listen to her, after all...they white same as Manners.

JUDY: I resent that!

BILL: I do too, Shel.

JUDY: I've had an awful lot of digs thrown at me...remarks about white, white...and I do resent it.

JOHN: (*To* JUDY. *He means what can you expect from* SHELDON.) Sheldon.

BILL: (*To* JUDY) I'm glad you said that.

SHELDON: I'm sorry, I won't say nothin' 'bout white. (*To* WILETTA) Look here, Hoskins, Manners, and Bronson...they got things in...er...common, you know what I mean?

WILETTA: Leave me alone…and suit yourselves.

MILLIE: I know what's right but I need this job.

SHELDON: There you go…talk.

WILETTA: Thought your husband doesn't want you to work.

MILLIE: He doesn't but I have to anyway.

JUDY: But you'll still be in New York. If this falls through I'll have to go back to Bridgeport…before I even get started.

JOHN: Maybe I'll never get another job.

MILLIE: Like Al Manners says, there's more to this life than the truth. (*To* JUDY) You'll have to go to Bridgeport. Oh, how I wish I had a Bridgeport.

BILL: Okay, enough, *I'm* the villain. I get plenty of work, forgive me.

JUDY: Life scares me, honestly it does.

SHELDON: When you kick up a disturbance, the man's in his rights to call the cops…police car will come rollin' up here, next thing you know…you'll be servin' time.

MILLIE: Don't threaten her!

JOHN: Why don't you call a cop *for* him…try it.

(HENRY *enters carrying a paper bag.*)

HENRY: I got Mr. Manners some nice Danish, cheese and prune.

MILLIE: He can't eat it right now…leave it there.

(EDDIE *enters with a shaken but stern attitude.*)

EDDIE: Attention company. You are all dismissed for the day. I'll telephone you about tomorrow's rehearsal.

SHELDON: Tell Mr. Manners I'm gonna memorize my first act.

(EDDIE *exits and* SHELDON *talks to company.*)

I still owe the doctor money…and I can't lift no heavy boxes or be scrubbin' no floors. If I was a drinkin' man I'd get drunk.

MILLIE: Tomorrow is another day. Maybe everybody will be in better condition to…talk…just talk it all out. Let's go to the corner for coffee and a calm chat. (*Suddenly solicitous with* JUDY) How about you, honey, wouldn't you like to relax and look over the situation? Bill?

BILL: I have to study for my soap opera…but thanks.

JUDY: Yes, let's go talk.

MILLIE: John? Wiletta, honey, let's go for coffee.

WILETTA: I'll be there after a while. Go on.

JOHN: We couldn't go without you.

SHELDON: We don't want to leave you by yourself in this old theater.

WILETTA: There are times when you got to be alone. *This is mine.*
(JOHN *indicates they should leave.* MILLIE, SHELDON, JUDY,
JOHN *and* BILL *exit.*)

HENRY: Are you cryin'?

WILETTA: Yes.

HENRY: Ah, don't do that. It's too nice a day. (*Sits near tape recorder*)
I started to throw coffee at him that time when he kicked up a
fuss, but you got to take a lotta things in this life.

WILETTA: Divide and conquer…that's the way they get the upper
hand. A telephone call for tomorrow's rehearsal…they won't
call me…. But I'm gonna show up any damn way. The next
move is his. He'll have to fire me.

HENRY: Whatcha say?

WILETTA: We have to go further and do better.

HENRY: That's a good one. I'll remember that. What's on this,
music?

WILETTA: (*Turns the machine on and down. The applause plays.*)
Canned applause. When you need a bit of instant praise…you
turn it on…and there you are.
(*He tries it.*)

HENRY: Canned applause. They got everything these days. Time
flies. I bet you can't guess how old I am.

WILETTA: Not more than sixty.

HENRY: I'm seventy-eight.

WILETTA: Imagine that. A fine-lookin' man like you.
(*Sound of police siren in street*)

HENRY: What's that?

WILETTA: Police siren.

HENRY: They got a fire engine house next to where I live. God-in-
heaven, you never heard such a noise…and I'm kinda deaf….
Didn't know that, did you?

WILETTA: No, I didn't. Some live by what they call great truths.
Henry, I've always wanted to do somethin' real grand…in the
theater…to stand forth at my best…to stand up here and do
anything I want….

HENRY: Like my father…he was in vaudeville…doin' the softshoe
and tippin' his hat to the ladies….

WILETTA: Yes, somethin' grand.

HENRY: (*Adjusting the tape recorder to play applause*) Do it…do it. I'm
the audience.

WILETTA: I don't remember anything grand…I can't recall.

HENRY: Say somethin' from the Bible...like the twenty-third psalm.

WILETTA: Oh, I know. (*She comes downstage and recites beautifully from Psalm 133.*) Behold how good and how pleasant it is for brethren to dwell together in unity. It is like the precious ointment upon the head, that ran down upon the beard, even Aaron's beard; that went down to the skirts of his garment; as the dew of Hermon, and as the dew that descended upon the mountains of Zion; for there the Lord commanded the blessing, even life forevermore.

(HENRY *turns on applause as* WILETTA *stands tall for the CURTAIN.*)

CURTAIN